The Real
George
Washington

"I was summoned by my country, whose voice I can never hear but with veneration and love."

G. Washington

Volume 3 of the
AMERICAN CLASSIC SERIES

The Real George Washington

Part I
George Washington: The Man Who United America
(A History of His Life)
By *Jay A. Parry and Andrew M. Allison*

Part II
Timeless Treasures from George Washington
(Selections from His Writings)
*Prepared by Andrew M. Allison, Jay A. Parry,
and W. Cleon Skousen*

National Center for Constitutional Studies

Library of Congress Cataloging-in-Publication Data

The Real George Washington.
    (Vol. 3 of the American Classic Series)
    Includes bibliographical references.
    Contents: Part 1. George Washington: the man who united America (a history of his life)/ by Jay A. Parry and Andrew M. Allison. Part 2. Timeless treasures from George Washington (selections from his writings) / prepared by Andrew M. Allison, Jay A. Parry, and W. Cleon Skousen.
    Includes index.
    1. Washington, George, 1732-1799. 2. Presidents—United States—Biography. 3. Generals—United States—Biography 4. United States—Continental Army—Biography. 5. United States—History—Revolution, 1775-1783—Campaigns. 6. United States—Politics and government—1789-1797. 7. United States—Politics and government—1783-1789. I. Allison, Andrew M., 1949– . II. Washington, George, 1732-1799. Selections. 1991. III. Title. IV. Series: American Classic Series (National Center for Constitutional Studies (U.S.)); v.3.
E312.P23   1991
973.4'1'092—dc20   90-5607
[B]   CIP

ISBN 10: 0-88080-014-3
ISBN 13: 978-0-88080-014-3

Cover image courtesy of The Granger Collection, New York.
Used with permission.
Printed in the United States of America

National Center for
Constitutional Studies
www.nccs.net

Contents

A compilation of the most important passages from Washington's writings, arranged alphabetically by subject matter. See pages 629–34 for a brief introduction and a note on sources.

Illustrations

Preface

"There is properly no history; only biography," wrote Ralph Waldo Emerson.[1]

If that is true of the general run of mankind, it is particularly applicable to George Washington. The story of his life is the story of the founding of America. His was the dominant personality in three of the most critical events in that founding: the Revolutionary War, the Constitutional Convention, and the first national administration. Had he not served as America's leader in those three events, all three would likely have failed. And America as we know it today would not exist.

Washington's contributions were clear to his contemporaries. He was called "The Father of His Country" as early as 1779, in Francis Bailey's *Lancaster Almanac.*[2] Those who knew him well joined in the praise. Benjamin Rush, a Congressman who served with Washington, wrote in 1775, "General Washington...seems to be one of those illustrious heroes whom Providence raises up once in three or four hundred years to save a nation from ruin.... There is not a king in Europe that would not look like a valet de chambre by his side."[3]

Francis Hopkinson, one of Washington's military aides, wrote: "To him the title of Excellency is applied with particular propriety. He is the best and greatest man the world ever knew.... He retreats like a General, and attacks like a Hero. Had he lived in the days of idolatry, he had been worshipped as a God."[4]

And Thomas Jefferson wrote in 1782, long before the Constitutional Convention and Washington's presidency, "[Washington's] memory will be adored while liberty shall have votaries, whose name shall triumph over time, and will in future ages assume its just station among the most celebrated worthies of the world."[5]

That high regard for Washington—and fascination with his life—has continued through the years, as reflected in the numerous studies done by both historians and journalists. A survey of the current *Books in Print,* which lists all available books from major publishers in the United States, reveals that more than one hundred studies of Washington's life and place in history are presently in print.[6] Literally thousands more, now out of print, can still be found on the shelves of libraries across the country.[7] Added to that total are the many collections of Washington's writings, which come in the aggregate to more than eighty volumes.[8]

Washington has been scrutinized and analyzed from every direction. Authors and scholars have looked at his private life, his religious life, his skills as a farmer, his military accomplishments, his ability as President. Complete volumes have been devoted to subjects as diverse as Washington's childhood, foreign policy, and role in forming the Constitution. Some researchers have written for very special interests, producing books on Washington's chinaware, his involvement in Masonry, and the music in his family. Other volumes discuss Washington and money, Washington and the law, Washington and the theatre, Washington as an employer and importer of labor, and Washington's pedigree.

Some have delighted in digging for dirty refuse in the rubble of history, seeking for ways to discredit our first President. Some have implied that Washington was improperly enamored of his best friend's wife, Sally Fairfax. Others have claimed that General Washington padded his Revolutionary War expense account, enriching himself while his country suffered impending bankruptcy.

Washington could swear a violent blue streak, they say, Washington took pleasure in the charms at his slave quarters. Washington was stern, humorless, ice cold. Such are the claims of some authors who take more pains to seek (or manufacture) Washington's foibles and failures than they take to learn who he really was.

In the face of the truth, such accusations turn to dust. As biographer James Thomas Flexner put it, "Most of the brickbats now being thrown at Washington are figments of the modern imagination."[8]

Who was the real George Washington? What was he really like? To find the answers to those questions, we have gone to the best source available, to the person who knew him best: Washington himself. Rather than analyze and dissect the man until nothing remains but faulty interpretations, we have told his story in simple terms, allowing him the privilege to present himself throughout.

The evidence leaves no doubt that Washington the man is entirely worthy of Washington the myth. Douglas Southall Freeman concluded the same after some nine years spent in researching and writing six volumes on Washington's life. In an introduction to the sixth volume, Dumas Malone wrote: "By the slow and painstaking processes of scholarship [Freeman] examined, verified, and preserved a major legend. . . . Some may have wondered then [during Washington's life] and some may wonder now if the man could have been as irreproachable, as inflexibly just, as dedicated a patriot as he seemed to be. The verdict of the scrupulous historian after years of unremitting inquiry is that, as nearly as can be in human life, the legend and the man were identical."[9]

Historian James Flexner, who wrote five volumes on Washington's life, came to a similar conclusion. Washington, he wrote, truly was "a great and good man." He added, "In all history, few men who possessed unassailable power have used that power so gently and self-effacingly for what their best instincts told them was the welfare of their neighbors and all mankind."[10]

In order to fully present both the life and thought of George Washington, we have divided this volume into two parts. Part I consists of the biography, and Part II contains selected quotations from Washington's writings and speeches. Together they provide a more meaningful and more complete portrait of George Washington. In both sections the passages quoted from Washington are carefully documented from original sources. A number of the sources for Part I, which are found in the Notes and References section, are accompanied by further explanatory material and editorial comments.

This book is published by the National Center for Constitutional Studies, an educational foundation dedicated to teaching Americans the principles of freedom in the tradition of our Founding Fathers. The AMERICAN CLASSIC SERIES, of which this volume is a part, is designed to help Americans understand and appreciate the Founders and the remarkable system of free government which they gave us.

The political, economic, and social challenges currently facing the United States have sparked an urgent and widespread search for "modern solutions." Ironically, the solutions have been readily available for more than two hundred years in the writings of our Founding Fathers. A careful analysis of recent U.S. history reveals that virtually every serious problem now confronting American society can be traced to a departure from the sound principles taught by these great statesmen. The citizen of today who turns to the Founders' writings is often surprised by their timeless relevance—and reminded that the self-evident truths which made us the freest and most prosperous country on earth can, with renewed attention, be put back to work again.

It is our earnest hope that the AMERICAN CLASSIC SERIES will prove to be an inspiration and a valuable resource to those who believe that this nation can yet fulfill its "manifest destiny" as a bulwark of freedom in the world.

JAY A. PARRY

Acknowledgments

We are indebted to many persons for their contributions to the preparation of this volume. The staffs of the J. Willard Marriott Library at the University of Utah and the Harold B. Lee Library at Brigham Young University, both of which house excellent collections in American history and biography, have been helpful and cooperative in identifying and making available many of the sources used in writing the biography and collecting the quotations for Part II. Dr. W. Cleon Skousen, founder of the National Center for Constitutional Studies and co-compiler of Part II, read the entire biography and made many valuable suggestions. Those who provided essential support have also been much appreciated: Lisa Carpenter, W. Glen Fairclough, Jr., and Rachel Williams did the typesetting; Vicki Parry and Suzanne Brady assisted with proofreading; and Susan Igo and E. Kay Watson handled the layout of the book. Sharon Norris designed the cover, and Paul David Thompson and Susan Igo conceived the graphic design.

We also express thanks to the many devoted Americans who have contributed financially to support the work of the National Center for Constitutional Studies, thus making this and other publications possible. Zeldon and Mary Lynne Nelson and LeRoy and Lillian Nelson have been particularly generous in supporting the publication of this volume.

Finally, each of us owes a debt of gratitude to a patient and loving wife and to other family members who have encouraged us and sacrificed to help us complete this endeavor.

George Washington: Biographical Highlights

1732 Born at Bridges Creek, Westmoreland County, Virginia, on February 22 (Old Style, February 11).

1743 His father, Augustine Washington, died April 12 at age 49 (age 11).

1749 Appointed official surveyor of Culpepper County, Virginia, on July 20 (age 17).

1751-52 Accompanied his older half-brother, Lawrence, to Barbados from September to March; while there, George contracted smallpox (ages 19–20).

1752 Appointed district adjutant general of the Virginia Militia on November 6, with the rank of major (age 20).

1753 Carried an official message to the French on the Ohio River, warning them to leave British territory; the journey lasted from October 31, 1753, to January 16, 1754 (age 21).

1754 Fought a battle with the French on May 28, the first engagement of the French and Indian War (age 22).

1755 On July 9, fought with General Edward Braddock and his army in a battle on the Monongahela River (age 23).

1755-58 Served as commander of the Virginia forces protecting the frontier from Indians (ages 23–26).

1759 Married Martha Custis on January 6 (age 26).

1759 Took his seat in the Virginia House of Burgesses on February 22; he served there until 1774 (age 27).

1774 Attended the First Continental Congress in Philadelphia in September and October (age 42).

1775 Attended the Second Continental Congress in Philadelphia beginning May 10; on June 15 was elected commander of the American army (age 43).

1776 Forced the British from Boston in March (age 44).

1776 From August to November, the British drove the Americans from Long Island, Harlem Heights, White Plains, Fort Washington, and Fort Lee (age 44).

1776 Washington and his forces defeated the British at Trenton, New Jersey, on December 26 (age 44).

1777 Met the British in battle at Princeton, New Jersey, in January (age 44); and at Brandywine and Germantown, Pennsylvania, in September and October (age 45).

1777 Began the terrible winter at Valley Forge on December 19 (age 45).

1778 Won an important victory at Monmouth, New Jersey, on June 28 (age 46).

1779 Established winter quarters at Morristown, New Jersey, in December where conditions were as extreme as those at Valley Forge (age 47).

1781 Besieged the British at Yorktown, Virginia, leading to a major British surrender on October 19 (age 49).

1783 Prevented an army coup through his famous Newburgh address on March 15 (age 51).

1783 Resigned his commission to Congress on December 23; two days later he and Martha celebrated Christmas at Mount Vernon for the first time in nine years (age 51).

1787 From May to September, presided at the Constitutional Convention in Philadelphia (age 55).

1789 Inaugurated President of the United States on April 30, after having been unanimously elected (age 57).

1789 On August 25 his mother, Mary Ball Washington, died at the age of 81 (age 57).

1793 Began second term as President on March 4 (age 61).

1793 Issued the proclamation of neutrality on April 22, declaring America neutral in European affairs (age 61).

1794 In September and October, called out the militia in response to the Whiskey Rebellion (age 62).

1795 On June 8, submitted to Congress the Jay Treaty, designed to resolve conflicts with England; the Senate ratified the treaty on August 18 (age 63).

1796 Issued his Farewell Address on September 17 (age 64).

1797 Attended the inauguration of his successor and former Vice-President, John Adams, on March 4 (age 65).

1798 On July 4, appointed commander of the American forces when war with France threatened; the difficulties were eventually solved without conflict (age 66).

1799 Died in his room at Mount Vernon on December 14, after a short illness; he was buried at Mount Vernon four days later (age 67); Martha died 2½ years later.

PART I

George Washington:
The Man Who United America

Jay A. Parry

and

Andrew M. Allison

Chapter 1

A Virginia Boyhood

After the frantic opening shots of the Revolutionary War were fired at Lexington and Concord in April 1775, volunteers for an American army swarmed into a rude encampment at Cambridge, outside of Boston. By July the newly appointed commander in chief, General George Washington, had journeyed up from Philadelphia to assume command. He soon found his greatest task to be suppressing the bitter jealousies, constant quarreling, and contention among his colonial troops. "Connecticut wants no Massachusetts man in their corps," he lamented in November. "Massachusetts thinks there is no necessity for Rhode Island men to be introduced among them; and New Hampshire says it's very hard that her valuable and experienced officers... should be discarded."[1] The squabbling never let up.

The Indispensable American

One wintry day Colonel John Glover raced up to the General's headquarters and reported breathlessly that fighting had erupted between his Massachusetts regiment and Daniel Morgan's crack Virginia riflemen. The incident had begun with some hard words and an angry exchange of snowballs; within minutes more than a thousand men were slugging it out in the open, snow-covered field. The camp officers desperately tried to restore order, but the brawl ignited pent-up passions that had been smoldering for months. Soon the rioting was completely out of control.

Without waiting to hear the whole story, Washington leaped onto his saddled horse outside the door and started off at a full gallop toward Glover's camp. His stallion flew over the pasture bars into the midst of the rioting troops. In an instant the six-foot, three-and-a-half-inch General was on the ground, rushing into the fray. He "seized two tall, brawny riflemen by the throat, keeping them at arm's length," and shook them in his powerful grip while thundering commands at their fellow soldiers. Immediately the tumult ceased.

"From the moment [I] saw Washington leap the bars at Cambridge," reflected a prominent colonial leader who witnessed the incident, "and realized his personal ascendancy over the turbulent tempers of his men in their moments of wildest excitement, [I] never faltered in the faith that we had the right man to lead the cause of American liberty."[2]

It is impossible to fully calculate the influence of George Washington on the formation and early development of the United States. In our own day historians wonder whether any other figure in its history could have done what he did to unite first a fractious army, then thirteen wrangling and strongly independent states. One historian has declared: "If there ever was an indispensable leader at a critical moment in history, it was George Washington. In the formative years of the American republic, roughly between 1776 and 1796, the man, the moment, and the crisis coincided. It was the sheer personality of Washington that was the decisive element in the three crucial events of early America—the Revolutionary War, the Constitutional Convention, and the first national administration."[3]

A Virginian of Royal Descent

The blood of natural command was pulsing through George Washington's veins: some genealogists have traced his descent through fifty-five generations from Odin, the heroic founder of the great Viking kingdom of Scandinavia. According to one source, Odin's "life and character were so great and glorious that his people deified himself and [his] family, and thus established a Scandinavian mythology of equal magnitude and grandeur with that of ancient Greece and Egypt.... By his superior military talents Odin had endeared himself to his...subjects. He was successful in every combat, whence his warriors believed that victory hung on his arm. When he sent forth his soldiers to any expedition he laid his hands upon them and blessed them; they then believed themselves invincible."[4]

Many years later the Washington family of England was founded by Thorfin the Dane, a descendant of Odin through the royal line of Denmark. The family derived its name from the ancient village of Wassyngton in the county of Yorkshire, where many of Thorfin's descendants lived during the eleventh and twelfth centuries. [5] One of the family members, a young man named John Washington, sailed from England in the 1650s, crossing the wide Atlantic to America. He landed in the British colony of Virginia, where he accumulated a sizable estate, reared a family, and eventually served as a lieutenant colonel in the militia. In addition, like his great-grandson after him, he was elected to the first popular assembly in America, the Virginia House of Burgesses.[6]

Most of the Washington lands in Virginia lay along the "Northern Neck," a long peninsula reaching into Chesapeake Bay between the Potomac and Rappahannock rivers. One of these properties was the Pope's Creek farm (later called "Wakefield"), a small tract on the south bank of the Potomac. There, in a modest four-room house, lived John Washington's grandson Augustine. Augustine married Jane Butler and fathered four children, but only two of them—Lawrence

George Washington's birthplace, Pope's Creek farm, on the south bank of the Potomac River in Virginia. George lived here until he was three years old, then moved with his family to the property that later became Mount Vernon.

and Augustine—survived and grew to maturity. When Jane died after bearing her fourth child, Augustine married a second time in 1730. At ten o'clock in the morning of February 22, 1732, his new wife, Mary Ball, presented Augustine with their firstborn, a large-boned, healthy boy. They named him George Washington. [7]

Growing Up on the Farm

George's father was called "Gus" by his friends. According to one of them, he was "blond, of fine proportions and great physical strength, and stood six feet in his stockings." [8] Like his grandfather, John Washington, he became a skillful land trader. In 1735, Gus moved his family to a property he had acquired forty miles up the Potomac, a 2,500-acre farm on Little Hunting Creek called Epsewasson.

This site, later renamed Mount Vernon, was probably the scene of young George's first memories. When the boy became a man, he inherited the farm and built his now-famous home there. Ten miles farther up the river was a swampy area where a beautiful city would someday rise to become the seat of the American government and make the name of Washington famous worldwide.

But those great events were all in the distant future as curious three-year-old George Washington first began to explore the new world of Little Hunting Creek. We know very little of his earliest years. [9] Epsewasson was in an isolated part of the country, so George was acquainted with very few people outside his family circle. He was the oldest child at home because his two older half-brothers, Lawrence and Augustine (called Austin), were away at a boarding school in England, and his half-sister Jane had died shortly before his third birthday. However, other siblings came quickly during these years, and before long George had acquired a younger sister, Betty, and three younger brothers: Samuel, John Augustine ("Jack"), and Charles. In later life he remembered Jack, four years his junior, as "the intimate companion of my youth."[10] The two remained close until Jack died in 1787.

Caring for numerous farm animals and performing the drudgery of daily chores undoubtedly consumed much of George's time while he was growing up. A few weeks before he turned seven years of age, the static routine of his life was interrupted by a new adventure. The family moved again, this time to a recently purchased 260-acre tract on the north bank of the Rappahannock. They called their new home Ferry Farm, and just across the river was something George had never seen before—a town. His parents said it was named Fredericksburg.

Entering the World of Knowledge

The historical record is almost silent about the education of George Washington. What schooling he did receive seems to have begun soon after the move to Ferry Farm, and continued off and on for six to eight years. There is some evidence that George may have been instructed part of the time by a hired tutor, and he may have been enrolled briefly in a school at Fredericksburg.[11] But he appears to have received most of his early training from his father and his half-brother Lawrence, both of whom had studied at the reputable Appleby School in Westmoreland, England.[12]

Whatever the sources of his schooling, George struggled throughout his life under a "consciousness of a defective education."[13] He learned none of the classical or European languages, and although he had a natural appreciation for music, he could neither sing nor play an instrument.[14]

However, his surviving written exercises show that he gained early proficiency in handwriting and "ciphering" (computing arithmetically), and soon advanced into plane trigonometry, geometry, and surveying. His skills as a surveyor were of major importance to him later on.

Young Washington also studied geography, climatology, astronomy, and history, and spent a good deal of time reading popular books of the day. One of these was Joseph Addison's *The Tragedy of Cato.* This book engendered in Washington a love for the theater and fostered his lifelong commitment to the principles of republican government. [15]

The "Rules of Civility and Decent Behavior"

Perhaps the most interesting and revealing item found in young Washington's exercise books is a collection of 110 polite maxims under the title "Rules of Civility and Decent Behavior in Company and Conversation." Taken from a sixteenth-century French Jesuit publication, this list included some quaint but highly pertinent advice for people attempting to exhibit a few basic refinements in a frontier culture. For example:

> In the presence of others, sing not to yourself with a humming noise nor drum with your fingers or feet.
>
> Kill no vermin, as fleas, lice, ticks, etc., in the sight of others.
>
> Spit not into the fire,... nor set your feet upon the fire, especially if there be meat before it.
>
> Cleanse not your teeth with the tablecloth, napkin, fork, or knife.

Others of these rules dealt with weightier matters, and when the boy became a man their influence was reflected in his life and demeanor. Here are additional samples of the bits of wisdom taken from his copybook:

Let your countenance be pleasant, but in serious matters somewhat grave.

Show not yourself glad at the misfortune of another, though he were your enemy.

In writing or speaking, give to every person his due title according to his degree and the custom of the place.

When a man does all he can, though it succeeds not well, blame not him that did it.

Strive not with your superiors in argument, but always submit your judgment to others with modesty.

Associate yourself with men of good quality if you esteem your own reputation; for 'tis better to be alone than in bad company.

Let your conversation be without malice or envy.... And in all causes of passion admit reason to govern.

Undertake not what you cannot perform, but be careful to keep your promise.

When you speak of God and his attributes, let it be seriously and with reverence. Honor and obey your natural parents although they be poor.

Let your recreations be manful, not sinful.

Labor to keep alive in your breast that little spark of celestial fire called conscience. [16]

The Distant Winds of War

In 1738, just about the time George was receiving his first lessons in reading and writing, his half-brother Lawrence returned from his schooling in England. He had sailed from Virginia before his father's second marriage, so this was his first introduction to George and the younger siblings. Now twenty years old, Lawrence was a well-educated young gentleman of aristocratic bearing, and he immediately became a hero in the eyes of his admiring six-year-old half-brother.

Opening another chapter in an endless series of European wars, in 1840 England entered into an angry squabble with Spain, and the resulting patriotic fervor spread to the British colonists in North America. Within two years after his return, Lawrence Washington was commissioned as a captain over one of the four Virginia companies in the so-called American Regiment. Soon thereafter he was appointed to join Admiral Edward Vernon's expedition to South America for a planned assault on the Spanish stronghold of Cartagena (located on what is now the northeast coast of Colombia).

George eagerly looked forward to Lawrence's letters to the family. "War is horrid in fact, but much more so in imagination," Lawrence reported in one. "We there have learned to live on ordinary diet; to watch much and disregard the noise or shot of cannon."[17] It was easy for an impressionable George to envision the glories of the battlefield, and he probably dreamed of the day when he too could enjoy the flash of cannon and the bright colors of a soldier's uniform.

Tragedy Strikes the Washington Household

Admiral Vernon's expedition was unsuccessful, but Lawrence returned safely in 1742. George continued his studies and his farm chores, and when the weather permitted he was also allowed to spend time with some of his cousins across the peninsula, in the Chotank district of the Potomac. Their boyish laughter rang through the forests as they raced horses, went swimming, and shared the excitement of canoeing.

On one of these happy days at Chotank in the spring of 1743, an agitated horseman pulled up with an urgent message: George was to return home at once; his father was dangerously ill. The boy rushed back to Ferry Farm, where he saw his powerful father lying helpless in his bed, surrounded by grieving family members. On April 12, at the age of forty-nine, Gus Washington was gone. [18] George was only eleven years old, and the agony of his emotions in losing his father left an emptiness that lasted for years to come.

Uplifting Influences During the Teenage Years

With his father gone, Washington was left in the care of his mother. She was a demanding, strong-willed woman, and young George sometimes found himself at odds with her. Nevertheless, in later life he spoke affectionately of "my reverend mother, by whose maternal hand (early deprived of a father) I was led from childhood." [19]

Mary Ball Washington, George's mother. Mary had five children— George, Betty, Samuel, John, and Charles—before her husband died in 1743. She lived long enough to see her oldest son become the first President of the United States.

He was drawn even closer to his half-brother Lawrence, who evidently served as his principal teacher from this time on. Having inherited the Little Hunting Creek property, Lawrence built a comfortable new home there and renamed the estate Mount Vernon, in honor of his respected former military commander. This was the same farm where George had lived for several years as a small boy. He now spent much of his time at Mount Vernon, studying under Lawrence and riding with him in the management of the plantation. Though he did not yet know it, someday Mount Vernon would belong to him.

In the summer of 1743 Lawrence married wealthy Anne Fairfax. Anne's father, Colonel William Fairfax, was the cousin and personal agent of Thomas, Lord Fairfax, the proprietor of a vast tract of Virginia land covering more than five million acres between the Potomac and the Rappahannock. The aristocratic Fairfax family, living in an attractive mansion less than five miles from Mount Vernon, became an important cultural influence in George's life. It is likely that his early exposure to the Fairfaxes helped him develop the polished manners and dignified bearing that later won the admiration and respect of so many of his contemporaries.

The Sea Beckons

As a young teenager, George Washington was already large for his age. By the time of his fourteenth birthday he was probably approaching his father's full height, and before long he would be even taller.

Besides his large frame and physical strength, he also exhibited an admirable degree of soberness and emotional maturity. He had progressed very well in his studies, and the time soon arrived when he began to think seriously about what he would do with his life.

One exciting possibility presented itself in September

1746, while George was at Ferry Farm with his mother. A letter from Lawrence announced that a midshipman was needed on a Royal Navy vessel now stationed off the Virginia coast, and that Colonel William Fairfax and others were willing to help George secure the appointment. Lawrence also included a letter to George's mother, urging her approval.

Mary Ball Washington was not eager to see her oldest son go to sea. Some of the friends she consulted thought it was an excellent idea, and at one point she softened so much that George actually had his "baggage prepared for embarkation."[20] But a neighbor noted that "she offers several trifling objections, . . . and I find that one word against [George's] going has more weight than ten for it."[21] Soon thereafter, the whole scheme "was abandoned in consequence of [her] earnest solicitations."[22] There are some indications that George felt deeply disappointed in missing this opportunity, but one cannot help wondering today how American history might have changed if Mary Ball Washington had launched her son on a career as a British sailor in the king's service.

Chapter 2

Expanding Horizons

Having been denied a naval career, George dusted off his father's surveying instruments and went to work. By the end of the summer of 1747, at the age of fifteen, he had acquired a good deal of experience and was proving himself a skillful surveyor in his own right. He enjoyed the independence and satisfaction of earning his own money, and occasionally he was even able to loan small amounts—without interest—to friends and relatives who were out of funds. [1]

Another winter passed slowly, and when the weather began to ease up George was ready to head back into the woods. Just about the time he turned sixteen in February 1748, he was invited to join a surveying expedition for Lord Fairfax which was assigned to explore the South Branch of the Potomac River in northwest Virginia. He eagerly accepted the invitation.

First Adventure on the Virginia Frontier

On March 11 the surveyors began their trek toward the Virginia frontier. An entry George wrote in his diary four days later suggests that he had not yet fully adjusted to the inconveniences of the primitive life in the wilderness. He wrote:

> We ... worked hard till night and then returned to [Isaac] Pennington's. We got our suppers and were lighted into a room; and I, not being so good a woodsman as the rest of my company, stripped myself very orderly and went into the bed, as they called it, when to my surprise I found it to be nothing but a little straw matted together without sheets or anything else, but only one threadbare blanket with double its weight of vermin, such as lice, fleas, etc. I was glad to get up (as soon as the light was carried from us) and put on my clothes and lie as my companions. Had we not ... been very tired, I am sure we should not have slept much that night. I made a promise not to sleep [in the same manner] from that time forward, choosing rather to sleep in the open air before a fire. [2]

After the next day's labors they scrubbed themselves thoroughly "to get rid of the game we had caught the night before" and somehow managed to find lodging which offered "a good feather bed with clean sheets, which was ... very agreeable." [3]

As they continued westward, George and his companions swam their horses across swollen rivers, slept under the stars and feasted on wild turkeys cooked over open campfires, had their tents carried away twice by high winds, and on one occasion awoke to find their straw beds in flames. But through it all they successfully surveyed or "ran off" hundreds of acres along the South Branch.

George described traveling over "the worst road that ever was trod by man or beast,"[4] where they met an Indian war party "with only one scalp."[5] The Indians entertained them with a vigorous war dance—which George considered more "comical" than frightening. During the return trip, he and one of the other young men got lost for a time in the Blue Ridge Mountains and encountered a rattlesnake, "the first we had seen in all our journey."[6] But by April 13 George was back at Mount Vernon, glad to be home with the comforts of civilization. [7]

"An Ardent Wish to See the Right of Questions"

The expedition had been hampered by constant, heavy rainfall, but George and his fellow surveyors had faithfully carried out their assignment. Undeterred by rain-soaked clothing, mud, threatening river crossings, and potentially violent Indians, they had faced off the danger and emerged victorious. This wilderness adventure, which lasted only a month, was an experience Washington never forgot. And it bore useful fruit in the years that followed. It gave him a knowledge of the frontier which later proved invaluable in launching his military career, and it enabled him to further develop the skills and the personal maturity which were essential as he advanced into adulthood.

At the age of sixteen, George already had the respect of many of the adults who knew him. One of them, a Buckner Stith, described him as "a sound looking, modest, large-boned young man."[7] And even the critical Lord Fairfax, who had hired George to take part in the surveying expedition, spoke of him in quite complimentary terms:

He is strong and hardy, and as good a master of a horse as any could desire. His education might have been bettered, but what he has is accurate and inclines him to much life out of doors. He is very grave for one of his age, and reserved in his intercourse; not a great talker at any time. His mind appears to me to act slowly, but, on the whole, to reach just conclusions, and he has an ardent wish to see the right of questions. [8]

Youthful Diversions

While it is true that the teenaged Washington was "very grave for... his age," he also enjoyed lighter moments. He occasionally visited Yorktown to do shopping for his mother, and on leisurely days he played billiards and other games with Lawrence and a few of the neighbors. He also demonstrated a natural ability at "riding to hounds." In the fall of 1748 he even paid for some dancing lessons. [9] Several months later he complained that he was unable to get away from Ferry Farm to attend the dances because he lacked enough money to buy corn for his horse. [10]

Virginia colonial life encouraged gregarious, festive activity, so young Washington had adequate opportunity to mingle with his peers at special gatherings and practice his social graces. Through such contacts he began to take an increasing interest in the opposite sex. His earliest romantic encounters were not always satisfactory, however, as is shown in this note to a "dear friend":

> My place of residence is at present at his Lordship's, where I might, were my heart disengaged, pass my time very pleasantly, as there's a very agreeable young lady [who] lives in the same house.... But as that's only adding fuel to [the] fire, it makes me the more uneasy, for by often and unavoidably being in company with her, [it] revives my former passion for your Lowland Beauty; whereas were I

to live more retired from young women, I might in some measure alleviate my sorrows by burying that chaste and troublesome passion in the grave of oblivion....

That's the only antidote or remedy that I ever shall be relieved by...as I am well convinced [that] were I ever to attempt anything, I should only get a denial, which would be only adding grief to uneasiness. [11]

"The Foundation of a Noble Estate"

Whether it was to forget about the young ladies or to earn the money he needed to feed his horse, George spent more and more time away from home on surveying assignments. In the summer of 1749 he helped survey the lots and drew up the plans for the new town of Alexandria. Shortly afterward he received a surveyor's commission from the College of William and Mary, and in November he was appointed to head a survey team for Lord Fairfax in the Shenandoah Valley. The following spring found him there again for the same purpose. He was maturing rapidly and beginning to feel like a man of affairs, at least on the frontier.

As his earnings accumulated, George soon found better use for them than the weekend dances. In October 1750, at age eighteen, he began buying his own land in western Virginia. First came the small "Bullskin plantation" in Shenandoah. Later he purchased a nearby 453-acre tract, then another 550 acres in the town of Frederick (later Winchester). Other acquisitions followed in the next few months, and before long he was leasing some of his properties to new settlers. George looked on these land purchases as "the foundation of a noble estate," [12] and indeed this was only the beginning. During his lifetime he would eventually own over 60,000 acres.

A Voyage to Barbados

Lawrence Washington had been appointed adjutant of the Virginia militia after his return from the Cartagena expedition in 1742, and since 1744 he had also served as a member of the House of Burgesses in Williamsburg. But his attention to these duties was increasingly limited by his poor health. He had to request a leave of absence from the meeting of the Burgesses in 1748, and again the next year. His incessant coughing led to fears of "consumption," or tuberculosis, and the diagnosis proved to be correct.

Lawrence Washington, George's oldest half-brother, fourteen years his senior. Their father died when George was only eleven, and Lawrence became a sort of substitute father. Lawrence himself died nine years later.

In July 1749 Lawrence sailed across the Atlantic to consult physicians in London, but their crude treatments gave him no relief whatever. Neither did his visits to the warm springs of Berkeley on the upper Potomac in 1750 and 1751. Hoping that his ailing lungs might benefit from a milder climate, he decided in the fall of 1751 to journey to Barbados Island in the West Indies. George agreed to accompany him, and the two set out together in late September.

About five weeks later they landed at Bridgetown, the principal settlement and capital of Barbados. They found lodgings in the nearby countryside, where George was "perfectly enraptured with the beautiful prospects which every side presented to our view—the fields of cane, corn, fruit trees, etc., in a delightful green."[13] When not attending to Lawrence's needs, he was out exploring this tropical paradise and seeing what Bridgetown had to offer. Within the first few days after their arrival he paid his first visit to a military fortification, attended a stage play at the local theater, and sampled pineapples and other tropical taste delights for the first time.

A Bout with Smallpox

Then something happened that stopped George's explorations short: he was "strongly attacked"[14] by the dangerous and often fatal disease of smallpox, aptly described by the medical profession as a "scourge." During a widespread epidemic it had been known to wipe out a third of the population. The first symptoms occurred on November 17, and the physician who attended George did not finally release him until December 12. The pain and the fever he suffered were no doubt severe, but the only visible marks of his struggle were several light facial scars, which in later years were hardly noticeable. Far outweighing the physical suffering, however, was young Washington's subsequent immunity to the dreaded disease. This immunity proved to be a valuable protection to him during the Revolutionary War, when smallpox sometimes stalked the camps of the American soldiers.

With the passing of time Lawrence became discouraged. Despite assurances from the medical experts he visited in Barbados, he did not improve. Believing that his stay might be a long one, he sent his younger half-brother back to Virginia to resume his surveying career. George embarked on December 22, and the next day he recorded in his diary: "Met with a brisk trade wind and pretty large swell, which made the ship roll much and [made] me very sick."[15] (Perhaps it was just as well that he had not become a sailor at age fourteen!) He arrived safely at Yorktown, Virginia, on January 28, 1752. As he disembarked at the wharf, he could not have imagined the monumental events which would bring him to this place many years later. In a few days he was home at Mount Vernon.

Lawrence Returns to Die

About three months after George's departure from Barbados, Lawrence traveled to Bermuda, still in search of a cure. In April he sent a letter to his wife suggesting that she and their infant daughter might have George accompany them to Bermuda later in the year. But his next letter suspended any such plans and caused great uneasiness in the family: "If I grow worse," he said, "I shall hurry home to my grave."[16] Sometime in June he did arrive at Mount Vernon, and it was obvious that he would not last long. He spent his painful last days with those he loved most, prepared his will, and passed away on July 26, 1752.

Lawrence was only thirty-four years old at the time of his death, and the profound grief which George Washington felt in the loss of this beloved half-brother was reminiscent of his feelings at the tragic loss of his father nine years before.

"All Washingtons Are Born Old"

During his short twenty years, George also experienced his own share of serious physical ailments. Besides his bout with smallpox in Barbados, he had been stricken by "ague and fever...to extremity"[17] in late 1749, and by "a violent pleurisy which has reduced me very low"[18] in the spring of 1752.[19] But his strong constitution enabled him to rebound quickly from these attacks, and as soon as he had recuperated he was back in the woodlands with his surveying instruments.

George's love for the outdoors was matched by an ardent desire for a military career. He longed to follow in the footsteps of the older half-brother whom he had admired so devoutly since early childhood. Ironically, it was Lawrence's death that opened the way for his dream to be realized. As noted earlier, Lawrence had served for several years as adjutant of the Virginia militia. In late 1752 Governor Robert Dinwiddie and his council decided to divide the adjutancy among four men. Partly due to the influence of the Fairfax family, one of these posts was given to George. Even though he was not quite twenty-one years of age when he took the oath of office in early February 1753, he was commissioned to the rank of major. When complaints were heard that he was too young for such a responsible position, one of the Fairfaxes reportedly answered, "All Washingtons are born old."[20]

Chapter 3

A Dangerous Journey

I n 1753 developing international events involved the young Major Washington in a wilderness journey that became the greatest adventure of his early life. In the middle of that year word reached Governor Dinwiddie in Virginia that the French were building forts in the Ohio Valley, which was part of Virginia's chartered territory. The French, on the other hand, considered this area part of the Mississippi Basin, all of which their early explorers had claimed for France.

Already the British and the French had clashed in several major wars, and now the seeds were being sown for another. The French began their incursions in the early spring of 1753, building their first fort on the southern shore of Lake Erie, the site of present-day Erie, Pennsylvania. They then cut a road through ten miles of dense forest and built Fort Le Boeuf where modern Waterford, Pennsylvania, is located. Proceeding farther south they came to the Allegheny River, where they ousted the only settler, an English trapper and trader. There they planned to build Fort Venango the following year.

The Governor's Emissary

After receiving instructions from London, Governor Dinwiddie decided to send a stern message to the French commandant, warning him to evacuate the entire Ohio Valley immediately. When Washington heard of the governor's intention he rode all the way to Williamsburg to volunteer to carry the message. Governor Dinwiddie was pleased with his young major's enthusiasm and promptly commissioned him to deliver the warning. On the last day of October, Washington set forth on his thousand-mile journey.

Governor Robert Dinwiddie of Virginia. When Washington was twenty-one, Dinwiddie sent him into the Virginia frontier to warn the French away from British territory. Three years later, Dinwiddie named Washington commander in chief of Virginia's militia.

At first he traveled northwest along the Potomac River, until the trail led upward through the Blue Ridge Mountains. Then he passed down into the beautiful Shenandoah Valley and, after following it in a northerly direction, crossed the Allegheny Mountains to reach the broad expanse of the Ohio Valley.

En route, Washington engaged the services of an interpreter, a prominent frontier guide named Christopher Gist, and also hired several men to assist with the horses and baggage. On November 23, 1753, the major reached the point where the Allegheny and Monongahela rivers come together and flow into the great Ohio. As Washington studied the terrain he made careful note to recommend this spot as an ideal place to build a British fort. It subsequently became Fort Pitt and even later a major metropolis, the city of Pittsburgh.

Traveling fifteen miles down the Ohio to an Indian settlement called Logstown, Washington conferred with the powerful Seneca chief, Half King, who had recently visited the French to protest any further troop movements or the building of forts. Half King and several other Indians agreed to accompany Washington on his mission.

They started up the Allegheny toward Fort Le Boeuf, the French headquarters. On December 4 they arrived in Venango, the trading post formerly occupied by the English trapper.

At Venango they sat at supper with several French soldiers stationed there. "The wine," wrote Washington, "as they dosed themselves pretty plentifully with it, soon banished the restraint which at first appeared in their conversation, and gave license to their tongues to reveal their sentiments more freely. They told me it was their absolute design to take possession of the Ohio, and by G-- they would do it."[1]

Facing the French Commandant

Finally, on December 11, Major Washington and his party

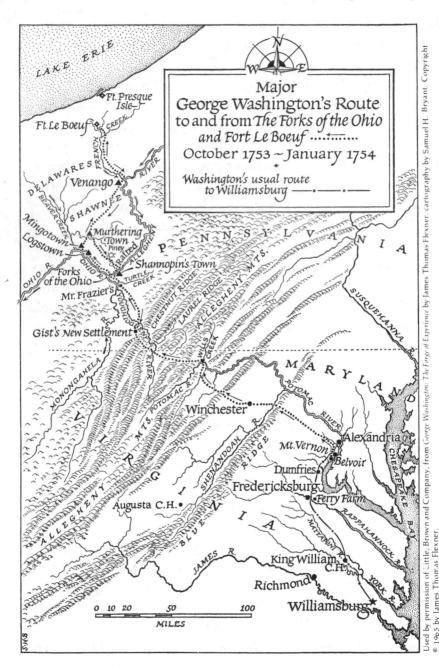

Major
George Washington's Route
to and from The Forks of the Ohio
and Fort Le Boeuf ...⋅......
October 1753 ~ January 1754

Washington's usual route
to Williamsburg ——⋅——⋅——

reached Fort Le Boeuf. The next day he met the elderly French commandant, Jacques Le Gardeur de Saint-Pierre, and delivered Governor Dinwiddie's letter. Saint-Pierre received the tall, young Virginian with cordiality, but it soon became obvious that the French had no intention of bending to the British demands. Washington perceived exactly what they had in mind when he counted more than two hundred canoes waiting by the river's edge for a major descent on the valley at the first sign of spring thaw.

Meanwhile, for two full days Saint-Pierre put off making a formal reply to Washington. His reason for the delay was easily apparent; as Washington noted with some distress, "Every stratagem that the most fruitful brain could invent was practiced to get the Half King won to their interest."[2]

Of course, all European military leaders knew that the favor or cooperation of the native Americans could be a decisive factor in any territorial conflicts in the New World. Therefore, while Saint-Pierre stalled in giving his reply, the French officers and even the commandant himself tried every way possible to entice the Indians to remain with them when Washington left. They repeatedly offered to supply them with guns, liquor, and other articles or gifts.

Nevertheless, when Saint-Pierre finally turned over the sealed packet containing his reply, Major Washington induced Half King and his tribesmen to return with him.[3] They left on December 16, but several French soldiers trailed along behind in canoes to offer the Indians still more liquor to buy their support. Again they were unsuccessful. Interpreter Christopher Gist recorded gleefully in his journal that "we had the pleasure of seeing the French [canoes] overset, and the brandy and wine floating in the creek.... [We] left them to shift for themselves."[4]

A Close Brush with Death

Half King and his warriors separated from the white men
on December 22, and Major Washington's party continued
their journey homeward. The weather was bitterly cold, and
by the day after Christmas three of the men were so
frostbitten and the horses were so weary that they could go
no farther. Nevertheless, Washington felt compelled to press
on. "As I was uneasy to get back to make a report of my
proceedings to his honor the Governor," Washington wrote,
"I determined to prosecute my journey the nearest way
through the woods on foot."[5] Gist consented to go with him,
so they wrapped themselves in "match coats" and covered
eighteen miles that afternoon.

The next day they engaged an Indian guide, but after he
had led them several miles through the woods he suddenly
wheeled around in a snowy meadow and fired his rifle
straight at them. Fortunately the bullet rustled harmlessly
through the bushes, and they both rushed him as he stood
behind a tree to reload. Gist wanted to kill the treacherous
Indian, but Washington prevented him, letting their attacker
go free. But what if he returned with murderous accomplices?
With fear spurring them on, Washington and Gist pushed on
through the forest, racing into the dark night without daring
even to stop and light a fire.[6]

Most of the creeks were frozen over, but when Washington and Gist reached the Allegheny on the morning of
December 29 they found the frigid waters still flowing at a
tremendous pace. With only a single hatchet, they spent the
entire day constructing a crude raft to cross the ice-choked
river. The task was completed just after sundown. In the
evening gloom the two men placed their packs on the heavy
structure and poled away from the bank. Within seconds they

George Washington and Christopher Gist cross the Allegheny River. As they crossed, a chunk of ice rammed into Washington's pole with such force that it threw him into the water, nearly drowning him.

knew they were in trouble. Washington wrote:

> Before we got half over, we were jammed in the ice in such a manner that we expected every moment our raft would sink and we [would] perish. I put out my setting pole to try to stop the raft that the ice might pass by, when the rapidity of the stream threw it with so much violence against the pole that it jerked me into ten feet [of] water. But I fortunately saved myself by catching hold of one of the raft logs. [7]

The major's powerful arms quickly pulled him back onto the raft, but the force of the river made it impossible to reach either shore. With great effort the two men maneuvered to a tiny island, where, without a fire, they shivered through the freezing night. Washington was soaked to the skin and unable to dry off, but, amazingly, neither he nor Gist succumbed to the sub-zero temperatures. Still, "the cold was so extremely severe that Mr. Gist got all his fingers and some of his toes frozen."[8] Gist acknowledged, however, that "the cold did us some service, for in the morning [the river] was frozen hard enough for us to pass over on the ice."[9]

Stepping onto the International Stage

Reaching Gist's settlement by January 2, 1754, Washington purchased a horse and saddle, then sped toward Williamsburg alone. On January 16 he appeared before Governor Dinwiddie and handed him Saint-Pierre's letter, which denied the British claims to the Ohio and rejected Dinwiddie's demand for the withdrawal of the French forces. Washington described what he had seen at Fort Le Boeuf—the strength of French defenses, the preparations being made for further troop movements, and the attitudes of the officers and Indians with whom he had spoken.

Impressed by Washington's verbal account of his long journey, the Governor asked for a written report to be prepared for the next day's executive council meeting. The young major hurriedly assembled a narrative of the trek based on the rough notes he had penned during the past three months. It was printed and distributed by order of the governor under the title *The Journal of Major George Washington.* The publication included the letter of Dinwiddie to Saint-Pierre and his disdainful reply.[10] This small volume caused great excitement in the American colonies and was soon reprinted in London, where it also created considerable alarm.

Thus, at the age of twenty-one, Washington had achieved a

measure of renown on both sides of the Atlantic. Although he could not have fully realized it at the time, he had already begun to play an important role on the world stage. One far-reaching contribution was his recommendation to Governor Dinwiddie that a fort be built at the junction of the Monongahela and Allegheny rivers, a step which later proved to be "the prime cause of the outbreak of hostilities in the French and Indian War."[11] And George Washington himself, as it turned out, was leader of the force that would fire the opening shots of that international conflict.

Chapter 4

The Thick of Battle

Acting on Washington's suggestion that a fort be built at the forks of the Ohio, Governor Dinwiddie sent a Captain William Trent in February 1754 to erect a stockade where the Allegheny and Monongahela rivers merged into the Ohio. The following month Dinwiddie promoted Major Washington to lieutenant colonel and placed him at the head of an advanced guard to protect the new fortification against French troops in the area. After recruiting over a hundred men in the vicinity of Alexandria, Lieutenant Colonel Washington trained and organized his small regiment, collected needed provisions, and on April 2 marched his militia into the wilderness. This advanced guard was to be joined as soon as possible by the main body of the expedition, under the command of experienced Colonel Joshua Fry.

During these weeks of recruiting, training, organizing, and outfitting his men, Washington got a bitter foretaste of the problems over which he would someday agonize as commander in chief of the American army. He encountered numerous objections to enlistment, many utterly ridiculous. Then he found that many who had enlisted were "without shoes, others want stockings, some are without shirts, and not a few... have scarce a coat or waistcoat to their backs."[1] He also learned that it was a "fatiguing" experience to manage "a number of self-willed, ungovernable people."[2]

Upon completing the first leg of his march to the Ohio, the lieutenant colonel was distressed to discover that the additional horses, wagons, and provisions which were supposed to be waiting at the Wills Creek settlement had not been collected. Even worse, he received word that the French had just captured and strengthened Captain Trent's new British fortification. It was now occupied by over a thousand French troops and renamed Fort Duquesne. Troubled but undaunted, Washington gathered what further supplies he could procure and continued his march, still feeling a "glowing zeal"[3] and believing that the fort could be retaken upon the arrival of Colonel Fry's forces. In the meantime he planned to have his advanced guard hold a position from which they could move on the enemy when Fry's forces joined him.

"I Heard the Bullets Whistle"

Washington's resolve to continue toward the Ohio was bolstered by an urgent plea from Half King, the Seneca chief who had accompanied him to Fort Le Boeuf the previous winter. "Come as soon as possible," urged Chief Half King. "You will find us as ready to encounter with [the French] as you are yourselves.... If you do not come to our assistance now, we are entirely undone."[4] He seemed to have particular confidence in the abilities of Lieutenant Colonel Washington to lead the attack, calling him "Caunotaucarius" (Devourer of Villages).[5]

Washington and about forty of his men pushed ahead to a site near Redstone Creek, where they met Half King and six or seven other Indians on the night of May 27. They had known for two days that a French scouting party of about fifty was somewhere nearby, and early the next morning two Seneca braves discovered the Frenchmen lurking in the woods. Acting without delay, Washington and Half King ordered their men to silently surround the enemy camp, and upon the lieutenant colonel's signal they discharged their rifles. The French soldiers desperately returned the fire, but their commander lay dying and within minutes they had given up the fight. Those who had not been killed were taken as prisoners.

For a few tense moments Washington had difficulty preventing his fierce ally, Half King, from killing and scalping the prisoners. Half King swore he would be avenged of the French for allowing their Indian allies to kill, boil, and eat his father. The earnest young Virginian eventually prevailed over the furious Indian, and the frightened French prisoners remained safe.

As he looked back on the brief engagement, Washington confessed that he had been exhilarated by the noise and smoke of his first victory in battle. Three days afterward he wrote naively to his brother Jack, "I heard the bullets whistle, and, believe me, there is something charming in the sound."[6] And in a letter to Governor Dinwiddie, he declared his eagerness to press forward with the campaign: "If the whole detachment of the French behave with no more resolution than this chosen party did, I flatter myself we shall have no great trouble in driving them to...Montreal."[7]

"We Expect Every Hour to Be Attacked"

Little more could be done, however, until Colonel Fry came up with his main contingent of troops. While awaiting their arrival, Washington's advanced force backtracked several miles and hastily erected a fortification in Great Meadows, where they had found a position protected by natural entrenchments on each side. The lieutenant colonel appropriately named this rude stockade Fort Necessity. Believing that the French would soon be there in force, he sent an urgent note to Fry, who was still over a week's journey away: "If there does not come a sufficient reinforcement, we must either quit our ground and retreat to you, or fight very unequal numbers, which I will do before I will give up one inch of what we have gained."[8] By the last day of May the tension was almost unbearable: "We expect every hour to be attacked by superior force."[9]

But just as Washington was writing these words, Colonel Fry was breathing his last. Several days before, he had suffered an agonizing fall from his horse, and on May 31 he died at Wills Creek. With Fry's untimely death, Washington was elevated to full colonel, becoming the senior field officer of the Virginia militia—despite his complete lack of experience. Feeling alone and inadequate, he continued his preparations against the large French force rumored to be marching toward Great Meadows. However, an entire month dragged by without any sign of the enemy. This provided time for the arrival of reinforcements from Wills Creek, but Fry's "main force" turned out to be fewer than two hundred men—not the seven hundred or more Washington had been promised. Also missing was the heavy artillery Washington was expecting. The new troops did bring a few small swivel guns in addition to their personal arms, but every day the new commander's frightening sense of vulnerability grew. Nevertheless, Washington made ready the best he could.

The Surrender of Fort Necessity

About eleven o'clock on the morning of July 3, after several hours of drenching rain, long columns of French soldiers and a sizable force of Indians began moving into Great Meadows—over seven hundred of them altogether. After their opening volley they broke their lines and scattered into the surrounding forest, where "from every little rising, tree, stump, stone, and bush," wrote Washington, they "kept up a constant, galling fire upon us."[10] The French had found the fort's fatal weakness: the men behind the trenches were dangerously exposed to fire from the surrounding bushy slopes. The battle was waged in "the most tremendous rain that can be conceived,"[11] and by late afternoon the trenches around the fort were nearly filled with water. As the downpour continued, the Virginians found it virtually impossible to keep their guns and powder dry enough to fire. One by one the men and their officers were picked off by the deadly barrage from the hillside. Bodies piled in the trenches; frightened soldiers sloshed frantically through the mud seeking an ever-safer position.

The murky afternoon passed and the evening sky began to darken. Then a clear French voice cried out of the gloomy woods: "*Voulez-vous parler?*"[12] No, replied Colonel Washington, he was not willing to parley—that would merely permit the enemy to get a better look at the stockade's defenses. Instead, he sent out an officer to receive a written proposal from the French commander. When it was brought back and translated, the document offered to allow the Americans to return home with their arms if they would surrender the fort. Washington's plight was desperate: more than a third of his original fighting force of 284 had been killed or wounded, his weapons were now almost useless, and the flour and bacon left in the stores would feed his troops only three more days. The terms of surrender were generous—probably because the confrontation had been only a disastrous skirmish; no war had yet been declared. He wearily signed the capitulation papers later that night. The next morning the heartsick survivors marched out of Fort Necessity, carrying their wounded with them. It was the fourth of July, 1754.

Colonel Washington Resigns His Commission

More than three months passed before Washington reached Virginia's capital to report the distressing details of his unsuccessful mission. Surprisingly, however, the loss of Fort Necessity did not diminish the young colonel's reputation in the eyes of the public. All opinion makers seemed to agree that the outcome of the expedition would have been quite different if the promised reinforcements had been provided. Washington was enthusiastically welcomed in Alexandria and elsewhere after he emerged from the wilderness, and the House of Burgesses voted a resolution of thanks to him and his officers for their courageous endeavors on behalf of the British Crown. [13]

Then came an announcement that shook the earth under Washington's feet: Governor Dinwiddie had decided to reorganize the entire Virginia militia and to reduce the rank of all officers above captain! This was a move to placate the officers from England, those of the "regular establishment," who were incensed at having to serve under colonials appointed as their superiors. "In short," wrote Washington, "every captain bearing the King's commission, every half-pay officer or other appearing with such a commission, would rank before me."[14]

Considering this a deliberate insult to his fellow Virginia countrymen and to himself personally, he submitted his resignation. Yet he made no secret of his "reluctance to quit the service. . . . My inclinations," he said, "are strongly bent to arms."[15] Even though Washington's hopes to make a career of military service seemed to waft away on the winds of this foolish policy, he was not yet ready to abandon the glories of military life. Despite his resignation, he had already determined to "serve the next campaign as a volunteer."[16]

"A Young Man of Extraordinary and Exalted Character"

In December 1754 Washington leased Mount Vernon from Lawrence's widow, Anne. She was now remarried and had little use for the property. His venture into farming had lasted only a few months, however, when a letter came in March that unexpectedly propelled him back into military service. Two regiments of British regulars had recently landed in Virginia under the command of Major General Edward Braddock; their assignment was to march to the Ohio and retake Fort Duquesne from the French. Washington personally was unknown to Braddock, but his reputation certainly was not. The young Virginian (now twenty-three years old) was one of the few military men in the colonies who was familiar with the rugged route to be traveled by Braddock's army. It was predictable, then, that soon after the troops landed he was invited to join the general's personal staff as an aide-de-camp.

Washington's behavior soon convinced those around him that he was no commonplace soldier. "He strikes me," one wrote, "as being a young man of extraordinary and exalted character, and is destined to make no inconsiderable figure in our country."[17]

Major General Edward Braddock, the commander of the ill-fated British expedition against the French at Fort Duquesne. Washington, at age twenty-three, served as an aide-de-camp to Braddock.

Knowing that he had the confidence of General Braddock, Washington felt free to express his views with openness and candor. For example, Braddock repeatedly and vehemently denounced the "supineness" of the American colonists because of the inadequate number of teams and wagons supplied to transport his army's provisions over the mountains. According to one eyewitness, Braddock's tirades led the tall officer from Virginia to "put his two thumbs up into the armpits of his vest" and bluntly contend that the general should place the blame on those who had contracted to supply the wagons—not the colonists as a whole.[18] Braddock was quite surprised at being contradicted with such firmness by one of his subordinates. Throwing up his hands, he turned to his other officers and protested: "What think you of this from a young hand—a beardless boy?"[19]

The Manner of War

Young Colonel Washington was soon to learn that Major General Edward Braddock ran his army by the inflexible "rule of the book." Military discipline, European style, was harsh, unbending, and sometimes inhumanly cruel. The recent development of the flintlock musket with a socket bayonet had led commanders to develop "incessantly" drilled regulars who could "wheel and dress ranks amid the very smoke and stress of battle."[20] The slightest deviation, insubordination, or failure to perform could bring down upon the hapless culprit an avalanche of punishment which the modern military commander would find almost impossible to believe. A scant fifty years before Washington's day, "a British guardsman was sentenced to 12,600 lashes and nearly died after he received the first 1,800."[21]

As in his disciplinary measures, Braddock was also of the old school in military training, tactics, and procedures. He was not accustomed to taking advice from an aide. Had he done so, the young colonel from Virginia could have taught him more about fighting in the forests of America than all the wisdom of European militarists combined. Instead of resorting to the massive "fire without aiming" techniques of a European army, Colonel Washington would have ordered his men to quickly disperse, take cover, and then pick off specific enemy targets.

Once his staff was assembled, General Braddock proceeded toward Fort Duquesne with more than 2,000 men—1,400 British regulars in bright red coats, around 450 members of the Virginia militia, and some 300 axmen who were expert in cutting roads through the forests. Accompanying them, traveling mostly among the trees alongside the army, was an unknown number of Indians who were recommended to

Braddock as British allies.

In addition to George Washington, three of the officers in Braddock's army were later commanders in the War of Independence: Thomas Gage, who commanded the British in Boston, and American generals Horatio Gates and Charles Lee.

"I Was Seized with Violent Fevers"

In mid-June 1755, after the army had left Fort Cumberland on Wills Creek and traveled several miles, Washington fell seriously ill with the "bloody flux," which was moving with virulence through the troops. "I was seized with violent fevers and pains in my head, which continued without the least intermission.... My illness was too violent to suffer me to ride; therefore I was indebted to a covered wagon for some part of my transportation."[22] The camp surgeon, in fact, warned him that if he did not halt to rest a few days his life would be at risk. When Braddock heard the doctor's prescription, he ordered his disappointed aide to remain behind while an advanced column of over 1,400 men moved on toward its objective. Before the troops pulled out, however, Washington extracted "the General's word of honor, pledged in the most solemn manner, that I should be brought up before he arrived at [Fort] Duquesne."[23]

The fever worsened, racking his body, and at times he became delirious. But by the first week in July he was able to lie in a wagon again, jostling painfully along the rough wilderness road which led toward Braddock's camp. On July 8 he finally reached the advanced force, only about ten miles from the forks of the Ohio.

The morning of July 9, 1755, seemed to hold bright promise for the British regiment now closing in on Fort Duquesne.

Washington was especially eager to see the English flag planted there again, vindicating his unsuccessful mission of the previous year. Though weak and still in great discomfort, he tied pillows to his saddle and managed to mount a horse for the first time in several weeks. He rode out of camp with the general and his other aides, the well-dressed column moving smartly forward, their spirits high.

"They Broke and Ran as Sheep Pursued by Dogs"

In the early afternoon, just a few miles from Fort Duquesne, Braddock's army marched straight into disaster. With no warning, a deafening volley of gunfire from the surrounding forest leveled scores of officers and men on the front lines. From that moment on, the air was filled with the incessant sounds of musket fire and whining bullets, coupled with the screams of wounded soldiers. Nearly nine hundred French soldiers and Indians had been hiding in the woods, waiting for the right moment to strike.

The British troops, trained for regimented warfare on the open fields of Europe, were panic-stricken to see their ranks being mowed down by the gunfire coming from among the trees. Here and there they caught the sun's reflection on a scalping knife and heard the eerie yelping of half-naked savages. The redcoats fired aimlessly into the forest, then quickly reloaded and fired again, sometimes shooting their own men in the terrifying confusion.

Most of the survivors soon dropped their weapons and fled. "The English soldiers ... behaved with more cowardice than it is possible to conceive," Washington wrote later. "The dastardly behavior of those they call regulars exposed all others that were inclined to do their duty to almost certain death; and at last, in spite of all the efforts of the officers to

The French and Indians ambush General Braddock and his soldiers. Two-thirds of the British force, including Braddock himself, were either killed or wounded in the engagement. Washington emerged from the battle a hero.

the contrary, they broke and ran as sheep pursued by dogs."[24]

As soon as the first volley rang out, General Braddock and his personal staff raced to the front to direct the fighting. Most of the mounted officers, being easy marks for the hidden enemy, were shot down within minutes. Braddock himself was severely wounded, and every one of his aides also fell—except George Washington. In the frightening melee the big Virginian had two horses shot out from under him and miraculously was unharmed as a bullet rushed through his hat and three more passed through his coat! He later wrote that he survived only "by the miraculous care of Providence, that protected me beyond all human expectation."[25]

Heedless of his debilitating sickness, Washington ranged all over the battlefield, delivering orders from his bleeding commander and desperately urging the men to regroup and "engage the enemy in their own way."[26] But he found that the British regulars were "struck with such a panic that . . . it was impossible to rally them,"[27] and before long the entire regiment was in retreat. Both Thomas Gage and Horatio Gates were among the wounded.

"We Have Been Beaten, Most Shamefully Beaten"

As the surviving British troops fled the field of battle, Washington and a few other officers placed the fallen Braddock in a small cart and carried him away from further danger. Sadly, his wound proved fatal. After four days of suffering he took his last painful gasp. Washington took charge of the burial service, then ordered the retreating footmen and wagons to pass over the unmarked grave so the Indians would not find and scalp the body.

When the remnants of the army reached Fort Cumberland, Washington's "weak and feeble state of health" forced him to remain there "for two or three days to recover a little strength, that I may thereby be enabled to proceed homeward with more ease."[28] During this stay he received an amazing report and immediately wrote to his brother Jack: "As I have heard since my arrival at this place a circumstantial account of my death and dying speech, I take this early opportunity of contradicting both and of assuring you that I now exist and appear in the land of the living."[29]

He rejoiced to have been spared, while mourning the loss of so many of his companions in arms. Of the total advanced force of 1,459 who had met the enemy near Fort Duquesne, 977 men—including 63 officers—had been killed or wounded.[30] Washington's reaction to the tragedy matched the "unbelief and indignation" with which the people of America and England received the bitter news. After reaching Mount Vernon again near the end of July, he lamented:

> We have been beaten, most shamefully beaten, by a handful of men who only intended to molest and disturb our march. Victory was their smallest expectation. But see the wondrous works of Providence! the uncertainty of human things! . . .
>
> Had I not been witness to the fact on that fatal day, I should scarcely give credit to it now.[31]

"He Cannot Die in Battle"

A little-known sidelight connected with Braddock's defeat was an "Indian prophecy" pronounced fifteen years later by an aged Indian chief. In the fall of 1770, Washington and several other men traveled to the Ohio to examine some of the western lands that had been granted to colonial veterans of the French and Indian War. During that journey the men were met by an Indian trader who "declared that he was conducting a party which consisted of a grand sachem and some attendant warriors; that the chief was a very great man among the northwestern tribes, and the same who [had] commanded the Indians on the fall of Braddock.... Hearing of the visit of Colonel Washington to the western country, this chief had set out on a mission, the object of which [he] himself would make known."[32] After the two groups had arranged themselves around a council fire, the old Indian rose and spoke to the group through an interpreter:

> I am a chief, and the ruler over many tribes. My influence extends to the waters of the great lakes, and to the far blue mountains. I have traveled a long and weary path that I might see the young warrior of the great battle.
>
> It was on the day when the white man's blood mixed with the streams of our forest that I first beheld this chief. I called to my young men and said, Mark yon tall and daring warrior? He is not of the red-coat tribe—he hath an Indian's wisdom, and his warriors fight as we do—himself is alone exposed. Quick, let your aim be certain, and he dies. Our rifles were levelled, rifles which but for him knew not how to miss—'twas all in vain; a power mightier far than we shielded him from harm. He cannot die in battle.
>
> I am old, and soon shall be gathered to the great council fire of my fathers in the land of shades; but ere I go there is something bids me speak in the voice of prophecy. Listen! *The Great Spirit protects that man, and guides his destinies—he will become the chief of nations, and a people yet unborn will hail him as the founder of a mighty empire!*[33]

Washington left no record of his reaction to these words. But his good friend Dr. James Craik, who witnessed this remarkable scene, later recounted the incident to soldiers in the Revolutionary War on several occasions when their commander in chief dangerously exposed himself to enemy fire on the battlefield.

Praise and Frustration

Other voices were praising Washington's heroism even before he returned from the tragic encounter near Fort Duquesne. Captain Robert Orme, one of the regular officers on Braddock's staff who had been wounded in the battle, reported that "Mr. Washington had two horses shot under him and his clothes shot through in several places, behaving the whole time with the greatest courage and resolution."[34] An inhabitant of Williamsburg noted that "scarce anything else is talked of here."[35] And frontiersman Christopher Gist, who had accompanied Washington on the difficult journey to Fort Le Boeuf in 1753–54, wrote to tell him that Benjamin Franklin and other Pennsylvanians had spoken very highly of him. "Your name is more talked of in Pennsylvania than any other person in the army, and everybody seems willing to venture under your command."[36]

Even clergymen sought to honor him. That August the Reverend Samuel Davies of Hanover County, Virginia, delivered a sermon in which he mentioned "that heroic youth, Colonel Washington, whom I cannot but hope Providence has hitherto preserved in so signal a manner for some important service to his country."[37] Others offered similar sentiments.

As to the outcome of Braddock's expedition itself, however, Englishmen on both sides of the Atlantic were deeply disturbed—and none more than the man who was being acclaimed as the hero of the campaign. The haunting reality was that the forks of the Ohio had still not been reclaimed, and the defeat suffered by the well-trained British troops was "so scandalous," Washington said, "that I hate to have it mentioned."[38] His former admiration for the military might of Great Britain was permanently altered by this disaster.

Chapter 5

Defending the Frontier

Now that the regular army was no longer in place to protect the Virginia frontier against encroachment by the French and the Indians, the western settlements were in a frantic state of alarm. Governor Dinwiddie and the House of Burgesses, recognizing the urgency of the crisis, moved quickly to reorganize and strengthen colonial defenses. George Washington, even though he was only twenty-three years old, was the obvious choice to be commander of the new forces. He hesitated at the prospect, as he explained in a private letter to one of his relatives:

> I wish . . . it were more in my power than it is to answer the favorable opinion my friends have conceived of my abilities. Let them not be deceived; I am unequal to the task, and do assure you it requires more experience than I am master of to conduct an affair of the importance that this is now arisen to. [1]

Whatever Washington may have thought of his own limitations, the authorities in Williamsburg were convinced that his leadership was essential. On August 14, 1755, the governor appointed him as "colonel of the Virginia Regiment and commander in chief of all the forces now raised and to be raised for the defense of His Majesty's colony." He was also given "full power and authority to act defensively or offensively, as you shall think for the good and welfare of the service."[2] Despite deep feelings of inadequacy, Colonel Washington accepted the commission and plunged into his new responsibilities. The assignment was the most difficult challenge thus far in his military experience.

"A Willing Offering to Savage Fury"

Most of Washington's next three years were spent along the Virginia frontier, straining every resource to protect the western settlers against the brutal savagery of the Indians. "Not an hour, nay scarcely a minute, passes that does not produce fresh alarms and melancholy accounts," he wrote in April 1756. "Three families were murdered the night before last, . . . and every day we have accounts of such cruelties and barbarities as are shocking to human nature."[3] A few days later he wrote plaintively of "the cries of the hungry, who have fled for refuge to [our military stockades] with nothing more than they carry on their backs."[4] In deep feelings of sympathy for the victims of the frontier massacres he cried out, "What can I do? If bleeding, dying! would glut their insatiate revenge, I would be a willing offering to savage fury, and die by inches to save a people!" He continued:

> I *see* their situation, know their danger, and participate
> [in] their sufferings without having it in my power to give
> them further relief than uncertain promises. . . .

The supplicating tears of the women, and moving petitions from the men, melt me into such deadly sorrow that I solemnly declare, if I know my own mind, I could offer myself a willing sacrifice to the butchering enemy, provided that would contribute to the people's ease.[5]

But his weak army was perpetually outnumbered by the enemy. Woeful shortages in recruiting and frequent desertions from the ranks left him with a perennially feeble force. His forces were never strong enough to end "the murder of poor, innocent babes and helpless families."[6] In 1757 he lamented bitterly: "I exert every means in my power to protect a much distressed country, but it is a task too arduous. To think of defending a frontier as ours is, of more than three hundred and fifty miles' extent, with only seven hundred men, is vain and idle."[7]

A Collision in Alexandria

Despite a life on the rough frontier, the record shows that Washington was physically assaulted by another man only once in his life—and that was not in a dangerous military conflict, but during a hotly contested political election. The incident reveals much about the character of the future President.

In December 1755, just four months after he was appointed to lead the Virginia Regiment, Washington visited Alexandria to vote for close friend George William Fairfax, a candidate for the House of Burgesses. During his visit, he chanced to meet a Mr. William Payne, a rabid supporter of a rival candidate. Their conversation deteriorated from congenial to argumentative—not atypical for political campaigns then or now. In the heat of temper, Payne suddenly lifted his walking stick and slammed Washington to the ground.

George William Fairfax as a young man. George Fairfax and George Washington were close friends from Washington's boyhood until the Fairfaxes moved to England in 1773. The Fairfaxes were among the most influential families in Virginia.

The officers of Washington's regiment promptly stepped forward to avenge their leader's wounded honor—and bruised body—but the young colonel calmed them down and "retired to his lodgings in a public house. From thence he wrote a note to Mr. Payne, requesting that he would meet him next morning at the tavern, as he wished to see him in reference to their recent disagreement."

Payne, a comparatively short man, went to the tavern expecting the worst. Instead Washington graciously apologized for an "offense given in an unguarded moment," asking Payne's forgiveness. "It is needless to say that Payne witnessed with admiration this triumph of principle over passion, and that a friendship was kindled in his bosom which he did not cease to cherish as long as he lived."[8]

Problems of Military Command

As commander in chief of Virginia's defense forces, Washington encountered the same distressing difficulties he would later struggle with during the Revolutionary War. The relentless problem of recruiting new troops was worsened considerably by the meager pay allowed by the General Assembly. "Our soldiers complain," Washington notified the Speaker of the House of Burgesses, "that their pay is insufficient even to furnish shoes, shirts, stockings, etc., which their officers, in order to keep them fit for duty, oblige them to provide. This, they say, deprives them of the means of purchasing any of the conveniences or necessaries of life, and obliges them to drag through a disagreeable service in the most disagreeable manner. . . . And this is the reason why the men have always been so naked and bare of clothes."[9] At the same time, he said, a regular pension system must be established for those who might be "maimed and wounded" in battle; certainly it was not right that they should be simply discharged as soon as they were "unfit for service . . . and turned upon an uncharitable world to beg, steal, or starve!"[10]

His letters to Virginia leaders seemed to fall on deaf ears. Again and again he wrote pleading for adequate provisions for his men. Seeing the horrible cost in human suffering, he desperately demanded both men and money for the erection of forts along the frontier. The royal governor and his bureaucratic cohorts approved the plan, but failed to give it adequate support.

Another sore spot was the inequality between officers of the regular army and those of the colonial forces. When a British Captain Dagworthy from Maryland arrogantly claimed superiority over all colonial officers by virtue of his royal commission, Colonel Washington rode all the way to Boston to have the matter settled by Governor William Shirley (then the acting commander in chief of all British forces in North America).[11] Shirley's ruling was so unsatisfactory that Washington briefly toyed with the idea of resigning. But when he considered the plight of the frontier settlers, he decided to continue in their service.

Despite Washington's personal sacrifice, the western settlers themselves—the very people Washington was protecting—were surprisingly unwilling to support the war effort. Heedless, they refused to fight, to work, or to assist with supplies for the ragged soldiers. On one occasion a small band of Indians moved with brutality and bloodshed toward a place called Winchester, where Washington had bought some land as a young surveyor. He wrote:

> I was desirous of proceeding immediately at the head of some militia to put a stop to the ravages of the enemy, believing their numbers to be few; but was told . . . that it was impossible to get above twenty or twenty-five men, they having absolutely refused to stir, choosing, as they say, to die with their wives and families. . . .
>
> In all things I meet with the greatest opposition. No orders are obeyed but what a party of soldiers or my own drawn sword enforces; without this, a single horse for the most urgent occasion cannot be had. To such a pitch has the insolence of these people arrived, by having every point hitherto submitted to them; however, I have given up none, where His Majesty's service requires the contrary, and where my proceedings are justified by my instructions; nor will I, unless they execute what they threaten—i.e., "to blow out my brains."[12]

Twenty-five Lashes for Profanity

An equally serious problem was the utter lack of discipline among the troops. But Washington knew what it took to build a creditable army. He wrote: "I have, both by threats and persuasive means, endeavored to discountenance gaming, drinking, swearing, and irregularities of every other kind; while I have, on the other hand, practiced every artifice to inspire a laudable emulation in the officers for the service of their country, and to encourage the soldiers in the unerring exercise of their duty."[13]

He strongly insisted on order and decency in the Virginia Regiment. Officers were instructed to administer twenty-five lashes for profanity,[14] fifty for feigned illness,[15] one hundred for drunkenness, and five hundred for fighting with another soldier.[16] As for deserters: "Any soldier who shall desert, though he return again, shall be hanged without mercy." Such punishments were in accordance with the harsh British military code of the times.[17]

In an effort to promote a general atmosphere of morality, the colonel engaged chaplains wherever he could and ordered that "divine service" be conducted on Sunday mornings and the troops marched to prayers.[18] He also encouraged his officers "in the strongest manner ... to devote some part of your leisure hours to the study of your profession"— particularly if they sought to earn "merit or applause." "Discipline," he told them, "is the soul of an army."[19]

"The Terror of These Colonies"

As the Virginia frontier was pushed farther and farther eastward by determined Indian warriors, who were allies of the French, Washington urged another offensive march against Fort Duquesne. "I have always thought it the best and *only* method to put a stop to the incursions of the enemy," he wrote, "as they would *then* be obliged to stay at home to defend their own possessions."[20]

He knew that the small Virginia Regiment could not manage the dangerous undertaking alone, but if he could add the Pennsylvania and Maryland troops to his own forces, he felt the expedition would certainly succeed.

That an offensive scheme of action is necessary, if it can be executed, is quite obvious. Our all, in a manner, depends upon it. The French grow more and more formidable by their alliances, while our friendly Indians are deserting our interest. Our treasury is exhausting, and our country depopulating. . . .

I am firmly persuaded that three thousand men under good regulation (and surely the three middle colonies could easily raise and support that number) might . . . take possession of [the Ohio], cut off the communication between Fort Duquesne and the [Great] Lakes, and . . . make themselves masters of that fortress, which is now become the terror of these colonies. [21]

After Braddock's defeat in 1755, the major theater of the French and Indian War had moved into the northern territories, and it was not until the summer of 1758 that the British government authorized another campaign against the fort at the forks of the Ohio. This expedition was to be under the command of Brigadier General John Forbes, a fifty-year-old Scotsman, and the Virginia Regiment was invited to participate. Washington was ready. At last the humiliating disaster of three years before would be avenged.

On November 24, 1758, after a tedious and difficult overland march of several months, the six-thousand-strong joint expeditionary force came within a single day of Fort Duquesne. That night a scout raced into Forbes's camp and reported that a great column of billowing smoke was now rising from the French stronghold—the enemy had set the torch to their prized fortress and, like so many mice fleeing the cat, had run in retreat toward Canada! The strategic site, now an English possession once again, was renamed Fort Pitt (later Pittsburgh). For Virginia, the worst of the war was over.

"Reduced to Great Extremity"

While part of the Virginia Regiment remained behind to hold Fort Pitt, Colonel Washington was ordered to travel to Williamsburg to obtain additional funding for their winter supplies. However, after fulfilling his assignment there, he abruptly submitted his resignation.

The decision had been forced on him by a continuing bout with perilously ill health. More than a year earlier, in the late summer of 1757, he had suffered a resurgence of his previous attack of dysentery or "bloody flux," which was common among soldiers in the American wilderness. The symptoms worsened until he was so weak he could barely walk, and that November his camp physicians warned him that he would risk grave danger if he did not suspend all activity and seek a "change of air."[22] Taking their advice, he rode to Mount Vernon and remained there through the winter to convalesce. In March 1758, eight months before the Forbes expedition, he wrote to a friend:

> I have never been able to return to my command [on the frontier] since I wrote to you last, my disorder at times returning obstinately upon me, in spite of the efforts of all the [physicians] whom I have hitherto consulted. At certain periods I have been reduced to great extremity, and have now too much reason to apprehend an approaching decay, being visited with several symptoms of such a disease....
>
> My constitution is certainly impaired; and as nothing can retrieve it but the greatest care and the most circumspect conduct,... and as I despair of rendering that immediate service which my country may require from the person commanding their troops, I have some thoughts of quitting my command and retiring from all public business, leaving my post to be filled by some other person more capable of

the task, and who may, perhaps, have his endeavors crowned with better success than mine have been. [23]

He did not resign at that time, however. Subsequent medical treatments he received must have been temporarily successful, for within a few weeks he was strong enough to ride back to the frontier and resume command of his troops. But now, following the successful Forbes expedition against Fort Duquesne, his health had declined again. By the time he got back to Williamsburg in December 1758 and had purchased the needed supplies, his condition was "precarious." [24] According to a would-be biographer who discussed the episode with Washington several years later, "his constitution became much impaired, and many symptoms menaced him . . . seriously with consumption." [25] The specter of his half-brother Lawrence floated grimly before his eyes; Lawrence had tragically died of that same consumption at the age of thirty-four. Wanting to avoid such a fate, at twenty-six Washington reluctantly gave up the military life he so cherished and retired to his home on the Potomac.

"How Great the Loss of Such a Man!"

Upon learning of Colonel Washington's resignation, the distraught officers of the Virginia Regiment sent him a lengthy address "to express our great concern at the disagreeable news we have received. . . . The happiness we have enjoyed and the honor we have acquired, together with the mutual regard that has always subsisted between you and your officers, have implanted so sensible an affection in the minds of us all that we cannot be silent on this critical occasion."

They then spoke of their leader with words that show how highly Washington was esteemed, even in his twenties:

In our earliest infancy you took us under your tuition
[and] trained us up in the practice of that discipline which
alone can constitute good troops, from the punctual observance of which you never suffered the least deviation.
Your steady adherence to impartial justice, your quick discernment and invariable regard to merit, wisely intended to
inculcate those genuine sentiments of true honor and passion for glory from which the great military achievements
have been derived, . . . heightened our natural emulation
and our desire to excel. . . .

Judge, then, how sensibly we must be affected with the
loss of such an excellent commander, such a sincere friend,
and so affable a companion. How rare is it to find those
amiable qualifications blended together in one man! How
great the loss of such a man! Adieu to that superiority
which the enemy have granted us over other troops, and
which even the regulars and provincials have done us the
honor publicly to acknowledge! Adieu to that strict
discipline and order which you have always maintained!
Adieu to that happy union and harmony which has been
our principal cement![26]

Washington's reply, sent ten days later, was written from
the deepest wellsprings of his heart:

If I had words that could express the deep sense I
entertain of your most obliging and affectionate address to
me, I should endeavor to show you that *gratitude* is not the
smallest ingredient of a character you have been pleased to
celebrate. . . .

That I have for some years (under uncommon difficulties
which few were thoroughly acquainted with) been able to
conduct myself so much to your satisfaction affords the
greatest pleasure I am capable of feeling. . . . Your approbation of my conduct during my command of the Virginia

troops I must esteem an honor that will constitute the greatest happiness of my life, and afford in my latest hours the most pleasing reflections....

In thanking you, gentlemen, with uncommon sincerity and true affection for the honor you have done me—for if I have acquired any reputation, it is from you I derive it—I thank you also for the love and regard you have all along shown me. It is in this I am rewarded; it is herein I glory. [27]

But in spite of "the pangs I have felt at parting with a regiment that has shared my toils and experienced every hardship and danger which I have encountered,"[28] Washington's ill health forced him to refuse a request from the officers that he remain at the helm another year. With this farewell, he withdrew completely from active involvement in the French and Indian War. British victory was secured by late 1760, and fifteen more years would pass before George Washington would return to the battlefield—not to lead the forces of Virginia, but to command the entire army of a continent.

Chapter 6

Marrying into a Ready-Made Family

Washington was just short of twenty-seven years old when he returned to civilian life in January 1759. His years in the rugged wilderness combined with his large frame and dignified character to make him a truly impressive figure. One who knew him well has left us an excellent pen portrait of his appearance at that time:

> He may be described as being straight as an Indian, measuring six feet two inches in his stockings and weighing 175 pounds...in 1759.[1] His frame is padded with well-developed muscles, indicating great strength. His bones and joints are large, as are his hands and feet.[2] He is wide shouldered, but has not a deep or round chest; is neat waisted, but is broad across the hips and has rather long legs and arms.[3]
>
> His head is well shaped, though not large, but is gracefully poised on a superb neck. [He has] a large and

straight rather than a prominent nose; blue-gray, penetrating eyes which are widely separated and overhung by a heavy brow. His face is long rather than broad, with high, round cheekbones, and terminates in a good firm chin. He has a clear though rather colorless pale skin, which burns with the sun, a pleasing and benevolent though a commanding countenance, [and] dark brown hair which he wears in a cue. His mouth is large and generally firmly closed, but which from time to time discloses some defective teeth.[4]

His features are regular and placid with all the muscles of his face under perfect control, though flexible and expressive of deep feeling when moved by emotions. In conversation, he looks you full in the face [and] is deliberate, deferential, and engaging. His demeanor [is] at all times composed and dignified. His movements and gestures are graceful, his walk majestic, and he is a splendid horseman.[5]

"A Votary of Love"

Washington must have loomed like a giant over most of his contemporaries, as the men of that day were typically several inches shorter than those of our generation. Tall, handsome, distinguished—the young military hero was certainly one of the most eligible bachelors in Virginia, yet he seemed awkward and unsure when he was courting. Still, he felt the normal physical attractions of the typical young man, and he enjoyed his share of innocent romances. We have already noted his interest in an unidentified "Lowland Beauty" a few years earlier; he had also made an unsuccessful attempt for the hand of an Elizabeth Fauntleroy in 1752, and he had paid some attentions to the wealthy Mary Eliza Philipse of New York City during his 1756 journey to Boston.[6]

But the relationship that has most intrigued many imaginative biographers, novelists, and magazine writers has been the enigmatic friendship of Washington and Sarah Cary Fairfax. In December 1748 George William Fairfax brought his eighteen-year-old bride Sarah—known as Sally—to the family estate of Belvoir, not far from Mount Vernon. Washington, two years younger than Sally, frequently visited the couple when he was not away surveying or soldiering, and over the years they became very good friends. During his

Sarah (Sally) Fairfax, the wife of George William Fairfax and a good friend of George Washington. Some historians have speculated that Washington had a love affair with Sally, but the historical record gives little support to such a view.

military campaigns the tall colonel found relaxation in newsy and sometimes witty correspondence with the Fairfaxes and other close associates. These communications generally make interesting reading, but one in particular—a letter Washington purportedly sent to Sally in 1758—has captured the attention of some historians. It has led a number of Washington scholars to claim that he was "passionately in love with Mrs.

Fairfax,"[7] while others have reached entirely different conclusions. Washington reportedly wrote:

> I profess myself a votary of love. I acknowledge that a
> lady is in the case, and I further confess that this lady is
> known to you. Yes, Madam, as well as she is to one who is
> too sensible of her charms to deny the power whose
> influence he feels and must ever submit to. I feel the force
> of her amiable beauties in the recollection of a thousand
> tender passages that I could wish to obliterate, till I am bid
> to revive them. But experience, alas! sadly reminds me how
> impossible this is, and evinces an opinion which I have long
> entertained, that there is a Destiny which has the control of
> our actions, not to be resisted by the strongest efforts of
> human nature.
>
> You have drawn me, dear Madam, or rather I have
> drawn myself, into an honest confession of a simple fact.
> Misconstrue not my meaning; doubt it not, nor expose it.
> The world has no business to know the object of my love,
> declared in this manner to you, when I want to conceal it.
> One thing above all things in this world I wish to know, and
> only one person of your acquaintance can [tell] me that, or
> guess my meaning. But adieu to this.... [8]

In the eighteenth century, matters of the heart were
guarded with a reserve that seems quite strained to our
generation. This letter is couched in such veiled and obscure
language that it is difficult—perhaps impossible—to identify
the "lady" about whom Washington was writing (if he did
indeed write the letter; a discussion on that issue is found
below). Several biographers have decided that she was
Martha Dandridge Custis, the quiet young widow to whom
he was then engaged.[9] Some suggest that he had not yet
conquered his affection for Sally's younger sister, Mary Cary,

who had recently rejected his proposal of marriage.[10] Many believe that he was alluding to Sally herself.[11]

Was Washington Ever in Love with Sally Fairfax?

It is true that Sally Fairfax was a vivacious and flirtatious young wife. After Washington had returned from the Braddock disaster, for instance, he sent a letter to Belvoir telling George William and Sally of his safe return and inviting them to call on him. He was utterly exhausted, both physically and emotionally, and had too little energy even for the short ride to Belvoir. George William replied with a warm welcome home, then Sally added a saucy postscript to her husband's note:

> Dear Sir—After thanking heaven for your safe return I must accuse you of great unkindness in refusing us the pleasure of seeing you this night. I do assure you nothing but our being satisfied that our company would be disagreeable should prevent us from trying if our legs would not carry us to Mount Vernon this night; but if you will not come to us, tomorrow morning very early we shall be at Mount Vernon.[12]

The postscript was signed by Sally and two friends who were staying with her at Belvoir. Such a letter from a married woman definitely borders on the inappropriate. Few other communications from Sally Fairfax to George Washington remain, so it is impossible to know if she was accustomed to playing the coquette in her letters. She may have been a woman who loved to test her charms for the inner thrill of proving her attractiveness without intending any serious romantic consequences.

If she was such a woman, her sauciness coupled with her

beauty, vivaciousness, worldliness, and womanly maturity may have created an enticing combination for George Washington. He had never enjoyed much success with the girls he had courted—and now one seemed to be making subtle approaches to him. Perhaps George, even at twenty-six, was still naive and unsure of his feelings. Perhaps he was attracted to Sally, even though she was the wife of one of his earliest and closest friends.

However, such things cannot be postulated with any certainty. We have little to go on, little to tell us of George's feelings for any woman before he found Martha Custis, the one who was to be his heart's companion for life. Even the obscure letter quoted above, in which Washington confesses himself a "votary of love," is difficult to interpret. After carefully reading the letter, all that one can say for certain is that Washington was in love and that he was confiding his secret to his friend, Sally, who knew the "lady" Washington had given his heart to. But who was she? We don't know.

That letter holds another problem, every bit as difficult as its internal vagueness. The letter remained undiscovered for more than a hundred years, until March 1877, when it was published in the New York Herald. The next day it was sold at an auction—but in neither case was it subjected by a known authority to the usual authenticating tests. Was the letter a forgery? Was it written by someone else? Was it quoted correctly? None of these questions can be answered, since the letter has long since been lost, never having been subjected to the necessary tests of handwriting, paper, and ink.

When scholar John Fitzpatrick was collecting Washington's writings into a huge and exhaustive thirty-seven-volume set earlier in this century, he seriously considered omitting this letter, since its validity is so questionable. In the end he included it—but only with a warning that one must consider it with caution.

If the letter was authentic, if Sally was a flirt with George, if the young colonel was indeed attracted to his friend's wife—all these combined give us an opportunity to see the depth of George Washington's character, even at that early age. All evidence suggests that, regardless of his personal feelings, he chose to conduct himself properly, keeping himself entirely free from any immoral or improper encounter with the wife of his neighbor and close friend.

As the eminent scholar Douglas Southall Freeman has noted, "There survives not one echo of the gossip that would have been audible all along the Potomac had there been anything amiss in their relations."[13]

After the young military hero was married to Martha Custis, the Washingtons and the Fairfaxes often exchanged visits and enjoyed one another's company at dinners and parties. They remained close until George and Sally Fairfax moved to England in 1773, never to return. However, even then George and Martha Washington continued to write to their old friends.[14]

"An Agreeable Consort for Life"

It is recorded that George Washington first met the delightful Martha Custis in March 1758 while journeying to the provincial capital of Williamsburg.[15] Martha's first husband had died the previous July, leaving her to care for their two small children and a large estate on the Pamunkey, a branch of the York River.[16] It was here that the colonel of the Virginia Regiment began to court the "young and charming widow"[17] who was at least a foot shorter than he. We are told that they were "mutually pleased on . . . their first interview;

nor is it remarkable, [for] they were of an age when impressions are strongest. The lady was fair to behold, of fascinating manners, and splendidly endowed with worldly benefits. The hero [was] fresh from his early fields, redolent of fame, and with a form on which 'every god did seem to set his seal, to give the world assurance of a man.'"[18]

George Washington proposes marriage to Martha Custis. Martha was a widow with two small children (two others had died before she met Washington). She was shorter than George by more than a foot.

Their courtship was brief, and although they had very little time together, George seemed to know he had found the one his heart had been searching for. Martha likewise welcomed his attentions, sensing that he was well fitted to serve as a loving father to her young children—and to fill the emotional void which her first husband's death had left in her own heart. The couple were engaged soon after meeting. In early May Washington ordered a ring from Philadelphia— most probably a wedding ring. [19] Back in the field that summer to join the final march on Fort Duquesne, he sent this tender note to his fiancee:

> We have begun our march for the Ohio. A courier is starting for Williamsburg, and I embrace the opportunity to send a few words to one whose life is now inseparable from mine. Since that happy hour when we made our pledges to each other, my thoughts have been continually going to you as to another self. That an all-powerful Providence may keep us both in safety is the prayer of your ever faithful and affectionate friend. [20]

Thus, when the 1758 campaign ended with the ousting of the French, Colonel Washington had another reason besides ill health to retire from the service. Soon after returning from the frontier and completing his official duties in Williamsburg, he rode to the Custis estate to claim his bride. It was probably at Martha's home, known as the "White House," that the wedding ceremony took place on January 6, 1759. [21] A servant who was present on that occasion remembered in later years that the distinguished bridegroom was "so tall, so straight! And then he sat [upon] a horse and rode with such an air! Ah, sir, he was like no one else! Many of the grandest gentlemen in their gold lace were at the wedding, but none looked like the man himself!" [22]

No one was more pleased with the match than Martha, who saved two mementos to remind her of the happy event—a piece of her wedding gown, which was of gleaming white brocaded satin threaded with silver, and the huge, starched white military gloves worn by her new husband. [23] Several months later, Washington wrote contentedly to a relative: "I am now, I believe, fixed at this seat with an agreeable consort for life, and hope to find more happiness in retirement than I ever experienced amidst a wide and bustling world."[24] Circumstances had forced him to give up the military life he so long had labored for—but what he received in return compensated him a thousandfold and more.

Washington in the House of Burgesses

Washington did not immediately take his bride and her two children to his broad estate on the Potomac. Following a brief honeymoon at the "White House," he remained in the region to assume his duties as a new member of the Virginia House of Burgesses.[25] He had been elected a delegate the previous summer, beating his incumbent opponent soundly even though Washington was away on the Forbes expedition at the time. He took his seat on February 22, 1759, his twenty-seventh birthday.

Four days later the Burgesses enthusiastically passed a resolution "that the thanks of the House be given to George Washington, Esquire, a member of this House [and] late Colonel of the First Virginia Regiment, for his faithful services to his Majesty and this colony, and for his brave and steady behavior, from the first encroachments and hostilities of the French and their Indians to his resignation after the happy reduction of Fort Duquesne."[26] According to the traditional account of this incident, Washington "rose to express his acknowledgments for the honor; but such was his trepidation and confusion that he could not give distinct utterance to a single syllable. He blushed, stammered, and trembled for a second, when the Speaker [of the House, John Robinson] relieved him by a stroke of address that would have done honor to Louis XIV in his proudest and happiest moment. 'Sit down, Mr. Washington,' said he with a conciliating smile, 'your modesty is equal to your valor, and that surpasses the power of any language that I possess.'"[27]

Indeed, Washington could claim little renown as a public speaker, but in private conversations he was impressive and persuasive. He often exercised his greatest influence in committee meetings or in personal contacts behind the scenes. In 1762, for example, his colleagues consented to his repeated urgings for a statute to prevent mutiny and desertions by Virginia soldiers. And despite his natural reticence, during his years as a Burgess he always took an active part in discussing those matters which related to the county he represented. But he was not the Patrick Henry type. He was not an orator. His own practice as a legislator is reflected in the thoughtful advice he later gave to a nephew who served in the Virginia House of Delegates after the Revolution:

> Speak seldom but to important subjects, except such as particularly relate to your constituents, and in the former case make yourself *perfectly* master of the subject. Never exceed a *decent* warmth, and submit your sentiments with diffidence. A dictatorial style, though it may carry conviction, is always accompanied with disgust.[28]

Enlarging and Beautifying the Mount Vernon Mansion

After completing several busy weeks of service in the House of Burgesses, Washington prepared to move his new family northward to Mount Vernon. He wrote ahead to his estate manager to ensure that everything would be in order for their arrival:

> You must have the house very well cleaned, and were you to make fires in the rooms below it would air them.

You must get two of the best bedsteads put up, one in the hall room and the other in the little dining room that used to be, and have beds made on them [before] we come. You must also get out the chairs and tables and have them very well rubbed and cleaned; the staircase ought also to be polished in order to make it look well.

Inquire about in the neighborhood and get some eggs and chickens, and prepare in the best manner you can for our coming.[29]

In early April 1759 he reached Mount Vernon with Martha and the children. The home had been greatly expanded since the previous year. Washington himself had designed the changes, relying on English architectural manuals and borrowing ideas from other structures in the area. His friend George William Fairfax had served as his construction supervisor while he made the 1758 expedition to Fort Duquesne.

In accordance with Washington's plans, the roof of the old farmhouse was raised atop a new second story, and a handsome staircase was built in the central hallway. Palisades mounted on low brick walls connected four service buildings to the main residence, creating the impression of a larger mansion. The wooden exterior of the house was given the illusion of stone blocks by an ingenious innovation: vertical grooves were cut into the horizontal boards used for siding, and sand was mixed with the paint to produce a roughened surface. At least part of the interior was also redecorated. The west parlor, for instance, was now adorned with rich paneling, a marble chimneypiece and an oil landscape imported from London, and columns and pediments around the doorways.[30]

Additional improvements would come in the years that

A view of Mount Vernon from the air. At the time of Washington's marriage, the estate con sisted of more than nine thousand acres, about half of which were in woodlands.

followed. As the number of guests at Mount Vernon increased, the length of the home was gradually doubled— first by an extension on the west end which included a first-floor library and several second-floor bedrooms, and later by an extension on the east end that boasted a large, high-ceilinged reception hall. Following the Revolutionary War, the appearance of the home was further enhanced by the placement of an attractive pediment over the northern front and a cupola in the center of the roof. And constructed along the entire length of the south side, which overlooked the stately Potomac River, was "the first extensive colonnaded two-story porch in Virginia, presag[ing] what became almost the hallmark of Southern pre-Civil War architecture."[31]

Besides serving as his own architect, Washington also filled the role of landscape designer. On the grounds around the mansion he arranged for beautiful flower and vegetable gardens bordered by decorative paths and hedges. Over the years he transplanted many varieties of shrubs and trees from the western territories, and he even imported numerous exotic plants from Europe. Throughout his eventful life Washington preferred his "small villa" at Mount Vernon above all other places on the continent. When the completion of public obligations permitted him to return home, he wished for nothing more than to enjoy "domestic ease under the shadow of my own vine and my own fig tree, . . . with the implements of husbandry . . . around me."[32]

Chapter 7

A Gentleman Farmer

Washington had leased Mount Vernon from his half-brother's widow beginning in 1754, and upon her death in 1761 it passed entirely into his hands. "No estate in united America is more pleasantly situated than this," he wrote in his later years.[1] Bounded on the east and south by the wide Potomac, it was nestled in one of the most scenic areas of Virginia's northern coast. From the time of his marriage Washington gradually increased the size of the estate by successive purchases of surrounding lands, until eventually it consisted of more than nine thousand acres.

One of Virginia's Largest Landholders

In addition to Mount Vernon and the extensive properties which came to him through Martha's late husband, Washington steadily acquired vast landholdings elsewhere in Virginia and in the western territories. He participated in several land speculation efforts, including a petition for a large tract on the Mississippi River, and in an ambitious reclamation project at the Great Dismal Swamp in the southeast corner of Virginia. When the lands promised to veterans of the French and Indian War were finally granted in the 1770s—due largely to Washington's own efforts—he owned over thirty-two thousand acres altogether. This figure was nearly doubled by the end of his life. It has been observed by one historian, "Had not the Revolution intervened, George Washington might have been known to history not as the father of his country but as one of the great entrepreneurs of the West, [purchasing] and settling lands to the far horizon."[2]

"The Life of the Husbandman . . . Is the Most Delectable"

During the next sixteen years, from 1759 to 1775, Washington devoted his time almost exclusively to agriculture and the management of his rapidly expanding estate. Of course, he was reelected to the Virginia House of Burgesses repeatedly during these years, and he conscientiously attended the regular legislative sessions in the late fall and the early spring. Otherwise he was free to manage the Mount Vernon estate and the Custis farms, and to look after his other lands which were in their early stages of development. Farming soon became his favorite pastime and rewarded him with a certain degree of congenial prosperity. "The life of the husbandman, of all others, is the most delectable," he once wrote. "It is honorable, it is amusing, and with judicious management it is profitable."[3]

But the profits did not come easily, as it turned out. Mount Vernon had been mismanaged by neglectful relatives and

Washington at work on one of his Mount Vernon farms. "The life of the husbandman, of all others, is the most delectable," he once wrote.

others during Washington's years in the military service, and after he married and settled there he faced a hard struggle to restore and improve his well-nigh intractable lands. In 1763 he wrote a friend that he "had provisions of all kinds to buy for the first two or three years, and my plantation to stock, in short, with everything; buildings to make, and other matters which swallowed up, before I well knew where I was, all the money I got by marriage—nay, more, brought me in debt."[4]

Like other farmers, he also encountered frustrating problems with the soil, the weather, and swarms of destructive pests. His acreage at Mount Vernon, he said, had "an understratum of hard clay impervious to water, which, penetrating that far and unable to descend lower, sweeps off the upper soil."[5] In the winter of 1763–64 he recorded wearily that his tobacco crop for the previous year had been "vastly deficient.... A wet spring, a dry summer, and early frosts have quite demolished me."[6] He met these challenges with the firm determination of a professional farmer and sometimes with a touch of good humor. In a note to Martha's brother-in-law he wrote, "Our . . . tobacco is assailed by every villainous worm that has had an existence since the days of Noah (how unkind it was of Noah, now I have mentioned his name, to suffer such a brood of vermin to get a berth in the ark), but perhaps you may be as well off as we are—that is, have no tobacco for them to eat."[7]

He also had struggles of another nature—these with his own soul. To compete in the Virginia agricultural economy he had little choice but to own slaves. Free farm laborers were so scarce a plantation owner could not survive using only their help. Yet it was morally reprehensible to Washington for one man to own another. He struggled with his unhappy dilemma through the years. Finally he found a solution that enabled him to feel at peace with himself. He chose to neither buy nor sell slaves, even when natural reproduction gave him far more than his plantation could support. He proposed legislation in the Virginia House of Burgesses to halt the importation of slaves. And in his will he set all his slaves free.

With or without the help of slaves, Washington had no illusions about the difficulty of succeeding at his "most delectable" of all pursuits. "The nature of a Virginia estate," he observed in 1775, "[is] such that without close application it never fails bringing the proprietors in debt annually, as Negroes must be clothed and fed, taxes paid, etc., etc., whether anything is made or not."[8]

"America's First Scientific Farmer"
Succeed he did, however, because it was not in his nature to accept defeat. The more irksome his challenges, the more

tenacious and industrious he proved to be. As the Mount Vernon plantation expanded through successive land purchases, he carefully divided it into five separate farms, each with its own resident overseer. The number of slaves and hired workers climbed at the same time, ultimately mounting to several hundred. Washington faithfully rose at four o'clock each morning to handle his correspondence and account books and to review the detailed weekly reports he required of his overseers. He then spent most of the day riding over his farms to inspect operations and make further plans for improvement. Sometimes he pulled off his coat, rolled up his sleeves, and joined his slaves and hired men in the sweat of ordinary labor.

Washington's orders for goods from London soon included the latest books on agricultural science and farm management. He studied these thoughtfully, applying their principles to the unique conditions at Mount Vernon. By 1764 he concluded that the tobacco culture common to Virginia estates should give way to other crops. The demanding tobacco plant quickly exhausted the fragile soil; its single growing season placed farmers too much at the mercy of the unpredictable weather; and its shipment to British ports led to an unhealthy dependence on the temperamental English market, where prices for American imports were depressed as often as not.

Within another year he had launched a series of innovative crop-rotation experiments that would continue throughout his life. Wheat replaced tobacco as the main crop on his Potomac farms, while other acreage was devoted to corn, hemp, and flax. Washington also experimented with various combinations of soils and fertilizers; the treatment of seeds before planting; plant grafting; land drainage systems; and the raising and breeding of horses, mules, sheep, cattle, and other animals (including the buffalo). He even invented an ingenious drill plow that automatically dropped seeds in furrows, and he designed a many-sided barn in which thirty men could thresh wheat (a grain that was usually treaded by horses outdoors, suffering much damage in the process). For these and other agricultural innovations, he has justly been called "America's first 'scientific farmer.'"[9]

After 1765, in a move that distinguished him from the typical American colonist, Washington began to rely very little on capricious British merchants. He sold his yearly harvest on the local market and bought his luxury goods from artisans and importers in Philadelphia and other large American cities. Most necessities were created in the extensive production facilities right at Mount Vernon. He gave his farm overseers standing instructions to purchase nothing that could be made on the plantation itself. A water-powered flour mill was built, with surplus flour being marketed in Alexandria and elsewhere. Fisheries were established along the banks of the Potomac. Carpenters, masons, coopers, spinners, weavers, and shoemakers were either hired or trained from among the servants. Peach and apple orchards were grown, and a cider press was set up. Eventually a greenhouse, a blacksmith shop, brick and charcoal kilns, and several other facilities were in operation; altogether there were about thirty buildings on the Mount Vernon estate.

As a modern biographer has noted, all of these concerns functioned "with organization that singularly resembled that of an army. There was a chain of command from the leader of a work gang up to the manager of an individual farm, on to various staff officers, and finally to the proprietor.... With his unbounded energy and his gift for detail, Washington was at Mount Vernon an efficient commander in chief."[10]

Washington's Stepchildren

Those busy years at Mount Vernon were filled with more concerns than simply agriculture. The young retired colonel of the Virginia Regiment had pressing domestic responsibilities as well. It is perhaps ironic that the "father of his country" never had any offspring of his own, yet he certainly became a father to Martha's two children.

John Parke ("Jacky") Custis was four years old, and little Martha ("Patsy") only two, when their mother married Washington. He welcomed them into his household as though they were his own. They took to him right away, calling him "Poppa" and responding to his kindness and gifts with genuine affection. "Poppa" Washington proved to be thoughtful and conscientious in his treatment of the children. He wrote reflectively in 1771, "I conceive there is much greater circumspection to [be observed] by a guardian than a natural parent, who is only accountable to his own conscience for his conduct."[11] He considered it his duty to be "generous and attentive" to the children,[12] and these convictions guided his actions as long as they lived with him.

Soon after his marriage, Washington's orders for goods from London began to include such things as "ten shillings' worth of toys," "six little books for children beginning to read," and "one fashionably dressed baby [doll]."[13] In the years that followed he took special pains to obtain proper clothing and other articles for the two youngsters. He ordered the best books for them to study and engaged well-qualified tutors to instruct them.

"The Lowest Ebb of Misery"

Jacky proved to be indolent and prissy. With hopes that both his mind and his character would improve, his stepfather enrolled him, at age fourteen, in a private academy. At about the same time an alarming event cast a dark cloud of concern over the troubled family: Patsy, now a budding twelve-year-old, suffered the first in a series of epileptic convulsions that plagued her off and on for five years, until her death. The best medical authorities of the day were baffled by the disorder; they could identify neither cause nor cure.

Jacky and Patsy Custis in 1772, two of Martha Washington's children from her first marriage. Patsy died a year after this portrait was taken; Jack died in 1781. Two other children had died in infancy.

Patsy's final tragic seizure came in the evening of June 19, 1773. "She rose from dinner about four o'clock," Washington explained to a relative, "in better health and spirits than she appeared to have been in for some time; soon after which she was seized with one of her usual fits, and expired in it in less than two minutes without uttering a word, a groan, or scarce a sigh. This sudden and unexpected blow...has almost reduced my poor wife to the lowest ebb of misery."[14] Washington, too, was deeply affected by the loss of his stepdaughter, but his sorrow was somewhat assuaged by his belief that "the sweet, innocent girl [has] entered into a more happy and peaceful abode than any she has met with in the afflicted path she hitherto has trod."[15]

He was also strengthened by a conviction he had expressed to another grieving parent just two months earlier: "The ways of Providence being inscrutable, and the justice of it [i.e., of a loved one's death] not to be scanned by the shallow eye of humanity, nor to be counteracted by the utmost efforts of human power or wisdom, resignation and, as far as the strength of our reason and religion can carry us, a cheerful acquiescence to the Divine Will [are] what we are to aim [for]."[16]

The mournful news reached Patsy's brother through the sluggish mails—he had entered King's College (later Columbia University) in New York City only a few weeks before. When Jack returned home in December for Christmas vacation, he pleaded with his stepfather for permission to leave school and marry Eleanor ("Nelly") Calvert, a local belle to whom he had become engaged the previous spring. Washington would have preferred that Jack, now nineteen years of age, complete his studies before marrying.

"But having his own inclination, the desire of his mother, and the acquiescence of almost all his relatives to encounter," Washington wrote, "I did not care...to push my opposition too far, and therefore have submitted to a kind of necessity."[17] The decision seemed to have but one advantage to recommend it: perhaps Martha, still grieving over Patsy, would be comforted by having her only surviving child closer to home. Martha was indeed comforted. She revealed her feelings in a brief but touching letter to her future daughter-in-law:

> My dear Nelly: God took from me a daughter when June roses were blooming. He has now given me another daughter about her age when winter winds are blowing, to warm my heart again. I am as happy as one so afflicted and so blessed can be. Pray receive my benediction and a wish that you may long live the loving wife of my happy son, and a loving daughter of
>
> Your affectionate mother,
> M. Washington [18]

Diversions of a Gentleman Farmer

During his quiet domestic years, the master of Mount Vernon always found time amid his many duties to relax and enjoy the rich company of friends. He relished the pleasing diversions of house parties, picnics, barbecues, and clambakes. It has been estimated that the Washingtons entertained about two thousand guests between 1768 and 1775, [19] and most of these ate freely at their dinner table or stayed overnight. Washington was especially fond of dancing. He attended a number of concerts and stage plays in Williamsburg and Alexandria. Occasionally he paid to see such traveling spectacles as circuses, cockfights, puppet shows, and exhibitions of wild animals.

Cards and billiards with neighboring gentlemen sometimes provided recreation during the long winter months, but strenuous outdoor activities were more frequent and more enjoyable. Washington participated in horse races, boat races, shooting matches, and various other contests of skill or strength. Of all these, his great love was hunting—particularly fox hunting. About half of the vast Mount Vernon estate consisted of woodlands; Washington enjoyed gathering a group of friends on horseback at the edge of the trees and unleashing his pack of carefully bred and well-trained hounds.

A modern biographer has graphically described the excitement of these outings: "By far the most engaging pictures of the life at Mount Vernon are those of the fox-hunting days. Washington took keen delight in the headlong dash of riding to hounds, and though his diaries record only the bare and sober facts of the hunts, sometimes several in the same week, these facts justify the color and verve of hard-riding, fence-jumping chases.... The hunts lasted at times for hours."[20]

Partially because of his fondness for hunting, Washington always kept a number of dogs and horses around him. Both horse and hound were counted as beloved friends. His affection can be seen in a few of the inventive names he gave his dogs: Jupiter, Drunkard, Vulcan, Truelove, and Sweetlips.

"Very Near My Last Gasp"

On one occasion, about two years after his marriage to Martha, Washington's newfound serenity was suddenly interrupted by a debilitating illness reminiscent of those he had suffered in his younger days. In the spring of 1761, while visiting some of his legislative constituents in the town of Frederick, he contracted a violent cold. This produced a fever and stirred up old maladies that stubbornly persisted for five or six months. Gradually he sank into "a very low and dangerous state"[21] that resisted every remedy he tried. He consulted with several local physicians and sent for advice from others as far away as Philadelphia. But in late July he despaired that he had "found so little benefit from any advice yet received that I am [of] more than half of the mind to take a trip to England for the recovery of that invaluable blessing, health."[22] The old mortality reasserted itself, and once again Washington saw visions of an unhappy early death like that suffered by his brother and father before him.

He never took the voyage to England, but in August he did journey with his family to the Berkeley springs, where his dying half-brother Lawrence had sought recovery ten years earlier. When he returned to his home the following month he seemed to be improving. He wrote in October: "I have in appearance been very near my last gasp.... I once thought the grim king would certainly master my utmost efforts, and that I must sink in spite of a noble struggle. But, thank God, I have now got the better of the disorder and shall soon be restored, I hope, to perfect health again."[23]

"Pitching the Bar"

Once again Washington's powerful body prevailed against the devastations of disease, and his hope of health was soon realized. This was evidently the only severe illness Washington experienced in the long period between his marriage and the Revolutionary War. After 1761 he was remarkably robust and active, and visitors often commented on his prodigious physical strength. For example, Charles Willson Peale, the popular American artist who traveled to Mount Vernon in 1772 to paint the first portrait of Washington, recorded this charming incident:

> One afternoon, several young gentlemen, visitors at Mount Vernon, and myself were engaged in pitching the

bar, one of the athletic sports common in those times, when suddenly the Colonel appeared among us. He requested to be shown the pegs that marked the bounds of our effort; then, smiling, and without putting off his coat, held out his hand for the missile.

No sooner did the heavy iron bar feel the grasp of his mighty hand than it lost the power of gravitation and whizzed through the air, striking the ground far, very far, beyond our utmost limits. We were indeed amazed, as we stood around all stripped to the buff with shirt sleeves rolled up, and having thought ourselves very clever fellows, while the Colonel, on retiring, pleasantly observed, "When you beat my pitch, young gentlemen, I'll try again."[24]

"I Would Advise You to Be Cautious"

When not tending to his farms or handling legislative duties, Washington took pains to cultivate his mental as well as his physical vitality. He acquired several hundred volumes in his library—this in a day when books were an expensive luxury—studying a good number very closely. In the first years after his marriage he purchased primarily books dealing with agriculture or military affairs, but as relations between Great Britain and the American colonies deteriorated he purchased an increasing number of works on history and government. "A knowledge of books," he believed, "is the basis upon which other knowledge is to be built."[25]

Included in his reading was the Bible—he considered religious and moral education an essential part of life's learning. In addition to study, he often attended services of the Episcopal church; in 1762 he was elected a vestryman of the local Truro Parish, and afterward was elevated to the position of warden. In these capacities he was assigned to handle parish collections and to help supervise the construction of a new church building.

His secular responsibilities were also expanded about this time. In 1766 he was named a trustee of Alexandria, the city he had helped to survey and lay out as a youth. Two years later he was appointed to serve as a justice of the Fairfax County Court.

In 1770 Washington agreed to represent the colonial veterans of the 1754 military campaign and attempt to secure the western bounty lands which had been promised to them by former Governor Dinwiddie. That fall he led several men on horseback as they undertook a hazardous journey to the Ohio to identify and examine the properties in question. (It was during this journey that an old Indian chief uttered the remarkable "Indian prophecy" described earlier.)

The group returned from the wilderness in late December, and on the basis of Washington's report the Virginia government finally issued the land grants in late 1772—nearly twenty years delinquent. As a field officer of the 1754 campaign, Washington was awarded some fifteen thousand acres, a third more than the regular militiamen. He offered, though, to relinquish part or all of this claim if complaints arose from other veterans that there should be a reallotment. But the complaints had to come from deserving veterans. One soldier who had behaved with cowardice at Fort Necessity charged that he had been cheated out of his fair share and apparently put the blame on his former commander. Washington's angry reply revealed a seldom-seen fire in his normally cool personality:

> Your impertinent letter...was delivered to me yesterday.... As I am not accustomed to receive such from any man, nor would have taken the same language from you

personally without letting you feel some marks of my resentment, I would advise you to be cautious in writing me a second of the same tenor. For though I understand you were drunk when you did it, yet give me leave to tell you that drunkenness is no excuse for rudeness, and that, but for your stupidity and sottishness, you might have known by attending to the public gazettes ... that you had your full quantity of ten thousand acres of land allowed you....

All my concern is that I ever engaged in behalf of so ungrateful and dirty a fellow as you are, ... as I do not think you merit the least assistance from

G. Washington[26]

"Scarce a Moment That I Can...Call My Own"

There were several other instances during Washington's domestic years when the heat of his temper flared at those who discourteously imposed on his good nature or his property. On one occasion, for example, he was hauling in a catch of fish from the Potomac when he almost lost his day's labor because of "an oyster man who had lain at my landing and plagued me a good deal by his disorderly behavior."[27] Three days later the troublesome poacher still had not left, and Washington's wrath boiled over. He "was obliged in the most peremptory manner to order him and his company away."[28]

Characteristically, however, he was a very amiable and generous man—not only to his friends and neighbors, but also to destitute transients who came to Mount Vernon begging for food or money. His nature would not permit him to turn away such people "without feeling inexpressible uneasiness."[29] Even while he was absent during the Revolutionary War, he instructed the manager of his estate to "let no one go hungry away" and to give "my money in charity to the amount of forty or fifty pounds a year."[30] In his later years he counseled Martha's grandson in the principle of liberality that had always guided his actions: "Never let an indigent person ask without receiving *something*, if you have the means, always recollecting in what light the widow's mite was viewed."[31]

Washington's generosity reached out to touch the lives of many, including several relatives and a large number of his former comrades in arms. Cash entries in his personal account books frequently carried such terse but meaningful notations as "To an old soldier," "To a wounded soldier," and "To a Virginia soldier."[32] In 1769 he volunteered to cover the expenses of a college education for the son of a friend—with no obligations attached. As he wrote to the boy's father, "No other return is expected or wished for this offer than that you will accept it with the same freedom and good will with which it is made, and that you may not even consider it in the light of an obligation, or mention it as such; for be assured that from me it will never be known."[33]

Nearby farmers, widows, and others in need increasingly called on him for advice and assistance. Because of his reputation for good judgment and sterling integrity, he was often asked to counsel acquaintances in financial distress or to serve as the executor of a deceased neighbor's estate. Such requests became so frequent that they grew burdensome. At the opening of 1775, Washington described how frustratingly busy he had been trying to meet the many obligations he had accepted:

> For this year or two past, there has been scarce a moment that I can properly call my own. . . . My own business, my present ward's [i.e., the estate of Jack Custis], my mother's (which is wholly in my hands), Colonel Colvill's, Mrs. Savage's, Colonel Fairfax's, Colonel Mercer's, . . . and the little assistance I have undertaken to give in the manage-

ment of my brother Augustine's affairs...keep me, together with the share I take in public affairs, constantly engaged in writing letters, settling accounts, and negotiating one piece of business or another in behalf of one or other of these concerns; by which I have really been deprived of every kind of enjoyment. [34]

Little did he realize that within a few short months he would find himself engaged in a completely different realm of activities—on a much larger scale—that would make these domestic concerns seem utterly tranquil by comparison. Circumstances were already combining that would thrust George Washington prominently onto the international stage.

Chapter 8

Seeds of Rebellion

King George III ascended to the throne of England in 1760, the year after Washington married and retired to private life at Mount Vernon. King George III was the first English-born, English-educated ruler of the British Empire since Queen Anne, who died in 1714. Queen Anne's successor, George I (1714-27), was an elector of Hanover, Germany, who seldom visited England, never learned English, and was never popular with the people. He was succeeded by his son, George II, who also spent most of his time in Germany. George II ruled so long (1727-60) that his crown prince died and the throne therefore passed to a grandson in 1760.

The British people on both sides of the Atlantic hailed George III as the first native English king they had had in forty-four years. He was born and educated in England, and he spoke the language without a German accent. He was also admired as a "family man," ultimately boasting a total of fifteen children.

Unfortunately, he was plagued by periods of mental illness throughout his adult life, until, in his later years, he became totally incompetent.

King George's stubborn and hot-tempered personality soon strained and eventually alienated the affections of the American colonists. Furthermore, the financial burden created by the French and Indian War led the king's ministers to initiate economic measures which, in time, provoked the Americans beyond endurance.

King George III, the British monarch whose policies led to the Declaration of Independence and the Revolutionary War. The Americans repeatedly petitioned the king and Parliament for a just government, but the petitions were uniformly ignored. George III, who reigned from 1760 to 1811, became deaf, blind, and insane before his death in 1820.

But America was not lit by a short fuse. Resentment had been building among the colonists for many years. The British government had long granted English merchants a monopoly on American raw materials, while manufactured goods generally had to be imported from Great Britain. These and other commercial restrictions were a galling irritation to American farmers and consumers alike, a painful sliver under their skin. Outrageous prices and shoddy workmanship combined with shipping damages and undelivered goods to heighten tensions and heat up tempers.

"Mean in Quality But Not in Price"

As he settled into the life of a Virginia gentleman, George Washington readily discerned the extreme disadvantages of the existing trade relations with the mother country. In August 1760 he wrote to the English factors who supplied orders for his estate: "I cannot forbear ushering in a complaint of the exorbitant prices of my goods this year.... Woolens, linens, nails, etc. are mean in quality but not in price, for in this they excel indeed, far above any I have ever had."[1]

He sent another protest the following month:

> Instead of getting things good and fashionable in their several kinds, we often have articles sent us that could only have been used by our forefathers in the days of yore. 'Tis a custom, I have some reason to believe, with many shopkeepers and tradesmen in London, when they know goods are bespoken for exportation, to palm sometimes old, and sometimes very slight and indifferent goods upon us, taking care at the same time to advance 10, 15, or perhaps 20 percent upon them.[2]

Like other frustrated Virginia planters, Washington chafed under Britain's discriminatory trade practices, which caught him in an impossible trap of debt. The problem began when he consistently received deflated prices for his exported tobacco crop. Since the crop would not support him, he was forced to obtain credit for the goods he ordered. But the credit proved to be more bane than blessing, since English lenders charged criminally excessive interest rates. In the spring of 1764 he was stunned to learn that his indebtedness to the overseas merchants was nearly £12,000. Even when he sought relief through crop rotation, home manufactures, and land investments, he found that most of his financial transactions were still controlled to a large extent by the narrow-minded British Parliament.

"This Unconstitutional Method of Taxation"

In the year 1765, colonial trade was disrupted by a controversial and unprecedented move on the part of the British government. Seeking new ways to reduce the pressing war debt, Parliament passed an ill-considered measure known as the Stamp Act, which required that government-issued stamps be purchased and placed on legal documents, newspapers, and many other articles that were sold or distributed within the colonies.

The colonists were outraged—the Stamp Act was a blatant violation of their rights as Englishmen. Up to this time, they had voted their own taxes in response to specific requests from the Crown; never before had taxes been levied upon them by the British Parliament. And since the colonies had no representation in Parliament, that ancient body had no legal authority, under long-standing English law, to pass taxes for America.

The Stamp Act was fiercely resisted in the colonies. Even before it went into effect, many Americans rioted in the streets, smuggled or boycotted British goods, and threatened the lives of the frightened officers appointed to enforce the act. The king and Parliament were flooded by a deluge of protests, petitions, and resolutions passed by town meetings, colonial assemblies, and an intercolonial Stamp Act Congress that met in New York in October 1765. Meanwhile, the tax stamps moldered unused in American seaport warehouses.

The floodgates of protest were first opened in the Virginia House of Burgesses, of which Washington was a prominent member. Writing privately to one of his wife's English relatives, he reflected the anxiety of most of his countrymen:

> The Stamp Act . . . engrosses the conversation of the speculative part of the colonists, who look upon this unconstitutional method of taxation as a direful attack upon their liberties, and loudly exclaim against the violation.
>
> What may be the result of this and some other (I think I may add) ill-judged measures, I will not undertake to determine. But this I may venture to affirm, that the advantage accruing to the mother country will fall greatly short of the expectations of the ministry; for certain it is [that] our whole substance does already in a manner flow to Great Britain, and that whatsoever contributes to lessen our importations must be hurtful to their manufacturers. And the eyes of our people, already beginning to open, will perceive that many luxuries which we lavish our substance to Great Britain for can well be dispensed with, while the necessaries of life are (mostly) to be had within ourselves. . . . Where, then, is the utility of these restrictions? . . .
>
> Our courts of judicature must inevitably be shut up; for it is impossible (or next of kin to it) under our present circumstances that the act of Parliament can be complied with, were we ever so willing to enforce the execution, for . . . we have not money to pay [for] the stamps, [and] there are many other cogent reasons to prevent it. And if a stop be

put to our judicial proceedings, I fancy the merchants of
Great Britain trading to the colonies will not be among the
last to wish for a repeal. [3]

Just as he predicted, the British merchants were soon
pleading with Parliament to do away with the Stamp Act.
These efforts, combined with the colonists' angry remonstrances, brought about a repeal of the hated measure in early
1766. Like other Americans, Washington was much relieved
that the storm had apparently passed. "The repeal of the
Stamp Act, to whatsoever causes owing, ought much to be
rejoiced at; for had the Parliament of Great Britain resolved
upon enforcing it, the consequences, I conceive, would have
been more direful than is generally apprehended, both to the
mother country and her colonies. All, therefore, who were
instrumental in procuring the repeal are entitled to the
thanks of every British subject, and have mine cordially." [4]

"Arms ... Should Be the Last Resource"

It was soon evident, however, that the colonists would
enjoy only a brief respite. During the same session in which it
revoked the Stamp Act, Parliament eased its humiliation by
passing a Declaratory Act asserting that it still had "full
power and authority to make laws and statutes of sufficient
force and validity to bind the colonies and people of America,
subjects of the Crown of Great Britain, in all cases whatsoever"—including taxation. [5]

Nerves were taut through the remainder of 1766 and into
1767. Americans had seen the bared teeth of the British lion
and were waiting fearfully for it to strike. In 1767 Parliament
made its move, passing the Townshend Act, which imposed
duties on various imports to the provinces. America was soon
invaded by a host of English customs officials sent to collect

the duties and prevent smuggling. These overzealous and often corrupt bureaucrats quickly became symbols of British oppression, and the colonists' resentment toward the royal government steadily intensified. As an additional sore spot, British troops that were expected to guard the frontier remained in the ports to support the collection of revenues. By the spring of 1769 a few were already thinking the unthinkable. One of these was thirty-seven-year-old George Washington:

> At a time when our lordly masters in Great Britain will be satisfied with nothing less than the deprication [sic] of American freedom, it seems highly necessary that something should be done to avert the stroke and maintain the liberty which we have derived from our ancestors; but the manner of doing it to answer the purpose effectually is the point in question.
>
> That no man should scruple or hesitate a moment to use arms in defense of so valuable a blessing, on which all the good and evil of life depends, is clearly my opinion. Yet arms, I would beg leave to add, should be the last resource. [6]

Washington was one of the first on the continent to openly speak of the dreaded possibility of using arms to defend the precious rights of his countrymen. Although most Americans would have been horrified at the thought, Washington did not shrink from the idea of military conflict with Great Britain. But such a course must be viewed only as the last alternative, after every other option had been exhausted. "Addresses to the throne and remonstrances to Parliament we have already . . . proved the inefficacy of," he wrote. "How far, then, their attention to our rights and privileges is to be awakened or alarmed by [our] starving their trade and manufactures remains to be tried." [7]

The Virginia Nonimportation Association

The idea of "starving" the English merchants by refusing to purchase their imported goods was appealing to an increasing number of discontented colonists. Perhaps that would prove an effective, bloodless alternative to the use of arms. When Washington traveled to Williamsburg for the May 1769 session of the House of Burgesses, he carried with him a nonimportation proposal for Virginia drawn up by his Potomac neighbor George Mason, a former Burgess. Some of the northern colonies had already implemented such a boycott. Now Washington wanted to see Virginia, most populous of all the colonies, join her voice in doing the same.

One of the first acts of the session was to call upon the king for a redress of grievances. When Lord Botetourt, then the royal governor of Virginia, heard of the act he promptly dissolved the assembly for their impertinence. Undeterred, the Burgesses adjourned to the nearby Raleigh Tavern, where they reconvened unofficially. There the discussion turned to nonimportation schemes, and Washington presented Mason's plan to put the proposal into action. The assembly was pleased with the basic idea, and appointed a committee (which included Washington) to draft recommendations for the entire body to consider.

Working from Mason's paper, the committee proposed a voluntary association of Virginia citizens to boycott all taxed articles from England. The Burgesses knew that about one out of every four Englishmen was residing in America, and hoped that a boycott of British products would motivate British merchants to join the colonists in their demands for a tax repeal. With the merchants and colonists banding together, the high-handed members of Parliament might be brought to their senses. Such reasoning won the day, and the

Virginia Burgesses voted to approve the resolutions.

Washington acted almost immediately on the plan. He spent the early part of the summer visiting estates in Fairfax and Prince William counties, seeking additional support for the boycott. And in late July, when he sent his annual order for goods from London, he clearly noted his personal intentions:

> If there are any articles contained in either of the [enclosed] invoices . . . which are taxed by act of Parliament for the purpose of raising a revenue in America, it is my express desire and request that they not be sent, as I have very heartily entered into an association . . . not to import any article which now is or hereafter shall be taxed for this purpose, until the said act or acts are repealed. I am therefore particular in mentioning this matter, as I am fully determined to adhere religiously to it, and may perhaps have written for some things unwittingly which may be under these circumstances. [8]

"Heavy Calamity . . . Threatens Destruction to Our Civil Rights"

Trouble was also brewing elsewhere, particularly in Boston and a few other port cities. In Boston, for example, the populace was so unruly that the king sent British troops to occupy the city and keep the peace there. Unfortunately, the occupation troops added to the tension, and in March 1770 feelings erupted into violence with the infamous Boston Massacre. The incident probably started when mischievous boys pelted British soldiers with snowballs; it ended when the gathering Bostonians were answered with a roar of gunfire that left five Americans dead and several others wounded.

Boston's Samuel Adams lost little time proclaiming what

the British had done in his hometown.

After nearly three years of stiff resistance among the colonists (including such tragedies as the Boston Massacre), Parliament bent to the pressure, repealing most of the Townshend Act in April 1770. The duty on tea was retained, but with the other changes relations between the provinces and the mother country entered a brief period of relative quiet.

The calm was deceptive. Churning under still waters were the old resentments many colonists held toward Great Britain. In late 1773, the bitterness burst through to the surface. Until that point Americans had largely ignored the tea duty by smuggling tea in from the Dutch. But in 1773 the British cracked down, trying to force compliance. On the night of December 16 a large group of zealous Bostonians, meeting compulsion with bold resistance, peremptorily dumped three hundred expensive chests of imported tea into Boston harbor. Parliament was stunned, and retaliated by passing a series of stringent laws that became known as the "Intolerable Acts." The most severe of these laws closed the port of Boston and essentially abrogated the charter of Massachusetts, effectively putting the state under British martial law. General Gage, one of Washington's comrades in arms during the French and Indian War, was made military governor of Massachusetts.

Washington first learned of these harsh measures in May 1774, while he was once again in Williamsburg attending the Virginia House of Burgesses. Feeling deep empathy for the plight of his brothers in Massachusetts, according to one source he rose to his feet on the assembly floor and solemnly offered to "raise a thousand men, subsist them at my own expense, and march . . . at their head for the relief of Boston."[9]

The colonial capitol at Williamsburg, Virginia. Washington served in the Virginia House of Burgesses there for almost twenty years before the Revolutionary War.

His appreciative colleagues were not ready to authorize such a daring move, but the story of Washington's "eloquent speech" quickly spread throughout the other provinces. The American people had not forgotten his reputation as a military hero.

Washington's courageous solution was ahead of its time, but the Burgesses did vote a resolution setting aside "the first day of June... as a day of fasting, humiliation, and prayer, devoutly to implore the divine interposition for averting the heavy calamity which threatens destruction to our civil rights and the evils of civil war."[10] Edgy at the mere mention of civil war, even in a context of praying that it not come, the royal governor, Lord Dunmore, dissolved the legislative body. As before, the Burgesses moved down the street to the Raleigh Tavern. Once settled in a large, private room, they adopted a paper urging all the American colonies to appoint delegates "to meet in general congress, at such place annually as shall be thought most convenient, there to deliberate on those general measures which the united interests of America may from time to time require."[11]

Washington, characteristically, took the resolution very seriously. On June 1, in words pregnant with meaning, he jotted in his diary, "Went to church and fasted all day."[12] A few days afterward he wrote to his old friend George William Fairfax, who had moved to England the preceding year:

> The [British] ministry may rely on it that Americans will never be taxed without their own consent; that the cause of Boston—the despotic measures in respect to it, I mean— now is and ever will be considered as the cause of America (not that we approve their conduct in destroying the tea); and that we shall not suffer ourselves to be sacrificed by piecemeal, though God only knows what is to become of us...while those from whom we have a right to seek protection are endeavoring by every piece of art and despotism to fix the shackles of slavery upon us.[13]

"Shall We...Whine and Cry for Relief?"

With the legislative session closed, Washington returned to his beloved haven, Mount Vernon. There he took precious time from his agricultural duties to write other letters propounding his developing political ideas. In one of these, he answered a correspondent who argued that "a humble and dutiful petition to the throne" would produce better results than Virginia's nonimportation scheme. Fuming, Washington replied: "Have we not tried this already? Have we not addressed the Lords and remonstrated to the Commons? And to what end? Did they deign to look at our petitions?

Does it not appear, as clear as the sun in its meridian bright-ness, that there is a regular, systematic plan formed to fix the right and practice of taxation upon us?... Ought we not, then, to put our virtue and fortitude to the severest test?"[14]

Two weeks later he bluntly told the same correspondent that "the Parliament of Great Britain have no more right to put their hands into my pocket, without my consent, than I have to put my hands into yours for money."[15] Then he reinforced his earlier point:

> As... I observe that [the British] government is pursuing a regular plan at the expense of law and justice to overthrow our constitutional rights and liberties, how can I expect any redress from a measure which has been ineffectually tried already?... Shall we, after this, whine and cry for relief when we have already tried it in vain? Or shall we supinely sit and see one province after another fall a prey to despotism?...
>
> I am convinced, as much as I am of my existence, that there is no relief but in their [the British government's] distress; and I think, at least I hope, that there is public virtue enough left among us to deny ourselves everything but the bare necessaries of life to accomplish this end. This we have a right to do, and no power upon earth can compel us to do otherwise till they have first reduced us to the most abject state of slavery that ever was designed for man-kind.[16]

In another letter written soon afterward he said, speaking with the assurance of one who has truly tried his feelings in the fire, "An innate spirit of freedom first told me that the measures which [the] administration have for some time been and now are most violently pursuing are repugnant to every principle of natural justice."

For my own part, I shall not undertake to say where the line between Great Britain and the colonies should be drawn; but I am clearly of opinion that one ought to be drawn, and our rights clearly ascertained. I could wish, I own, that the dispute had been left to posterity to determine, but the crisis is arrived when we must assert our rights or submit to every imposition that can be heaped upon us, till custom and use make us...tame and abject slaves. [17]

Chapter 9

America Protests

I n late May 1774 the House of Burgesses had requested that Virginia's counties hold citizens' meetings on the rapidly deteriorating state of Anglo-American relations. They recognized the vital need for a grass-roots movement, for an increased stirring in the hearts of the citizenry. Only then could America unite. Only then would an arrogant Crown—a stubborn Parliament—listen.

The Fairfax County gathering was set for July 18 in Alexandria, with George Washington chosen to preside. Under his direction, the "freeholders and inhabitants" of Fairfax voted to adopt a series of resolutions (drafted by Washington's neighbor George Mason) which vigorously protested recent acts of British oppression and urged additional nonimportation measures.

The Fairfax Resolutions

Many papers were issued from county meetings throughout Virginia during that summer of 1774, but the Fairfax
Resolutions were decidedly the most influential on American
political thought. Included in the document was a carefully
worded statement on the limited powers of Parliament and
the rights of freemen:

> *Resolved* that ... our ancestors, when they left their native
> land and settled in America, brought with them (even if the
> same had not been confirmed by charters) the civil
> constitution and form of government of the country they
> came from, and were by the laws of nature and nations
> entitled to all its privileges, immunities, and advantages;
> which have descended to us, their posterity, and ought of
> right to be as fully enjoyed as if we had still continued
> within the realm of England.
>
> *Resolved* that ... the most important and valuable part of
> the British constitution, upon which its very existence
> depends, is the fundamental principle of the people's being
> governed by no laws to which they have not given their
> consent, by representatives freely chosen by themselves. ...
>
> *Resolved* therefore, as the inhabitants of the American
> colonies are not, and from their situation cannot be,
> represented in the British Parliament, that the legislative
> power here can of right be exercised only by our own
> provincial assemblies or parliaments, subject to the assent
> or negative of the British Crown, to be declared within
> some proper limited time. ...
>
> *Resolved* that the claim lately assumed and exercised by the
> British Parliament, of making all such laws as they think fit
> to govern the people of these colonies, and to extort from
> us our money without our consent, is not only diametri-
> cally contrary to the first principles of the constitution

and the original compacts by which we are dependent upon the British Crown and government, but is totally incompatible with the privileges of a free people and the natural rights of mankind. [1]

In addition to the Fairfax Resolutions, the Fairfax County meeting appointed Washington as their delegate to a special convention of former Burgesses to be held in Williamsburg on August 1, 1774. There, as they met to determine what steps should next be taken in the mounting political crisis, the former Burgesses voted to accept proposals from several other provinces that the upcoming "general congress" meet at Philadelphia on September 5. Not surprisingly, George Washington was chosen as one of the seven delegates to attend. It was a turning point in a life which was already rich and eventful. As one modern biographer has written, Washington "could not have realized, by any power of human reason, what that relatively unimportant incident of being chosen one of seven delegates to a new, experimental Congress was to mean in his life." [2]

The Beginning Days of Congress

Traveling with fellow delegates Patrick Henry and Edmund Pendleton, Washington rode into the Quaker city on a quiet Sunday, September 4, 1774. The next morning he joined the other delegates at Carpenters' Hall, and the proceedings of the First Continental Congress were soon under way. The session stretched out nearly two full months.

As the days passed, Washington acquainted himself with many of the bright stars of the American provinces, men he had known before only by reputation—Samuel and John Adams of Massachusetts, John Jay of New York, and others whose names were equally familiar. In all, the assembly consisted of over fifty delegates, several of whom took occasion to record in their journals and private letters their cool-eyed impressions of one another's abilities. Washington was not mentioned as frequently as some of his illustrious colleagues, probably because he was usually silent in debate, saying little before the entire body of Congress. But Patrick Henry, whose unsurpassed oratorical powers had already made him something of a legend, knew the stuff of which the tall, quiet planter from Mount Vernon was made. Observed Henry in honest praise, "Colonel Washington, who has no pretensions to eloquence, is a man of more solid judgment and information than any man on the floor."[3]

As the debates progressed, the Congressmen formed a Continental Association, modeled after the one in Virginia, in which they agreed to join in a broad nonimportation pact. Merchants throughout the colonies were advised that they should avoid ordering any goods whatsoever from England until further notice—or be considered traitors to the patriot cause.

While the Congress was still in session, Paul Revere, a silversmith and sometime express rider, galloped down from Boston with the electrifying Suffolk Resolves. Authored by patriot Dr. Joseph Warren and adopted by the riled citizens of Suffolk County, Massachusetts, the Suffolk Resolves put the British on notice that the American people would no longer submit peaceably to British oppression. "Reprisal would be the answer to arrest, . . . scuffs would be returned as blows and, if need be, . . . war would be met with war," as one author has aptly paraphrased it.[4]

After scarcely any debate, on September 17, 1774, Congress unanimously accepted the Suffolk Resolves. "This assembly," they wrote, "deeply feels the suffering of their countrymen in the Massachusetts Bay, under the operation of the late unjust, cruel, and oppressive acts of the British Parliament." Furthermore, the Congress proclaimed that its members "most thoroughly approve the wisdom and fortitude with which opposition to these wicked ministerial measures has hitherto been conducted."[5]

On the same day, Congress passed a resolution calling for relief of the poor in Boston, who were suffering greatly from Great Britain's inhumane blockade.

Broadening Horizons

A good part of the first two weeks of the Congress were taken up with committee meetings. Since Washington had received no committee assignments, he likely spent some of his time studying the several political pamphlets he had purchased. He also made studious efforts to learn more about Virginia's sister colonies. He had visited Boston only once, and had several times been to Philadelphia, but virtually all of his travels as a youth had been into the frontier. His horizons had been narrow, and he knew it. Now he had an opportunity to learn more of the colonies surrounding Virginia. He sat long hours with other delegates, asking questions, probing, and listening thoughtfully.

Each colony had traditionally viewed itself as relatively independent from all the others, connected only by language, allegiance to Great Britain, proximity, and commercial concerns. But now a Congress of delegates from each of the states had voluntarily gathered together, bringing the colonies into a new relationship. Perhaps seeds of a new order were beginning to sprout.

On October 1, someone proposed that the Congress send another address to the king, pleading for justice in taxation.

Arguments boiled; like Washington, many of the delegates felt that repeated petitions were both futile and humiliating. All that the colonies wanted were their natural rights. Why should it be needful to beg for what was theirs *by right?* But Washington and other dissenters were eventually overruled, and the plea for relief was sent.

"Blood Will Be Spilt"

While Washington was still attending Congress, he received a disturbing letter from an old friend, Captain Robert Mackenzie, who had served under him during the French and Indian War. Mackenzie had since received a royal commission in the British army and was serving with his new compatriots in the military occupation of Boston. He had written Washington with a number of complaints about the rebellious citizens of Boston. Their minds had been twisted and deceived, he said. In their search for liberty they were seeking to overthrow the order of established government. The occupation of the British had been necessary to protect the better class of people in Boston.

Some of Mackenzie's arguments sounded good on the surface, but Washington knew his friend had utterly misread the circumstances in Boston. He responded with firmness:

> Though you are led to believe by venal men ... that the people of Massachusetts are rebellious, setting up for independence and what not, give me leave, my good friend, to tell you that you are abused, grossly abused. ...
>
> It is not the wish or interest of that government or any other upon this continent, separately or collectively, to set up for independence. But this you may at the same time rely on, that none of them will ever submit to the loss of those valuable rights and privileges which are essential to

the happiness of every free state, and without which life, liberty, and property are rendered totally insecure.

These, sir, being [the] certain consequences which must naturally result from the late acts of Parliament relative to America in general, and the government of Massachusetts Bay in particular, is it to be wondered at ... that men who wish to avert the impending blow should attempt to oppose it in its progress, or prepare for their defense if it cannot be diverted? Surely I may be allowed to answer in the negative; and again give me leave to add, as my opinion, that more blood will be spilt on this occasion, if the ministry are determined to push matters to extremity, than history has ever yet furnished instances of in the annals of North America.[6]

Washington's appointment to the First Continental Congress was a critical milestone in his public career. During his eight-week stay in Philadelphia he frequently dined with prominent men of the city, and everywhere he was received with great respect. He could not boast the gifts for speaking or writing possessed by many of the other delegates, who were some of the most eloquent in the colonies. He was appointed to no committees and rarely participated in the debates. But colonial leaders who had long esteemed his military reputation found on meeting him that Washington was a man of commanding presence and mature judgment. Moreover, his perspectives were broadened as he conversed with other leading patriots from all over America. It has aptly been observed that "his view now was increasingly continental."[7] He was not alone in his gradual yet inexorable shift in attitude from provincialism. Others too began to think not only of Virginia or Massachusetts or Pennsylvania, but of America. The powerful pull of common cause had already begun its slow work of bonding.

"To Devote My Life and Fortune"

Washington returned home at the end of October 1774. The plight of the colonies continued to weigh heavily on his mind. After a quiet Christmas season, he met in mid-January with George Mason and others to establish a military association in Fairfax County. Many other colonial militias were established at the same time, as local leaders responded to the resolves of Congress. During the next two months, Washington several times made the eight-mile trip to Alexandria to drill the green Fairfax militia.

On March 20, 1775, representatives of all the counties in Virginia met in Richmond to review the recommendations of the First Continental Congress, and to select delegates for a second Congress to be held in Philadelphia that May. Debates on how to deal with continuing British oppression raged through the halls. On the fourth day of the Richmond convention, fiery Patrick Henry stood to address a special meeting in a nearby church. His voice swelled in majesty as he concluded his stunning address:

> Gentlemen may cry, "Peace, peace!"—but there is no peace. The war is actually begun. The next gale that sweeps from the north will bring to our ears the clash of resounding arms! [The shots at Lexington and Concord were fired less than one month later.] Our brethren are already in the field! Why stand we here idle? . . . Is life so dear, or peace so sweet, as to be purchased at the price of chains and slavery? Forbid it, Almighty God! I know not what course others may take; but as for me, give me liberty or give me death![8]

The effect of Henry's speech was electric, spreading like a rippling wind through the chapel. Sitting in the audience was a tall, distinguished-looking man with classic features—

George Washington. He agreed with the strong words of his friend. With Patrick Henry, he felt he could say that peace, however sweet, was not worth "the price of chains and slavery."

Patrick Henry argued fiercely that the entire province must be put into "a posture of defense." The Virginia legislators agreed, appointing Henry to a committee that was to recommend defensive measures. To serve with Henry, among others, they selected George Washington, the most experienced military man of them all.

Two days later the Richmond convention selected its delegates to the Second Continental Congress, choosing the same seven they had sent the previous fall. As in 1774, the largest number of votes went to Peyton Randolph, long-time Speaker of the House of Burgesses and president of the First Continental Congress. Running a close second was George Washington. He accepted the responsibility without hesitation, having already committed himself fully to the righting of British wrongs. In a note he sent his brother Jack on the day of the election, he stated his position: "It is my full intention to devote my life and fortune in the cause we are engaged in."9

Bloodshed at Lexington and Concord

As Washington prepared to make another journey up to Philadelphia, the sullen undercurrent of strain in Massachusetts threatened to break out into open strife. Hoping to weaken the menace of his rebel enemies, Massachusetts Royal Governor Thomas Gage, who also served as commanding general of the British occupation army, planned a mission to seize their stock of arms at Concord. He also had warrants of arrest for Samuel Adams and John Hancock, leaders of the

General Thomas Gage, governor of Massachusetts and commander in chief of the British forces until 1775. He was removed from both of these positions after the Battle of Bunker Hill, where he lost half of his assault troops.

resistance movement. Gage's destination was secret, as was the day of the mission, though all Boston could see that a major movement was afoot. Through careful surveillance work, the Boston rebels uncovered Gage's plans and sent Paul Revere and Billy Dawes to warn the people along the way: the British were coming, and they intended to confiscate the stores at Concord.

The word spread like seeds on a gusty wind, and American minutemen from miles around responded to the call. Farmers, merchants, tradesmen, teachers, ministers—all dropped their work, picked up their guns, and began to move toward the British route. The first shots were fired at Lexington on April 19, 1775, in a sudden and bloody confrontation that reverberated "'round the world." After another brief battle at Concord, the British hastily retreated, leaving their wounded moaning on the ground and abandoning their dead where they had fallen.

It was to have been a routine mission, protected by a shroud of secrecy. But the secret was out, and as the British marched in terror back toward Boston, they ran a twenty-two-mile gauntlet through a bitter, endless hell of American gunfire. When the horror of the day was over, the British had 70 dead and 170 wounded—and Massachusetts was unequivocally committed to war.

The shocking news traveled quickly southward, stunning all who heard it. The scent of war was in the air as Washington and Richard Henry Lee set out in Washington's new coach to attend the Second Continental Congress in Philadelphia. After five days of traveling, they arrived on May 9. Five hundred horsemen met them on the outskirts of Philadelphia and escorted them, as honored visitors, into the city.

Within another week more news came from the north. Colonel Ethan Allen and the "Green Mountain Boys" of Vermont had just captured Fort Ticonderoga from the British. "You must surrender," Allen had commanded them, proclaiming that he acted "in the name of the great Jehovah and the Continental Congress."[10] After the British were evacuated Allen burned the fort to the ground.

"Can a Virtuous Man Hesitate?"

The Second Continental Congress convened on May 10, meeting at the Pennsylvania State House (later designated Independence Hall). During the 1774 session of Congress Washington had not been appointed to a single committee. But recent disturbing events placed his military experience in great demand.

His first assignment was to chair a committee charged with

planning defenses for New York City. Serving with him were Samuel Adams of Massachusetts, Thomas Lynch of South Carolina, and the entire New York delegation. Washington had barely launched into this work when he was asked, as chairman of another committee, to recommend means of supplying the colonies' great potential needs for ammunition and military stores. He was next appointed to help draw up guidelines for the strict regulation of an American army. There were other committee assignments as well.

While Washington attended the daily session of Congress, he chose an unusual form of dress—his old red-and-blue uniform from the French and Indian War. He left no record of his reason, but likely he wished to convey his profound, unhappy conviction that the time had come for fighting. [11]

Washington's ever-dignified appearance and his superior performance as chairman of several committees combined to make a deep impression on the other colonial representatives in Philadelphia. He was not the political philosopher that John Adams was, nor had he the broad European experience of fellow delegate Benjamin Franklin. But his military background was widely respected, and the others readily leaned on his wisdom. As John Adams noted, "Colonel Washington, . . . by his great experience and abilities in military matters, is of much service to us." [12]

Washington was among a growing number who felt that the British had gone too far, that Anglo-American relations had reached a tragic point of no return. His heart ached to think that relations with the mother country had degenerated to the point of armed conflict. But no other options remained. On the last day of May 1775 he wrote dismally to his old friend, George William Fairfax, now permanently in England:

Unhappy it is...to reflect that a brother's sword has been sheathed in a brother's breast, and that the once happy and peaceful plains of America are either to be drenched with blood or inhabited by slaves. Sad alternative! But can a virtuous man hesitate in his choice? [13]

Chapter 10

A General to the Generals

Boston was essentially in a state of siege, with determined militiamen camped outside the city and a distraught British army hesitant to move. Yet the rebellion was still a local affair, a noose around the necks of Massachusetts and her neighbors. In early June the congressional delegates began to consider a proposal from Massachusetts that the Congress assume direction of the growing American army. Volunteers from neighboring colonies were marching into the Boston area. Congress had issued resolutions indicating their firm support. Now it was time, people said, for words to be replaced by action and for the combined colonial forces to be organized on a continental basis. Another committee was appointed, again with Washington as a member, to resolve the sticky issue of financing such an army. Several days later Congress authorized the raising of ten companies from Pennsylvania, Maryland, and Virginia.

Choosing a Commander in Chief

By mid-June it was apparent that the question of a commander in chief for the amalgamated American forces could no longer be deferred. The matter had been discussed behind the scenes for nearly a month, and many of the delegates had already formed their opinions regarding this crucial appointment. Most of those from the northeastern colonies preferred an officer who would be familiar with their region. How could a southerner command a northern army in northern territory? John Adams, however, whose influence among New Englanders was substantial, was more politically astute than many of his fellows. Looking at the issue from a broad perspective, he understood that the colonies would stumble along in continued disunity if divergent interests were not brought together in the army.

As John Adams discussed the problem with his second cousin Samuel Adams and other delegates, the answer became increasingly clear. Most of them agreed that an army from the north combined with a commander from the south would create a thread that could run from the bottom of the colonies to the top, tying them together. As the delegates considered their options, they mentioned one name over and over again: George Washington. He was not only from the south, but was the closest thing to a *national* hero the colonies had. Furthermore, he was a skilled and experienced commander of battles against the French and the Indians in the years gone by. As discussions continued, there began to be a consensus that "the beloved Colonel Washington"[1] was the ideal man for the post.

Washington himself was fully aware of the discussions buzzing around him, and he made no secret of his deep reluctance to assume command of the army. He felt his training and abilities were inadequate for such an awesome responsibility—and he did all he could to restrain his friends in Congress from advocating his nomination. It appears that he even persuaded a fellow Virginia delegate to directly oppose his election.[2] This was the situation when John Adams rose on June 14 to introduce a motion that the Congress formally adopt the army in Massachusetts and appoint a commander in chief. Adams later described what happened:

> I had no hesitation to declare that I had but one gentleman in my mind for that important command, and that was a gentleman from Virginia who was among us and very well known to all of us, a gentleman whose talents and excellent universal character would command the approbation of all America, and unite the cordial exertions of all the colonies better than any other person in the Union.
>
> Mr. Washington, who happened to sit near the door, as soon as he heard me allude to him, from his usual modesty darted into the library room.[3]

Washington did not want the delegates to embarrass themselves by having to discuss his qualifications while he was sitting among them. He was still absent the following day when his colleagues unanimously elected him "to command all the continental forces raised or to be raised for the defense of American liberty."[4] They stipulated a salary of five hundred dollars per month. Through this action the new commander in chief became, for a time, the only man actually enlisted in the Continental Army. He was to take the reins of an unorganized military force to fight an undeclared war in behalf of a nation that did not yet exist. Realizing the extreme difficulty of these circumstances, the delegates afterward declared with courage and commitment that "this Congress... will maintain and assist him, and adhere to him, the said George Washington, Esquire, with their lives and fortunes in the same cause."[5]

"I Do Not Think Myself Equal to the Command"

When the day's proceedings closed, Washington heard the distressing, bittersweet news of his election. The next morning, June 16, 1775, he stood on the floor of Congress and accepted the commission, describing his nagging feelings of inadequacy but firmly pledging himself to the cause of liberty:

> Mr. President: Though I am truly sensible of the high honor done me in this appointment, yet I feel great distress from a consciousness that my abilities and military experience may not be equal to the extensive and important trust. However, as the Congress desires, I will enter upon the momentous duty and exert every power I possess in their service for the support of the glorious cause; I beg they will accept my most cordial thanks for this distinguished testimony of their approbation.
>
> But lest some unlucky event should happen unfavorable to my reputation, I beg it may be remembered by every gentleman in the room that I this day declare, with the utmost sincerity, I do not think myself equal to the command I am honored with.[6]
>
> As to pay, Sir, I beg leave to assure the Congress that, as no pecuniary consideration could have tempted me to have accepted this arduous employment at the expense of my domestic ease and happiness, I do not wish to make any profit from it. I will keep an exact account of my expenses; those I doubt not they will discharge, and that is all I desire.[7]

Washington's gracious, unassuming speech impressed all present. Here, clearly, was a man who sought neither riches nor fame, but was guided by a brighter star. Here, indeed, was a man who would "command the approbation of all America." With swelling hopes that they had made the right decision, John Adams wrote of his great confidence in their new commanding general, "This appointment will have a great effect in cementing and securing the union of these colonies."[8] It was a view shared by many.

"A Kind of Destiny...Has Thrown Me Upon This Service"

Washington was much less optimistic. His troubled reaction is clearly evident in his private letters to those he loved. To his brother Jack he acknowledged a disturbing apprehension that he had "embarked on a wide ocean, boundless in its prospect, and from whence perhaps no safe harbor is to be found."[9] It was his "first wish," he said, to "discharge the trust to the satisfaction of my employers,"[10] but in surveying the spiny challenges that lay ahead he knew he could promise only three things—"a firm belief [in] the justice of our cause, close attention in the prosecution of it, and the strictest integrity. If these cannot supply the place of ability and experience, the cause will suffer.... But it will be remembered, I hope, that no desire or insinuation of mine placed me in this situation."[11]

His anxious state of mind was best revealed in a painful letter he wrote to Martha. He was uneasy about how she would receive the news and carefully sought to reassure her—and possibly himself at the same time.

> My dearest: I am now set down to write to you on a subject which fills me with inexpressible concern, and this concern is greatly aggravated and increased when I reflect upon the uneasiness I know it will give you. It has been

determined in Congress that the whole army raised for the defense of the American cause shall be put under my care, and that it is necessary for me to proceed immediately to Boston to take upon me the command of it.

You may believe me, my dear Patsy, when I assure you in the most solemn manner that, so far from seeking this appointment, I have used every endeavor in my power to avoid it, not only from my unwillingness to part with you and the family, but from a consciousness of its being a trust too great for my capacity—and that I should enjoy more real happiness in one month with you at home than I have the most distant prospect of finding abroad, if my stay were to be seven times seven years.

But as it has been a kind of destiny that has thrown me upon this service, I shall hope that my undertaking it is designed to answer some good purpose....I shall rely, therefore, confidently on that Providence which has heretofore preserved and been bountiful to me, not doubting but that I shall return safe to you in the fall.

I shall feel no pain from the toil or the danger of the campaign; my unhappiness will flow from the uneasiness I know you will feel from being left alone. I therefore beg that you will summon your whole fortitude and pass your time as agreeably as possible. Nothing will give me so much sincere satisfaction as to hear this, and to hear it from your own pen. [12]

With this letter, Washington soberly enclosed his will. "Life is always uncertain," he explained, "and common prudence dictates to every man the necessity of settling his temporal concerns while it is in his power." [13]

Washington's Generals

After accepting his commission, the new commander in chief tarried in Philadelphia for a week to put his personal

affairs in order and to assist Congress in organizing the
Continental Army. Finally, on the morning of June 23, 1775,
after jotting a brief note to reassure Martha of his
"unalterable affection... which neither time nor distance can
change,"[14] he mounted his horse and started toward Boston.
Riding with him were two of his recently appointed major
generals, Charles Lee and Philip Schuyler.

Lee, a former British army officer, had seen extensive
"duty under fire" in various parts of Europe as well as in the
French and Indian War in America. He had served with
Washington under Braddock and had subsequently settled in
Virginia. When the conflict with England reached the crisis
stage he volunteered his services to Congress, who made him
third in command. The members of Congress were delighted
to have so experienced an officer in their service.

Lee's pride and eccentric personality, however, soon
revealed him to be something less than an asset. Foul-
mouthed, ragged, unwashed, and unkempt, Lee was said to
prefer the company of his dogs to that of humans. It rankled
him that Washington, rather than he, had been made the
commander in chief. At the very least, Lee felt, he should
have been made second in command; but since Artemas Ward
was the commander already in place in Massachusetts, Lee
had to settle for third. For a time Washington's high respect
for Lee's broad military experience somewhat blinded him to
Lee's character deficiencies, as well as his disloyalty to his
commander.

Major General Philip Schuyler seemed to be the opposite of
Lee in almost every way. Rather than being a professional
military man, Schuyler was a rich and aristocratic Dutch-
American landowner from New York. His dress and speech
were impeccable. He also had served during the French and

Indian War, and was a member of the Continental Congress
when he was appointed fourth in command under Washington.

Bad News from Boston

Just as Washington, Lee, and Schuyler were preparing to
leave Philadelphia, they received an alarming report which
greatly increased the urgency of their journey northward.
Although sketchy in details, the report described the first
major battle between the Americans and the British, a
shocking confrontation at Breed's Hill and Bunker Hill just
across the river from Boston. After the frightening bloodshed at Lexington and Concord only a few weeks earlier, the
Americans had entrenched themselves in a semicircle around
Boston. Two of these entrenchments were on small hills
overlooking Boston from across the Charles River to the
north. Fearing the potential strength of the American position, the British commander, General Thomas Gage, had
ordered some two thousand regulars to cross the river and
"scatter the rebels."

Washington knew Thomas Gage. They had served together under Braddock. He was a tough, determined professional. Washington also recognized the names of some of the
British military brass serving with Gage. The Breed's Hill
attack on the Americans had been led by General William
Howe, a member of Parliament and a hero of the 1759 Battle
of Quebec, which had wrenched Canada away from France.
Next in command was veteran Henry Clinton, who had just
arrived from England with Howe. He had been in the king's
service for twenty-four years; his father had been the royal
governor of New York from 1741 to 1751. Finally there was
"Gentleman Johnny" Burgoyne, who also had just arrived

from England. He was a member of Parliament, a well-known playwright, and a favorite in the high society of London.

These four—Gage, Howe, Clinton, and Burgoyne—were the military principals in what became known as the Battle of Bunker Hill. The battle had taken place on June 17, 1775. It began with a direct assault on Breed's Hill, with the British troops in full regalia marching three deep, shoulder-to-shoulder, directly up to the American trenches on the summit. The Americans, equipped primarily with old-fashioned muskets they had supplied themselves, held their fire until the British were so close they could "see the whites of their eyes." When the withering blast raked the British at close range, nearly five hundred redcoats were brought down. General William Howe never forgot the horrifying sight of his carefully disciplined, magnificently uniformed British regulars suddenly collapsing in a heap of crumpled bodies while the survivors raced back to the bottom of the hill in wild confusion.

But William Howe was a stubborn man. He regrouped the terrified soldiers and ordered a second assault. Once again the effort produced a catastrophic percentage of casualties, with the panicked survivors scrambling back down the hill.

Furious, Howe ordered his soldiers to attack once more. General Henry Clinton personally led the assault. Trembling in fear, the British soldiers marched back up the hill. But by now the Americans had virtually run out of ammunition. When the enraged British came over the top of their trenches with fixed bayonets, the slaughter was terrible, and the Americans abandoned their position.

The subsequent statistics depicted both the tragedy and the triumph of this bloody encounter. The Americans had

441 killed and wounded while the British lost 1,054. The British gained their point—but this Pyrrhic victory, with a loss of over a thousand professional soldiers, cost Thomas Gage his command. William Howe replaced him.

The Battle of Bunker Hill burned into the consciousness of the British command the unhappy reality of the emerging conflict. Americans would fight. To Washington, however, there was another reality, a very instructive one. If the Americans had been organized under a unified command, they would have been able to hold Breed's Hill. The soldiers waiting on Bunker Hill, only a few hundred yards away, had plenty of powder and ball. Had there been an organized command, the supplies could have been rushed in from the back side of Bunker Hill, saving over four hundred Americans from being killed or wounded.

When he heard the sorrowful tale of Bunker Hill, Washington's instinct for defensive combat surged in his breast. He hurried with greater urgency to get to his post of duty.

"When We Assumed the Soldier, We Did Not Lay Aside the Citizen"

When the General and his companions rode into New York City in the afternoon of June 25, after three hot days of travel from Philadelphia, they were surprised to be met by a great crowd of cheering citizens. The next morning a delegation from the New York Provincial Congress appeared at Washington's quarters, honoring him with an address from the legislators. His thoughtful reply was afterward circulated widely in colonial newspapers, helping to shape a strong and positive image of the new American commander in chief.

Gentlemen: At the same time that with you I deplore the unhappy necessity of such an appointment as that with which I am now honored, I cannot but feel sentiments of the highest gratitude for this affecting instance of distinction and regard.

May your every wish be realized in the success of America at this important and interesting period; and be assured that the every exertion of my worthy colleagues and myself will be equally extended to the reestablishment of peace and harmony between the mother country and the colonies, as to the fatal but necessary operations of war.

When we assumed the soldier, we did not lay aside the citizen; and we shall most sincerely rejoice with you in that happy hour when the establishment of American liberty, upon the most firm and solid foundations, shall enable us to return to our private stations in the bosom of a free, peaceful, and happy country. [15]

To what "happy country" did he refer? British America, which he expected would remain both British and free after a brief confrontation that would induce the Parliament to abandon its abusive policies. In mid-1775 Washington and most other Americans regarded the war not as a bold revolution or a romantic struggle for independence, but as a drastic effort to reestablish "peace and harmony between the mother country and the colonies." Although Americans were bitterly opposed to the tyrannical measures concocted by the ministers of George III and enacted by Parliament, they still looked upon themselves as loyal subjects of the British Crown. They sought liberty from injustice and oppression, not from allegiance to the king. For several months thereafter, Washington and his soldiers respectfully referred to the redcoats in Boston as "the ministerial troops." As Washington expressed it, "We . . . cannot yet prevail upon ourselves to call them the King's troops." [16]

But all of that would soon change.

"A Mixed Multitude of People...
Under Very Little Discipline"

Washington left General Schuyler behind with instructions for the defense of New York, a strategically important yet vulnerable city. He then proceeded with his party to the camp outside Boston, arriving on Sunday, July 2. After a cordial greeting from the Massachusetts officers who had assembled to meet him, Washington rode out for a first look at the fortifications. "The enemy," he wrote, were "in possession of a place called Bunker Hill on Charlestown Neck, strongly entrenched and fortifying themselves. I found part of our army on two hills...about a mile and a quarter from the enemy on Bunker Hill, in a very insecure state; I found another part of the army at [Cambridge], and a third part at Roxbury, guarding the entrance in and out of Boston."[17] The colonials were attempting to contain the redcoats within "a semicircle of eight or nine miles, to guard every part of which we are obliged to be equally attentive; while [the British], situated as it were in the center of the semicircle, can bend their whole force (having the entire command of the water) against any one part of it with equal facility." The Americans were thus in a precarious position. As Washington concluded in a somewhat dour understatement, "This renders our situation not very agreeable, though necessary."[18]

It was out of the question for the weak, thinly spread Americans to attempt an offensive. Such a move would simply be a species of suicide, and they would lose the ground they held. Instead, Washington wisely decided to strengthen his lines of defense in order to further protect his own men and keep the enemy bottled up. His major objective was to buy precious time. Every day he raced to gather much-needed supplies while urgently organizing, training, and disciplining

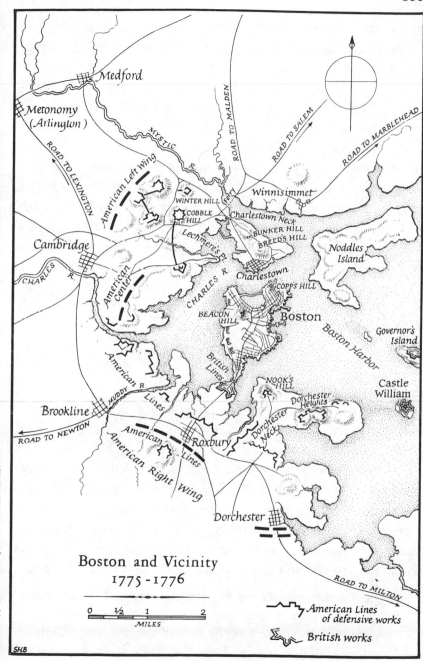

Boston and Vicinity
1775-1776

0   ½   1   2
MILES

⌐⌐⌐ *American Lines of defensive works*

〰 *British works*

SHB

the newborn Continental Army.

The magnitude of the task was overwhelming. Washington's heart sank as he surveyed his troops, "a mixed multitude of people ... under very little discipline, order, or government."[19] They had come to the field green and untrained, and green they had remained. On the day Washington arrived at his Cambridge headquarters, a committee from the Massachusetts Provincial Congress made an official visit, apologizing for the army's deficiencies. The poor condition of the army was unavoidable, they explained, given "the hurry with which it was necessarily collected." The majority of the troops "have never before seen service," they continued, "and although naturally brave and of good understanding, yet, for want of experience in military life, have but little knowledge of divers things most essential to the preservation of health and even life."[20]

"We Shall Work Up These Raw Materials into Good Stuff"

To fashion this "mixed multitude" of some 14,500 farmers and a few shopkeepers into an effective fighting machine would require something of a miracle, but the new commander in chief knew he must venture it. Several days after his arrival he cheerfully wrote to John Hancock, president of Congress, that he believed he had "materials for a good army, a great number of men able-bodied, active, zealous in the cause, and of unquestionable courage."[21] His first appeal to the soldiers was for unity and strict discipline:

> The Continental Congress having now taken all the troops of the several colonies ... into their pay and service, they are now the troops of the United Provinces of North America; and it is to be hoped that all distinctions of

colonies will be laid aside, so that one and the same spirit may animate the whole, and the only contest be who shall render, on this great and trying occasion, the most essential service to the great and common cause in which we are all engaged.

It is required and expected that exact discipline be observed and due subordination prevail through the whole army, as a failure in these most essential points must necessarily produce extreme hazard, disorder, and confusion, and end in shameful disappointment and disgrace. [22]

In addition to his general instructions, Washington concerned himself with specifics. He believed, as the English proverb says, that "great engines turn on small pivots." He ordered all officers "to pay diligent attention to keep their men neat and clean"; forbade "profane cursing, swearing, and drunkenness"; and required all who were off duty on the Sabbath to punctually attend "divine service to implore the blessings of heaven upon the means used for our safety and defense." [23]

By riding among the troops to inspect their defensive works, and by frequently calling for verbal and written reports from his subordinate officers, Washington soon familiarized himself with the conditions of the army. In his daily general orders he established regulations governing sanitation and health measures, desertions and cowardice, the use of arms and ammunition, the distribution of supplies and provisions, and many other details, and these he enforced by imprisonment and other punishments. The significant impact of his aggressive leadership was described by one approving observer, who said:

There is a great overturning in camp as to order and regularity. New lords, new laws. The Generals Washington and Lee are upon the lines every day. New orders from his Excellency are read to the respective regiments every morning after prayers. The strictest government is taking place, and great distinction is made between officers and soldiers. Everyone is made to know his place and keep it, or be tied up and receive ... thirty or forty lashes according to his crime. Thousands are at work every day from four till eleven o'clock in the morning. It is surprising how much work has been done. [24]

Although the greatest "confusion and disorder [had] reigned in every department" at the time of his arrival, in late July Washington recorded with satisfaction that "we mend every day, and I flatter myself that in a little time we shall work up these raw materials into good stuff." [25]

A Complex Challenge

When Washington first met his troops, he realized he did not have an army at all. Instead, he found himself with a varied batch of independent-minded men from many different colonies, each trying to pull the army apart.

The troops truly were a heterogeneous hodgepodge. Some of the men had fought the French and Indians nearly twenty years before but were hardly prepared to meet the resolute British in a direct assault. Others had no military experience whatsoever. Uniforms were the exception rather than the rule. Some of the men had weapons generously provided by local patriots; others used guns they had brought with them; a few, surprisingly, had no weapons at all until something could be scrounged up for them.

Men who were accustomed to loose fighting in the forests had little experience with the fine art of military drill. Squadron commanders somewhat vainly attempted to correct the situation by drilling their men according to standard texts of the day, such as *The Norfolk Exercise*. Different books used different methods, however, and it was not unusual for neighboring regiments to engage in conflicting military drills.

Discipline was another worry. Some of the men were autonomous souls from the frontier, accustomed to an existence of bare survival and doing things on their own. Others not only prided themselves in being independent but were totally egalitarian—and they were less than excited about the idea of taking orders from someone else, no matter what his rank.

The long years of war did little to solve most of these problems, particularly since the makeup of the army was in a continuous state of flux. Washington recognized his major handicap to be a lack of discipline in the ranks, and he did what he could to cure it. He was repeatedly forced to issue orders against plundering. He sternly condemned profanity and gambling. He directed his regimental officers to require their men to wash their clothing, bodies, and hair, and to use proper toilet facilities. He continued the traditional British and European practice of whipping offenders, though modified in accordance with American sensibilities. He expected his men to be a credit to their cause as well as to themselves, and he treated them accordingly.

One month after assuming command Washington wrote soberly:

> I have made a pretty good slam among such kind of officers as the Massachusetts government abound in, . . . having broken one colonel and two captains for cowardly behavior in the action on Bunker Hill, two captains for drawing more provisions and pay than they had men in their company, and one for being absent from his post

when the enemy appeared there and burnt a house just by
it. Besides these, I have at this time one colonel, one major,
one captain, and two subalterns under arrest for trial. [26]

Short enlistments further aggravated the problem. Just as
soon as a group was trained and conditioned to army
discipline, their term of enlistment would expire and they
would be swiftly on their way back home. Recruiting was
impeded by abominably low pay and miserable living
conditions. As an additional complication, at the same time
Washington was trying to establish a more permanent
national army, the states were seeking recruits to fill their
temporary militia quotas. Both had to pull from a common
pool, with the men usually going to the highest bidder—and
even the poor states often had more money to spend than an
insolvent Congress did.

Uniforms remained in short supply throughout the war.
Even the barest essentials of clothing were sometimes
lacking, with soldiers suffering for want of shoes, coats, even
trousers.

"Poor Bloody Tommy"

The markedly superior British army stood in stark contrast. The Americans were rustic farmers and city-dwelling
craftsmen, taking time off from their normal quiet occupations to fight for their freedom. The British soldiers, on the
other hand, were highly trained professional troops. The
men were incessantly drilled, hour after hour, to teach them
the subtleties of synchronized movement. When they failed
to measure up, unfeeling officers flogged them into obedience.

"Poor bloody Tommy," as some called the British infan-
tryman, had to dress and powder his hair every day —or suf-

fer a stiff fine or brutal flogging. He was required to wear spotless white breeches, daily applying a moist paste called pipe clay to hide dirt and stains. The clay left poor Tommy's legs damp and uncomfortable. When the clay dried, it shrank the breeches, chafing his legs and cutting off circulation.

Pay for the British soldier was atrocious, and what he did earn was often siphoned away for his uniform and mandatory grooming. Food allotments were so meager that hunger loomed like a grim specter over every camp.

With such intolerable conditions, it is surprising that anyone enlisted at all. Conscription did not exist—but illegal press gangs did, and they were constantly active in finding new "recruits." Other soldiers came from the poor classes, the down-and-out, those viewed as society's unfortunate dregs. They included the unemployed and unemployable, men with no inheritance, ex-convicts (who could not find a suitable job elsewhere), the mentally deficient, and unhappy men who were given a bitter choice between armed service and jail.

The lot of the officers, predictably, was significantly better. Commissions were available for purchase by the wealthy, with one's rank often matching the price he was willing to pay. If one were truly rich and powerful, he could form an entirely new regiment, then hire out his troops to the king. It was viewed as a business arrangement, pure and simple.

Thus the privileged officers came almost invariably from the wealthy upper classes, while the troops enlisted from the lower classes. With such a system, it is amazing that the army was the efficient fighting machine that it was. Somehow they trained men to march unwaveringly into the ugly face of death—as they did when climbing the blood-soaked ground of Breed's Hill.

Despite British superiority, however, the Americans had one distinct advantage. British soldiers were fighting for their paltry pay, for fear of their officers, for duty to the Crown, for a portion of fickle glory. The Americans, conversely, were fighting for personal freedom and for independence from what they viewed as intolerable oppression. In the end, it was probably not so much the makeup of the armies, or their relative strengths and weaknesses, as it was the *reason* for which they were fighting that made the difference and determined the outcome.

Chapter 11

A Troubled Command

With the weakness of his command, Washington was grateful for a brief respite to begin to put his army in order. Despite the temporary lull in action, he was convinced that an enemy attack was imminent. On July 27, 1775, he noted apprehensively that "the [British] transports are all arrived and their whole reinforcement is landed, so that I can see no reason why they should not . . . come boldly out and put the matter to issue at once."[1] A week later he was perplexed. The redcoats had "lain much longer inactive than I expected," he wrote.[2] He feared a meeting of the forces, but at the same time he seemed almost eager to put his troops to the test.

"For Half an Hour He Did Not Utter a Word"

Then the roof fell in on his cautious optimism. He had been informed upon first reaching Cambridge that the local military stores contained 308 barrels of gunpowder, an ample supply. But when he tried in early August to distribute a portion among the troops, word came from the storehouse that only 36 barrels were left! The total would provide a scant nine cartridges per man. Washington was so dismayed when he heard this news that, according to one source, "for half an hour he did not utter a word."[3]

When he did speak he ordered the strictest secrecy. If the enemy should learn of their desperate plight before it could be corrected, he said, the consequences would be "terrible even in idea."[4] He sent urgent appeals to the nearby townships and neighboring colonies for more powder, and he wrote to the president of Congress that "the existence of the army and salvation of the country" depended on relief that was "both speedy and effectual."[5]

Colonial leaders responded, and within a few weeks the shortage was made up. By September 10 Washington could state with confidence that his forces were "in no fear or dread of the enemy, being... very securely entrenched, and wishing for nothing more than to see the enemy out of their strongholds that the dispute may come to an issue."[6] Weeks dragged on, and still the British made no advance. The tense state of inactivity was "exceedingly disagreeable," Washington wrote, "especially as we can see no end to it." Why the stagnation? Washington could not say—unless perhaps "the ministerial troops in Boston are waiting for [more] reinforcements." Otherwise, "I cannot devise what they are staying there after, and why (as they affect to despise the Americans) they do not come forth and put an end to the contest at once."[7]

"My Situation Is Inexpressibly Distressing"

The strain of constant waiting, with no action, was

aggravating to commander and men alike. Despite all Washington's efforts to train and discipline his men and to "make them watchful and vigilant," he found that it was "among the most difficult tasks I ever undertook in my life to induce these people to believe that there is, or can be, danger till the bayonet is pushed at their breasts."[8] The longer they sat idle, the more unruly they became. Insubordination and neglect of duty were rampant in some regiments, frequent requests for furloughs weakened the army's tenuous morale and numerical strength, and foolish intercolonial jealousies led to constant bickering among the officers and soldiers.

Further heightening the irritation were the vexing shortages of money, food, clothing, blankets, and other supplies. Even worse, the entire army would disband by the end of the year (December 31, 1775) unless enlistments could be extended or new troops recruited.[9] The combined challenges were overwhelming, even to such an optimist as George Washington. On September 21 he sent a pleading report to the president of Congress, describing the circumstances that were threatening to destroy the American army:

> My situation is inexpressibly distressing—to see the winter fast approaching upon a naked army, the time of their service within a few weeks of expiring, and no provision yet made for such important events. Added to this, the military chest is totally exhausted. The paymaster has not a single dollar in hand. The commissary general assures me he has strained his credit to the utmost for the subsistence of the army; the quartermaster general is precisely in the same situation, and the greater part of the army in a state not far from mutiny [because of the resulting] deduction from their stated allowance.[10]

The General was not seeking to place blame: "I know not to whom to impute this failure." But the woeful conclusion was inescapable: "I am of opinion [that] if the evil is not immediately remedied and more punctuality observed in [the] future, the army must absolutely break up."[11]

"Could I Have Foreseen..."

In addition to sending repeated pleas to Congress, Washington appealed directly to his soldiers. In late October, in warm and stirring words, he urged his men to stay on for the 1776 campaign.

> The times and the importance of the great cause we are engaged in allow no room for hesitation and delay. When life, liberty, and property are at stake; when our country is in danger of being a melancholy scene of bloodshed and desolation; when our towns are laid in ashes, and innocent women and children driven from their peaceful habitations, exposed to the rigor of an inclement season and to the hands of charity, perhaps, for a support—when calamities like these are staring us in the face, and a brutal, savage enemy... are threatening us and everything we hold dear with destruction from foreign troops, it little becomes the character of a soldier to shrink from danger.[12]

Despite such moving entreaties, some of the troops began departing for home even before their enlistments were up; these were forcibly apprehended and escorted back to their posts. Others temporarily refused to reenlist, holding out for offers of promotion or preferment, "[standing] aloof to see what advantage they could make for themselves."[13] Washington was both hurt and disgusted by such attitudes. Confiding to one of his personal aides, he said:

> Such a dearth of public spirit and want of virtue, such stock-jobbing and fertility in all the low arts to obtain advantages of one kind or another in this great change of

military arrangement, I never saw before and pray God I may never be witness to again.... Such a dirty, mercenary spirit pervades the whole that I should not be at all surprised at any disaster that may happen....

Could I have foreseen what I have [experienced], and am likely to experience, no consideration upon earth should have induced me to accept this command.[14]

Observers could readily see the heavy stress the commander in chief was laboring under. President James Warren of the Massachusetts Provincial Congress wrote, "I pity our good General, who has a greater burden on his shoulders and more difficulties to struggle with than I think should fall to the share of so good a man."[15] Washington agreed that his life at Cambridge brought "nothing else...but one continued round of annoyance and fatigue."[16] He knew his duty, however, and was determined to carry it out, whatever the personal costs. In early December he proclaimed his unyielding resolve: "I have met with difficulties...such as I never expected; but they must be borne with. The cause we are engaged in is so just and righteous that we must try to rise superior to every obstacle in its support."[17]

"The Best Man for the Place He Is...That Ever Lived"

In spite of the exasperation they brought him, officers and men of the Continental Army quickly developed a sincere respect for Washington. One officer, a mammoth twenty-five-year-old Bostonian named Henry Knox, wrote to his wife that "General Washington fills his place with vast ease and dignity, and dispenses happiness around him."[18] The growing devotion of the American troops toward their commander in chief resulted largely from his carefully balanced philosophy of military leadership, which he summarized in a letter to a young, inexperienced Virginia colonel who had asked for his counsel:

> The best general advice I can give . . . is to be strict in your discipline; that is, to require nothing unreasonable of your officers and men, but see that whatever is required be punctually complied with. Reward and punish every man according to his merit, without partiality or prejudice. Hear his complaints; if well founded, redress them; if otherwise, discourage them in order to prevent frivolous ones.
>
> Discourage vice in every shape, and impress upon the mind of every man, from the first to the lowest, the importance of the cause and what it is they are contending for. . . . Be easy and condescending in your deportment to your officers, but not too familiar, lest you subject yourself to a want of that respect which is necessary to support a proper command. [19]

Those outside the army were also impressed with the General's personality and bearing. Abigail Adams wrote to her husband, John, after a first meeting: "You had prepared me to entertain a favorable opinion of General Washington, but I thought the half was not told me. Dignity with ease and [complaisance], the gentleman and soldier, look agreeably blended in him. Modesty marks every line and feature of his face."[20] His appearance as well as his character prompted glowing praise. Surgeon James Thacher described him as "truly noble and majestic, being tall and well proportioned."[21] And Dr. Benjamin Rush of Philadelphia was even more exuberant: "General Washington . . . seems to be one of those illustrious heroes whom Providence raises up once in three or four hundred years to save a nation from ruin. . . . He has so much martial dignity in his deportment that you would distinguish him to be a general and a soldier from among ten thousand people. There is not a king in Europe that would not look like a *valet de chambre* by his side."[22]

As more and more Massachusetts colonists met him, they agreed with the president of their legislature in the high appraisal that Washington was "certainly the best man for the place he is in, important as it is, that ever lived."[23]

Martha Washington Comes to Cambridge

Both the irksome frustrations of command and the rich gratification of public praise were overshadowed by a happy event in mid-December: the General's wife, together with recently married Jack and Nelly Custis, arrived at his headquarters in Cambridge. Martha had never before ventured so far from home, and it took several weeks for her to muster the courage to make this long, demanding journey. En route she was surprised by the flattering attentions given to her; near Philadelphia, for example, she recorded that a delegation from the city met her "in as great pomp as if I had

Martha Washington in the early to mid-1770s, some twelve to fifteen years after her marriage to George. Martha once described herself as "steady as a clock, busy as a bee, and cheerful as a cricket."

been a very great somebody."[24]

The Washingtons had been separated for seven lonely months, and the reunion between the General and his travel-worn wife was undoubtedly filled with joy. Martha soon discovered, however, that military life took a heavy toll on her nerves. "I confess I shudder every time I hear the sound of a gun," she wrote candidly to a friend in Virginia. "But I endeavor to keep my fears to myself as well as I can."[25] Grateful to be with her husband even in such anxious circumstances, Martha resolved to remain through the winter, serving as hostess to visitors and making life more comfortable for George. The leading citizens of Massachusetts and others who came to headquarters seemed to agree that she was perfectly fitted for this role. One of these visitors said of Mrs. Washington, "The [complaisance] of her manners speaks at once the benevolence of her heart, and her affability, candor, and gentleness qualify her to soften the hours of private life, or to sweeten the cares of the hero and smooth the rugged pains of war."[26]

"Nothing But Confusion and Disorder"

Martha undoubtedly did much to "sweeten the cares of the hero," but she could not remove her husband's anguish over the army's rapidly deteriorating condition. As 1775 drew to a close, many soldiers had marched home already, and the remainder were enlisted only until the end of December. Provisions for new troops were frighteningly inadequate. On the last day of the year one of the Continental officers wrote in discouragement: "Nothing but confusion and disorder reign. . . . We never have been so weak as we shall be tomorrow."[27]

But the army did not entirely disintegrate with the

dawning of 1776, as Washington had feared. Almost half of the men decided to stay on for the next campaign, and desperately needed reinforcements began to arrive from New England and some of the other colonies. Still, in early January total enlistments amounted to a scant 8,200, and of these only 5,582 were actually present and fit for duty. [28] Even fewer had firearms.

General Washington felt he was trapped in a cycle of unhappy circumstance. "I have scarcely emerged from one difficulty before I have plunged into another," he wrote. "How it will end, God in his great goodness will direct. I am thankful for his protection to this time. We are told that we shall soon get the army completed, but I have been told so many things which have never come to pass that I distrust everything." [29] A few days later he restated his fears:

> Reflection on my situation, and that of this army, produces many an uneasy hour when all around me are wrapped in sleep. Few people know the predicament we are in. . . .
>
> I have often thought how much happier I should have been if, instead of accepting of a command under such circumstances, I had taken my musket on my shoulder and entered the ranks. . . . If I shall be able to rise superior to these and many other difficulties which might be enumerated, I shall most religiously believe that the finger of Providence is in it. [30]

Washington Proposes a Permanent Army

What distressed Washington most was the impossible requirement of maintaining a viable military force when Congress would authorize only voluntary, short-term enlistments. In a soundly reasoned letter to John Hancock, president of Congress, he explained the painful dilemma.

To [make] men well acquainted with the duties of a
soldier requires time; to bring them under proper discipline
and subordination not only requires time, but is a work of
great difficulty.... To expect, then, the same service from
raw and undisciplined recruits as from veteran soldiers is to
expect what never did and perhaps never will happen. Men
who are familiarized to danger meet it without shrinking,
whereas those who have never seen service often apprehend danger where no danger is....

But this is not all. Men engaged for a short, limited time
only have the officers too much in their power; for to obtain
a degree of popularity in order to induce a second enlistment, a kind of familiarity takes place which brings on a
relaxation of discipline, unlicensed furloughs, and other
indulgences incompatible with order and good government, by which means the latter part of the time for which
the soldier was engaged is spent in undoing what you were
aiming to inculcate in the first....

Congress...would save money and have infinitely
better troops if they were, even at the bounty of twenty,
thirty, or more dollars, to engage the men already
enlisted,...and such others as may be wanted to
complete...the establishment, for [the duration of] the
war....

The trouble and perplexity of disbanding one army and
raising another at the same instant, and in such a critical
situation as the last was, is scarcely in the power of words to
describe, and such as no man who has experienced it once
will ever undergo again.[31]

Despite such careful arguments, the same "trouble and
perplexity" continued for months and years before congressional delegates were able to overcome their deep-seated fear
of a large standing army.[32] (A large continental army was
authorized as early as July 1775, but the soldiers were all on

short-term enlistments. Long-term enlistments were approved in September 1776—but Congress had neither the means nor the will to make such enlistments attractive.) As a predictable but troublesome consequence, much of Washington's time and energy during the war was consumed in recruiting, arming, outfitting, and training new men to replace those who had enlisted for only a few months.

To make matters worse, for security reasons he had to keep the horrible secret of the army's true state of weakness from his own officers. As he confided in a trusted friend:

> My own situation feels so irksome to me at times that, if I did not consult the public good more than my own tranquility, I should long ere this have put everything to the cast of a die. So far from my having an army of twenty thousand men well armed, etc., I have been here with less than one half of it, including sick, furloughed, and on command, and those neither armed nor clothed as they should be. In short, my situation has been such that I have been obliged to use art to conceal it from my own officers. [33]

"The Spirit of Freedom Beats Too High in Us to Submit"

In the midst of Washington's mental agony over his feeble army, several events occurred which bolstered his resolve to win the war. Soon after the opening of the new year, 1776, he received a copy of a royal proclamation in which King George III vowed to utterly crush the colonial rebellion. The General reacted with dry humor. "We are at length favored with a sight of his Majesty's most gracious speech, breathing sentiments of tenderness and compassion for his deluded American subjects," he wrote sarcastically to a friend. Then, in the same tone: "By this time I presume [the redcoats] begin to think it strange that we have not made a formal surrender."[34]

A few days later his humor turned to wrath when he learned that Lord Dunmore, the royal governor of Virginia, had supervised the bombing and burning of Norfolk on January 1. Patriots in the city had refused to give provisions to Dunmore's troops, and the governor decided to teach them a lesson. That same January Washington read *Common Sense,* a new pamphlet by Thomas Paine, which developed a compelling argument for complete independence from Great Britain. Tens of thousands of copies of this forceful publication spread through the colonies almost overnight, exerting a tremendous influence on the thinking of the colonists. On the last day of January the commander in chief pulled these events together, writing insightfully:

> I hope my countrymen . . . will rise superior to any losses the whole navy of Great Britain can bring on them, and that the destruction of Norfolk and the threatened devastation of other places will have no other effect than to unite the whole country in one indissoluble band against a nation which seems to be lost to every sense of virtue. . . . A few more of such flaming arguments as were exhibited at Falmouth and Norfolk, added to the sound doctrine and unanswerable reasoning contained in the pamphlet *Common Sense,* will not leave numbers at a loss to decide upon the propriety of a separation.[35]

This was Washington's first indication that he had fully committed himself to the idea of American independence. Ten days later he confirmed this position when he declared that the British ministers must understand "that the spirit of freedom beats too high in us to submit to slavery, and that . . . we are determined to shake off all connections with a state so unjust and unnatural."[36]

Those first weeks of 1776 proved to be a turning point for George Washington. The real objective of the war was now clear: total separation from England. As this awesome realization settled upon him, his conviction deepened that the American soldiers were not simply fighting over a plot of real estate. Much more importantly, they were defending "the cause of virtue and [of] mankind." Divine Providence would not permit them to fail.[37]

The War Moves to Canada

In the summer of 1775 Congress had initiated a campaign to conquer Canada and woo the predominantly French population into an alliance with the American colonies. Washington had left Philip Schuyler to develop the defenses of New York, but Congress preempted his services and assigned him to head up the Canadian campaign with a highly competent former British officer, Richard Montgomery, as his aide.

Schuyler was less than enthusiastic about the mission. He wavered and stalled, finally resigning on account of illness. This left tall and graceful Montgomery on his own.

The skilled Montgomery moved against the British forts on the Richelieu River, capturing them after an extended siege. Then, with winter threatening, he attacked Montreal, capturing the city on November 12, 1775.

In the meantime, Benedict Arnold was busy on his own expedition against Canada. He had assisted Ethan Allen in the taking of Fort Ticonderoga the previous May, and that same month he had approached Congress about invading Canada. Miffed when Congress accepted his idea but appointed Schuyler, he rushed from Philadelphia to meet with Washington in Boston. He complained bitterly about the decision of Congress; after all, it was the fall of Fort Ticonderoga that opened Canada to conquest. To pacify the fiery Arnold, Washington agreed to let him march against Quebec while Montgomery was capturing Montreal. With him went young Aaron Burr, a green soldier with apparent natural ability, and Captain Daniel Morgan.

Daniel Morgan, a first cousin of Daniel Boone, was a battle-scarred old hand. At the age of nineteen he had served as a teamster under Braddock. In 1756 an officer had struck Morgan with the flat of his sword—and Morgan struck back. In payment he was given five hundred lashes with a whip. Two years later, in the Indian wars, an Indian bullet passed through his neck and mouth, knocking out all the teeth on one side. When Morgan heard news of Lexington and Concord, he gathered one hundred crack riflemen and marched them from the Virginia mountains to Boston. They covered six hundred miles in twenty-one days without losing a man.

Morgan soon became bored with the endless stalemate at Boston. When he learned that Benedict Arnold was marching up to take Quebec, he signed up. About a thousand others did the same.

Arnold's Incredible March

Benedict Arnold's trek to Quebec was an incredible ordeal from beginning to end. Because he started so late in the year, in the final days of September, his expedition carried a curse of doom almost from the first day. His route was to take him up to Maine; then he would push north up the Kennebec River until he could catch the Chaudiere River, which roared down to the St. Lawrence just across from Quebec. But the only boats available were made with green lumber and were poorly constructed. Many fell apart, drowning the hapless soldiers in pummeling waters. The remaining boats sometimes had to be hauled over swamps or rugged terrain. One stretch of swampy ground reached on for nearly 180 miles; the exhausted men had no choice but to wade across the entire distance.

> After provisions gave out, the Americans ate soap and hair grease. They boiled and roasted their bullet pouches, moccasins, and old leather breeches and devoured them. They killed and ate the dogs that accompanied them. There were dropouts and slow death and mass defections along the way. At one point Lieutenant Colonel Roger Enos refused to go on and withdrew his division of 300 men. Undaunted, Arnold pressed forward. On November 9 [one week after Montgomery had captured Montreal] his ragged band burst from snow-cloaked forests onto the south bank of the St. Lawrence. They marched upriver to Point Levi on the Isle of New Orleans. They were ragged and bearded. Their feet were shod in raw skins. Their clothes hung in tatters over bodies that were but bags of sticks. There were only 600 of them. They had taken 45 days, not the estimated 20, to cover 350, not 180, miles. But they had arrived, and they were going to attack Quebec. [38]

Arnold knew he was outnumbered two to one, and he sent urgent word for Montgomery to join him. Meanwhile, he moved ahead with his attack. The Americans met a troop of militia on the Plains of Abraham outside Quebec, beating them badly. But when a British commander arrived with eight hundred reinforcements, the Americans were forced to retreat.

Arnold's men were suffering severely from lack of food and clothing in the freezing Canadian winter. Then, on December

2, 1775, Montgomery arrived from Montreal with three hundred men and a boatload of food and warm clothes captured from the British—warm caps, moccasins for bare feet, heavy overalls, thick coats.

The Attack on Quebec

Now nearly a thousand strong, the combined American armies of Arnold and Montgomery moved against Quebec. It was truly a desperate gamble. The city was strongly fortified, and Sir Guy Carleton had brought in another six hundred reinforcements. A siege of the city to starve them out was impossible—the Americans themselves were facing starvation. To make matters worse, smallpox had broken out in the ranks. Arnold knew many of his men were already talking about going home when their enlistments expired at the end of the month. Under these circumstances, both Arnold and Montgomery concluded there was no other choice. They must attack.

The snow was falling as they marched against the city, dragging a cannon on a sled and carrying scaling ladders. Soon the snowfall turned into a blizzard. Soldiers floundered through drifts deeper than the men were tall.

Arnold attacked from the north, leading a small force that included Daniel Morgan. The British were ready for them. After only minutes of furious fighting Arnold was down— wounded with a bullet in the leg. The command passed to the huge Daniel Morgan. He took a bullet through his beard and another through his hat, but still he pushed on. His men successfully forced their way past the first barrier, then halted, waiting for Montgomery's group.

On the other side of the fortress, Montgomery and his men pulled at a barricade with their bare, freezing hands. His force was only sixty strong—hundreds had been lost in the storm. They tore the barrier down and moved ahead. Immediately in front of them was a blockhouse with three small cannon. They charged. Flame roared through the ports, a torrent of grapeshot coming with it. The men screamed, twisted, fell into the snow. Only a few, including Aaron Burr, escaped. Richard Montgomery, the man who had reluctantly left his new wife to go to war, lay dead, his blood staining the snow under his body.

Morgan was now in desperate trouble. He was greatly outnumbered, and more British were coming from the rear. Some of the Americans began to surrender. Morgan fought on, tears of disappointment and rage streaming down his face. Then he spotted a clergyman in the crowd. "Are you a priest?" he called out. The man nodded, and Morgan handed him his blade. "Then I give my sword to you," he said. "But not a scoundrel of these cowards shall take it out of my hands." Morgan was kept as a prisoner of war for nearly a year, then was exchanged. [39]

As Washington read the report from Canada he was heartsick. The attack on Quebec had been an utter disaster. The whipped American army was in full retreat, leaving behind the proud fortress of Quebec, eventually leaving behind the newly won Montreal, and in fact leaving behind all hopes of conquering Canada for the American cause.

Chapter 12

A Moment of Triumph

At the same time Ethan Allen was capturing Fort Ticonderoga in May 1775, Washington was chairing a congressional committee charged with finding ways to supply the unprepared colonies with guns and ammunition. Ticonderoga held eighty cannon and six mortars—very encouraging news for the entire committee. But now, in late 1775, General Washington faced an occupied Boston in the midst of a cold and snowy winter, and the cannon remained an impossible three hundred frozen miles away.

The solution to his problem came in the person of Henry Knox, a former bookseller from Boston. Knox had learned a great deal about artillery from his voracious reading; and in November 1775 Washington named him chief of the artillery corps. Knox's first task was to get the cannon from faraway Ticonderoga.

When Knox arrived at the fort, he was dismayed to find that many of the cannon were old and damaged beyond repair. He selected about sixty of the best, and had his men drag them onto boats to float across Lake George. The largest guns weighed 2,000 pounds apiece, making the total cargo (including ammunition) some 120,000 pounds.

The trip to Ticonderoga had been exhausting, but Knox's adventure was only beginning. Fierce winds pressed them hard as the crews strained to row across the boisterous lake.

Henry Knox hauls captured British cannon from Fort Ticonderoga to Boston. Washington installed the cannon on Dorchester Heights and used them to drive the British out of Boston.

Then the largest scow struck a rock. The tired men wanted to weep when they saw several of the largest cannon bubble down into the water. But Knox was undeterred. He had the priceless guns raised from the water, and he repaired the scow. With numb hands in the freezing weather, the men worked as quickly as they could—but not as quickly as they wished. With no further mishap they reached the southern end of the lake and loaded the guns onto sleds for the

General Henry Knox, a 300-pound Boston bookseller who became Washington's artillery chief. After the war Knox took Washington's place as commander in chief, and he later became President Washington's first Secretary of War.

overland journey. Using his own money, Knox hired teamsters and 160 oxen to pull them across the mountains ahead. They were forced to cross the Hudson four times. They fought their way through the winds and two-foot snows, laboriously making their way over hills and swamps. They climbed through the rolling Toconics, then the higher Berkshire Hills, descending onto the floor of the Connecticut River valley. Then the ground began to thaw, making the sleds useless. But Knox and his men waited for a new freeze and pressed on.

Finally, after a grueling forty-day struggle, in late January Knox arrived at his destination, Cambridge, Massachusetts. He had spent $2,500 of his own money and had thoroughly worn out himself and his men. But his mission had been a success.

"A Most Astonishing Night's Work"

Knox's heroic achievement gave new fire to Washington's determination to oust the redcoats from Boston. For four months Washington had been honing plans for an offensive strike, but he agreed with the generals in his council of war that the Americans were too weak to move ahead. The commander in chief grew impatient as time dragged by. Just four days before Knox arrived, he fretted that "no opportunity [for an attack on Boston] can present itself earlier than my wishes."[1] Now, the arrival of Fort Ticonderoga's artillery nourished his hopes. He immediately issued a call for militia from the surrounding provinces. Reinforcements soon began to appear, and within six weeks the time was ripe for a decisive move.

"We are preparing," wrote the General on February 28, "to take possession of a post ... which will, it is generally thought, bring on a rumpus between us and the enemy."[2] That post was strategic Dorchester Heights, an unoccupied elevation overlooking Boston from the south. Detailed plans were carefully laid and communicated to only a few key officers to prevent the secret from reaching the itching ears of the British, and on the night of March 2 the Americans moved into action. Cloaked by blackness of night, three thousand shadows slipped onto Dorchester Heights. The hard, resistant ground was too frozen for digging fortifications, but the Americans came prepared: using wagons, they hauled heavy bundles of sticks and wooden frames to build stout ramparts against the hill.

The troops worked until early morning, setting the fortifications in place, dragging the largest of Knox's cannon onto the Heights. They finally returned to camp at three o'clock in the morning, while twenty-four hundred fresh soldiers moved in to take their places in the newly established stronghold.

At dawn the waking British were astounded. The embattlements were "a most astonishing night's work," their engineering officers exclaimed, estimating that the work must have required the efforts of fifteen to twenty thousand men. Another officer was even more extravagant, crediting the work to "the genie belonging to Aladdin's wonderful lamp."[3]

The Taking of Boston

Whatever their amazement, the British quickly prepared to attack. The American position was too dangerous to ignore. Washington and his men were ready. He only hoped the soldiers on Dorchester Heights could show the spirit Americans had displayed a year earlier at Breed's Hill. And this time they would have plenty of ammunition.

But the General was not prepared to simply sit and wait. While many of the redcoats were pushing against the Heights, Washington planned a surprise assault against Boston itself, with four thousand men attacking by small boats and another strong contingent entering by land. Perhaps the patriots could crush the British in one great, smashing blow.

Before Washington could give his troops the order to move, however, the skies darkened and a tremendous storm lowered over the area. Washington cautiously held back; the advancing British regiments retreated. The storm passed harmlessly away, but the surprise of the moment was lost. The British saw it was foolish to attack the Heights, and with the full contingent of British troops back in Boston, Washington no longer dared press his own attack.

Hours passed. Uneasy, the British officers considered those menacing dark holes in the barrels of Knox's guns staring down at them from the nearby hills. Unable to attack, unable to maintain their threatened position, in the ensuing days the British scrambled to their ships and sailed out of the bay, dumping many of their heavy cannon into the water to keep them from the Americans. A thousand frightened Tories insisted on clambering aboard with them, thereby displacing tons of badly needed stores. As Washington described it, they "resolved upon a retreat, and accordingly embarked in as much hurry, precipitation, and confusion as ever troops did."[4] The Americans had won their first major victory—and had done it without the shedding of blood.

The Fortifications of Boston

With the British gone, the Americans moved in on Boston. There they discovered some valuable booty—cannon, small arms, and other stores that had been left by the British. The city itself was ghostly and quiet; since the battles of Lexington and Concord, some ten thousand of the city's original population of seventeen thousand had fled. Many who remained were loyalists, totally dismayed at the turn of events.

Washington felt a real sense of bitterness toward these American loyalists who had in some cases betrayed their former neighbors to aid the British occupation of Boston. "One or two of them have done what a great many of them

*George Washington at Boston.
Washington's first victory of the
war consisted in driving the
British out of Boston. He took
the city without shedding blood.*

ought to have done long ago—committed suicide," he wrote. [5]
But in a letter the next day, Washington wrote of the
loyalists: "Unhappy wretches! Deluded mortals! Would it not
be good policy to grant a general amnesty and conquer these
people by a generous forgiveness?"[6]

The Americans must have been surprised if not shocked to
see the overwhelming strength of the British fortifications in
Boston. Perhaps Washington was grateful he had not
attacked after all. While inspecting the city, he noted that it
was "almost impregnable, every avenue fortified." And when
he saw the excellent barricades on Bunker Hill he said, almost
in awe, "Twenty thousand men could not have carried it
against one thousand."[7]

What would have happened if that storm had not arisen,
and Washington had attacked Boston? One historian has
speculated:

Had Howe known of Washington's plan [to attack], he
might well have cursed rather than blessed the storm. The

American commander had yet to learn that in hand-to-hand fighting his farmboys, who considered their bayonets principally useful for roasting meat over campfires, were no match for England's professional killers. He was to be taught this lesson on terrains where the Americans could save their lives by running away. But had most of his army been trapped with the murderous British on Boston Neck, Washington might then and there have lost the war.

In Homeric times, it would have been assumed that some pro-American god had ridden the storm, procuring time for the amateur American commander to learn how to conquer. [8]

"We Expect a Very Bloody Summer of It"

The members of Congress were ecstatic when they received the news of the Boston victory, and they promptly passed a resolution thanking General Washington and honoring him with a gold medal for his successful command. But medals were not what Washington was after. He wrote: "It will ever be my highest ambition to approve myself a faithful servant of the public.... The only reward I wish to receive [is] the affection and esteem of my countrymen." [9]

In May, Washington traveled to Philadelphia to confer with Congress about the war. They informed him that the army was to defend New York and hold "every foot of ground" occupied by the Americans in Canada. [10] Much too short-handed for any such assignment, Washington urged them to enlist regular soldiers for a period of years, enticing them with bounties, but once again Congress stubbornly refused.

The meeting with Congress did little to reassure the General. Benedict Arnold had recovered from his leg wound and was making a desperate effort to hold Montreal. Meanwhile, the British were getting ready to attack New York.

"We expect a very bloody summer of it at New York and Canada...," Washington wrote, "and I am sorry to say that we are not, either in men or arms, prepared for it."[11] But he was not ready to concede defeat. "If our troops behave well,...they [the British] will have to wade through much blood and slaughter before they carry our works, if they can carry them at all."[12]

Tory Uprising in the South

The challenges in the north were not the only problems Washington faced. He was well aware of the strong loyalists in the south, who clung fiercely to their allegiance to the Crown. Most of these Tories were recent immigrants from Scotland and Ireland. Washington was particularly alarmed when fifteen hundred Scottish Tories staged an uprising in Charleston (the most important port south of Philadelphia) in February 1776, attempting to establish a beachhead for a British invasion. Charleston patriots put down the uprising, but the British military received a clear signal: loyalists in the south were willing to fight.

Washington dispatched gaunt General Charles Lee to Charleston to take command of six thousand volunteers who poured in to man the fortifications around the Charleston harbor. The main defense structure was built to the north of the harbor on Sullivan's Island. It was called Fort Moultrie after the ingenious man who had built a sandwich-like fortress wall with palmetto logs holding up a dirt barricade sixteen feet thick. It was manned with 450 men and 30 guns.

The Charleston fortifications were barely in place in June 1776 when the many masts of the British fleet under Henry Clinton and Sir Peter Parker pierced the eastern horizon. After preliminary maneuvering and several excursions with unsuccessful landing parties, the entire fleet concentrated on Sullivan's Island and Fort Moultrie.

With nine ships and a total of 260 guns, the British were confident that Fort Moultrie, with its unimpressive 30 guns, did not have a prayer. Thus a bombardment began.

The British were relying heavily on a bomb ketch, appropriately called *Thunder,* to hurl its explosives inside the fort while other ships battered down the fortress wall. But the British commander soon saw that his shells were falling short. He dared not move closer, fearing the accuracy of the Moultrie guns, so he decided to increase the powder charge in his own guns. It was a foolish move. The increased powder was too much for the mortar beds and they violently burst asunder, rendering the cannon useless.

Meanwhile, the guns of Fort Moultrie continued to belch fire and iron in a near-deafening roar. Two ships whose cables were shot away listed dangerously into the water. Three other ships, trying to maneuver into better position, ran aground. One eventually exploded into fire from Fort Moultrie's ceaseless shells.

Finally, near midnight, the British turned their ships and limped out of the harbor, embarrassed and humiliated. Their guns had outnumbered the fort's almost seven to one—and they had been defeated.

Plots and Providence

The stirring victories in the south were heartening to George Washington, especially in light of distressing events closer to home. In late June 1776 a plot to assassinate General Washington was uncovered. Rumors flew about the country on swift wings. One said that Washington had declined to eat a dish of peas that were subsequently fed to some chickens—

and killed them. Another reported that one of the American drummers had agreed to stab Washington when the British drew near. The drummer's traitorous cohorts, the story said, were then to sweep away their fellow Americans with a murderous burst of cannon fire.

These rumors were probably false; such assassination plots most likely never got beyond the idle planning stage. But one frightening plot was actually set into motion. The British arranged with Sergeant Thomas Hickey, one of Washington's personal bodyguards, to kill the General, and Hickey even accepted his blood money for that purpose. Luckily, Hickey's plans were discovered, and on June 26, 1776, he was tried at a court martial. (Thirteen others were arrested but never tried.) Hickey was convicted and hanged two days later, with some twenty thousand people, including the army, witnessing the execution.

Afterward, Washington issued general orders giving a solemn "warning to every soldier in the army to avoid those crimes...so disgraceful to the character of a soldier and pernicious to his country, whose pay he receives and bread he eats."[13]

Such difficulties served to strengthen Washington's dependence on divine help throughout the war. As he wrote to a clergyman friend, "No man has a more perfect reliance on the all-wise and powerful dispensations of the Supreme Being than I have, nor thinks His aid more necessary."[14]

In July Washington ordered the appointment of a chaplain for each regiment. "The blessing and protection of heaven are at all times necessary," he explained to his men in a general order, "but especially so in times of public distress and danger. The General hopes and trusts that every officer and man will endeavor so to live and act as becomes a Christian soldier defending the dearest rights and liberties of his country."[15]

Washington gave more than lip service to such ideas. His faith in God ran deep. On a number of occasions people witnessed him in the act of private prayer. According to some contemporaries, at Valley Forge he frequently retired to a grove where he could be alone in prayer. And he often repeated his deep conviction that God maintained dominion over America and that He was directing events for the ultimate good of the Union.[16]

"A Freeman Contending for Liberty"

In the spring of 1776, Washington noted with pleasure that Thomas Paine's masterful *Common Sense* "is working a powerful change...in the minds of many men."[17] That change was clearly manifest a month later when Virginia instructed its delegates in the Continental Congress to propose a resolution calling for complete independence from Britain. Washington delighted in their action, calling it "noble" and concurring in its vital necessity. "Things have come to that pass now as to convince us that we have nothing more to expect from the justice of Great Britain," he wrote. Those who advocated a more moderate course were blind, deceiving themselves. Such were "many members of Congress... [who] are still feeding themselves upon the dainty food of reconciliation."[18]

On July 2 Washington sent a stirring communication to his men that the time for commitment had arrived, that Americans could no longer suffer complacently under Britain's tyrannical rule. Unbeknown to the General, on that very day Congress had voted almost unanimously in favor of a resolution for independence. (Two days later, on July 4, Congress approved the actual Declaration of Independence, which had been drafted by Thomas Jefferson.) Acting on his own instincts, Washington issued orders that said:

> The time is now near at hand which must probably determine whether Americans are to be freemen or slaves, whether they are to have any property they can call their own, whether their houses and farms are to be pillaged and destroyed, and they consigned to a state of wretchedness from which no human efforts will probably deliver them. The fate of unborn millions will now depend, under God, on the courage and conduct of this army. Our cruel and unrelenting enemy leaves us no choice but a brave resistance or the most abject submission. This is all we can expect. We have therefore to resolve to conquer or die. Our own country's honor [calls] upon us for a vigorous and manly exertion, and if we now shamefully fail we shall become infamous to the whole world. Let us therefore rely upon the goodness of the cause, and the aid of the Supreme Being in whose hands victory is, to animate and encourage us to great and noble actions. The eyes of all our countrymen are now upon us, and we shall have their blessings and praises if, happily, we are the instrument of saving them from the tyranny meditated against them. Let us therefore animate and encourage each other and show the whole world that a freeman contending for LIBERTY on his own ground is superior to any slavish mercenary on earth. [19]

Congress Declares American Independence

Exactly one week later, General Washington joyously announced to his troops that Congress had issued a formal Declaration of Independence. "This important event," he said, should "serve as a fresh incentive to every officer and soldier to act with fidelity and courage, as knowing that now the peace and safety of his country depends (under God) solely on the success of our arms."[20]

America's response to the Declaration of Independence was electrifying. Celebrations from north to south were marked by huge bonfires and incessantly tolling bells. Excited patriots in Savannah burned King George in effigy. Those in New York pulled down a statue of the king astride a horse, broke it in pieces, and sent the fragments to Connecticut, where they were melted and remolded into bullets. Bostonians, never known to be slackers, pulled down every image of the king they could find, creating a huge pile which they burned amid raucous cheers and rejoicing.

But not everyone rejoiced. John Adams estimated later that only one-third of the country's population was actively in favor of the revolution. Another third had mixed feelings, by turns swinging from patriot to loyalist according to the times and circumstances. The final third was staunchly opposed to independence—and certainly they faced the national celebrations with troubled spirits, with outrage and mourning.[21]

Still, in July 1776 the voice of the majority had spoken for independence. Now it was Washington's duty to make that independence secure.

"On Our Side the War Should Be Defensive"

By the time of the Declaration of Independence, Washington had been in command for precisely one year. During that time he had developed a cautious strategy that he felt would ultimately win the war. That strategy, one primarily of defense, was born of sober necessity.

Washington could have been more aggressive, of course, had he been able to command a bona fide army. But Congress insisted on using state militia, even though the General argued repeatedly that regular troops would be much more reliable. "No dependence could be in a militia or other troops than those enlisted and embodied for a longer period than our regulations have heretofore prescribed," he wrote, frustrated. "I am persuaded, and as fully convinced as I am of any one fact that has happened, that our liberties must of necessity be greatly hazarded, if not entirely lost, if their defense is left to any but a permanent standing army."[22] This issue became a prickling thorn in Washington's side; in the end the policies of Congress forced him to fight the entire war with inadequately trained, short-term troops taken in large part from the state militia.

Given the weak composition of his army, Washington felt he had no other choice: "On our side the war should be defensive," he wrote to Congress. "We should on all occasions avoid a general action or put anything to the risk unless compelled by necessity, into which we ought never to be drawn." He then explained that his troops were decidedly inferior to the British "both in number and discipline," and noted that it was foolish to try to hold a post "at all hazards.... The honor of making a brave defense does not seem to be a sufficient stimulus when the success is very doubtful and the falling into the enemy's hands probable."[23]

By fighting defensively and retreating when necessary, the American army would survive to fight another day—instead of being killed or captured. Some members of Congress were strongly opposed to this approach, but history has proven that Washington used the wisdom of expediency. Some of Washington's learned contemporaries even began to call him "Fabius," after Rome's Quintus Fabius Maximus, known as "the delayer." Fabius successfully used the strike-and-retreat method of warfare against Hannibal during the Second Punic War.

Washington knew that an essential element of effective defensive warfare is superior intelligence. The Americans needed to know at all times where the British were and what they were doing—and what they planned to do. When the British were weak, Washington could strike suddenly and powerfully (as at Trenton and Monmouth). When the British were strong, the Americans could safely keep their distance (as in the retreat across New Jersey).

In addition to the gradual establishment of an elaborate spy network (Nathan Hale was Washington's most famous spy), Washington created a smooth system of counterintelligence, through which he fed a stream of false information to British agents. Some fabrications were sent to the British through three or four different sources—all seemingly reliable—and some bits of false information bore the ultimate mark of authenticity: Washington's own handwriting. [24]

Chapter 13

Disaster at New York

While America was celebrating the Declaration of Independence, Washington was uneasily planning the defense of New York. The British had pinpointed that crucial port city as a key target in their strategy to end the war, and in the summer of 1776 General William Howe began to mass his troops there. By July "the largest expeditionary force of the eighteenth century"[1] had ominously gathered off Staten Island, with more than one hundred vessels and thirty-two thousand men. One astonished American rifleman wrote: "This morning...I spied, as I peeped out the bay, something resembling a wood of pine trees trimmed.... In about ten minutes the whole bay was as full of shipping as ever it could be.... I thought all London was in afloat."[2]

In mid-July Admiral Richard Howe, William Howe's brother, nicknamed "Black Dick" because of his dark complexion, sent a message to "Mr. Washington." The message proposed negotiations for a peaceable settlement between the king and the colonists. Washington refused the letter without even looking at it. As his aide explained, no such person as "Mr. Washington" served in the American army. Howe tried again, this time addressing the message to "George Washington, Esq.," but it also was refused. A third time Howe sent a message, this time to "His Excellency, General Washington." Satisfied that Howe recognized him as the leader of an opposing military force, Washington finally accepted the message.

The exchange led to a meeting between Washington and a representative of Britain, Lt. Col. James Patterson. But negotiations broke down when Washington discerned that Great Britain was interested only in bringing America back to the fold through a general offer of amnesty. Washington firmly declined the offer. America was now an independent nation. Why should its citizens seek pardon from another country?

Preparing for Battle

In the weeks that followed, the Howes marked time, quietly waiting for the remainder of their forces to arrive. The Americans watched with a stifling sense of desperation. They were outmanned by nine thousand men (23,000 Americans were facing 32,000 British), up to a third of the Americans were unfit for duty, and, unlike the Americans, the British were highly trained. In addition, Admiral Howe had a fleet of ten ships of the line, twenty frigates with twelve hundred guns, and hundreds of transports, all assembled at the unprecedented expenditure of £850,000. In the face of such odds, Washington felt it was true folly to try to defend

New York. But he remained loyal to the wishes of Congress and sought to build a similar feeling of loyalty and unity among his men. "[There is] no way to assist our cruel enemies more effectually than making division among ourselves," he said in his general orders of August 1. "The honor and success of the army, the safety of our bleeding country, depend upon [our] harmony and good agreement with each other.... The provinces are all united to oppose the common enemy, [with] all distinctions sunk in the name of an American."[3]

Washington also sought to prepare his men in other ways for the frightful impending contest. Two days later, in issuing orders against "the foolish and wicked practice of profane swearing," he shared his conviction that "we can have but little hopes of the blessing of heaven on our arms if we insult it by our impiety and folly."[4] He was to repeat his orders against profanity many times in the long years of war that followed.

As humid days passed with no action, tensions heightened. Washington buoyed up his men with repeated encouragements, seeking to get them mentally ready for the coming battle. "Remember that liberty, property, life, and honor are all at stake," he wrote, reminding them that "the hopes of their bleeding and insulted country" rested upon their "courage and conduct. [Your] wives, children, and parents expect safety from [you]," he said, "and ... we have every reason to expect heaven will crown with success so just a cause."[5]

"The Scene of a Bloody Conflict"

Weeks dragged by, and still the British did not attack. Washington prepared feverishly. He divided his force into five divisions, putting one in northern Manhattan Island, three in the southern end of the island, and one across the East River on Long Island. Anxious about the safety of New York's civilians, on August 17 he wrote the New York legislature, "When I consider that the city of New York will in all probability very soon be the scene of a bloody conflict, I cannot but view the great numbers of women, children, and infirm persons remaining in it with the most melancholy concern." To ensure their protection, Washington suggested that the legislators "immediately ... form and execute some plan for their removal and relief." The General would cooperate in the effort "to the utmost of my power," he said. [6]

On August 19 Washington was feeling increasingly optimistic; Britain's powerful force had not attacked and showed little sign of movement. "We are now past the middle of August," he wrote to his cousin, Lund Washington, "and they are in possession of an island only [Staten Island], which it never was in our power or intention to dispute their landing on. This is but a small step toward the conquest of this continent." [7]

But three days later the British made a boldly aggressive move. Twenty thousand British troops disembarked on Long Island and advanced to within three miles of the outer American positions. Determined to stop the British short, Washington stationed six battalions of American troops, about five thousand men, in Brooklyn to form a front-line defense. Several thousand more were placed in a fort at Brooklyn Heights. Perhaps the British would attack the fort in a foolish frontal assault, enabling the Americans to enjoy a repeat performance of Breed's Hill (with no shortage of ammunition).

Early in the morning of August 27, 1776, as the Americans waited for the impending attack, Washington spoke sternly

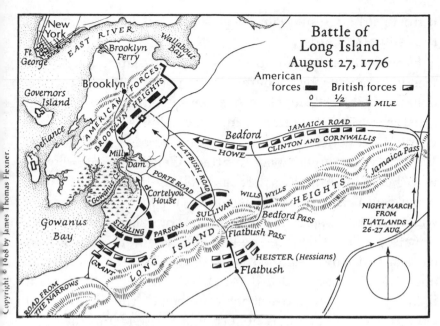

to a nervous group near him. "If I see any man turn his back today, I will shoot him through. I have two pistols loaded." Then his tone softened. "But I will not ask any man to go farther than I do. I will fight as long as I have a leg or an arm."[8]

The British Move into Position

Hours earlier, Britain's William Howe had separated his men into three divisions. Then, with the night for a cover, they began to move. The first group, under Major General James Grant, was to attack the American right, which was commanded by Lord Stirling. Grant hated Americans and threatened to torture all the males he could capture. His threat backfired, however, frightening Stirling's patriots into fighting more fiercely, afraid to surrender. Stirling, American-born but heir to a British title, was born William Alexander. Stirling is probably the only American peer in British history, although his claim to this title was later rejected by the House of Lords.

Howe's second group, composed of Hessian mercenaries, was commanded by General Philip von Heister, the commander in chief of the Hessian troops in America until 1777. Heister, a crippled veteran of many wars, was nearly seventy years of age when he led his Hessians across Long Island in 1776. His assignment was to attack General John Sullivan, who held the American left, as well as the main body of Americans under Israel Putnam. Putnam, a longtime veteran, was about five-and-a-half feet tall and built like a bull. Affectionately called "Old Put," he had survived numerous Indian battles, had barely escaped being burned at the stake, was once shipwrecked, and had fought at Bunker Hill. General Sullivan, a lawyer and former member of the Continental Congress, later served as governor of New Hampshire.

The third British division, led by Howe himself, secretly circled around the Americans by way of the unguarded Jamaica Pass and prepared to attack from the rear.

"What Brave Fellows I Must This Day Lose!"

Grant was the first to strike, attacking while it was still dark. Stirling and his men fought desperately, repelling the British in a series of engagements from midnight until dawn. On the American left, Sullivan's men resisted repeated heavy blows from the Hessians. Then General Howe moved up with shattering firepower from the rear. Confused and frightened at being surrounded, many men panicked and ran; others dropped their arms and surrendered.

The Hessians gave no quarter. They had been indoctrinated to believe that the Americans tortured and killed their captives, and they were prepared to return in kind.

Many of the surrendering Americans were mercilessly slaughtered.

While the devastated main body of the American army was either surrendering or retreating, a solitary Maryland regiment stubbornly held its ground. On seeing such courage, Washington reportedly exclaimed, "Good God! What brave fellows I must this day lose!"[9] Of that regiment, 256 men out of 684 were lost that day to death, serious wounds, or capture.

The British victory was stunningly decisive. The Americans lost nearly 2,000 men, while British losses were a mere 380. The fleeing Americans sought refuge in the sturdy fort at Brooklyn Heights, where additional troops, commanded by Washington himself, waited to make a brilliant last stand. They would have much the advantage over the British in the event of the expected headlong frontal assault. But, with ghastly visions of Bunker Hill still in his mind, Howe refused to storm the stronghold. Instead he began to dig in, planning to move with slow, steady advances toward the fort. He knew Washington was trapped; with a wise strategy, perhaps the British could win the war with a single siege.

The Evacuation of Long Island

Caged up in the fort on Brooklyn Heights, Washington knew he was in a desperate situation. His plan had tragically backfired; now his only hope was to get his troops out of the fort and off Long Island. It was an impossible hope: both the fort and the island were heavily guarded by the enemy. In the face of such odds, Washington reached into his magician's hat and pulled out "a wonderful feat; . . . a military movement [that] has had no equal in the history of America."[10] In the evening of August 28 Washington called his senior officers to a secret council of war. They urgently discussed the crisis and the emergency options available if they were to save themselves. By the next night, Washington was ready to make his move.

> At ten on the night of 29 August he began to draw his men off in acute precision from their places in the lines—a silent move of men in the shadows, each line slipping into the place vacated by the one before, keeping up a false front to the watching British of a solid and undisturbed defense. At the ferry, the troops found a vast array of small craft— summoned in haste the day previous—lined up on the shore. All night the boats kept up their silent and incessant relays, bringing boatload after boatload to safety on Manhattan, as [Washington] kept his watch between the beach and trenches and the lines behind the row of soldiers thinned. About three there was a ghastly moment: a regiment had gone off early under mistaken orders, leaving a gaping hole in the front lines. [Washington's] reaction was short and violent: "Good God!... I am afraid you have ruined us." There was a brief flurry, and the regiment came back into the lines.
>
> A few of the last troops were still in the trenches as a perilous light began to leak in from the east. Then a fog began to drift in from the river, covering both camps in a blanket that the rising sun turned only into a brighter and more incandescent haze. It began to lift, giving scant visibility, just as Washington stepped into the last boat to leave the shore. Two hours later the British swarmed into the empty trenches as Howe's ships, the wind having altered, sailed up the river's narrow sleeve. The arms had closed around an empty shell.[11]

That night, in less than a dozen hours, Washington soundlessly ferried between eight thousand and twelve thousand men across the East River—and he did it within a few hundred yards of the unsuspecting enemy. It was a masterful retreat. But the disastrous defeat that preceded it demoralized the troops, and many began to desert, skulking back to their homes. The Connecticut militia, for example, shrank from eight thousand to two thousand after the Long Island defeat. Washington noted sadly, "The check our detachment sustained...dispirited too great a proportion of our troops and filled their minds with apprehension and despair."[12]

Disaster at Kip's Bay

With his depleted and discouraged army, General Washington faced an overwhelming new challenge: the defense of Manhattan. Militarily, the best course was simply to burn the city. Nearly two-thirds of the citizens were staunch Tories, openly sympathetic and all too helpful to the British. And the city itself would be an inviting, comfortable haven for the enemy in winter. But Congress had ordered him to hold the city "at every hazard,"[13] and Washington obeyed.

The British hesitated for two weeks, strengthening their foothold on Long Island and waiting to see if the Americans would surrender after their disastrous defeat. Washington had no such intentions. He stationed his men in three areas on Manhattan Island: nine thousand around Fort Washington on Harlem Heights, a bluff on the northern end of the island; five thousand in New York City itself; and five thousand in the lowlands between the Heights and the city.

On a hot September 15, the British landed off Kip's Bay, protected by a barrage of heavy naval guns. Washington heard the guns, and galloped toward the sound—only to find, to his "great surprise and mortification," that his men were

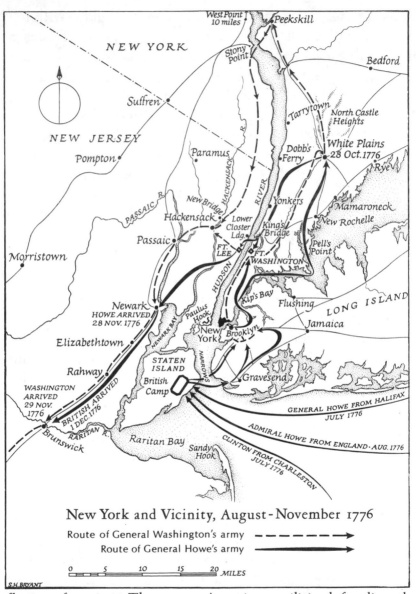

New York and Vicinity, August - November 1776

Route of General Washington's army ‑ ‑ ‑ ‑ ‑ ➤
Route of General Howe's army ━━━━━➤

0   5   10   15   20 MILES

fleeing, frantic.[14] The green American militia defending the landing area had paused only a moment in their shallow trenches, then, in the face of hundreds of close-ranked, bayonet-bearing Englishmen, panicked and ran without firing a shot.

A second group of soldiers rushed up to the trenches. But when an advance contingent of sixty to seventy redcoats appeared, the entire American force—consisting of several hundred men—cowered, broke, and ran, dropping guns and knapsacks behind them. Using his riding whip, Washington struck at several men in their flight, futilely trying to stop them. They veered in their course, but ran on. In furious exasperation, he dashed his hat to the ground and exclaimed, "Are these the men I am to defend America with?"[15]

His men having fled like frightened chickens, the General angrily faced the advancing British troops alone, without so much as a musket to defend himself. As General Nathanael Greene wrote, he was "so vexed at the infamous conduct of his troops that he sought death rather than life."[16] Washington's stunned aides watched, frozen in place, as their unprotected leader confronted the approaching enemy. Finally, seeing that his beloved commander in chief had no intention of moving, one aide rode up, grabbed the drooping bridle of Washington's horse, and quickly led him to safety.

The Battle of Harlem Heights

As the long day dragged on, countless small groups of American troops slipped through the brush and woods to the refuge at Harlem Heights, until some ten thousand were crowded there. The British, busy consolidating their gains, let them go without interference. But the next day, the King's troops sent out a scouting party, led by a bugler taunting the Americans with notes of a fox hunt. Washington was indignant about the insult. He promptly dispatched two groups to clamp the redcoats in a deadly vise. The British, spying the trap, scrambled away through the trees. The Americans chased after them, fox becoming hunter, while Washington sent in reinforcements. Then Washington heard the deep boom of cannon and knew the British had also received reinforcements. Eventually five thousand redcoats were gathered in the field.

Despite the threat, the Americans, now numbering eighteen hundred men, firmly stood their ground. Even those who had cowered at Kip's Bay showed a determination to hold their positions. After two hours of close fighting, the British supply of ammunition was depleted, and they began to fall back. The Americans shouted and pursued, then were called off before new British reinforcements could be sent in.

On the whole it was a relatively minor encounter, engaging only 6 percent of the American forces. Fatalities were low: the killed and wounded totaled 60 for the Americans, 168 for the British. But the significance of the Battle of Harlem Heights reaches far deeper than the size of the engagement. The battle once again showed the British that the Americans were able to stand up to them. And it demonstrated to the dejected Americans that they did indeed have the backbone to fight. As Washington wrote, "The affair seems to have greatly inspirited the whole of our troops."[17]

In the face of such resistance, cautious General Howe did not attack again for over a month.

The Burning of New York

Howe returned to Manhattan in a spirit of triumph. Even though he had lost the final small skirmish, he gloried in his success in driving the Americans off Long Island and into Harlem Heights. The rebels might fight courageously on occasion, but overall the ragged American volunteers were

General William Howe, commander in chief of the British army from 1775 to 1778. Howe's tenure took the British through some of the most significant battles of the war, including those at Long Island, Fort Washington, Trenton, Princeton, Germantown, and Saratoga.

no match for his seasoned regulars!

Howe's British troops received a hero's welcome from the American Tories as they marched back down to the lower end of Manhattan to the town site of New York. Weeping, cheering citizens thronged the redcoats as they strutted along the main street. Officers were carried on the shoulders of shouting men and women. The hated rebel standard was torn down and the British flag triumphantly raised in its place. But the celebration was short-lived.

Congress had ordered Washington not to burn the city. He obediently complied with their wishes. But a few New York patriots had vowed to reduce the city to ashes before they allowed the British to occupy it. Whether they really tried or not is difficult to tell. Perhaps it was just a strange coincidence, an accident—but by the early morning hours of September 20, 1776, New York City was afire. The flames rapidly grew out of control and became a ravenous monster consuming everything in its path. The fire is believed to have started in a shed near Whitehall Slip; lashed by high winds, it quickly spread from block to block, taking shacks and mansions, wharves, warehouses, and churches. An eyewitness left this graphic account:

> It is almost impossible to conceive a scene of more horror and distress. . . . The sick, the aged, women, and children half naked were seen going they knew not where, and taking refuge in houses which were at a distance from the fire, but from whence they were in several instances driven a second and even a third time by the devouring element, and at last in a state of despair laying themselves down on the Common. The terror was increased by the horrid noise of the burning and falling houses, the pulling down of such wooden buildings as served to conduct the fire, . . . the rattling of above 100 wagons, sent in from the army and which were constantly employed in conveying to the Common such goods and effects as could be saved. The confused voices of so many men, the shrieks and cries of the women and children, the seeing the fire break out unexpectedly in places at a distance, which manifested a design of totally destroying the city, with numberless other circumstances of private misery and distress, made this one of the most tremendous and affecting scenes I ever beheld. [18]

Panic-stricken citizens and soldiers rushed out to stop the hungry flames, but buckets were too few and water was too dear. With all hope of quenching the holocaust gone, outraged Tories turned on their patriot neighbors, accusing them of setting the fire. The patriots protested their innocence, but the Tories closed their ears, hanging some on the spot, without trial, and throwing others screaming into the flames.

Finally, nature did what men could not do. The wind turned and the flames died down. Nearly five hundred houses had been destroyed, estimated by General Howe to be about one-quarter of the town.

At midnight Washington saw a bright red glow lighting up the city to the south. "Providence, or some good honest fellow," he said, "has done more for us than we were disposed to do for ourselves." [19]

Courageous Captain Hale

The next day General Howe met face-to-face with an American officer, Captain Nathan Hale, who had been captured on Long Island dressed as a teamster and having damning intelligence notes and sketches on his person. Obviously the man was a spy. The young, twenty-one-year-old American freely admitted he was observing the British troops for General Washington. Howe heard him briefly, then ordered him hanged, not allowing him a formal hearing or a trial.

Captain Hale asked for the benefit of a minister. The British refused. He asked for a Bible. They refused. A gallows was thrown together. The young man was led to the spot, and the noose was tightened around his neck. Nathan Hale had something important to say before he died. In a piercing voice he cried out, "I only regret that I have but one life to lose for my country!" Then the rope jerked and, after a brief struggle, Nathan Hale was dead. [20]

Chapter 14

"I Shall Continue to Retreat"

I n mid-October 1776, after a month of inactivity, the British finally were on the move again, sailing three ships up the Hudson between Fort Washington and Fort Lee. Washington had tried to prevent such a move by sinking broad hulks in the river, then constructing a tight network of chains and booms across the water. But his barriers proved ineffective. The British broke through and passed upriver, where they were in a good position to attack the American right flank. But they did not attack.

Three days later, under cover of fog, Howe sailed the main body of his troops out the East River through Hell Gate and landed them on the mainland north of Manhattan. Fearing they would seek to cut him off from the northernmost colonies, Washington shifted the bulk of his troops northward to White Plains. At the same time, he left a significant defensive garrison of two thousand men at Fort Washington and four thousand at Fort Lee, which was directly across the Hudson on the New Jersey shore.

On October 28, after a stiff engagement, the British took a ridge overlooking Washington's position. The British had the distinct advantage, and if they had moved promptly they perhaps could have finished off the Americans in a single sweep. But they hesitated, then were delayed by heavy rains. During the night of November 1 Washington quietly moved his troops to the higher hills near New Castle. Howe thereby lost once again his immediate chance for a final victory, as he had done both on Long Island and on Manhattan. The British later turned south and lumbered down along the Hudson River. Washington trailed them with about two thousand troops, ready to present a barrier to an invasion of New Jersey. At the same time, just in case Howe was feinting again, seeking advantage through trickery and deceit, Washington left behind him another seven thousand troops under the leadership of General Charles Lee. Lee's powerful presence would discourage a British movement northward into vulnerable New England.

General Washington was scheduled to pick up five thousand additional recruits when he marched into New Jersey. But when he arrived at Fort Lee, he was chagrined to learn that very few men had actually been recruited. His army, always too small, was now spread precariously over hundreds of square miles. Desperate, he wrote to Congress, urgently reminding them "how essential it is to keep up some show of force and shadow of an army."[1] And he pleaded with the states for additional militia. Tragically, the response was too little and too late.

The Battle of Lake Champlain

While Washington was struggling to contain the British in New York, Benedict Arnold was fighting far to the north at Lake Champlain. Sir Guy Carleton (who would later serve as British commander in chief during the closing days of the war), was building a strong fleet to advance on the bastion at Ticonderoga. In response, Arnold hastily constructed a makeshift fleet of galleys and gundalows (barges), manned them with amateur sailors, and went out to meet him.

Arnold soon found he was hopelessly mismatched against the British ships. The Americans had a scant fifteen vessels to challenge a large British fleet of four sailing ships, two schooners, a large gundalow, twenty gunboats, four long-boats, and twenty-four provision boats. Furthermore, the American fleet was crudely made of heavy, green wood—a disaster in water, while the British were aboard fine craft made of seasoned lumber. As for manpower, the American forces were mostly unskilled at naval warfare, while the British sailors had been trained in the strongest navy in the world. In addition, the British were supported by nine thousand infantry, a legion of Indians on the shore, and a huge raft aptly named *Thunderer*. The *Thunderer* was a floating fortress, with heavy wooden walls rising upward along its sides, having only portholes for the huge guns mounted on its deck.

But Arnold was determined to move ahead at all costs. Congress had recently questioned his integrity, demanding an accounting of public funds for which he had been responsible, and Arnold wanted a chance to prove himself. At the same time, he was itching for revenge of his defeat at Quebec. The bullet scar on his leg was a constant reminder of his earlier pain and humiliation at the hands of the British.

The British might have the *Thunderer*, but the Americans

had an angry Arnold. It was almost enough to even the odds.

On October 11 the two forces met head on, firing at close range. The two navies raked each other with shot, while the Indians fired at the Americans from the shore. Arnold commanded the flagship *Congress* until it caught fire and became unseaworthy. Finally he and his men abandoned it for another boat.

Although the Americans fought bravely, the British gradually asserted their superiority. One after another, Arnold's ships were sunk. After a long day's battle, fighting from noon until dark, Arnold retreated, salvaging only six of his fifteen vessels. Throughout the next day Arnold varied between attack and retreat, trying to hold the British off while he escaped. When he saw such an effort was impossible, he beached and burned the ships to keep them from British hands, and marched through the wilderness back to Ticonderoga. The British had not lost a single boat.

Even though Arnold had been thoroughly defeated, his engagement of Carleton was extremely important. It delayed the British commander in his southward movement, prevented him from making a possible move on Ticonderoga, and made it impossible for him to capture the upper Hudson, which would have cut off New England. Instead, concerned about the coming winter, Carleton moved back to Montreal to wait for the following spring.

Fort Washington and Fort Lee

Fort Lee was located on the New Jersey side of the Hudson, directly across the river from Fort Washington on the New York side. As Washington moved southward, dogging the British, he stopped briefly at Fort Lee and then decided to press on toward Philadelphia. He feared the British might seek to occupy the new nation's capital city, which would strike deeply at the morale of patriot and soldier alike. He had just begun the trek when he received word that the British were marching in force on Fort Washington.

At that point Fort Washington had little strategic value. Originally the two facing forts on the Hudson River had been designed to prevent the British fleet from sailing up the river. When that purpose had failed, Washington felt that Fort Washington should be evacuated. But other generals argued in favor of maintaining the fort, and he left the final decision to the commander in that area, General Nathanael Greene.

Nathanael Greene was a patriotic Quaker who had been read out of his congregation after joining the army. Local militia officials refused him a commission because of a limp he had suffered since childhood, but he quickly rose to a brigadier under Washington. The commander in chief considered Greene to be one of his most able generals, and many historians feel he was second only to Washington. Still, Greene's decision to remain at the fort on the Hudson was a costly, major mistake.

To the inexperienced Americans, Fort Washington appeared to be as good as impregnable; the commandant of the fort, Colonel Robert Magaw, boasted he could hold it, unassisted, for a full two months. Yet it was deceptively weak, with no moat, casements, or palisade. Its outworks were so poor that they were extremely vulnerable and therefore virtually useless. To make the situation even worse, the fort's cannon were trained over the river to repel attack from that direction. They were worthless against an infantry attack coming from the inland side.

Magaw said he was ready for a two-month siege, yet the fort was hardly good for a single day.

The Fall of the Forts

The British might not have attacked at all except for an unfortunate incident. Howe had been pushing up the Hudson, when he suddenly turned southward and moved against Fort Washington. Why did he change the entire plan of his campaign? The answer is to be found in the person of William Demont.

Demont was an ensign in Magaw's forces, stationed at Fort Washington. On the second of November, 1776, he deserted his post and went over to the enemy, carrying with him the complete plans of the fort—which clearly revealed its ill-advised construction. Despite the huge numbers of men stationed there, the British began to see a strategy by which they could easily take the fort. The attack took place on November 16.

When the American commander in chief heard that Fort Washington was being threatened, he rushed back to Fort Lee, but he dared not cross the river. He helplessly watched the struggle of the American forces as thirteen thousand British and Hessian troops attacked the fort from all four sides. Cannon from two men-of-war in the river bombarded the fort's walls. Throngs of infantry menaced by land. The Americans found themselves in a deadly trap, hemmed in with no means of escape. As the day drew on, their options became depressingly clear: either surrender or be totally destroyed. Before the sun had set, Magaw chose to surrender.

The loss of Fort Washington was a terrible blow, but even worse was the tremendous loss of some 3,000 American troops (most of whom were captured). The British and Hessians lost 458. As Washington considered the problems of short enlistments, unqualified troops, and lack of support from the states—now coupled with the loss of Fort Washington, he was weighed down with discouragement. "I am wearied almost to death with the retrograde motions of things,"[2] he lamented.

During the next four days, Washington worked tirelessly to get the valuable stores shipped out of Fort Lee, which was now indefensible. He was only partially successful. When the British attacked on the fifth day, Washington led his men in a safe retreat, but the total losses were staggering. In addition to losing two strategic forts and 3,000 men, the Americans lost 146 cannon, nearly 3,000 muskets, 400,000 cartridges, a number of tents, and quantities of valuable tools.

After that week's work, a British officer wrote confidently to a friend, "You see, my dear sir, that I have not been mistaken in my judgment of this people.... The fact is that their army is broken all to pieces, and the spirit of their leaders and their abettors is also broken.... I think one may venture to pronounce that it is well nigh over with them."[3] Cornwallis is said to have begun loading his furniture aboard ship preparatory to returning to England. A little mopping up, he felt, and the war would be over.

"Playing at Bo Peep"

Without Washington the war might indeed have been over. The American forces west of the Hudson were deplorably weak, and enlistments were about to lapse. Washington decided to risk a British invasion of New England and consolidate the entire American army in New Jersey. He therefore ordered Lee to bring his seven thousand troops from New York. Lee deliberately delayed, making a series of artificial excuses. The British soon pressed forward against Washington, and the small American army with him was forced to fall back from one position to another as it retreated across New Jersey. Day after day Washington watched anxiously for Lee's reinforcements, and day after day they failed to come. With only three thousand men fit for duty, Washington could do little more than keep his army out of reach of the British. He confided his plan to General Lee: "I shall continue to retreat before them so as to lull them into security."[4] Then, when Lee's troops finally came, the Americans would suddenly fight back.

One British officer described those days in late November and early December, when Washington's tactics provoked the British to utter frustration:

> As we go forward into the country the rebels fly before us, and when we come back they always follow us. 'Tis almost impossible to catch them. They will neither fight nor totally run away, but they keep at such a distance that we are always a day's march from them. We seem to be playing at bo peep.[5]

"I Will Not ... Despair"

On November 30, 1776, a personal letter arrived from General Charles Lee. It was addressed, not to Washington, but rather to Joseph Reed, the adjutant general. Since Reed was absent, and Washington had been expecting word from Lee, he opened the letter hoping it would give some word of Lee's planned arrival. Instead he found a letter bitterly criticizing Washington for a "fatal indecision of mind which in war is a much greater disqualification than stupidity." Lee advised Reed that he had no intention of coming to the assistance of Washington with his troops and thanked Reed for an earlier note in which Reed had apparently criticized his commander.[6]

Though the words in the letter were rude and insubordinate, Washington simply forwarded the epistle to Reed with an apology for having opened it. He offered no hint of censure for Reed's disloyalty toward him as commander in chief. Amazingly, the friendship of the two men survived Reed's foolish indiscretion, and Reed subsequently gave valuable service to the General at Trenton, at Princeton, and in several other battles.

That same day, after all that had happened in the previous weeks—the tragic loss of New York City, the fall of Fort Washington and Fort Lee, the fearsome advances of the British, the plotting of Lee and Reed—Washington nevertheless wrote, "I will not ... despair."[7]

Still, he recognized the overwhelming realities of his situation. The next day the enlistments were up for more than two thousand of his fifty-four hundred troops. Unless there was a "speedy enlistment of a new army," he said, "I think the game will be pretty well up."[8]

The diary of one of Washington's men reveals the same troubling fears. Solomon Clift wrote, "We are in a terrible situation, with the enemy close upon us and whole regiments ... leaving us."[9]

One of the men present during the New Jersey retreat was a fiery young patriot named Thomas Paine. One night, sitting by the campfire for light and using a drumhead for support, he penned a passage that later became enshrined in America's classics. He wrote:

> These are the times that try men's souls. The summer soldier and the sunshine patriot will, in this crisis, shrink from the service of their country; but he that stands it now deserves the love and thanks of man and woman. Tyranny, like hell, is not easily conquered; yet we have this consolation with us, that the harder the conflict, the more

glorious the triumph.... Heaven knows how to put a
proper price upon its goods; and it would be strange indeed
if so celestial an article as FREEDOM should not be highly
rated. [10]

Jealousy or Duplicity?

No one knows for certain why Lee refused to obey orders
and reinforce Washington with his troops. It was brazen
insubordination—but was the cause jealousy or duplicity?
Lee viewed himself as the most capable officer in the entire
American army, none excepted, and he resented being
subordinate to Washington, whom he viewed as a bungling
amateur. Though he was now second in command (the
previous second, Artemas Ward, had resigned), that was not
good enough for Lee. He wanted to be the commander in
chief, and clearly hinted as much to a number of
Congressmen from the beginning. But Congress was not
interested in replacing Washington. Despite the reverses, he
could be trusted.

*General Charles Lee,
Washington's second in command
who was insubordinate and disobedient to Washington's orders.
Even worse, he initiated communications with the British that
bordered on betrayal. Because of
his actions, Congress removed him
from office for a year and he never
returned.*

Lee felt that he was the only man who could win the
American war for freedom. And now circumstances had
virtually made him an independent general commanding

several thousand men, the largest part of the army. Was he thinking that perhaps by remaining behind he would have the opportunity to gain distinction by striking a telling blow against Howe with his own force? Or was he entertaining a more sinister scheme to remain behind so that without his assistance Washington might be defeated?

Whatever his thoughts or his motivation might have been, Lee's disregard for his commander's orders to march south jeopardized the safety of the entire American military campaign—and Washington was forced to retreat across New Jersey with Lord Charles Cornwallis close behind. Cornwallis was an affable, thickset member of a wealthy family. He was among Britain's greatest military leaders and remained in the forefront of the Revolutionary War from Long Island to Yorktown. In later years he would be appointed governor-general of India and then of Ireland. But in the winter of 1776, he was chasing across New Jersey trying to catch Washington.

The late-autumn rains turned the roads to mud. Cold winds came out of the north as winter approached. Pulling their cloaks more closely about them, Washington's tired army fled through the Watchung Mountains, through Newark, through New Brunswick, all the while with Cornwallis stalking, feinting, thrusting. Finally the patriots reached Trenton. Washington immediately gathered boats from up and down the river to carry his retreating troops across the Delaware. Anxious dispatches went out to Lee: *Where are you? Why won't you come?* Lee, smug in his designs, determined to make a name for himself, dawdled and dallied and made excuses. Washington led his men across the Delaware, taking all the boats with him. Howe soon showed up on the other side, furious at being unable to cross. Again and again Washington wrote Lee: *I need you. Help me avoid a disaster. Come immediately!*

Lee did not come.

A Schemer Is Captured

Having risked court-martial for his inexcusable conduct, Major General Charles Lee finally broke camp in New York and drifted southward into New Jersey. On December 12 Lee's army camped a few miles south of Morristown. General Lee then carelessly left the troops and rode four miles to seek the comforts of a tavern, where he stayed the night. With him went a guard of about fifteen men and four other officers. On that same day, Cornwallis, with his British forces thirty miles to the south, sent out a small reconnaissance party to locate Lee's errant army and try to determine their direction.

The next morning, Friday the thirteenth, Lee had a leisurely breakfast at the tavern, then sat down to write a letter to General Horatio Gates. He was still carping against his commander, writing, "The ingenious maneuver of Fort Washington has unhinged the goodly fabric we had been building. There never was so damned a stroke." Then he drove in the final spike, speaking in conspiratorial confidence: "*Entre nous,*" he wrote, "a certain great man is most damnably deficient."[11]

Lee had just finished the letter when his aide, James Wilkinson, cried out that a troop of British cavalry were closing in on them. The British scouting party, led by Lieutenant Colonel William Harcourt, had learned that Lee had separated himself from his army and gone to the tavern. It was an opportunity almost too good to be true. Lee's guards resisted only briefly and with little effect. In the skirmish, two were killed and two were wounded. With the guards out of the way, Harcourt shouted that he would burn down the house if Lee did not surrender in five minutes. One minute passed. Two minutes. Then a dejected Lee appeared at the door, suffering the deep humiliation of turning himself over to Harcourt, who had been under Lee's command years earlier in Portugal.

Harcourt, on the other hand, was jubilant. The coup of Lee's capture helped him win a general's star.

When the news of Lee's capture reached Washington, he was devastated. Lee's misadventure resulted in a great loss, he felt, since Lee was America's most experienced officer in European warfare. In light of Lee's later plottings, however, his capture may have been a blessing in disguise. As eminent historian John C. Fitzpatrick wrote humorously, "The Tory informer [who told Harcourt where Lee was] should have been pensioned by Congress as a public benefactor." Instead of trying to protect Lee when the British later threatened to hang him, Fitzpatrick said, "the Congress should have sent Howe a good strong rope!"[12]

With Lee out of the way, General John Sullivan, Lee's second in command, took control of the troops and, knowing of Washington's desperate need, marched the entire army to the aid of his commander in chief. But the arrival of the northern army was not quite the godsend Washington had hoped for. After severe losses from desertions and terminated enlistments, Sullivan's army had dwindled to little more than two thousand men.

Chapter 15

A Season of Success
and Suffering

With the arrival of Sullivan's troops, Washington decided to make one last strike against the British before the year's end. Most of his six thousand men were due to go home at the end of December, barely a week away, and Washington wanted to utilize them one more time. General Howe, assuming that Washington would sit out the winter now that he was safely across the Delaware, retired to New York, leaving a series of posts to hold New Jersey. One of those posts became Washington's target: the Hessian stronghold at Trenton. It would be a dangerous move—the entire American army would be at risk, and if they failed in the venture, retreat would be virtually impossible. But "necessity, dire necessity, will, nay must, justify an attack," Washington said. [1]

On December 23 Washington had his men form in ranks

and, seeking to prepare their tremulous hearts for the coming battle, ordered the first of Thomas Paine's stirring *Crisis* papers read to them. "These are the times that try men's souls," it began. These agonizing words captivated the cold and hungry soldiers. They had indeed been tried. Paine's words vividly recalled to mind the loss of Long Island, New York, Fort Washington, Fort Lee, the march across New Jersey, and the difficulty to "both officers and men," who, "though greatly harassed and fatigued, frequently without rest, covering, or provision, the inevitable consequences of a long retreat, bore it with a manly and martial spirit."[2]

Paine's *Crisis* had the desired effect. The harsh cold of the New Jersey winter blew through their fragile garments—but the men resolved to bear up with manly spirits and be everything Paine's eloquent lines had attributed to them.

Washington divided up his forces carefully for the attack on Trenton. Brigadier General James Ewing was to take about nine hundred men, cross the Delaware directly opposite Trenton, and capture a bridge, sealing off the Hessian retreat to the south. General John Cadwalader, with about two thousand men, was to cross downriver. There he would engage the Hessians stationed in Bordentown, preventing them from assisting their fellows in Trenton to the north. Washington chose to lead the dangerous main attack personally. With some twenty-four hundred men, he would cross upriver and march down to Trenton, arriving an hour before dawn. The chosen day of attack was December 26.

Perilous Crossing

The Americans celebrated apprehensively on Christmas Day, but the Hessians were carefree and self-secure. Colonel Johann Rall, commander of the Hessians at Trenton and a hero from the capture of Fort Washington, spent Christmas evening in a supper party, then called for wine and cards. The night storm howled around the home of the wealthy local merchant with whom he was visiting, but Rall paid it no heed. Was not this the night of the Nativity, the time for gaiety and celebration? He put the cares of war far from him. He had sentries posted along the roads, and they would certainly notify him if the Americans made a move. Besides, what army would be foolish enough to venture out on a stormy night like this?

As the cold evening darkened, Washington and his men began to move. Boats were waiting for Washington's contingent at McKonkey's Ferry, about nine miles above Trenton. The oarsmen, wrapped in heavy blue coats, were John Glover's skilled Marbleheaders, a remarkable corps of fishermen from Massachusetts who were more comfortable on water than on land. Glover, a heavyset redhead, had led his men in performing the phenomenal evacuation of Long Island; now they would perform a similar feat in taking Washington's twenty-four hundred men across the Delaware, this time fighting a heavy storm and sub-zero temperatures.

The men stood stoically on the river banks, waiting their turn to cross. The sleet mixed with snow pelted their faces, dripped under their collars. Some had covered the firelocks of their muskets with rags, attempting to keep them dry for the battle. Others, having no rags—or no foresight—watched miserably as their muskets became useless burdens.

Ice floated down the river, smashing against the boats and threatening to dump the passengers into the river. Hour after long hour passed, rows of weary men shifting in place as they waited on both sides of the freezing water. Washington

Washington crosses the Delaware River, a dangerous prelude to the attack on Trenton, New Jersey. It took most of the night for Washington to get his 2,400 men across the icy river.

hoped to have the crossing completed by midnight, but the stormy weather and ice-choked river slowed the movement. It wasn't until four in the morning that the army was ready to march.

Four hours earlier, an American Tory had stopped at the home of Colonel Rall's host. The Tory said he had a vitally important message for the Hessian commander. Rall refused to see him. Nothing of great importance could be happening out in that storm, nothing that could not wait until morning. The Tory, desperate to convey his message, wrote Rall a note that could have undone everything Washington had so painfully planned. In substance it said, "The Americans are on the move, coming toward Trenton." A servant passed the note to Rall. He disdainfully stuck it into his pocket without even looking at it and returned to his wine.

While Washington was struggling across the Delaware, Cadwalader and Ewing, commanders of the support contingents, were holding back. Ewing briefly agonized about crossing the icy water, then shook his head and decided not to attempt it. The river was impassable, he said. Cadwalader at least made the attempt. He successfully shipped men across for several hours, but when he tried to transport the heavy cannon, the riverbanks were too slick, too perilously coated with ice. Some of the cannon slid out of control and disappeared into the water. He finally recalled his men and canceled the march.

A Bloodstained March

With one lone contingent left for the attack—but unaware of Cadwalader's and Ewing's failure—General Washington organized his men into two divisions and began to march. John Sullivan's division was to march along the river and attack the town from below. Nathanael Greene's division, which Washington accompanied, was to enter the town from above.

The men had a nine-mile march ahead of them, traveling slick, icy roads. Lowering their heads and pulling their wraps tight against the storm that whipped about them, the men forged ahead. One officer scribbled in his journal, "It is fearfully cold and raw and a snowstorm setting in. The wind . . . beats in the faces of the men. It will be a terrible night for the soldiers who have no shoes."[3]

The officer's words proved to be sadly prophetic. Jagged ice on the road cut through worn-out shoes and threadbare stockings. The next day, Major James Wilkinson, coming behind, could follow their route by the bloodstains in the snow.

As the soldiers marched, a worried report came to Washington that the sleet was wetting their muskets. For some, even the precautionary rags were proving inadequate. Washington's determined reply: "Use the bayonet. I am resolved to take Trenton."[4]

Victory at Trenton

Shortly after daybreak, about eight o'clock, the two columns converged on the town. Shocked Hessians had no time to prepare. Rall hurriedly dressed and formed a regiment on King Street. Another regiment, wearing scarlet uniforms, formed on the parallel Queen Street. The American artillery was waiting for them. Both armies hesitated, and time seemed to stand still. Then the gunners, under a slender young American officer named Alexander Hamilton, lit the touchholes of the cannon. Grapeshot roared from the cannons' mouths and the screaming Hessians fell back.

On Queen Street the Hessians rolled out their own cannon and fired back. Bayonets at ready, a troop of Virginians

George Washington at Trenton. The Americans took the Hessian army at Trenton by surprise and won a significant victory.

sprinted toward the enemy, racing straight at the cannon. Captain William Washington, cousin of the commander in chief, and Lieutenant James Monroe courageously led the charge. In only moments the Americans had captured the cannon—but both Captain Washington and Lieutenant Monroe had fallen with serious wounds. Monroe likely would have bled to death had a doctor not been present. Through the doctor's careful ministerings, Monroe survived to become the fifth President of the United States.

Sullivan's men fought their way across town to meet Greene's group. Their muskets generally useless because of wet firelocks, the untrained, awkward Americans were forced to rely on the bayonet. Frustrated, some wisely crept into houses and stores and dried their firelocks. When Rall formed a counterattack they were ready, dropping the Hessian commander from his horse with two well-aimed slugs.

It was a glorious and almost unbelievable victory for the beleaguered American commander and his troops. Nearly 1,000 Hessians were taken captive; another 115 were killed or wounded. Four Americans had been wounded, but not a single one was lost in battle—although in the fierce night before, two had tragically frozen to death.

"The enemy have fled before us in the greatest panic that ever was known," one of the patriot soldiers wrote after the victory. "Never were men in higher spirits than our whole army is."[5]

On December 27 General Washington sent a detailed letter to Congress reporting the victory. The attack had been successful, he explained, but still had fallen short of his secret hopes. "Could the troops under Generals Ewing and Cadwalader have passed the river, I should have been able, with their assistance, to have driven the enemy from all their posts below Trenton."[6] But he was nevertheless proud of his men and what they had accomplished: "Their behavior upon this occasion reflects the highest honor upon them. The difficulty of passing the river in a very severe night, and their march through a violent storm of snow and hail, did not in the least abate their ardor. But when they came to the charge, each seemed to vie with the other in pressing forward."[7]

"Desperate Diseases Require Desperate Remedies"

At the same time Washington was planning his attack on Trenton, he was also taking other steps to keep his straggling army alive. Even though Washington was commander in chief, Congress retained a tight grip on many critical decisions. This tragic flaw in organization severely limited the General's effectiveness in both strategy and logistics. With a measured argument, Washington applied to Congress for greater powers:

> Ten days more will put an end to the existence of our army.... If therefore, in the short interval we have to... make these great and arduous preparations, every matter... is to be referred to Congress, at a distance of 130 or 140 miles, so much time must necessarily elapse as to defeat the end in view. It may be said that this is an application for powers that are too dangerous to be entrusted; I can only add that desperate diseases require desperate remedies, and with truth declare that I have no lust after power, but wish with as much fervency as any man upon this wide, extended continent for an opportunity of turning the sword into a plowshare. But my feelings as an officer and a man have been such as to force me to say that no person ever had a greater choice of difficulties to contend with than I have.[8]

One week later, on December 27, Congress voted to give Washington sweeping emergency powers for six months. (They repeated this act on September 7, 1777.) With full congressional authorization, Washington could raise and equip sixteen additional regiments (bringing the total number of regiments in the permanent army to 104). He could also set up a system of promotions in the army; arrange for supplies; and arrest hindering, disloyal citizens.

Washington accepted the new authority with sober spirit: "Instead of thinking myself freed from all *civil* obligations by this mark of... confidence, I shall constantly bear in mind that as the sword was the last resort for the preservation of our liberties, so it ought to be the first to be laid aside when those liberties are firmly established."[9]

"Scarce a Pair of Breeches"

Even with his broadened authority, Washington could do little to relieve the tragic physical state of his men—a condition that continued throughout most of the war. Many of the men were clothed in garments that were woefully inadequate for the severe winter weather; the combining of men from many different colonies brought a deadly combination of contagious diseases into the camp; and food supplies were sometimes so scarce that the starving men had to plunder the countryside to stay alive.

These conditions were not beyond notice of the well-supplied enemy. Earlier in 1776 a British officer, in describing the retreat of the Americans across New Jersey, noted that "many of the rebels who were killed were without shoes or stockings."[10]

Of this period during the war, historian Douglas Southall Freeman wrote, "To have called [Washington's] situation desperate would have been to brighten the picture." Then he enumerated the dreadful problems Washington and his troops faced:

Scores of tents had been lost in the evacuation of New York; incoming militia, as usual, brought none with them. Compelled to sleep on the ground, where ice was formed as early as November 2, many of the recruits fell sick and went to hospitals which were worse, if possible, than camps. Some of the troops had no cooking utensils; others had to man the works all night when they were weary and were shivering for lack of clothing. "There are few coats among them," a British officer said of the Americans, "but what are out at elbows, and in a whole regiment there is scarce a pair of breeches." Homesickness afflicted hundreds of new-comers to the Army.... In September, when tents were not available for all, Washington's recourse had been to direct that the troops be "stored thicker." That would not now suffice. "The men," said a Connecticut chaplain of patriotic stock, "are worried in a manner to death and are treated with great hardship and severity."[11]

"A Receptacle for Ragamuffins"

Such conditions did little to encourage new recruits, and Washington was constantly battling the fluctuating size and mixed constitution of his army. His problems were basically twofold: "short enlistments and a dependence upon militia." These conditions, Washington warned, might well "prove the downfall of our cause."[12] "It is a ... painful consideration," he wrote to Congress in September 1776, " . . . to be forming armies constantly, and to be left by troops just when they begin to deserve the name, or perhaps at a moment when an important blow is expected."[13]

Many short-term enlistees were farmers who planted in

the spring, came to war for the summer, then left in the fall to harvest their crops. Others simply were not interested in a career of precarious and rigorous army life. As patriots, they would serve a term—but, having served, they then wanted to go home.

Washington found himself forced into the dangerous position of planning his military strategy around the varied schedules of his men: "We dare not in the beginning of a campaign attempt enterprises on account of the rawness of the men, nor at the latter end of it because they are about to leave us."[14] In December 1776, thoroughly disgruntled, he wrote, "If 40,000 men had been kept in constant pay...and the militia had been excused,...the continent would have saved money."[15]

The state militia were a festering thorn in Washington's side. "They come in you cannot tell how, go you cannot tell when, and act you cannot tell where; consume your provisions, exhaust your stores, and leave you at last in a critical moment."[16] "To place any dependence upon the militia," Washington candidly wrote to Congress, "is assuredly resting upon a broken staff." Members of the militia, having been "just dragged from the tender scenes of domestic life" and therefore being "unaccustomed to the din of arms," were "ready to fly from their own shadows." They stubbornly resisted necessary army discipline, and "scandalous desertions among themselves...infuses the like spirit in others."[17]

Washington was not the only officer with anxious concerns about the army. Artillery officer Colonel Henry Knox, for example, wrote harshly in September 1776: "The bulk of the officers are a parcel of ignorant, stupid men.... As the army now stands, it is only a receptacle for ragamuffins."[18]

Washington's frustration with short-term enlistments and an unreliable militia was so deep that he lamented in late

September 1776, "Such is my situation that if I were to wish the bitterest curse to any enemy on this side of the grave, I should put him in my stead."[19] And to another correspondent, soberly: "Fifty thousand pounds should not induce me again to undergo what I have done."[20]

Obstacles to Strengthening the Army

Despite the General's many urgent, even desperate requests, Congress was unbelievably slow to respond. Part of the reason was financing—there simply were not enough funds, they said, to maintain a standing army. But that was largely just an excuse, as on other occasions the early Congress (just as the Congress of today) seemed not the least bit hesitant to spend money they did not have. Much more critical were two imposing political roadblocks that stood in the way of the army Washington wanted.

First, the "nation" in 1776 was a loose confederation of independent states. Many Americans at that time had no thought of continuing in close union beyond the war. To create a standing army, with troops from many states, could cement a unity that might not be desired.

Second, and perhaps more important, the Congress had an inherent fear of standing armies. They knew the oppressive power a standing army could wield—and many Congressmen feared giving that power to anyone, even Washington.

Nevertheless, Washington's repeated urgings slowly began to bring the desired effect. After more than a year of putting Washington off, Congress finally responded, approving an expansion of the standing army, authorizing three-year enlistments, and giving greater bounties (both in land and in money) as inducements to those who would enlist. But their action came too late for the troops serving in 1776. On

December 22, 1776, the General wrote to Robert Morris, president of Congress, reminding him that the American army would be reduced to a scant twelve hundred men by January 1. He said, "You may as well attempt to stop the winds from blowing" as to attempt to keep troops after their term has expired. The British were waiting only for the ice on the Delaware to thicken before attacking "the poor remains of our debilitated army," he warned. [21]

Faced with certain failure if he lost his army as enlistments expired, Washington made a bold move. Four days before the bulk of the army was to disband, the General met with several regiments of regulars and entreated them to stay. If they would remain for just six weeks, he would give them a generous ten-dollar bounty as well as a continuance of pay. Flushed with excitement over the victory at Trenton and enticed by the extra money, many agreed to stay. Washington had no authority from Congress thus to pledge public funds—but fortunately an express arrived the next day giving him that power.

Chapter 16

Vexations and Perplexities

One day after the new year dawned, on January 2, 1777, Lord Cornwallis marched on Trenton. He brought five thousand men from Princeton, leaving behind a rear guard of twelve hundred under Lieutenant Colonel Charles Mawhood. The smaller group was to join Cornwallis the next day. It was dusk when the British saw the distant campfires of the Americans. As the British moved in, Cornwallis could see that Washington was as good as trapped. In front of the American general was the enemy; to his rear was the icy Delaware. It was a bad spot.

Some of Cornwallis's aides advised the British commander to attack immediately. One warned that the wily Washington might be gone in the morning if they gave him the chance. But Cornwallis rejected their counsels. The British regulars were exhausted from their long march—and, anyway, how could Washington escape?

As the evening sky grew ever darker, Washington called his highest officers around him in a tense council of war. The success at Trenton was fresh in their memories, and heroic imagination suggested they could do the same thing with Cornwallis as they had with the Hessians. But such fanciful illusions soon gave way to reality, and Washington knew they must flee. He was not content, however, for them merely to stick their tails between their legs and run yelping from the fearsome redcoats. No—they would escape, but on the way they would take Princeton. And beyond that lay the inviting British war chest of £70,000, carefully guarded at New Brunswick.

Four hundred men were assigned to stay behind, keeping fires burning and providing a cover by loudly digging earthworks within earshot of the British. At one o'clock in the morning the dark march began, tired Americans slipping around the left flank of the sleeping British. Noise of the departing wagons was muffled by rags wrapped around the wheels. The march was a nightmare for the fatigued and hungry rebels, chilled to the bone in the winter cold. But by dawn they had nearly reached their destination, while in Trenton the unsuspecting Cornwallis was still dreaming of the wonderful victory he expected to achieve that day.

"A Fine Fox Chase"

As Washington neared Stony Brook Bridge, two miles outside Princeton, he sent an advance guard under General Hugh Mercer to secure the bridge. Mercer, a former Scottish surgeon, promptly moved through the trees to carry out the order. But he arrived just in time to see Colonel Mawhood's British troops coming over the bridge. Mercer's men took position in an orchard, temporarily holding the British off with their muskets. Then Mawhood ordered his redcoats to charge with fixed bayonets. Mercer stood up to rally his men, but a redcoat smashed him to the ground with the butt of his gun. Mercer arose, drawing his sword. Seven British soldiers thrust their bayonets into his body, and he fell dying to the ground. His frightened brigade hastily retreated toward Washington's advancing American vanguard.

The battle of Princeton. The American victory at Princeton came only one week after their victory at Trenton and greatly inspirited Washington's troops. (Painting by John Trumbull, a Revolutionary War soldier.)

When the General perceived what was happening, he spurred his magnificent white horse into a fast gallop, waving his hat and calling his men forward. As Washington raced heedlessly toward the enemy, the astonished redcoats lifted their muskets, pointed at the man on the horse, and fired. Smoke filled the air, and neither side could see what had become of the General. Then the smoke lifted—miraculously, Washington still sat astride his great horse, urgently calling his men to battle. Sullivan's troops raced into the fray, and soon the British began to retreat. "After them, my boys," General Washington shouted. "It's a fine fox chase!"[1]

Five hundred British were killed, wounded, or captured in the engagement. The Americans lost fewer than fifty. Altogether, the main action of the battle had lasted barely fifteen minutes Once the enemy was in hand, the victorious Americans immediately set about exchanging their old, worn blankets and gear for new British supplies, but Washington drove off several Americans who were robbing a wounded British soldier on the field. He ordered one of his men to stand guard until an American doctor arrived.

"A Most Infernal Sweat"

By mid-morning Cornwallis was hot on Washington's trail, furious at having been duped. Washington knew his men were too weary to fight another battle. They had marched half the night and had spent the morning fighting and rounding up prisoners. This forced the General into a painful dilemma.

Just eighteen miles away was New Brunswick, with vast British supplies and a war chest worth a small fortune. From a strategic standpoint, the capture of New Brunswick could have been the biggest break of the war. From a practical standpoint, it was impossible. As Washington mournfully wrote to Congress afterwards: "Six or eight hundred fresh troops, upon a forced march, would have destroyed all their stores and magazines, taken... their military chest,... and put an end to the war."[2]

Tragically, Washington had no fresh troops, only a few thousand famished, exhausted, soiled, and ragged scarecrows. Weary and worn to near collapse, they trailed off toward Morristown, following their disappointed General.

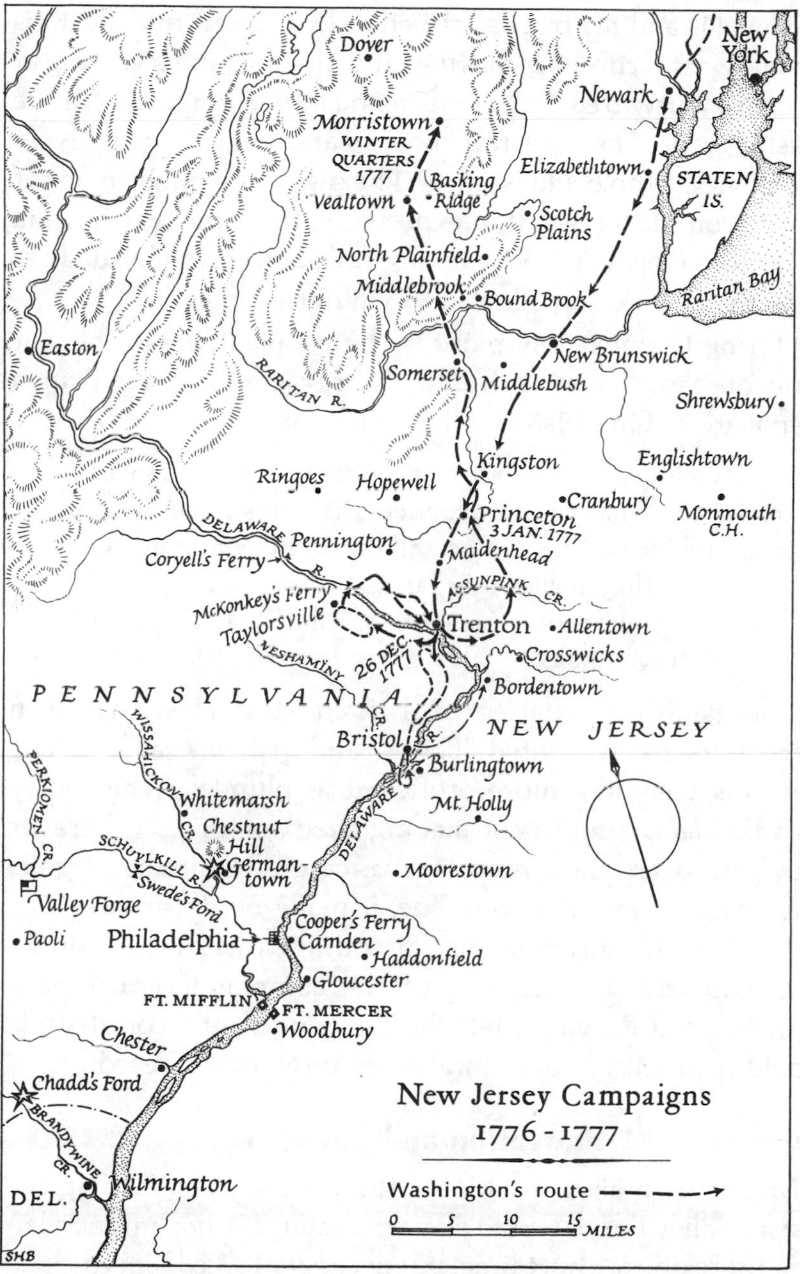

Dover
New York
Newark
Morristown
WINTER QUARTERS 1777
Elizabethtown
STATEN IS.
Basking Ridge
Vealtown
Scotch Plains
North Plainfield
Middlebrook
Bound Brook
Raritan Bay
Easton
New Brunswick
RARITAN R.
Somerset
Middlebush
Shrewsbury
Kingston
Englishtown
Ringoes
Hopewell
Cranbury
Princeton 3 JAN. 1777
Monmouth C.H.
DELAWARE R.
Pennington
Coryell's Ferry
Maidenhead
ASSUNPINK CR.
McKonkey's Ferry
Taylorsville
Trenton
Allentown
NESHAMINY CR.
26 DEC. 1777
Crosswicks
PENNSYLVANIA
Bordentown
Bristol
NEW JERSEY
Burlingtown
PERKIOMEN CR.
WISSAHICKON CR.
Whitemarsh
Mt. Holly
Chestnut Hill
SCHUYLKILL R.
Germantown
DELAWARE
Moorestown
Swede's Ford
Valley Forge
Cooper's Ferry
Paoli
Philadelphia
Camden
Haddonfield
Gloucester
FT. MIFFLIN
FT. MERCER
Woodbury
Chester
Chadd's Ford
BRANDYWINE CR.
Wilmington
DEL.
SHB
New Jersey Campaigns 1776 - 1777
Washington's route
0 5 10 15 MILES

Cornwallis and his troops arrived at Princeton "in a most infernal sweat—running, puffing, and blowing and swearing at being so outwitted."[3] But he made no attempt to pursue Washington. His greatest immediate anxiety was New Brunswick. Who could be sure? The cagey Washington might sneak around and take it unexpectedly, the same way he took Princeton. Cornwallis was taking no chances. He headed for New Brunswick and allowed Washington to escape.

During the next few months the people living in the war zone of New Jersey suffered the ravages of cruel British despoliation. One historian has written:

> Claiming the miserable eighteenth-century soldier's privilege of pillage and plunder, the British and Hessian regulars burned and looted and raped the winter away. In Princeton they maliciously burned all the firewood available to inhabitants,... slaughtered and carried off cattle and destroyed mills. [4]

The paid mercenaries of Britain—the Hessians from Germany—freely looted Tories and patriots alike: "The Hessians were the more proficient at plunder, which they regarded as the means of making their fortunes. Wherever they passed, anything movable was carefully piled on wagons and carried away. Friend or foe, it made no difference."[5]

The British officers did not discourage this pillaging of the local populace. In fact, one of the commanders, decadent Francis, Lord Rawdon, felt the ravaging of the countryside would help teach "these infatuated wretches" a lesson. [6]

Starvation and Smallpox

Morristown always haunted the memory of Washington, just as Valley Forge would do a year later. He had intended to stop there only a short time, but necessity forced him to make it the site of the American army's winter encampment. The collapse of practically all support from the states and from much of Congress almost proved fatal. With only about three thousand soldiers left after most enlistments expired, Washington still could not get sufficient food, tents, and clothing to provide even for the most basic human needs. The starving, freezing veterans of the great victories at Trenton and Princeton shuffled about their camp as though they were the offscourings of humanity. In desperation Washington finally felt compelled to use the emergency powers Congress had given him in order to commandeer provisions and survive.

Then came the smallpox.

The General knew of only one way to halt the plague. He ordered every member of the encampment to be inoculated. Because of primitive techniques, however, more than one-third of the men became seriously ill as a result of their inoculations. To save the lives of his men, Washington had to lodge many of them in the homes of the complaining townspeople. Had the British attacked at any time during this critical period, the whole patriot army under Washington would likely have collapsed and been captured or destroyed.

The New Image of Washington

In spite of neglect, hunger, and freezing at Morristown, the slow leaven of public opinion was sweetening future prospects for the General and his woeful, ragamuffin army. The victories at Trenton and Princeton did something for the morale of the whole country. For example, British traveler Nicholas Cresswell wrote: "Volunteer companies are collecting in every country on the continent, and in a few months the rascals will be stronger than ever.... Damn them all."[7]

The American victories also caught the attention of the British military brass. Lieutenant Colonel William Harcourt of the British army (captor of General Charles Lee) wrote, "Though it was once the fashion of this army to treat them in the most contemptible light, they are now become a formidable enemy."[8]

In the wake of the recent triumphs of the patriot army, many Americans began to proclaim high praise for General Washington. His brother-in-law, Bartholomew Dandridge, seemed to echo the feelings of many when he wrote: "It is plain [that] Providence designed you as the favorite instrument in working out the salvation of America. It is you alone that can defend us.... I am sure you have no idea of your real value to us."[9]

An article in the *Pennsylvania Journal,* published about six weeks after the victory at Princeton, described Washington in glowing terms:

> In his public character he commands universal respect and admiration. Conscious that the principles on which he acts are indeed founded on virtue, he steadily and coolly pursues those principles, with a mind neither depressed by disappointments nor elated by success, giving full exercise to that discretion and wisdom which he so eminently possesses. He retreats like a general and acts like a hero. If there are spots in his character, they are like the spots in the sun, only discernible by the magnifying powers of a telescope.[10]

Washington was indeed beginning to be viewed as a hero in the eyes of many. His countrymen had been given a closer look at the capabilities of their commanding general, and they liked what they saw.

Washington's Phantom Army

Surprisingly, Washington did not react favorably to this rising tide of popularity and praise. "Everybody seems to be lulled into ease and security," he wrote. They needed to be shocked into the possibility of a potential disaster: "I think we are now in one of the most critical periods which America ever saw."[11] His greatest worry, of course, was how to keep his feeble army together. A sufficient number of new enlistments remained almost impossible to come by. Many who had enlisted began to desert as the freezing winter progressed and disastrous weather conditions wore them down. At the end of December 1776, 1,200 militia had agreed to stay with the army for six weeks; but by mid-January only 800 remained. The problem reached such troubling proportions that on January 31 the General wrote to Congress that if desertions continued at the same rate, "we shall be obliged to detach one half of the army to bring back the other."[12] By March the American army numbered about 4,500, though on paper the numbers were shown to be 17,812. The British had 27,000.

There were a number of disturbing problems that combined to make enlistments increasingly difficult and desertions a scandal. First and foremost was the miserable condition of the army in the field. Not only was the American soldier risking his life in a battle against superior troops, but he suffered from little or no bedding, insufficient clothing, and extremely poor rations. He was subject to long marches, night watches, and much fatigue, exacerbated by restless nights on the cold, hard ground, often with a rag for a blanket and no tent for a covering. Pay was grossly inadequate, frequently late, and sometimes didn't come at all. What pay he received often came in the form of Continental dollars or state notes which the merchants rejected as worthless.

Added to these problems was the general feeling among those who served that they had to bear an unfair share of the burden of the war. Most of the citizens of the new United States stayed at home, comfortable and safe, enjoying their families, selling produce to the British, or otherwise making money from their occupations.

Enlistments were further discouraged by the stories of troops who returned through desertion or upon completion of their tour of duty. All felt keenly the hardships they had endured, and some even felt ill-used. In gatherings with friends, sitting in shops, enjoying a drink at the tavern, these former soldiers shared the last horrible detail of their trials, often with colorful exaggeration. (The unadorned truth was bad enough!) No doubt most of these veterans wanted to magnify their own self-image rather than deter others from enlisting, but the results were the same. Many patriots, though convinced of the cause, decided they were not quite ready to sacrifice the comforts of home—and perhaps their lives—for such a frightening mission with so many trials and tribulations.

Such problems left Washington with haunting nightmares and sleepless nights. Meanwhile, Congress continued to issue orders as though the "heroic Washington" could single-handedly accomplish the impossible. He complained that Congress seemed to think it could say, "Presto, begone, and everything is done."[13]

"The Thing...Most Fatal to Our Interests"

By April 1777 it appeared that the British were beginning to move out of their winter quarters. Washington was deeply troubled, even alarmed, because his troops were still suffering from the recent ravages at Morristown. "The campaign is opening," he recorded, "and we have no men for the field."[14]

In late May General Washington moved his headquarters to Middle Brook, New Jersey, only seven miles northwest of the British headquarters at Brunswick. His worn-out troops had to be close enough to respond quickly if the British began to move.

While he waited, Washington issued strict orders to ensure that his troops were preparing themselves spiritually for the coming difficulties. "All chaplains are to perform divine service...every...Sunday," he declared, and he ordered "officers of all ranks" to set an example by attending. "The commander in chief expects an exact compliance with this order, and that it be observed in the future as an invariable rule of practice. And every neglect will be considered not only as a breach of orders, but a disregard to decency, virtue, and religion."[15]

In the early summer the redcoats made a series of forays up the Raritan River in New Jersey, but each time they were successfully repulsed. Washington feared a major frontal attack, but it never came. Such an assault could have spelled utter disaster, but then, as on other occasions, Washington felt the blessings of a benevolent Providence hovering over his fragmented forces.

Then something rather amazing happened. The British suddenly pulled up stakes. They stopped briefly at Perth Amboy, and then moved out of New Jersey altogether. The Americans soon learned that the British headquarters had once more been established on Staten Island across the bay from New York Harbor.

This left New Jersey entirely in the hands of Washington, a

heartening prospect for America's tired patriots. From Congress, John Hancock wrote optimistically to the General that this was a clear signal and "the most explicit declaration to the whole world that the conquest of America is not only a very distant, but an unattainable object."[16]

But Washington was not convinced. He knew this was not really an American military victory. Something puzzling was brewing in the British War Office. Why had Howe withdrawn his forces? What new campaign was being mapped out? Still, the General welcomed this temporary period of relief, during which he could continue to plead for support and supplies. Almost in a state of despondency, he warned Congress that the troops under his command had provisions for less than a week, leading to deep-seated fears that "this army must be disbanded.... If the present difficulties continue, it is impossible it can exist."[17]

The only bright spot in the midst of the gloom was the arrival of a young French nobleman, the Marquis de Lafayette. Although only nineteen, he had equipped his own ship and brought eleven companions, including a German-turned-Frenchman, Baron Jean de Kalb, to fight with Washington. Washington was also cheered by the arrival of some unexpected French supplies, which included twenty-two thousand muskets. The supplies had barely reached camp before a trickle of reinforcements also began to arrive from several of the states. Before long, Washington had an army of around nine thousand soldiers, and General Horatio Gates had an additional force of several thousand men to guard Fort Ticonderoga and the lake-and-river chain leading to Canada.

The New British Strategy

It was not long before Washington learned why the British had concentrated their forces back in New York. The British

War Office in London had agreed to a plan proposed by General "Gentleman Johnny" Burgoyne. He had offered to lead a force down from Canada while General Howe went up the Hudson from New York. By meeting at Albany, the two generals could neatly cut off New England from the rest of the states, and then conquer the American revolutionary forces region by region.

The Burgoyne plan was in operation almost before the Americans realized what was happening. Coming down from Montreal with around eight thousand troops (7,200 regulars—half British, half Hessian; about 400 Indians; and around 250 Canadian and Tory volunteers), Burgoyne arrived at Fort Ticonderoga on July 2, 1777. Unfortunately, the fort was poorly manned—generals Horatio Gates and Philip Schuyler had been quarreling instead of preparing. Benedict Arnold, still recovering from the leg wound suffered at Quebec, wisely suggested precautions but was overruled, and Ticonderoga had to be abandoned.

Washington was greatly disturbed when he received the news. The loss of Fort Ticonderoga was "among the most unfortunate [events] that could have befallen us,"[18] he wrote. When King George heard the news, he danced into the queen's dressing room shouting, "I have beat them! I have beat all the Americans!"[19] What he did not know was that after the news had been sent to the king, there had been a strange turn of events in America.

"A State of Constant Perplexity"

Instead of sailing up the Hudson to meet Burgoyne, on July 24 Howe sailed out of New York Harbor with 15,000 soldiers aboard 260 ships and took to the open sea. It turned out that General Howe and his brother, Admiral Richard Howe, had changed their minds about supporting Gentleman Johnny

Burgoyne in his heroic quest for glory. They had a plan of glory of their own. At first, however, it was not at all clear to Washington just what the Howe brothers were up to. Would they sail north and attack Boston, or sail south to attack Philadelphia?

For more than a month Howe's ships moved here, then there, playing cat and mouse with the weary Continentals. Washington wrote, "The amazing advantage the enemy derive from their ships and the command of the water keeps us in a state of constant perplexity and the most anxious conjecture."[20]

Finally spies and other intelligence sources convinced Washington that Howe's huge fleet was headed for Charleston, South Carolina, much too far for Washington to reach in time. Washington therefore decided in a high-level council of war that he would march north with the main part of the army and confront the advancing forces of Burgoyne. But within hours his intelligence changed: Howe was not heading for South Carolina. He had changed course and was sailing up the Chesapeake Bay. From the head of Chesapeake Bay the British would have an easy fifty-five-mile march north to capture Philadelphia!

Washington hastily moved south to meet them. On the way he marched his Continental brigades through the city of Philadelphia to reassure the patriots and impress the Tories. "It was a gallant and, at the same time, a pathetic two-hour display of what the troops were and were not," one historian has observed.[21]

Washington's troops were a ragged and tired lot—poorly fed, poorly clothed, and poorly equipped. Their march through Philadelphia did not exactly inspire confidence.

Vexations at Brandywine

As Washington drove south, General Howe was engaged at the north end of Chesapeake Bay, disembarking the largest contingent of British forces in North America. This huge military entourage took up its line of march northward and first encountered Washington's advance guard near Brandywine Creek, about thirty miles southwest of Philadelphia. Screened by heavy forests, the British moved up along the west side of the creek on the morning of September 11, 1777. Washington, on the east side, finalized careful efforts to guard the many shallow crossings of the creek.

Around mid-morning, Washington learned that five thousand Hessians under General Wilhelm von Knyphausen ere taking up a position just opposite the main body of Americans at Chad's Ford. Within moments the German cannon began a thunderous bombardment of the American position. The Americans returned the fire, but neither side was able to wreak significant damage on the other.

Washington waited anxiously for reports on the whereabouts of Howe and the main body of his army. At eleven o'clock an excited messenger brought some disturbing news—the British were marching toward Trimble's Ford, seven miles upstream. Feelings of distress and regret raced through Washington's being—Trimble's Ford was the one crossing he had failed to adequately cover. Then Washington saw an opportunity to capitalize on his earlier oversight. If Howe had divided his forces from the Hessians, both would be substantially weaker.

Washington countered by dividing his own forces. He ordered one division to march northward to intercept the British and commanded the other division to cross the creek and attack the now-weakened Hessian forces. Just as both divisions were starting to move, a contrary message came from General John Sullivan on Washington's right. He reported that the road to Trimble's Ford was empty; the British were nowhere in sight. Perplexed and disconcerted, Washington commanded all his forces to hold.

Disaster and Defeat

The hours dragged by, punctuated with the meaningless cannon exchange across the creek. Then, at two o'clock in the afternoon, another message came from Sullivan, now frantic: the British had crossed the creek and were pushing in. Washington ordered Sullivan to march to Birmingham Meeting House, a mile away, and hold the British (if at all possible) until reinforcements could arrive. Sullivan moved swiftly, occupying a hill that blocked the British advance. But it scarcely slowed the determined redcoats. They charged forward with bayonets mounted on their guns, forcing the outnumbered Americans to fall back.

At the same time, Knyphausen finally thrust his British regiments across Chad's Ford, his five thousand men sweeping into the forces commanded by General Anthony Wayne. A handsome Pennsylvania tanner, Wayne was called "Mad Anthony" by his troops, a soldier's way of expressing awe at his rashness in battle. Trusting the reliable Wayne to handle Knyphausen, Washington took over General Nathanael Greene and his troops and rushed off to assist Sullivan.

The Americans at Birmingham were fighting valiantly, but the British had twice their number and were supported by four powerful cannon. Five times they drove the Americans off their position on the hill, with dead and wounded covering the ground; but five times the Americans forced their way back.

General Anthony Wayne, who earned the nickname "Mad Anthony" for his rashness in battle.

When Washington and Greene came in sight of the battlefield, a murderous assault by British and Hessian soldiers was once again forcing Sullivan back. The sturdy Americans under Sullivan had been fighting an enormous force of redcoats for two hours straight; now they could hold on no longer.

Seemingly at the last minute, just as Sullivan was about to crumble, Greene rushed in with his reinforcements. They surrounded their brothers, pushed in beside them, took their places in battle, and allowed Sullivan's exhausted troops to disengage and withdraw. By nightfall, however, Greene had fallen back under the pressure of the British onslaught. Mad Anthony Wayne had been forced to flee from the Hessians some time earlier. When darkness finally descended on the scene, the Hessians left off their pursuit. The disaster at Brandywine was over.

Washington agonized over the defeat. Earlier in the day he had thought there was a singular opportunity to attack the British and fight their divided forces on his own terms, but poor reconnaissance of the terrain and faulty intelligence had forced him to remain motionless until it was too late. The Americans lost about twelve hundred soldiers that day, four hundred of which were captured. The British lost only half that number.

The Paoli Massacre

Ten days later the Americans suffered another tragic setback. On September 20 General Anthony Wayne and his division camped outside Paoli's Tavern (near Pennsylvania's Valley Forge). Long after dark, British General Charles Grey and his men appeared seemingly out of nowhere. Silently rushing from the darkness, they savagely attacked the unsuspecting Americans with the cold steel of their bayonets, while invisible snipers shot at any unfortunate Americans who happened to be silhouetted in front of their campfires.

The engagement began shortly after midnight and was soon over, Wayne hastily leading his men to safety. The British killed some two hundred and captured one hundred more. British losses were minimal: six killed and some twenty wounded.

News of the "Paoli Massacre" spread quickly, infuriating and frightening the Americans. Meanwhile, the British triumphantly marched toward Philadelphia, seeking the prize of the nation's capital. Members of Congress hastened to the safety of York, Pennsylvania, terrified at the prospect of being captured. On September 26 Howe and his soldiers took possession of Philadelphia, completely unopposed.

In traditional European warfare, successfully taking the enemy's capital city was usually considered tantamount to final victory. By occupying the seat of government, an army could bring most of the nation's business to a standstill and break the back of the government. Howe had hopes of accomplishing exactly that when he proudly marched his troops into the American capital.

But America was not Europe, and the national government during the war was only nominally located in Philadelphia. In fact, the national government was so weak that most Americans would hardly have noted its demise. Though Howe did not realize it, Philadelphia was important symbolically but not strategically. The seat of America was not there, but in the capitals of thirteen different colonies, stretching twelve hundred miles from New Hampshire to Georgia.

When General Howe entered Philadelphia, the excited Tories gave him a glorious victor's welcome. Howe reveled in the festivities, preparing to settle in for a comfortable winter. He felt secure and safe among these loyalist friends. Where better could he stay? After surveying the city, he decided to divide his forces for the winter season, leaving a contingent in Philadelphia itself and moving the main army to nearby Germantown.

Meanwhile, Washington received regular reports from patriots and spies. He watched closely and began to make plans.

The Attack on Germantown

The day after the British occupied Philadelphia, Washington received some welcome reinforcements from the northern command, boosting his total forces to eight thousand regulars and three thousand militia. With a command some eleven thousand strong, his spirits began to lift: "I am in hopes it will not be long before we are in a situation to repair the consequences of our late ill success," he said. 22

On October 3 he took fate into his own hands and sought to create such a situation. That night he marched his men fifteen miles through the chilly darkness to surprise the major British encampment at Germantown, about five miles north of Philadelphia. This time the odds would be on the side of the Americans—Washington's eleven thousand were to face nine thousand Britons.

Before beginning the march, Washington issued a stirring challenge to his men:

> Let it never be said that in a day of action you turned your backs on the foe. Let the enemy no longer triumph. They brand you with ignominious epithets. Will you patiently endure that reproach? Will you suffer the wounds given to your country to go unrevenged? Will you resign your parents, wives, children, and friends to be the wretched vassals of a proud, insulting foe? And your own necks to the halter? . . . Nothing, then, remains but nobly to contend for all that is dear to us. Every motive that can touch the human breast calls us to the most vigorous exertions. Our dearest rights, our dearest friends, and our own lives, honor, glory, and even shame urge us to fight. And my fellow soldiers, when an opportunity presents, be firm, be brave. Show yourselves men, and the victory is yours. 23

The weary American troops arrived in the early daylight hours. A thick morning fog had lowered over the countryside, blanketing the enemy camp and obscuring the American view. The fog was so dense Washington could not see the vanguard of his troops as they fell on the surprised British. But he could hear them—and he was exhilarated to hear the sounds of battle recede as he moved ahead. His men were

The battle at Germantown. The Americans nearly won this battle but lost the victory through confusion and lack of communication.

driving the British army back! It was the first major British withdrawal of the war.

The fighting pushed through the widespread camp, with Generals Sullivan and Wayne in the center. Wayne's men fought savagely, crying, "Have at the bloodhounds! Revenge the Paoli Massacre!"[24] As he followed the din of battle, Washington passed a heavy stone house, the home of Justice Benjamin Chew, in which 120 British soldiers were prepared to make their last stand. The General left a small detachment to take the house and continued on with his rear guard. His army was approaching the critical point where Howe was personally headquartered. Victory surely was theirs.

Suddenly, inexplicably, the tide turned. The front guard of American soldiers turned in frantic retreat, with eager British troops nipping at their heels. Then the main body of Americans heard the frightening sound of firing behind them. Were they being surrounded? Panic spread, and soon the entire American army was on the run. Washington, by now near the front, had no choice but to follow, trying vainly to put some semblance of order into their reckless flight. His momentary jubilation had turned to anger and frustration.

"The Day Was . . . Unfortunate"

Afterward, Washington unraveled the tangled web of events that had so cruelly ruined their certain victory. The soldiers in the vanguard, who had been fighting the longest, had run out of ammunition. They had to withdraw or die defenseless. The troops behind them, unaware of the true reason for the withdrawal, assumed the worst and stampeded away from the British. Others heard the firing of General Greene's troops—who had been delayed as they came in on another road—and the booming cannon shots at the stone house, and they falsely supposed they were being surrounded. Soon the entire American force, confused and frightened, was scrambling up the road in retreat.

"Upon the whole," Washington later reported to Congress, "it may be said the day was rather unfortunate than injurious."[25] Yet later he learned it was a good deal more injurious than he had initially supposed: nearly eleven hundred Americans were killed, wounded, or captured in the Germantown battle.

Nevertheless, the near success of the day was ample cause for optimism. The Americans had learned, Washington told his careworn troops, that "the enemy are not proof against a vigorous attack, and may be put to flight when boldly pushed."[26] And he expressed his abiding trust that "a superintending Providence is ordering everything for the best and that in due time all will end well."[27]

That hope was to sustain him in the coming dark winter at Valley Forge.

Chapter 17

Surrender at Saratoga

Throughout his days of planning and executing the battle at Germantown, Washington worried about the British threat in the north. He could not personally be present at the northern theater, and he worried that a defeat there might be catastrophic to the American effort as a whole.

Burgoyne's movements in northern New York heightened Washington's anxiety. After retaking Fort Ticonderoga in July, Gentleman Johnny continued to push south, grasping more and more territory for the British. His destination: Albany, New York, where he expected to join his eight thousand men with General Howe's fifteen thousand.

"A Labyrinthine Hell"

Unknown to Washington, however, Burgoyne's expedition was meeting overwhelming difficulties in its struggle southward. Fate seemed to throw up a hedge and a barrier in front of Burgoyne's every step. Fearing an American flotilla (which did not exist) on the waterways, he chose to travel overland to Fort Edward, a route that was nearly impassable. America's General Schuyler, not satisfied with the region's impressive natural barriers, sent a thousand axmen to fell trees and "make Burgoyne's straight way crooked. They felled huge trees 'as plenty as lamp-posts upon a highway about London.'"[1]

General John Burgoyne, known as "Gentleman Johnny" because of his fine dress and manner, was the British commanding general at the battle of Saratoga in 1777. His surrender removed 5,000 British troops from the war.

The rebels dug numerous ditches to slow the British troops; and they searched out every bridge to destroy it, compelling Burgoyne's tired engineers to build forty bridges to cross streams and deep ravines. In one place the British were forced to a long halt while they constructed a makeshift two-mile causeway.

To intensify the British supply problems, Schuyler warned the locals to drive their cattle elsewhere and even convinced a number of local patriots to burn their unharvested grain. "He made a labyrinthine hell and a scorched earth of Burgoyne's southward path."[2]

Schuyler's sabotage was potently effective: Burgoyne and his men were able to travel but twenty-three miles in twenty days. And by the time Burgoyne arrived at Fort Edward on July 29, 1777, the defending Americans had disappeared, having moved to Stillwater, New York, nestled along the shores of the Hudson.

That trek was only the beginning of Burgoyne's grief.

Stark's Victory at Bennington

The exhausted British delayed at Fort Edward for two weeks, resting and recuperating from their march. But with eight thousand men to feed, his supplies quickly dwindled; and in mid-August Burgoyne sent a party of about five hundred Germans, Indians, and Tories (under the Hessian Lieutenant Colonel Friedrich Baum) to plunder the countryside. Their target was the fertile Connecticut River valley in nearby Vermont.

They had barely moved from the fort when the local American militia began harassing them from all sides. A nervous Baum immediately sent back for reinforcements, and Burgoyne dispatched Lieutenant Colonel Heinrich von Breymann with 650 men. Foolishly using parade-ground formations as they marched through the woods, Breymann covered a scant one mile per hour.

The local militia was not the only threat lurking in those woods. Outside of Bennington, Baum stumbled onto a large body of New Hampshire militia under General John Stark. Stark, an old hand from the Battle of Bunker Hill, was equally surprised to meet the British. But he had led fifteen hundred patriots to that area to find and engage the British, and now he had his opportunity.

On a rainy August 15, 1777, Baum dug in. Stark watched and waited, devising his strategy. The next day, resisting the urge to make a frontal attack on the British, Stark chose instead a quiet course of subterfuge. He dressed a contingent of his best men in civilian clothing, putting the loyalist white-paper badge on their hats, and sent them over to the other side. Stark's phony loyalists played their parts so well that a British major accompanying Baum accepted them without suspicion. He verified that these men were indeed Tories, apparently coming to help him against their hated rebel neighbors.

Unchallenged, the disguised Americans sauntered nonchalantly past the Hessians, stationing themselves on their flank and rear. Then Stark reportedly cried out: "There, my boys, are your enemies.... You must beat them—or Molly Stark is a widow tonight!"[3]

Once they saw they were virtually surrounded, most of Baum's Indians and Tories fled. But the sturdy Hessian regulars stood firm, fighting until their ammunition was gone. Then they charged with pulled swords, trying to hack their way to safety. Stark and his men would have none of it. They kept the Hessians penned in until noon, making it almost impossible for any to escape. When it was all over, Baum lay in agony, suffering from a mortal wound. Altogether, 365 Hessians were either killed or captured that day. Only nine escaped.

Just at the moment when Stark was mopping up his operations, Breymann suddenly marched up with Baum's reinforcements. At almost the same time, Colonel Seth Warner and his Green Mountain Boys arrived with their reinforcements for Stark. The battle started afresh, ferocious and bloody. Combining their efforts, Stark and Warner sent Breymann reeling back. Breymann's casualties amounted to 230 dead, wounded, or captured, while Stark, in both actions, lost only 30 dead and 40 wounded.

The Siege of Fort Stanwix

Burgoyne could hardly believe the news of Baum's and Breymann's defeat. These Americans were supposed to be amateurs fighting against his professionals! Then additional depressing news came from the west, from which direction Burgoyne thought a large contingent of reinforcements was rushing to his support.

When Burgoyne first took the southward route from Canada, he had sent a secondary expedition, under General Barry St. Leger, to come in from the west along Lake Ontario. St. Leger had been in his country's service for more than half of his forty years; he was a man who could be trusted. Burgoyne gave St. Leger a force of more than 1,800 troops, combining British regulars, Hessians, Tories, French Canadians, and some 900 Indians. His task was to march toward Albany to join Burgoyne, capturing Fort Stanwix, on the way. Stanwix, he was told, could easily be taken. The fort was old and decaying and was reportedly held by only 60 Americans.

On August 3, 1777, St. Leger calmly surrounded the fort, unaware that inside were 750 men—more than twelve times the number he expected. Their commander was young Colonel Peter Gansevoort. An Indian who was friendly to the Americans took word of the siege to nearby patriots, and 800 New York militia, under staunch General Nicholas Herkimer, rushed to the scene. Meanwhile, however, St. Leger's spies warned him of Herkimer's coming, and the British prepared an ambush of Indians and Tories in the woods.

As the unsuspecting Americans marched through the woods toward the fort, their front ranks were cut down by a horrifying rake of musket fire. Herkimer fell with many of his troops, seriously wounded, but he continued to direct the battle with his back to a tree and his pipe in his mouth. Under Herkimer's leadership, the Americans rallied and struck back against the enemy skulking behind the trees. (Unfortunately, Herkimer never recovered from his wounds and died soon after the battle.)

Back at Fort Stanwix, St. Leger had left but a small force to maintain the siege. Discovering the weakness of the enemy camp, Gansevoort sent Lieutenant Colonel Marinus Willet out of the fort to attack. The few British defenders fled in fright when Willet and his 250 men approached. Willet looted the enemy encampment, carrying off twenty-one wagonloads of valuable supplies, including muskets, ammunition, blankets, and clothing. What he could not carry away, he destroyed. Then he scurried back to the fort before St. Leger could return.

At the ambush site, St. Leger's Indians and Tories had heard the gunfire coming from back near the fort. Fearing an attack from their rear, they melted into the woods. Herkimer's men were thus relieved of further fighting and limped back the way they had come.

Despite the failed ambush, and despite the devastating loss of his camp supplies, St. Leger was determined to take Fort Stanwix. He set his jaw and renewed the siege.

The Coming of Arnold

Word of the siege eventually reached General Schuyler, who was preparing to face Burgoyne in New York. He knew that with Fort Stanwix in British hands, his western flank would be vulnerable. Who, Schuyler asked, would volunteer to forestall that danger by leading a force against St. Leger? Only one man stepped forward. It was Benedict Arnold. He was now a major general and eager to prove himself. With one thousand volunteers he raced toward Fort Stanwix, taking pains to ensure that news of his coming preceded him—and to create the impression that his force was much larger than it actually was.

First he sent a half-crazy Indian named Hon-Yost Schuyler to tell St. Leger that a huge force of Americans was on the move. "How many?" St. Leger asked. Hon-Yost was unable to speak his answer, but he pointed at the thousands of leaves on the trees above him. This simple gesture spoke volumes to the leery St. Leger. Hon-Yost had scarcely delivered his message before a second Indian arrived, also secretly sent by General Arnold. He assured St. Leger that the Americans were indeed coming with a powerful force.

St. Leger's Indians did not wait for further confirmation, nor did they wait for orders. Frightened by the reports of an invincible army on the way, they grabbed up any available stores of clothing, plus a plentiful supply of rum, and fled into the forest. Anxious Tory volunteers soon followed. With his troops so thoroughly depleted, St. Leger's options narrowed to one: retreat. Discouraged and disappointed, he unhappily returned to his British base at Oswego.

The Battle of Bemis Heights

Back at his Hudson River headquarters, General Burgoyne was growing desperate. He had received word that Howe had decided not to meet him in Albany. Howe was going to take Philadelphia instead. This shocking news, plus the report that

General Horatio Gates, a former British officer who led the Americans to victory at Saratoga and only days later became a co-conspirator in the Conway Cabal. In 1780 Gates retreated in disgrace from the battle of Camden and was forced from service for two full years.

St. Leger had returned to Oswego, was a crushing blow to Burgoyne. At the same time, the opposing American forces were swelling in number and becoming stronger every day.

On August 19, 1777, General Horatio Gates arrived at Stillwater to replace Schuyler. Congress, disturbed about the loss of Ticonderoga under Schuyler's command, had sent Gates to bail the northern colonies out of the fix in which they found themselves. Ruddy-faced Gates was a snob of the first order, a godson of Horace Walpole and a man who forever resented his servant-class background. Impatient at having been subordinate to Schuyler for so long, Gates was aching to meet and beat the boastful Burgoyne. He had his first opportunity six miles north of Stillwater, on the rolling hills of Bemis Heights, New York.

On September 19 the two forces met, with Gates and his seven thousand Americans entrenched at Bemis Heights. When the rebels saw the redcoats through the trees, Arnold, who had now returned to join Gates's northern command, begged permission to attack. Gates refused. Safely hidden behind his earthworks, he wanted to force Burgoyne to come to him. But Arnold persisted until Gates finally agreed. Arnold could lead Daniel Morgan's sharpshooters and a New Hampshire regiment in an attack on the British at Freeman's Farm.

Arnold flew at the enemy. Morgan's skilled riflemen picked off the advance guard, giving the Americans the initial advantage and driving the British back. Then reinforcements bolstered the ranks of the redcoats, and the Americans were forced to retreat. Tears of frustration flowed down Morgan's rugged face as he sounded his famous turkey call to bring his men back. Disheartened, they returned and regrouped.

Overconfident British artillery moved forward, certain that victory soon would be theirs. But American riflemen climbed surrounding trees and began to scour them with a lethal rain of bullets. Every British artillery officer but one was struck down; thirty-six out of forty-eight artillerymen were wounded or killed. In desperation the British ordered a bayonet charge. Again they were forced back.

Arnold now saw his chance for a killing blow. But he needed more men. *Send reinforcements!* he begged Gates. Mule-headed, Gates refused, still relying on his tidy entrenchments against the hill. Eventually Gates changed his mind, but it was too late. Hessian reinforcements were arriving, and the Americans were soon repulsed. Night fell with the British still on the field and the Americans retreating to their camp. British losses in the battle were five to six hundred; the Americans had lost three hundred.

The Confrontation Is Renewed

Burgoyne was sorely weakened by the engagement, and he felt his troops, worn down after three troublesome months in the wilderness, were near the end of their rope. Nevertheless he decided, against the heated counsel of some of his generals, to make one last stab at the Americans. His strategy was to send about fifteen hundred men against the left wing of the American entrenchments on Bemis Heights. If success looked possible, he would send additional men in to support them. Of course, if the Americans resisted in strength, he would call for a general retreat and pull his entire army out of range.

On the morning of October 7, the British established a strong position on a gentle rise north of the Americans. They had at least one thousand yards of clear range over which to fire their ten cannon. Like stern sentries those cannon guarded the field and it was expected that if the Americans tried to attack the British position, they would be mowed down. Meanwhile, the crimson-coated infantry began their drive toward the American lines.

Gates immediately approved a counterattack, but he refused to send Benedict Arnold at the head of the troops. For two weeks the two men had been quarreling bitterly over Gates's official report of the previous battle—Gates had taken all credit for the victory—and Arnold had been relieved of any command in the field. Instead of using Arnold, Gates sent out Daniel Morgan against one flank of the British and New Hampshire General Enoch Poor against the other. Stealthily attacking from the woods rather than from the open fields, both divisions fought heroically in the face of incessant enemy artillery. Finally the Americans pushed in so close that the British felt compelled to order a bayonet attack—their favorite tactic in close fighting. Undaunted, the Americans answered with a thunderous volley from their muskets. This took its toll. The commander of the British grenadiers, General John Ackland, received a shot through both legs and was quickly and unceremoniously captured.

When Burgoyne saw his soldiers falter and begin to fall back, he called for a retreat. An urgent message was sent forward with Sir Francis Clerke, but Clerke was wounded and captured before he could deliver the message. The British and their Hessian mercenaries fought on.

At this point the frustrated Benedict Arnold suddenly came racing up on a tall brown horse and, even though he had no authority to do it, began to take command of the tired American forces. The men cheered as Arnold came onto the field. First, he drove against a German unit, where he saw a weakness in the line, and they collapsed. Then he saw British General Simon Fraser rallying the redcoats. Arnold turned to Morgan and asked him to have one of his sharpshooters bring Fraser down. Tim Murphy received the assignment. He climbed a tree with his double-barreled rifle, and on the third shot Fraser fell dead.

With the loss of their leader, the British pulled back to some nearby earthworks. Arnold and his men vigorously attacked, but they were repulsed. Arnold spurred his horse around to the other side, commandeered the troops of another general, and ordered them to attack the earthworks in force. Before long they had swept over the top and had driven the enemy from their stronghold.

Surrender at Saratoga

The last British holdout was a strong redoubt on the British right, commanded by Breymann. Arnold gathered two more regiments and drove his combined forces against this stronghold. The brutal Breymann, determined to keep his men from retreating or surrendering, ran four slackers through with his saber. One of their comrades, sickened by Breymann's work, shot him dead. The redoubt crumbled.

With the battle virtually over, a messenger raced from Gates to Arnold, ordering the disobedient Arnold back to camp. Arnold willingly obeyed: In the attack on Breymann's stronghold a bullet had fractured his thigh bone—on the same leg that was injured at Quebec. He was carried off the field on a litter.

The battle gradually died out. Burgoyne had lost 600 men, while the Americans lost only 150. In addition, Burgoyne had 500 sick and wounded. His once proud forces were depleted and beaten. He pulled back to nearby Saratoga, leaving his sick and wounded in the field behind him.

Gates, who until this point had remained a safe observer, now moved decisively. He gradually began to encircle Gentleman Johnny's remnant of an army, his strong pincers closing in around the British army's neck. In three days Burgoyne was surrounded. All avenues for victory or escape were closed. On October 13, after four desperate councils of war, Burgoyne proposed that he and Gates negotiate. On October 17 Burgoyne and his five thousand men laid down their arms. After more than two years of grinding war, the Americans had finally won a major victory. [4]

Saratoga's Significance

The surrender at Saratoga proved to be a pivotal point in the war, bringing to George Washington and his American army a series of significant benefits. Prior to that fateful October, the states had been united only by a Declaration of Independence and a crucial common cause. Now a sizable portion of the mighty British army had been defeated and a resurgence of hope swelled the breasts of Americans. The victory prompted Congress to solidify the Union by adopting the Articles of Confederation and sending them to the states for ratification.

Other vital benefits came from overseas. For more than a year, aging statesman Benjamin Franklin had been negotiating with the French, seeking their open support of America's war for independence. France had agreed in principle with the American effort, and even admitted that they would welcome an opportunity to strike at their age-old enemy, the British. But in practical terms the French felt it doubtful that the Americans could ever win their war—especially when one considered the string of defeats they had suffered during the first two years of conflict. The French were not eager to throw their money (and possibly their troops) into the sinkhole of an unwinnable war.

But now the sentiments of the French began to change. It was obvious the Americans had won an astounding major victory. Perhaps these ragged Americans were indeed a worthy foe of the seasoned British army. Saratoga proved to be a turning point for the French, and they soon agreed to give both financial and tactical support to America's army.

Unfortunately, however, some of Saratoga's results were not so positive. Benedict Arnold had been instrumental in the victories, but the glory-seeking Gates grabbed the credit, giving Arnold just one more reason to hold a grudge against his superior—and against Congress, who simply accepted Gates's report.

In a way, Washington also was adversely affected by Gates's victory. Of course he rejoiced when he received word of Burgoyne's surrender. But he did not then know that it would provide dangerous ammunition for enemies he thought were his friends.

Chapter 18

The Conway Cabal

Though Washington was revered by many, almost worshipped by some, he had his detractors. Armchair generals were quick to compare Gates's impressive victory at Saratoga with Washington's disappointing string of failures. It was curious, they said, that Washington had not yet won many battles, let alone the war. Tongues began to wag; whispers spread from the halls of Congress to the streets. Unaware that Arnold was the true genius behind Burgoyne's surrender, or that Gates had the terrain on his side, or that Washington had weakened his own forces by sending Gates reinforcements at the critical moment— unaware of any of the actual conditions of the war—some began to wonder aloud: Was Washington really the right man to command the American armies? If Gates could conquer Burgoyne, then perhaps he could also beat Howe. If Gates could so readily defeat a major army in the north, perhaps he could likewise repulse the rest of the British and bring the tiresome war to a close. Like little demons sitting on a person's shoulder and whispering lies into a person's ear, these armchair generals moved from group to group, freely sharing their malicious "wisdom."

Gates took note of the chatter, adding his own fuel to the fire. He deliberately turned his back on the proper line of authority and took the opportunity to demonstrate his independence from Washington by sending his report of the victory at Saratoga directly to Congress. Was he not the equal of George Washington? Perhaps he was even superior to Washington! Why should he have to answer to the commander in chief?

Jealousy and Plots

Then General Thomas Conway began his own whisperings. Conway, born in Ireland, was an officer from France who had joined the American forces earlier in the year. A true soldier of fortune, he had served nearly thirty years with the French in Europe and fancied himself the most valuable officer in the American army. As time passed, Conway became increasingly critical of the "inept" Washington. He slyly suggested that Gates would be a much more qualified commander in chief—with Conway at his side, of course. Conway wrote that Washington's "talents for the command of an army . . . were miserable indeed."[1] Charles Lee, meanwhile, wrote from the security of his position as a British prisoner that George Washington was "not fit to lead a sergeant's command."[2]

In October 1777 Conway wrote Gates a letter filled with burning criticism of General Washington: "Heaven has

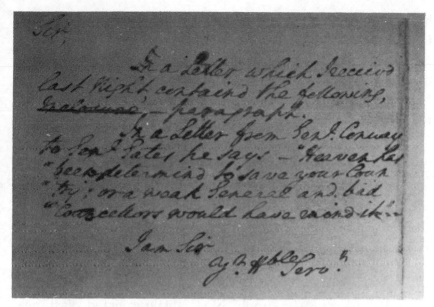

Washington's note to General Thomas Conway, who was involved in a plot to force Washington from the army. In one of Conway's letters to a fellow conspirator, which fell into Washington's hands, he said, "Heaven has been determined to save your country, or a weak general and bad counselors would have ruined it."

determined to save your country, or [otherwise] a weak general and bad counselors would have ruined it." Washington chanced to learn of the letter's condemnations through a third party and decided to confront Conway with it. But rather than make an official charge against Conway, Washington simply sent him a note that included the quotation.[3] Conway denied everything, and sought to underscore his innocence by submitting his resignation to Congress.

The Congress of late 1777 was very different from the seasoned and distinguished assembly that had nominated and supported Washington in 1775. Only two Congressmen now remained of the earlier group, and since most of the new representatives had never met Washington, they were scarcely able or competent to judge either his qualifications or his character. In their ignorance, the Congress wondered if Conway's negative assessment of Washington might be correct. No doubt time would tell. In the meantime, they felt it would be foolish to lose such a splendid general as Thomas Conway, and therefore they refused to accept his proffered resignation.

An Insidious Board of War

General Thomas Mifflin, one of Washington's original advisers and a man who had his own dreams of ambition, now saw a personal opportunity to gain ascendancy over the General. Earlier, tired of dealing with ephemeral congressional committees, Washington had suggested that a standing Board of War be created, with power to assist the army in crucial matters of war supply. Now Mifflin twisted Washington's original idea around and urged Congress to create such a board but give it supreme war powers, presiding over even Washington. The board was set up with five members, all critics of Washington, including Gates and Mifflin himself. Gates was made president of the board, while retaining his field command. The board's inspector general was to be none other than Thomas Conway.

Congress had thus unwittingly made Gates, Mifflin, and Conway all superior to Washington. In their new positions, each of these men was now only a step away from supplanting Washington as the commander in chief—and all harbored the secret desire of doing just that.

When Dr. James Craik, Washington's ever-faithful friend and ally, saw what was happening in the "Conway Cabal," he was sick with concern and wrote, "They dare not appear openly as your enemies, but . . . will throw such obstacles and other difficulties in your way as to force you to resign."[4]

*General Thomas Conway, leader
of a plot to force Washington to
resign as commander in chief.
Conway wrote in late 1777 that
Washington's "talents for the
command of an army... were
miserable indeed."*

"The Man I Deem My Enemy"

The problem dragged on through the brutal winter of Valley Forge. In his role as inspector general, Conway twice visited Washington at his Valley Forge headquarters. Both times he was so coolly received that he protested, venting his complaints in writing. Washington forwarded the correspondence to the president of Congress, freely admitting that there was some truth to Conway's charge. "I am [not] capable of the arts of dissimulation," he wrote. "My feelings will not permit me to make professions of friendship to the man I deem my enemy and whose system of conduct forbids it. At the same time, truth authorizes me to say that he was received and treated with proper respect to his official character."[5]

In the meantime, Gates vainly tried to extricate himself from the whole mess. He insisted that he had no designs on Washington's job and that the reported collusion between himself and Conway simply did not exist. Washington was not convinced. He declared that if Gates were innocent, he should make Conway's letter public.

As for the numerous talents Conway claimed for himself, Washington wrote sarcastically, "The United States have lost much from that unseasonable diffidence which prevented his embracing the numerous opportunities he had in council of displaying those rich treasures of knowledge and experience he has since so freely laid open to you." Then his sarcasm turned to anger. Conway was a man "capable of all the malignity of detraction and all the meanness of intrigue to gratify the absurd resentment of disappointed vanity, or to answer the purposes of personal aggrandizement and promote the interests of faction."[6]

It was all very discouraging to the weary commander. Not only was he assailed from too many sides by untrue subordinates, but he could not even defend himself. To do so would require that he reveal top-secret military information, and that would be of great detriment to the American cause. "My enemies take an ungenerous advantage of me," he explained to Henry Laurens, president of Congress. "They know I cannot combat their insinuations . . . without disclosing secrets it is of the utmost moment to conceal."[7]

At the same time, Washington once again acknowledged that he was a fallible human being and perhaps actually deserved some of the criticism that was being heaped upon him. He wrote: "Why should I expect to be exempt from censure, the unfailing lot of an elevated station? . . . My heart tells me it has been my unremitted aim to do the best circumstances would permit. Yet I may have been very often mistaken in my judgment of the means and may, in many instances, deserve the imputation of error."[8]

On more than one occasion he made it very clear that "I did not solicit the command but accepted it after much entreaty." He continued:

> [Nevertheless,] I pursued the great line of my duty and the object in view (as far as my judgment could direct) as pointedly as the needle to the pole. So soon, then, as the public gets dissatisfied with my services, or a person is found better qualified to answer her expectation, I shall quit the helm with as much satisfaction and retire to a private station with as much content as ever the wearied pilgrim felt upon his safe arrival in the Holy Land or haven of hope; and shall wish most devoutly that those who come after may meet with more prosperous gales than I have done, and less difficulty. [9]

End of the Cabal

Gradually, word spread that a plot was under way to oust Washington. Members of the army cried out in anger, and Congress, when it reconvened in the spring of 1778, was newly supportive of Washington. Conway, miffed at not receiving an expected promotion, again threatened in April to resign—and was stunned when Congress accepted his resignation without argument.

By May 1778 the dangerous threat of the Conway Cabal was over. Conway himself was gone. The Board of War steadily fell into disrepute. Those powerful politicians and generals who had deceitfully attempted to depose the commanding general saw their influence fading rather than growing. In the end Washington stood taller than ever.

Through it all, Washington remained philosophic. To Lafayette he wrote that after the war "we shall laugh at our past difficulties and the folly of others." [10]

When Gates finally apologized, Washington generously responded that he wished to bury the whole affair in "silence, and as far as future events will permit, oblivion. My temper leads me to peace and harmony with all men; and it is particularly my wish to avoid any personal feuds or dissensions with those who are embarked in the same great national interest with myself, as every difference of this kind must in its consequences be very injurious."[11]

Chapter 19

The Depths of Valley Forge

Despite Washington's concerns about the looming clouds of the Conway Cabal, the winter of 1777–78 brought a problem that was even more menacing: his army was ill-fed and shabbily clothed as they prepared to move to their winter quarters. In November Washington wrote soberly, "There are now in this army . . . four thousand men wanting blankets, near two thousand of which have never had one, although some of them have been twelve months in service."[1] Another thousand men stumbled along without shoes.

These problems threatened disastrous consequences. As General Nathanael Greene wrote in distress, "I think I never saw the army so near dissolving since I have belonged to it."[2] Particularly alarming about the army's condition was the fact that these problems were not new. The army was continually undersupplied and ever on the verge of dissolution.

"I Searched for Water Till I Was Weary"

These were only the "beginning of sorrows." A month later, in mid-December, Washington marched with about ten thousand men into Valley Forge, Pennsylvania, to wait out the winter. In matter-of-fact language, a Connecticut private recorded the biting pain of that march to Valley Forge, a march that many made without shoes and all made with very little food:

Washington leads his army into Valley Forge. He described his men as "without clothes, ... without blankets, ... without shoes, ... without provisions, ... without a house or hut to cover them."

The army was now not only starved but naked; the greatest part were not only shirtless and barefoot, but destitute of all other clothing, especially blankets. I procured a small piece of raw cowhide and made myself a pair of moccasins, which kept my feet (while they lasted) from the frozen ground, although, as I well remember, the hard edges so galled my ankles while on a march that it was with much difficulty and pain that I could wear them afterwards. But the only alternative I had was to endure this inconvenience or go barefoot, as hundreds of my companions had to, till they might be tracked by their blood upon the rough, frozen ground. But hunger, nakedness, and sore shins were not the only difficulties we had at that time to encounter; we had hard duty to perform and little or no strength to perform it with....

We arrived at the Valley Forge in the evening. It was dark, there was no water to be found, and I was perishing with thirst. I searched for water till I was weary, and came to my tent without finding any; fatigue and thirst, joined with hunger, almost made me desperate. I felt at that instant as if I would have taken victuals or drink from the best friend I had on earth by force.... Just after I arrived at my tent, two soldiers, whom I did not know, passed by. They had some water in their canteens which they told me they had found a good distance off, but could not direct me to the place, as it was very dark. I tried to beg a draft of water from them, but they were as rigid as Arabs. At length I persuaded them to sell me a drink for three pence, Pennsylvania currency, which was every cent of property I could then call my own, so great was the necessity I was then reduced to.[3]

"The Army...Begins to Grow Sickly"

History has preserved other poignant, firsthand accounts of some of the valiant men who suffered through that wretched winter. Surgeon Albigence Waldo, for example, left us this pitiable record of the first days at Valley Forge. Sadly, conditions only worsened as the horrible days dragged on.

December 14—... The army, which has been surprisingly healthy hitherto, now begins to grow sickly from the continued fatigues they have suffered this campaign.... I am sick, discontented, and out of humor. Poor food, hard lodging, cold weather, fatigue, nasty clothes, nasty cookery, vomit half my time, smoked out of my senses—the devil's in it; I can't endure it. Why are we sent here to starve and freeze? What sweet felicities have I left at home: A charming wife, pretty children, good beds, good food, good cooking—all agreeable, all harmonious! Here all confusion, smoke and cold, hunger and filthiness—a pox on my bad luck! There comes a bowl of beef soup, full of burnt leaves and dirt, sickish enough to make a Hector spew—away with it, boys! I'll live like the chameleon upon air. . . .

There comes a soldier: his bare feet are seen through his worn-out shoes, his legs nearly naked from the tattered remains of an only pair of stockings, his breeches not sufficient to cover his nakedness, his shirt hanging in strings, his hair dishevelled, his face meager. His whole appearance pictures a person forsaken and discouraged. He comes and cries with an air of wretchedness and despair, "I am sick, my feet lame, my legs are sore, my constitution is broken. . . . I fail fast; I shall soon be no more!" . . .

December 16— . . . For the first time since we have been here the tents were pitched, to keep the men more comfortable.

"Good morning, Brother Soldier," says one to another, "how are you?"

"All wet I thank'e, hope you are so," says the other. . . .

December 21— . . . A general cry through the camp this evening among the soldiers, "No meat! No meat!" . . .

What have you for your dinners, boys? "Nothing but fire cake and water, sir." At night: "Gentlemen, the supper is ready." What is your supper, lads? "Fire cake and water, sir." . . .

December 22— . . . What have you got for breakfast, lads? "Fire cake and water, sir." The Lord send that our Commissary of Purchases may live [on] fire cake and water till their glutted guts are turned to pasteboard. . . . But why do I talk of hunger and hard usage, when so many in the world have not even fire cake and water to eat?[4]

No Clothes, No Shoes, No Blankets, No Shelter

The winter was well designed for a work of brutal destruction, nearly crushing the American army through intense starvation and cold. Washington grieved at the terrible hardship of his troops, but locating them at Valley Forge was a strategic necessity. Valley Forge, a wooded region south of the Schuylkill River, was only eighteen miles northwest of British-occupied Philadelphia. Washington was therefore close enough to keep an eye on the British while still being far enough to forestall a surprise attack. Furthermore, with the American army there, British raiding parties could not as easily rove about seeking food and supplies, nor could they make a major march of any kind. As for the security of the American forces, Washington knew his troops would be safe at Valley Forge: the windy hills of the area provided terrain that could easily be defended.

As they began their stay there, the men lived in cold, drafty tents. In the weeks that followed they gradually built huts, fourteen feet wide by sixteen feet long, each housing twelve men. The huts, ready by mid-January, were crowded—but the number of men in each one contributed much-welcomed body warmth.

Washington voiced high praise for his ragamuffin army when he wrote:

No history now extant can furnish an instance of an army's suffering such uncommon hardships as ours has done. To see men without clothes to cover their nakedness, without blankets to lie on, without shoes (for the want of which their marches might be traced by the blood from their feet), and almost as often without provisions as with them, marching through the frost and snow, and at Christmas taking up their winter quarters within a day's march from the enemy, without a house or hut to cover them till they could be built, and submitting to it without a murmur, is a proof of patience and obedience which in my opinion can scarce be paralleled.[5]

As he moved among the suffering troops, Washington assured them that he himself would "share in the hardship and partake of every inconvenience." And knowing that great strength would come through unity and perseverance, he admonished "the officers and soldiers with one heart and one mind [to] resolve to surmount every difficulty with a fortitude and patience becoming their profession and the sacred cause in which they are engaged."[6]

But he knew such admonitions were inadequate to meet the army's ultimate needs. Infinitely more important than wise counsel were physical warmth, food in the belly, trousers on shivering legs. Immediately after arriving at Valley Forge, Washington begged Congress to take action to relieve the army's horrible condition. "My feelings are every day wounded" by the army's dire situation, he wrote on December 22.[7]

An Army "Made of Stocks and Stones"

The next day he warned that "unless some great and capital change suddenly takes place, . . . this army must inevitably be reduced to . . . starve, dissolve, or disperse in order to obtain subsistence in the best manner they can. . . . Three or four days' bad weather would prove our destruction." Nearly three thousand of his men were unfit for service because "they are barefoot and otherwise naked." Thoroughly disgruntled, he reported to Congress that he had ordered troops out to meet a British foraging party, and then learned they could not go because of inadequate supplies!

With growing indignation, he wrote that it was easy, while sitting in a "comfortable room by a good fireside," to imagine that the army was "made of stocks and stones and equally insensible of frost and snow." But Washington's sense of compassion made these circumstances almost beyond his capacity to endure. He wrote, "Although [many] seem to have little feeling for the naked and distressed soldier, I feel superabundantly for them, and from my soul pity those miseries which it is neither in my power to relieve or prevent."[8]

Despite Washington's emotional appeals, Congress seemed totally powerless to take immediate action. Their hands were shackled by the defaulting states, many of which claimed they were drained by the war already. At the end of the year, Washington's summary of the army's condition was even darker than before. In righteous rage he spoke vehemently about "our sick naked, our well naked, our unfortunate men in captivity naked!"[9] Eventually some of the men's clothing grew so ragged that it literally fell off their gaunt bodies, leaving them with only a blanket to cover their nakedness. With no clothes to wear, the men were too embarrassed even to leave their quarters.

The trials continued well into February 1778. One officer wrote pitifully, "It would melt the heart of a savage to see the state we are in."[10]

Martha Washington joined her husband at the Valley Forge encampment on February 10, following her usual custom of spending at least part of the winter season with the General. She was immediately struck with the terrible destitution of the soldiers and began to take steps to help them. One eyewitness recorded:

> I never in my life knew a woman so busy from early morning until late at night as was Lady Washington, providing comforts for the sick soldiers. Every day, excepting Sunday, the wives of officers in camp, and sometimes other women, were invited to Mr. Potts' [where the Washingtons were staying] to assist her in knitting socks, patching garments, and making shirts for the poor soldiers, when materials could be procured. Every fair day she might be seen, with basket in hand and with a single attendant, going among the huts seeking the keenest and most needy sufferer, and giving all the comforts to them in her power. [11]

During those months at Valley Forge, hundreds of horses died of starvation. (Despite their own destitution, the men could not bear to eat them. The rotting carcasses, which could not be buried in the frozen earth, contributed to the growing problem of disease.) More tragic, about twenty-five hundred troops—a full one-quarter of Washington's army—died of cold, starvation, and disease. Several thousand more deserted, some two thousand of which joined the British in order to secure the basic necessities of food and warm clothing which were virtually nonexistent in the American camp. Yet those who stayed gave new vitality to the American army. They knew they had looked death full in the face without quavering. Those who survived came out of the winter far stronger than they were when they went into it.

Emerging from the Winter

By spring, conditions had improved measurably. The frozen ground began to thaw. Drafty chinks in the roofs and walls of the men's huts leaked less with cold air. Clothing remained in short supply, but the need for warm, protective covering was not as great. And food became more abundant: each man received a daily allotment of a pound and a half of bread, a pound of meat or pork and beans, and a gill (just over a cup) of whiskey. In addition, the spring run of shad up the Schuylkill was so bountiful that men long accustomed to hunger gorged themselves, eating to satiety and then eating more. Hundreds of barrels of the succulent fish were salted for future use.

George Washington gratefully credited God with preserving the American army through the trials of such a devastating winter. Deep thanks, he wrote, are "due to the great Author of all the care and good that have been extended in relieving us in difficulties and distress."[12]

Washington had pled repeatedly with that "great Author," seeking relief for his suffering men. Those prayers at Valley Forge, romantically preserved in art, have almost been given the status of legend. Yet the General really did pray during that dark winter. According to the record, two eyewitnesses (General Henry Knox and the man with whom Washington was quartered at Valley Forge, Isaac Potts) tell of the General retiring to a quiet grove where he could be alone to seek the help of God.[13]

But this man of great faith was not motivated to pray at Valley Forge simply because of the horrors of that winter. Washington prayed at Valley Forge in large part because it was his habit to pray. As his grandson, George Washington Parke Custis, later wrote, "Throughout the war, as it was understood in his military family, he gave a part of every day to private prayer and devotion."[14] George Washington prayed from the time of his youth, and he apparently continued that practice throughout his life.[15] His prayers at

Valley Forge, then, were but one strand in a lifetime of devotion.

One bright spot in Valley Forge's bleak winter was the welcome arrival of a crack drillmaster. About mid-February a stocky man rode into camp and announced himself as Lieutenant General Friedrich Wilhelm Ludolf Gerhard Augustin Baron von Steuben. Von Steuben had served in the Prussian army under Frederick the Great, and now he wished to join the Americans in their great cause of liberty. Though in reality he was neither a baron nor a lieutenant general, he soon proved to be a superb drillmaster who was adaptable to the needs of the Americans. During the spring of 1778 he taught the patriot troops how to march and maneuver in ranks, as well as how to effectively use their bayonets, a skill much needed against the British.

The Baron von Steuben, a former Prussian officer who joined the American army at Valley Forge. Von Steuben became the drillmaster for the American troops, teaching them how to march and maneuver in ranks, as well as how to effectively use their bayonets.

The colorful von Steuben spoke very little English, but the Americans learned well under his style of teaching. He began by teaching one hundred carefully picked men; he then used them to help him teach the new skills to additional groups. Under his tutelage, the American army began to discover for the first time how to beat the British at their own game. Largely because of von Steuben, the American troops finally became an army with the ability to fight as a cohesive unit.

The Culprits of Valley Forge

What was the underlying cause of the grueling trial at Valley Forge? Was Washington a poor commander, choosing a disastrous wintering position? Was the weather unusually severe? Did the British consistently intercept supply shipments, leaving the suffering Americans destitute?

Actually, the army's greatest enemy during that wretched winter was none of these. Instead, the responsibility for so much death and hardship at Valley Forge rested primarily on the shoulders of those whom the army was trying to serve: their fellow Americans.

At the top of the list must go the notorious name of Thomas Mifflin, one of the devious participants in the Conway Cabal. Mifflin served as the quartermaster general through most of the period from August 1775 to March 1778. His duties were straightforward. Along with the commissary general, he was to procure and distribute the food, clothing, and supplies so urgently needed by the army. Easily distracted by other concerns, he was absent from his post throughout most of 1777, and in October he submitted his resignation. Congress asked him to continue in his position until he could be replaced, even though he was not functioning. He reluctantly agreed.

Thus, Washington and his army entered the difficult winter of Valley Forge without an effective quartermaster general. How could they get the supplies they needed when their quartermaster was either absent or delinquent in his duties most of the time?

It must be noted that the members of Congress were equally guilty. They persistently refused to appoint an aggressive and committed officer to the post of quartermaster general. To make matters worse, they not only left Mifflin in this badly neglected position but, as discussed earlier, appointed him to the Board of War. So Mifflin was plotting against Washington and taking on new duties when he should have been attending to the needs of the shivering army in Valley Forge.

The states also must bear much of the blame. Each state was given the responsibility of providing a certain amount of food and clothing to the army. Often, however, the state performed inadequately or not at all. Washington repeatedly wrote to the state governors, pleading with them to send their allotment of supplies. But his requests usually seemed to fall on deaf ears.

Others also are culpable. For example, while the men at Valley Forge were slowly starving on fire cakes and water, the farmers of Pennsylvania were making a tidy profit on their products by selling them for hard cash to the British in Philadelphia. Farmers and merchants in the state of New York were doing the same thing in selling their products to the occupation troops in the New York City area. Furthermore, "private contractors reaped a golden harvest by sending hundreds of government wagons north from Pennsylvania loaded with flour and iron while pork in Jersey awaiting shipment to the army spoiled for lack of transport."[16]

Of course, these farmers and private contractors had a right to choose their own customers, and it is equally true that they would have been virtually giving away their products for worthless American scrip if they had sold it to the army. Still, it is a shameful chapter in revolutionary history that the army was allowed to suffer such extremities while nearby civilians turned their eyes away and made a profit by trafficking with the British forces.

Eventually, Mifflin was so negligent in his performance as quartermaster that Washington demanded that he be replaced by a trusted military leader, General Nathanael Greene. Greene was reluctant to take the job, knowing the enormity of the task. But Washington persisted, and finally Greene accepted. He began at Valley Forge by sending army details into the surrounding countryside with orders to collect all the food they could, both in produce and "on the hoof." In exchange for the items they took, these foraging parties left a receipt with the farmers, to be redeemed in better times. Greene continued as quartermaster general from March 1778 until August 1780. Through that period he demonstrated that the quartermaster general could surmount many of the great difficulties plaguing the army if a competent officer was in charge.

As good weather returned and supplies were replenished, the army began to recuperate from its long and dreadful winter. Washington knew it was time for the Americans to put Valley Forge behind them—another bloody season of war lay ahead.

Chapter 20

A Year of Hope and Deceit

I n the months that followed Valley Forge, a new challenge loomed from an unexpected source: the British
began to propose a "reconciliation." Washington dis-
trusted them thoroughly, having seen their craftiness and
deceit all too often. When he learned of their proposal he
wrote to Henry Laurens, president of Congress, "The enemy
are determined to try us by force and by fraud." The fraud
they were trying to perpetrate was appealing—they were
suggesting that an easy peace could be had. But Washington
clearly saw the diplomatic deceit behind their proposal. In disgust he reminded Congress that the British were cunningly
"versed in the arts of dissimulation."

He knew that even the slightest hint of reconciliation could
drain the strength and steal the momentum from the freedom movement. Then the British could regain their crushing
grip on the colonies. With firmness, Washington wrote:

It appears to me that nothing short of independence can possibly do. The injuries we have received from Britain can never be forgotten, and a peace upon other terms would be the source of perpetual feuds and animosities. Besides, should Britain from her love of tyranny and lawless domination attempt again to bend our necks to the yoke of slavery, and there is no doubt but that she would, for her pride and ambition are unconquerable, no nation would credit our professions nor grant us aid. At any rate, their favors would be obtained upon the most . . . dishonorable terms. [1]

Congress stood foursquare behind their commanding general. Rather than be tempted by the British proposal, Congress adopted its own prerequisites for peace. First, Great Britain must withdraw her troops from the continental United States; and second, Great Britain must announce to all the world that she fully recognized the independence of the American colonies.

The British decided they were not interested in peace after all.

The Budding French Alliance

On April 30, 1778, Washington received the cheering news that France had agreed to assist in the war effort. After three years of struggling alone, at last America would have an ally. His enthusiasm evident, Washington wrote to Congress, "I believe no event was ever received with more heartfelt joy." [2] He readily credited the help of God—a practice he often followed—in the formation of the all-important alliance. "It having pleased the Almighty Ruler of the Universe propitiously to defend the cause of the united American states," he wrote to his troops, "and finally, by raising us up a powerful friend among the princes of the earth, to establish our liberty and independence [upon] lasting foundations, it becomes us to set apart a day [May 7] for gratefully acknowledging the divine goodness and celebrating the important event which we owe to his benign interposition."[3]

King Louis XVI, the ruler of France who supported the American Revolutionary War by sending troops, ships, and money. Later, during the "reign of terror" in France's revolution, Louis XVI lost his head at the guillotine.

The French alliance was the result of long months of painstaking effort by Benjamin Franklin, who was a superb statesman. Franklin had arrived in France in late 1776, suffering from gout and discomfort at the age of seventy; he was one of a three-member commission appointed to negotiate a treaty. (The other two commissioners were Arthur Lee and Silas Deane.) The public immediately lionized the great inventor, publisher, and thinker—but the French government could not officially receive him, since they had not yet recognized the young American government. Still, the French were sympathetic with the American cause. The foreign minister, Charles Vergennes, began meeting secretly with Franklin, but refused to see the other two commissioners.

Vergennes had a long-standing hatred of the British, a fire

that was fanned to white heat by the French humiliation in the recent French and Indian War. That conflict had extended from America to Europe and involved many countries. However, the prime actors had been England and France, and England had come off the proud victor.

Bitter memories of that war increased Vergennes's desire to answer America's cries for help. Nevertheless, France would be taking grave risks by engaging England in another conflict. It was true that a combination of the French and the Americans might eventually defeat the powerful British. But what if the Americans became reconciled with the British after France had become involved? Then England, enraged at France's involvement in the war, would be free to turn the full force of her arms against a meddling rival. If that event happened, the results could be disastrous for France. It would probably lead to bankruptcy through war, humiliating defeat, even loss of sovereignty. All of these considerations turned Vergennes into a stone pillar of caution.

Rather than commit himself openly, he began by setting up a secret fund to help the Americans pay for their expensive war. Through the fictitious business firm of Hortalez and Cie, Vergennes funneled several million livres (one million livres equalled $200,000) worth of financial aid to the United States.

Franklin's Diplomacy

While Vergennes was watching the flow of events in America, Franklin practiced a unique style of low-key diplomacy that proved to be precisely right for the occasion. He never pushed or cajoled or threatened. He quietly argued practicalities, carefully reasoned on the basis of principle—then he left to tour the famous Paris museums or to explore ideas with some French philosopher while his suggestions had time to sink deeply into the French minister's consciousness.

Time was the critical factor in Franklin's plan, and time eventually convinced Vergennes that America's commitment to independence was indeed irrevocable. The French minister was impressed with Washington's well-planned victories at Trenton and Princeton. He even received the report of the battle at Germantown without being overly alarmed. Although the Americans had technically lost that battle, Vergennes could see encouraging promise in the American army.

Then came the astounding victory at Saratoga. A major British force of more than five thousand had been cowed into surrendering to the rough-hewn Americans. From a European vantage point, it almost seemed like a cat bowing meekly before a tiny mouse. The French were impressed by America's stunning achievement at Saratoga, and finally Vergennes was able to persuade his reluctant government to join an open alliance with the Americans. After a year of untiring effort, Franklin's patient diplomacy, plus the sensational victory at Saratoga, had won over a powerful ally to the American cause.

Though Washington rejoiced at the news, he soon learned, to his frustration and chagrin, that the French were not nearly as useful as he had hoped they would be. It took four years of fighting together before the French and the Americans were finally able to effectively coordinate their forces.

Howe Retires from the Scene

Washington's primary opponent almost from the beginning had been Sir William Howe. He was an aristocrat with a brilliant war record when he first took over the command of the British troops from General Thomas Gage in 1775.

However, as commander in chief, Howe was mediocre or worse during most of his American tenure, and two years of tedious war gradually wore him down. In October 1777 he asked the British government to relieve him of the command. The slow-moving British government finally named his replacement in May 1778. It turned out to be Sir Henry Clinton, Howe's second in command.

Howe's failure to quash the American patriots seems puzzling. He had nearly every advantage over Washington— a large force of well-trained troops, adequate food and supplies, a formidable navy, help from American loyalists— yet he continually failed. Perhaps the advantages he lacked— character and cause—were enough to make the critical difference.

After Howe left for England, the forward-speaking Charles Lee, who as a prisoner of war in New York City had some opportunity to observe the British commander, drew this uncomplimentary sketch of him:

> From my first acquaintance with Mr. Howe I liked him. . . He is . . . [however] the most indolent of mortals. . . . He is naturally good humored, complaisant, but illiterate and indolent to the last degree. . . . His understanding is . . . rather good than otherwise, but was totally confounded and stupefied by the immensity of the task imposed upon him. He shut his eyes, fought his battles, drank his bottle, had [his mistress, the pretty, married Betsy Loring], advised with his counselors, received his orders from [British ministers] North and Germain (one more absurd than the other), took Galloway's opinion, shut his eyes, fought again, and is now, I suppose, to be called to account for acting according to instructions. [4]

Sir Henry Clinton, Howe's replacement, harshly criticized his former commander and listed half a dozen ways in which

Howe could have achieved a decisive British victory. He
wrote:

> Had Sir William Howe fortified the hills around Boston,
> he could not have been disgracefully driven from it. Had he
> pursued his victory at Long Island, he had ended the
> rebellion. Had he landed above the lines at New York, not a
> man could have escaped him. Had he fought the Americans
> at Brunswick he was sure of victory. Had he cooperated
> with the northern army, he had saved it, or had he gone to
> Philadelphia by land, he had ruined Mr. Washington and his
> forces. But as he did none of these things, had he gone to
> the Devil before he was sent to America, it had been a
> saving of infamy to himself and indelible dishonor to this
> country. [5]

*General Henry Clinton, who
served as the British commander
in chief longer than any other
officer during the war, from
1778 to 1782. He was removed
from his command and returned to
England following the British loss
at Yorktown.*

Hindsight seemed to give Clinton incredibly clear vision,
but now the future beckoned him to prove his own abilities.

Henry Clinton assumed his high commanding role with
great expectations. He was a small, paunchy man of
aristocratic lineage who had been present at the Battle of

Bunker Hill. History records that he seriously bungled the attack on Charleston and Fort Moultrie, but he planned the successful capture of Long Island, and for that he received his knighthood. In Clinton's eyes, Washington's survival was simply a matter of pure luck. And Clinton planned to make 1778 the year when that luck would abruptly come to a halt.

The Treachery of Charles Lee

One month before Howe sailed for Great Britain, Washington welcomed the return of Charles Lee, who had been exchanged for a British prisoner of war in April 1778. Washington was so happy to receive back his old second-in-command that he rode out several miles from his camp to greet him, then embraced him as a long-lost brother.

What Washington did not know—in fact, the truth remained hidden for almost a hundred years—was that Lee was returning as a secret traitor. His loyalty to his country had always seemed secondary to his own self-interest and now he had sold out, trying to gain favor with the British.

On March 29, 1777, three months after his capture, Lee had unfolded to General William Howe a plan for the certain defeat of the Americans. The British were going to win the war anyway, Lee explained, and his "conscience" required him to try to diminish the bloodshed on both sides by bringing the conflict to a speedy conclusion. Howe ignored Lee's ideas, however, because he had plans of his own.

The following January, Washington learned that the British might be interested in exchanging Lee. He sent an emissary, Elias Boudinot, to New York to negotiate. While in the city, Boudinot met with Lee himself—and was shocked when Lee proposed that the Americans prepare to flee their own country, since they could never defeat the powerful British.

Shortly after Lee's release in late April 1778 he sent a letter to British General James Robertson, which was then passed on to Clinton. In his letter, Lee suggested that the British proclaim a general pardon for all Americans, without exception, and renounce their right to tax the American people. In turn, America should forget the idea of independence and return to her old allegiance. If the British agreed, Lee said, they should let him know, and he would use his broad influence to bring the war to an end. The British did not deign to reply.

Lee's treachery reached its pinnacle on June 4, more than a month after his release from British captivity. On that day he sent a curious letter to Clinton, congratulating him on his promotion to commander in chief. "General Lee presents his most sincere and humble respects to Sir Henry Clinton. He wishes him all possible happiness and health and begs, whatever may be the event of the present unfortunate contest, that he will believe General Lee to be his most respectful and obliged humble servant."[6]

To what extent was Lee willing to oblige Clinton as his "humble servant"? Perhaps we will never know. Certainly his fraternizing with the enemy could have had no good effect. Lee appears to have been trying to play both sides—then he would be on the winning team no matter what happened. Whatever his motives, we do know this: less than one month after sending that incriminating letter, Lee met Clinton on the battlefield at Monmouth, and his disgraceful behavior in that conflict nearly created a major disaster for the American army.

Clinton Begins to Move

Clinton's first order of business as commander in chief was to evacuate Philadelphia, which had proven worthless as a military prize. He ordered his ten thousand troops back to New York, a strategic base that was infinitely more valuable than Philadelphia and one which needed strengthening before the arrival of the French.

In late June 1778 Clinton transported his Philadelphia regiments across the Delaware and slowly marched them into New Jersey. The army, with its vast train of baggage and camp followers, was strung out long miles across the countryside. Progress was slowed further by destroyed bridges and strategic obstructions in the road (carefully placed by the Jersey militia). Day by day, the army's ponderous artillery and fifteen hundred supply wagons fell farther and farther behind. Washington's spies informed him that Clinton was unwittingly giving the Americans an ideal target for a surprise attack. As they saw it, Washington could strike against the rear of the army before the main body, miles away, could come back in time to rescue them.

A Divided Council of War

Washington called his foremost officers into a council of war. Lee, admittedly fearful of open battle with the British, spoke vociferously against an attack. He argued that if they struck against the professional British troops, the raw American volunteers would be annihilated. When someone mentioned the careful training the men had received under von Steuben, Lee scoffed at it, saying such training was worthless.

The other officers in the council listened attentively, and

most were swayed by Lee's persuasive arguments. But not all. Alexander Hamilton was thoroughly disgusted. The council's decision, he said with scorn, "would have done honor to the most honorable society of midwives."[7]

A few others agreed with Hamilton that Lee was wrong; Washington should attack. Nathanael Greene, Lafayette, and Anthony Wayne all lobbied privately with the commander in chief. They believed the stretched-out British troops were so vulnerable that it would be positively foolish not to strike. Washington agreed. He decided to overrule his council of war and get ready for an attack.

Lee was offered the commanding position, but he brusquely declined, miffed that his advice was not being followed. Washington thereupon assigned the command to Lafayette and sent him ahead with five thousand troops. But at the last minute Lee changed his mind. He had apparently decided that an engagement with five thousand troops was too significant to his military career to ignore. He therefore mounted his horse and raced after Lafayette, relieving him of his command in the field.

Under Lee's direction, the American forces trailed after Clinton for several days, watching for an opportune moment to attack. On June 27, Lee and his troops camped six miles from the British rear. Washington, with the main body of the army, about eight thousand soldiers, was three miles farther back. On June 28, at four in the morning, the British began to march from Monmouth Court House (now called Freehold, New Jersey). Lee waited until seven o'clock, then began to follow. When Lee reached Monmouth, he found that Clinton had left behind a large rear guard of about two thousand troops. Apparently intending to cut them off from the main body, Lee ordered an attack.

The Battle of Monmouth

The attack began about ten o'clock on a sweltering, muggy morning. Unfortunately, Lee failed to prepare a coherent plan of assault, and the Americans pushed into battle willy-nilly. As the battle was joined, Clinton heard the explosion of shots far behind him and rushed back with several regiments to help his troops. The reinforced rear guard drove the Americans back until Lee, confused and feeling over-whelmed, ordered a general retreat.

Washington, meanwhile, arose early that morning and marched his men toward Monmouth. As they neared Monmouth Court House they began to hear the vigorous sounds of active fighting. It was music to Washington's ears. At last the enemy had been engaged! Washington rushed forward but was shocked a short time later to meet some of Lee's troops running toward him in retreat. What could be wrong? Leaving Greene in command, he charged ahead on his tall white horse to discover what was happening. Soon he saw Lee riding in retreat with some of his officers, chatting gaily with them. Washington pulled up his panting horse and demanded, "What is all this confusion for, and retreat?"

Lee began a litany of weak excuses—he had received conflicting intelligence reports, some of his troops had disobeyed him, the geography had been disadvantageous. Besides, he concluded, he had advised against an attack in the first place.

Washington exploded. "All this may be true, sir, but you ought not to have undertaken it unless you intended to go through with it!"[8]

Lee began to voice further excuses, but Washington would have none of it. He wheeled his horse to return to the troops, hoping to put some semblance of order into the jumbled retreat. He had barely begun the task when he was stopped by a messenger—the British were advancing rapidly and would arrive in minutes. Not only had Lee fled the field of battle, but the redcoats were in hot pursuit. Lee's retreat could prove "fatal to the [whole] army."[9]

Washington rallies his troops at Monmouth. British vulnerability would have given the Americans an easy victory, but General Charles Lee, inexplicably, had begun a retreat.

Washington hastily reorganized his troops. He ordered two regiments to charge forward and hold Clinton's army while he re-formed the American line on high ground. There he determined to make a stand. Lafayette was fascinated as he watched the American commander move into action. "General Washington appeared to arrest fortune by one glance," he wrote. "His presence stopped the retreat.... His graceful bearing on horseback, his calm and dignified deportment, which still retained some trace of ... displeasure, ... were all calculated to excite the highest degree of enthusiasm.... I thought then as now that I had never beheld so superb a man."[10]

In stifling 100-degree heat the British pushed relentlessly forward. They charged up the slope where Washington's troops were, but they were repulsed. They charged again. The Americans still stood firm, while von Steuben beamed at their performance. It was the first test of their training, and they were standing like seasoned professional soldiers. Throughout the day, the two sides exchanged volley after volley. At least six times the British tested the American lines, sometimes engaging in pitched hand-to-hand battles that lasted more than an hour. Men on both sides slumped to the ground under the boiling sun; a number died of heat prostration. Finally the British drew back to a secure position, unable to sustain further losses. Still, they continued to bombard the American position with sixteen cannon. But Washington was

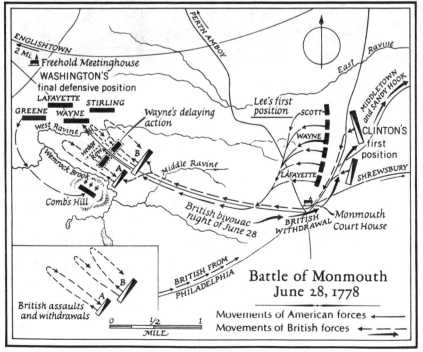

Battle of Monmouth
June 28, 1778

Movements of American forces
Movements of British forces

not intimidated. Instead of moving back, he ordered several regiments to drive forward with fixed bayonets in a massive counterattack. The British saw what was coming, broke ranks, and were soon on the run.

But before the Americans could catch the fleeing redcoats, the day's light failed them. With dusk deepening both armies collapsed in their tracks, suffering from heat, thirst, and exhaustion. Washington's troops spent the night in the open field, sleeping on their arms.

Long before dawn, however, Clinton and his British troops "stole off as silent as the grave."[11] The exhausted Americans slept right through the night, oblivious of their noiseless departure.

The British losses in the battle amounted to more than twelve hundred; the Americans lost substantially less—some two to three hundred. At least one hundred men from both sides died of sunstroke, and many more had to withdraw from the battle because of total exhaustion. In addition, more than six hundred British deserters—most of them German mercenaries—slipped away from the battle, straggling back to take refuge in Philadelphia during the next few days.

Aftermath of Monmouth

In the midst of all the confusion and chaos, just as Lafayette had seen, Washington's coolness and determination had saved the day. Of course, he was disappointed that his army had not achieved the major victory it would have enjoyed had it not been for Lee's ill-advised retreat. But he nevertheless rejoiced that his brave soldiers had more or less won the day. At least they had sent the British sneaking off in the dark toward New York. Afterwards, Alexander Hamilton wrote that Washington had been a "master workman." "A general rout, dismay, and disgrace would have attended the whole army in any other hands but his."[12]

The General was aided by the discipline of his men. After a season of training under von Steuben at Valley Forge, the army was better prepared for battle than ever before. "The officers of the army seemed to vie with each other in manifesting their zeal and bravery," Washington reported to Congress. "The behavior of the troops in general, after they recovered from the first surprise occasioned by the retreat of the advanced corps, was such as could not be surpassed."[13] Monmouth was Washington's last major battle before the closing engagement of the war at Yorktown. His men—save the traitorous Charles Lee—had served the cause of freedom valiantly.

Two days after the battle, Washington displayed his usual gratitude to Deity. In general orders he said: "The men are to wash themselves this afternoon and appear as clean and decent as possible... that we may publicly unite in thanksgiving to the Supreme Disposer of human events for the victory which was obtained... over the flower of the British troops."[14]

In the days that followed, an angry Charles Lee insisted he had done nothing wrong and demanded that a court-martial be held to clear his name. The trial began on July 2, four days after the battle. A little more than a month later the court found Lee guilty of disobedience to orders, misbehavior before the enemy, and disrespect toward his commander in chief. He was suspended from any command in the American army for a twelve-month period. In December, Congress voted to uphold both the verdict and the sentence. When he heard his sentence Lee reportedly exclaimed, "O that I were a dog, that I might not call man my brother."[15] He never returned to active service in the Continental army again.

Chapter 21

Help from Abroad, Troubles at Home

The American troops celebrated the second anniversary of the Declaration of Independence with great optimism. For once, the circumstances of their infant nation seemed favorable: The army had survived the deadly winter of Valley Forge, emerging to best the British in a major battle at Monmouth. At the same time, the union proposed in the Articles of Confederation was receiving broad acceptance. Nine states had ratified the Articles, and it appeared the others would eventually do the same.

Another event also gave bright hope: a strong French fleet had arrived off the American coast under Vice Admiral Count d'Estaing. The handsome and energetic French admiral was inexperienced in naval warfare, but he promised vigorous support for the American cause. Washington was hopeful that that would indeed be the case.

In mid-July Washington proposed to d'Estaing that they jointly attack the British garrison at Rhode Island, but adverse weather conditions as well as diplomatic problems raised an insurmountable barrier, and the plan had to be abandoned. D'Estaing moved up to Boston Harbor to repair several ships that had been damaged in a storm—and to salve feelings that had been hurt by an undiplomatic American general, John Sullivan, who had taken the liberty to issue orders to the French admiral as though he were his commander.

D'Estaing's temperamental response to Sullivan's indiscretion underscored a host of problems Washington was beginning to have with many of the foreign officers who had joined the American army. These veterans from faraway places all too frequently got embroiled in petty wranglings and jealousies over place and position. In fact, the problem became so serious that in 1778 Washington exploded, "I do most sincerely wish that we had not a single foreigner among us, except the Marquis de Lafayette, who acts upon very different principles from those which govern the rest."

He then described the selfish, grasping motives that prevailed with most veterans from Europe: "In the first instance, [they] tell you they wish for nothing more than the honor of serving so glorious a cause as volunteers, the next day they solicit rank without pay, the day following want money advanced to them, and in the course of a week want further promotion and are not satisfied with anything you can do for them." These volunteers were "military fortune-hunters," Washington said—but Lafayette was refreshingly different.[1]

The Marquis de Lafayette

Marie Joseph Paul Yves Roch Gilbert du Motier, the Marquis de Lafayette, was a true aristocrat whose father had been killed in military combat before Lafayette had reached the age of two. Tragically, his mother also died before he was thirteen, and his grandfather—who had become his guardian—died a few weeks later. Thus, Lafayette became a wealthy orphan while barely a teenager.

He was only sixteen when a marriage was arranged for him with Marie Francoise de Noailles. His marriage brought him into one of the most powerful families in France.

The Marquis de Lafayette in 1779. Lafayette was a French aristocrat who joined the American army in their fight for freedom. He and Washington were very close, like a son and his father. Washington wrote, "I do not know a more noble soul, . . . and I love him as my own son."

One month before his eighteenth birthday, in August 1775, an event occurred that changed his life. Lafayette attended a dinner party at which England's Duke of Gloucester praised the Americans for their magnificent struggle for freedom. Lafayette was impressed with the Duke's attitude that liberty is such a precious prize that men should be willing to fight for it. Beginning at that moment, Lafayette became inflamed with the noble heroism of the American cause and resolved to somehow become a part of it. Within a short time he had purchased his own ship, paid for his own crew, and was on his way to America. Congress was amazed when this boyish French aristocrat presented himself to them and offered to serve without pay in Washington's army. He was not quite twenty years old.

Almost from the moment when Lafayette first appeared in Washington's camp in August 1777, the General and the French youth were drawn to each other. Lafayette seemed to become for Washington the son he had never had, and Washington became as the father Lafayette had never known. In fact, Washington once remarked, "I do not know a more noble soul, more honest, and I love him as my own son."[2]

In September 1777 Lafayette was seriously wounded in the battle at Brandywine, but his senses were so absorbed in the fierce fighting that he was unaware of the injury until his boot had filled with blood. When Washington learned of the wound, he said to the surgeon, speaking with great tenderness, "Treat him as if he were my son, for I love him as if he were."[3]

A year later, Washington wrote a letter to the young Lafayette in which he poured out some of his deepest feelings:

> The sentiments of affection and attachment which breathe so conspicuously in all your letters to me are at once pleasing and honorable and afford me abundant cause to rejoice at the happiness of my acquaintance with you. Your love of liberty, the just sense you entertain of this valuable blessing, and your noble and disinterested exertions in this cause of it, added to the innate goodness of your heart, conspire to render you dear to me, and I think myself happy in being linked with you in bonds of strictest friendship.[4]

Within six months after their first meeting, Lafayette affectionately called Washington his "adopted father." Later, Lafayette was invited to dine with members of the "Conway Cabal." During the meal he sensed the subversive spirit of these men and shocked them by raising his glass in a toast to

Washington's health. The embarrassed conspirators had little choice but to join in.

Lafayette was deeply committed to the vision of a free America. When Congress bestowed on him the position of honorary major general, he responded with these words: "The moment I heard of America, I loved her; the moment I knew she was fighting for freedom, I burned with a desire of bleeding for her; and the moment I shall be able to serve her at any time, or in any part of the world, will be the happiest one of my life."5

Lafayette's son-father relationship with Washington was undoubtedly a rich blessing to the commanding general throughout the long years of war, but Lafayette also benefited the United States in another way. Historians have agreed that Lafayette's strong influence with the French court was a significant factor in bringing France and the United States together. When the French officials at Versailles hesitated in becoming open allies with the infant United States, Lafayette helped convince them that they should send a major force to help the Americans.

Lafayette and Washington—the beloved orphan "son" and the loving "father"—remained close friends until the end of Washington's life.

A Motionless Summer and Fall

With the British holed up in New York City, Washington moved to White Plains, New York, which he made his headquarters. Just two years earlier the British had driven him from that very spot. He remembered the event all too well, remarking, "It is not a little pleasing, nor less wonderful to contemplate, that after two years' maneuvering and undergoing the strangest vicissitudes that perhaps ever attended one contest since the creation, both armies are brought back to the very point they set out from." He noted with pleasure that the British army, which had formerly been on the offensive, was "now reduced to the use of the spade and pickax for defense." And, as always, he thanked God for the blessing: "The hand of Providence has been so conspicuous in all this that he must be worse than an infidel that lacks faith, and more than wicked that has not gratitude enough to acknowledge his obligations."[6]

In the months that followed, Washington waited expectantly for the British to make a move, but Clinton seemed contented with total inaction. The British "are indecisive and foolish," Washington wrote.[7] Their lack of movement wore on his nerves. "I am every day more and more at a loss [as to what I should do]."[8]

Finally, convinced that the British were going to linger in New York through both summer and fall, Washington began to turn to other plans. He temporarily wondered about staging an invasion into Canada. Lafayette had worked out a detailed plan for making such an assault, and in November Congress proposed an invasion strategy that involved French assistance. But after thoughtful consideration Washington concluded such plans were impractical and quashed the whole idea.

In November and December the General moved his troops into winter quarters, forming them in a loose semicircle around New York, with pivotal camps in New Jersey, New York, and Connecticut. Then he traveled to Philadelphia to confer with Congress. His stay was brief. Some of his friends encouraged him to stay in Philadelphia for the entire winter, but Washington declined. "Were I to give in to private conveniency and amusement, I should not be able to resist the invitation of my friends," he said. "But the affairs of the army require my constant attention and presence ... to keep it from crumbling."[9]

The Loss of Savannah

While Washington was holding Clinton at bay in New York, the British shipped a large force south to fight in Georgia. There, under the direction of Lieutenant Colonel Archibald Campbell, some thirty-five hundred regulars and Tories were assigned to take the coveted port of Savannah. Capturing Savannah would give the British a critical entrance to the rest of the South as well as a closer link with their supply source in the West Indies.

Campbell's American opposition came in the person of a feisty and determined American general named Robert Howe. Unfortunately, Howe was far outnumbered, having only a thousand inexperienced militiamen to defend Savannah. On December 29, Howe positioned his troops between the British and Savannah, placing his men on a road that ran between a spread of flooded rice paddies on one side and a swamp on the other. It was an ideal position, chosen carefully to negate Britain's great advantage in numbers. Campbell immediately realized that, with no available way around Howe, the British had no choice but to make a bloody frontal assault on the narrow road.

But luck was with Campbell. Before he sent his men into battle, he learned of an old Negro, Quamino Dolly, who knew the area intimately and was willing to act as a guide for the British. Dolly showed them a hidden path through the swamps, over which Campbell sent a detachment of light infantry to attack the Americans from the rear. The surprise attack caught the Americans unaware and diverted their attention just as Campbell began his assault from the front.

The fighting was brisk but brief. The outmanned Americans were soon threatened with extinction, and Howe ordered a general retreat across a swampy causeway. The engagement turned out to be costly for the Americans: 83 were killed in fighting or drowned in the retreat, while 453 were captured. The British losses consisted of three killed and ten wounded.

Savannah was easily occupied, and the British then moved to secure the rest of Georgia. A month later, they took Augusta, which helped them establish a solid base of operations for a long campaign in the south.

The Capture of Stony Point

For Washington, the early part of the year 1779 was a time of frustrating stagnation. Since Washington was determined to fight a defensive war—except where he had the strength to do otherwise—he remained dependent on the British initiative. He carefully watched for signs of any movements, but under an entrenched Clinton, the British did not seem to be much interested in moving anywhere.

Finally, in late May, six thousand British and Hessian troops unexpectedly sailed up the Hudson and attacked two American outposts—Verplanck's Point and Stony Point—crushing the weak American resistance. Alarmed at the loss of these important strategic positions, Washington sent Mad Anthony Wayne downriver from West Point with twelve hundred men to recapture Stony Point and rout or capture the six hundred British garrisoned there. After dark on July 15, 1779, Wayne's troops began moving into the area, taking local inhabitants into custody to prevent any loyalists from warning the British. Dogs were bayoneted to assure silence on the march.

The men filed along the riverbank and across a water-filled marsh, sloshing in water up to their knees. They arrived at the fort just after midnight. Wayne was leading a column on the right when a sentry spotted him and fired. The bullet grazed his skull and knocked him to the earth, stunned. Angry and frightened, Wayne's men raced forward, yelling in fury; using axes they smashed against the walls of the fort, broke through, and attacked the British with bayonets. Within thirty minutes the fighting was over, and the fort was once more in American hands. The Americans lost 95 men in the brief engagement, 80 of whom were only wounded. The British lost 133, while 543 were captured.

It was a skillful, daring raid, and Wayne was awarded a gold medal by a grateful Congress. After touring Stony Point, Washington determined it would be too costly to maintain, and the Americans therefore abandoned it to the British. But the moral victory had been significant, inspiriting both the American troops and the Congress.

The Pestilence of Indian Raids

Except for the brief escapade at Stony Point, Washington spent the year troubled by a foe other than the British. During 1778 and 1779, the Indians in Pennsylvania and New York were led by Tories to engage in brutal raids against patriots on the frontier. Frequently, the victims of these raids were tortured and mutilated for several days before they were finally killed. In response to these bloody activities, Washington sent General John Sullivan and five thousand men against the Iroquois settlements in those states.

Sullivan moved like an avenging angel up the Susquehanna River from the Wyoming Valley in Pennsylvania. Another American general, James Clinton, pushed through the

Mohawk Valley of New York with his force. The scorched-earth tactics used by these two generals was devastating and thorough. They destroyed granaries and standing crops, slashed down orchards, and burned forty Iroquois towns to the ground. The following winter was uncommonly severe, and hundreds of Indian families were wiped out by slow starvation and exposure to the bitter cold.

The blow was one from which the Iroquois nation never completely recovered.

In addition to fighting redcoats and Indians, Washington and his generals spent 1779 and 1780 struggling to overcome their usual logistical adversaries: sickness, death, desertion, inadequate supplies, the expiration of enlistments. The enemies within the ranks were at least as devastating as the British, and they seemed to plague the American commander in ever-recurring cycles. Weary of the struggle, Washington warned the Congress and the people that unless the states cooperated to strengthen and supply the army "our affairs are irretrievably lost."[10]

The winter of 1779–80 seemed determined to prove the truth of his prediction.

"Every Kind of Horse Food But Hay"

After a year of uneasy and indecisive activity, General Washington moved the main army back to Morristown, New Jersey, and set up winter quarters. What happened during the next few months was even worse than the experience at Valley Forge. Never before had Washington seen such extremely cold weather. The New York harbor froze over. Roads were buried under four feet of snow, drifting as high as twelve feet. It was the coldest winter in the memory of local inhabitants.

In the face of such trials the hungry, ill-clad men shivered in their tents and struggled to build huts. In December Washington received reports that five thousand British had sailed to the southern theater, but he was unable to respond because, as he said, "the most pressing exigency" facing him at that moment was the lack of shoes for his soldiers. [11]

During that winter, Washington noted pathetically, his soldiers ate "every kind of horse food but hay," [12] and he warned the governors of the middle states that, unless aid was given immediately, "there is every appearance that the army will infallibly disband in a fornight." [13]

In January 1780 additional snowstorms added to their plight. With commissaries empty, marauding bands of soldiers roamed through the darkness and robbed nearby farms for food. That month Nathanael Greene wrote: "Poor fellows! They exhibit a picture truly distressing—more than half naked and two-thirds starved. A country overflowing with plenty are now suffering an army, employed for the defense of everything that is dear and valuable, to perish for want of food." [14]

As Greene correctly observed, the problem was not a fundamental lack of food or clothing among Americans. Instead, the army had only worthless money with which to buy that food, and the farmers and merchants were loath to let their products go for nothing. Eventually Washington sent out squads to commandeer food from the surrounding countryside. In exchange for produce and beef, the squads left a written promise to pay at some unspecified time in the future when Continental money had regained its value. Even these extreme tactics forestalled hunger only temporarily.

Eight Months of Privation

A brief survey of comments and incidents from those

months reveals how horribly desperate the army's condition had become:

January 1—Surgeon James Thacher: "The sufferings of the poor soldiers can scarcely be described—while on duty they are unavoidably exposed to all the inclemency of storms and severe cold; at night they now have a bed of straw on the ground and a single blanket to each man; they are badly clad, and some are destitute of shoes.... The snow is now from four to six feet deep."[15]

February 6—Joseph Walker: "Many a good lad [has] nothing to cover him, from his hips to his toes, save his blanket."[16]

February—Baron de Kalb: "It is so cold that the ink freezes on my pen, while I am sitting close to the fire."[17]

March 25—George Washington: "The army is now upon a most scanty allowance, and is seldom at the expiration of one day certain of a morsel of bread for the next."[18]

April 12—George Washington: "We have not at this day one ounce of meat, fresh or salt, in the magazine."[19]

May 10—A committee of congressional delegates, after visiting the winter camp: "Their patience is exhausted.... Their starving condition, their want of pay, and the variety of hardships they have been driven to sustain [have] soured their tempers and produced a spirit of discontent which begins to display itself under a complexion of the most alarming hue."[20]

May 25—With the supply of meat totally exhausted— and having received no pay for five months—two Connecticut regiments marched in armed mutiny. One officer was stabbed with a bayonet. Only with difficulty was the uprising put down.

May 28—George Washington, seeking aid from Pennsylvania's Executive Council: "Every idea you can form of our distresses will fall short of the reality.... We see in every line of the army the most serious features of mutiny and sedition.... We have everything to dread. Indeed, I have almost ceased to hope."[21]

May 31—Lafayette: "An army that is reduced to nothing, that wants provisions, that has not one of the necessary means to make war, such is the situation wherein I found our troops, and however prepared I could have been to this unhappy sight by our past distresses, I confess I had no idea of such an extremity."[22]

July 7—Ebenezer Huntington: "I despise my countrymen. I wish I could say I was not born in America. I once gloried in it but now am ashamed of it.... The insults and neglects which the Army have met with from the country beggars all description.... I am in rags, have lain in the rain on the ground for 40 hours past, and only a junk of fresh beef and that without salt to dine on this day, received no pay since last December...and all this for my cowardly countrymen who flinch at the very time when their exertions are wanted, and hold their purse strings as though they would damn the world rather than part with a dollar to their army."[23]

August 27—George Washington: "Either the army must disband, or what is, if possible, worse, subsist upon the plunder of the people."[24]

These difficulties at Morristown were extreme even for an army hardened and inured to suffering. After having survived the enormous travail of Valley Forge, Washington still could write in the early days of Morristown, "We have never experienced a like extremity at any period of the war."[25]

A Crumbling Economy

It is remarkable that the crucible of Morristown continued all the way into August. Long after winter was over, Washington's men were still scrabbling for the barest subsistence.

The difficulty was aggravated by a severe economic decline, which came primarily as a result of the collapse of the national monetary system. From the beginning the monetary system was seriously defective. In the Articles of Confederation, Congress had been given the power to print and release money, but the states withheld from the federal legislators the right to tax. In order to fund an expensive war, Congress was therefore compelled to print paper money with nothing to back it up. It did not take American citizens long to discover that almost anything was more reliable than the congressional legal tender, called Continental dollars. To further complicate the problem, each of the states began printing its own paper money, which competed with the Continental currency. The British also sent over tons of counterfeit bills to add to the money supply. Before long public confidence in all forms of paper money had totally disappeared.

This had a disastrous effect on the American economy in general, but the army was particularly hard hit. Washington watched helplessly as his commissarians tried to purchase food with money that nobody wanted. And the soldiers were angered at being paid with virtually worthless currency. In October 1778 Washington wrote to Gouverneur Morris in Congress, complaining of their plight. "What funds can stand the present expenses of the army?" he queried. "And what officer can bear the weight of prices that every necessary article is now got to? A rat in the shape of a horse is not to be bought at this time for less than two hundred pounds, a saddle under thirty or forty, boots twenty, and shoes and other articles in like proportion. How is it possible, therefore, for officers to stand this without an increase in pay?" He pointed out that the price of other essentials, including flour, hay, and beef, had also become discouragingly prohibitive. [26]

The Board of War shared Washington's anxiety. They worried that they had to spend fifteen times more in paper than the same items would have cost in gold, silver, or British currency. The American dollar gradually depreciated to the ratio of forty to one, and soon after was worth less than two cents. In May 1780, Baron de Kalb fumed that for "a bad supper and grog," and a night's lodging for himself and six others, he had to pay $850. [27] In January 1781 Allen McLane had to pay an outrageous $600 for a pair of boots and $900 for six yards of chintz. [28] Finally the Board issued this warning: "We believe in a very short period, unless some extraordinary event takes place, the present currency will cease to be a medium of commerce." [29] Their dire prophecy came to pass all too soon: by April 1781 the value of the Continental dollar was quoted at zero.

The nation's runaway finances were crushing to Washington personally. He wanted to set a worthy example by using the new national currency—but through this noble gesture of patriotism he soon saw his personal finances melting away. A number of opportunists who owed him large, longtime debts now descended upon him to pay all they owed in virtually worthless, depreciated currency. For a time he generously accepted the money and canceled the debts. Then he advised his business manager, kinsman Lund Washington at Mount Vernon, to reevaluate that ruinous policy. He wrote that Lund should find out what his most patriotic and honorable neighbors were doing, and then do the same.

A "Host of Infamous Harpies"

Since Washington was giving so unstintingly of his time, his energy, and his personal fortune, it rankled his soul to see others deceitfully growing rich from the misfortunes of war. In April 1779 he decried the "decay of public virtue" that led to the "host of infamous harpies who, to acquire a little pelf, would involve this great continent in inextricable ruin."[30]

A month later he reiterated his indignation. He wrote, "I cannot with any degree of patience behold the infamous practices of speculators, monopolizers, and all that class of gentry which are preying upon our very vitals and, for the sake of a little dirty pelf, are putting the rights and liberties of the country into the most imminent danger."[31]

Speculators and monopolizers were the unprincipled lot who heaped so much tribulation on the army throughout the war years. The monopolizers were those merchants who secretly colluded with one another in raising prices ever higher and higher. The speculators, meanwhile, sought to "corner" the market on items in short supply and then name their own extravagant price. Some of these amassed incredible fortunes during the war years, greedily building their future on the misfortunes of those who were fighting the war.

Conditions finally deteriorated to the lowest possible point. As General Washington put it, "a wagon load of money will scarcely purchase a wagon load of provision."[32] Soldiers and working people suffered gravely, unable to obtain the barest necessities. An officer's salary of $400 bought goods that would have cost him only $10 before the war. Then the bottom dropped out entirely. Congress itself, growing desperate, repudiated the Continental dollar both as a medium of exchange and as the basis for making assessments on the states. One loyalist poet, gleefully observing the condition of the country's currency, wrote in scorn:

Mock-money and mock-states shall melt away,
And the mock troops disband for want of pay. [33]

As the war dragged on, it looked as though he might very well be right.

Chapter 22

"A History of False Hopes"

The army of American militia recruited in the south enjoyed a much easier winter than Washington's army did, but they were soon to have troubles of their own. Word arrived that the British were coming in force.

The south was strongly loyalist and therefore teeming with Tories. Through luck and pluck the Americans had successfully defended Charleston in 1776 when the British attacked Fort Moultrie, but in 1780, bolstered by broad Tory support, Sir Henry Clinton expected to emerge conqueror. As mentioned earlier, Savannah and Augusta had been captured a year before, and Clinton intended to use them as a solid base from which to invade the Carolinas. Then he hoped to subjugate Virginia and, with his army fully expanded by southern Tories, to push north and bring the war at last to a conclusion.

General Benjamin Lincoln, the commander at Charleston whose misjudgment led to the greatest American loss of the war. Lincoln was Washington's second in command at Yorktown, where he officially received the British sword of surrender.

A Tragic Surrender

Clinton arrived at Charleston on February 11, 1780, bringing with him some six thousand regulars. But he seemed to be in no hurry to move into action. In fact, he had been on the site nearly a month before he began to erect batteries opposite the town. American General Benjamin Lincoln, who had been severely wounded at Saratoga, was now serving as commander at Charleston, and he welcomed the delay. Lincoln consolidated his force of five thousand men (including two thousand Washington had sent from the north), and marched them into Charleston to better protect the city. Little did he know that he was putting their heads into a noose.

George Washington, more than seven hundred sea miles away, saw Lincoln's danger and repeatedly sent warnings. The burden of his messages was this: *Do not allow yourself to be trapped with your troops in Charleston. Remember the awful debacle at Fort Washington. We could hardly bear another such blow.*[1] Tragically, Washington's letters did not arrive in time.

Meanwhile, Tories were greatly expanding Clinton's army, just as he had hoped they would. With ten thousand men under his command, he deployed them around Charleston and cut off all means of escape or reinforcement to the Americans. He first secured the Ashley River south of Charleston, then the Cooper River to the north. During a fierce thunderstorm the British fleet slipped past that sturdy guardian of the water front, Fort Moultrie, and anchored menacingly just outside the town.

With his batteries in place by April 10, Clinton attacked Charleston from a safe distance, sending a continual bombardment of bombs and red-hot round shot into the center of town. Fires erupted throughout the city, and the violence of the spreading flames distracted soldiers and citizens alike. On May 7 the British invaded Fort Moultrie with sailors and marines, and the two hundred disheartened American defenders surrendered without a fight. On May 8 Clinton invited the beleaguered Lincoln to surrender, but the American commander insisted on terms that were patently unacceptable to the British. He wanted the American army to be allowed to march safely away from Charleston and take their arms with them!

Rejecting Lincoln's terms, Clinton redoubled his artillery assault, methodically destroying the American's will to resist. After a night of seeming hellfire, which rained incessantly upon their heads through the early darkness of May 10, the Americans agreed to surrender. On May 12, to the muted sounds of a Turkish march, 5,466 Continentals, militia, and armed citizens marched out of the city, delivering themselves into the hands of the British. For the Americans, it was the worst disaster of the entire war.

"Tarleton's Quarter"

Lincoln's surrender was devastating to the American cause. He had not only lost the city but had removed his five thousand men from future activity in the war. At the same time, Clinton's victory brought the increased support for which he had been hoping. After Charleston surrendered, two thousand additional Tories signed up to fight with him.

After years of persecution as traitors to the patriot cause, the Tories rejoiced to finally find themselves with the upper hand. Guerrilla groups of Tories struck out in ways that were fierce and dreadful, murdering their patriot neighbors in their beds or in the streets. Patriot guerrillas responded in kind. Blood seeped deep into South Carolina soil as brother fought against brother.

Colonel Banastre Tarleton, a British cavalry leader of American Tories in the South. In May 1780 Tarleton violated a truce and attacked American soldiers who had grounded their arms. This and other such actions earned him the nickname "Bloody Ban."

On May 29, 1780, British Colonel Banastre Tarleton, a cocky and brutal cavalry leader, violated a truce and led a group of mounted Tories against an American cavalry force under Colonel Abraham Buford. When Buford saw all was lost, he surrendered, raised a white flag, and ordered his men to ground their arms. But surrender was not what Tarleton's bloody Tories wanted. With sword and bayonet, they began hacking away at the unarmed Americans. The Americans pled for quarter, but their cries went unheeded. Even those who had fallen wounded were run through.

This incident of British treachery and perfidy became known in patriot circles as "Tarleton's Quarter." It was not soon forgotten.

Gates in the South

Pleased with the British gains in South Carolina, Clinton sailed back to New York, leaving Cornwallis with twenty-five hundred soldiers and a command to mop up the south. General Cornwallis was distinguished, competent, and affable. In appearance he was impressive, except for a permanent cast in one eye resulting from a boyhood accident. In military circles, Cornwallis was regarded as an experienced warrior, and Clinton expected him to take the entire south in very short order.

Baron de Kalb, a one-time Bavarian peasant boy who was a veteran of European wars and later joined the American forces, began the formidable task of reassembling a southern force. But de Kalb was a foreigner and was essentially unknown to the members of Congress. Another commander was needed. Washington recommended one of his most experienced field commanders, Nathanael Greene, but Congress chose instead the self-proclaimed hero of Saratoga, Horatio Gates.

When Gates arrived to take command in South Carolina during late July of 1780, he found an army of five thousand men waiting for him. They were mostly volunteers, a people's militia, outraged by Tory atrocities in the south. The main body of the British army had left their marauding and had returned to Charleston, but a large contingent under Lord Rawdon (a British lieutenant colonel who had distinguished himself at Bunker Hill) had remained to guard Camden, South Carolina. Gates decided that Camden would be the showpiece of his new campaign and the target of his first attack.

The march against Camden was set to begin at ten o'clock at night on August 15, 1780. A count of the troops revealed that only about thirty-one hundred were present and fit for duty. To gain strength before they began the march the Americans ate a special supper of meat, bread, and dessert. But the meat was half-cooked, the bread was half-baked, and the dessert was cornmeal mush mixed with molasses. Even though it was unappetizing in the extreme, the ravenous soldiers, who had been existing on short rations, ate it with gusto. But as they moved out into the hot, dark night, the men began to cramp and many became miserably sick. The mush and molasses mix functioned as a severe purgative, so that one by one the distraught soldiers broke ranks and slipped out into the trees to relieve themselves. By the time they reached Camden almost the entire body of troops was sick, weak, and very weary.

Disaster at Camden

British spies had warned Cornwallis of the impending attack, and he had rushed back to his troops in Camden. There he lay in wait for Gates, knowing the British were greatly outnumbered. The two forces met under a moonless sky at two in the morning of August 16, converging in a forest bordered by swamps. The cavalry clashed briefly, then both sides withdrew, waiting for daylight.

At dawn, the British light infantry struck at the untrained militia on the left, advancing with bayonets at ready. The militia barely had time to get off one shot before the bayonets were pricking at their bellies. Then, inexperienced, unseasoned, and utterly dispirited, the militia panicked and ran. With the battle scarcely begun, twenty-five hundred terror-stricken Virginians and North Carolinians, "like an un-dammed torrent," ran in shameful retreat, "raving along the roads and bypaths towards the north."[2]

All that remained were de Kalb's Continentals from Maryland and Delaware, along with a lone regiment of North Carolina militia. The British swung around and assaulted de Kalb's troops from the rear, bringing the full force of their two thousand against the tiny band of six hundred Americans. A shot felled de Kalb's horse; he stood and fought on foot. A saber sliced his head open; he blinked against the pain and continued to battle. He called his men to charge the British with bayonets. Cheering, they rushed forward, thrusting as they went, nearly breaking through the swarm of redcoats that girdled them. But the Americans were too few and they were driven back.

De Kalb, bulking over his men and pressing forward relentlessly, stood out as the prime target of British sharpshooters. They shot him with ball after ball, straining to bring him down. Still he fought on, manfully swinging his sword and shouting at his men. Then he was wounded for the eleventh time. He stabbed a British soldier and brought him down, then fell dying on the turf.

Meanwhile, unaware of the retreat of the militia, and having no orders from Gates to retire, de Kalb's men bravely fought on, advancing a final time, and then repelling a final British charge. At that moment, Tarleton's sword-swinging cavalry returned from hounding the retreating American militia and swept through the remaining American ranks, breaking and confusing them. Within minutes the battle was over.

But what had happened to the proud General Horatio Gates—the hero judged to be de Kalb's superior in command—what of him during this battle? When the militia fled, Gates chased after them, trying to rally them against the British. But he was unable to stop them in their mad, headlong flight, and at that point he made a fateful choice. He panicked, and like a frightened rabbit, he fled after them, passed them, and then continued north. With the help of fresh horses, he covered an impressive 240 miles in three days of hard riding. Alexander Hamilton was thoroughly amazed when he heard the news. He wrote: "Was there ever an instance of a general running away as Gates has done from his whole army? And was there ever so precipitous a flight?" Referring to the number of miles Gates covered so quickly, Hamilton added sarcastically, "It does admirable credit to the activity of a man at his time of life."[3]

Figures for the losses at Camden vary greatly. The best authorities suggest that some 2,500 of the total 3,100 Americans in the battle fled at the outset. Of those who remained to fight, virtually all were wounded, captured, or killed. The British lost a total of 324.[4]

Two days later Colonel Banastre Tarleton was prowling about with his cavalry and came upon General Thomas Sumter, the "Carolina Gamecock," and his small band of militia (700 men) at Fishing Creek, North Carolina. The Americans, caught with inadequate sentry posts, were taken completely by surprise. Some were sleeping, some cooking, some bathing in the creek. Sumter himself was asleep under his wagon. Tarleton charged into the camp with no warning, devastating Sumter's unarmed forces. With the loss of only 16 men, Tarleton killed 150 Americans and captured another 300. He also released 150 British prisoners and captured 44 wagons of supplies.

"Do Not Depend on These People"

With loss after heartbreaking loss, the American cause appeared to be dead in the south. But Washington was heartened by word from another part of the world. Two days before the fall of Charleston he received some welcome news from Lafayette. The exuberant young Frenchman had just returned from a mission to his homeland—and he was delighted to report that six French ships and six thousand troops, under the command of the Comte de Rochambeau, were on their way from France. Rochambeau, who spoke no English, was a proven commander with broad experience from the European wars. Washington had long dreamed of attacking Britain's New York stronghold and ending the war in the process. Now, with the help of Rochambeau and his six thousand, that elusive dream might become a reality.

But by June the General's optimism was waning. The twin threats of inadequate troops and scanty supplies had resurfaced. As he saw the subverting of this great opportunity by the neglect of the states, he wrote sternly: "If we do not strenuously embrace the favorable opportunity which now presents itself, we shall perhaps set down with the melancholy reflection that we lost the prize for which we long,

The Comte de Rochambeau, the commander of the French forces in America who helped to orchestrate the great victory at Yorktown.

nobly, and virtuously contended, by want only of a proper use and direction of the means which we have within our power, at the last critical moment."[5]

A little later he wrote the governors of the states, pleading for new recruits and refreshed supplies. How could they expect France to help America when the Americans themselves were not prepared to fight? With fervent intensity he wrote: "Our allies would be chagrined were they to arrive today, to find that we have but a handful of men in the field, and would doubt, it is more than probable, whether we had any serious intentions to prosecute measures with vigor.... If we do not avail ourselves of their succor by the most decisive and energetic steps on our part, the aid they so generously bring may prove our ruin."[6]

On July 11, 1780, Rochambeau anchored off Rhode Island. Washington assigned Lafayette, his trusted go-between with the French, to convey plans for the attack of New York. But the French fleet proved to be markedly inferior to the British fleet in New York Harbor (a second division of French warships was expected later), and Washington's own army was still inadequate to the task. Again, circumstances forced the General into a frustrating waiting game.

As Washington feared, the French were dismayed by the feeble state of the American army. French commander Rochambeau wrote home that the American government was "in consternation." He reported that Washington had only three thousand men and that depreciation had all but destroyed the economy. "Send us troops, ships, and money, but do not depend upon these people nor upon their means; they have neither money nor credit; their means of resistance are only momentary, and called forth when they are attacked in their own homes."[7]

"We Are Hastening Our Ruin"

Rochambeau's harsh assessment would have come as no surprise to Washington. He had battled such problems from the very beginning. For five long years he had been frustrated by the states in his efforts to build and sustain a standing army. "The contest among the different states now is not which shall do most for the common cause, but which shall do least," he wrote in July 1780.[8] Too often it seemed as though he were stumbling backward rather than running forward. "I see nothing before us but accumulating distress," he wrote that fall.[9]

Most officials in the individual states seemed to have a selfish, do-as-little-as-possible attitude. "It won't hurt if we don't send enough men, or if we fall short on our supply requisitions," they seemed to say. "The other states will surely fill in the gap. Besides, haven't we already done more than our share?"

It had been a long and wearing war. Victory seemed no closer in 1780 than in 1775. Who could know when the end would come? In 1775 many had expected the British to be driven away in a matter of months, perhaps in a year or two. But the hostilities dragged on and on, continuing from year to year as surely and incessantly as the cycle of the seasons. The cause was just, all patriots agreed—but could the states be drained of their resources indefinitely?

That fear led Washington to record once more his perennial complaint: "We are without money, and have been so for a great length of time, without provision and forage except what is taken by impress, without clothing, and shortly shall be (in a manner) without men. In a word, we have lived upon expedients till we can live no longer; and it may truly be said that the history of this war is a history of false hopes and temporary devices, instead of system and economy."[10]

In February 1780 a call for thirty-five thousand regulars had been issued; in June Washington called for seventeen thousand militia. By July few had come. By mid-August things were looking up: six thousand of the militia had been raised. But an additional forty-five hundred coming from Pennsylvania had to be turned back for lack of provisions.

Adding to Washington's frustration was the sorry truth that these were not new problems. Washington had faced them time and time again. He had long argued and pleaded with Congress and the states, almost to the point of embarrassment—but conditions never seemed to improve. "It has ever been our conduct and misfortune to slumber and sleep while we should be diligent in preparation, and when pressed by irresistible necessity and when we can delay no longer, then to bring ourselves to the brink of destruction by expensive and temporary expedients. In a word, we have no system and seem determined not to profit by experience."

He then bemoaned the fact that they seemed to be trapped in a destructive cycle:

> We are, during the winter, dreaming of independence and peace, without using the means to [achieve them]. In the spring, when our recruits should be with the army and in training, we have just discovered the necessity of calling for them; and by the fall, after a distressed and inglorious campaign for want of them, we begin to get a few men, which come in just in time enough to eat our provisions and consume our stores without rendering any service. Thus it is, one year rolls over another, and without some change we are hastening our ruin. [11]

"An Entire New Plan"

The commander in chief was not content, however, simply to complain about tangled problems without making any real effort to unravel them. Even though he knew his recommendations would likely be unpopular with the states, he suggested solutions that drove straight to the heart of the nation's power structure:

> If we mean to continue our struggles (and it is to be hoped we shall not relinquish our claim), we must do it upon an entire new plan. We must have a permanent force, not a force that is constantly fluctuating and sliding from under us as a pedestal of ice would do from a statue in a summer's day.... We must at the same time contrive ways and means to aid our taxes by loans and put our finance[s] upon a more certain and stable footing than they are at present. Our civil government must likewise undergo a reform; ample powers must be lodged in Congress as the head of the federal union, adequate to all the purposes of

war. Unless these things are done, our efforts will be in vain, and only serve to accumulate expense, add to our perplexities, and dissatisfy the people without a prospect of obtaining the prize in view. [12]

On another occasion he exploded: "Unless Congress speaks in a more decisive tone, unless they are vested with powers by the several states competent to the great purposes of war, or assume them as a matter of right, . . . our cause is lost. We can no longer drudge on in the old way." Dealing with the states was a losing cause: "One state will comply, . . . another neglects, . . . a third executes it by halves." His feeling for the necessity of a powerful Congress, Washington noted, "is the result of long thinking, close application, and strict observation." He felt that if Congress were not strengthened, the worst was to be feared: "I see one head gradually changing into thirteen." [13]

At Washington's fervent urging, Congress did slowly begin to adopt some reforms. They approved a plan to enlist infantry for the duration of the war. One-year recruits could augment the standing army if needed. Officers who served through the war would be given a small pension when they retired.

But such attempts only scratched the surface. Troops were still notoriously hard to come by, and the financial problems lingered on. In December 1780 Washington urgently needed to send an express to Rhode Island—but doubted whether there was enough money in the whole army to pay for it. At the same time, the Board of Treasury in Philadelphia faced eviction from their quarters—they were unable to pay their rent!

"We have neither money nor credit adequate to the purchase of a few boards for doors to our log huts,"

Washington worried in the fall. "It would be well for the troops if, like chameleons, they could live on air or, like the bear, suck their paws for sustenance during the rigor of the approaching winter."[14]

With these boundless problems, which Washington and his men faced month after month and even year after year, it is a wonder that the army continued to exist at all. It is even more miraculous that the following year, 1781, they aroused their spirits and delivered a killing blow to the mightiest army on earth.

Chapter 23

Treachery in the North,
Battles in the South

The fall of 1780 gave birth to one of the most tragic episodes of the entire war, a startling event that touched Washington deeply. In the month of September General Benedict Arnold, one of the preeminent field officers in the American army, became a traitor to his commander, his country, and his trust.

The Benedict Arnold Tragedy

Of course, the seed of deceit had been planted long before. As early as 1777 Washington had expressed misgivings when five officers, all Arnold's juniors, were promoted above him. Sternly criticizing the action of Congress, Washington spoke high praise of Arnold and said, "It is not to be presumed... that he will continue in service under such a slight."[1] Arnold later received the promotion he deserved, but only after much damage to his spirits.

In March 1778, when Arnold was in command of Philadelphia, he used public monies for personal speculation—and in the process broke the law by buying and selling certain restricted goods. In addition, he began to court Peggy Shippen, whose family were well-known British sympathizers. Arnold's illegal speculative practices became so serious that in April 1780 charges were brought against him, and Congress ordered a court-martial. Solid evidence was difficult to come by, however, and Arnold escaped with merely a reprimand.

Washington grieved that so good a soldier should have been caught in so thick a mire. In the official reprimand, given in carefully chosen words, Washington reflected the true sorrow he felt. He wrote, "The commander in chief would have been much happier in an occasion of bestowing commendations on an officer who has rendered such distinguished services to his country." Then he was compelled to pronounce the judgment. He stated that Benedict Arnold's behavior had been "peculiarly reprehensible."[2] There was no anger in these words, only the sorrow of one great soldier for the conduct of another who had also once been great.

Arnold exhibited little remorse for what he had done. Instead, he nursed his pride and bitterness until it completely obscured his previous rich feelings of loyalty and love toward both his country and his commander.

This is all the more astonishing in light of the brilliant career Benedict Arnold had carved for himself in the cause of American freedom. Back in 1775 he had helped Ethan Allen and the Green Mountain Boys capture and burn Fort Ticonderoga. Later that same year he accepted a commission from Washington to make a hazardous trek through Maine and into Canada to capture Quebec. Although the mission failed and Arnold was wounded, his conduct was heroic.

In the American flight from Canada in the fall of 1776, Arnold had supervised the building of a makeshift fleet of ships and then held off the strong British armada, significantly delaying their southward movement. When General John Burgoyne followed him down from Canada the next season, Arnold spurred the Americans to victory against him, leading to the astounding British surrender at Saratoga. But Arnold left that battlefield with two scars, one physical, the other psychic, both slow to heal: He was so seriously wounded in the leg that it was noticeably shortened, and it appeared for a time that he might be permanently crippled. Even more painful was the injury to his soul when Horatio Gates falsely took the hero's laurels for their great victory.

Eventually Arnold did gain some recognition from Congress and was made the American commander in Philadelphia. It was there that he met and married socialite Peggy Shippen. Peggy was a Tory and was well known among the British; some were even considered her closest friends. One of her most valuable connections was the dashing John Andre, the adjutant general in charge of British intelligence. Perhaps encouraged by Andre, Peggy stoked the fire of her husband's grievances, all the while arguing for the British cause. Ultimately, the seeds began to take root. Arnold began to rationalize that maybe she was right. At the same time, Arnold found himself in difficult financial circumstances. Peggy's high style of living demanded much more money than Arnold's modest officer's income could provide. Finally he agreed to offer his services to Andre in exchange for £20,000. Andre accepted on one condition: Arnold must hand over the crucial American fort at West Point. Possession of that strategic position would fulfill the long-held British dream to have command of the Hudson River—and thus cut the thirteen American states in half.

"My Mind Misgave Me"

By the summer of 1780 Arnold had been recuperating from his wounded leg for nearly three years, and Washington hoped to send him back into action. Instead, Arnold surprised him by asking for the command of West Point. In August 1780, as a personal favor to Arnold, Washington gave him what he sought. Arnold triumphantly pursued his secret plans.

General Benedict Arnold in 1777. Arnold was a brilliant leader in the early years of the war, but pride, a loyalist wife, and financial troubles combined to lead to his betrayal of the American cause in 1780. He later fought with the British forces in the South.

In late September Washington notified Arnold that he wished to inspect the defenses of West Point. When Washington arrived on the twenty-fifth, however, Arnold was nowhere to be found. The commander in chief inspected the fort alone, wondering where Arnold could be. "My mind misgave me," he recalled years later, but "I had not the least idea of the real cause."[3]

Later that day Washington was given a packet of papers taken from a man captured on the road to New York. The documents, which the man had hidden in his shoes, contained detailed plans for the capture of West Point—and they were in the handwriting of Benedict Arnold. The prisoner, who had been dressed as a civilian, turned out to be none other than the adjutant general of the British army, John Andre.

As soon as Washington recovered from the shock of these disclosures, he dispatched Alexander Hamilton to try to intercept the fleeing Arnold. But Arnold, fearing such pursuit, rushed to safe haven on a British ship. Although his plan to betray West Point had failed, Arnold received 6,315 pounds sterling for his perfidy, as well as a command post in the British army. He later fought against the Americans in the south; after the war he made his way to England, where he died in 1801.

Andre did not fare so well. After a short, formal hearing before a board of generals, he was ordered to be hanged as a spy. That sentence was difficult to pronounce, and for Washington it was a difficult task to carry out. Andre was a young and handsome officer who had conducted himself with great dignity throughout the days of his captivity. But Washington knew he must send a clear message to all—both British and Americans. Spying and treason would not be tolerated!

The hanging took place on October 2, 1780. Andre was twenty-nine years old.

Washington counted the capture of Andre and the saving of West Point as nothing less than providential. In a message to his troops issued on September 26, Washington described the events of the previous day and declared that the loss of West Point would have "given the American cause a deadly wound, if not a fatal stab. Happily," he continued, "the treason has been timely discovered to prevent the fatal misfortune. The providential train of circumstances which led to it affords the most convincing proof that the liberties of America are the object of divine protection."[4] Three weeks later he reiterated those feelings, saying, "In no instance since the commencement of the war has the interposition of Providence appeared more conspicuous than in the rescue of . . . West Point from Arnold's villainous perfidy."[5]

The Battle of King's Mountain

Just after the near-fatal disaster in the north had been avoided by the discovery of Arnold's treachery, the tide in the south began to turn. Lord Cornwallis, flushed with his victory at Camden, began to march up toward North Carolina, which was the next step on his ladder of conquests. As he pressed forward, his inland flank was covered by a Scottish officer named Major Patrick Ferguson. Major Ferguson was the inventor of an amazing breech-loading rifle that was usable in wet weather and could be fired five or six times a minute.

Ferguson was zealous in his duties. As he marched through the countryside, he pillaged and burned patriots' homes, raising the ire of people all through the Carolinas, Virginia, and across the mountains in what is now called Tennessee. As the people's rage grew, an army of one thousand men gradually gathered to teach Major Ferguson an unforgettable lesson. The two forces met on October 7, 1780, at King's Mountain in South Carolina.

Ferguson established himself and his twelve hundred Tory volunteers atop the mountain and felt so secure that he defied "God Almighty and all the rebels out of hell to overcome him."[6]

The rebels certainly had not come "out of hell," but they

took up the challenge. Organized in nine different parties, they laboriously climbed the steep mountainside, surrounding the Tories. When they reached the top, one of the patriot officers, Colonel William Campbell, called, "Here they are, boys! Shout like hell, and fight like devils!"[7] The Tories answered him with a bayonet charge that pushed the Americans back. Then a number of frontier sharpshooters with long rifles saw another strategy: they climbed the tall trees surrounding Ferguson's position and began a rain of terror on the Tory troops.

One of the frightened Tories raised a white flag of surrender, but Ferguson angrily cut it down. The balls continued to fall on the Tory ranks, now tightly pinned down on the mountaintop. Another white flag went up, and again Ferguson knocked it down. Finally Ferguson himself was shot. He died while being dragged with one foot caught in the stirrup of his terrified mount.

With their commander gone and their position hopeless, the Tories cried for quarter. But the enraged patriots recognized the faces of some of those who had slaughtered American prisoners without mercy. They charged in and cut them down with bullets and bayonets, crying, "Tarleton's Quarter! Tarleton's Quarter!"

Campbell could not stand it. He rode through the American ranks screaming, "For God's sake, quit! It's murder to shoot any more!"[8] Finally they desisted, stopping barely in time to preserve the honor of their victory.

In the Battle of King's Mountain, the patriots of the south had repeated the famous Bennington victory of their brothers to the north. The losses to the Americans totaled 28 killed and 64 wounded. The Tories lost 157 killed, 163 wounded, and 698 captured. Among those who were captured, nine were later hanged for their atrocities.

The victory at King's Mountain seriously blunted the British campaign in the south. Rumors quickly magnified the scope of the battle, and Cornwallis, frightened by what he heard, abandoned his plans for the conquest of North Carolina and retreated south.

The Morristown Mutiny

News of the victory at King's Mountain was much welcomed at Washington's headquarters. It came as the first encouraging word from the south since the fall of Charleston. But Washington had little time to rejoice. All his energies were turned to the task of preparing his own troops for the rigors of the oncoming winter.

By mid-November 1780, Washington began settling his troops in winter quarters at several strategic locations ranging from Morristown in New Jersey to the Hudson Highlands in New York to the hills of Connecticut. Predictably, as temperatures dropped many of the agonizing problems of previous winters began to be repeated. The men were ill-housed, poorly clothed, and almost always on short rations.

Given the deplorable conditions the American troops were compelled to endure, it was probably inevitable that some of them would eventually mutiny. They had been hungry and cold for too long. They had gone month after month with no pay. They had stoically suffered while watching merchants in the city grow fat and rich.

On New Year's Day, January 1, 1781, after a night and a day of too much drink, the Pennsylvania troops erupted in mutiny at Morristown, New Jersey. Furious at the conditions of their service, some twenty-four hundred men rose up in arms, captured the artillery, killed one officer, and wounded two others. Then they began marching toward Philadelphia, pulling a cannon behind them, determined to lay their demands at the feet of Congress. Some simply wanted livable conditions and their long-promised pay. Others had signed up for three years or the duration of the war, and since three years had now passed, they insisted that they be allowed to go home.

The mutineers reached Princeton on January 3, and they were now near enough to Philadelphia to begin raising a clamor to see a representative of Congress. Washington, who was headquartered at New Windsor, New York, received word of the mutiny that same day. He had long dreaded such an outbreak, but his anticipations did little to prepare his mind for the actual event. He rushed word to Congress that they must not flee. If the mutineers found them gone, they might sack the city. Then he began hasty preparations to send a thousand carefully chosen soldiers to quash the mutiny. Underlying his preparatory efforts was a deep concern, unspoken except to a few confidants, that the soldiers in his own camp had the same compelling complaints. What if they also rose up in mutiny?

His apprehensions were never put to the test. Acting on behalf of Congress, Joseph Reed, the president of Pennsylvania, hammered out an agreement by January 10. The soldiers discontinued their march on Philadelphia, but the cost of Reed's agreement was overwhelming to an already struggling army. Half the mutineers had been granted a discharge, and the other half had been given a three-month furlough. A number of financial concessions were also granted.

Britain's General Clinton, headquartered in New York City, got word of the mutiny and immediately seized the opportunity to send two spies to the camp. Clinton's emissaries offered hard cash to any American soldier who would change his allegiance. Outraged that their intentions were being misunderstood, the mutineers imprisoned the spies and handed them over for trial. They were both hanged on January 11.

Grievances of the Mutineers

Even though their methodology was flawed, the Pennsylvanians' grievances were real. Two weeks before the mutiny, General Anthony Wayne had described their depressing plight to Joseph Reed. "We are reduced to dry bread and beef for our food," he complained, "and to cold water for our drink.... This, together with the old worn-out coats and tattered linen overalls, and what was once a poor substitute for a blanket (now divided among three soldiers), is but very wretched living and shelter against the winter's piercing cold, drifting snows and chilling sleets."

The matter of payment was equally grave: "Our soldiery ... have now served their country with fidelity for near five years, poorly clothed, badly fed and worse paid; ... they have not seen a paper dollar in the way of pay for near twelve months."

Wayne then issued a sober warning: "If something is not immediately done ... to quiet their minds, we have not yet seen the worst side of the picture."⁹

The Pennsylvania mutiny had barely been quelled when a crowd of New Jersey troops rose up. This mutiny was much smaller, involving but two hundred angry men who marched on the state capital of Trenton. This time there would be no parleying; a stern precedent had to be set. Washington sent six hundred men from West Point in swift pursuit. Faced with a decidedly larger force, the New Jersey men threw down their arms and surrendered. Their rabble-rousing leaders were tried and convicted on the spot. Two were ordered executed, and a dozen of their most vocal followers were forced, with tears streaming down their faces, to serve as the firing squad.

Washington sorrowed over the cruel hardships his army was compelled to endure, but he knew the spreading spirit of mutiny would be fatal to their cause. In a general message issued after the New Jersey uprising, he said: "The General is deeply sensible of the sufferings of the army. He leaves no expedient unessayed to relieve them.... But it is our duty to bear present evils with fortitude, looking forward to the period when our country will have it more in its power to reward our services."[10]

The Southern Campaign Continues

Beginning in 1779 the war was fought almost entirely in the south, far from the position of General Washington and the main body of the American troops. Although Washington was technically the commander in chief of all the American armies, he was only nominally in charge of the troops in the south. Hampered by sluggish eighteenth-century communications and transportation, he had to trust the commanders of the southern theater to win their battles on their own.

Unfortunately, as we have seen, this trust was sometimes violated. The army in the south had twice been depleted through bad generalship, once under Lincoln and once under Gates. In the closing weeks of 1780, fretful about British gains in South Carolina, Washington assigned Nathanael Greene to take the command. This time Congress approved the appointment. (Greene had also been Washington's choice for the position earlier when Congress had named Gates.) Washington knew that Greene was a superbly qualified officer with three years of hard fighting under his belt. Perhaps he could succeed where Lincoln and Gates had so miserably failed.

Greene's first challenge was to organize an effective army. After Gates's disastrous defeat at Camden, less than a thousand regulars remained in the south. Another thousand militiamen were available, but these were mostly ill-trained, and fewer than eight hundred of that total were properly clothed and equipped. In January 1781 Greene recorded his initial shock on arriving at his new command: "The appearance of the troops was wretched beyond description, and their distress on account of [lack of] provisions was little less than their suffering for want of clothing and other necessaries." Just as disturbing, they had lost "all their discipline" and were "so addicted to plundering that they were a terror to the inhabitants."[11]

Greene knew that his ragged troops would be no match for Cornwallis and his well-supplied regiments of more than four thousand men. With his back thus against the wall, Greene made an astounding decision. Rather than combine his unimpressive troops together as a single unit, he decided to seek victory by dividing them! He realized he was breaking the oldest rule in the book of war, but he saw one possible way of finding success. Instead of risking an all-out confrontation with the powerful main body of Cornwallis's troops, he worked out a strategy of attack against their unprotected flanks.

The Battle of Cowpens

Greene's strategy was like a classic move in a game of chess. He sent Daniel Morgan west from Charlotte to serve as a lure. Cornwallis immediately saw that if he moved against Greene on his right, he would leave Camden open to Morgan. On the other hand, if he moved against Morgan on his left, he would leave Charleston open to Greene.

Captain Daniel Morgan, the leader of the sharp-shooting Virginia frontiersmen who led his riflemen in the battle at Saratoga and commanded the brilliant victory at the battle of Cowpens.

The two players paused momentarily in stalemate, neither making a move. Then Cornwallis broke the stalemate by sending out Banastre ("Bloody Ban") Tarleton and eleven hundred horsemen and ground troops against Morgan and his thousand. They clashed on January 17, 1781, on high, rolling ground that had traditionally been used as winter pasture for cattle, a place named Cowpens, South Carolina.

Morgan chose this battlefield shrewdly. Standing on a broad plain with his back to a river, it seemed to be a dangerous site, almost a trap. But a good number of Morgan's men were raw recruits, new to battle. He knew that if he placed them near a swamp they would melt away as the dew evaporates under the summer sun. And if he crossed the river his men would vanish when the fighting became intense. So his position was a trap, and that was how he wanted it. He knew that in this precarious cowpen his trapped men would fight for their very lives.

The astute American commander established his men in

several lines. First, he placed 150 sharpshooters up front, ready to fire at the enemy when they moved into range. He ordered them to focus their sights especially on "the men with the epaulets."[12] After delivering two volleys the sharpshooters were to fall back 150 yards to the next line, where 300 militia waited. The militia were to shoot off two volleys, then backpedal to the main line of 400 Continentals, who stood on the crest of a hill. Behind another hill waited 100 cavalrymen under the command of heavy William Washington, the kinsman of the commander in chief who had been wounded with James Monroe at Trenton.

Tarleton rode boldly into the battle, heading straight for the sharpshooters. The rifles flashed and fifteen saddles were emptied. Tarleton's Tories, confused and frightened, abandoned the field and refused to reenter the battle. Still the main body of British regulars marched forward, bayonets at ready. This would surely put the American militia to flight! But the militia stood firm, obeying their orders, firing once, calmly reloading, and firing again. Then, once more obeying orders, they turned and ran.

The British exultantly saw the withdrawal as a retreat. Their dragoons spurred their horses to a gallop to ride down the fleeing Americans. But suddenly, from behind a hill, William Washington and his mounted soldiers were upon them, sabers singing through the air. While the dragoons were engaged with Washington's cavalry, the British footmen charged up the hill at the American Continentals. The Americans were ready. They knelt and sent a scathing fire through their enemy.

Tarleton ordered his Highlanders to swing around to the left. The Americans changed position to meet them, then at the last moment faced about and fired, sending a surprised troop of redcoats crumpling to the earth. They followed up with a cheer and a bayonet charge, ready to give the British some of their own sharp medicine. At the same moment Washington's cavalry smashed through the enemy rear, moving like hell's furies against the British.

Bloody Ban Tarleton narrowly escaped, taking with him the few troops he could salvage. But his defeat had been incredible. He had lost 90 percent of his forces through either death or capture. The Americans had twelve dead and sixty wounded.

From a military standpoint, Cowpens was undoubtedly the best American battle of the entire revolution. And it was fought by a band of rustic backwoodsmen against one of Britain's brightest commanders. It showed the British that the Americans were not just a bunch of bumpkins—or if they were, at least they were bumpkins of which the British must beware!

The Race for the Dan

Cornwallis was enraged when he heard of Morgan's astonishing victory. Determined to punish the American rebels, he pulled together three thousand troops and began to pursue the old soldier with a vengeance. Morgan's lead initially seemed far too great, but Cornwallis would not give up. He burned all his tents, destroyed his wagons (except a few to carry ammunition, salt, medical supplies, and the injured), packed a few provisions into haversacks, and destroyed the rest of the provisions so he could travel faster. However, Morgan moved too swiftly for the British, and Cornwallis was not able to catch him. On January 30, 1781, Morgan triumphantly rejoined Greene and the rest of the American troops. Cornwallis cursed his luck. His prey had slipped between his fingers, while he had destroyed a mountain of his own supplies foolishly trying to avenge himself.

Nevertheless, Cornwallis did not waver, but turned his anger on Greene. Now it was Greene's turn to be pursued. Greene chose to play a clever game of cat and mouse with Cornwallis—with the mouse in control. Cornwallis tried to catch Greene at the Catawba River, but arrived too late. He was again too late when Greene crossed the Yadkin. But the Dan River—that would be another matter. The British were certain that the fleeing rebels, lacking the necessary boats to cross the lower Dan, would have to cross at a ford upstream. Cornwallis was confident the British would bag their quarry there.

Both sides began a wild race for the Dan. The Americans arose at three each morning and slogged all day through thick mud, stopping only for one brief meal. In their rear was Henry ("Light-Horse Harry") Lee, a young Virginian with manifest brilliance in commanding cavalry. Lee was charged with keeping the enemy somewhat at bay as the two armies marched along. Hopelessly outmanned, Lee's dog-weary troops averaged six hours of sleep every forty-eight hours, half the force being on duty every night. Meanwhile, Greene furtively sent ahead to the Dan to have boats waiting for him on the lower portion of the river, warning his messengers to carefully avoid detection by spies.

By February 13, 1781, both armies were forty miles from the river. The British stopped briefly after dark to rest, and the Americans stopped as well. But at midnight the king's troops took off in pursuit once again, and Greene was forced to hurriedly lead his men off into the night. The weather was cold and wet on the fourteenth, the muddy roads glistening with frost. During the morning both sides stopped for an hour to rest, then marched on. Exhausted though they were, the British covered the final forty miles in twenty-four hours—but the Americans arrived eight hours earlier. Their boats were waiting; they crossed safely into Virginia while the British, frustrated and cursing, stumbled along at a weary pace several miles away.

Greene had covered two hundred miles in fifteen days, keeping his troops in orderly retreat the entire time. On paper, it appeared that Cornwallis had driven him from the south—not a single Continental soldier remained south of Virginia—but in reality Greene had scored two momentous victories. He had kept his army together and out of the hands of Cornwallis, and he had seriously weakened the British forces by goading Cornwallis into making a precipitous launch away from the security of his southern holdings.

These victories were substantial and far-reaching. If Cornwallis, with his superior force, had been able to catch Greene, he almost certainly would have demolished him and his untried troops. Then Cornwallis could have joined Benedict Arnold, who was commanding a major force in northern Virginia. The two of them, with their combined forces, could have liberated the five thousand prisoners of war from Saratoga who were located at Charlottesville, Virginia. They also could have liberated the six hundred Cowpens prisoners and thereby assembled a formidable army. Fortunately, Greene outfoxed and outran the British, and Cornwallis found himself stuck on the banks of the Dan River with no boats to get across. The fords upstream were easily defended by Greene. Cornwallis finally decided to take the only sensible course. He withdrew and crawled with his exhausted troops back to Hillsboro, North Carolina.

The Battle of Guilford Courthouse

Greene rested with his Americans on the Virginia side of the Dan for several days. While they were recuperating he went out to gather reinforcements. With these in hand, he marched back into North Carolina and began to close in on Cornwallis. By mid-March 1781, his original body of fourteen hundred troops had increased to forty-four hundred, and he grew ever bolder as he came within striking distance of the British. Greene finally stationed himself in the woody area around Guilford Courthouse, North Carolina, which was tantamount to inviting Cornwallis to attack. The British, who were only twelve miles away, were low on supplies, and Cornwallis knew he had to either strike or retreat eastward toward the sea. The British commander was badly outnumbered, but he knew that most of Greene's troops were raw recruits who had never fought. He expected his seasoned veterans could make the difference.

General Nathanael Greene, who became Washington's most trusted general by the end of war. Greene served as commissary general when supplies and provisions were particularly difficult to obtain. Later, through his superior strategy, he forced the British out of their stronghold in the South.

At dawn on March 15, without even waiting for breakfast, the British began to move forward. Greene was ready for them, having put his men in a formation much like that used by Morgan at Cowpens. The British moved into sight around noon, greeted by cannon blasts from the American artillery. The British continued to advance, smooth and disciplined, their red coats and well-burnished arms visible more than a mile away. Finally the two armies clashed. The advantage in battle seesawed for three hours, then the wise mouse withdrew from the fierce, hungry cat once again; Greene retreated to fight another day. The Americans lost between 300 and 400 men in the battle (killed, wounded, or missing), while the British lost 750. The more experienced British troops held the field, demonstrating that they were indeed superior—but they had to pay a dreadful price to prove it.

Strike-and-Run Warfare

After two days' rest, Cornwallis moved south to Wilmington, North Carolina, leaving behind his many wounded. The well-manned British post in Camden was closer and safer, but Cornwallis feared a move to Camden would acknowledge the failure of his campaign against Greene.

Camden was commanded by the dark, tall, and ruthless Lord Rawdon, who had some two thousand troops serving under him. He also had access to an additional six thousand men scattered about in various posts. Greene, on the other hand, was reduced to fifteen hundred men because his militia had been released to go home. But he had the assistance of a number of southern partisan leaders, all of them experts at strike-and-run warfare and thoroughly seasoned at harassing the British. Those leaders included Francis Marion, the legendary "Swamp Fox," who had once been chased by Tarleton for seven hours across twenty-six miles of swamps without the British cavalryman once catching sight of his foe.

There was also Thomas Sumter, the "Carolina Gamecock," who had been humiliated by Tarleton at Fishing Creek just after the defeat at Camden. Finally, there was Andrew Pickens, who had been an important figure in the American victory at Cowpens. Greene also knew he could expect yeoman service from the valiant Light-Horse Harry Lee.

Beginning in mid-April 1781, Greene and his American compatriots met in a series of confrontations with Lord Rawdon and his British forces out of Camden. Many of these skirmishes were disappointments for the Americans, but Greene's strategy was to keep pecking at the British. "We fight, get beat, rise, and fight again," he said. [13]

Under Greene's incessant harassment, the British hold on the south began to slip away. In April the British lost Fort Watson; in May it was Fort Motte and Fort Granby. They even lost Camden and Georgetown. In June the Americans brought the enemy garrison in Augusta to its knees by a paralyzing siege, and they almost did the same at a town called Ninety-six (which the British subsequently abandoned). By July, after having been in the southern theater for less than eight months, Greene had recaptured all of the south with the exception of Savannah and the Charleston area. In those eight months his army had marched just short of a thousand miles, had fought three full battles and numerous smaller engagements. They had captured nine posts, and had taken nearly three thousand prisoners.

The victories had not come easily. Cornwallis was doggedly aggressive in pushing his opponent, and Rawdon was an excellent strategist. But Greene's overall strategies proved to be superior. Though he lost a number of engagements, he won the campaign, and his little army held the region while the redcoats ultimately withdrew.

Confrontation at Eutaw Springs

With the British pulling back, Greene moved into the nearby Santee Hills for six weeks to escape the fierce South Carolina heat and to rest and reinforce his troops. On August 22 he marched out of the hills with twenty-four hundred soldiers and swept after the two thousand men under Lieutenant Colonel Alexander Stewart, who had replaced the ailing Lord Rawdon. On September 8, 1781, the two armies collided at Eutaw Springs, South Carolina. The bloody fighting stretched out long hours under the torturous southern sun. Finally the Americans carried the day, driving the British back and earning a hard-won victory. With the British on the run, the tired Americans trooped into the British camp, where they found ample supplies of food and rum. Heedless of their danger, the hungry, thirsty soldiers fell on the food and drink with a vengeance. While the Americans were gorging themselves, the British regrouped and attacked. This time the Americans were forced to retreat.

The losses on both sides were all out of proportion to the numbers in the opposing armies. The Americans suffered losses of 522, while the British lost an incredible 866. In this, the last major engagement before Yorktown, the British troops lost a greater percentage of men (43 percent) than at any other time in the entire war except for Burgoyne's surrender at Saratoga. Weakened and weary, Stewart's army fled to Charleston, and Greene marched back into the hills.

Meanwhile, Cornwallis had virtually surrendered the rest of the south and had marched up to Virginia to join forces with Benedict Arnold. But he never made the connection. Unbeknown to Cornwallis, Lafayette lay in wait, and he forced Cornwallis away from Arnold and toward the Atlantic coast. Finally the British took refuge in a quiet little port called

Yorktown. If worse came to worst, Cornwallis knew he could always exit aboard British ships at Chesapeake Bay. [14]

Chapter 24

The Great Strike at Yorktown

H ow loud are our calls from every quarter for a decisive
naval superiority," Washington cried in early 1781,
"and how might the enemy be crushed if we had it!"[1]
Through the entire six years of the war, Washington had
been hamstrung by inadequate naval support. Too many opportunities had slipped away because Great Britain controlled
America's sea lanes. Washington had hoped the French
would challenge the English, but their promise wilted and
faded as a rose in the frost.

In 1781, however, the Americans did achieve naval superiority, although only for a moment. The British fleet had been
severely damaged by a storm, while, providentially, the
French fleet had been spared. At that particular season, Benedict Arnold and his British troops had left off pillaging Virginia to winter over at Portsmouth. Arnold had felt protected

and secure in this coastal refuge as long as Britain maintained dominance over the seaways. But with the British fleet damaged he was suddenly vulnerable. When Washington saw Arnold's predicament, he hoped that perhaps the Americans could capture him and destroy his army in one sudden swoop. He asked the French to move their fleet down to Chesapeake Bay.

By the time his message had arrived, the French had already set sail. Acting on their own initiative, the French commanders had sent a small group of ships down to torment and harass Arnold. The French captured a British frigate and six smaller vessels, taking five hundred prisoners. But without the full French force behind them, their strength proved inadequate. Before they could call for reinforcements, the British fleet, now repaired, was ready once again to enter the fight. Another propitious opportunity had vanished.

Arnold's presence in Virginia was a threat to Washington personally. Washington's own lands and property were placed in immediate jeopardy—and the vengeful Arnold was one who freely burned the properties of his enemies. The British threat was so great that at one point Washington's well-meaning caretaker even felt it necessary to buy protection for Mount Vernon by taking goods onto a British ship. Washington was infuriated when he learned of the caretaker's action. Rather than treat with the enemy, Washington wrote, he would much rather "they had burnt my house and laid the plantation in ruins."[2]

"The Game Is Yet in Our Hands"

Washington's moods swung up and down as the war dragged on through 1781, his inner feelings undulating from brightness to shadow. In March he wrote with optimistic spirit, "The many remarkable interpositions of the divine government in the hours of our deepest distress and darkness have been too luminous to suffer me to doubt the happy issue of the present contest." But then he added a dreary qualification: that "happy issue" might be far in the future. "The period for its accomplishment may be too far distant for a person of my years."[3]

In April, still concerned about the enduring hunger and nakedness of his troops, he wrote ominously, "It may be declared in a word that we are at the end of our tether, and that now or never our deliverance must come."[4]

A letter in June showed more hope, though his eyes remained open to the challenges: "We must not despair. The game is yet in our hands; to play it well is all we have to do.... A cloud may yet pass over us; individuals may be ruined; and the country at large, or particular states, undergo temporary distress. But certain I am that it is in our power to bring the war to a happy conclusion."[5]

Money, as always, presented an alarming complication. In May the congressional currency depreciated to utter worthlessness, and carried in its wake ruinous collapse from one end of the country to the other. With few exceptions, hard money was the only medium of exchange accepted in the marketplace. To bolster the economy, Congress sent valiant, twice-wounded John Laurens (shot at Germantown and later at Monmouth) to France seeking a loan. Eventually Laurens returned with the triumphant news that, with the help of Benjamin Franklin, he had been able to secure 6 million livres from King Louis XVI. Upon its arrival from France, the money was transported from Boston to the congressional leaders in an oxcart.

It was a measure of the high esteem which the French held

for the American commander that this large loan was approved. Benjamin Franklin, the ambassador to France, emphasized the warm sentiments of the French in a letter to Washington. "You would, on this side of the sea," he wrote, "enjoy the great reputation you have acquired.... I frequently hear the old generals of this martial country, who study maps of America and mark upon them all your operations, speak with sincere approbation and great applause of your conduct, and join in giving you the character of one of the greatest captains of the age."[6]

June and July brought additional welcome news to Washington's wearied soul: a series of victories had occurred in the south. General Greene had maneuvered the British out of all their positions in Georgia except Savannah, and he had nearly taken over South Carolina as well. Cornwallis had repaired to Virginia, where Lafayette and his troops had gradually pushed him across the state, pinning him down at

The Comte de Grasse, the French admiral who was instrumental in the successful siege of Yorktown. While Washington trapped the British troops by land, de Grasse prevented the British fleet from evacuating them by sea.

Yorktown. Now all Washington lacked for a decisive strike was a strong navy. In mid-August he received word that he might finally have one. The tall, handsome Comte de Grasse was coming with a powerful French fleet from the West Indies, bringing twenty-nine warships and three thousand troops. A new door of opportunity had swung wide, and Washington began to make expansive plans. A sudden, unexpected blow against the British at Yorktown might have significant consequences.

"Come to Catch the Bird"

Secrecy was of utmost importance. Washington's plans had been foiled before by security leaks. This time he was determined to stop even the tiniest trickle of unauthorized communication. His intentions were kept so close that even his own troops knew only that a march had been ordered. Where? Bets were made in camp—would they attack Clinton in New York or Cornwallis in Virginia? To further confuse the issue, Washington finally did leak some selected bits of intelligence—but it was either false or of no consequence. Surprise, he knew, could be one of his most effective weapons.

"The moment is critical, the opportunity precious, the prospects most happily favorable," Washington wrote to the governor of Maryland.[7] With the help of his allies, success would surely come.

Through a controlled stream of bogus intelligence, Washington had Clinton and his British advisers convinced that the Americans were going to sneak through New Jersey, then fall upon New York from the rear. To undergird that interpretation, Washington prepared a siege camp on Staten Island, strictly as a diversionary ploy. Workers patched and smoothed

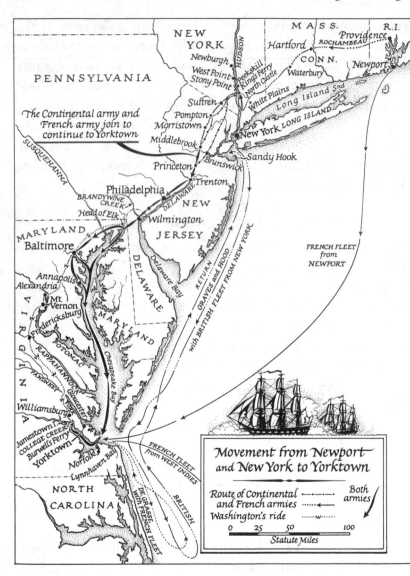

Used by permission of Little, Brown and Company, from *George Washington in the American Revolution* by James Thomas Flexner, cartography by Samuel H. Bryant. Copyright © 1968 by James Thomas Flexner.

strategic roads on the island; French troops across the way in New Jersey built huge ovens capable of baking bread for thousands of hungry soldiers. Clinton took the bait and was frightened into action—he had Cornwallis send him two thousand men as reinforcements. The senior British commander was so intently concentrating his attention on Staten Island that Washington and Rochambeau were able to march their troops quietly out of New Jersey without being detected, and three days passed before Clinton even realized they were gone. As a result, Cornwallis received no warning that Washington was coming and that the British must flee Yorktown.

When General Greene heard that Washington's army was trekking south he was exuberant. "We have been beating the bush," he exclaimed, "and the General has come to catch the bird."[8]

As Washington marched south, however, an ugly fear danced at the edges of his consciousness: What if de Grasse didn't come? The French admiral should have already arrived, but he was inexplicably tardy. Could the American plans once again be dashed to the ground?

On September 5, Washington received the glorious news that de Grasse's fleet had sailed into Chesapeake Bay. Lafayette had straitjacketed Cornwallis by land; now de Grasse was holding him back by sea. The siege could begin.

The messenger had barely announced the good news before Washington wheeled his horse and galloped back three miles to inform Rochambeau that the admiral had come. Overflowing with joy, Washington impulsively embraced the surprised French commander. French officers standing nearby were charmed by Washington's uncharacteristic effusiveness. "A child whose every wish had been granted could not have revealed a livelier emotion," said one. Observed another, "I have never seen a man moved by a greater or sincerer joy."[9]

Four days later, Washington tingled with a different kind of excitement as he rode into Mount Vernon. It was the first time he had been home in more than six years. Circumstances permitted him to stay three nights. After the forced march south, he was temporarily at peace in a country lacerated by war, relishing Martha's loving companionship and enjoying the warm comforts of his own fireside. Also staying at the mansion were Rochambeau and the staffs of both men. Then, the brief respite over, Washington and his men rode off once again toward their fateful encounter at Yorktown, Virginia.

The Decisive Blow

When Cornwallis first settled in at Yorktown, he felt comfortably secure. Lafayette was pressing him from the west, but the town was well fortified and could be taken only by a protracted siege. Furthermore, so long as the British controlled the Chesapeake, the peerless British navy could give him all the supplies and reinforcements he might need. And should the unthinkable happen, Cornwallis had an escape hatch: his naval compatriots could evacuate him.

Lord Charles Cornwallis, the British general who allowed his troops to become trapped at Yorktown in 1781. The siege at Yorktown was the last significant battle of the war, ending in the surrender of 8,000 British soldiers.

Suddenly, however, the French fleet loomed up in Chesapeake Bay. Cornwallis saw his escape path begin to close. See-

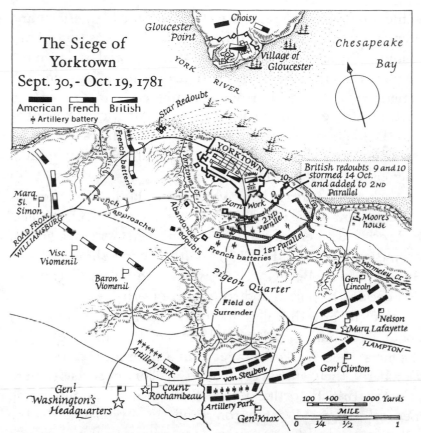

The Siege of
Yorktown
Sept. 30,- Oct. 19, 1781

American French British
⊹ Artillery battery

ing his nasty predicament, the British fleet rushed to his aid. But the British soon found themselves outmanned and out-gunned by de Grasse, and after suffering heavy damages the British finally gave up the fight. The Union Jack disappeared over the horizon as the ships limped off toward New York, leaving Cornwallis to his unhappy fate.

But Cornwallis was far from ready to acknowledge defeat. He stubbornly resisted for three anxious weeks. Then on September 30 he made a surprising move, abandoning the outer redoubts that curved around Yorktown like a huge shell on the landward side. Amazed at this partial British withdrawal, on that same day the combined American and French forces began to shift into a siege position. They followed Rochambeau's expert instructions and occupied the fortified redoubts the British had just vacated. Together, the American and French troops numbered some seventeen thousand (nine thousand of whom were American Continentals). In addition, nineteen thousand French sailors stood wait on de Grasse's ships. Cornwallis, trapped in Yorktown, had only eight thousand men.

Washington learned later why Cornwallis had forsaken his all-important outer perimeter. On September 29 Cornwallis had received an encouraging dispatch from General Clinton, promising an evacuation force with several ships and five thousand men. Believing help was on the way, Cornwallis had decided to pull in and consolidate his forces.

On October 6 the allies dug their first fortification trench about six hundred yards from the town. Sweating heavily in the moist heat, workers dragged bulky guns into position. On October 9, the trenches completed, artillery experts began to pelt the British fortifications of Yorktown. Commanding General George Washington fired the first shot. By the following night fifty-two guns were battering the town in a ceaseless roar. Dr. James Thacher, an American army surgeon at the siege, described the wonder and horror of it all:

> The siege is daily becoming more and more formidable and alarming, and his lordship [Cornwallis] must view his situation as extremely critical, if not desperate. Being in the trenches every other night and day, I have a fine opportunity of witnessing the sublime and stupendous scene which is continually exhibiting. The bombshells from the besiegers and the besieged are incessantly crossing each other's path in the air. They are clearly visible in the form of a black ball in the day, but in the night they appear like a

fiery meteor with a blazing tail, most beautifully brilliant, ascending majestically from the mortar to a certain altitude and gradually descending to the spot where they are destined to execute their work of destruction.

It is astonishing with what accuracy an experienced gunner will make his calculations, that a shell shall fall within a few feet of a given point, and burst at the precise time, though at a great distance. When a shell falls, it whirls round, burrows, and excavates the earth to a considerable extent and, bursting, makes dreadful havoc around. I have more than once witnessed fragments of the mangled bodies and limbs of the British soldiers thrown into the air by the bursting of our shells; and by one from the enemy, Captain White... and one soldier were killed and another wounded near where I was standing. [10]

Failed Rescue, Failed Escape

Cornwallis eventually accepted the hopelessness of his position. He wrote to Clinton, "Many of our works are considerably damaged; with such works on disadvantageous ground, against so powerful an attack, we cannot hope to make a very long resistance." Then, in a chilling postscript, he added later: "We continue to lose men very fast." [11]

Clinton was not indifferent to Cornwallis's plight. He commanded shipworkers to labor long hours to repair and strengthen the fleet, which a month earlier had struggled into port like a flock of wounded birds. Repairmen promised Clinton they would be finished by October 5. Then they postponed the deadline to the eighth, then the twelfth. Finally, on October 17, the ships were crammed with seven thousand troops and set sail for the south. But unfavorable tides and winds delayed them two more days—while the black night of failure was collapsing around the miserable Cornwallis.

The Americans and French had no intention of waiting meekly for Clinton and his rescue operation. To further discomfit Cornwallis, Washington commanded von Steuben and his engineers to establish their second parallel only three hundred yards from Yorktown. But when the engineers set to work, they were met by a scathing spray of fire from two British redoubts nestled against the York River. Washington ordered the redoubts eliminated and sent a small division to storm each redoubt—four hundred French on the left and an equal number of Americans (under Lieutenant Colonel Alexander Hamilton) on the right.

The two divisions attacked simultaneously on the evening of October 14. They smashed over the abatis (barriers of trees placed with the branches facing the attackers) and stormed the parapets in the face of heavy fire. Then, with

Alexander Hamilton and his troops storm a parapet at Yorktown. Hamilton's courage contributed to the greatest American victory of the war.

bayonets fixed, they charged over the parapets to engage in hand-to-hand combat. Within half an hour, both redoubts had been captured.

With these obstructions out of the way, the construction crews continued feverishly through the night to complete the essential second siege parallel. By morning, the siege trench had been extended to include the two redoubts leading down to the river.

When Cornwallis looked out upon the completed parallel, he sent an urgent message to Clinton. "My situation now becomes very critical," he wrote. "We dare not show a gun to their old batteries, and I expect that their new ones will open tomorrow morning.... The safety of the place is, therefore, so precarious that I cannot recommend that the fleet and army should run great risk in endeavoring to save us."[12]

On the night of the sixteenth, a desperate Cornwallis tried to lead a mass escape across the quarter-mile-wide York River. But the small British boats were hindered by a sudden, violent storm, and many of the boats were swept downstream. The frantic British, trapped along the river front behind their own useless fortifications, now found themselves with no way out.

Early the next morning, as a Hessian soldier recalled with an apparent shudder, "the bombardment began again from the enemy side even more horribly than before. They fired from all redoubts without stopping. Our detachment, which stood in the hornwork, could scarcely avoid the enemy's bombs, howitzer shot, and cannonballs anymore. One saw nothing but bombs and balls raining on our whole line."[13]

"The World Turned Upside Down"

Later, on that same morning of October 17, the British finally ran out of ammunition, and Lord Cornwallis was compelled to call for a truce. (This was the day Clinton's evacuation force left New York; it arrived, fruitlessly, a full week later.) By October 19 the terms of an almost unconditional surrender had been agreed upon, though the British signed only with the utmost reluctance. The terms of surrender dictated that Cornwallis and his troops would be taken as prisoners of war, their arms and stores would be given to the American army, and the British would be accorded exactly the "same honors" that had been imposed upon Benjamin Lincoln and his surrendering American garrison at Charleston. [14]

The last condition was the hardest to accept. The Americans at Charleston had been treated rudely and disgracefully when they surrendered. The traditional "honors of war" had been scornfully refused. Now Cornwallis indignantly protested against such treatment, but Washington would not yield.

The formal surrender was set for two o'clock in the afternoon on October 19, 1781. Rather than face his disgrace, Cornwallis chose not to attend, sending instead his deputy, Brigadier General Charles O'Hara. Cornwallis used the excuse that he was indisposed.

As a traditional gesture of surrender, O'Hara directed his horse to Rochambeau, preparing to offer him his sword. Rochambeau refused the sword, indicating that Washington was the commanding general of the allied forces. O'Hara turned to surrender to Washington, but he also declined. He nodded toward General Benjamin Lincoln. If Britain was going to use a deputy to offer the surrender, Washington would use a deputy to receive it. The British general handed his sword to Lincoln, who accepted it and then handed it back. The surrender ceremony had begun.

Out marched the British in their red coats and the Hessians in their blue and green, striding between the long lines of smartly dressed French soldiers on one side and the more ragged Americans on the other. The Germans grounded their arms neatly, but the British, many of whom were weeping, smashed their muskets down and marched sullenly off. Through it all the British fife-and-drum corps played a doleful tune called "The World Turned Upside Down."

The surrender at Yorktown in October 1781. Washington's victory over General Cornwallis at Yorktown marked the end of active fighting in the Revolutionary War. (Painting by John Trumbull, a Revolutionary War soldier.)

"Jumping and Dancing and Singing"

Local patriots were overjoyed to see the surrender. According to one account, they "rushed into each other's arms and wept for gladness."[15] The American troops were equally demonstrative. One American colonel recalled, "The officers and soldiers could scarcely talk for laughing, and they could scarcely walk for jumping and dancing and singing as they went about."[16] An unnamed patriot, with obvious delight, wrote a comic song about the Yorktown victory. The lyrics describe Cornwallis's ill fortune from the moment he and Nathanael Greene first clashed:

> Cornwallis led a country dance, the like was never seen, sir,
> Much retrograde and much advance and all with General Greene, sir.
> They rambled up and rambled down, joined hands and then they run, sir,
> Our General Greene to Charlestown and the Earl to Wilmington, sir....
>
> Now housed in York he challenged all to minuets so spritely,
> And lessons for a courtly ball his soldiers studied nightly,
> His challenge heard, full soon there came a set who knew the dance, sir,
> De Grasse and Rochambeau, whose fame proved certain to advance, sir.
>
> And Washington, Columbia's son, whom easy nature taught, sir,
> That grace which can't by pains be won, nor monarch's gold be bought, sir,
> Now hand in hand they circle round, this ever-dancing pair, sir,
> Their gentle movements soon confound the Earl, as they draw near, sir.
>
> His music he forgets to play, his feet can move no more, sir,
> And all his soldiers curse the day they jiggled to our shore, sir,

Now, Tories all, what will you say? Come, is this not a griper?
That while your hopes are danced away, 'tis you must pay the piper.[17]

Immediately after the surrender, Washington rushed a dispatch to Congress telling, in carefully restrained language, of "a reduction of the British army . . . at an earlier period than my most sanguine hope had induced me to expect."[18]

American and British Reactions to Yorktown

Washington's reaction to the great victory at Yorktown was typical of his nature. After the sword ceremony, after the British and Hessian troops had been claimed as prisoners, after the arms had been grounded, Washington turned his thoughts to thanksgiving. In general orders issued the day after the formal surrender he "earnestly" recommended that all troops not on duty attend "divine service," and that they do so "with that seriousness of deportment and gratitude of heart which the recognition of such reiterated and astonishing interpositions of Providence demands of us."[19]

Congress was of a like mind: after receiving news of Washington's momentous victory, that body went en masse to a Lutheran church in Philadelphia for a service of thanksgiving.

Cornwallis visited Washington at his tent the day after the surrender. The disgrace of the ceremony behind him, the British commander could now afford to be cordial. In keeping with European customs of "civilized warfare," Washington and Rochambeau subsequently hosted a dinner for Cornwallis and his chief officers. Rochambeau grandly offered a toast to the king of France. Cornwallis lifted his glass and repeated, "To the king."

"Of England," Washington interrupted cleverly. "Confine

him there and I'll drink him a full bumper."[20]

The British received the news of Yorktown with dark dismay. Lord North, the prime minister, took the news "as he would have taken a ball in his breast," crying out repeatedly, "O God! it is all over!"[21] King George III was so discomposed that he considered abdicating; he even prepared his abdication message, but never delivered it. Lord North languished in the deepest misery for several months and finally resigned from his post the following March. His replacement was the Marquis of Rockingham, who was friendlier to the American cause. (Fifteen years earlier, Rockingham had been the prime minister who helped obtain repeal of the oppressive Stamp Act.)

"A State of Languor"

Although Yorktown was a momentous victory, it by no means signified a final triumph for America. Cornwallis's troops were a mere one-quarter of the British forces on American soil. Those who remained still outnumbered—and outclassed—the American army. Furthermore, de Grasse was determined to sail back to the West Indies with his ships and troops before the hurricane season prevented it.

Under these circumstances, Washington was well aware of the clouds of danger that still loomed ahead. "My only apprehension," he wrote to Virginia's Governor Thomas Nelson, "...is lest the late important success, instead of exciting our exertions as it ought to do, should produce such a relaxation in the prosecution of the war as will prolong the calamities of it."[22]

To avoid a decline in morale and resolution, Washington hoped to strike again while the momentum was with his forces. He pleaded with Admiral de Grasse to join him in an attack on the British forces in Charleston, where the Tories had been cornered by General Greene. But de Grasse declined.

It was painful to let such an opportunity pass. With the British stunned and reeling from Yorktown, Washington believed another blow would drive them to their knees. The president of Congress, John Hanson, applauded the idea. The members of Congress, he said, were "fixed" in their purpose "to draw every advantage from [the victory] by exhorting the states in the strongest terms to the most vigorous and timely exertions."[23]

But congressional actions did not support congressional promises. Washington shared his apprehensions with General Greene: "My greatest fear is that Congress, viewing this stroke in too important a point of light, may think our work too nearly closed, and fall...into a state of languor and relaxation." That, he warned, would be a "fatal mistake."[24]

Washington was determined to prevent such a fatal mistake. Even though Yorktown proved to be the last great battle of the war, another two years dragged past before General Washington and his men were able to lay down their arms. British soldiers did not leave American shores until late 1783, several months after a peace treaty was finally signed. Never knowing their true intentions, and always fearing the possibility of another attack, Washington kept his army in a state of constant readiness. If the British chose to prolong the war, the Americans must be prepared to repel them.

Washington's Courage

Washington's peerless courage during the siege of Yorktown was completely in character with what the American army had come to expect. At one point in early October he stood in the siege trenches with the engineering troops, the enemy lines a scant two hundred yards away. A cannonball exploded so close that it showered the General and his party with flying dirt. Washington, single-minded in his study of the British fortifications through field glasses, did not even turn his head to look. The chaplain was astounded at the General's composure and grabbed off his own hat to show the General the spray of dirt that covered it. Washington simply smiled. "Mr. Evans," he said, "you had better carry that home and show it to your wife and children."[25]

A few days later General Washington was standing in an exposed position as British fire poured heavily over the American trenches. Colonel David Cobb, one of the General's aides, "solicitous for his safety, said to his Excellency, 'Sir, you are too much exposed here. Had you not better step a little back?'

" 'Colonel Cobb,' replied his Excellency, 'if you are afraid, you have liberty to step back.' "[26]

Such incidents were not limited to Yorktown. At the Battle of Princeton in 1777 Washington galloped within thirty yards of the enemy before shouting the order to fire. The ensuing volley raised such a thick cloud of smoke that visibility was cut to near zero. The men could scarcely see each other, let alone their commander. When the smoke cleared, Washington's aides feared they would see their beloved General lying lifeless on the ground. Instead he remained solidly on his horse, unscathed. "Thank God, your Excellency is safe," his aide Edward Fitzgerald exclaimed, then burst into tears of relief. Washington took him by the hand to reassure him. "Away, my dear colonel, and bring up the troops. The day is our own."[27]

Washington's courage sometimes seemed to be sheer

recklessness and aroused deep anxieties in those around him. Wrote Benjamin Harrison, "Every officer complains of his exposing himself too much."[28]

One American officer wrote from Morristown in early 1777: "Our army love their General very much, but they have one thing against him, which is the little care he takes of himself in any action. His personal bravery, and the desire he has of animating his troops by example, make him fearless of danger. This occasions us much uneasiness. But Heaven, which has hitherto been his shield, I hope will still continue to guard so valuable a life."[29]

Many Americans were convinced that the loss of Washington would be the ultimate disaster. In December 1777 Lafayette conveyed to Washington his deepest fears, writing, "If you were lost for America, there is nobody who could keep the army and the revolution for six months."[30] And the Reverend Jacob Duche, a Philadelphia cleric, wrote, "The whole world knows that [the army's] only existence depends upon you; that your death or captivity disperses it in a moment, and that there is not a man . . . in America capable of succeeding you."[31]

Washington's courage, shown repeatedly and dramatically throughout the war, had a strong inspiriting effect on his army. With this quality of his character he not only motivated his men during earlier battles but also led them to victory in the all-important siege of Yorktown.

The Death of Jack Custis

After arranging for troops and stores to be moved from Yorktown back to a base on the Hudson River, Washington made an unhurried journey to a relative's home in Eltham, Virginia, where his stepson, Jack Custis, had been sent to recover from an illness. Although the twenty-five-year-old Jack had sat out most of the war, he had joined Washington at Yorktown, volunteering to serve as one of the General's aides. Lacking immunity to the many deadly camp diseases, however, he soon became sick and had to leave the battle site. Washington had barely arrived in Eltham when he learned, to his great surprise, that rather than recovering Jack was grievously ill. Within hours of Washington's arrival, Jack died.

Jack's demise diminished Washington's exultation in the Yorktown triumph. The bright glow of victory was dimmed by this sudden tragedy in his private life. With heavy heart, the General spent several days taking care of Jack's funeral arrangements, then moved on to Mount Vernon. He had much business to take care of after his long absence, but he spared only one week. Then he left for Philadelphia to meet with Congress. Martha accompanied him, seeking by a change of surroundings to take her mind off her mournful thoughts. In the years following, the General virtually adopted two of Jack's four children, Eleanor and George Washington Parke Custis.

Washington's deliberations with Congress took the entire winter, as he sought once again to improve the strength of the army and the lot of his men. He met weekly with an "executive committee" of Congress, composed of Secretary of Finance Robert Morris, Foreign Affairs Secretary Robert Livingston, and Secretary of War Benjamin Lincoln. In hours of leisure, he attended parties and plays, but suffered genuine embarrassment on frequent occasions when he was feted almost to the point of being idolized.

A Shocking Proposal

In May 1782, after returning to his headquarters at Newburgh, New York, Washington received a horrifying proposal. Colonel Lewis Nicola, commander of the Invalid Regiment, wrote a detailed letter reciting the chronic grievances of the army. They had gone too long with inadequate food and scanty clothing, he said—and when would they be paid? Nicola placed the blame for their sorry condition directly at the feet of the present form of government. Congress was too weak. The states were unwilling to relinquish adequate power to a centralized government. Only one solution would work: the army must establish a new monarchy—and George Washington was the man who should be crowned king.

Nicola's suggestion was not as outrageous as it may seem to the modern mind. A monarchical government was the form found throughout the world in the eighteenth century, and it had been so through all the centuries before.

But the idea of having an American king was profoundly distasteful to Washington. It was a slap in the face to everything he had given his life and fortune to achieve. His reply to Nicola was stern and uncompromising: "No occurrence in the course of the war has given me more painful sensations than your information of there being such ideas existing in the army, . . . and [these] I must view with abhorrence and reprehend with severity." Such ideas, he continued, were "big with the greatest mischiefs that can befall my country. . . . You could not have found a person to whom your schemes are more disagreeable." He then urged Nicola from the depths of his soul: "If you have any regard for your country, concern for yourself or posterity, or respect for me, . . . banish these thoughts from your mind, and never communicate, as from yourself or anyone else, a sentiment of the like nature."

The matter of the grievances of the army was terribly real, of course. Washington acknowledged the continuing validity of those concerns, and promised Nicola that he would use his "powers and influence...to the utmost of my abilities" to bring an acceptable solution. But that solution, he emphasized, must come in a "constitutional way."[32]

A month after quashing Nicola's plan, Washington reiterated his honest lack of desire for power or position, yearning instead for a return to the idyllic life he once so much enjoyed: "The first wish of my soul is to return speedily into the bosom of that country which gave me birth and, in the sweet enjoyment of domestic happiness and the company of a few friends, to end my days in quiet."[33]

Uncertain Prospects for Peace

Throughout the winter of 1781–82, rumors of peace flew through the colonies on swift wings. It was said the British were going to recognize the independence of America and cease all hostilities. But six years of war had taught Washington not to trust rumor. Infinitely more reliable, he said, was "an old and true maxim that to make a good peace, you ought to be well prepared to carry on the war."[34]

Sir Guy Carleton, the last commander in chief of the British forces during the war. Many historians feel he was the most capable of all the British commanders, but he arrived on the scene too late (in February 1782) to prove himself.

In May 1782 Sir Guy Carleton replaced Clinton as commander of the British forces. Clinton went home to Britain self-righteously placing all the blame for his misfortunes on Cornwallis. Meanwhile, Carleton made no sign of wishing to move against the Americans, and in August he sent Washington an official notice: a peace conference was under way in Paris. A letter sent shortly thereafter notified Washington that hostilities had been "suspended." Carleton set about removing his troops from their southern holdings, with the last detachment leaving Charleston in December. "The evacuation is not a matter of choice," Carleton wrote to another correspondent, "but of deplorable necessity in consequence of an unsuccessful war."[35]

But word came from Britain that Prime Minister Lord Rockingham had died; and his successor (the Earl of Shelburne) was markedly less liberal-minded. Washington grew pessimistic. "Our prospect of peace is vanishing.... That the king will push the war as long as the nation will find men or money admits not a doubt in my mind.... If we are wise, let us prepare for the worst." He then repeated "a doctrine I have endeavored ... to inculcate"—and one he was certain would prove true. Said he: "There is nothing which will so soon produce a speedy and honorable peace as a state of preparation for war, and we must either do this or lay our account for a patched-up, inglorious peace, after all the toil, blood and treasure we have spent."[36]

In December 1782 the British fleet sailed from New York Harbor, but a major land force lingered in New York City. When would they leave—if at all? Again rumors flew, but the rumors brought no change. "With respect to peace," Washington complained to his brother Jack, "we are held in a very disagreeable state of suspense."[37] And to Thomas Jefferson he expressed his nagging fears: "At present, the prospect of peace absorbs... every other consideration among us, and would, it is to be feared, leave us in a very unprepared state to continue the war."[38] He was quick to point out that peace should be diligently sought, but until that peace was secured, Washington had a continuing responsibility to make sure the Americans were ready to press on in winning the war.

He dared not attack, however. With de Grasse in the West Indies, and with the American forces already diminishing, Washington's main desire was simply to hold the semblance of an army together. Accordingly, as the months after Yorktown dragged by, the Americans and the British saw little armed contact. "Our summer was inactive," Washington wrote to Lafayette at the end of 1782, "and, more than probably, the winter will be tranquil."[39]

Chapter 25

"A Gulf of Civil Horror"

E
ven though 1782 was relatively calm on the battle-front, the year was one of deep disquiet in the American camps. The bitter frustrations Colonel Nicola had so clearly painted continued to nag the soldiers. The commander in chief pushed Congress for satisfactory solutions, but results tottered in so slowly that they seemed not to come at all. "The patience, the fortitude, the long and great suffering of this army is unexampled in history," he wrote to James McHenry, Congressman from Virginia. "But there is an end to all things, and I fear we are very near to this."[1] He fearfully envisioned mass mutiny, or worse, an uprising of angry troops against a helpless government.

He had hoped to spend the winter at Mount Vernon, but the army's mood shackled him to the camp. He must stay with the troops through the winter, he told McHenry, "to prevent, if possible, the disorders getting to an incurable height."[2]

The Secretary of War, Benjamin Lincoln, received a similarly alarming message: If the army was not paid soon, "I cannot help apprehending that a train of evils will follow, of a very serious and distressing nature. . . . While in the field, I think it may be kept from breaking out into acts of outrage, but when we retire into winter quarters . . . I cannot be at ease."[3]

As the months dragged on, the officers feared that Congress would violate its trust and default on promises of payment, land, and pension. "The temper of the army is much soured," Washington wrote in December. They were "more irritable than at any period since the commencement of the war." Congress must "dictate soothing measures" without delay. [4]

When the new year arrived without promise of change, the army grew increasingly restless. Washington's worries also increased: "The army, as usual, are without pay, and a great part of the soldiery without shirts; and . . . [their] patience . . . is equally threadbare." He spoke sarcastically of "those at a distance" who seemed to feel that "the army had contracted such a habit of encountering distresses and difficulties, and of living without money, that it would be impolitic and injurious to introduce other customs in it!"[5]

In early March 1783, Washington wrote with heaviness of soul to Alexander Hamilton, who was then in Congress. He spoke of deep "forebodings of evil." Troubles seemed to lap around his feet like ocean waves in a rising tide. It seemed inevitable that the situation would deteriorate to "events

which are more to be deprecated than prevented."[6]
In barely a week his forebodings proved true.

Feelings in Ferment

Washington's anxieties were not new to Hamilton. In mid
February Hamilton had written a strange and curious letter
to Washington, who was then headquartered at Newburgh,
New York. He confidentially informed Washington that the
army was through with waiting for Congress to make good
on unredeemed promises, and that many were prepared to
resort to the sword "to procure justice." Some of the army felt
that Washington had failed them, that he was not representing their cause before Congress with sufficient fervor. If the
army took the law into its own iron hands, Hamilton warned,
it would be virtually impossible to keep them "within the
bounds of moderation."

But there was a solution, Hamilton said. If Washington
would not "discountenance their endeavors to procure redress, but [would] take the direction of them," the army
might be able to obtain their just rewards from the states.
"Should any commotions unhappily ensue," he felt Washington could use his influence "to moderate the pretensions of
the army and make their conduct correspond with their
duty."[7]

Washington stewed about the letter for several days,
seeking answers to the problem it posed. Finally he wrote
back to Hamilton: "The predicament in which I stand as citizen and soldier is as critical and delicate as can well be conceived. It has been the subject of many contemplative hours.
The sufferings of a complaining army on the one hand and
tardiness of the states on the other," he feared, represented a
dilemma that could bring a truly disastrous result. Still,

Hamilton's suggestion that Washington and the army become the arbiters of the law was a reckless, heedless solution
—even though Hamilton would have the army act in moderation. "No observations are necessary to evince the fatal
tendency of such a measure. . . . It would at this day be
productive of civil commotions and end in blood. Unhappy
situation this! God forbid that we should be involved in it."[8]

A Dangerous Circular

Nevertheless, many others concurred with Hamilton's
pessimistic outlook, and a number of the army's officers were
unwilling to wait for the blessing of their commander in chief.

On March 10, 1783, Washington learned that an unauthorized meeting of general and field officers had been
called by an anonymous circular. At the same time, he was
handed a fiery message to all officers, encouraging them to
forcibly seek redress from a long-delinquent Congress. The
author of the address was later identified as Major John
Armstrong of General Gates's staff. He spoke eloquently of
the crisis point the army had reached. His words were not designed to soothe, but were incendiary, deliberately designed
to inflame and incite. The men in the army, already at the end
of their emotional rope, were ripe for such a message.

After thoroughly whipping up the raw feelings of the
soldiers, Armstrong concluded by saying that the troops had
selflessly placed America "in the chair of independency; and
peace returns again to bless—whom?"

> A country willing to redress your wrongs, cherish your
> worth, and reward your services? A country courting your
> return to private life with tears of gratitude and smiles of
> adoration—longing to divide with you that independency
> which your gallantry has given, and those riches which

your wounds have preserved? Is this the case? Or is it rather a country that tramples upon your rights, disdains your cries, and insults your distresses? Have you not more than once suggested your wishes and made known your wants to Congress? ...

Can you ... consent to be the only sufferers by this revolution, and, retiring from the field, grow old in poverty, wretchedness, and contempt? Can you consent to wade through the vile mire of dependency and owe the miserable remnant of that life to charity which has hitherto been spent in honor? ...

Tell [Congress] that ... the wound often irritated and never healed may at length become incurable.

Armstrong exhorted the men to "discover" and "oppose ... tyranny under whatever garb it may assume, whether it be the plain coat of republicanism or the splendid robe of royalty. ... Redress yourselves. If the present moment be lost, every future effort is in vain, and your threats then will be as empty as your entreaties now."[9]

Washington was stunned by the inflammatory appeal. Members of his army were advocating use of arms to force their way upon Congress and the states. It was a dangerous and horrifying prospect! He immediately issued strict orders condemning the meeting and calling for another meeting to be held on the fifteenth of March. At that time the officers could openly discuss their many grievances and come to a more intelligent solution to their problems.

"A Gulf of Civil Horror"

Even though Washington had taken this preliminary step, he instinctively knew that the situation could still explode out of control. Only through vigorous action would he be able "to arrest on the spot the foot that stood wavering on a tremendous precipice, to prevent the officers from being taken by surprise while the passions were all inflamed, and to rescue them from plunging themselves into a gulf of civil horror from which there might be no receding."[10] Initially, he had hoped to let the officers work out their grievances on their own, but on careful reflection he decided to address the meeting himself.

After a fitful, sleepless night, Washington arose on the fifteenth with the fears of the day looming ominously before him. At the appointed time, he strode to the large wooden dance hall his soldiers had erected a few weeks before and without formal introduction took over the crude lectern at the front. He began by apologizing for attending personally; such had not been his original intention, but he finally realized he must. He disparaged the paper that had circulated, characterizing it as "addressed more to the feelings and passions than to the reason and judgment of the army. The author of the piece is entitled to much credit for the goodness of his pen, and I could wish he had as much credit for the rectitude of his heart."

Then he referred to those who felt he had not done enough to help the army in its extremity. He said:

> If my conduct heretofore has not evinced to you that I have been a faithful friend to the army, my declaration of it at this time would be equally unavailing and improper. But as I was among the first who embarked in the cause of our common country; as I have never left your side one moment, but when called from you on public duty; as I have been the constant companion and witness of your distresses . . . ; as I have ever considered my military reputation as inseparably connected with that of the army; as my heart has ever expanded with joy when I have heard its praises, and my indignation has arisen when the mouth of detrac-

tion has been opened against it, it can scarcely be supposed, at this late stage of the war, that I am indifferent to its interests.

But apparently there was some disagreement about how best to promote those interests. The first method proposed by the anonymous circular was to "remove into the unsettled country . . . and leave an ungrateful country to defend itself. But who are they to defend? Our wives, our children, our farms and other property, which we leave behind us?" Or would the soldiers perhaps take their wives and children with them—"to perish in a wilderness with hunger, cold, and nakedness?"

Perhaps another course would be even more satisfactory, if the ideas in the anonymous letter were to be followed. Washington summarized them: "Never sheathe your swords, says he, until you have obtained full and ample justice." The commander's comment on such an approach was terse: "This dreadful alternative of either deserting our country in the extremest hour of her distress, or turning our arms against it . . . unless Congress can be compelled into instant compliance, has something so shocking in it that humanity revolts at the idea."

"Unexampled Patriotism and Patient Virtue"

Washington agreed that Congress was shackled. But he insisted it was peopled by honorable men who eventually would be certain to do the army "complete justice." He had respect for these men and said the labor of Congress "to discover and establish funds for this purpose has been unwearied and will not cease till they have succeeded. . . . Why, then, should we distrust them and . . . adopt measures which may cast a shade over that glory which has been so justly acquired, and tarnish the reputation of an army which is celebrated through all Europe for its fortitude and patriotism?"

Washington solemnly pledged to continue to promote the army's cause "to the utmost extent of my abilities." But he added that both officers and soldiers must continue to be patient while Congress was addressing these problems.

> Let me entreat you, gentlemen, on your part, not to take any measure which, viewed in the calm light of reason, will lessen the dignity and sully the glory you have hitherto maintained. . . . And let me conjure you, in the name of our common country, as you value your own sacred honor, as you respect the rights of humanity, and as you regard the military and national character of America, to express your utmost horror and detestation of the man who wishes, under any specious pretenses, to overturn the liberties of our country, and who wickedly attempts to open the floodgates of civil discord and deluge our rising empire in blood. By thus . . . acting, you will . . . give one more distinguished proof of unexampled patriotism and patient virtue, rising superior to the pressure of the most complicated sufferings; and you will, by the dignity of your conduct, afford occasion for posterity to say, when speaking of the glorious example you have exhibited to mankind, "Had this day been wanting, the world had never seen the last stage of perfection to which human nature is capable of attaining."[11]

"I Have Grown Gray in Your Service"

Thus Washington concluded his carefully prepared remarks. Some of the men had been swayed, but others continued to stare with hardened faces and were determined not to bend. Then, almost as an afterthought, the General pulled from his pocket a letter he had received from Joseph Jones, a Congressman from Virginia who expressed deep sympathy toward the army and pledged his help. Perhaps if he read aloud selected parts of that letter, Washington thought, it would underscore the things he had been saying.

He opened the letter and tried to read it, but stumbled badly. He paused, then pulled from his pocket a pair of new spectacles, which only his closest aides had ever seen him wear. He fumbled to put them on, but seemed to have difficulty. Finally, he said simply, "Gentlemen, you must pardon me. I have grown gray in your service and now find myself growing blind."[12]

That humble, honest statement suddenly made a difference. Stern faces softened and strong soldiers wept.

Major Samuel Shaw recalled the commanding power of this moment:

> On other occasions, [Washington] had been supported by the exertions of an army and the countenance of his friends; but in this he stood single and alone. There was no saying where the passions of an army, which were not a little inflamed, might lead.... Under these circumstances he appeared, not at the head of his troops, but as it were in opposition to them; and for a dreadful moment the interests of the army and its General seemed to be in competition! He spoke—every doubt was dispelled, and the tide of patriotism rolled again in its wonted course. Illustrious man! What he says of the army may with equal justice be applied to his own character. "Had this day been wanting, the world had never seen the last stage of perfection to which human nature is capable of attaining."[13]

After Washington left the room, the officers voted to sustain their beloved commander in chief and to wait patiently on Congress. No one voted nay, and there was only one abstention.

Washington was relieved and gratified by the officers' response. He wrote to his cousin, "The good sense, the virtue and patient forbearance of the army on this, as upon every other trying occasion... has again triumphed."[14]

But he could not let Congress close its eyes to the deadly peril he had momentarily averted. He wrote that they must act speedily to fulfill all their promises. He further stated that should they fail, "then shall I have learned what ingratitude is; then shall I have realized a tale which will embitter every moment of my future life." He trusted, however, that he need not worry. "A country rescued by their arms from impending ruin will never leave unpaid the debt of gratitude."[15]

In retrospect, historians have recognized how critical these decisive actions by Washington truly were. As one writer observed, "Americans can never be adequately grateful that George Washington possessed the power and the will to intervene effectively in what may well have been the most dangerous hour the United States has ever known."[16] If Washington had not intervened—or had his efforts been ineffective—the army might very well have made good on their angry threat to use armed force. Had they done so, a new military dictatorship could have been born.

A year later, in 1784, Jefferson acclaimed Washington's decisive actions in the Newburgh crisis: "The moderation and virtue of a single character have probably prevented this revolution from being closed, as most others have been, by a subversion of that liberty it was intended to establish."[17]

Chapter 26

The Closing Days of War

The Newburgh crisis had just been resolved when Washington received the most welcome news of the entire eight-year war. Far overshadowing the victories at Ticonderoga, Boston, Trenton, and Princeton, Saratoga, Monmouth, King's Mountain, Cowpens, and even Yorktown was the glorious news that now came floating across the Atlantic. At last a formal peace treaty had been signed between the United States and England! Preliminary articles had been approved as early as the previous November, but now the treaty was final and official. Keeping his flood of emotions under careful control, Washington wrote, "The news has filled my mind with inexpressible satisfaction."[1]

On April 18, 1783, Washington joyfully informed the army of "the cessation of hostilities" between the United States and Great Britain. The final attainment of peace, he continued, "opens the prospect to a more splendid scene, and, like another morning star, promises the approach of a brighter day than hath hitherto illuminated the western hemisphere." He emphasized that the troops deserved the highest praise for "the dignified part they have been called to act (under the smiles of Providence) on the stage of human affairs; for happy, thrice happy, shall they be pronounced hereafter who have contributed anything, who have performed the meanest office in erecting this stupendous fabric of freedom and empire on the broad basis of independence." They had stood together, firm and unyielding, in "protecting the rights of human nature and establishing an asylum for the poor and oppressed of all nations and religions."[2]

On the following day—the eighth anniversary of the battles at Lexington and Concord—Washington asked his chaplains and soldiers to put a fitting crown on the news of peace by "render[ing] thanks to Almighty God for all His mercies, particularly for His overruling the wrath of man to His own glory, and causing the rage of war to cease among the nations."[3]

The war had persisted for eight long years. During those eight years the army had grappled with inadequate support from both Congress and the states. It had suffered constantly for lack of funds and supplies. And for eight years Washington had struggled with Congress, trying to gain approval for more troops, for continental troops rather than militia, and for troops with longer enlistments.

Washington knew the annals of the Revolutionary War would read more like fiction than history. He wrote, "It will not be believed that such a force as Great Britain . . . could be baffled . . . by numbers infinitely less, composed of men oftentimes half-starved, always in rags, without pay, and experiencing, at times, every species of distress which human nature is capable of undergoing."[4]

A Time of Waiting

Even though a peace treaty had been announced, Washington insisted on continuing vigilance so long as any British forces remained on American soil. Congress sent most of the army home in order to save money, but Washington clung to the rest, dragging through seven months of "distressing tedium" as they waited for the British to evacuate.[5]

In May and June Washington sought temporary relief from his ever-present dental problems. A visiting French dentist treated the General for persistent pain and, possibly, gum disease. Washington also attempted, unsuccessfully, to have some of his previously pulled teeth replaced in a bridge. In spite of the pain and general discomfort from his teeth, Washington utilized the month of June 1783 to explore 750 miles of New York frontier on horseback, by canoe, and on foot. He examined the defenses of the region and, with great satisfaction, inspected the site of Burgoyne's defeat.

June was the month he wrote his momentous Circular to the States, sometimes called "Washington's Legacy." This letter, his last official communication to the states as commander in chief, is a vivid demonstration of Washington's keen-sighted views on both politics and war. He began by observing that he was "now preparing to resign" his commission as commander of the American forces "and return to that domestic retirement which, it is well known, I left with greatest reluctance, a retirement for which I have never ceased to sigh through a long and painful absence." He hoped, he said, "to pass the remainder of life in a state of undisturbed repose." Before that retirement began, however, he expressed a desire "to offer my sentiments respecting some important subjects... and to give my final blessing to that country in whose service I have spent the prime of my life, for whose sake I have consumed so many anxious days and watchful nights, and whose happiness, being extremely dear to me, will always constitute no inconsiderable part of my own."

He said America was an exceedingly choice land, and the United States had come into being during an "auspicious period" of history. Yet he predicted it would be the character and conduct of America's citizens that would determine "whether they will be respectable and prosperous or contemptible and miserable as a nation."

> This is the favorable moment to give such a tone to our federal government as will enable it to answer the ends of its institution, or this may be the ill-fated moment for relaxing the powers of the Union, annihilating the cement of the Confederation, and exposing us to become the sport of European politics, which may play one state against another to prevent their growing importance, and serve their own interested purposes. For, according to the system of policy the states shall adopt at this moment, they will stand or fall, and by their confirmation or lapse it is yet to be decided whether the revolution must ultimately be considered as a blessing or a curse—a blessing or a curse not to the present age alone, for with our fate will the destiny of unborn millions be involved.

"Pillars... of Our Independence"

Believing as he did that the moment was pivotal, Washington felt that for him to remain silent on certain important issues "would be a crime." He then listed four foundational elements "which I humbly conceive are essential

to the well-being, I may even venture to say, to the existence
of the United States as an independent power":

> First, an indissoluble union of the states under one
> federal head.
> Secondly, a sacred regard to public justice.
> Thirdly, the adoption of a proper peace establishment.
> And, fourthly, the prevalence of that pacific and friendly
> disposition among the people of the United States which
> will induce them to forget their local prejudices and policies,
> to make those mutual concessions which are requisite to
> the general prosperity, and, in some instances, to sacrifice
> their individual advantages to the interest of the com-
> munity.
> These are the pillars on which the glorious fabric of our
> independence and national character must be supported;
> liberty is the basis, and whoever would dare to sap the
> foundation or overturn the structure, under whatever
> specious pretexts he may attempt it, will merit the bitterest
> execration and the severest punishment which can be
> inflicted by his injured country.

In elaborating on the need for "public justice," Washington
spoke emphatically of the responsibility of Congress to pay
the soldiers as promised, pleading particularly for those who
had been permanently disabled while in service. "Nothing but
a punctual payment of their annual allowance can rescue
them from the most complicated misery, and nothing could
be a more melancholy and distressing sight than to behold
those who have shed their blood or lost their limbs in the
service of their country, without a shelter, without a friend,
and without the means of obtaining any of the necessaries or
comforts of life, compelled to beg their daily bread from door
to door!"

392 The Real George Washington

Characteristically, Washington closed with a strong reiteration of his faith:

> I now make it my earnest prayer that God would have you, and the state over which you preside, in his holy protection, that he would incline the hearts of the citizens to cultivate a spirit of subordination and obedience to government, to entertain a brotherly affection and love for one another; ... and finally, that he would most graciously be pleased to dispose us all to do justice, to love mercy, and to demean ourselves with that charity, humility, and pacific temper of mind which were the characteristics of the Divine Author of our blessed religion, and without an humble imitation of whose example in these things we can never hope to be a happy nation. [6]

Final Orders to a Departing Army

Despite the tension of waiting for the British to leave, Washington began to feel more relaxed than he had in years. One friend found the change in his facial expression remarkable, describing it as "uncommonly open and pleasant. The contracted, pensive [face], betokening deep thought and much care, ... is done away, and a pleasant smile and sparkling vivacity of wit and humor succeed." [7]

That wit, always a subtle part of Washington's personality, now began to surface more frequently. Washington was normally rather reserved when he was not among close friends or family. But when the president of Congress lamented that the public financier had his hands full, Washington quipped, "[I wish] he had his *pockets* full, too." [8]

On November 2, 1873, Washington issued his final orders to the army, speaking as a concerned father to a body of much-beloved sons. He wrote, "Before the commander in chief takes his final leave of those he holds most dear, he wishes to bid them an affectionate, a long farewell." Together they had trudged through "almost every possible suffering and discouragement." Their unswerving constancy had been "little short of a standing miracle." Now, the war over, his men must "prove themselves not less virtuous and useful as citizens than they have been persevering and victorious as soldiers.... The private virtues of economy, prudence, and industry will not be less amiable in civil life than the more splendid qualities of valor, perseverance, and enterprise were in the field." The soldiers could do much to help cement the Union; they must join hands with their fellow citizens in the great cause.

Again he closed with a prayer: "May ample justice be done them [the war veterans] here, and may the choicest of heaven's favors, both here and hereafter, attend those who, under the divine auspices, have secured innumerable blessings for others."[9]

Departure of the British

By mid-November Washington received word that the British would leave New York by the end of the month. As he moved toward the city, planning to be present to ensure order, great crowds gathered to cheer his coming. One woman compared the American to the British troops, saying the Americans "were ill-clad and weather beaten, and made a forlorn appearance." Yet, ultimately, that did not matter, the woman added proudly, because "they were *our* troops!"[10]

The British boarded their ships in New York Harbor on November 25, 1783. The next day Washington received a formal message from the "long-suffering exiles," loyal patriots who had been forced from New York by the British occupation and were now returning to their homes. They declared, "In this place, and at this moment of exultation and triumph,... we look up to you our deliverer with unusual transports of gratitude and joy." The city had been "long torn from us by the hard hand of oppression, but now, by your wisdom and energy, under the guidance of Providence, [the city is] once more the seat of peace and freedom.... Permit us, therefore, to approach your Excellency with the dignity and sincerity of freemen, and to assure you that we shall preserve, with our last breath, our gratitude for your services and veneration for your character."[11]

A Tearful Farewell

Washington had promised the troops at Newburgh that they would be taken care of, but Congress now sent them home with a simple resolution of thanks and nothing more.

Anger about empty congressional promises, bitter thoughts of long years of desperate privation, exultation at a successful conclusion to the war—all combined in a strange mixture as military comrades began to break camp and straggle off toward their homes.

Feelings ran high as Washington joined his remaining few officers for a final farewell at Fraunces' Tavern in New York. One of the officers, Lieutenant Colonel Benjamin Tallmadge, recorded in his journal a touching account of that meeting:

> We had been assembled but a few moments when His Excellency entered the room. His emotion, too strong to be concealed, seemed to be reciprocated by every officer present.
>
> After partaking of a slight refreshment, in almost breathless silence, the General filled his glass with wine and, turning to his officers, he said, "With a heart full of love and gratitude, I now take leave of you. I most devoutly

wish that your latter days may be as prosperous and happy as your former ones have been glorious and honorable."

After the officers had taken a glass of wine, General Washington said, "I cannot come to each of you, but shall feel obliged if each of you will come and take me by the hand."

General Knox, being nearest to him, turned to the Commander in Chief, who, suffused in tears, was incapable of utterance, but grasped his hand, when they embraced each other in silence. In the same affectionate manner, every officer in the room marched up to, kissed, and parted with his General-in-Chief.

Such a scene of sorrow and weeping I had never before witnessed, and hope I may never be called upon to witness again. . . . Not a word was uttered to break the solemn silence . . . or to interrupt the tenderness of the . . . scene. [12]

Washington bids farewell to his officers at the end of the Revolutionary War. An eyewitness to the event, which took place at Fraunces' Tavern in New York, wrote, "Such a scene of sorrow and weeping I had never before witnessed."

"A Prodigious Crowd Had Assembled"

After leaving the gathering, Washington walked down to a barge that was waiting to take him to Philadelphia. Tallmadge wrote, "We all followed in mournful silence to the wharf, where a prodigious crowd had assembled to witness the departure of the man who, under God, had been the great agent in establishing the glory and independence of these United States."[13]

Every square foot of the wharf seemed to be occupied by New Yorkers who had come to see their beloved General. Some held up their little children to give them a glimpse of the tall hero who had led America's victorious struggle for independence. As he passed, his tense face suggested that only with the greatest effort was he able to keep his emotions under control.

Tallmadge described the final scene: "As soon as he was seated, the barge put off into the river, and when out in the stream, our great and beloved General waved his hat and bid us a silent adieu." The sober crowd waved in return, then strained to keep sight of him as he slowly vanished in the distance. "The simple thought that we were [parting] from the man who had conducted us through a long and bloody war, and under whose conduct the glory and independence of our country had been achieved, and that we should see his face no more in this world, seemed to me utterly [insupportable]."[14]

Chapter 27

Victory Over the
Mighty British Empire

Many people in 1783—both in America and in Europe— were stunned by America's victory over Great Britain. Since then, historians have expended barrels of ink in trying to explain how America could have bested the British in war. How did it happen?

The thirteen American colonies knew they faced stiff resistance when they declared their independence from Great Britain. They were well aware that bearding a vicious lion can be frightfully risky business. Nevertheless, by July 4, 1776, the Americans had already driven the king's troops from Boston; they had formed a small, stubborn army; and they had a commander in chief who had pledged his life and fortune to the cause. But no one could have foreseen the ultimate cost of that declaration of independence. Who could have known that the British would send wave after wave of soldiers to the colonies, trying to whip the rebels into subjection?

And who would ever have supposed that those feeble colonies would eventually be able to beat back the mightiest nation on earth?

On a superficial level, America won its victory by outlasting the British, by winning the last crucial battle at Yorktown, and by wearing down the British will to fight. But the British Empire was powerful and rich. Why did they give in to a much weaker foe? What really enabled the new American nation to win?

There is much to the story of Washington's glorious victory that commonly remains untold. Yet understanding these elements of the war and of its final peace help open the doors to a richer comprehension of General George Washington and his world.

The Strength of the British

The eighteenth-century British were a strong and prosperous people. Though some labored under the weight of oppressive poverty, many enjoyed a standard of living far superior to most of the rest of the world. In 1775 Great Britain claimed 8 million people. The American colonies had somewhat over 2 million, not counting the Indian tribes (which were considered independent nations). The British tallied some 2 million men they could call on to bear arms against America, ten times the potential military manpower of the Americans themselves (estimated at 300,000).

London in 1776 had 750,000 people. Philadelphia, the largest city in America (and second largest city in the British empire), had a mere 34,000. Other prominent cities were considerably smaller: New York City had 22,000; Boston, 15,000; Charleston, 12,000. With such a marked difference in population, it is a wonder indeed that the Americans could beat the British in a war. [1]

The wonder becomes even greater when the resources of the two combatants are compared. Great Britain boasted a carefully trained and well-equipped army and navy. The colonies had neither. British financial resources were literally a thousand times greater than those available to the colonies. The British currency was strong and vital. After the Americans declared their independence they were forced to rely on their own currency, which quickly inflated to near worthlessness. The British enjoyed a long tradition of skilled manufacturing. Colonial manufacturing was still in its infancy; Americans typically sent to Great Britain and its European neighbors for almost everything they needed. After the war began the British set up a naval blockade to keep essential war materials from the colonies. For a time this created even greater shortages in America.

But not all factors were on the side of the king. Though the Americans had few professional soldiers, they did have a number of men who had seen valuable combat service in the French and Indian War. They also received as volunteers a variety of officers well schooled in foreign service, such as Charles Lee, von Steuben, and de Kalb.

Geography also favored the Americans. The British had to send communications and supplies thousands of miles across an unfriendly ocean. The Americans were fighting on their own territory, in terrain that generally was familiar to them.

British Opposition

One element that confused and complicated the war in both nations was the mixed public opinion. The British, to a man, have commonly been painted as haters of American independence, while most colonial Americans have been pictured as unitedly for independence. Both representations are highly inaccurate.

In Great Britain the Parliament was generally in favor of pummeling the upstart Americans into submission. On the other hand, there were a number of eloquent dissenters, primarily from the Whig party. Their names are worthy of remembrance: Edmund Burke, one of the most clear-sighted philosophers of his day; William Pitt, the Earl of Chatham, who had emerged from retirement to fight his own battles in the war, using Parliament as his battleground; Charles James Fox, who was dismissed from Lord North's cabinet for his public denunciations of British policy; John Wilkes, champion of the common people, who had twice been imprisoned and had to live for years in exile because of his opposition to the king. These men, and dozens of others, spoke clearly and forcefully in behalf of the Americans, not often advocating independence, but certainly decrying war and proffering the idea of an open British commonwealth from which all would benefit. Yet they were always in the minority; their views were invariably the views of the opposition.

Nevertheless, their eloquence had its influence. The many common people in England who were opposed to the war were delighted to hear their views expressed in Parliament. Most such commoners did not approve of American independence, but they stoutly disagreed with an expensive, bloody war to keep the colonies servile. In contrast, British merchant barons, who faced tremendous losses if the Americans became independent, shuddered when leaders of the opposition rose to speak. [2]

British Recruitment Woes

The mixed popular opinion was reflected in the resistance to recruiting. Parliament had approved an army of 55,000 men to fight the Americans, but a draft was illegal and most of the king's "loyal subjects" were not interested in fighting an unpopular war in the American wilderness. The British army constantly fell short of its full allotment of soldiers, and its troops all too often were England's "undesirables," having come from the persistently poor or criminal classes, or having been illegally impressed into service.

The men who did enter the army's ranks faced a life of inadequate food (though their rations were impressive compared to what American soldiers often received) and meager pay, along with a somewhat dubious adventure. Their first great challenge was the dangerous Atlantic crossing (another powerful deterrent to enlistments). Once on board, the soldier "and his fellows were 'pressed and packed like sardines' in bunks between decks, so that in storm, with portholes made tight, they gasped for air as if 'buried alive in coffins.'"

> These were the horrors of the night, but the day was often worse. Kicked and caned by the mate or sergeant, branded, pilloried and starved, the soldier arrived at the voyage's end only to be robbed by the purser or paymaster.... For food, the soldier on a transport had oatmeal, often sour and weevily, boiled in ship water full of worms.... His daily bread was often full of vermin, his bacon sometimes four or five years old.... It was under such conditions that English armies must be flung three thousand miles to fight their fellow subjects. [3]

If the winds were right, the journey would last two months. Otherwise, it could go two or three weeks longer.

Some prominent British military leaders actually refused to serve in the war. Sir Jeffrey Amherst, the distinguished commander in chief of all the British land forces, was repeatedly begged to oversee the war in America, but he refused the king's offers. Admiral Keppel of the Royal Navy likewise decided against battling in American waters. Lord Frederick Cavendish, a seasoned lieutenant general who had fought with distinction in the Seven Years' War, also sat out the war with America. Even General William Howe promised his parliamentary constituents that he would not accept a post in America; when he finally did so it was with lingering reluctance and out of a firm sense of public duty. [4]

The British, therefore, with their much larger population and vast resources, were greatly limited in what they could do. The king wanted a war; the Parliament wanted a war; certain classes of citizens wanted a war. But the broad spectrum of the people wanted peace, being unwilling to fight in such a cause. The apparent advantages of population and resources were in reality advantages only on paper.

Loyalists in America

While the British were engaged in their great debates, the Americans also were having theirs. Many Americans were violently opposed to separation from England, and they were eager to stand on the side of their king.

Loyalists have typically been presented as treasonous and unpatriotic. It is implied that they were weak in character and lacking in moral courage. Such a view is unfair, of course. The loyalists, or Tories, were as patriotic and moral as their rebel counterparts—they simply rested their loyalty in the king. The Tories insisted it was the rebels who were treasonous. Had Britain won the war, historical scholars probably would have agreed with them.

How many Tories were there in America? It is difficult to tell for certain—no official counts were ever taken. The best estimates suggest that a full third of the colonists were loyal to the king. Another third were active in backing the revolution. The final third were either undecided or decidedly neutral.[5]

The Tories generally followed geographical and class patterns. They were stronger in the middle states than in New England, stronger in the south than in the north, and strongest of all in New York. The greatest number seemed to be wealthy merchants and the landed gentry, who had the most to lose from a war. However, many notable exceptions can be found (John Hancock and George Washington, for example).[6]

The political differences between Americans led to extreme emotional divisiveness. A large number of Tories—some estimates say fifty thousand—were so committed to Great Britain that they actually joined the British to fight against their fellow Americans. Although the number of loyalists who served their king in the war is impressive, it quickly pales when compared to the 250,000 Americans who fought for freedom and independence. Eighty to one hundred thousand Tories left the country either during or after the war.[7] Most of them fled to Canada.

Yet the British reliance on loyalists proved to be more of a detriment than a help. Too often a British general planned his campaign around the expected support of the loyalist population in the area—as Cornwallis did in the south—only to be bitterly disappointed by the local response.

There were also a number of reasons why this was so. Foremost among these was the fact that, despite their anger over the rebellion, the loyalists remained relatively unorganized throughout the war. The patriots, on the other hand, were years ahead when it came to organization. Most of them could trace their lineage of resistance back to the Sons of Liberty of the 1760s, the committees of correspondence, the minutemen.

In many ways, life was a horror for loyalists during the war. They were almost everywhere persecuted, violently subjected to tarring and feathering, whipping, fines, confiscation of property, and banishment. As the war progressed, most of the colonies passed laws requiring loyalty oaths. Under threat of prosecution, a suspected Tory was required to swear, before God, that he was loyal to the new American government. The British military authorities responded in kind, requiring those under their jurisdiction to declare absolute loyalty to the king. [8]

Opposition to the war persisted on both sides of the Atlantic throughout the entire revolution, though for widely different reasons. Loyalists in America wished to preserve their status as English citizens, even though they resented the abuses which had reduced Americans to second-class status. Meanwhile, dissenters in Parliament were troubled about the morality and advisability of the war, speaking out repeatedly and forcefully in their effort to change the prevailing policy.

These two forces—loyalists in America and dissenters in England—did not quite counterbalance each other. The dissenters effectively prevented the king's armies from recruiting as many soldiers as they needed. And the popular British outcry about financial losses, combined with fears of invasion from France and Spain, served to force the king and his ministers to reconsider their policies. At the same time, although the loyalists could be loudly vocal, they were not nearly as effective in America as their opponents were.

Help from France and Germany

Even during the early stages of the war, both countries felt compelled to seek help from friendly allies. The British were unable to persuade enough of their own men to fight the war, so they contracted with several German princes to buy the services of their soldiers. As a result, the British forces were usually composed of about 50 percent British soldiers, 35 percent German mercenaries, and 15 percent loyalist volunteers. [9]

The Americans, on the other hand, diligently sought the help of France. At first, the French limited their help to secretly provided funds and supplies. Later, when the Americans showed themselves to be both persistent and successful, France openly recognized American independence and sent thousands of troops and a fleet of ships to provide active naval support. The Americans also received a small measure of financial support from Spain. (Holland helped the United States in the form of loans, but the war was essentially over before the money arrived.)

The reinforcements from the French came as angels to the beleaguered Washington. While 1778 saw the largest number of Continental soldiers ever to serve at a given time during the war—35,000 divided among several commands—the combined army was typically much smaller. The total number of soldiers, both regular and militia, serving throughout the war is estimated to have been about 250,000. [10] Most of these served for brief periods, some as little as thirty days, then were released or simply went home. Because Congress would not allow Washington to field a permanent professional army, the Americans were consistently outnumbered by the more stable British forces. The arrival of the French helped to even the odds.

As a general rule, neither the French nor the Germans spoke English. (The Germans were often called Hessians, since most were mercenaries of the Landgrave of Hesse-Cassel.)

Both the French and the Germans contributed to the war in their own unique way. The French, motivated by their long-standing hatred of the British, were effective in forcing the war to a conclusion at Yorktown. By contrast, the Germans, though excellent professional soldiers, were serving primarily for duty, simply obeying the command of their rulers. (They were paid the same as their British counterparts, but that was no significant amount. The German rulers, however, were paid handsomely.) German mercenaries bore their part in strengthening the British forces, but they never generated enough additional momentum to help the British win.

Of the 30,000 German mercenaries who left their homeland, only 60 percent returned. Of the remainder, 7,754 were killed either in battle or by disease, while 5,000 deserted to make a new life in America. [11]

Battles Outside the Colonies

With allied countries entering the fray, it was inevitable that the war would erupt on other fronts. The British enlisted the help of the Indians and opened brutal warfare on the western frontier. At one time more than five thousand American troops were diverted from fighting the British to put down the depredations of the Indians in the west. Some Canadians—though far too few for England's liking—signed up to fight under Burgoyne in the north.

Most of the battles occurring outside the colonies, however, were on the high seas. Great Britain boasted the most powerful navy in the world, but France was eager to challenge her whenever they met. French and British fleets clashed furiously off the coast of Europe and in the West Indies. In 1779 France and Spain even plotted to conquer the

British Isles themselves; and they might have succeeded if the French had not stumbled through a series of ill-advised decisions. Fighting occurred even in faraway India.

Americans also sought to wage war on the high seas. John Paul Jones won his spectacular engagement with a larger and stronger British ship through sheer doggedness. More significant were the efforts of American privateers, raiders who had congressional approval to prey on British merchant ships. Approximately a thousand American privateers, with crews averaging one hundred men, took to the seas during the years of the war, capturing six hundred British merchant ships and their cargoes, worth $18 million. They also captured sixteen British warships. [12]

The immediate effect of the privateers was relatively small. But over the years British merchants became increasingly wary about setting sail, anxious about further financial losses they might suffer. Fearing bankruptcy, many eventually raised a loud outcry for an end of the war, adding their voices to those of the Whigs.

The Horrors of War

Boiling at the center of all the issues surrounding the war was the bloody conflict itself. Logistics, political philosophies, conflict of personalities—all these were forgotten when enemy faced enemy with bared bayonets.

In battle there is always the smell of fear, the dripping sweat, the filthy clothes, the gray, pungent smoke from exploding shells. And there are fleeting thoughts of mother, wife, and children, images of tall-grass pastures, a warm fireside, perhaps a bustling merchant's shop or one's faithful dog. But when muskets roar a scant hundred yards away and balls whistle past one's ears, a single, consuming passion takes over the mind—the instinct for survival.

What were a soldier's deepest feelings in the Revolutionary War? For the British, the prime emotion was often a deep and chilling fear: "I hope I get out of here alive." The Americans experienced the same terror, but it was mixed with another powerful feeling: "My homeland is at risk, my freedom and peace."

These contrasting emotions and attitudes played a critical role in the outcome of the war. The fears and thoughts the Americans experienced in the heat of battle gave them a subtle edge over their opponents and helped many Americans to persevere through the long and weary years of war.

The methods of fighting wars in the eighteenth century were brutal and personal. The prime weapons were the musket and the bayonet, both of which were used in close contact with the enemy. The musket could kill a man at three hundred yards, but only with a lucky shot. To hit the target with any consistent accuracy, the soldier had to be within fifty yards of his enemy.

The typical order of battle involved the following: The men marched onto the field to the cadence of the drums, which were placed in the rear. When the infantry were about fifty yards from the enemy, at a command from the drums they raised their muskets, pointed (but did not aim), and fired. Aiming was ineffective and was discouraged—commanders sought to weaken the enemy by the force of repeated volleys rather than by careful shooting. Quantity rather than quality was the desired object. The musket could be reloaded and fired successively about three times per minute. When the front line was broken by wounded or killed soldiers, a back-up line was ready to step into the gaps.

All this occurred with the enemy close enough that one

could see his eyes, scrutinize the expression on his face, hear his curses and prayers. It was not a form of battle for the squeamish.

After two or three volleys, the soldiers rushed the enemy with their bayonets. From this point on the battle became even more personal, the infantry entering into sword-to-sword, bayonet-to-bayonet, hand-to-hand combat. Each soldier could feel the resistance as the bayonet went into the flesh of his opponent; he could feel the heat of his opponent's breath on his cheek; he could hear the dying man's exclamation (in his own language, unless he was fighting Frenchmen or Hessians); he could see the red stain growing in the enemy's gut, the blood dripping from his own bayonet. [13]

It is no wonder that thousands of raw militia, not being accustomed to hard camp life nor being prepared for the rigors of battle, quickly found a short route to the safety of their own hearths.

In the eight years of war, forty-four hundred American men were killed in battle by the methods just described, as well as from the grape and mortar from artillery. Another sixty-two hundred suffered nonfatal wounds. Many of these were sent to the hospital, which too often was little more than a living hell for the dying. [14]

The Deadly Hospital

Generally, only the severely wounded were sent to a hospital. In many cases the wounded were already suffering from the malnutrition and disease that stalked the camps, and their distress was further compounded by the hospital itself. Staffs were poorly trained, and some were not trained at all. In 1775 the colonies could find only about thirty-five hundred doctors, and of these only two hundred had medical degrees. [15]

In the hands of such practitioners, it is no exaggeration to say that the soldiers were sometimes safer on the battlefield than in the hospital. A man already gasping from the pain of a wound would be carved open with no anesthetic and no sterilization. Amputation was often the only remedy for limbs mutilated by the large-diameter, three-quarter-inch musket balls. After surgery, if the man did not bleed to death, he might die of shock. If he did not die of shock, he could easily catch infection from dirty surgical instruments. If he did not die of infection, he would be subject to the many diseases present in and around the hospital—principally smallpox, but also typhus, mumps, diphtheria, dysentery, malaria, measles, and scurvy. As one observer wrote, "It would make a heart of stone melt to hear the moans and see the distresses of the sick and dying."[16]

During the eight years of war, sixty thousand American soldiers died from disease, exposure, or malnutrition. It is a marvel that so many survived.[17]

Prisoners of War

Those who escaped death and the hospitals were at risk of being captured. The British captured some ten thousand men after major battles; the Americans captured about fifteen thousand. But neither side was prepared to hold prisoners of war. What could be done with all the captives?

The Americans handled the problem by setting large numbers loose on parole or exchanging them for patriot prisoners. The British, on the other hand, transformed churches and warehouses and barracks into prisons. When those became overcrowded, the redcoats began to place their captives in prison ships. In theory, they thought, the ships would be cleaner and more secure against escape. In reality they were neither. The ships were far too crowded to be clean. And any soldier who could swim—and who was not too weakened by fatigue, disease, malnutrition, and abuse—could often find a means of escape.

The prison ships soon became evil death ships. The British were not intentionally seeking to be cruel, but they killed more Americans through their flawed prison system than they did on the battlefield: between eight and ten thousand Americans died in the stench and disease of the prison ships anchored in the Hudson off New York City. [18]

The diary of one soldier provides a stark description of the circumstances on board the transport *Grosvenor*. He was put on the ship on December 2, 1776, with about five hundred other men:

> Friday, 13th of December 1776. We drawed bisd [bisquits?] and butter. A little water broth. We now see nothing but the mercy of God to intercede for us. Sorrowful times, all faces look pale, discouraged, discouraged.
>
> Saturday, 14th. We drawed bisd. Times look dark. Deaths prevail among us.... At night suffer cold and hunger. Nights very long and tiresome, weakness prevails.
>
> Sunday, 15th. Drawed bisd. Paleness attends all faces. The melancholiest day I ever saw. At noon drawed meat and peas. Sunday gone and comfort. As sorrowful times as I ever saw.
>
> Monday, 16th of December 1776.... Sorrow increases. The tender mercies of men are cruelty.
>
> Tuesday, 17th. Drawed bisd. At noon meat and rice. No fire. Suffer with cold and hunger. We are treated worse than cattle and hogs....
>
> Sunday, 22nd. Last night nothing but groans all night of sick and dying. Men amazing to behold. Such hardness,

sickness prevails fast. Deaths multiply. Drawed bisd. At noon meat and peas. Weather cold. Sunday gone and no comfort. Had nothing but sorrow and sadness. All faces sad.

Monday, 23rd. Drawed bisd and butter.... About 20 gone from here today that enlisted in the king's service. [These were deserters who accepted the offer to escape the horrible conditions by changing allegiances, a not uncommon practice.] Times look very dark. But we are in hopes of an exchange. One dies almost every day....

Wednesday, 25th. [Christmas Day] Last night was a sorrowful night. Nothing but groans and cries all night.... Sad times.

Thursday, 26th. Last night was spent in dying groans and cries. I now grow poorly.... Very cold and stormy.

Friday, 27th. Three men of our battalion died last night. The most melancholiest night I ever saw. Smallpox increases fast. This day I was blooded. Drawed bisd and butter. Stomach all gone....

Saturday, 28th. Drawed bisd.... Ensign Smith [an American] come here with orders to take me ashore [in a prisoner exchange]. We got to shore about sunset. I now feel glad. Coffee and bread and cheese....[19]

Britain's inhumane treatment of their prisoners had a powerful effect on the minds and hearts of Americans. Escaped or exchanged prisoners often rejoined the army with bitter hatred of the enemy. And when others heard of the atrocious prison conditions, they fought with greater vigor, both to avoid capture and to avenge the wrongs done to their American brothers.

The Place of America's Commander

In the preceding pages we have discussed many elements that combined to help the Americans win the war. All were important, but none of these factors would have amounted to much without the most important factor of all: the tenacity and courage with which George Washington wore the redcoats down through eight long years of war.

In the two centuries which have passed since the British defeat at Yorktown, historians and scholars have provided their evaluation of Washington's merits as a general. The cynicism of modern scholarship is reflected in the writings of a small school of historians who sneer at the traditional portrayal of Washington as a truly great man. They claim he would have quickly been defeated by any opposing general worthy of the title. Washington did not win the war, they say—the British simply bungled themselves to a loss. Of course, other historians hold the opposite position, ranking General Washington with Alexander the Great, Hannibal, Julius Caesar, and Napoleon.

What kind of military leader was George Washington? His record during the war gives a clear answer.

When the British army entered America, its commanders came as skilled professionals expecting to defeat the rank American amateurs in short order. Their approach to victory was the traditional one: push the enemy from point to point until you have conquered the territory in question. Essentially they came to fight a war over real estate. With that as an overall strategy they began to drive forward, ever successful, pushing Washington and his beleaguered army from Long Island to Manhattan, from lower Manhattan to Harlem Heights, from there to White Plains. They forced him from Fort Washington and Fort Lee. They occupied Philadelphia, the capital city of the entire nation. By all rights they should have been winning the war.

Washington, on the other hand, was determined but not so

self-assured. Feeling inadequate, inexperienced, and un-schooled, he was overwhelmed by the task before him. What strategy should he follow? How could he and his ragged army survive against the strong and disciplined troops they faced?

The Greatness of General Washington

It was in that emotional setting that Washington's genius began to bud and blossom. He studied military texts from every source. He consulted with his most experienced offi-cers, principally British-trained Horatio Gates and Charles Lee. He listened carefully, observed, meditated, adapted, re-vised, and studied some more. He moved ahead with what he had—raw, untrained, undisciplined troops—and lost battle after battle, almost lost his army, but learned from experience and tried again.

General Washington during the Revolutionary War.

He learned that a war can be won by tactics different from those used by his opponents. He used his militia, unreliable otherwise, to harass small British foraging parties and Tory volunteers. He used expert sharpshooters as snipers to slow the movement of major British marches and to attack smaller outposts. He used his main army to strike the enemy at their weak points, always avoiding a head-to-head confrontation until conditions seemed particularly favorable. He knew that to succeed he must jealously preserve his army and wait for the ideal moment to assail the redcoats. He learned that the superior mobility of his army was vital to that effort.

Therein lay Washington's genius. He was not a great general in the European style of fighting, nor were his troops adequate for such a task. But he gradually developed creative ways to work with his terrain, his troops, his lack of funds and resources. By the sheer force of his personality he kept the army together for an amazing eight years, often with inadequate food and clothing and nonexistent pay. The British were unable to adapt to the unique conditions in America. But Washington, recognizing his inexperience, learned assiduously, adapted his new knowledge to special circumstances, and moved ahead with courageous tenacity.

Washington was facing the best Britain had to offer. No one has suggested that William Howe, John Burgoyne, Henry Clinton, or Lord Cornwallis were inexperienced and few have claimed they were incompetent. They had learned well the craft of generalship. But they knew only what they had been taught, and they discovered to their chagrin that they were unable to apply their knowledge in America. As a result, rather than attempt other approaches, they pulled back. Washington, in contrast, was a great adapter. When one approach did not work he tried another. Through trial and error he found ingenious solutions to the immense, almost insurmountable, problems that faced him throughout the war.

By the end of the war most of Washington's expert

advisers had long since vanished. Gates alone remained, and he had been disgraced by his cowardly flight from Camden after abandoning his army. In the place of such advisers Washington had substituted men who shared his desire and ability to learn, men like Nathanael Greene, perhaps second only to Washington in military ability; Henry Knox, who so wanted to learn the art of artillery that he spent countless hours with his books; Lafayette and Hamilton, both very young officers who showed brilliance at critical times.

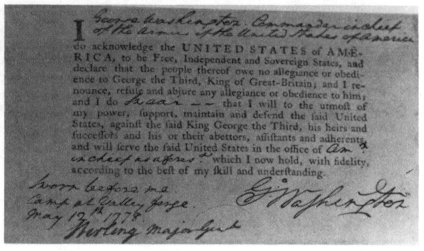

Washington's oath of allegiance, signed in May 1778. During the Revolutionary War so many Americans remained loyal to Great Britain that it was sometimes difficult to tell the patriots from the loyalists. The oath of allegiance was one way to make the distinction.

So we conclude by returning to our original question. How did the Americans win the war against such heavy odds and a far superior force? The reasons are varied and numerous, but rising above them all is the figure of George Washington. Washington was the force that kept a ragtag army together through unthinkable trials; Washington's was the mind that saw the way to victory. With faith and steadfastness he varied neither to the right nor to the left. He pursued the ideal of liberty despite the dreadful trials of hunger, death, and freezing winter, despite mutiny and inconstant militia, despite deceit and severe financial loss. If Washington had done nothing more than lead his countrymen to victory, if his public life had begun and ended with the turbulent years of the Revolutionary War, his name would deserve to be celebrated and revered for countless generations to come.[20]

Victory with the Help of Providence

While historians regard General George Washington as the primary reason why the Americans were able to win the war, Washington himself saw a higher source of victory. Again and again, in letters to friends, acquaintances, governors, and members of Congress, Washington reiterated his conviction that America was successful because God willed it so.

In 1778, for example, he wrote, "Providence has a ... claim to my humble and grateful thanks for its protection and direction of me through the many difficult and intricate scenes which this contest has produced, and for the constant interposition in our behalf when the clouds were heaviest and seemed ready to burst upon us."[21]

Later, to the Reverend William Gordon, Washington repeated the same idea. He wrote: "We have ... abundant reason to thank Providence for its many favorable interpositions in our behalf. It has at times been my only dependence, for all other resources seemed to have failed us."[22]

After the war was long past he continued to voice the same feelings. "I was but the humble agent of favoring Heaven," he wrote in 1789, "whose benign interference was so often manifested in our behalf, and to whom the praise of victory alone is due."[23]

And in 1795, as his second term as President began to wind down, he reminded his countrymen that "to the great Ruler of events, not to any exertions of mine, is to be ascribed the favorable termination of our late contest for liberty. I never considered the fortunate issue of any measure in any other light than as the ordering of a kind Providence."[24]

Chapter 28

Whatever Became of the Leaders in the War?

After the war was over, the characters who had long dominated America's center stage quickly dispersed and began pursuing their own private paths. What became of these prime actors in the Revolutionary War, these men who had been so much a part of Washington's life during the extended years of conflict? Here is an alphabetical roll call, separated into the British and American camps.

Leaders on the British Side

Benedict Arnold (1741–1801) became one of Washington's foremost field commanders in the early days of the war. But in 1779 he turned redcoat and not only received a huge bribe, but was commissioned a brigadier general in the British army. He thereafter led a series of raids in Virginia's countryside during the final stages of the war. He sailed to

London in December 1781 and began to advise the king and his ministers on American matters. This assignment was a great disappointment to Arnold. He received little respect, and in 1785 moved to New Brunswick, Canada. He set himself up as a merchant shipper in an effort to make a quick fortune, but failed and returned to England in 1791. It was there he died ten years later, deeply disappointed, deeply in debt, and plagued by lawsuits.

John "Gentleman Johnny" Burgoyne (1722-92), after surrendering at Saratoga, was returned on parole to England, promising never to fight against America again. Although temporarily disgraced, Burgoyne served briefly as commander in chief in Ireland. This was essentially a political assignment and not at all satisfying to his own sense of importance. He therefore turned from politics to the literary life. In 1786 he enjoyed a major success with his play *The Heiress,* which went through ten editions in one year and was even performed on the Continent. It may be of interest to some that between the years 1782 and 1788 he fathered four illegitimate children by singer Susan Caulfield. His eldest son by Miss Caulfield became Field Marshal Sir John Fox Burgoyne, who served as chief engineer in the Battle of New Orleans in 1815.

Archibald Campbell (1739-91), who captured Savannah in 1778 and Augusta, Georgia, a month later, had earlier been a prisoner of war for two years. He resumed active duty after being exchanged for Ethan Allen. Following his singular success in the south he returned on leave to England, and subsequently served as governor of Jamaica. He was knighted in 1785.

Sir Guy Carleton (1724-1808) was the last commander in chief of the British forces, having been appointed in February 1782. He returned to his post as Canadian governor after the war and served until 1796. He then retired to England, where he eventually died. Many military historians feel he was the most capable of all the British commanders but had the misfortune of entering the war too late to genuinely prove himself.

Henry Clinton (1738?-95) served as the British commander in chief longer than any other officer during the war (1778-82). He was relieved of his command in 1782 and returned to England as the unhappy scapegoat for the Yorktown defeat. In 1790 he was reelected to Parliament, and in 1794 he was appointed governor of Gibraltar. He died a year later while serving in that position.

Charles Cornwallis (1738-1805) was the commander who surrendered at Yorktown. He was exchanged in 1782 for the American envoy Henry Laurens, who had been held for some time in the Tower of London. In 1786 Cornwallis was appointed governor general of India, and in 1797 he was made governor general of Ireland. In 1805 he was reassigned to India, but died shortly after arriving.

Thomas Gage (1719?-87) served as commander in chief from 1763 to 1775 and as governor of Massachusetts from 1774 to 1775. He was removed from both of these positions following the Battle of Bunker Hill, wherein he lost half of his assault troops—around 1,000 killed or wounded. He continued in military service in England until his final illness and death in 1787.

King George III (1738-1820) reigned as the English sovereign from 1760 to 1811. He suffered brief fits of insanity after 1765 and in 1788 became so ill that he was fully expected to die. He recovered both his sanity and his popularity, but lost his mind again in 1811 and never recovered. His son, the Prince of Wales (later King George IV), became the regent.

George III also became deaf and blind before he finally died.

Richard "Black Dick" Howe (1726–99) was admiral and commander in chief of the Royal Navy in America from 1776 to 1778. Interestingly, he was much more prominent in British history than his brother William. After leaving America in 1778 he went into a brief retirement because he refused to serve longer under the existing British ministry. Later he commanded the navy in the English Channel, a vital and important post. He was appointed First Lord of the Admiralty from 1783 to 1788 and was named both baron and earl before his death.

William Howe (1729–1814) was commander in chief of the British army in America from 1775 to 1778. After capturing Philadelphia, he and his brother, Admiral Howe, resigned their posts because of their deep disgust with the decisions of the British leaders. Back in England, he was promoted to full general in 1793 and was given an important command in England when Napoleon threatened the island. In 1799, after the death of his brother, he succeeded to the Irish title of Fifth Viscount Howe. He died in 1814 after a long and painful illness.

Baron von Knyphausen (1716–1800) came to America as commander in chief of the Hessian mercenaries. He was a veteran of battles at Fort Washington, Brandywine, and Monmouth. After losing an eye, he retired from service in 1782 and returned to Germany. He subsequently served as military governor of Cassel.

Lord Rawdon (Francis Rawdon-Hastings) (1754–1826) was prominent in the British southern campaign against Greene. He was captured by a French privateer on his way home to England in 1781 and was held prisoner for many months. In 1783 he was named a baron; ten years later he succeeded his father as an earl. That same year, 1793, he served as a major general in the war against Napoleon, leading ten thousand men in Belgium and the Netherlands. From 1813 to 1826 he distinguished himself as governor general and commander in chief of India.

Bunastre "Bloody Ban" Tarleton (1754–1833) was the hard-riding cavalry leader of the Tories in the south, the man who "gave no quarter." He was captured at the Yorktown surrender and was thereafter returned to England on parole. In 1781 he published a history of his involvement in the war, speaking very critically of Lord Cornwallis. He was in and out of Parliament from 1790 to 1806, and in 1812 he was made a full general. In 1820 he was knighted.

Leaders on the American Side

Ethan Allen (1738–89) was the leader of the "Green Mountain Boys" and captor of Fort Ticonderoga in May 1775. He was captured in Montreal later that same year. After two years as a prisoner in England and British-occupied New York City, he was exchanged for Colonel Archibald Campbell. In 1779 he published *A Narrative of Col. Allen's Captivity*, which was followed by a number of other books and pamphlets.

John Cadwalader (1742–86) was one of the commanders who failed in his assignment to cross the Delaware to assist Washington at Trenton, but he proved more helpful at Princeton. He also fought at Brandywine, Germantown, and Monmouth. In 1778, while defending the honor of George Washington, he fought a duel with Thomas Conway and shot him in the mouth. After the war he became a state legislator in Maryland. He died at the relatively young age of forty-three, leaving a large fortune.

George Clinton (1739–1812) was a general of the Continental army and governor of the state of New York for six consecutive terms beginning in 1777. He later opposed the new Constitution on the issue of states' rights and the absence of a bill of rights. He was elected Vice President of the United States in 1804, serving with Thomas Jefferson. He was elected James Madison's Vice President in 1808; he died in 1812 while still in office.

Thomas Conway (1733–1800?) was an outspoken critic of George Washington and a key member of the Conway Cabal. As indicated above, he was shot in a duel with John Cadwalader and was severely wounded in the mouth. Thinking himself mortally wounded, Conway rushed off an awkward letter of apology to Washington. He later recovered, however, and in 1779 served as an officer with the French army in Flanders. In 1787 he was named governor general of the French forces in India. Two years later he commanded all French forces beyond the Cape of Good Hope. By 1793, he was back in France, but he was compelled to flee from the revolutionaries because of his royalist affiliations. He died in exile around 1800.

Comte d'Estaing (1729–94) was the rather inept French admiral who served in America from 1778 to 1780 and then returned to France to argue that the government should send over a larger force. His counsel, combined with that of Lafayette, influenced the French to send Rochambeau with his thousands. D'Estaing was later elected to the Assembly of Notables in 1787 and became commandant of the National Guard in 1789. He testified in behalf of Marie Antoinette during the French Revolution, which contributed to his own execution in 1794.

Horatio Gates (1728–1806) was a former British officer. He was the nominal commander of the great victory at Saratoga, taking more than his share of credit. He retired in disgrace for two years after his shameful retreat from Camden. Finally he was cleared by Congress in 1782 and rejoined the army for the closing days of the war. His wife died in 1784, and in 1786 he married a woman with a large fortune. To his credit, he used much of this money to assist impoverished veterans. Four years later he freed his slaves and moved from Virginia to New York City, where he died in 1806.

Comte de Grasse (1722–88) was the French admiral who was instrumental in the successful siege of Yorktown. During a subsequent naval battle with the British in late 1781, he was captured in the West Indies. While on parole in France he helped to arrange the preliminary phase of the peace negotiations between France and England. He died on the eve of the French Revolution, in January 1788. During the revolution his home was destroyed by mobs, and four cannon from Yorktown, which were given to him as gifts from Congress, were dragged off and melted down into revolutionary coin.

Nathanael Greene (1742–86) was Washington's most trusted general by the end of the war. He returned home in 1783 to disentangle a web of serious financial troubles which had accumulated during the war. He eventually lost his property in his home state of Rhode Island and was forced to move to Georgia to live on land donated by that state's government. He died of sunstroke in 1786 at the age of forty-four.

Alexander Hamilton (1757–1804) was the fiery young aide to Washington during the war. He served in Congress from 1782 to 1783 and then practiced law in New York. He pushed constantly for a new federal constitution, then worked tirelessly to get it ratified. More than half of the *Federalist Papers* came from his pen. He was the first Secretary of the

Treasury, from 1789 to 1795, then resumed his law practice. He died at age forty-seven following a duel with U.S. Vice President Aaron Burr.

Henry Knox (1750–1806) was the three-hundred-pound chief of artillery for the American forces. He briefly succeeded Washington as commander in chief in 1783–84. From 1785 to 1794 he was Secretary of War. He was the father of twelve children. He choked to death on a chicken bone at the age of fifty-six.

Marquis de Lafayette (1757–1834) was the beloved French volunteer in the American army who became a commander under Washington. After the battle at Yorktown in December 1781, he returned to his homeland. Throughout the years he retained close ties with many of his friends in America, particularly Washington. He greatly assisted Thomas Jefferson while the latter was serving as U.S. minister to France. In 1787 he was named a member of the Assembly of Notables, and in 1789 he was appointed commander of the newly established National Guard. That same year he saved the royal family from the Paris mob. In 1792, while serving as commander of the 52,000-man Army of the Center during the war against Austria, he was captured and held in a dungeon for five years. He was liberated by Napoleon in 1797. In subsequent years he declined high honors offered to him by both Napoleon and Jefferson. In 1824 and 1825 he toured the United States and was celebrated with elaborate festivities wherever he went.

Charles Lee (1731–82) was Washington's second in command who fraternized with the British and led the near-disastrous retreat at Monmouth. He returned to his Virginia estate in 1779 and, after a court martial, was officially dismissed from service a year later. He then moved to Philadelphia, where he died in 1782.

Henry "Light-Horse Harry" Lee (1756–1818) was one of the great American cavalrymen. In early 1781 he was forced to leave the service as a result of severe battle fatigue. He married his cousin, and served in Congress from 1785 to 1788. Later, during the 1790s, he was governor of Virginia for three years. He commanded fifteen thousand troops during the Whiskey Rebellion, and returned to Congress in 1799. At Washington's death he described his former commander in chief as "first in war, first in peace, and first in the hearts of his countrymen."[1] Through bad investments he sank heavily into debt and was eventually thrown into debtor's prison. In 1813 he went to the Caribbean to recover from an illness and stayed for several years. He died on his way back home. Lee's famous son, Robert E. Lee, was born in 1807.

Benjamin Lincoln (1733–1810) was Washington's second in command at the siege of Yorktown. He became Secretary of War from 1781 to 1783, and led Massachusetts troops against Shays's Rebellion in 1787. In 1788 Lincoln worked for the ratification of the new Constitution; and in 1789 he became collector of the port of Boston. He was a member of the American Academy of Arts and Sciences and of the Massachusetts Historical Society.

King Louis XVI (1754–93), who generously approved French aid to the Americans during the Revolutionary War, was guillotined in the Reign of Terror during the French Revolution.

Daniel "Old Wagoner" Morgan (1736–1802) was the leader of the crack-shooting frontiersmen and the victorious commander at the battle of Cowpens. He commanded militia troops during the Whiskey Rebellion of 1794 and was elected to Congress in 1797.

Thomas Paine (1737–1809), who inflamed America with his writings, was impoverished by his sacrifices to the war cause. To assist him, New York gave him a confiscated estate after the war, where he lived until 1787. In that year he moved to France to champion the budding cause of freedom there. He published *The Rights of Man* in 1791 and 1792. By 1793 it had sold 200,000 copies. In December 1793 he was imprisoned as an English alien and remained in prison for eleven months. He was finally rescued by U.S. minister James Monroe. After attacking organized religion and the hero status of George Washington he fell into disrepute and spent his final years, in America, in poverty and ostracism.

Israel "Old Put" Putnam (1718–90) was the strength of the American leadership at Bunker Hill and commander of a wing on Long Island. He suffered a paralytic stroke in 1779 and retired from the service.

Comte de Rochambeau (1725–1807), commander of the French forces in America, became a Marshal of France in 1791. During the Reign of Terror he was arrested and slated for execution, but his life was spared by the sudden death of the murderous Robespierre, which ended the widespread use of the guillotine.

Philip Schuyler (1733–1804), commander in the northern department, resigned in 1779, disgruntled by the lack of congressional support. He held public office continuously from 1780 to 1798, including membership in Congress and on the Board of Commissioners for Indian Affairs. He became the father-in-law of Alexander Hamilton in 1780 when Hamilton married his daughter, Elizabeth Schuyler.

Baron von Steuben (1730–94) helped the American troops

learn how to effectively fight the trained British. He did not return to his native land, but became an American citizen in 1783. Always a bachelor, he struggled under heavy financial burdens until Alexander Hamilton and other friends rescued him in 1786.

Lord Stirling (1726–83) was present as a subordinate commander at most of Washington's major battles (including Long Island, Trenton, Brandywine, Germantown, and Monmouth). He died of gout shortly before reaching his fifty-seventh birthday, still in the service of his country.

John Sullivan (1740–95), who led columns at battles from Trenton to Germantown, resigned because of poor health in 1779. He subsequently served in Congress, as governor of New Hampshire, and as a federal judge. [2]

Chapter 29

The General Retires

With the British finally gone from America's shores the American army disbanded, the farmer returning to his farm, the merchant to his shop.

Washington, too, prepared to lay aside his sword. His thoughts were filled with memories of the war's long march through the eight previous years, but his heart rejoiced as he contemplated his return to beautiful Mount Vernon. He rode south to Annapolis, where Congress was sitting, to formally resign and surrender his commission. On the way he stopped in Philadelphia to settle accounts with the comptroller of the treasury, James Milligan. Washington had refused the congressional offer of a salary, but kept detailed accounts for the agreed-upon reimbursement of his expenditures. An audit showed that his record keeping was honest, accurate, and complete. Along with his records, Washington delivered to

Milligan the $27,770 of public money that remained in the military chest.

On December 22, a great ball was held in honor of the commander in chief. His spirits were high, the music was exhilarating, and the General did not miss a dance.

"This Last Solemn Act of My Official Life"

On the twenty-third, exactly at noon, he presented himself at the door of the congressional chamber of the Maryland State House. The nineteen or twenty Congressmen who remained at the session sat soberly in their places with their hats on. After Washington was escorted into the room, the doors of the chamber were opened and leading Maryland citizens were allowed to enter. They soon filled the gallery to overflowing.

Washington resigns his commission to Congress, December 1783. The active fighting had ceased some two years before, and the peace treaty had been signed for months, but Washington remained on duty until the British finally departed America's shores. (Painting by contemporary artist John Trumbull.)

Secretary of Congress Charles Thomson ordered silence, and an expectant hush filled the room. President Thomas Mifflin then addressed Washington: "Sir, the United States in Congress assembled are prepared to receive your communications."[1]

Washington stood and bowed with dignity toward the members of Congress. The Congressmen responded by lifting their hats. He drew from his pocket his prepared resignation speech and held it in front of him. His hand shook, and his voice trembled slightly. It was only with effort that he was able to begin.

> Mr. President: The great events on which my resignation depended having at length taken place, I have now the honor of... presenting myself before [Congress] to surrender into their hands the trust committed to me, and to claim the indulgence of retiring from the service of my country.
>
> Happy in the confirmation of our independence and sovereignty and pleased with the opportunity afforded the United States of becoming a respectable nation, I resign with satisfaction the appointment I accepted with diffidence—a diffidence in my abilities to accomplish so arduous a task, which, however, was superseded by a confidence in the rectitude of our cause, the support of the supreme power of the union, and the patronage of Heaven.
>
> The successful termination of the war has verified the most sanguine expectations, and my gratitude for the interposition of Providence, and [for] the assurance I have received from my countrymen, increases with every review of the momentous contest.[2]

The General then spoke of his deep appreciation for the officers who had served with him, but his emotions welled up inside him and he found it difficult to continue. Finally, holding the paper with both hands to steady it, he was able to read on.

"I consider it an indispensable duty to close this last solemn act of my official life by commending the interests of our dearest country to the protection of Almighty God, and those who have the superintendence of them, to his holy keeping."

He was scarcely able to complete the sentence—his throat tightened and tears came brimming to the surface. As Congressman James McHenry recalled, "His voice faltered and sank, and the whole house felt his agitations." The feeling in the room was so intense that "the spectators all wept, and there was hardly a member of Congress who did not drop tears."[3]

After a pause Washington regained control. "Having now finished the work assigned me, I retire from the great theatre of action; and bidding an affectionate farewell to this august body under whose orders I have so long acted, I here offer my commission and take my leave of all the employments of public life."[4]

Mifflin replied with a brief speech of his own, complimenting Washington on his superb leadership and his marked respect for civil authority. When the ceremony was completed, Washington bowed once again, then turned and walked from the chamber.

Congress adjourned moments later. With the formalities over, Washington reentered the room and shook hands with each of the delegates, bidding them a bittersweet farewell.

The Hearth and Home

His horse was waiting outside the building. Washington and his companions set off immediately, pressing on toward

Mount Vernon. They doubtless spent the night in some tavern along the way.

> The next morning, December 24, Washington rode rapidly past the gates of Maryland friends by whose fireside he would in other circumstances have been delighted to linger for an hour. Home was the magnet that drew him, home the haven he sought, home the years'-long dream that now was near fulfilment. Every delay was a vexation and every halt a denial. At last the cold, clear waters of the Potomac came in sight, then the ferry and after that the blusterous passage, the last swift stage of the ride, the beloved trees, the yard, the doorway, Martha's embrace and the shrill, excited voices of "Jack" Custis's younger children—all this a richer reward than the addresses of cities, the salute of cannon and the approving words of the President of Congress. [5]

He had arrived home barely in time for Christmas dinner with Martha and the grandchildren.

As he closed the chapter on his impressive military career, Washington wrote, "My first wish is to see this plague to mankind [war] banished from off the earth, and the sons and daughters of this world employed in more pleasing and innocent amusements than in preparing implements and exercising them for the destruction of mankind."[6]

To another correspondent he wrote feelingly, "My first wish is . . . to see the whole world in peace, and the inhabitants of it as one band of brothers, striving who should contribute most to the happiness of mankind."[7]

This temperate man of peace had been wonderfully suited to meet the ugly realities of war, however. Writing from the vantage of one who could see with crystal vision, Thomas Jefferson remarked years later that George Washington had been "the fittest man on earth for directing so great a contest under so great difficulties."[8]

Now he could enjoy the fruits of that labor.

Home at Last

Throughout the waning months of the war, Washington's restless yearning for home had increased. He had been gone far too long; he longed for "that repose and tranquility to which I have been an entire stranger for more than eight years."[9] During those years, his mind had been "constantly on the stretch." He had fought the war with a "halter" around his neck, never knowing if the British might catch and hang him, never confident that he had enough men or supplies.[10]

Letters came too infrequently. When Martha joined him in his winter quarters each year, she became a welcome and stabilizing influence. Her annual journeys to be with the General were so extensive that she described herself as "a kind of walking perambulator."[11] She said she heard the first and last guns of every season, marching home when the year's new campaign was about to open. Washington eagerly anticipated her visits—but she was gone all too soon, and then the old homesickness returned.

In December 1783 he wrote that he was "hastening with unspeakable delight to the still and placid walks of domestic life."[12] But his return was not without its cares. He expressed deep concerns to his Mount Vernon caretaker, a cousin named Lund Washington, that "worse than going home to empty coffers and expensive living, I shall be encumbered with debt. . . . My private concerns," he fretted with quiet understatement, "do not wear the most smiling countenance."[13]

Nevertheless, despite his anxieties about financial

pressures, Washington would not seek reimbursement for his earlier service as commander in chief. "You ask how I am to be rewarded for all this?" he wrote to Lund. "There is one reward that nothing can deprive me of, and that is the consciousness of having done my duty with the strictest rectitude and most scrupulous exactness."[14] The "greatest of rewards," he told the mayor of Annapolis, was "the approbation and affection of a free people."[15] That approbation, he wrote to Jefferson, "is the height of my ambition and will be a full compensation for all my toils and sufferings in the long and painful contest [in which] we have been engaged."[16]

The General now put the war behind him. His desire was a quiet life at Mount Vernon, and "henceforward my mind shall be unbent, and I will endeavor to glide down the stream of life till I come to that abyss from whence no traveler is permitted to return."[17] But he had no thought of spending the rest of his life in utter repose. He would renew old friendships with his neighbors. He would tend his farm, long neglected. And he hoped to take "a more contemplative and extensive view of the vast inland navigation of these United States.... I shall not rest contented till I have explored the western country, and traversed those lines (or a great part of them) which have given bounds to a new empire."[18] Such were the plans of this fifty-one-year-old retired soldier as he once again assumed the role of a gentleman farmer.

On December 28, three days after his return home, he wrote to Governor George Clinton of New York: "The scene is at last closed. I feel myself eased of a load of public care. I hope to spend the remainder of my days in cultivating the affections of good men, and in the practice of the domestic virtues."[19]

"The Foundation Is Badly Laid"

The peace and tranquility Washington had hoped to enjoy were clouded by the realization that the Articles of Confederation were not adequate to meet the needs of the Union. Even as the war began to wind down in 1782 and 1783, Washington turned his mind more and more to the knotty problem of maintaining the Union. He concluded, fearfully, that dissolution would surely occur unless a stronger central government were created. Those fears became a recurring theme in his letters throughout 1783.

He wrote to Alexander Hamilton that unless Congress were given adequate powers to govern, "the blood we have spilt... will avail us nothing."[20] Such feelings ran deep. "All my private letters have teemed with these sentiments," Washington said. "Almost the whole of the difficulties and distresses of the army have their origin" in the present, defective form of government.[21]

Some of his most pointed remarks went to his young confidant, Lafayette. "I fear," said Washington, "... that local or state politics will interfere too much with that more liberal and extensive plan of government which wisdom and foresight... would dictate." Of course they would make "blunders" in developing the character of the national government, but they must persist at all costs. He declared, "To form a constitution that will give consistency, stability, and dignity to the Union... is a duty which is incumbent upon every man... and will meet with my aid as far as it can be rendered."[22]

Such thoughts were clear echoes of sentiments Washington had expressed years before. In 1776, a month before the Declaration of Independence, Washington wrote to his brother, Jack, who was involved in preparing the formative constitution for an independent Virginia:

> To form a new government requires infinite care and unbounded attention, for if the foundation is badly laid the superstructure must be bad.... My fear is ... that you will patch up some kind of constitution as defective as the present. This should be avoided; every man should consider that he is lending his aid to frame a constitution which is to render millions happy, or miserable, and that a matter of such moment cannot be the work of a day. [23]

By July 1783 Washington was calling for "a convention of the people" to establish "a federal constitution" which would strengthen the national government. [24] It was a call he would make repeatedly in the months and years to come. Yet four troublous years would pass before such a convention was finally assembled.

Chapter 30

Life at Mount Vernon

At length...I am become a private citizen on the banks of the Potomac," Washington wrote in February 1784. Finally he was "under the shadow of my own vine and my own fig tree, free from the bustle of a camp and the busy scenes of public life,...solacing myself with...tranquil enjoyments."[1]

He had long dreamed of retiring permanently from the public stage, and had even announced his determination publicly. But nerves long wrought up did not readily relax. After being home for two full months he still could say, "I am just beginning to experience that ease and freedom from public cares which, however desirable, takes some time to realize.... I feel now...as I conceive a wearied traveler must do who, after treading many a painful step with a heavy burden on his shoulders, is eased of the latter, having reached the goal."[2]

Burdens Upon Burdens

Woeful financial affairs contributed to Washington's continuing feeling of disquietude. He had predicted that he would come home from the war "with empty pockets,"[3] and that was very nearly true. When nephew Fielding Lewis begged for a loan, Washington sadly responded, "I made no money from my estate during the nine years I was absent from it, and brought none home with me."[4] Some have estimated that Washington's cumulative financial losses from the war—from neglect of his lands, noncollection from delinquent debtors and tenants, stoppage of exportation, and rapid depreciation of paper money—rose to some $120,000.[5]

Unfortunately, his financial troubles were slow to improve. Four years later, in 1787, he still had ample cause to lament, "My estate for the last eleven years has not been able to make both ends meet."[6]

Adding to the oppressive burden were the numerous visitors to Mount Vernon, many of whom freely expected meals and overnight lodging. So thickly did the crowds come, in fact, that Washington wrote that Mount Vernon had essentially become "a well-resorted tavern, as scarcely any strangers who are going from north to south, or from south to north, do not spend a day or two at it."[7] Dining without visitors became the exception rather than the rule. Washington confided to his diary in June 1785, "Dined with only Mrs. Washington, which I believe is the first instance of it since my retirement from public life."[8]

Correspondents also made heavy demands on his time and energy, preventing him from fully working his estate. "At no period of the war have I been obliged ... to go through more drudgery in writing," he explained to old friend George William Fairfax. "Strange as it may seem, ... I have been able since I came home to give very little attention to my own concerns."[9] He complained of the many "letters (often of an unmeaning nature) from foreigners; inquiries after Dick, Tom, and Harry who may have been in some part or at some time in the Continental service; . . . introductions; applications for copies of papers; references [to] a thousand old matters with which I ought not to be troubled more than the Great Mogul."[10]

Still, despite the presumptuous imposition, to Washington's way of thinking each request deserved some answer. Struggling under such a burden, Washington finally hired a

Tobias Lear, Washington's personal secretary from 1786 to 1793. Lear, a Harvard graduate, was paid $200 a year and lived with the Washington family. Historian Douglas Southall Freeman described him as "personable, industrious, discreet, and highly intelligent." In his eight years of service, Lear became Washington's closest associate.

private secretary, Harvard-educated Tobias Lear. With the competent Lear behind the desk, Washington joyfully rode out onto his estate again.

"Every Experiment Is a Treasure"

Returning to the farm was a source of "great satisfaction," Washington said.[11] "To see plants rise from the earth and flourish by the superior skill and bounty of the laborer fills a contemplative mind with ideas which are more easy to be conceived than expressed."[12]

Still, he acknowledged modestly that he had "never possessed much skill in the art, and nine years' total inattention to it has added nothing to a knowledge which is best understood from practice."[13] Hoping that he could perfect his farming skills, he opened a fruitful, long-lasting correspondence with famed English agriculturalist Arthur Young.

Washington found real pleasure in experimenting with his farming. He divided his holdings into six plantations, placing an overseer over each; he then visited each plantation every weekday, making the twenty-mile round trip with his horse at a canter. In order to get the most out of his poor soil, he developed a six-year rotation system for his plantations. The staples of his farms were corn, wheat, and fish (tobacco had been abandoned before the war), but in 1785 Washington began experimenting with other crops, from barley and clover to carrots, cabbage, and pumpkins. He received seeds and cuttings from all around the world to assist him in his experiments, then reciprocated in kind; France's King Louis XVI, for example, Washington's old ally, received Kentucky seeds for his exotic gardens at Versailles.

One of Washington's long-held goals was to improve Virginia's flawed agricultural practices. "I never ride to my plantations without seeing something which makes me regret having continued so long in the ruinous mode of farming which we are in," he wrote.[14] The land was "gullied and exhausted" throughout the entire state.[15] He wished the larger landholders would begin to experiment to find better solutions. The typical farmer certainly would not "hazard" to move "from the old road till the new one is made so plain and easy that he is sure it cannot be mistaken"—but someone must lead the way.[16] To that end, "every experiment is a treasure."[17]

Following his own counsel, Washington continued to experiment. He grew grass for grazing, tried different kinds of fertilizers, worked at breeding a superior line of mules. He carefully planned drainage to preserve precious, thin topsoil. He planted neat rows of hedges, which he called his "live fences."[18] He built a greenhouse. And he received a silver cup from an agricultural society in South Carolina "as a premium for raising the largest jackass."[19]

"The First Farmer in America"

In November 1785 Robert Hunter, a curious Englishman, visited Mount Vernon and recorded his impressions in his diary. Washington, he noted, dressed in a plain blue coat, white cashmere waistcoat, black knee breeches, and black boots. When meeting guests, he changed to a clean shirt, plain dark coat, white waistcoat, and white silk stockings, with his hair neatly powdered.

"His greatest pride now," Hunter wrote, "is to be thought the first farmer in America. He...often works with his men himself—strips off his coat and labors like a common man."

Hunter commented on Washington's bent for "mechanics"—he created minor inventions and supervised the erection of farm buildings, "condescending even to measure things himself, that all may be perfectly uniform."[20]

In 1785, anxious for additional help, Washington asked George William Fairfax, who now lived in England, to find him "a thoroughbred practical English farmer...who understands the best course of crops, how to plow, to sow," and so forth. The man's most important qualification Washington described thus: he must be able, "Midas-like," to "convert everything he touches into manure as the first transmutation towards gold."[21] That "thoroughbred" English farmer came a year later and stayed until 1790.

Washington and Slavery

Though Washington greatly enjoyed the life of a plantation owner, one aspect of the business was a constant, festering sore, causing him considerable anguish of soul. That sore, grown raw over the years, was the economic order that essentially locked farmers into the practice of owning slaves. Washington's slave holdings eventually extended to several hundred—but he was never comfortable with the prevailing notion that one man could own another. As early as 1769 he had begun to take legislative action to severely limit slavery: in the Virginia House of Burgesses he sponsored a bill to forbid further importation of new slaves after November of that year.

Nine years later, in the midst of the war, Washington confided to his estate manager, "I every day long more to get clear of [my slaves]."[22] But, unfortunately, hired labor was almost impossible to find in Virginia.[23] Given the economic system in America at that time, the only way Washington could discontinue his use of slaves would be to abandon his plantation altogether.

Feeling trapped in a narrow box, Washington continued to farm with slaves. But his humane policies toward them nearly ruined him financially. As his slaves had children, his slave holdings expanded and grew far beyond his need. Many ate his goods without being able to contribute to the well-being of the plantation. "One good field hand was worth as much as a small city lot," one historian has observed. "By selling a single slave Washington could have paid for two years all the taxes he so complained about."[24] But he stood firm on his moral principles, refusing to sell any of his slaves. He could not bring himself to "traffic in the human species."[25]

"There is not a man living who wishes more sincerely than

I do to see a plan adopted for the abolition of [slavery]," Washington wrote in 1786. But only "legislative authority" could effectively accomplish the desired end—that he knew. [26]

That same year Lafayette proposed a bold idea to Washington: he would buy an estate in French Guiana and some black slaves to go with it. Then he would free the blacks and place them on the estate as tenants. It was only a small step in the right direction, but Washington was enthusiastic: "Would to God a like spirit might diffuse itself generally into the minds of the people of this country! But I despair of seeing it."[27]

Four months later the problem still weighed heavily on his mind. "I never mean...to possess another slave by purchase," he then vowed, "it being among my first wishes" that slavery be "abolished by slow, sure, imperceptible degrees."[28] If possible, he hoped "to lay a foundation to prepare the rising generation [of blacks] for a destiny different from that in which they were born."[29]

As the years passed, he saw with remarkable clarity that emancipation must come. In 1798 he reportedly said with prophetic insight, "I can clearly foresee that nothing but the rooting out of slavery can perpetuate the existence of our union, by consolidating it in a common bond of principle."[30]

In the last year of his life Washington wrote a will providing that his slaves be set free at Martha's death.

Life at Home

Washington called the years 1784 to 1789 his "furlough."[31] Those were the years when, in addition to his agricultural pursuits, he was at last able to enjoy his family. When Martha's son John Parke ("Jackie") Custis died, his younger two children, Eleanor ("Nelly") and George Washington

The east front of Mount Vernon. Washington regarded his days at Mount Vernon as the happiest in his life.

Parke ("Tub" or "Little Washington"), went to live with their loving grandparents at Mount Vernon. (Jackie's two older children, Elizabeth and Martha, remained with their mother and a new stepfather.) And when George Washington's brother Samuel died in the early 1780s, his daughter Harriot also found a home in George's family circle.

The focus of that circle was his beloved Martha. She was the "partner of all my domestic enjoyments," he wrote,[32] and in many ways she was the creator of them.

The peaceful days at Mount Vernon provided an opportunity for Washington to reveal a spark in his personality that had lain dormant during most of the war. One visitor was pleased on one occasion to observe Washington becoming "quite merry, and, being with his intimate friends, [he] laughed and talked a good deal."[33] James Madison said of

Washington that "no man seemed more to enjoy gay conversation, though he took little part in it himself. He was particularly pleased with the jokes, good humor, and hilarity of his companions."[34]

A homely experience of one of Mount Vernon's guests, Elkanah Watson, illuminates another warm characteristic of Washington's complex personality. Watson had arrived at Mount Vernon with a discomforting cold and severe cough. Washington offered home remedies, but Watson declined. During the night, however, Watson coughed so violently he could not sleep. Then he heard the door to his room quietly open. "On drawing my bed-curtains, to my utter astonishment, I beheld Washington himself, standing at my bedside, with a bowl of hot tea in his hand.... This little incident, occurring in common life with an ordinary man, would not have been noticed; but as a trait of the benevolence and private virtue of Washington, [it] deserves to be recorded."[35]

While sharing himself with those in his own household, Washington did not forget the ever-pressing needs of his less fortunate neighbors. One of the Mount Vernon overseers recalled later:

> I had orders from General Washington to fill a cornhouse every year for the sole use of the poor in my neighborhood, to whom it was a most seasonable and precious relief, saving numbers of poor women and children from extreme want, and blessing them with plenty.... He owned several fishing stations on the Potomac.... For [the] accommodation [of the poor] he appropriated a station, one of the best he had, and furnished it with all the necessary apparatus for taking herring.[36]

Scenes from a Quiet Life

The retired General constantly received requests to sit for paintings. Initially he was reluctant, but gradually he softened. He wrote to one artist:

> I am so hackneyed to the touches of the painter's pencil that I am now altogether at their beck, and sit like patience on a monument while they are delineating the lines of my face.... At first, I was as impatient at the request and as restive under the operation as a colt is of the saddle. The next time I submitted very reluctantly, but with less flouncing. Now no dray moves more readily to the [pole] than I do to the painter's chair. [37]

In 1784 Washington became involved in a project to establish a water route between the Potomac and Ohio rivers. Such a route would create a waterway that would stretch inland from Virginia and Maryland all the way to the Great Lakes—a significant trade boon to those states. In September he set out with Dr. James Craik, a longtime friend, to examine Washington's western lands and to identify a viable route between the two rivers. Their round trip extended 680 miles. Though the journey was cut short because of growing Indian unrest, they were able to find an acceptable passage.

In November Washington traveled to Richmond, Virginia's capital city, to meet with Governor Benjamin Harrison and the General Assembly. Several improvements were vitally needed on the Potomac and James rivers; Washington reviewed the issues with the assembly, then proposed specific legislation, which they subsequently passed.

In December Lafayette, who was on an extended visit to Mount Vernon, reluctantly departed for France. Sorry to see him go, Washington accompanied him almost to Baltimore, a one-way distance of at least fifty miles. Later Washington wrote his beloved friend: "I often asked myself...whether that was the last sight I ever should have of you. And though I wished to say no, my fears answered yes."[38] Unhappily, his fears proved to be right.

Earlier that same year, Dr. Craik asked for privileged access to Washington's private papers, hoping to write his biography. Even though Craik was a close and trusted friend, Washington refused:

> I will frankly declare to you, my dear doctor, that any memoirs of my life, distinct and unconnected with the general history of the war, would rather hurt my feelings than tickle my pride while I lived. I had rather glide gently down the stream of life, leaving it to posterity to think and say what they please of me, than by any act of mine to have vanity or ostentation imputed to me.... I do not think vanity is a trait of my character.[39]

A year later, former aide David Humphreys suggested that Washington write his own history of the Revolutionary War. Washington was blunt in response: "If I had talents for it, I have not leisure to turn my thoughts to commentaries. A consciousness of a defective education, and a certainty of the want of time, unfit me for such an undertaking."[40]

Washington was sensitive about his lack of a formal education. Writing was ever a chore, and he frequently leaned on others to help him. Still, he was not willing to use others as a crutch forever. He read, observed, and forced himself to practice and improve. Timothy Pickering, who later became Washington's Secretary of War, wrote, "When I first became acquainted with the General [in 1777] his writing was defective in grammar and even in spelling, owing to the insufficiency of his early education." Of course, Washington's shortcomings in this respect were typical of the

John Augustine ("Jack")
Washington, one of George's
younger brothers. In later life,
George referred to Jack as "the
intimate companion of my youth."

times, more the rule than the exception. Pickering explained, however, that Washington "gradually got the better [of these limitations] in subsequent years of his life, by the official perusal of some excellent models, particularly those of Hamilton; by writing with care and patient attention; and reading numerous, indeed multitudes, of letters to and from his friends and correspondents."[41]

Losses, Pains, and Difficulties

In 1786, Washington was stunned as several close friends died, some of them still relatively young. These included stalwart, reliable General Nathanael Greene. In January 1787, Washington also lost his favorite brother, John Augustine, to whom he always affectionately referred as "Jack." Of the five brothers who had lived to adulthood, three were now dead. Only two brothers and one sister still survived. Washington began to feel the reality of his own mortality more and more—a feeling that was heightened by his own illness. In the fall of 1786 he suffered a "violent attack" of "fever and ague"—perhaps a return of the deadly malaria of his youth. [42] The next April found him enduring severe discomfort from "a rheumatic complaint which has followed me more than six months. [It] is frequently so bad that it is with difficulty I can, at times, raise my hand to my head or turn myself in bed." [43] When he was finally able to struggle out of bed, he had to carry his arm in a sling for several days.

During these years Washington honestly felt that he was "descending the hill" of life. Though he had been "blessed with a good constitution," he was "of a short-lived family." [44] Now past "the noon-tide of life," he was moving "gently down a stream which no human effort can ascend." [45] (Fortunately for America, Washington lived another thirteen years. It gave him time to preside over the drafting of a brilliant new constitution and to serve two triumphant terms as the first President of the United States.)

Severe financial problems continued to burden him. [46] He lamented in 1787 that he owed "more than £500...and I know not where or when I shall receive one shilling with which to pay it." When he thought of a source of money it brought only disappointment: "I am not able to pay debts unless I could sell land," he wrote, "which I have publicly advertised without finding bidders." [47]

More than a year later his financial woes still plagued him: "I never felt the want of money so sensibly since I was a boy of fifteen years old as I have done for the last twelve months, and probably shall do for twelve months more to come." [48] He was deeply embarrassed that he owed money for medical services, and he had to put the sheriff off three times when he came to collect taxes. Washington also received a polite letter seeking prompt payment of overdue rent for his pew at the church.

Although health problems and financial worries sometimes dominated his thoughts, Washington still felt it possible to find happiness without either health or wealth. "Happiness depends more upon the internal frame of a person's mind than on the externals in the world," he concluded. [49] "It is assuredly better to go laughing than crying through the rough journey of life." [50]

Chapter 31

"A Half-Starved, Limping Government"

A dded to the burden of his personal problems was Washington's anxiety over the survival of his new nation. Its potential, of course, was wonderful to contemplate. He wrote that with "a little political wisdom" the nation might eventually become as "populous and happy" as its territory was extensive. [1] But were the people prepared to exercise that wisdom? Washington was not certain.

"Like a young heir come prematurely to a large inheritance, we shall wanton and run riot until we have brought our reputation to the brink of ruin," he feared. [2]

The problem, as always, was the enervating weakness of the Union. "The Confederation [of states] appears to me to be little more than a shadow without the substance," he said. [3] And the foundation of the problem was the jealous, mistrustful states: "The disinclination of the individual states to yield competent powers to Congress for the federal government...will, if there is not a change in the system, be our downfall as a nation. This is as clear to me as the A, B, C."[4]

"A Rope of Sand"

This theme runs like an unbroken thread through Washington's correspondence. He had other concerns, and he talked about other matters, but the overwhelming need for union and a strong central government was his constant plea.

To Nathanael Greene he wrote in 1783: "It remains only for the states to be wise and to establish their independence on that basis of inviolable, efficacious union and firm confederation which may prevent their being made the sport of European policy. May heaven give them the wisdom to adopt the measures still necessary for this important purpose."[5]

To Benjamin Harrison in 1784: "[I] predict the worst consequences from a half-starved, limping government that appears always moving upon crutches and tottering at every step."[6]

To Henry Knox in 1785: "Contracted ideas, local pursuits, and absurd jealousy are continually leading us from those great and fundamental principles which are characteristic of wise and powerful nations, and without which we are no more than a rope of sand, and shall as easily be broken."[7]

To James Madison in 1785: "We are either a united people or we are not. If the former,...let us...act as a nation, which [has] national objects to promote and a national character to support. If we are not, let us no longer act a farce by pretending to it."[8]

To James Warren in 1785: "To me...it is one of the most

extraordinary things in nature that we should confederate as a nation, and yet be afraid to give the rulers of that nation, who are the creatures of our making, . . . sufficient powers to order and direct the affairs of the same. By such policy as this the wheels of government are clogged, and our brightest prospects, and that high expectation which was entertained of us by the wondering world, are turned into astonishment; and from the high ground on which we stood we are descending into the vale of confusion and darkness."[9]

To David Stuart in 1785: "If we are afraid to trust one another under qualified powers, there is an end of the Union."[10]

To John Jay in 1786: "Our affairs are drawing rapidly to a crisis. . . . I do not conceive we can exist long as a nation without having lodged somewhere a power which will pervade the whole Union in as energetic a manner as the authority of the state governments extends over the several states. To be fearful of investing Congress, constituted as that body is, with ample authorities for national purposes, appears to me the very climax of popular absurdity and madness."[11]

The Weak Confederation

Washington was not alone in his fears about the weakness of their original constitution, the Articles of Confederation. Other thinkers of his day made equally dire predictions about America's dim future under the Articles. All acknowledged that throughout the war Congress had been tightly shackled by an ineffectual federal constitution. (It had been in effect essentially since 1776, even though it was not ratified by all of the states until 1781.) In fact, Washington repeatedly placed blame for the war's long continuation on the weakness of the national government. Now, in a tenuous peacetime, the confederation was as ineffectual as ever.

For example, under the Articles of Confederation, Congress had no power to enforce treaties or to wage war. Yet the new nation was being threatened from virtually all sides. Flexing their muscles, the Spanish had closed the Mississippi to American navigation; the British were illegally holding posts in the western territories; thousands of armed Tories who had fled to Canada were massing along the American border—who knew what they planned?

Under the Articles, Congress was greatly handicapped in dealing with other nations. Distinguished envoys such as John Adams and Thomas Jefferson were sent to England and France, but they were treated indifferently. No European power expected the American union to survive very long.

In 1783, seeking to strengthen British merchants and upset the American economy, England's Privy Council closed the British West Indies to American ships and sailors. Other orders of the council prohibited American ships from trading at Newfoundland and Nova Scotia. Oppressively high duties were imposed on American trade with the British Isles. Congress was powerless to counteract such arbitrary acts.

Britain's measures nearly crippled the American economy. Exports to the West Indies of fish alone dropped from $448,000 to $284,000. America's whaling industry, having lost its only foreign market for whalebone and whale oil, saw exports plummet to a third of their prewar level. The balance of trade for the United States in 1786 tipped at a lopsided £.9 million in exports to £2.3 million in imports. Congress saw the critical need to swing the balance in the direction of America's favor, but the Articles of Confederation gave them no power to deal effectively with foreign governments.

Under the confederation, Congress had no authority to

regulate commerce. Every state could freely impose its own duties on imports from other nations. In their fear of insolvency, many states even went to the extreme of charging duties on goods "imported" from other states—which further widened the rift between themselves and their neighbors.

Under the confederation, Congress had a hopelessly flawed means of gathering revenue. It was essentially limited to requesting money from the states—and a state could pay or not pay as it chose. The nation's debt was so heavy that Congress was unable to keep up even with the interest. But the states consistently dragged their feet in paying their assessments or otherwise helping.

To further complicate matters, the states issued competing forms of currency. This contributed to the deadly rash of inflation by flooding the marketplace with paper money.

All of these flaws in the Articles of Confederation were exacerbated by the impossible amending provision: no amendment could take effect until all thirteen states had ratified it. This rule of unanimous consent tied the hands of the majority; on more than one occasion twelve states approved a needed amendment and one state killed it.

When all the weaknesses of the Articles were added together, it seemed to Washington and others that the sweet promise of freedom was rapidly slipping through their fingers. What was worse, under the Articles of Confederation, Congress was powerless to stop it.

Shays's Rebellion

Washington's deep concern for America alternated with a more optimistic outlook. "It is not the part of the good citizen to despair of the republic," he said. In a letter to one of his

French correspondents, he noted some of America's weaknesses, then said:

> In other respects our internal governments are daily acquiring strength. The laws have their fullest energy; justice is well administered; robbery, violence, or murder is not heard of from New Hampshire to Georgia.... Economy begins, partly from necessity and partly from choice and habit, to prevail.... It is wonderful to see how soon the ravages of war are repaired. Houses are rebuilt, fields enclosed, stocks of cattle which were destroyed are replaced, and many a desolated territory assumes again the cheerful appearance of cultivation.... The arts of peace, such as clearing rivers, building bridges, and establishing conveniences for traveling, etc., are assiduously promoted. In short, the foundation of a great empire is laid, and I please myself with a persuasion that Providence will not leave its work imperfect. [12]

Despite his expressions of optimism in this letter, Washington wrote to other correspondents about the dark fears that continued to play at the back of his mind. The Union was indeed "imperfect"—and he worried that the slightest nudge could push it over the precipice.

Unknown to Washington and most others, those fears were about to become realities. Seeds of unrest had earlier been sown that now began to sprout. The Massachusetts legislature had foolishly levied heavy taxes, payable in gold, at a time when the economy was weak and the working class could not pay. Particularly hard hit were the farmers, who were struggling just to make a living. Rather than alleviate the tax burden, Massachusetts leaders strictly enforced tax collection. When a farmer was unable to pay taxes or debts or loans, cattle and property were sold to raise the money that was due. Some farmers were even thrown into debtor's prison.

Angered to action, in 1786 Massachusetts farmers began to march on the courthouses where foreclosure proceedings were being held. Through threats and intimidation the farmers were able to prevent many courts from sitting. Eventually the men chose a leader, a Revolutionary War veteran named Daniel Shays. He and his followers began to make grandiose plans, including a daring assault on a nearby arsenal. There they would obtain arms to enforce their wishes on the state legislature.

Washington shuddered at the horrifying prospects. Anarchy in one state might lead to rebellion elsewhere. Fortunately, before Shays and his followers were able to make good on their threats, a small, privately organized force frightened them into disbanding. Demoralized, Shays's army melted into the countryside, while Shays himself fled to Vermont.

"Verging to Anarchy and Confusion"

Although the uprising had been brief, it left a perceptible mark on many Americans. Washington pleaded more than ever for a stronger government—before it was too late.

"What stronger evidence can be given of the want of energy in our governments than these disorders?" he asked James Madison. "If there exists not a power to check them, what security has a man for life, liberty, or property?" He complained that the states were little more than "thirteen sovereignties pulling against each other, and all tugging at the federal head." Such a condition, he warned, "will soon bring ruin on the whole."

"Let us look to our national character," Washington

challenged, "and to things beyond the present period. No morn ever dawned more favorably than ours did; and no day was ever more clouded than the present!... Without some alteration in our political creed, the superstructure we have been seven years raising at the expense of so much blood and treasure must fall. We are fast verging to anarchy and confusion!"[13]

Anarchy and confusion were precisely what Europeans had predicted would result from the American experiment. The idea of a republic, of people's rule, was untried in modern times, and those schooled in history and government prophesied it would never work. Washington was well aware of European sentiments, and lamented, "How melancholy is the reflection that in so short a space we should have made such large strides towards fulfilling the prediction of our transatlantic foe!"[14] He felt they had reached a low point of public humiliation: "To be more exposed in the eyes of the world, and more contemptible than we already are, is hardly possible."[15]

At the height of the crisis, Henry "Light-Horse Harry" Lee, then in Congress, begged Washington to step in with his influence. But individual influence, Washington knew, was a sorry substitute for a strong and effective government. In stern tones he wrote to Lee: "You talk, my good sir, of employing influence to appease the present tumults in Massachusetts. I know not where that influence is to be found.... Influence is no government. Let us have one by which our lives, liberties, and properties will be secured, or let us know the worst at once."

At the same time, Washington warned against the spirit that would carelessly disregard the legal authorities established by the Articles of Confederation: "Precedents are dangerous things," he said. "Let the reins of government then be braced and held with a steady hand, and every violation of the constitution be reprehended; if defective, then let it be amended, but not suffered to be trampled upon while it has an existence."[16]

Invitation to a Convention

While some of the disorderly elements of American society were raging to the point of rebellion, a far more powerful and decisive move for reform was quietly under way. It began in March 1785 when a group of commissioners for the Potomac Canal project, representing Virginia and Maryland, met at Mount Vernon. George Washington, as president of the Potomac Company, presided at the meeting.

The commissioners declared that the Potomac would be an open waterway not only for both Maryland and Virginia but for all the states and their allies. In addition, in an unprecedented show of unity, the commissioners recommended that the money of the two states have the same value, and that duties and exports be the same for both states.

The focus of the conference was on a set of proposed canals that would link the Potomac River with the Ohio River, and the Chesapeake Bay with the Delaware River. The commissioners realized that the success of the project would require the cooperation of Pennsylvania and Delaware, and they recommended that a meeting be held with all four states present.

The Virginia legislature considered the "Mount Vernon Conference" recommendations the following January. James Madison proposed that all thirteen states be invited to the meeting, and the legislature acted accordingly. They called for all the states to come together in September 1786 to discuss the commercial challenges they shared.

Only five states attended that September trade conference, held at Annapolis, Maryland. But their discussions on the pitiful state of the nation's economy led to a recommendation that reverberated across America. Led by James Madison and Alexander Hamilton, two of the youngest delegates present, the Annapolis conference proposed that a national convention be held in Philadelphia the following May (1787). The purpose of the conference was to revise the Articles of Confederation. The delegates argued that only by revamping the government itself could America begin to resolve its deep-rooted commercial problems. The convention, they said, would "devise such...provisions as shall appear to them necessary to render the constitution of the federal government adequate to the exigencies of the Union."[17]

After years of personally urging just such a change, Washington was delighted by this broad-based call for a convention. He promptly wrote to James Madison, a member of Virginia's House of Delegates, urging that Virginia appoint representatives. Madison responded that representatives had already been named—and that George Washington headed the list.

Washington was flattered at Madison's news, but it left him in a difficult situation. He cherished his life as a private citizen; he had declared to the entire nation in 1783 that he was retiring from public life—and now friends were trying to thrust him into the battle once again. Only three months earlier he had written to John Jay: "Retired as I am from the world, I frankly acknowledge I cannot feel myself an unconcerned spectator. Yet, having happily assisted in bringing the ship into port, and having been fairly discharged, it is not my business to embark again on a sea of troubles."[18]

Washington had other compelling reasons not to attend the convention: he was president of the veterans' Society of the Cincinnati—and he had already notified that group he could not attend their Philadelphia meeting in May 1787. His reasons ranged from his debilitating rheumatism (which was so painful he had to wear his arm in a sling) to Potomac Company responsibilities to pressing private affairs. "Under these circumstances," he told Madison, "...I could not appear" at the federal convention "without giving offense."[19]

Under the weight of these concerns, Washington wrote to Virginia's Governor Edmund Randolph and declined the nomination. "Some other character, on whom greater reliance can be had, may be substituted in my place, the probability of my nonattendance being too great to continue my appointment."[20]

He remained, of course, fully committed to the need for a better constitution. But was it necessary that he be personally involved? He thought not—his day was past. As he explained to Jay, humbly: "Nor could it be expected that my sentiments and opinions would have much weight on the minds of my countrymen. They have been neglected, though given as a last legacy in the most solemn manner. I had then perhaps some claims to public attention. I consider myself as having none at present."[21]

Fears and Hesitations

It was not until February 1787 that Congress got around to approving the proposed convention. It stated that the convention was "for the sole and express purpose of revising the Articles of Confederation."[22] Despite Washington's previous objections, Randolph, Madison, and others continued to urge him to go. As late as March, however, Washington still wrote that he was certain he would not be able to attend. Henry Knox joined the chorus of those trying to encourage him. "It is the general wish that you should attend," he said. "It is conceived to be highly important to the success of the ... convention." If Washington did not attend, Knox argued, the people might assume that Washington wanted some other means of altering the defective Articles—perhaps force. "The unbounded confidence the people have of your tried patriotism and wisdom would exceedingly facilitate ... a convention of which you were a member," he concluded. 23

Martha's wishes pulled strongly in the other direction. She confessed that no one could "blame" George if he chose to go, acting "according to his ideals." But she added passionately that she had never thought "any circumstances could possibly [call him] into public life again [after returning from the war]. I had anticipated that from this moment we should have been left to grow old in solitude and tranquillity together." 24

Washington also considered the possibility—all too likely— that the convention might fail in its purpose. If it did, the reputations of those associated with it would doubtless be damaged. Washington knew that a reputation is not easily earned and must not thoughtlessly be put at risk.

But in spite of all the reasons for not going, Washington could not get Shays's Rebellion out of his mind. He could not forget his painful struggles during the war—trying to keep an army alive with too little support from a weak and ineffective government. He had given some of the best years of his life for America, gradually wresting her from the grasp of foreign domination—now perhaps he could help cement that freedom by creating a strong government. He vacillated and wavered, then finally wrote to Governor Randolph announcing his change of mind. He would go to the convention.

Even though Washington had reconciled himself to attending the convention, he still remained doubtful that the convention would enjoy a positive outcome. "I see little prospect ... of our agreeing upon any other [constitution], or that we should remain long satisfied under it if we could," he wrote. "Yet I would wish anything and everything essayed to prevent the effusion of blood and to avert the humiliating and contemptible figure we are about to make in the annals of mankind."[25]

"New Luster to His Character"

George Washington, as Virginia's most prominent delegate, approached the convention with strong opinions about the kind of changes he would like to see in the Articles of Confederation. The government must be made strong enough to enforce its policies—but federal officials must always be answerable to the people, subject to recall any time there was cause. A monarchy, which some were suggesting, would be absolutely unacceptable. If seriously pursued, such a proposal would shake "the peace of this country to its foundation."[26] The people simply would not stand for such a form of government— nor should they. Instead, Washington favored a careful separation of powers, with three branches (executive, legislative, judicial) in the federal government.

In sum, "a thorough reform of the present system is indispensable, ... and with hand (and heart) I hope the business will be essayed in a full convention." All the states must be represented. And Washington hoped the delegates would come without "fetters ... as my wish is that the convention may adopt no temporizing expedient, but probe the defects of the [Articles of Confederation] to the bottom and provide radical cures."[27]

When James Monroe learned that Washington planned to attend the convention, he was exuberant. A letter to Jefferson expressed his praise of Washington's character: "To forsake the honorable retreat to which he [Washington] had retired, and risk the reputation he had so deservedly acquired, manifested a zeal for the public interest that could, after so many and illustrious services, scarcely have been expected of him."[28]

Henry Knox also appreciated what was at stake when Washington made his decision to attend. He wrote: "General Washington's attendance at the convention adds . . . new luster to his character. Secure as he was in his fame, he has again committed it to the mercy of events. Nothing but the critical situation of his country would have induced him to so hazardous a conduct. But its happiness being in danger, he disregards all personal considerations."[29]

The *Pennsylvania Herald* put it more succinctly: "This great patriot will never think his duty performed while anything remains to be done."[30]

Chapter 32

Forming a New Constitution

After a five-day carriage ride, Washington arrived in Philadelphia on May 13, 1787, one day before the convention was to open. The next day he expected to join the other delegates and get to work—but he soon learned that only two states had a full delegation present, Virginia and the host state of Pennsylvania. Muddy spring roads combined with an old habit of arriving late for Congress (transferred to the convention) to delay the other delegates. While they waited for a quorum from the other states, Washington and his fellow Virginia delegates met for private discussions on revising the Articles of Confederation. Washington, Madison, and Randolph had come prepared with proposals for a completely new constitution. Working together over the next two weeks, the Virginia delegates hammered out a plan of government which they intended to present to the convention as a whole. Though the plan (called the Virginia Plan) was prepared primarily by Madison, Washington's experience and common sense were doubtless helpful in determining what was needed and what would work.

By May 25 delegates from seven states were present, and the convention officially began at the Pennsylvania State House. The square-faced, sturdy building held many profound memories for George Washington. There, in 1774, he had attended the First Continental Congress, sitting long hours through warm autumn days. Seven months later he had returned to the Second Continental Congress—and had been both pleased and dismayed to be named commander of the American armies. In this same state house, while Washington was engaged in the field, the Declaration of Indepen-

The Pennsylvania State House, or "Independence Hall," where the Declaration of Independence was debated and the United States Constitution was framed. Here Washington attended the Second Continental Congress and, eight years later, resigned his commission as commander in chief.

dence had been signed, thereafter giving the building a new name: Independence Hall.

The meetings of the convention, for the most part, were held in the East Room of the hall, a room about forty feet square. The delegates were seated at round tables covered with green woolen cloths, three or four to a table. Tall windows gave light from each side of the room.

Eventually, representatives came from all thirteen states except Rhode Island (known with some irritation as "Rogue Island"). The leaders of that tiny state wanted nothing to do with a stronger system of government and boycotted the convention. Some of the most esteemed citizens from each of the other states were there, but two stood out above the rest: Benjamin Franklin and George Washington.

Franklin was known and loved throughout the states as a writer, scientist, philosopher, statesman, and newspaper publisher. His *Poor Richard's Almanack* was one of the best-selling publications of its time. He had served in the Continental Congress and had been an influential diplomat during the war, helping to persuade France to come to America's aid. Earlier, Franklin had fathered a plan for national union that had eventually influenced the creation of the Articles of Confederation. Now he was at the Constitutional Convention to perfect the work. A fellow delegate, William Pierce, characterized Franklin as "the greatest philosopher of the present age. He is [eighty-one] years old, and possesses an activity of mind equal to a youth of twenty-five."[1] As president (i.e., governor) of Pennsylvania, Franklin was essentially the host of the convention.

At the time of the convention Franklin was in poor health and had to be carried to the meetings in a sedan chair he had purchased during one of his missions to France. The chair, which was borne by four convicts, was the first such chair ever seen in the United States.

Washington, of course, was esteemed as America's most loved war hero. People remembered that he had fought in the French and Indian War, had served in Congress, and had sacrificed greatly for eight years to lead America to victory in the Revolutionary War. His steady, resolute character had been acclaimed throughout the nation. He was known as a man who could take firm grip on the reins of power without becoming corrupted or dictatorial. Pierce said of Washington: "Having conducted these states to independence and peace, he now appears to assist in framing a government to make the people happy.... He may be said to be the deliverer of his country."[2]

"An Assembly of Demigods"

The convention included so many leading figures in America that Jefferson characterized it as "an assembly of demigods."[3] Attending the convention were such distinguished leaders as the following:

John Dickinson of Delaware, nicknamed the "penman of the Revolution," who had written the initial draft of the Articles of Confederation and had served as a brigadier general during the Revolutionary War. "Famed through all America," Pierce wrote, "... [Dickinson] will be ever considered one of the most important characters in the United States."[4]

Alexander Hamilton of New York, who had been one of Washington's aides in the Revolutionary War, as well as a heroic leader in his own right. Along with James Madison, he was the guiding force in the Annapolis Convention, which led directly to the Constitutional Convention. Pierce wrote of

Hamilton: "Colo. Hamilton requires time to think; he enquires into every part of his subject with the searching of philosophy, and when he comes forward he comes highly charged with interesting matter; there is no skimming over the surfaces of a subject with him; he must sink to the bottom to see what foundation it rests on."[5]

James Madison, primary author of the Virginia Plan, unofficial recorder of the convention debates, and later coauthor of the *Federalist Papers,* which were written to promote the Constitution's ratification in New York. "Every person seems to acknowledge his greatness," Pierce said of Madison. "He blends together the profound politician with the scholar.... [Of] the affairs of the United States, he perhaps has the most correct knowledge of any man in the Union."[6]

George Mason, a prominent politician from Virginia who had authored the 1774 Fairfax Resolves, the Virginia Constitution, and Virginia's Bill of Rights. Pierce observed that Mason was "a gentleman of remarkable strong powers, and possesses a clear and copious understanding. He is able and convincing in debate, steady and firm in his principles, and undoubtedly one of the best politicians in America."[7]

Gouverneur Morris of Pennsylvania, who had been a member of the Continental Congress and had helped to devise America's monetary system. Of Morris, Pierce wrote, "One of the geniuses in whom every species of talents combine.... No man has more wit... than Mr. Morris."[8] It was Gouverneur Morris who wrote most of the final draft of the Constitution, including its preamble.

Robert Morris, also of Pennsylvania, known as the financier of the Revolution. Morris had been a member of the Continental Congress and chairman of its important Committee of

Safety during the war. He was one of the signers of the Declaration of Independence. "Robert Morris is a merchant of great eminence and wealth, an able financier, and a worthy patriot," Pierce wrote. "He has an understanding equal to any public object, and possesses an energy of mind that few men can boast of."[9] Morris's attractive three-story home was considered the finest mansion in Philadelphia. Although Washington had originally lodged at a boardinghouse, Morris finally persuaded him to stay at his house during the convention.

Charles Cotesworth Pinckney of South Carolina, a major general during the war and two years a prisoner of war, had been a distinguished leader in South Carolina politics. "He has received the advantage of a liberal education," Pierce wrote, "and possesses a very extensive degree of legal knowledge."[10]

Edmund Randolph, the governor of Virginia, presided over the nation's most populous state of over half a million. Randolph had served as aide-de-camp to General Washington during part of the Revolutionary War. Later he served in the Continental Congress and for several years as Virginia's attorney general. Pierce described him as "a young gentleman in whom unite all the accomplishments of the scholar and the statesman."[11]

Roger Sherman of Connecticut, a former shoemaker who had finally achieved distinction in the legal profession. He was the only American who had signed the Declaration of Rights and Grievances (the formal protest of the Stamp Act Congress), the Declaration of Independence, the Articles of Confederation, and the Constitution. Sherman was for several years a member of Congress and served on the committees to draft the Declaration of Independence and the Articles of Confederation. Pierce wrote that Sherman "deserves infinite praise.

No man has a better heart or a clearer head."[12]

James Wilson of Pennsylvania, a distinguished lawyer and long-time member of Congress. In 1779 he served as Advocate-General for France. "Mr. Wilson ranks among the foremost in legal and political knowledge," Pierce wrote. "He has joined to a fine genius all that can set him off and show him to advantage. He is well acquainted with man, and understands all the passions that influence him. . . . No man is more clear, copious, and comprehensive than Mr. Wilson."[13]

George Wythe of Virginia, who had distinguished himself as the first professor of law in America. He had been a former member of the Continental Congress and had trained some of the nation's early leaders in the legal profession: Thomas Jefferson, John Marshall, James Monroe, Henry Clay, and others. Wythe also had signed the Declaration of Independence. Pierce described him as "one of the most learned legal characters of the present age. He is remarked for his exemplary life and universally esteemed for his good principles. No man, it is said, understands the history of government better than Mr. Wythe—nor [is there] anyone who understands the fluctuating conditions to which all societies are liable better than he does."[14] Unfortunately, Wythe was able to stay at the convention for only a few days. Then he was called home to his wife, who was seriously ill. She subsequently died, and Wythe never returned to the convention.

Those who gathered at the convention were unquestionably members of a prestigious group: eight had signed the Declaration of Independence; seven had been governors of their states; forty-two had served in one of the gatherings of Congress (including the Stamp Act Congress and the Continental Congress); thirty-one were either lawyers or judges; almost all had broad political experience on the state level.

Thirty of the fifty-five delegates had been officers under Washington's command in the Revolutionary War, and three had served as close, trusted aides. The average age of the delegates was forty-four.

Famed historian Samuel Eliot Morison wrote of the convention's delegates, "Practically every American who had useful ideas on political science was there except John Adams and Thomas Jefferson, on foreign missions, and John Jay, busy with the foreign relations of the Confederation. Jefferson contributed indirectly by shipping to Madison and Wythe from Paris sets of Polybius and other ancient publicists who discoursed on the theory of 'mixed government' on which the Constitution was based."[15] Adams also made an important contribution, authoring *A Defence of the Constitutions of Government of the United States of America,* which was carefully read by some of the delegates and often quoted during the convention debates.

"Banish from Your Bosoms Those Demons"

Once the convention came to order on May 25, the first matter of business was to choose a presiding officer. Franklin, old and gout-ridden, intended to nominate Washington as president of the convention, but the aging statesman was too ill to attend that day. Acting in Franklin's place, Robert Morris, also of Philadelphia, made the nomination. John Rutledge of South Carolina seconded the motion, and the delegates voted their unanimous approval. Washington was not accustomed to presiding over civil convocations, and he apologized in advance for any mistakes he might make. He had been hesitant even to attend—now, suddenly, he had been pushed to the forefront of the whole affair.

With Washington seated on the podium, the convention

Washington presiding at the Constitutional Convention of 1787. The convention delegates, whom Jefferson called "an assembly of demigods," made it their first order of business to unanimously elect George Washington the president of the convention.

proceeded to establish their rules of order. Each state was given one vote in the convention, following the pattern used in Congress. All comments were to be addressed to the president or chairman, thus diminishing the possibility of arguments erupting among the delegates. No delegate was to be allowed to speak more than twice on a given issue unless he received special permission from the other members of the convention.

The most important rule of all: the proceedings of the convention must be kept strictly secret until final adjournment. The delegates did not want preliminary reports of their deliberations to leak out before their final decisions were reached. They wanted to be able to speak freely, to discuss ideas and philosophies openly, to discard or further develop theories and approaches without fear of popular reaction. To ensure security, they kept all doors and windows closed throughout that long, hot Philadelphia summer. Sentries were posted outside the building to keep out those who did not belong. No one was admitted without signed, authenticated credentials.

Unrelated to security, but designed to aid the concentration of the delegates, the cobblestone street in front of the State House was covered with straw and sand to diminish the noise of passing carriages and wagons.

Washington soon learned that the delegates varied widely in their expectations of the convention. "Much is expected from it by some, but little by others, and nothing by a few," he wrote to Thomas Jefferson. However, "that something is necessary all will agree, for the situation of the general government (if it can be called a government) is shaken to its foundation, and liable to be overset by every blast. In a word, it is at an end . . . unless a remedy is soon applied."[16]

Congress had authorized a convention to merely revise the Articles of Confederation. But the delegates had barely convened when they decided to scrap the flawed Articles and start afresh. Rather than sew a new patch of cloth on a rotten garment, they agreed to tailor a completely new suit. "The sentiments of the different members seem to accord more than I expected they would, as far as we have yet gone," Washington observed hopefully in the early days of the convention.[17]

This approach to the convention's appointed task was more radical than it might at first seem. In many ways the United States were more independent than united. The Articles of Confederation had served to bring under one central government thirteen independent and sovereign states. Yet the Articles of Confederation removed little of the sovereignty of the states. The central government was weak, with very limited powers, and most of the real powers remained with the states.

What Washington, Madison, and others were proposing, then, was not a simple rewriting of the nation's charter. They were suggesting that America adopt a completely different form of government, one in which the national government would be much stronger and the states would in many ways hold a subordinate position.

As rumors of the convention's actions began to circulate (despite the strict rule of secrecy), a number of Americans grew increasingly anxious. What if the convention usurped power from the states? What if the delegates decided to establish a monarchy? Could Americans really trust these men to write a new constitution? The *Massachusetts Centinel* took pains to put minds at rest. "Ye men of America," the paper editorialized, "banish from your bosoms those demons, *suspicion* and *distrust*.... Be assured the men you have delegated ... are men in whom ye may confide.... Consider, they have at their head a Washington."[18]

Debating the Virginia Plan

Some of the delegates were unwilling to go beyond the mandate given by Congress—to revise the Articles of Confederation. But most felt the nation's situation was so desperate that other options must be considered. Accordingly, on May 29 Virginia's Edmund Randolph rose from his chair and presented the plan his state's delegates had earlier devised. The "Virginia Plan" or "fifteen resolves" called for a government with power balanced between three branches: legislative, executive, and judicial. The legislature would have two houses, one with representatives to be elected by the people of each state, the other with representatives chosen by the first house. The legislative branch would have all the powers granted to Congress by the Articles of Confederation, as well as authority to pass laws on matters of general (as opposed to local) importance. Any state law that contradicted the proposed constitution could be negated by an act of Congress.

The executive branch would wield the executive powers Congress had held under the Articles of Confederation, as well as "a general authority to execute the national laws."

The judiciary was to resolve all "questions which may involve the national peace and harmony."[19]

After hearing Randolph's lengthy speech, the convention decided to move into a committee of the whole, chaired by Judge Nathaniel Gorham of Massachusetts (a highly respected former president of Congress), to discuss the Virginia Plan. The committee of the whole was designed to allow the delegates to freely debate the issues without reaching any conclusions that would be binding on the convention. The committee meeting started the following morning, May 30. Each morning and afternoon Washington opened the session, then turned his gavel over to Gorham and took his place among the other Virginia delegates.

As the delegates considered the provisions of the Virginia Plan, according to William Pierce, each man was given a copy of "these propositions, . . . with the injunction to keep everything a profound secret." One morning a delegate dropped his copy, which was subsequently picked up by Thomas Mifflin and given to Washington. Pierce recorded what happened next:

After the debates of the day were over, and the question for adjournment was called for, the General arose from his seat and, previous to his putting the question, addressed the convention in the following manner—

"Gentlemen: I am sorry to find that some one member of this body has been so neglectful of the secrets of the convention as to drop in the State House a copy of their proceedings, which by accident was picked up and delivered to me this morning. I must entreat [the] gentlemen to be more careful, lest our transactions get into the newspapers and disturb the public repose by premature speculations. I know not whose paper it is, but there it is (throwing it down on the table), let him who owns it take it."

At the same time he bowed, picked up his hat, and quitted the room with a dignity so severe that every person seemed alarmed. . . . It is something remarkable that no person ever owned the paper.[20]

The committee of the whole methodically debated item after item of the Virginia Plan, approving the basic ideas as they went. Their approach was to first find the points of agreement and to defer the areas of disagreement until later on. At the end of each day's session, Gorham stepped down, Washington resumed the chair, and Gorham reported on the debates of the day. On June 13 Judge Gorham reported the conclusions of the committee of the whole: the Virginia Plan had merit and should be considered by the convention.

"I See No End to My Staying Here"

Washington again took the chair, and the debates began anew. Surprisingly, the discussions proceeded almost as though the delegates had not already considered the same issues in the committee of the whole. Unfortunately, the warm amity they had enjoyed earlier now burst into bitter divisiveness. The primary point of conflict was how the Congress should be organized. Under the Articles of Confederation, each state had been allowed one vote in Congress. Should that be continued, or should the larger states be given additional votes based on population? Should the Senators be appointed by the other legislative house, or should they be elected by the people or by the state legislatures? Was it really desirable to allow Congress to negate state laws that conflicted with the new constitution?

On June 15 William Paterson, an influential lawyer from New Jersey, proposed an alternative that strongly appealed to the smaller states. Rather than create a new constitution, he said, why not simply amend the Articles of Confederation to give Congress greater power? Each state could still have one vote, but the body would have more authority over the states and thus each vote would count for more. Response to Paterson's proposal was heated, with impassioned arguments being advanced on both sides of the issue. When a vote was finally taken on June 19, the plan lost: three states for the Paterson plan, seven states against. (Two states did not vote: The delegates from New Hampshire did not arrive until the end of July, and there were too few delegates from New York to constitute a voting quorum.) This vote was particularly significant. It confirmed the delegates' desire to consider the creation of a new form of government, rather than to amend the existing form.

As the convention returned to their consideration of the Virginia Plan, the stormy debates lengthened. Despairing of a speedy conclusion to the convention, Washington wrote home for more clothes. "I see no end to my staying here," he said. [21]

The Convention Reaches an Impasse

By early June the delegates had come to agreement on one important point: "A national government ought to be established, consisting of a supreme legislative, executive, and judiciary." [22] But there the agreement stopped. They still could not reach consensus on how each branch should be chosen. The more populous states wanted representation based on population. Standing stoutly in opposition, the smaller states prophesied that under such an arrangement their interests would not be represented at all. They would forever be outvoted by the larger states. The two sides soon reached a stalemate.

By June 28 tempers were so high that Franklin recommended daily prayer in their meetings. Man's wisdom was obviously insufficient for the task at hand, he explained— perhaps they ought to seek some wisdom from God. The proposal was voted down, primarily because the convention had no funds with which to pay a minister, and Washington grew discouraged. "I almost despair of seeing a favorable issue to the proceedings of our convention," he wrote to Hamilton, who, also discouraged, had temporarily returned to his home in New York. [23]

On June 29 a decision on the lower house was finally reached, the smaller states being outvoted six to four: the House of Representatives would have membership in proportion to the population of each state. Having lost the battle over the House, the smaller states opened debate on the membership of the second chamber with increased vigor. Washington disagreed with their point of view, as did the other delegates from Virginia, preferring that the upper chamber also have membership according to each state's population. But the need for compromise was critical,

Washington knew. What would be accomplished if the larger states won their point—and the smaller states abruptly walked out? Where would the Union be then?

On July 2 another vote was taken. The result was a tie: five states were for equal representation in the second chamber, five were for representation according to population, and one was divided. (New York at this point had no representation.) Deadlocked, neither side would yield. Then South Carolinian Charles Cotesworth Pinckney proposed that a committee be appointed (a "grand committee," as some called it), with one delegate from each state, to work out a compromise. [24] The convention approved and, to allow time for the committee to work, adjourned over the third and fourth of July.

Conflict and Compromise

During the two-day break, Washington attended patriotic services at the Reformed Calvinist Church and dined at the state house with the Pennsylvania chapter of the Order of Cincinnati. But despite the welcome distractions, he was constantly preoccupied with apprehension and worry about the stalemate in the convention—it seemed all too probable that the delegates would drag home in sorry defeat.

On the morning of July 5 the delegates reconvened, anxious to hear the compromise committee's proposal. They learned that at first the wrangling had continued unabated, but finally Franklin had brought the group to agreement: Representation in the first chamber of Congress (the House of Representatives) would be by population, as decided earlier. That chamber would have exclusive authority to originate bills levying taxes, appropriating money, and fixing congressional salaries. The second chamber (the Senate) could not alter or amend the appropriation and taxation bills of the first, but it would not be subordinate to the first in any other legislation. In the Senate each state would have an equal vote. Senators were to be chosen by the respective state legislatures; members of the House would be elected by the people in each state. In essence, the House would represent the people, while the Senate would represent the states.

The small states were delighted, but some of the more populous states were unhappy with the compromise plan. They felt it gave too much power in the Senate to the few people who populated the small states. James Madison and Gouverneur Morris attacked the plan with emotion and energy, seeking to sway the undecided states to their view. But Washington was more open to such innovations, and through the long days of debate he grew increasingly exasperated. Too many delegates on both sides of the issue, he complained, were "narrow-minded politicians...or under the influence of local views."[25]

Finally, on July 16, another vote was taken. The result: five states for the plan, four against, one divided. The compromise had carried.

The large states still were not satisfied, but they could not agree on an alternative proposal. As they further discussed the compromise in informal settings, a broad spirit of accommodation slowly began to set in. Finally the body of delegates found themselves coming to agreement.

"To Please All Is Impossible"

Washington was not altogether happy with the solution, but, as he wisely wrote, "To please all is impossible, and to attempt it would be vain. The only way, therefore, is... to form such a government as will bear the scrutinizing eye of criticism, and trust it to the good sense and patriotism of the people to carry it into effect."[20]

In the days that followed, the convention made rapid progress. The delegates voted that the new Congress would not be able to negate state laws, although its acts would be the "supreme law of the respective states."[27] They defined the basic form and function of the judiciary, the means of admitting new states, the means of electing the executive, and the veto power of the executive.

But other particulars regarding the executive branch stopped them short. Some delegates favored a three-man presidency; others stubbornly held for a one-man executive. Many felt a one-man executive smacked of monarchy; they shrank from the painful memories of England's George III and his excesses. Others saw a committee-type executive as cumbersome and unreliable. Committees do not make decisions quickly—and they find it all too easy to defer responsibility for faulty judgments.

Despite the aversion of many to a single executive, the majority of the delegates finally accepted the idea. Perhaps they were willing to give so much power to one man because they had seen in one of their own countrymen a compelling model of the judicious use of power. "Many of the members cast their eyes towards General Washington as President," explained Pierce Butler of South Carolina, "and shaped their ideas of the powers to be given to a President by their opinions of his virtue."[28]

Moving Toward a Final Draft

On July 26 the convention adjourned again, leaving only a "Committee on Detail" to create an initial draft of the constitution the delegates had been hammering out. (The committee members were John Rutledge, Edmund Randolph, Nathaniel Gorham, Oliver Ellsworth, and James Wilson.) During the ten-day break allowed for that purpose, Washington went fishing for perch on the Delaware and made a melancholy visit to Valley Forge. It was a refreshing, contemplative change from the long, hot summer days cramped in a tight hall with thirty to fifty men.

When the delegates reconvened on August 6, the draft of the Committee on Detail was printed and ready. With Washington presiding, the group went over the proposed constitution word by word, line by line, paragraph by paragraph, slowly, laboriously, meticulously. Every day, six days a week (breaking only for Sunday), the delegates met from ten in the morning to four in the afternoon, carefully discussing and debating the specific issues that had been raised. They argued about federal assumption of state debts, the problem of national defense, the ethics and economics of slave trade. Whenever they found themselves locked in an impasse, they sent the problems to committees for recommendations.

By Saturday, September 8, all were agreed on the specific content of the new Constitution. It represented a consensus of the delegates' best thinking, incorporating the best of the political philosophies of Polybius, John Locke, Baron Charles de Montesquieu, and other classical and contemporary writers. On that day the Constitution was sent to a committee of five skilled writers and clear thinkers, jointly assigned to create a final version. The five chosen for the Committee on Style, all lawyers, were superbly qualified for the task—Dr. William Samuel Johnson of Connecticut, an elderly man of great understanding and an old-school gentleman in every way; Alexander Hamilton of New York, only thirty years old but generally viewed as brilliant; Gouverneur

Morris of Pennsylvania, a one-legged financial genius with an enviable flair for expression; James Madison of Virginia, noted in the convention for his forceful and incisive arguments in debate; and Rufus King of Massachusetts, a man with a rich classical background.

The committee on style (principally Gouverneur Morris) went back over the Constitution like precise copy editors, refining the language and checking the grammar. Gouverneur Morris also wrote a new preamble. On September 12 the polished document was sent to the printer, who made a copy for each delegate to review.

It seemed that nothing could now stand in the way of a speedy and successful conclusion to the convention. But on Saturday the fifteenth, in the midst of last-minute suggestions, Virginia's Edmund Randolph suddenly stood to be recognized by the chair. During the preceding months he had wavered back and forth in his support for the proposed Constitution. On more than one occasion he had threatened not to support the work of the convention unless certain changes were made. Now he was making good on his threat, proclaiming that he would not sign the Constitution unless another general convention were scheduled to create what we now know as the Bill of Rights. Sixty-two-year-old George Mason, one of Washington's neighbors and a scrupulous, seasoned politician, spoke out in support of Randolph. Elbridge Gerry of Massachusetts also voiced some deep concerns about the Constitution and announced that he too would not sign.

The hall buzzed in response. Most agreed that the points were well taken; the additional amendments were indeed desirable and necessary. But the proposed Constitution already allowed for needed amendments, and to close the first convention by establishing another would be to jeopardize all that had gone before. One by one, in unanimous judgment, the states voted no to Randolph's motion.

It was now nearly six o'clock, two hours past the agreed upon adjournment time. The final proposed change had been presented and debated. With the discussions closed, Washington stood, calling for a roll of the states. Would they or would they not accept the Constitution they had created? Down the roll they went, calling the names of the states from north to south: New Hampshire? "Aye." Massachusetts? "Aye." Connecticut? "Aye." New Jersey? "Aye." Down the roll to the end, with the last state being Georgia, and again the answer was "Aye."

Of the states represented at the convention, none voted in dissent. With a unanimous recommendation of the states, the Constitution would now be sent to Congress for action. Convention president George Washington lifted his gavel, then let it fall.

"A Unique Creation"

The following Monday, September 17, 1787, the delegates gathered for the last time, emotions welling near the surface. For four long months they had labored together; now, at last, it was time to send their precious creation out into the world.

Before the delegates signed the document, Nathaniel Gorham stood and proposed a last-minute change: that the clause declaring "the number of Representatives shall not exceed one for every forty thousand" be changed by striking out "forty thousand" and inserting "thirty thousand." He apologized for making such a proposal after all the debates had supposedly been concluded, but felt it was necessary "for the purpose of lessening objections to the Constitution."[29]

Washington then arose from his chair and began to speak. It was the only speech on a specific issue he delivered in the entire convention. James Madison recorded:

> When the President rose, ... he said that although his situation had hitherto restrained him from offering his sentiments on questions depending in the House and, it might be thought, ought now to impose silence on him, yet he could not forbear expressing his wish that the alteration proposed might take place. It was much to be desired that the [states'] objections to the plan recommended might be made as few as possible. The smallness of the proportion of representatives had been considered by many members of the Convention [to be] an insufficient security for the rights and interests of the people. He acknowledged that it had always appeared to himself among the exceptionable parts of the plan; and late as the present moment was for admitting amendments, he thought this of so much consequence that it would give much satisfaction to see it adopted.
>
> No opposition was made to the proposition of Mr. Gorham and it was agreed to unanimously.[30]

Finally, each taking his turn, the delegates picked up the quill pen, dipped it into the ink bottle, and grandly signed the new Constitution, with only three standing in dissent: Edmund Randolph, George Mason, and Elbridge Gerry. At the top of the list of signers, written in bold form, was the name of the man who had helped to make it all happen, the man who had contributed so much by his very presence: George Washington, president and deputy from Virginia.

Washington was solemn when he signed his name to the document. "Should the states reject this excellent constitu-

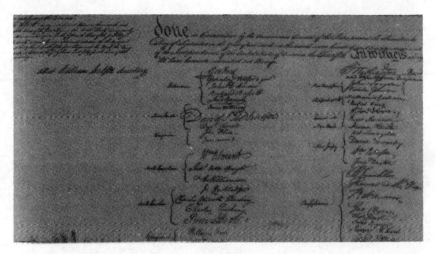

The signatures on the Constitution of the United States. The Constitution was signed on September 17, 1787, by 39 of the original 55 delegates. Washington's signature is at the top of the right-hand column of names. He signed the document "Go. Washington, Presidnt. and deputy from Virginia."

tion," he said, "the probability is that an opportunity will never again offer to cancel another in peace—the next will be drawn in blood."[31]

Madison noted that "whilst the last members were signing" the Constitution, Benjamin Franklin made a quiet comment to those who were nearest him. "Looking towards the President's chair [the one from which Washington had presided], at the back of which a...sun happened to be painted, [he] observed...that painters had found it difficult to distinguish in their art a rising from a setting sun. I have, said he, often and often in the course of the session, and the vicissitudes of my hopes and fears as to its issue, looked at that [sun depicted on Washington's chair] without being able to tell whether it was rising or setting. But now at length I have the happiness to know that it is a rising and not a setting sun."[32]

That night Washington "retired to meditate on the momentous work which had been executed."[33] The Constitution, he knew, was a unique creation in the political history of the world—

> a government of the people; that is to say, a government in which all power is derived from and, at stated periods, reverts to them; and...in its operation, it is purely a government of laws made and executed by the fair substitutes of the people alone.... It is clear to my conception that no government before introduced among mankind ever contained so many checks and such efficacious restraints to prevent it from degenerating into any species of oppression.[34]

After a final night in Philadelphia, he dallied no longer; the following morning saw him on his way home, eager for a long-awaited rest and reunion with Martha.

The Miracle of the Constitution

A number of the delegates regarded the successful creation (and later ratification) of the Constitution as nothing less than a miracle. James Madison wrote in a letter to Thomas Jefferson, who was then serving as minister to France, that it was "impossible to consider the degree of concord which ultimately prevailed as less than a miracle."[35]

And Washington wrote to Lafayette in early 1788, "It appears to me...little short of a miracle that the delegates from so many different states (which states you know are also different from each other in their manners, circumstances, and prejudices) should unite in forming a system of national government."[36]

In the two hundred years that have passed since the Constitution became the foundation of our government, its principles have helped America to stay strong and free. Our form of government (and the freedoms it ensures) is a key reason why we were able to grow from a tiny, infant nation in 1776 to the richest and most powerful country in the world.

What is this Constitution that our Founders labored so hard to create? What sets it apart from other forms of government in the world?

As might be expected, the document itself gives us some vital clues. The Constitution is divided into seven articles: Article I deals with the legislature, Article II with the executive branch, and Article III with the judicial branch. As a protection against tyranny, the Founders created a federal government in which power was balanced, separated, divided, and distributed. No branch of the government could fully function without the others; at the same time, each branch was to have a certain amount of autonomy, having authority to act unilaterally in certain areas. Political scientists call these aspects of our government "separation of powers" and "checks and balances." These are essential and vital elements of American constitutionalism.

A Limited Government

Article I also defines the limitations on the lawmaking powers of Congress. Since neither the executive nor the judicial branch was to pass laws for the United States, the limitations on Congress are restrictions on the federal government in general. Section 8 of Article I contains a fairly specific list of areas in which the federal government may legislate. These include a power to "lay and collect taxes," "to borrow money," "to regulate commerce with foreign nations," "to coin money," "to establish post offices and post roads," "to declare war," and so forth.

The specific list in Article I, section 8, tells us that the

Founders intended the federal government to be a limited government, restricted in its powers. As they later clarified in the Tenth Amendment, "The powers not delegated to the United States by the Constitution, nor prohibited by it to the states, are reserved to the states respectively, or to the people."

James Madison explained in *The Federalist*:

> The powers delegated by the proposed Constitution to the federal government are few and defined. Those which are to remain in the State governments are numerous and indefinite. The former will be exercised principally on external objects, as war, peace, negotiation, and foreign commerce; with which last the power of taxation will, for the most part, be connected. The powers reserved to the several States will extend to all the objects which, in the ordinary course of affairs, concern the lives, liberties, and properties of the people, and the internal order, improvement, and prosperity of the State.[37]

James Madison, "The Father of the Constitution." He was the primary author of the Virginia Plan (which served as the framework for debate in the Constitutional Convention), was active in debate at the convention, kept the most thorough record of the convention's proceedings, coauthored The Federalist Papers, *led the ratification debates in Virginia, and acted as main architect of the Bill of Rights.*

Elsewhere Madison said, "This is not an indefinite government ... but a limited government, tied down to the specified powers which explain and define the general terms."[38] And Jefferson wrote, "Congress [has] not unlimited powers to provide for the general welfare, but [is] restrained to those specifically enumerated."[39]

The Founding Fathers had had enough of an overly powerful government under King George III. They felt that both the public good and the liberties of the people required that the American system of government feature a vertical separation of powers as well as a horizontal separation. The horizontal separation was the division of powers on the federal level. The vertical separation was the division of powers between the federal government and the states. The Constitution makes clear that the federal government was to be more limited in power than the states were—and that, in the end, all power resided in the people themselves.

Article IV of the Constitution deals with relationships between the states, as well as some restrictions placed on them. Article V describes the amendment process. Article VI provides that the Constitution will be the supreme law of the land. And Article VII specifies the ratification procedure.

The Preamble to the Constitution, written by Gouverneur Morris, describes the purpose of the Constitution: "We the people of the United States, in order to form a more perfect Union, establish justice, insure domestic tranquility, provide for the common defense, promote the general welfare, and secure the blessings of liberty to ourselves and our posterity, do ordain and establish this Constitution for the United States of America."

Elements of the Foundation

Underlying the Constitution are some unspoken assumptions that help form its foundation. Without such a foundation the Constitution would not have the meaning and power it does. Four pillars in the foundation of the Constitution are:

First, it recognizes the existence of natural law. In the Declaration of Independence Thomas Jefferson referred to "the laws of Nature and of Nature's God." Natural law recognizes the existence of God and acknowledges that God has established a natural order of things for this earth and the people of this earth. The concept of unalienable rights is based on an understanding of natural law, as are the three principles below.

Second, the Constitution is based on the principle that the citizens of a republican nation must be virtuous and moral. Benjamin Franklin wrote: "Only a virtuous people are capable of freedom. As nations become corrupt and vicious, they have more need of masters."[40]

Washington held deep feelings about the need for morality and virtue among Americans. He wrote to Lafayette that America's constitutional government would protect us only "so long as there shall remain any virtue in the body of the people."[41] And in his Farewell Address he emphasized, "Of all the dispositions and habits which lead to political prosperity, religion and morality are indispensable supports."[42]

Third, the Constitution acknowledges that the people are the true sovereigns in a republican government. The Founders rejected the notion that a king has a "divine right" to rule. Under natural law, no man has a right to rule over another, unless the subject gives his consent.

Alexander Hamilton emphasized this in *The Federalist:* "The fabric of American empire ought to rest on the solid basis of the consent of the people. The streams of national power ought to flow immediately from that pure, original fountain of all legitimate authority."[43] And James Madison added, "The ultimate authority, wherever the derivative may be found, resides in the people alone."[44] Washington concurred: "The power under the Constitution will always be in the people," he wrote in 1787.[45]

Fourth, the Constitution was created on the assumption that America would function under a free-market economy, recognizing and protecting property rights. John Adams wrote: "All men are born free and *independent*, and have certain natural, essential, and unalienable rights, among which may be reckoned the right of enjoying and defending their lives and liberties; that of acquiring, possessing, and protecting property; in fine, that of seeking and obtaining their safety and happiness."[46]

These, then, are the elements that make the Constitution what it is. It is a federal government of limited powers, with those powers divided both horizontally and vertically. The horizontal separation of powers is between the bicameral legislature, the executive, and the judiciary, each with checks and balances on the others; the vertical separation is between the federal government and the states.

It is a government based on principles of natural law, assuming a populace that is moral and virtuous, and recognizing the people as sovereigns. It is a government built to function in a free-market economy.

These were all ideas and principles that were important to George Washington. It is no wonder that he was enthusiastic as he penned his name in large letters at the top of the list of signatures on the Constitution.

Washington's Influence in the Convention

Washington's role in the convention was significant, though quiet. Although he was viewed as a strong, determined leader, he was reticent when it came to speaking in public, especially extemporaneously. Further, in the convention setting, he felt his role as president enjoined silence. He thus spoke only rarely before the convention or the committee of the whole.

But he found subtle ways to influence the delegates just the same. According to the rules of order, all remarks were addressed to Washington as president of the convention (except, of course, when the delegates were meeting as a committee of the whole). In the small room, generally with no more than thirty delegates present at one time, all could clearly see his face, which openly conveyed his feelings. When rancor reigned and the delegates seemed unwilling to compromise, Washington's face bore an expression of "anxious solicitude." When the compromise finally came and the problem was fruitfully resolved, his "countenance . . . brightened, and a cheering ray seemed to break in upon the gloom."[47] Washington was thus able to communicate with the delegates even when he wasn't speaking.

Washington's influence may also have been felt in another way. In afternoons and evenings, when they left the convention chambers, the delegates often mingled socially. Some historians suspect that Washington took that opportunity to informally discuss problems and philosophies and points of view, helping his fellow delegates find amity where previously there had been only discord. It is impossible to fully measure the impact Washington had in these casual settings, but it is likely that it was great.[48]

Even though he often saw measurable progress, the responsibility of the convention weighed heavily on Washington. The convention leader "seemed pressed down in thought" when seen in public.[49] Washington wrote gloomily,

"There are seeds of discontent in every part of the Union, ready to produce other disorders if the wisdom of the present convention should not be able to devise, and the good sense of the people be found ready to adopt, a more vigorous and energetic government."[50]

Gouverneur Morris later recalled one critical point when the convention delegates seemed unable to agree. He noted that Washington's "countenance had more than usual solemnity. His eye was fixed, and seemed to look into futurity. 'It is (said he) too probable that no plan we propose will be adopted. Perhaps another dreadful conflict is to be sustained. If, to please the people, we offer what we ourselves disapprove, how can we afterwards defend our work? Let us raise a standard to which the wise and the honest can repair. The event is in the hand of God.'"[51]

Washington's lofty ideals were a comfort to the anxious American public, who were still kept in the dark about the convention's proceedings. One paper reported, "A Washington surely will never stoop to tarnish the luster of his former actions by having an agency in anything capable of reflecting dishonor on himself or his countrymen."[52]

Another observed: "In 1775, we beheld [Washington] at the head of the armies of America, arresting the progress of British tyranny. In the year 1787, we behold him at the head of a chosen band of patriots and heroes, arresting the progress of American anarchy, and taking the lead in laying a deep foundation for preserving that liberty, by a good government, which he had acquired for his country by his sword."[53]

But Washington's work was not yet finished. The new Constitution must now pass the test of public opinion—and that opinion would be based in part on the views held by George Washington.

Chapter 33

The Ratification Fight

The new Constitution was sent first to Congress for approval. Congress was openly pleased with the convention's work and, after only eight days of deliberation, voted unanimously to transmit the new Constitution to the people of the states for ratification. Washington looked to the coming months with deep anxiety. Would the people accept the new form of government? Or would the Union continue to disintegrate until there was open anarchy?

The Constitution "is now a child of fortune," Washington observed, "to be fostered by some and buffeted by others."[1] He soon saw the highly emotional form that most of the objections were taking. They were, he noted, "better calculated to alarm the fears than to convince the judgment."

[Opponents] build their objections upon principles that do not exist, which the Constitution does not support them in, and the existence of which has been, by an appeal to the Constitution itself, flatly denied; and then, as if they were unanswerable, draw all the dreadful consequences that are necessary to alarm the apprehensions of the ignorant or unthinking. It is not the interest of the major part of those characters to be convinced, nor will their local views yield to arguments which do not accord with their present or future prospects. [2]

Firm in his support for the convention's work, Washington would not budge. Had the convention not aggressively altered the Articles of Confederation, he wrote, "anarchy would soon have ensued, the seeds being richly sown in every soil." [3]

He thought it remarkable that the Constitution had even come into existence. "It appears to me... little short of a miracle that the delegates from so many states,... different from each other in their manners, circumstances, and prejudices, should unite in forming a system of national government so little liable to well-founded objections." [4]

"A Fair and Dispassionate Investigation"

With the Constitution before the states, Washington decided to refrain from public involvement in the ratification process. Regardless of the consequences, he resolved to let the people decide for themselves. "I did not incline to appear as a partisan...," he explained later. "It was my sincere wish that the Constitution... might, after a fair and dispassionate investigation, stand or fall according to its merits or demerits." [5]

That attitude, however, did not prevent him from expressing his strong personal views in private or in letters to his regular correspondents. At several critical times in the ratification fight, he wrote to friends in a number of states, urging them to stand firm against the powerful, eloquent enemies who had risen up against the new Constitution. As might have been expected, many of his letters found their way into the American press. Washington made no objection. For example, in a masterful letter to Lafayette he expressed his deep appreciation for the "merits of the new Constitution." Then he declared, "I will disclose [my sentiments] without reserve, although by passing through the post offices they should become known to all the world; ... I have nothing to conceal on that subject." He then said, for Lafayette and "all the world" to read:

> My creed is simply:
> First, that the general government is not invested with more powers than are indispensably necessary. ...
> Secondly, that these powers ... are so distributed among the legislative, executive, and judicial branches that it can never be in danger of degenerating into a monarchy ... so long as there shall remain any virtue in the body of the people. ...
> The proposed Constitution ... is provided with more checks and barriers against the introduction of tyranny ... than any government hitherto instituted among mortals. ͦ

Determining "the Political Fate of America"

Washington had initially felt that a public noninvolvement in the ratification battles was the prudent stance to take. But the heated struggle sometimes gave him second thoughts. On one occasion when it appeared that the Constitution was in genuine danger of defeat, he wondered aloud if he had not "meddled ... in this political dispute less ... than a man so thoroughly persuaded as I am ... ought to have done."⁷

But even where Washington tried to keep himself out of the fight, others freely thrust him into it. Avid supporters of the Constitution constantly used his name as a sharp knife to cut down the arguments of dissenters. For example, one newspaper noted, "The arguments . . . most insisted upon in favor of the proposed Constitution are that if the plan is not a good one, it is impossible that either General Washington or Doctor Franklin would have recommended it."[8]

Another asked pointedly, "Is it possible that the deliverer of our country would have recommended an unsafe form of government for that liberty for which he had for eight long years contended with such unexampled firmness, consistency, and magnanimity?"[9]

As with the reprinting of his letters, Washington did not object to such arguments. If the use of his name helped the new Constitution pass the ratification hurdle, so much the better.

By February 1788 six of the required nine states had ratified the Constitution. Several of those that remained seemed to be waiting to see what Virginia would do. That state had both strong supporters, such as Washington and Madison, and strong opponents, including Patrick Henry and one of the convention delegates who had refused to sign, George Mason. (Governor Edmund Randolph had also refused to sign, but now he favored ratification.) In spite of the opposition, Washington was optimistic. "No doubt, from the first, has been entertained in my mind of the acceptance here [in Virginia]," he wrote, "notwithstanding the indefatigable pains which some very influential characters take to oppose it."[10]

After eight states had ratified, Washington wrote to Lafayette, "A few short weeks will determine the political fate of America for the present generation and ... a long succession of ages to come."[11]

Washington's expectation of a favorable outcome came true. On June 21 New Hampshire became the ninth state to accept the Constitution. Four days later, unaware of New Hampshire's action, the Virginia convention at Richmond also ratified. In late July New York followed suit. In all three cases the vote had been close. A change of only six votes in New Hampshire would have defeated ratification there. In Virginia, only four votes made the difference; and in New York, two votes made victory possible.

But even though the margin of victory was narrow, the new Constitution nevertheless carried. The new government had been born.

"A Lasting Foundation for ... Happiness"

Boats floated up the Potomac to congratulate Washington, and cannons boomed to honor him on the ratification of the Constitution. He hailed the Constitution and its ratification as a "new phenomenon in the political and moral world, and an astonishing victory gained by enlightened reason over brute force."[12]

Washington exulted to his friends: "No one can rejoice more than I do at every step the people of this great country take to preserve the Union, establish good order and government, and to render the nation happy at home and respectable abroad. No country upon earth ever had it more in its power to attain these blessings than united America."[13]

And who had placed those blessings within America's reach?

> We may, with a kind of pious and grateful exultation,
> trace the fingers of Providence through those dark and

mysterious events which first induced the states to appoint a general convention, and then led them one after another ...into an adoption of the system recommended by that general convention, thereby, in all human probability, laying a lasting foundation for tranquility and happiness, when we had but too much reason to fear that confusion and misery were coming rapidly upon us. That the same good Providence may still continue to protect us, and prevent us from dashing the cup of national felicity just as it has been lifted to our lips, is [my] earnest prayer. [14]

With rich emotion, Washington celebrated the hand of God in the establishment of America—but even God must work through human agents. Those agents were many: James Madison, the guiding force behind the Constitution's basic scheme; Thomas Jefferson, Madison's mentor and philosophical guide; John Adams, whose *Defence of the Constitutions of Government of the United States* had a profound impact on the convention's delegates; Alexander Hamilton, whose *Federalist* writings (written in collaboration with Madison and John Jay) presented a cogent, convincing argument for the new Constitution; Robert Morris, Gouverneur Morris, James Wilson, Roger Sherman, John Rutledge, and a host of others who championed the Constitution, fighting for it with both heart and hand.

But no matter how brilliant the document, and no matter how eloquent the advocates who defended it, the Constitution would likely have failed without the backing of the nation's most popular leaders, George Washington and Benjamin Franklin. "Be assured," wrote James Monroe, perceptively putting into words what many others were feeling, "[Washington's] influence carried this government." [15]

Chapter 34

"Best Fitted" for the Presidency

With the Constitution ratified, Washington looked forward to ending his days in the quiet seclusion of his farm. But voices from all directions were calling for his continued leadership. The ink had scarcely dried on the proposed Constitution before David Humphreys, a friend and former military aide, wrote, "What will tend perhaps more than anything to the adoption of the new system will be a universal opinion of your being elected President of the United States and an expectation that you will accept it for a while."[1] Joining Humphreys were a host of newspapers, all confidently predicting that Washington would be the first chief executive. The *Pennsylvania Packet* even published a "new federal song," whose five verses each concluded with the words,

> Great Washington shall rule the land
> While Franklin's counsel aids his hand.[2]

With some insistency, Gouverneur Morris added his view that "should the idea prevail that you would not accept of the presidency, it should prove fatal in many parts. . . . Of all men, you are the best fitted to fill that office. Your cool, steady temper is indispensably necessary to give firm and manly tone to the new government. . . . You must, I repeat must, mount the seat."[3]

Despite the repeated recommendations of valued friends, Washington continued to resist the idea. He had several strong reasons to avoid the office, but foremost among them was his feeling that another person, someone more willing, could do the job as well as Washington could. He wrote:

> Notwithstanding my advanced season of life, my increasing fondness for agricultural amusements, and my growing love of retirement, . . . yet it will be no one of these motives, nor the hazard to which my former reputation might be exposed, or the terror of encountering new fatigues and troubles, that would deter me from an acceptance, but a belief that some other person, who had . . . less inclination to be excused, could execute all the duties [fully] as satisfactorily as myself.[4]

"Clouds and Darkness"

Throughout the year, Washington consistently rejected the suggestions of friends and admirers. "The presidency . . . has no enticing charms and no fascinating allurements for me," he wrote to Lafayette. His only wish, he said, was to live and die "an honest man on my own farm. Let those follow the pursuits of ambition and fame who have a keener relish for them, or who may have more years in store for the enjoyment."[5]

But many, including his longtime friend Alexander Hamilton, closed their ears to his stubborn resistance. They argued that America desperately needed a strong and recognized leader at the helm—specifically George Washington. Washington answered Hamilton by saying, "I should unfeignedly rejoice in case the electors, by giving their votes in favor of some other person, would save me from the dreaded dilemma of being forced to accept or refuse." He then revealed his deep, distressful feelings about the situation: "I have always felt a kind of gloom upon my mind . . . as I have been taught to expect I might . . . be called to make a decision."

Despite Washington's denials, however, Hamilton's hammering arguments had their effect. Earlier, Washington had flatly refused to even consider the Presidency. But now he was weakening. In the same letter he wrote, "If I should receive the appointment and if I should be prevailed upon to accept it, the acceptance would be attended with more diffidence and reluctance than I ever experienced before in my life."

If he did accept, he continued, "It would be . . . with a fixed and sole determination of lending whatever assistance might be in my power to promote the public weal, in hopes that at a convenient and early period my services might be dispensed with, and that I might be permitted once more to retire, to pass an unclouded evening after the stormy day of life, in the bosom of domestic tranquility."⁶

Three weeks later, he described his dark forebodings at the thought of assuming the presidency. Accepting that post, he wrote, "would be the greatest sacrifice of my personal feelings and wishes that ever I have been called upon to make. It would be to forgo repose and domestic enjoyment for trouble, perhaps for public obloquy, for I should consider myself as entering upon an unexplored field, enveloped on every side with clouds and darkness."

Despite his misgivings, Washington seemed to sense that a mantle of inescapable duty was descending upon his shoulders. He admitted he had reached the point where he could be prevailed upon to accept the position—but only under the compelling weight of "the conviction that the partiality of my countrymen had made my services absolutely necessary, joined to a fear that my refusal might induce a belief that I preferred the conservation of my own reputation and private ease to the good of my country."[7]

The problem bore down on the frustrated Washington for over a year. From the beginning of 1788 to the end, his fears and hesitations filled his waking thoughts each day and swirled through his dreams by night. December found him still wrestling with the decision. "May Heaven assist me in forming a judgment," he pleaded, "for at present I see nothing but clouds and darkness before me."[8]

"I Anticipated...Ten Thousand Embarrassments"

When 1789 arrived Washington knew the apprehensive waiting was almost over. The die was cast, whether he liked it or not. In early January 1789 the eleven states of the Union chose their presidential electors (North Carolina and Rhode Island had not yet ratified the Constitution). A month later the electors cast their votes and sent them to Congress, as required by the Constitution. Almost immediately, rumors began to sweep the country that Washington had been named President by a unanimous vote. The tally would not be formally announced until Congress met to make an official count—but Washington saw no reason to disbelieve what he had heard, and he began to make preparations. Still pressed by heavy debts, he sought a large loan from a private citizen so he could start afresh, and he borrowed additional money to fund the anticipated journey to the national capital of New York. Twice he visited his aged and ailing mother in Fredericksburg, hoping to prepare her for the extended absence which this new assignment would make necessary.

"The event which I have long dreaded I am at last constrained to believe is now likely to happen," he wrote. From the moment when his election appeared "inevitable, I anticipated, in a heart filled with distress, the ten thousand embarrassments, perplexities, and troubles to which I must again be exposed in the evening of a life already nearly consumed in public cares."[9]

Congress was to gather in New York on March 4 to count the ballots, but snowy, sloppy roads and stormy weather delayed them. It was early April before a quorum had finally assembled. Time plodded, tortoise-like, day after day, as Washington awaited word of his fate. In those long, emotionally charged days, Washington compared his agonized, fearful feelings to "those of a culprit who is going to the place of execution."[10]

Finally, on April 6, Congress opened the electors' ballots and proclaimed that George Washington was indeed the unanimous choice for President. John Adams was named Vice President.

Congress appointed Charles Thomson, secretary of the Congress, to carry the official news to the new President. Thomson, long a staunch patriot, had been secretary of Congress when Washington had been a member back in 1775. When Thomson arrived at the doorstep of Mount Vernon on April 14, he read the official notification from Congress, then listened intently as Washington, hardly able to keep the emotion from his voice, read his prepared response:

> I have been long accustomed to entertain so great a respect for the opinion of my fellow citizens that the knowledge of their unanimous suffrages having been given in my favor scarcely leaves me the alternative for an option.... While I realize the arduous nature of the task which is imposed upon me, and feel my own inability to perform it, I wish there may not be reason for regretting the choice. All I can promise is only that which can be accomplished by an honest zeal. [11]

Farewell to Private Life

Two days later, with his home affairs in order, Washington departed for New York by coach. Accompanying him were Charles Thomson and David Humphreys. "I bade adieu to Mount Vernon, to private life, and to domestic felicity," he recorded in his diary, "and with a mind oppressed with more anxious and painful sensations than I have words to express, set out for New York . . . with the best dispositions to render service to my country in obedience to its call, but with less hope of answering its expectations." [12]

As the new President journeyed northward, he was greeted by enthusiastic celebrations at every stop. Swarms of people lined the road to see his coach, while uniformed troops of local militia met him on the road and escorted him into each city and town. Leading citizens took delight in saluting their new leader with long speeches; town fathers honored him at festive banquets. Washington appreciated the affection and confidence expressed by his fellow citizens, but he felt pressed to push quickly toward his destination—some of the Congressmen had been waiting over a month for the new government to move into operation. Still, he patiently took time to respond to the warm American graciousness as he slowly moved northward.

His first stop was Alexandria, Virginia, where friends gave him a lavish dinner. In an affectionate address, Mayor Dennis Ramsay said: "Farewell! Go and make a grateful people happy, a people who will be doubly grateful when they contemplate this recent sacrifice for their interest. To that Being who maketh and unmaketh at His will, we commend you; and, after the accomplishment of the arduous business to which you are called, may He restore to us again the best of men and the most beloved fellow citizen."[13]

In a moving response, Washington admitted the deep feelings that burned inside. "Words, my fellow citizens, fail me," he said. "Unutterable sensations must then be left to more expressive silence, while, from an aching heart, I bid you all, my affectionate friends and kind neighbors, farewell!"[14]

The next day he arrived in Baltimore. Answering a laudatory speech offered there, he returned the compliment, noting that America's people were the foundation of the nation's future success: "It appears to me that little more than common sense and common honesty, in the transactions of the community at large, would be necessary to make us a great and a happy nation."[15]

When he rolled out of Baltimore at half past five the following morning, he was bidden farewell by roaring cannon. A troop of Baltimore militia accompanied him for seven full miles; finally, Washington climbed out of his coach and persuaded them to turn back.

"The Approaches Were Graced with ... Flags"

Two days later, as he neared Philadelphia, he was presented with a richly caparisoned white horse, on which he was to head a triumphal parade entering the city. As Washington approached the city, tall and imposing on his prancing mount, he was joined by scores of dignitaries and well-wishers from Philadelphia, including such distinguished gentlemen as Thomas Mifflin, president of the Supreme Executive Council of Pennsylvania, and Richard Peters, speaker of the Pennsylvania Assembly. Washington had known both men when they had served for long years on the Board of War during the revolution.

At Gray's Ferry outside of Philadelphia, Washington was surprised to see the bridge extravagantly decorated in his honor. After enlisting the services of Charles Willson Peale, the Gray brothers "had adorned amazingly the unstable structure. At each end of the bridge was an arch of laurel; the sides were lined with more of that shrub and with cedar.... All the approaches were graced with large flags— one that proclaimed 'The New Era,' another that portrayed the rising sun of empire."[16] The north side of the bridge displayed banners for each of the eleven states that had ratified the Constitution; the south side boasted the Union flag.

After crossing the Schuylkill to enter Philadelphia, Washington was deeply moved to see the enthusiastic reception that awaited him. "Every fence, field, and avenue" was lined with excited citizens, both young and old, rich and poor— more than twenty thousand in all—who had come to see their new President.[17] Cannon boomed, sending their message to far-distant towns.[18] Church bells rang out a greeting. The people cheered and clapped, and Washington bowed from his horse. The setting was in stark contrast to the ragged march he had taken through the city in August 1777, instructing his men to do their forlorn best to make a good impression—but understanding completely when they failed.

The appreciative citizens of Philadelphia were eager to hear their new President speak, and their many formal addresses provided him that opportunity. "When I contemplate the interposition of Providence in guiding us," he said, "...I feel myself...almost overwhelmed with a sense of divine munificence. I feel that nothing is due to my personal agency." He then gave voice to the deep faith that buttressed his view of the prospects ahead: "If I have distressing apprehensions,...I am supported...by a confidence that the most gracious Being, who has hitherto watched over the interests and averted the perils of the United States, will never suffer so fair an inheritance to become a prey to anarchy, despotism, or any other species of oppression." [19]

"Strew Your Hero's Way with Flowers"

Other cities and towns were just as demonstrative as Philadelphia. As Washington neared Trenton, mounted once again on a spirited charger given him for that purpose, he reined up in surprise as he approached the bridge over Assunpink Creek. The once-familiar bridge had been changed into a decorated monument, covered by an arch twelve feet long and twenty feet high. On the southern face of the arch he read, "The Defender of the Mothers Will Also Defend the Daughters."

Charmed and pleased, Washington began to advance across the bridge, but he was stopped by the stunning sight of dozens of little girls in white, teenagers in spring costume, and mothers and older matrons—all from Trenton—ranked on both sides of the road. As he looked on in astonishment, they burst into song:

Welcome, mighty Chief! once more
Welcome to this grateful shore!
Now no mercenary foe
Aims again the fatal blow—
Aims at thee the fatal blow.
Virgins fair, and Matrons grave,
Those thy conquering arms did save,
Build for thee triumphant bowers
Strew, ye fair, his way with flowers—
Strew your Hero's way with flowers. [20]

As the song concluded, young girls with baskets of flowers skipped forward and scattered blossoms along their hero's path. Washington's emotions welled. When the baskets were empty, he bowed deeply and thanked the children and women for their warm and thoughtful graciousness.

On April 23, at Elizabeth Town, New Jersey, he stepped into an expensive new barge, a forty-seven-foot sailboat with thirteen supplementary oars on each side, which had been provided especially for this occasion. Thomson, Humphreys, and a joint committee of Congress accompanied him. The entire population of Elizabeth Town, it seemed, had converged on the dock to see him depart on the final phase of his journey. As the barge slipped across the water toward New York City, an artillery salute rang through the air. Washington looked back to see the New Jersey militia still standing at attention on the dock.

"All the Guard I Want"

Despite the extravagant receptions Washington had encountered on his northward journey, nothing prepared him for the rich welcome awaiting him at New York. He was escorted across the bay by an assemblage of both large and small craft, all with colorful flags flying. The battery on Staten Island saluted him with thirteen guns as he passed. This was answered later by a thirteen-gun salute from a British packet and a Spanish sloop of war, the *Galveston*, which was ceremonially flying the flags of twenty different countries.

As the barge pulled near the wharf, Washington was stunned to see thousands upon thousands of New Yorkers crowded along the waterfront. He tried to hide the effusion of his emotion, but could not. Another thirteen cannon roared in greeting. The throng shouted out three huzzahs, and, at the appointed time, church bells began to ring for a full half hour.

Washington had barely stepped from the barge, climbing up the carpeted steps, when an officer moved forward, saluted, and announced that a military guard had been assigned to escort the General to his residence. Washington was hesitant and answered: "As to the present arrangement [of having an escort], I shall proceed as directed. But after this is over I hope you will give yourself no further trouble, as the affection of my fellow citizens"—and here he gestured toward the attentive crowd—"is all the guard I want."[21]

When the journey was over and Washington could finally relax, he recalled the amazing events in his diary. He reflected on the flowers, songs, and poems that had been offered him, the many laudatory speeches he had heard, and especially the elaborate ceremonies on his arrival at New York. The public had truly showered him with praise and affection—but through it all, in the secret recesses of his heart, he had continued to have doubts and misgivings. What if he proved inadequate to the task? What if he embarrassed himself with clumsy mistakes? What if he were forced to make critical decisions that then brought public condemnation because the people did not have all the facts? How often that had happened during the war!

Knowing how quickly cheers can change to criticism and scorn, Washington wrote in his diary:

"The display of boats, . . . the decorations of the ships, the roar of cannon, and the loud acclamations of the people . . . filled my mind with sensations as painful (considering the reverse of this scene, which may be the case after all my labors to do good) as they are pleasing."[22]

Chapter 35

"God Bless Our President!"

Apr il 30, 1789, was the day set for the President's inaugural. Washington arose early, had his hair powdered, and dressed himself in a Connecticut-manufactured suit of broadcloth, hoping thus to advertise the infant American textile business. Then he took his breakfast in his quarters.

Shortly after noon, he heard "the sound of horses' hoofs, the tramp of troops, and the grind of carriage wheels."[1] A joint committee of Congress had come to escort him to Federal Hall. At half past the hour, the General slowly rolled off in his grand coach pulled by four splendid horses. Preceding him in the presidential procession was a small contingent of troops, while riding behind him were his secretaries, leading representatives from the joint committee of Congress, and a few eminent citizens.

"Long Live George Washington!"

The inauguration ceremonies took place on a crowded Federal Hall portico that overlooked Wall and Broad streets. Excited throngs had gathered to watch, surrounding the portico on the ground, on rooftops, at windows, a sea of faces stretching as far as eye could see. When Washington stepped onto the portico and saw the vast extent of the crowds, he bowed to the people who had called him to serve, his face deadly sober. They erupted in cheers that could not be stopped until Washington had bowed again and again, his hand held over his heart.

When the crowd had quieted, President-elect George Washington and William Livingston, Chancellor of New York, faced each other near the portico's iron railing. Since no Supreme Court justices had yet been appointed, Livingston, New York's highest judicial officer, had been named to administer the oath of office. Samuel Otis, secretary of the United States Senate, lifted an ornate, leather-covered Bible, along with the plush red cushion it was resting on, and took his place between Washington and Livingston. When Washington saw that Livingston was ready, he placed his right hand on the Bible.

"Do you solemnly swear," the chancellor asked, "that you will faithfully execute the office of President of the United States and will, to the best of your ability, preserve, protect, and defend the Constitution of the United States?"

"I do solemnly swear that I will faithfully execute the office of President...," Washington answered, repeating the oath in first person. Then, the oath formally finished, Washington reverently added the words, "So help me, God," and bowed and kissed the Bible.

"It is done," Livingston said. Turning to the crowd, he

President George Washington
taking the oath of office on April
30, 1789, at Federal Hall in
New York City. Washington
repeated the oath after Robert R.
Livingston, chancellor of New
York, then added, "So help me
God," and bent and kissed
the Bible.

gestured toward their new President and shouted, "Long live George Washington, President of the United States!" The crowd responded with wild, joyful cheers: "Long live George Washington! Long live George Washington!" and, clearly, through the din came the shout, "God bless our President!"[2]

"A Reverence for the ... Rights of Freedom"

Washington had not intended to address the people, and he would not have been heard had he tried. Instead, he once again bowed his acknowledgment of the crowd's courtesy. They roared in response.

Washington paused a moment as the cheering continued, then stepped back into the Senate chamber of Federal Hall to read his inaugural address. His hands trembled as he began, speaking in a low, deep voice. He reminded the Congressmen assembled that it had been most difficult to accept the office of President. He was tired of the public battles, and he felt uncomfortably inadequate to the duties at hand. Yet the people had called him, and he had responded.

Now the new government must move forward with a national view. "No local pledges or attachments, no separate views nor party animosities" must "misdirect the comprehensive and equal eye which ought to watch over this great assemblage of communities and interests."

The new President had only one specific suggestion for the first Congress. With some "inquietude," the public was calling for amendments to the Constitution to more fully secure their rights. Certainly such amendments would be on the agenda of the first Congress. Washington said: "I assure myself that while you carefully avoid every alteration which might endanger the benefits of a united and effective government, or which ought to await the future lessons of experience, a reverence for the characteristic rights of freedom and a regard for the public harmony will sufficiently influence your deliberations on the question [of] how far the former can be more impregnably fortified, or the latter be safely and advantageously promoted."

He then turned to the issue of compensation. As he had in 1775, when he was named commander in chief, he voiced his willingness to serve without salary, asking only that his official expenses be paid. (Congress later declined his offer, voting him an annual salary of $25,000.)

The remainder of Washington's address, for the most part, dealt with his undeviating faith in God and the imperative need for national reliance on goodness and truth.

> It would be peculiarly improper to omit in this first official act my fervent supplications to that Almighty Being who rules over the universe, who presides in the councils of nations, and whose providential aids can supply every human defect, that his benediction may consecrate to the liberties and happiness of the people of the United States a

government instituted by themselves for these essential purposes, and may enable every instrument employed in its administration to execute with success the functions allotted to his charge.... No people can be bound to acknowledge and adore the invisible hand which conducts the affairs of men more than the people of the United States. Every step by which they have advanced to the character of an independent nation seems to have been distinguished by some token of providential agency....

There is no truth more thoroughly established than that there exists, in the economy and course of nature, an indissoluble union between virtue and happiness, between duty and advantage, between the genuine maxims of an honest and magnanimous policy and the solid rewards of public prosperity and felicity.... We ought to be no less persuaded that the propitious smiles of heaven can never be expected on a nation that disregards the eternal rules of order and right which heaven itself has ordained.

He concluded his remarks by "resorting once more to the benign Parent of the human race in humble supplication." As God had helped the people of America become free and establish a republican government, so Washington hoped that "his divine blessing [might] be equally conspicuous in the enlarged views, the temperate consultations, and the wise measures on which the success of this government must depend."[3]

The members of Congress were deeply affected by the President's address. Fisher Ames, perhaps the greatest orator in Congress, wrote: "It was a very touching scene and quite of the solemn kind. [Washington's] aspect grave, almost to sadness; his modesty, actually shaking; his voice deep, a little tremulous, and so low as to call for close attention; added to the series of objects presented to the mind, and overwhelming it, produced emotions of the most affecting kind upon the members. I . . . sat entranced. It seemed to me an allegory in which virtue was personified, and addressing those whom she would make her votaries."[4]

"An Ocean of Difficulties"

The speeches and festivities over, Washington turned himself to the heavy challenge of establishing a new government. He entered his high office unsure of himself. "I walk on untrodden ground," he fretted. None had gone before to show him the way; he was the pathfinder. To further complicate his situation, he walked along a precipice where serious mistakes could prove disastrous: "There is scarcely any part of my conduct which may not hereafter be drawn into precedent."[5] Since his precedents might well lead to critical turning points, he could only "devoutly" wish "that these precedents may be fixed on true principles."[6]

As he considered the broad complexities of his situation, he felt he faced "an ocean of difficulties . . . without that competency of skill, abilities, and inclination which is necessary to manage the helm."[7] As a result, he said, "I may err, notwithstanding my most strenuous efforts to execute the difficult trust with fidelity; . . . but my errors shall be of the head and not of the heart."[8] Despite his nagging feeling of inadequacy, he had one solid foundation on which to stand: "The Constitution of the United States, and the laws made under it, must mark the line of my official conduct."[9] Washington thus established a wise precedent, showing his successors the way to safeguard America's liberty.

Setting Up House

After concluding all her business at Mount Vernon, Martha joined her husband at the end of May. She also had been feted on her northward journey, enjoying crowds and escorts and thirteen-gun salutes. She was pleased when she saw the President's House on Cherry Street in New York, which had been provided by Congress. She noted it was "a very good one and...handsomely furnished all new for the General."[10] She soon found that she was pressed by visitors almost as constantly as was her husband. "I have not had one half-hour to myself since the day of my arrival," she groused good-naturedly to a niece two weeks after reaching New York.[11]

One of Martha's early visitors was Abigail Adams, wife of Washington's Vice President. "She received me with great ease and politeness," Mrs. Adams wrote. "She is plain in her dress, but that plainness is the best of every article.... Her hair is white, her teeth beautiful, her person rather short than otherwise.... Her manners are modest and unassuming, dignified and feminine, not the tincture of hauteur about her."[12]

In her next letter, Abigail continued her warm description of the new First Lady: "Mrs. Washington is one of those unassuming characters which create love and esteem. A most becoming pleasantness sits upon her countenance and an unaffected deportment which renders her the object of veneration and respect. With all these feelings and sensations I found myself much more deeply impressed than I ever did before their majesties of Britain."[13]

Martha doubtless would have shifted uncomfortably under such high praise. She viewed herself in a much more homely light; she was, she said, an "old-fashioned Virginia housekeeper, steady as a clock, busy as a bee, and cheerful as a cricket."[11]

However one describes her, Martha Washington was a gracious and effective hostess in the President's House. She

*Martha Washington in 1796.
Martha was gracious and unassuming as the First Lady, but,
like her husband, she preferred the
quiet life at Mount Vernon.*

ran the household with all the efficiency of a woman accustomed to overseeing the center of a large plantation; she supervised the servants and even planned many of the large, official dinners President Washington served.

The value of her presence was felt almost immediately. However, the day after her arrival, the President hosted an afternoon meal without giving Martha adequate time to prepare. "It was the least showy dinner that I ever saw at the President's," one Senator, usually easy to please, critically observed. But before the summer had passed, Martha was able to elicit high praise—even from Senators who were more wont to complain. Wrote one of an August 27 meal, "It was a great dinner, and the best of the kind I ever was at."[15]

Another visitor remembered the strict punctuality of those dinners. "When lagging members of Congress came in, as they often did, after the guests had sat down to dinner," he remembered, "the President's only apology was, 'Gentlemen (or sir), we are too punctual for you. I have a cook who never asks whether the company has come, but whether the hour has come.'"[16]

In addition to inviting dignitaries to dinner, the President left a standing order in behalf of his former comrades in war. If any Revolutionary War veteran should call, Washington told his staff, he was to be served a good meal and given a few dollars before he left.

"I Am Not Afraid to Die"

Martha's presence became particularly important in the summer of Washington's first year as President. In mid-June he began to suffer from a burning fever and a large, painful tumor on his left thigh. Doctors tried diligently to break the fever, but their usual methods brought no result. The tumor grew quickly and became fiery red. Rumors flew around the country that the life of Washington was in dire danger. The excruciating pain tortured the President day and night; ropes were stretched across Cherry Street and straw was spread on the sidewalk to diminish the noise of passing traffic so he could rest.

Martha tended her bedridden husband for several weeks, lovingly responding to his needs. Eventually the tumor showed itself to be an abscess. Dr. Samuel Bard, a noted New York practitioner, decided in consultation with his father, Dr. John Bard, that surgery would be required to save the President's life. Washington pressed Dr. Bard to tell him the truth about his condition. "Do not flatter me with vain hopes," he said. "I am not afraid to die, and therefore can bear the worst.... Whether tonight or twenty years hence makes no difference; I know that I am in the hands of a good Providence."[17]

With the medical practices of the day, Washington had to endure the operation without the benefit of anesthetic. The younger doctor made the long incision and found the tumor was larger than they had expected. Seeing it, his father exclaimed: "Cut away—deeper—deeper still! Don't be afraid. You see how well he bears it!"[18]

The entire tumor was removed, and five days later the fever was completely gone. But Washington struggled for weeks to regain his strength. He had his carriage restructured so he could lie down in it and feel the massaging motion of the carriage as it jostled over the cobblestone streets.

In September, after twelve tiresome weeks of fighting the stubborn illness, Washington confided to Dr. James Craik, "The want of regular exercise, with the cares of office, will, I have no doubt, hasten my departure for that country from whence no traveler returns." Still, concerns about health must be shoved aside: his primary concern must remain "a faithful discharge" of the trust he had accepted. [19] It was forty days before he could spend a few short hours at his desk, and four months before his wound was completely healed.

In addition to his own shattered health, Washington had another reason why death was on his mind: his mother died on August 25, a victim of the cancer that had long been an affliction to her. [20] Though George must have been deeply saddened by her passing, it did not come as a complete surprise. She had been ailing when he last saw her, and his "final leave" had been taken with the thought of "never expecting to see her more."[21]

In examining his inner feelings about his mother's death, Washington once again revealed the astonishing depth of his faith, a faith that held firm even when staring into the ghastly face of death: "Awful and affecting as the death of a parent is, there is consolation in knowing that Heaven has spared ours to an age beyond which few attain, and favored her with the full enjoyment of her mental faculties and as much bodily strength as usually falls to the lot of fourscore. Under these considerations and a hope that she is translated to a happier place, it is the duty of her relatives to yield due submission to the decrees of the Creator."[22]

Just a few months after recovering from the tumor, Washington suffered another serious illness, contracting a frightening form of pneumonia in May 1790. The sickness was "of threatening appearance," said Thomas Jefferson, his new Secretary of State. "Yesterday (which was the fifth day) he was thought by the physicians to be dying.... He continues mending today, and from total despair we are now in good hopes of him."[23]

After Washington recovered, Martha wrote to a friend that he "seemed less concerned himself as to the result than perhaps almost any other person in the United States."[21]

At the end of the year Washington reflected, "Within the last twelve months, I have undergone more and severer sickness than thirty preceding years afflicted me with, put it all together."[25]

"No Man Has Influence with the President"

Washington's election had not even been made official before scores of office seekers began to pester him for government appointments. "Scarcely a day passes in which applications of one kind or another do not arrive," he noted in March. [26] He early resolved to steel himself against the subtle influences of friendship and kinship in making appointments. To ensure fairness and equity, he established three criteria by which he would be guided:

1. The candidate must be fit to fill an office.

2. The person must have served well in other positions in the past.

3. As much as possible, all the states must be equally represented in the appointive positions.

He hated to disappoint people by rejecting their applications, but there were far more aspirants than there were positions. And the welfare of the country was infinitely more important than the desires of individuals were: "I should hold myself absolutely at liberty to act while in office with a sole reference to justice and the public good."[27]

One man, hoping to get a leg up on his competitors, approached Vice President John Adams for help in getting a public appointment from the President. Adams refused even to try. "No man, I believe, has influence with the President," he said. "He seeks information from all quarters and judges more independently than any man I ever knew."[28]

Washington hoped to get the executive branch organized quickly, but he was greatly hampered by the first Congress. That Congress had so much on its agenda that it was slow to establish the departments in the executive branch. By September, however, the way was clear for Washington to make his appointments for the major offices. He asked Thomas Jefferson to be Secretary of State, Alexander Hamilton to be Secretary of the Treasury, Edmund Randolph to be Attorney General, and Henry Knox to continue as Secretary of War. He also nominated John Jay as the first Chief Justice of the new Supreme Court.

For the most part, Washington dealt with his executive officers on an individual basis rather than as a group. The first formal Cabinet meeting (though that body was probably not called a Cabinet by Washington until 1793) was not held until November 1791, almost two years into Washington's first term. During that same period, however, the President dealt frequently with the individual Cabinet members, conferring in private meetings or through private letters.

When Cabinet members submitted items to the President's attention, he reviewed them carefully. "Generally, they were simply sent back after perusal," Jefferson recalled, "which signified his approbation. Sometimes he returned them with an informal note, suggesting an alteration or a query. If a doubt of any importance arose, he reserved it for conference." [29]

Working with a New Cabinet

The members of Washington's Cabinet were well suited to his exacting method of making decisions. As a rule, he tried to avoid reaching conclusions on important questions until he had consulted with those he trusted, hearing all sides of the issue. "I am anxious, always," he wrote, "to compare the opinions of those in whom I confide with one another, and those again (without being bound by them) with my own, that I may extract all the good I can." [30]

The President had strong confidence in his ability to discern the best course, particularly after he had considered all the options. But he never presumed to think he was a repository of all the correct answers. Early in his presidency he wrote:

> Shall I...set up my judgment as the standard of perfection?...Shall I arrogantly pronounce that whoever differs from me must discern the subject through a distorting medium, or be influenced by some nefarious design? The mind is so formed in different persons as to contemplate the same subject in different points of view. Hence originates the difference in questions of the greatest import, both human and divine. [31]

When he and Benjamin Harrison (a signer of the Declaration of Independence and later governor of Virginia) disagreed over an important constitutional issue, Washington reassured his friend:

> My friendship is not in the least lessened by the difference which has taken place in our political sentiments.... Men's minds are as variant as their faces, and where the motives of their actions are pure, the operation of the former is no more to be imputed to them as a crime than the appearance of the latter; for both, being the work of nature, are equally unavoidable. Liberality and charity... ought to govern all disputes.[32]

Even though he wisely sought the advice and counsel of others, Washington was never a puppet of others, never a figurehead President. The power to lead was his, and he exercised it firmly, although, always with his characteristic prudence. "He was always in accurate possession of all facts and proceedings in every part of the Union," Jefferson noted with admiration. Furthermore, he "formed a central point for the different branches, preserved a unity of object and action among them, exercised that participation in the suggestion of affairs which his office made incumbent on him, and met himself the due responsibility for whatever was done."[33]

Making the Presidency Respectable

In addition to his administrative approach, Washington brought a certain style and personality to the presidency itself. Unfortunately, that style sometimes collided with what some Americans considered appropriate for the "President of the people."

Americans as a group had mixed feelings about how the position should be treated. Some, including Washington, felt that the presidency should be accorded high respect; it was, after all, the most important single office in the entire republic. Others were concerned about the reestablishment of a monarchy, and any innovations that even suggested pomp or ceremony were completely repugnant to them.

Since Washington was plowing new ground, he made a conscious effort to make the presidency an office of dignity. He drove an expensive carriage, for instance, pulled by six cream-colored horses. When he rode on horseback, his tall white steed was covered with a leopard skin and a saddlecloth with gold binding. The entry to the President's House was manned by powdered servants, waiting to receive guests. Martha ran the house with the assistance of fourteen white servants and seven blacks from Virginia.

In the early days of the presidency, Washington was overwhelmed by countless visitors who dropped in at all hours to seek favors or simply to satisfy their curiosity. The President soon learned that he must limit such visits if he hoped to accomplish any of his important work. Accordingly, he

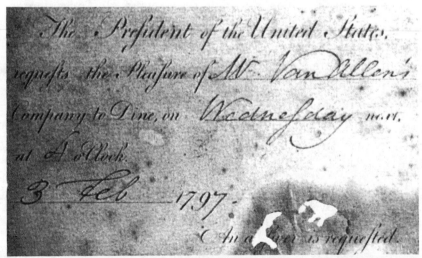

An invitation to dine with President and Martha Washington at the Executive Mansion in 1797. Every Tuesday night Washington held a "levee," where people could visit him without prior notice. But the many dinners he sponsored required an invitation.

established certain limited times when visitors could call without an appointment. Every Tuesday night, for instance, he held a "levee," where any respectably dressed person could come without an invitation and greet the President. Practical though his solution was, some criticized the President for separating himself from the people. Now that he was President, some carped, he thought himself too good for the common people.

Most, however, felt Washington was the dupe of evil, designing men behind him. One New England writer lamented that the "old General" was "being taken over" by high-hatted New Yorkers. In the homely words of the writer, "These fine folks would spoil our General if they could. He never was a greater man than when he rode among us with his dusty boots."[34]

Working with the First Congress

The people's uncertain feelings toward the presidency were reflected in one of the first actions of Congress. As that body considered what they should call the new chief executive, a majority of the Senate favored the title "His Highness, the President of the United States of America, and Protector of Their Liberties."[35] When Jefferson heard the proposal he scoffed, "The President's title as proposed by the Senate was the most superlatively ridiculous thing I ever heard of."[36]

Washington, mortified, agreed with Jefferson—he was embarrassed by the whole discussion. Having a fine carriage was one thing; being called "His Highness" was quite another. He was greatly relieved when the House of Representatives prevailed with their simpler title: "President of the United States."

Moving beyond the issue of titles, which was important in its implications, the first session of Congress boasted some laudable achievements. They passed the "impost bill," which finally established effective means by which the federal government could raise money. Continually strapped for funds, Congress knew this bill would be the first step to much-needed fiscal stability. Washington, ill at the time with the tumor, signed the bill from his sickbed.

The first Congress also approved the major departments of the executive branch, organized the federal court system, and directed the new Secretary of the Treasury to draft a plan for public credit, which he was to present in the next congressional session.

In many ways, the first Congress functioned as a second Constitutional Convention. Some of the states had ratified the Constitution with a strict proviso: certain amendments, particularly those delineating the basic rights of citizens, must be included as soon as possible. In September 1789 Congress approved twelve amendments to the Constitution and sent them to the states. Ten were ratified and became known as the Bill of Rights.

One amendment which the states rejected came back to haunt them later. This amendment provided that if the Congress gave itself a raise in pay (as the Constitution allowed), the raise could not take effect until after the next election. This gave the people a chance to defeat a Congress that tried to vote itself an extravagant pay raise. Amazingly, even though Congress approved the amendment, the states did not.

As the President looked back at the work of the first Congress, he was filled with praise. Shortly after they adjourned for the year, he wrote that the "national government is organized and, as far as my information goes, to the satisfaction of all parties.... Opposition to it is either no more, or hides its head."[37]

Chapter 36

"All Things ... Seem to Succeed"

The year 1789 closed with a bright and auspicious omen: North Carolina ratified the Constitution and joined the Union, becoming the twelfth state to send representatives to Congress. The nation, which had seemed incomplete with only eleven states, was beginning to be perfected. Four other states joined the Union during Washington's presidency: Rhode Island (May 1790), Vermont (March 1791), Kentucky (June 1792), and Tennessee (June 1796).

The country was also growing in other ways. In 1790 Washington signed a congressional bill providing for a national census every ten years. (This put into effect the constitutional mandate for a census found in Article I, section 2, clause 3.) The law went into effect immediately, yielding a figure for the population of the United States that year of 3,929,214. (According to modern estimates, the nation had

grown by well over a million inhabitants in the decade since
1780.) [1]

"The Surest Basis of Public Happiness"

In January 1790 Washington delivered his first State of the
Union address to Congress, a presidential report called for in
the Constitution. (He delivered such an address every year
thereafter, thus beginning the tradition of making the State
of the Union address an annual event.) As at his inaugural,
the President on this occasion dressed in a suit of broadcloth
manufactured in America, a relative rarity. He hoped that by
doing so he could encourage budding American manufacturers, even though "their broadcloths are not of the first
quality as yet." [2]

Washington began his address by congratulating Congress
"on the present favorable prospects of our public affairs." But
much room remained for growth and development. The
"common defense" was his first area of concern: "To be
prepared for war is one of the most effectual means of
preserving peace." It was vital that Americans become
independent of other nations in their manufacturing, "particularly for military supplies."

Washington's anxieties were not limited to possible
conflicts with Europe. "Certain hostile tribes of Indians" were
bringing "depredations" on "the inhabitants of our southern
and western frontiers," he said. Those citizens should be
protected, and, if necessary, the "aggressors" should be
punished.

Washington also spoke in his address of several pressing
needs: for uniformity in currency, weights, and measures; for
the advancement of agriculture and commerce; for improvement of the postal system; and for "the promotion of science
and literature."

"Knowledge is in every country the surest basis of public happiness," he said. [3]

Troubles with the Indians

Indian affairs were a continuing source of uneasiness. In July 1790 the President was forced to order troops against an uprising of the Miami and Wabash along the Ohio. At the same time, angry Creeks threatened whites over a boundary dispute in Georgia; Secretary of War Henry Knox judiciously negotiated a resolution.

The armed resistance on the Ohio brought only temporary relief. Problems boiled up repeatedly—some suspected that the British (who still held army posts in the area) were inciting Indian raids against American villages. Washington ordered further troop action in September 1791, but American success was spotty and dearly won.

The Indians were potentially America's most formidable enemy, as they held the entire western border of the United States. But they were unorganized, at odds with one another through tribal rivalries, and wholly dependent on the white man for their guns and ammunition.

As the bloodshed persisted year after year, Washington began to think there must be a better way to deal with the Indians than simply to fight them. He encouraged the courts to treat the Indians with justice, arguing that they should have the same civil rights as white men. He also pursued new treaties with the Indians and reevaluated, for fairness, the treaties that had been made in the past.

President Washington was far-seeing in his views of Indian relations, but he was swimming against the stream of public opinion. Unable to effectively sway the views of his fellow citizens, he was never truly successful in cementing his policies into place.

Hamilton's Fiscal Plan

Before the Constitution was ratified, the United States was indebted almost to the point of bankruptcy. Unfortunately, the simple act of signing a new charter of government did not suddenly make the new nation solvent. Constitutional principles first had to be applied.

Alexander Hamilton, the first Secretary of the Treasury. Hamilton had earlier served as Washington's aide in the Revolutionary War and as a delegate to the Constitutional Convention.

As a first step to solving the problem, in 1789 Congress asked Alexander Hamilton, Secretary of the Treasury, to submit a national fiscal plan for congressional consideration. Of particular concern were the war debts of both the Continental Congress and the states. Despite Washington's best efforts, most of the debts due the soldiers of the Revolutionary War, now long delinquent, still had not been paid. In addition, some $12 million was owed to foreign banks and other creditors (primarily in France and Holland), and more than $40 million was owed to U.S. creditors. The states themselves also owed some $25 million in war debts. [1] The combined burden was nothing less than crushing.

Still, Hamilton thought he could see light through the dark tunnel. His plan consisted of three parts. [5] First, he wished to borrow $12 million to redeem the foreign debts. Second, he recommended that existing currencies from the war be exchanged for new bonds, which could circulate as money.

Hamilton's third recommendation threw him into a maelstrom of angry controversy. The national government, he said, should assume the states' war debts, then pay them off by collecting taxes. President Washington supported the proposal: since the war had been a common effort, the costs should be borne by all.

An idea that made sense on the surface, however, was violently opposed by some of the states. Virginia, for instance, had paid off most of its debts. Why should Virginians have to help pay the debts of another state? Massachusetts, on the other hand, was much delinquent in paying its obligations. Hamilton's proposal was exactly what they had been hoping for.

Hamilton, astutely aware of the political storms that lay ahead for his plan, knew that sailing would be rough. In fact, feelings ran so deep during the debates in Congress that both Massachusetts and South Carolina threatened to secede from the Union if their debts were not assumed.

When it seemed that the fabric of the Union might completely tear apart, Jefferson introduced a new element that opened the door to a workable compromise. With the poor communication and slow transportation of the time, each region clamored for the advantage of having the national capital in its area. Using the capital as his bargaining chip, Jefferson worked up a trade: Virginia would support the assumption of state debts, and Massachusetts would agree to move the national capital to the Virginia/Maryland area. [6] (In the meantime, until the new city could be built, Congress voted that the capital should be in Philadelphia.) Hamilton's plan had been up and down in Congress for nine frustrating months; finally, with the compromise, all three of his steps were approved, though in modified form, and were passed into law.

Washington was pleased with the compromise, which enabled the passage of Hamilton's financial plan and brought the seat of the national government so near to his lifelong home. The happy solution to the congressional wranglings he had just witnessed brought fresh optimism to Washington's spirit as he wrote to the Comte de Rochambeau about the current state of the American government. "We have a good government in theory," he wrote, "and are carrying it pretty happily into practice. In a government which depends so much in its first stages on public opinion, much circumspection is still necessary for those who are engaged in its administration. Fortunately, the current of public sentiment runs with us, and all things hitherto seem to succeed according to our wishes."[7]

By August 1790 all the arrangements had been made for the transfer of the national capital from New York to Philadelphia. President Washington departed New York on August 30, 1790, and arrived in Philadelphia on September 2. The officials of Philadelphia had arranged for him to live in what may have been the finest mansion in the city—the Robert Morris home, where Washington had stayed during the Constitutional Convention three years earlier. Morris and his wife had graciously agreed to the idea and had found other quarters elsewhere. Washington had hoped to live on a farm in Philadelphia—he was ever homesick for Mount Vernon—but, upon inquiry, he learned that such a location would be impracticable.

The National Bank Furor

Congress finally assembled a quorum in the new capital by the first week of December 1790. They met in the Hall of Congress, a plain brick building at the southeast corner of Sixth and Chestnut streets. The hall had originally been built as a courthouse.

Shortly after Congress began their meetings, Hamilton dropped another potent bombshell, proposing the creation of a national bank "under a *private*, not a *public*, direction—under the guidance of *individual interest*, not of *public policy*."[8] Such a bank would have broad powers to serve the national government, lending it money and creating currency for circulation among the populace. The need was critical. When governments found themselves in a financial fix, Hamilton argued, they invariably came up with unwise and inflationary solutions. But private interests would seek to avoid inflation at all costs, thus doing more to keep the economy healthy.

The proposal passed Congress over Madison's strenuous objection that the whole idea was unconstitutional, arguing that Congress had no power to create any such entity as a bank. Washington had followed the debates closely, and when the bill reached his desk he was in a quandary. He had never used the veto; he felt the veto was to be used only to protect the Constitution. Was the bank really unconstitutional?

As was his practice, the President sought the counsel of his advisers. Secretary of State Thomas Jefferson wrote his firm conviction that Congress had no authority to create a bank. Attorney General Edmund Randolph, in a separate opinion, came to the same conclusion.

Washington then asked Secretary of the Treasury Hamilton to respond to the papers submitted by Jefferson and

Randolph. Hamilton answered in a fifteen-thousand-word paper, reiterating his support of the bank on constitutional grounds: "This general principle is inherent in the very definition of government . . . ," he wrote, "namely: That every power vested in a government is in its nature sovereign, and includes, by force of the term, a right to employ all the means requisite and fairly applicable to the attainment of the ends of such power, and which are not precluded by restrictions and exceptions specified in the Constitution."[9] (The Tenth Amendment, ratified ten months later, established a broad restriction on the federal government and underscored the Founders' intent to create a limited federal government, reserving most powers to the states and the people. The Tenth Amendment reads: "The powers not delegated to the United States by the Constitution, nor prohibited by it to the states, are reserved to the states respectively, or to the people." With the clarification the Tenth Amendment provided, such arguments as Hamilton's could no longer be considered valid.)

Washington's chief advisers were thus divided on the most fundamental principles. The best course proved to be elusive. Finally, the President signed the bill and gave birth to the bank, viewing it as only a temporary measure—the bank's charter was slated to expire after twenty years. Perhaps, in making the final decision, he took comfort in a passage from Jefferson's report:

> Unless the President's mind on a view of everything which is urged for and against this bill is tolerably clear that it is unauthorized by the Constitution—if the pro and the con hang so even as to balance his judgment—a just respect for the wisdom of the legislature would naturally decide the balance in favor of their opinion. It is chiefly for cases where they are clearly misled by error, ambition, or interest that

the Constitution has placed a check in the negative of the President. [10]

Even though Hamilton's scheme would perpetuate the national debt, Washington hoped to eliminate the debt as soon as possible. He urged Congress "to enter upon a systematic and effectual arrangement for the regular redemption and discharge of the public debt. . . . No measure can be more desirable," he explained, "whether viewed with an eye to its intrinsic importance or to the general sentiment and wish of the nation." [11]

Tours to North and South

Washington had been in office scarcely a month when he contemplated a "tour of the United States in order to become better acquainted with their principal characters and internal circumstances, as well as to be more accessible to numbers of well-informed persons who might give [me] useful information and advice on political subjects." [12] But his illness and the press of public business delayed him for a time.

He took his first tour in the fall of 1789. For nearly a month he traveled through the northeast, visiting every state in the north except Rhode Island, which had not yet joined the Union. (He visited Rhode Island the following year.) In a repeat of his triumphal journey to his inauguration, he was greeted by an endless stream of celebrations and fetes. At every opportunity, he spoke directly and simply in favor of the Constitution and a strong Union. The President's tour, one newspaper noted, "appears to have totally dissipated the fog of anti-Federalism." [13]

In the spring of 1791 he took a second tour, this time to the south. On the first leg of the trip he rode to the Potomac to examine the area selected for the new federal capital. It was his first of many visits to the site; over the years he repeatedly walked the land there, ordering surveys, buying property, and participating in ceremonies. Washington later wrote, "It was a pleasure indeed to find, in an infant country, such a display of architectural abilities."[14]

The southern tour took two full months. The President's object "was not to be received with parade and an ostentatious display of opulence. It was for a nobler purpose, . . . to learn on the spot the condition and disposition of our citizens."[15]

The itinerary for the journey was meticulously plotted and carefully followed. Washington wrote: "I performed a journey of 1,887 miles without meeting any interruption by sickness, bad weather, or any untoward accident. Indeed, so highly were we favored that we arrived at each place . . . on the very day I fixed upon before we set out. The same horses performed the whole tour, and, although much reduced in flesh, kept up their full spirits to the last day."

He was also gratified at the results of the journey. "It has enabled me to see with my own eyes the situation of the country through which we traveled," he explained, "and to learn more accurately the disposition of the people than I could have done by any information. The country appears to be in a very improving state. . . . Tranquility reigns among the people, with that disposition towards the general government which is likely to preserve it. They begin to feel the good effects of equal laws and equal protection."[16]

As part of his journey Washington took time to tour the sites of major southern battles of the Revolutionary War. His heart swelled as he thought of the great men who had led the American forces in those battles—and of the friends who had been lost.

Mount Vernon in 1792. Washington continued to be concerned with the administration of his plantation even while he was serving as President, and he periodically traveled there seeking a quiet refuge from the demands of his office.

On his return trip he lingered at Mount Vernon for two weeks, resting, relaxing, enjoying a chance to be home again. Then it was back on the road to Philadelphia. He found himself still en route on a Sunday, so he stopped to attend church in York, Pennsylvania. "There being no Episcopal minister present in the place, I went to hear morning service performed in the Dutch Reformed Church—which, being in that language (not a word of which I understood), I was in no danger of becoming a proselyte to its religion by the eloquence of the preacher."[17]

New Thoughts of Retirement

In 1792, the last full year of his first term, Washington turned his thoughts once again to retiring from public life. In a February conversation with Thomas Jefferson the President revealed that he "really felt himself growing old, his bodily health less firm, his memory, always bad, becoming worse, and perhaps the other faculties of his mind showing a decay to others of which he was insensible himself.... He found, moreover, his activity lessened, business therefore more irksome, and tranquility and retirement become an irresistible passion."[18] In addition, Jefferson noted, "he was sensible...of a decay of his hearing."[19]

In May 1792 Washington gave Madison a rough draft of a proposed farewell address, asking him to refine and polish it. In a letter to Madison he said, "I...still look forward to the fulfillment of my fondest and most ardent wishes to spend the remainder of my days (which I cannot expect will be many)...in ease and tranquility."

He continued, "Nothing short of conviction that my dereliction of the chair of government...would involve the country in serious disputes...could, in any wise, induce me to relinquish the determination I have formed."[20]

Madison was horrified to think that Washington might retire. The infant nation still needed his strong, steady hand to keep the country on course. Along with Hamilton, Jefferson, and others, Madison urged the President to continue for another term. Only by staying could he firmly establish America on the right footing.

In October Washington again confided his hesitations to Jefferson. The Secretary of State noted in his journal:

> As yet he was quite undecided whether to retire in March or not. His inclinations led him strongly to do it. Nobody disliked more the ceremonies of his office, and he had not the least taste or gratification in the execution of its functions.... He did not believe his presence necessary;... there were other characters who would do the business as well or better. Still, however, if his aid was thought

necessary to save the cause to which he had devoted his life principally, he would make the sacrifice of a longer continuance. [21]

Jefferson was ready with a powerful answer. He wrote to the President:

I consider your continuing at the head of affairs as of the last importance. The confidence of the whole Union is centered in you. Your being at the helm will be more than an answer to every argument which can be used to alarm and lead the people, in any quarter, into violence and secession. North and south will hang together if they have you to hang on. [22]

Washington thoughtfully listened to the sage counsel of the men he respected, then determined to say nothing publicly about his anxieties. If it was true that the country wanted and needed him so desperately, he would serve. In the months that followed he neither sought nor discouraged his election to a second term.

As most predicted, when the electoral votes were counted in February 1793 he was unanimously reelected. John Adams remained the Vice President. By the time Washington entered his second term on the fourth of March, he was a stout, but aging, sixty-one.

Chapter 37

The Jefferson-Hamilton Feud

President Washington's second term was clouded by storms and trouble. One of his greatest difficulties stemmed from two of his own friends and close fellow workers, Thomas Jefferson and Alexander Hamilton. These two men, each strong and forceful, found themselves holding political views that were much opposed, and every move one made seemed destined to raise the ire of the other.

Jefferson was the son of a well-established Virginia family. Hamilton had been born illegitimately in the West Indies. Jefferson was a product of an agricultural background, having grown up on the Virginia frontier. Hamilton was the archetypical businessman, feeling comfortable and at home when dealing with merchants and bankers in bustling New York City. Jefferson believed in the right and ability of the

people to rule themselves. Hamilton felt the common man
was incapable of self-rule. Jefferson was a strong proponent
of states' rights. Hamilton sought an ever-stronger central
government.

At first it seemed that the men would be able to work
together amicably. Near the beginning of his first term
Washington reflected, "I feel myself supported by able
coadjutors who harmonize extremely well together." [1] But as
the years wore on, Hamilton and Jefferson each began to fear
that the other was trying to destroy the Union. Eventually
they became implacable enemies.

The center point of their dissension was Hamilton's radical
fiscal policies. To Jefferson, the establishment of a national
bank was simply a means of enriching a few money men—
and Hamilton's other measures fell under the same censure.
Jefferson saw Hamilton's financial practices as harmful to the
poor and destructive to the national well-being. Hamilton, on
the other hand, insisted that his policies were essential to a
strong national economy. Yes, a few money men would
become wealthier—but, in a viable economy, so could
everyone else.

The Birth of Political Parties

Over time people began to polarize around the two points
of view. Jefferson's followers called themselves Republi-
cans—they stood for a true republic of the people, they said.
Hamilton's disciples, on the other hand, called themselves
Federalists—they sought to strengthen the federal Union.
That division proved to be the birth of political parties in the
United States.

The contention soon began to be played out in the pages of

the press. Hamiltonians established a national newspaper called the *Gazette of the United States,* while Jeffersonians founded the *National Gazette.* Each paper almost exclusively espoused the views of the party it represented. The *National Gazette* boldly accused Hamilton of "artifice and deception," of fostering a "revolution in favor of the few."[2] Hamilton, using a variety of aliases, struck back with well-honed pen, charging Jefferson with trying to lead the unsuspecting nation down the road to anarchy.

Washington carefully walked the middle path, seeing the need for balance between the two points of view. Some of Hamilton's measures were needful, despite Jefferson's objections. But other measures were untimely or were founded on false principles, just as Jefferson charged.

As the conflict deepened, Washington became increasingly disturbed by what he was reading in the press. "The newspapers," he noted, "are surcharged and some of them indecently communicative of charges that stand in need of evidence for their support."[3]

The *National Gazette* had stopped short of attacking the President personally, Washington noted, but in condemning his administration "they condemned him, for if they thought there were measures pursued contrary to his sentiment, they must conceive him too careless to attend to them or too stupid to understand them."[4]

Some observers, however, were more willing to attack Washington himself. William Maclay, a puritanical Senator from Pennsylvania who was violently outspoken in his reactionary beliefs, wrote: "Republicans are borne down by fashion and a fear of being charged with a want of respect to General Washington. If there is treason in the wish, I retract it, but would to God this same General Washington were in heaven! We would not then have him brought forward as the constant cover to every unconstitutional and irrepublican act."[5]

Attempts at Reconciliation

Throughout much of this time, Washington was shielded from the intense animosity that existed between Jefferson and Hamilton. The President was aware that these two members of his cabinet harbored strong differences of opinion—that was obvious even to the casual observer—but surely such differences would not prevent them from cooperating in the vital work of the Union. As Jefferson recorded in his journal, Washington "knew, indeed, that there was a marked difference in our political sentiments, but he had never suspected it had gone so far in producing a personal difference." Once he had learned of the depth of the

Thomas Jefferson, President Washington's first Secretary of State. Washington held the highest regard for Jefferson's "integrity and talents," but he was much saddened by Jefferson's ongoing feud with Alexander Hamilton, the Secretary of the Treasury.

problem in August 1792, Washington was earnest in his efforts to bring it to a quick and satisfactory conclusion. "He wished he could be the mediator to put an end to it," Jefferson wrote.[6]

When the President invited Jefferson to convey how he really felt, the Secretary of State opened his heart, venting his fearful feeling that Hamilton's "corrupt squadron" in Congress were making themselves rich while approving tax measures that would be "chained...about our necks for a great length of time." Hamilton was turning the nation from its safe and solid agricultural base to monetary speculation, Jefferson charged; his ultimate objective was to create a monarchy.[7]

Hamilton was not surprised at the accusations: "I know that I have been the object of uniform opposition from Mr. Jefferson," he said. But the Secretary of the Treasury had accusations of his own: "I have long seen a party formed in the legislature under his auspices bent on my subversion... which, in its consequences, would subvert the government."[8]

Washington dreaded the prospect of losing either man, each brilliant in his own right. "How unfortunate," he wrote, "...that internal dissensions should be harrowing and tearing at our vitals.... Without more charity...the fairest prospect of happiness and prosperity that ever was presented to man will be lost." He pleaded with each man to yield "liberal allowances, mutual forbearances" to the other.[9]

Two months later, in mid-October, the problem was still unresolved. Washington wrote Jefferson again:

> I will frankly and solemnly declare that I believe the views of both of you are pure and well meant, and that experience alone will decide with respect to the salubrity of measures which are the subject of dispute. Why, then, when some of

the best citizens in the United States—men of discernment, uniform and tried patriots, who have no sinister views to promote, but are chaste in their ways of thinking and acting—are to be found, some on one side and some on the other of the questions which have caused these agitations, should either of you be so tenacious of your opinions as to make no allowances for those of the other?... I have a great, a sincere esteem and regard for you both, and ardently wish that some line could be marked out by which both of you could walk. [10]

"An Arduous Duty"

Despite the great love and admiration both men held for the President, their mutual animosity ran too deep for reconciliation. After serving for nearly four years, Jefferson could stand it no longer, resigning at the end of 1793. Hamilton quit a year later. Washington retained warm feelings for both men, feelings that continued to the end of his life. He wrote to Jefferson just as the Secretary of State was leaving office, "The opinion which I had formed of your integrity and talents, and which dictated your original nomination, has been confirmed by the fullest experience." [11]

Jefferson, for his part, held the highest respect for the President. Three decades later, when George Washington was long dead, Jefferson recalled: "General Washington was himself sincerely a friend to the republican principles of our Constitution.... He repeatedly declared to me that he was determined it should have a fair chance for success, and that he would lose the last drop of his blood in its support against any attempt which might be made to change it from its republican form." [12]

Although Washington was deeply distressed by the widening split of two of his key men, he was equally disturbed by the parties that began to form around them. He himself was a man "of no party . . . whose sole wish is to pursue, with undeviating steps, a path which would lead this country to respectability, wealth, and happiness."[13] He wished others could walk the same path.

After Jefferson resigned as Secretary of State, the President offered the post to Attorney General Edmund Randolph. Randolph served until August 1795, then he also resigned. To replace Randolph, Washington offered the position to one man, then another, then a third—five times he offered the job and five times he was rejected. (The five candidates: William Paterson of New Jersey, a Supreme Court Justice and signer of the Constitution; Thomas Johnson, governor of Maryland; Charles Cotesworth Pinckney, a Revolutionary War general from South Carolina and a signer of the Constitution; Patrick Henry, the famous old patriot from Virginia; and Rufus King, an influential Senator from New York and another signer of the Constitution.)

Utterly frustrated by his inability to fill the all-important slot, Washington fretted to Alexander Hamilton, "What am I to do for a Secretary of State? . . . I find the selection of proper characters an arduous duty."[14] He was much relieved when Timothy Pickering, the Secretary of War, agreed to transfer to the State Department, though Pickering was less than excited about the switch. Then President Washington found himself having similar vexations in filling vacancies in the offices of Secretary of War, Attorney General, and Chief Justice of the Supreme Court.

When the Cabinet was once again fully staffed, John Adams wrote, "The offices are once more filled, but how differently than when Jefferson, Hamilton, Jay, etc., were here!"[15] Washington had found capable men who were willing to assist him in his administration—but the brilliant, shining stars, the men of true genius, were gone.

Chapter 38

Foreign Troubles, Domestic Strife

In the midst of the continuing strife between Jefferson and Hamilton, an international problem of frightening dimensions arose—which served as a heavy wedge to further widen the rift between the two men. The difficulty had its roots in an honest American disagreement with France.

Washington was favorable toward France, with warm, positive feelings that reached back to the Revolutionary War, and he was delighted to see the French experiment in republican government. The atrocities of the French war of independence troubled him deeply, but he hoped a more moderate leadership would be able to create a strong and just government of the people.

In early 1793, Washington approved an official declaration from the U.S. government to France, written by Jefferson:

"The government and the citizens of the United States...
consider the union of principles and pursuits between our
two countries as a link which binds still closer their interests
and affections. The genuine and general effusions of joy
which... overspread our country on seeing the liberties of
yours rise superior to foreign invasion and domestic trouble
have proved to you that our sympathies are great and sincere."[1]

"The Labyrinth of European Politics"

The feeling of amity was not to last, however. In April
Washington received word that war had broken out in
Europe. France had angrily declared war against England;
Spain and Holland had linked arms with England against
France. At this early stage of the French Revolution, most
Americans were sympathetic with the French cause, and
some urged the President to support them in their war. The
1778 treaty with France, these Americans said, implied an
obligation for the United States to become involved in the
war. According to the treaty, if the French were attacked in
the French West Indies, the United States was to come to
their assistance.

The President carefully reviewed the agreements in the
treaty and decided they no longer were binding. The French
were the aggressors in this case, and the monarchical
government with whom the United States had made the
treaty no longer existed. Further, involvement in another
war could prove disastrous to the budding young American
republic, barely on a solid footing itself. After conferring with
his Cabinet, Washington decided that the United States must
remain neutral in the conflict. His Neutrality Proclamation of
1793 warned American citizens to stay free of the European

dispute. "The duty and interest of the United States," the proclamation stated, "require that they should with sincerity and good faith adopt and pursue a conduct friendly and impartial towards the belligerent powers."[2]

Five years earlier Washington had written: "I hope the United States of America will be able to keep disengaged from the labyrinth of European politics and wars.... It should be the policy of united America to administer to their wants without being engaged in their quarrels."[3]

He repeated that sentiment in a 1795 letter to Patrick Henry. The purpose of the neutrality policy, he explained, was "to keep the United States free from political connections with every other country, to see them independent of all and under the influence of none. In a word, I want an American character, that the powers of Europe may be convinced we act for ourselves and not for others."[4]

The Neutrality Proclamation raised howls of outrage among many Republicans. A policy of neutrality could only help their monarchical British enemies and hurt their French friends, they shouted. Washington's action brought them to a damning conclusion: the President had sold out to their longtime British enemies.

Such accusations soon found their way into the press, some writers attacking with gleeful vigor. Washington tried to ignore the attacks, but gradually they wore him down both physically and emotionally. "The President is not well," Jefferson observed. "Little lingering fevers have been hanging about him for a week or ten days, and [have] affected his looks most remarkably. He is also extremely affected by the attacks made and kept up on him in the public papers. I think he feels those things more than any person I ever met with. I am sincerely sorry to see them."[5]

The Genet Fiasco

The fires of opposition to Washington's stance were growing when a new French minister, Edmond Charles Genet, arrived in the United States. Egalitarian "Citizen Genet," contemptuously disregarding standard protocol, refused to first visit the U.S. President. Instead, he disembarked at South Carolina and began to enlist privateers from among American citizens. The people thronged him in excitement; pro-French emotions ran high. Encouraged by his success, the energetic Genet decided to continue overland to enlist further support.

When Genet finally reached Philadelphia, Washington was formal but cold. Genet was undeterred, reasoning that the people's support could override Washington's neutral stance. The United States needed to rectify "the cowardly abandonment of their friends in the moment when danger menaces them," he declared.[6]

Edmond Genet, the French minister to the United States who sought to turn the American people against President Washington and his official policies. Though Jefferson was a committed friend to France, he said, "Never . . . was so calamitous an appointment made" as that of Genet. He described Genet as "hotheaded, all imagination, no judgment."

Americans responded to his call with enthusiasm. John Adams remembered years later, with some exaggeration, "the terrorism excited by Genet in 1793, when ten thousand people in the streets of Philadelphia, day after day, threatened to drag Washington out of his house," overthrow the government, and help France fight against Great Britain.[7]

Genet was delighted to see the power of the American government threatened. "The true republicans triumph," he wrote, "but *le vieux* [old] Washington, a man very different from the character emblazoned in history, cannot forgive me for my success.... He puts thousands of obstacles in my way, and makes it necessary for me to urge secretly a convocation of Congress—of whom a majority, led by the best minds of the American union, will be decidedly on our side."[8]

In a striking effort to strengthen French support, the Pennsylvania Democratic Society was formed; it was to be the first of many clubs whose purpose was to incite pro-French, anti-administration feeling throughout the nation. Washington became increasingly alarmed when he saw the dangerous growth of this movement. He wrote:

> There are in this [country], as well as in all other countries, discontented characters.... These characters are actuated by very different views: some good, from an opinion that the measures of the general government are impure; some bad, and (if I might be allowed to use so harsh an expression) diabolical, inasmuch as they are not only meant to impede the measures of that government generally, but more especially (as a great means towards the accomplishment of it) to destroy the confidence which it is necessary for the people to place (until they have unequivocal proof of demerit) in their public servants.[9]

When these "characters" joined in clubs, the results could be particularly pernicious. "I early gave it as my opinion...

that if these societies were not counteracted (not by prosecutions, the ready way to make them grow stronger), or did not fall into disesteem, . . . they would shake the government to its foundations."

The source of the clubs? Washington was not deceived. They stemmed directly from "their father, Genet."[10]

"He Had Rather Be in His Grave"

Though criticism of the President's neutrality proclamation continued to grow, Washington tried to stand above it. "I have a consolation within that no earthly efforts can deprive me of, and that is that neither ambitions nor interested motives have influenced my conduct," he explained. "The arrows of malevolence, therefore, however barbed and well pointed, can never reach the most vulnerable part of me." Still, he lamented that he was "up as a mark," fearing that he would remain a broad target as long as he was in the public eye.[11]

His determination to ignore this abuse was not always successful, however. On one occasion he was described as a vile aristocrat who should be guillotined for his evil crimes against the common man. The attack hurt the President deeply, according to Jefferson, who wrote in his journal that Washington defied "any man on earth to produce one single act of his since he had been in the government which was not done on the purest motives." The President said that "he had never repented but once having slipped the moment of resigning his office, and that was every moment since, and that by God he had rather be in his grave than in his present situation; that he had rather be on his farm than to be made emperor of the world, and yet that they were charging him with wanting to be king."[12]

Genet's Recall

Events came to a head in mid-July when Washington learned that the impulsive Genet had outfitted a former British brigantine (the *Little Sarah*) with an American crew and was making ready to sail it against British ships. Fearing government resistance, Genet publicly warned that his rough-and-ready sailors were armed, determined to fight off any attempts to hold them in the harbor.

Washington suspected that Genet's threat was more than idle words. In an emergency Cabinet meeting he presented America's options. Should they stop the ship, thus angering the French? Or should they let it go, thus angering the British? Discussions were still being held when they learned that their decision would be nothing more than academic: Genet had sailed his ship out to sea, unchallenged and unhindered.

Washington was furious at Genet's actions. From first to last the arrogant French minister had been a law unto himself. The President immediately sent a stern message to France demanding the recall of their minister. Meanwhile, the public had become aware of Genet's repeated disregard for the legal authority of the American government. Indignant at his obvious contempt for their national law, the American people swung their support firmly back to Washington.

Jefferson, too, though he had long been a steadfast friend to France, was angered by the French minister's precipitous actions. "Never, in my opinion, was so calamitous an appointment made as that of the present minister of France here," he said, describing Genet as "hotheaded, all imagination, no judgment."[13]

In a letter to James Madison, Jefferson offered advice to his own political allies, some of whom had earlier opposed Washington's policy. "In Congress," he wrote, "I believe that it will be true wisdom in the Republican party to approve unequivocally of a state of neutrality... [and] to abandon Genet entirely." Later in the same letter Jefferson said, "I adhered to him [Genet] as long as I could have a hope of getting him right.... Finding at length that the man was absolutely incorrigible, I saw the necessity of quitting a wreck which could not but sink all who should cling to it."[14]

Genet's replacement, the more proper Joseph Fauchet, arrived in February 1794. He brought with him an official request that Washington have Genet arrested and returned to France for punishment. Washington, however, once again showing the greatness of his heart, granted Genet's plea for asylum—he knew the Frenchman would lose his head if he were returned to his homeland. Genet subsequently married the daughter of New York Governor George Clinton and lived quietly in New York until his death in 1834.

In the midst of the Genet fiasco, the capital city of Philadelphia was beset by a deadly epidemic of yellow fever. Hordes of citizens fled, closing down shops and services across the city. Nevertheless, more than four thousand people died from the epidemic (which lasted from late summer 1793 to early fall); and a number of public officials, including Alexander Hamilton, were grievously afflicted. The government all but shut down. Washington functioned as President from Mount Vernon for a few weeks, then moved to Germantown, just outside of Philadelphia, for a month. Finally, on December 1, he moved his office back to Philadelphia.

The Whiskey Rebellion

The government had barely settled back from Genet's threat before another crisis loomed. Its seeds had been sown years before, in 1790, when the new government was just beginning. In that year, as a partial means of support for his fiscal policies, Hamilton pushed through Congress an excise tax on liquor. The measure was initially met with loud cries of outrage, but opponents of the tax soon quieted. In 1794, however, as the democratic societies spread, disaffection increased. Feelings erupted in the summer of that year in western Pennsylvania.

The rebellion began as a small uprising in the tiny frontier town of Pittsburgh, when a band of distillers, armed and angry, attacked the home of the local tax collector. An army platoon rushed to his rescue. In the brief struggle that ensued one man was killed—and the platoon was forced to surrender.

The local democratic societies exulted. They had met the government and had emerged victorious. Word quickly spread to other societies: "Rise up together, and we can force a weak government to repeal the tax."

When news reached Washington, he knew he had but one choice. For a republic to survive, a minority must not be able to dictate its wishes to a majority, especially by force. Should that be allowed, "there is put an end at one stroke to republican government, and nothing but anarchy and confusion is to be expected thereafter: for some other man or society may dislike another law and oppose it with equal propriety until all laws are prostrate and everyone... will carve for himself." [15]

The President ordered federal mediators to make one final

attempt to bring about a peaceful solution. In the meantime, fearful that the mediators would fail, he called for the enlistment of militia. The whiskey people mocked his plea, claiming that the public would not enlist—but more than sixty thousand stepped forward. Scores of thousands had to be turned away.

President Washington leads the American troops in the Whiskey Rebellion. When citizens in western Pennsylvania rose up in revolt against federal excise tax policies in 1794, Washington personally led the militia to help restore order.

When peaceful mediation did indeed fail, Washington left Philadelphia on September 30 and went personally to command the new army, which had gathered in Bedford, Pennsylvania. He journeyed for almost a full month, making certain the army was equipped and orderly, then returned to Philadelphia to be present for the next session of Congress. General Henry "Light-Horse Harry" Lee took his place as commander of the army of fifteen thousand.

In the face of such a formidable foe, the insurrectionists meekly surrendered. Lee sent eighteen of the most prominent leaders to Philadelphia for trial. Two were sentenced to death, but Washington revoked their sentences. Some Republicans feared that Washington would use the rebellion as an excuse to establish a standing army—but they did not know their President. As soon as the crisis was over, the men were discharged and the army ceased to be.

In his annual message that year, given in the very month the Whiskey Rebellion was quashed, Washington said that "certain self-created societies" had sought "to withstand by force of arms the authority of the United States, and thereby to extort a repeal of the laws of excise." He explained in careful detail the steps he had taken to deal with the rebellion, noting thoughtfully that "[to] yield to the treasonable fury of so small a portion of the United States would be to violate the fundamental principle of our Constitution, which enjoins that the will of the majority shall prevail."[16]

Private Concerns and Counsels

While critical world events and national crises were boiling all around him, Washington took warm refuge in home and family. He periodically visited Mount Vernon during the years of his presidency, checking with his overseer and seeking a respite from the cares of his office. Twice during these years his overseers died, leaving the plantation "as a body without a head."[17]

Debt continued to be an imposing challenge. To keep himself solvent, Washington was forced to sell some sections of his land and lease others. The weather seemed constantly to conspire against a good harvest. One year his overseer reported that the crops had been seriously damaged by a winter that was too wet and a spring that was too dry. Washington responded, "These being acts of Providence and not within our control, I never repine at them."[18]

During one visit to Mount Vernon he was hurt when his horse stumbled; the result was a painful back injury that hampered him for several weeks. He also continued to have dental problems. At one point he returned a set of his false teeth to his dentist for repair. They had become "uneasy in the mouth," Washington explained.[19]

Busy as he was during the years of his presidency, Washington found time to counsel with his friends and family, often in writing. He wrote to John Ehler, gardener at Mount Vernon, about the evils of drunkenness. "Consider how little a drunken man differs from a beast," he said. "The latter is not endowed with reason; the former deprives

The Washington family in 1796. The children shown are two of Martha's grandchildren, George Washington Parke Custis and Eleanor Parke Custis, who were raised by George and Martha.

himself of it and . . . acts like a brute, annoying and disturbing everyone around him."[20]

To a step-grandson he wrote about wise selection of friends. "Select the most deserving only," he advised, observing also that "true friendship is a plant of slow growth."[21]

And a step-granddaughter received these reflections on romantic love and marriage, born of the long experience of a happy, thirty-five-year union with Martha: "Love is a mighty pretty thing; but like all other delicious things, it is cloying; . . . love is too dainty a food to live upon alone, and ought not to be considered farther than as [one] necessary ingredient for that matrimonial happiness which results from a combination of causes."[22]

Chapter 39

The Controversial
Jay Treaty

The crisis with France had barely been resolved when a more dangerous crisis with England developed. In the war between Europe's two great powers, England wished to do everything possible to bring the French to their knees. A cornerstone in that effort was a parliamentary edict known as the Provision Order. Any vessel trading with the French, they decreed, would be subject to capture by British ships. Did that include the neutral Americans? Yes. But the Americans had purposely remained separate from the conflict. No matter, Great Britain said. Even trading with the French constituted an act of war against England.

Under the Provision Order American ships were not to be destroyed, but hundreds were captured, with their goods confiscated and their men either impressed into the British navy or imprisoned. In the face of such blatant British aggression, it seemed to many that another war with England was inevitable.

The Jay Treaty

Seeking to give U.S. officials a little time to consider options, Congress ordered a thirty-day embargo on all shipping. President Washington followed up with a suggestion that the United States send an envoy to negotiate a treaty with Great Britain. "A mission like this . . . ," he told the Senate, "will announce to the world a solicitude for friendly adjustment."[1]

Chief Justice John Jay was chosen to fill the mission. Not all agreed he was the best choice: his viewpoint was strongly Federalist, and the Republicans were apprehensive about what he might agree to. But he was eminently qualified, and at last his opponents acquiesced to the appointment. Jay sailed

John Jay, the minister to Great Britain who hammered out the controversial "Jay Treaty." Opposition to the treaty was so great that when Washington signed it, one newspaper editor wrote, "Better his hand had been cut off when his glory was at his height, before he blasted all his laurels!"

for England in May 1794.

Almost an entire year passed before Jay dispatched a copy of the proposed treaty. He was not entirely satisfied with the result, but he wrote to Secretary of State Edmund Randolph that he had "no reason to believe or conjecture that [a treaty] more favorable to us is attainable."[2] And to the President he said, "It must speak for itself.... To do more was not possible."[3]

Others shared Jay's lack of enthusiasm for the treaty. It specified that the British were to evacuate their posts along the American border—a much-desired concession. But the British did not have to leave until June 1796—a delay that greatly concerned many Americans. The treaty did nothing to stop the hostile British practice of seizing American ships. It placed no restrictions on impressing captured American sailors into British service. It left past American losses at sea to future arbitration.

In the main, the treaty was favorable to the British and inflammatory to the Americans. But it did seem to guarantee continued peace. To some, that was reason enough to approve it.

"The Most Tortured Interpretation"

Congress had adjourned just before the treaty arrived; it took another three months for the Senate to meet in a special session. As expected, the debate on the treaty was protracted and volatile. Eighteen exhausting days of debate passed before the Senate approved the treaty by the required two-thirds vote (twenty to ten), with nothing to spare. But the ratification was conditional: Article 12 of the treaty specified that the United States could trade with the British West Indies in small vessels only. That article, the Senate insisted, would be acceptable only after renegotiation.

By common agreement, at first the text of the treaty was kept secret. But then a disgruntled Virginia Senator leaked it to the press, triggering an explosive public uproar. How could Americans allow themselves to be so humiliated by the hated British? John Jay was burned in effigy in Philadelphia and other cities. Copies of the treaty were ripped apart and set afire. British consulates were defaced. At a town meeting in New York, riotous townspeople began throwing rocks and tomatoes, with one stone striking Alexander Hamilton in the head. Bleeding, he retired from the stage.

In the midst of the turmoil, Washington complained that Philadelphia was "suffocating" from the July heat and flew off to Mount Vernon. The "one great object of my visit to Mount Vernon is relaxation," he said. [4] But he found little relaxation there—or escape from the commotion. He was "extremely hurried with one dispatch after another" during the few days he was gone. [5]

When Washington had initially sought the Senate's "advice and consent," he had given no recommendation. Perhaps the Senators would kill the beast and the issue would be moot. But now that they had voted to ratify it, the problem was squarely back in the President's lap. Should he sign or not sign? He found himself caught on the sharp horns of a classical dilemma: rejection of the treaty might loose anew the dark angels of death, resulting in war with England. But signing the treaty could tear asunder an angry American nation.

His mind divided, he delayed the decision week after week, struggling in his thoughts and seeking counsel from his closest advisers. "The cry against the treaty is like that against a mad dog," he wrote to Hamilton, "and everyone, in a manner, seems engaged in running it down.... It has received the most tortured interpretation and... the most abominable misrepresentations."[6]

Finally, reluctantly, he made his decision. Writing to Randolph he said, "My opinion respecting the treaty is the same now that it was: namely, not favorable to it, but that it is better to ratify it in the manner the Senate have advised... than to suffer matters to remain as they are, unsettled."[7] He feared the consequences he was bringing upon himself, however, and explained sadly that he was "preparing my mind for the obloquy which disappointment and malice are collecting to heap upon my character."[8]

"Better His Hand Had Been Cut Off"

The expected condemnation came immediately, and was so widespread that Washington cried, "The affairs of this country are in a violent paroxysm."[9] One American wrote bitterly: "Washington now defies the whole sovereign [people] that made him what he is—and can unmake him again. Better his hand had been cut off when his glory was at his height, before he blasted all his laurels!"[10] The editor of a newspaper wrote vehemently that Washington was "a malediction on departed virtue" whose "false ambition" had taken the nation "to the precipice of destruction."[11]

Washington bore up solidly under the criticism, willing to stand by his action: "I have... been directed by the great principle which has governed all my public conduct: a sincere desire to promote and secure the true interests of my country."[12] Yes, the Jay Treaty was severely flawed—but its passage was the best possible means of ensuring America's safety.

Despite his self-assurance, though, Washington acknowledged once again a continuing sense of his own fallibility. In a personal note to Henry Knox he wrote:

> If any power on earth could, or the Great Power above would, erect the standard of infallibility in political opinions, there is no being that inhabits this terrestrial globe that would resort to it with more eagerness than myself, so long as I remain a servant of the public. But as I have found no better guide hitherto than upright intentions and close investigation, I shall adhere to these maxims while I keep the watch, leaving it to those who will come after me to explore new ways if they like or think them better. [13]

In the midst of the Jay Treaty furor came another grief for Washington, one that sliced to his very heart. With Hamilton and Jefferson gone, Washington had drawn close to his longtime friend and fellow Virginian, Edmund Randolph, making him his closest adviser. Randolph was steady and true, even if he lacked the brilliance of a Hamilton or a Jefferson, and the President came to lean heavily upon him in times of wearing stress.

Edmund Randolph, a close friend of Washington and Secretary of State in his Cabinet. In 1795 Randolph resigned in disgrace, having been accused of collaborating with the French to prevent the ratification of the Jay Treaty—but most historians agree he was innocent.

In August 1795 Washington was shocked to receive documents implicating Randolph in near-treasonous plotting with the French. The documents, sent from French minister Joseph Fauchet to his own government, had been captured by the British in the mid-Atlantic. Realizing their import, the British had gleefully forwarded the papers to Washington.

The papers fairly reeked of conspiracy and collusion. Between the lines—and with a little imagination—one could read that Randolph had been collaborating with the French to prevent the ratification of the Jay Treaty. Under the right circumstances, it was suggested, Randolph was even willing to accept bribes.

Washington was totally at a loss. Was this close personal friend a traitor to his country? The President had no way of knowing. But the very thought repelled him. Finally, heartsick, he confronted Randolph with the letters. Randolph denied everything: it was disinformation; he was completely innocent (most historians agree that he indeed was innocent). But later that day, feeling mistrusted and abused, Randolph submitted his resignation. Once again, sadly, Washington was without an able adviser. And the Jay Treaty controversy raged on.

Pressure from the House

According to the Constitution, all treaties are to be ratified by the Senate. But the Jay Treaty dealt extensively with matters of commerce, and the House of Representatives insisted that they, the controllers of the purse strings, should approve it also. In the spring of 1796, after the ratifications had been exchanged with England and final copies arrived back in the United States, the House directed Washington to give them "every document which might tend to throw light on the subject" of the treaty. They wanted, they said, to review "important constitutional questions."[14] Washington's reaction was masterfully captured by Vice President John Adams in grave understatement: "He is not at all pleased with this."[15]

After three weeks the President finally responded, sending only a brief note. "The power of making treaties is exclusively vested in the President," he reminded them, "by and with the advice and consent of the Senate.... It is perfectly clear to my understanding that the assent of the House...is not necessary to the validity of a treaty.... A just regard to the Constitution and to the duty of my office...forbids a compliance with your request."[16]

The members of the House were furious, and they petulantly threatened to withhold funds for the implementation of the treaty. But Washington stood firm, undeterred in his desire to let his actions be guided by the strict bounds set by the Constitution. After a month of angry resistance, the House weakened and complied.

In this issue, as always, Washington was deeply concerned with setting precedents. He felt strongly the need for a well-marked separation of powers in the national government. He had been careful not to trespass on the domain of either Congress or the courts[17]—and it was his constitutional duty to see that the prerogatives of the executive were equally defended.

After the House capitulated, another challenge arose: Washington received word that the French were demanding a recision of the treaty. Again, the President was unawed by such pressures. "We are an independent nation and act for ourselves," he proclaimed. "We will not be dictated to by the politics of any nation under heaven."[18]

"The Grossest ... Misrepresentations"

After refusing the House request, Washington was attacked with renewed intensity. His enemies shouted that not only had he agreed to a bad policy, but he was taking too much power to himself. To confidant David Humphreys Washington lamented:

> I am attacked for a steady opposition to every measure which has a tendency to disturb the peace and tranquility of [the country]. But these attacks, unjust and unpleasant as they are, will occasion no change in my conduct, nor will they work any other effect in my mind than to increase the anxious desire ... to enjoy in the shades of retirement the consolation of having rendered my country every service my abilities were competent to, uninfluenced by pecuniary or ambitious considerations. ... Malignity therefore may dart her shafts, but no earthly power can deprive me of the consolation of knowing that I have not in the course of my administration been guilty of a willful error, however numerous they may have been from other causes. [19]

He had not sought to promote any partisan cause; "truth and right decisions," he said, "were the sole objects of my pursuit." He explained to Jefferson that "I was no believer in the infallibility of the politics or measures of any man living.... I was no party man myself, and the first wish of my heart was, if parties did exist, to reconcile them." [20]

Still, the attacks on his motives and character wounded his feelings. "Until within the last year or two ago, I had no conception that parties would, or even could, go to the length I have been witness to; nor did I believe ... that every act of my administration would be tortured, and the grossest and most insidious misrepresentations of them be made." The opposition had a nasty habit of "giving one side only of a subject, and that, too, in such exaggerated and indecent terms as could scarcely be applied to a Nero, a notorious defaulter, or even to a common pickpocket."[21]

Despite the angry uproar, however, most Americans slowly began to accept the Jay Treaty, acknowledging that it had indeed kept them out of a disastrous war. Gradually Washington began to be vindicated. And the treaty had a beneficial aftereffect: For years the Americans had been trying to negotiate a treaty with Spain, while the Spanish stubbornly held back. But the Jay Treaty suggested prospects of a dangerous new cooperation between Great Britain and the United States. In order to protect their own interests, Spain quickly agreed to a treaty that resolved disputes over navigation of the Mississippi, Florida's boundary, and the issue of neutral rights.

Chapter 40

The End of Public Life

After the tumultuous years of Washington's second term, he was eager to retire from public life. "I can religiously aver that no man was ever more tired of public life, or more devoutly wished for retirement than I do," he wrote in January 1795, two full years short of his retirement date. [1] When all circumstances were added together, Washington's reasons for desiring retirement were truly compelling. He was tired and wished to get back to the farm he missed so much. He felt, somewhat sadly, that the nation no longer needed him; after passing through crisis upon crisis, often in the face of burning, biting criticism, he was ready to close the door. Surely the country must be ready for another leader.

At least as important as any other reason was Washington's concern about succession. The American public was accustomed to monarchical thinking—many expected Washington to serve as long as he lived, then choose an heir to succeed him in office. Washington wanted to set that notion at rest. His countrymen must freely choose another leader while he was still alive.

Alexander Hamilton, John Jay, and a number of others repeatedly urged Washington to serve another term. But he would not hear it. "[I will] close my public life on the fourth of March [1797]," he stated firmly. [2]

He wrote to John Jay of the "much concern" and "serious anxiety" that filled his thoughts. "Indeed, the troubles and perplexities,... added to the weight of years which have passed over me, have worn away my mind more than my body." [3]

The tiring of Washington's mind was coupled with the inevitable weakening of his powerful body. One who met the President described him as "considerably older" than his years. "The innumerable vexations he has met with... have very sensibly impaired the vigor of his constitution and given him an aged appearance." [4]

Another observer who met him that same year (1796), however, gathered quite a different impression:

> Washington has something uncommonly commanding and majestic in his walk, his address, his figure, and his countenance. His face is characterized more by intense and powerful thought than by quick and fiery conception. There is a mildness about its expression, and an air of reserve in his manner covers its tone still more.... He appeared to enjoy a humorous observation, and made several himself. He laughed heartily sometimes, and in a very good-humored manner. On the morning of my departure he treated me as if I had lived years in his house, with ease and attention. [5]

Washington's Farewell Address

Before the President retired he hoped to leave his fellow Americans a legacy of his counsel. Thus, in May 1796 he submitted a draft of a proposed farewell address to Alexander Hamilton, asking him to refine and polish it. (Madison had performed a similar function years earlier.) "My wish is that the whole may appear in a plain style and be handed to the public in an honest, unaffected, simple garb," he instructed Hamilton.[6]

Some have questioned who the author of that masterful address really was—Washington, Hamilton, or Madison? It is true that all three men had a significant impact on how the address was finally worded. But Washington was undoubtedly the creator and framer of the address; the ideas and most of the expressions are recognizably Washington's.[7]

Washington's farewell address was never given as a speech. Dated September 17, 1796 (the ninth anniversary of the signing of the Constitution), it was initially published on September 19 in Philadelphia's *American Daily Advertiser*, afterward appearing in many other newspapers. Washington offered it to his countrymen as the parting counsel of "an old and affectionate friend."

The President began by publicly announcing that he did not wish to be considered for a third term in the presidency. "I am influenced by no diminution of zeal for your future interest," he said, "no deficiency of grateful respect for your past kindness; but am supported by a full conviction that the step is compatible with both." He referred to his years of service and said:

> If benefits have resulted to our country from these services, let it always be remembered to your praise, and as an instructive example in our annals, that under circum-

stances in which the passions, agitated in every direction, were liable to mislead, amidst appearances sometimes dubious, [with] vicissitudes of fortune often discouraging, in situations in which not infrequently want of success has countenanced the spirit of criticism, the constancy of your support was the essential prop of the efforts and a guarantee of the plans by which they were effected.

He mentioned his desire to leave the people with some parting counsel, hoping they would receive it as "the disinterested warnings of a parting friend." The union of the states was vitally important, he reminded them—but cautioned that some would seek "to weaken in your minds the conviction of this truth." Americans must therefore watch "for its preservation with jealous anxiety, discountenancing whatever may suggest even a suspicion that it can in any event be abandoned, and indignantly frowning upon the first dawning of every attempt to alienate any portion of our country from the rest."

Though the different regions of the country often had different needs and interests, those should be considered in the light of their interdependencies. "Your Union ought to be considered as a main prop of your liberty, and . . . the love of the one ought to endear to you the preservation of the other."

The primary support of the Union, other than the people's commitment to liberty, was the Constitution. "Toward the preservation of your government and the permanency of your present happy state," he said, "it is requisite, not only that you steadily discountenance irregular oppositions to its acknowledged authority, but also that you resist with care the spirit of innovation upon its principles, however specious the pretexts. One method of assault may be to effect in the forms of the Constitution alterations which will impair the energy of the system, and thus to undermine what cannot be directly overthrown." The underlying principles of the Constitution, then, must be scrupulously guarded and protected and preserved.

If the people ever felt a "modification of the constitutional powers" to be necessary, "let it be [done] by an amendment in the way which the Constitution designates. But let there be no change by usurpation; for though this, in one instance, may be the instrument of good, it is the customary weapon by which free governments are destroyed."

"A Frightful Despotism"

Throughout Washington's presidency he was ceaselessly afflicted by the wranglings of the Federalist and Republican parties. He was usually successful in remaining aloof from the squabbling, doing what he felt was right despite the constant push and pull of opposing philosophies of government. But he feared the destructive influence of political parties, and he sought to warn his countrymen "in the most solemn manner against the baneful effects of the spirit of party.... This spirit, unfortunately, is inseparable from our nature, having its root in the strongest passions of the human mind....

"The alternate domination of one faction over another, sharpened by the spirit of revenge natural to party dissension,... is itself a frightful despotism.... A fire not to be quenched, it demands a uniform vigilance to prevent its bursting into a flame, lest, instead of warming, it should consume."

He then emphasized the vital need for morality in government:

Of all the dispositions and habits which lead to political prosperity, religion and morality are indispensable supports. In vain would that man claim the tribute of patriotism who should labor to subvert these great pillars of human happiness.... The mere politician, equally with the pious man, ought to respect and to cherish them. A volume could not trace all their connections with private and public felicity.... And let us with caution indulge the supposition that morality can be maintained without religion.... Reason and experience both forbid us to expect that national morality can prevail in exclusion of religious principle.

He encouraged "institutions for the general diffusion of knowledge." This was a recurring concern for him; he had repeatedly urged the establishment of an American university. He worried that American youth were being sent to Europe to be trained in nondemocratic ways of thinking.

"Unconscious of Intentional Error"

Another anxiety was the still-unresolved problem of public credit. "One method of preserving it is to use it as sparingly as possible,... avoiding... the accumulation of debt, not only by shunning occasions of expense, but by vigorous exertions in time of peace to discharge the debts which unavoidable wars may have occasioned, not ungenerously throwing upon posterity the burden which we ourselves ought to bear."

Taxes, of course, were necessary, and "no taxes can be devised which are not more or less inconvenient and unpleasant." But a public "spirit of acquiescence" toward needed taxes was important.

Alliances with other nations were to be approached with strict caution. Remembering the pro-French, anti-British sentiments he had just struggled through, Washington warned the people that "the nation which indulges toward another an habitual hatred or an habitual fondness is in some degree a slave. It is a slave to its animosity or to its affection, either of which is sufficient to lead it astray from its duty and its interest."

Washington concluded his farewell address humbly:

> Though, in reviewing the incidents of my administration, I am unconscious of intentional error, I am nevertheless too sensible of my defects not to think it probable that I may have committed many errors. Whatever they may be, I fervently beseech the Almighty to avert or mitigate the evils to which they may tend. I shall also carry with me the hope that my country will never cease to view them with indulgence; and that after forty-five years of my life dedicated to its service, with an upright zeal, the faults of incompetent abilities will be consigned to oblivion, as myself must soon be to the mansions of rest.
>
> ...I anticipate with pleasing expectations that retreat in which I promise myself to realize, without alloy, the sweet enjoyment of partaking, in the midst of my fellow citizens, the benign influence of good laws under a free government—the ever favorite object of my heart and the happy reward, as I trust, of our mutual cares, labors, and dangers. [8]

"The Wearied Traveler"

Two months after publishing his farewell address, Washington stood before the Congress to deliver his last annual message. "I cannot omit the occasion to congratulate you and my country on the success of the experiment," he said, "nor to repeat my fervent supplications to the Supreme Ruler of the Universe and Sovereign Arbiter of nations that his Providential care may still be extended to the United States, that the virtue and happiness of the people may be preserved, and that the government which they have instituted for the protection of their liberties may be perpetual."[9]

His presidency was almost over—but much still remained to be done. "As the curtain of my political life is about to drop, I am...a great deal hurried in the closing scenes of it," he wrote.[10] He wanted to leave the affairs of state in good order for John Adams, who had been elected to succeed him.

At the same time, the President was making hopeful plans for his private life. "To the wearied traveler who sees a resting place and is bending his body to lean thereon, I now compare myself," he wrote to Henry Knox. "I have not a wish to mix again in the great world or to partake in its politics. Yet I am not without regret at parting with (perhaps never more to meet) the few intimates whom I love. Among these, be assured, you are one." He then noted that "the remainder of my life (which in the course of nature cannot be long) will be occupied in rural amusements.... I shall seclude myself as much as possible from the noisy and bustling crowd."[11]

"Strong Nervous Sobs Broke Loose"

John Adams was inaugurated on March 4, 1797. Washington attended to give a short valedictory address. When he entered the hall, he was greeted with a tremendous outpouring of applause. Once he began to speak, as one witness remembered, "There was no cheering, no noise; the most profound silence greeted him, as if the great assembly desired to hear him breathe." The President was "perfectly composed and self-possessed, till the close of his address. Then, when strong nervous sobs broke loose, when tears covered the faces, then the great man was shaken. I never took my eyes from his face. Large drops came from his eyes."[12]

That afternoon Washington went to the Francis Hotel to

John Adams, Washington's Vice President and successor as President. In 1797, after Washington attended Adams's inauguration ceremony, Adams wrote, "Methought I heard him say, 'Ay! I am fairly out and you fairly in! See which of us will be happiest!'"

pay a courtesy call on the new President. A large throng of citizens followed at a distance, respectful and silent. After entering the building, Washington turned back and bowed to the crowd, his cheeks wet with tears.

The next day President John Adams described the inaugural ceremonies in a letter to his wife: "A solemn scene it was indeed, and it was made affecting to me by the presence of the General, whose countenance was as serene and unclouded as the day. He seemed to me to enjoy a triumph over me. Methought I heard him say, 'Ay! I am fairly out and you fairly in! See which of us will be happiest!'" [13]

Suspicion of Scandal

From time to time throughout Washington's career, enemies tried to tarnish his name. Always he emerged unscathed from the threatened scandal, his character and actions completely cleared of any reproach.

One such incident occurred early in the Revolutionary War. In 1775 General Benjamin Harrison wrote a letter to

Washington which was intercepted by the British. Hoping to embarrass (and perhaps ruin) the American commander, the British printed the letter in the *Gentleman's Magazine*—but only after inventing and inserting a damning additional paragraph. In that spurious paragraph, the British had Harrison refer to Washington's enjoyment of the "wonderful charms" to be found in Mount Vernon's slave quarters.

Washington's anger was deeply aroused. He wrote: "The arts of the enemy, and the low dirty tricks which they are daily practicing is an evincing proof that they will stick at nothing, however incompatible with truth and manliness, to carry their points."[14]

The truth was that Washington was strictly and unwaveringly faithful to Martha and his marriage vows. As one historian has put it, "Despite the snickering rumors that circulate, not one shred of conceivably authentic evidence has been discovered which links Washington sexually with any slave" —or with anyone else in an illicit relationship.[15]

In recent times, Washington has been accused of cheating on his Revolutionary War expense account. One author alleges that the General billed Congress for private items— and that he outrageously inflated the actual cost of expenses in his ledger.

The truth: When Washington handed in his expense account, it was carefully audited by professionals, and they found the record had been scrupulously and honestly kept. Rather than enriching himself through his war service, Washington actually lost many thousands of dollars. He invested money in bonds he knew could well become worthless (which they did). He lost additional thousands through inflation because he refused to engage in the base speculation that was so common among his countrymen.

Perhaps more than all else, as a true patriot, he gave freely of himself for his country, donating eight years of his life to the cause of liberty.[16]

A similar accusation was made during Washington's presidency. A rabid opposition newspaper, the *Aurora*, censured the President in 1795 for having overdrawn on his annual appropriation of $25,000. On the face of it, the charge was true. But investigators soon discovered that the extra money had been officially advanced to help the Washingtons with inordinate household expenses. The Treasury Department advance had not come at the President's request, and it had been done with congressional approval.

Those in the public eye are inevitably exposed to public attack—but such attacks do not always confirm the presence of wrongdoing. As historians have examined the various accusations of graft or immorality that have been leveled at George Washington, they have declared him completely innocent. In the last year of his life he could truthfully declare that he had "always walked a straight line and endeavored, as far as human frailties and perhaps strong passions would enable [me], to discharge the relative duties to [my] Maker and fellow man."[17] The record shows that where he had frailties he sought to overcome them, and where he had passions he bridled them.

As for accusations and scandal, Washington had a consistent policy that helped him remain stable when the fierce winds howled around him: "To persevere in one's duty and be silent is the best answer to calumny."[18]

Chapter 41

The Final Days

Washington was sixty-six when he retired, though "time had done nothing towards bending him out of his natural erectness."[1] He was elated to get back to his first love, farming. As granddaughter Nelly Custis put it, "Grandpapa is very well and much pleased with being once more 'Farmer Washington.'"[2]

This long-awaited time with George at home was precious to Martha. She wrote to a friend: "The General and I feel like children just released from school or from a hard taskmaster, and believe that nothing can tempt us to leave the sacred roof-tree again, except on private business or pleasure. We are so penurious with our enjoyment that we are loath to share it with anyone but dear friends; yet almost every day some stranger claims a portion of it, and we cannot refuse."[3]

"An Old Gentleman Riding Alone"

After so many years' absence from Mount Vernon, Washington's first desire was to put the plantation back in order. Everything, from fields to fences to buildings, had fallen into a state of ragged disrepair. "I have . . . scarcely anything . . . about me that does not require considerable repairs," he wrote. His surroundings were soon permeated with "the music of hammers, or the odoriferous smell of paint."[4]

As in Washington's previous retirement, the house was filled with a constant flow of visitors, as Martha noted. One was a child whose parents brought her to see the former President. She recalled that he sat her on his knee and sang to her. Martha, as always, was the consummate hostess. One visitor said graciously, "She possesses that amenity and manifests that attention to strangers which render hospitality so charming."[5]

Gradually, however, the visits upon visits became an unwelcome burden. Washington had been home only four months when, weary from the demands, he wrote to Lawrence Lewis, his nephew, inviting him to come live at Mount Vernon and serve as host to the many guests. "As both your aunt and I are in the decline of life," Washington explained, "and regular in our habits, especially in our hours of rising and going to bed, I require some person . . . to ease me of the trouble of entertaining company, particularly of nights."[6] (Nephew Lawrence accepted the invitation and eventually married Washington's granddaughter, Nelly Custis, who also lived at Mount Vernon.)

There was little pretension about the retired President. Not only did he refuse to hold court with his guests, but he wore ordinary clothes and took no entourage when he made his regular tour of his plantation. A person who did not know him might see him simply as an old farmer out on his horse. Grandson George Washington Parke Custis, in directing an "elderly stranger" to Washington at Mount Vernon, said, "You will meet, sir, with an old gentleman riding alone, in plain drab clothes, a broad-brimmed white hat, a hickory switch in his hand, and carrying an umbrella with a long staff, which is attached to his saddlebow—that person, sir, is General Washington!"[7] Washington toted the umbrella to protect his sensitive skin from the sun as he made the rounds of his farms.

"My Diurnal Course"

The days were busy for Washington. As he put it, "I am occupied from the rising of the sun to the setting of the same."[8] One friend received a detailed description of a typical day at Mount Vernon.

> I begin my diurnal course with the sun.... If my hirelings are not in their places at that time I send them messages expressive of my sorrow for their indisposition;... having put these wheels in motion, I examine the state of things further, and the more they are probed, the deeper I find the wounds are which my buildings have sustained by an absence and neglect of eight years. By the time I have accomplished these matters, breakfast...is ready;...this being over, I mount my horse and ride round my farms, which employs me until it is time to dress for dinner, at which I rarely miss seeing strange faces, come as they say out of respect for me. Pray, would not the word curiosity answer as well? And how different this from having a few social friends at a cheerful board! The usual time of sitting at table, a walk, and tea brings me within the dawn of candlelight; previous to which, if not prevented by company, I resolve that, as soon as the glimmering taper

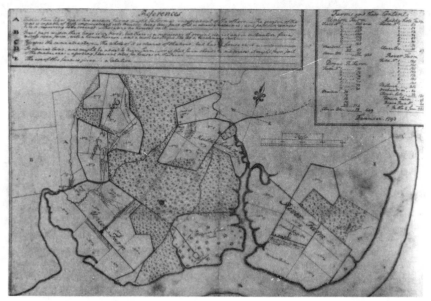

A map of the farms that made up the Mount Vernon plantation, drawn from field notes Washington made in 1793. The river that curves across the bottom and up the right side of the map is the Potomac.

supplies the place of the great luminary, I will retire to my writing table and acknowledge the letters I have received; but when the lights are brought, I feel tired and disinclined to engage in this work, conceiving that the next night will do as well. The next comes, and with it the same causes for postponement, and effect, and so on.

. . . Having given you the history of a day, it will serve for a year, and I am persuaded you will not require a second edition of it. But it may strike you that in this detail no mention is made of any portion of time allotted for reading. . . . I have not looked into a book since I came home, nor shall I be able to do it until I have discharged my workmen, probably not before the nights grow longer.⁹

Despite his inability to find time for personal reading, Washington's deep interest in education continued. During his later years he saw to the education (and support) of twenty-two nieces and nephews. He donated £1,000 to an academy in Alexandria. He also contributed to other charitable causes, and virtually every Christmas he anonymously donated several hundred dollars to the poor.

"The Venom of the Darts"

During these months of retirement Washington tried to remain personally uninvolved in public concerns. Even though some policies of his administration continued to be attacked, he said: "It is . . . a misconception if it be supposed that I feel the venom of the darts. Within me I have a consolation which proves an antidote against their utmost malignity, rendering my mind, in the retirement I have long panted after, perfectly tranquil."[10]

His deeply held interest in his country's well-being did not stop with his retirement, however. When French officials ordered harassment of American ships trading with Great Britain, he wrote anxious letters to his friends, but did nothing more, being willing to "leave it with those whose duty it is" to act for the nation. "As every good citizen ought to do," he would "conform to whatsoever the ruling powers decide."[11]

He still lamented the partisan, dependent attitude of many Americans, aligning themselves with one foreign power or another. "If our citizens . . . instead of being Frenchmen or Englishmen in politics . . . would be Americans," he said, America could prosper even in the face of confrontations with France and continuing tension with England.[12]

Despite his enduring solicitude for his country's welfare, however, he refused to let burning political controversies disrupt his retirement. "I shall view things in the calm light of mild philosophy," he said.[13]

Back into the Public Eye

"No consideration under heaven that I can foresee shall again withdraw me from the walks of private life," Washington wrote in June 1796. [14] And, a year later: "I do not think it probable that I shall go beyond the radius of twenty miles" from Mount Vernon again. [15]

Washington's desire to live a quiet life ran deep. But the unforeseen interrelationships of nations gradually intruded on his life, infringing on the ease of his retirement. In 1798 America's relations with France worsened and the clouds of war loomed darkly. Rumors began to filter out to Mount Vernon that Washington would be asked to command the nation's armies in the dreaded event of a conflict. In July the request became official: President John Adams asked the old General to resume the position of commander in chief.

Washington was disturbed and uneasy about the request. It would be painful "to quit the tranquil walks of retirement and enter the boundless field of responsibility and trouble," he wrote. But at the same time he could not in good conscience "remain an idle spectator under the plea of age or retirement." [16] He had not driven one European army from the American continent simply to make room for another. "As my whole life has been dedicated to my country in one shape or another, for the poor remains of it" he could not comfortably "contend for ease and quiet when all that is valuable in it is at stake." [17]

The General accepted the post under two conditions: first, he was not to be called to active duty until the army was assembled and in the field; second, he was to enjoy the prerogative of choosing his principal officers. Adams fully agreed to Washington's conditions—then he made appointments different from those Washington had requested. In the months that followed, the issue became a bitter point of conflict between the two men. On the one hand, Adams felt his authority as President was being threatened; on the other, Washington knew the critical importance of having trusted, hand-picked assistants in the field.

In the end the conflict with France was handled diplomatically, and Washington was never called to the field. His peace and freedom once again were preserved.

Just the same, he had been willing, despite his personal desires, to accept the call of his frightened country. "His accepting the command of the army in 1798 was the most patriotic act of all his patriotic life," one historian has observed. "His fame was bright and secure; he was comfortably established at Mount Vernon, where the infirmities of age were creeping up on him; he had everything to lose and nothing to gain. No man would be shrewder than Washington in understanding this; yet he was ready to sacrifice reputation and comfort because he thought that he might serve his country."[18]

Looking Back on Life

As George Washington's final years wound down, he doubtless engaged in some thoughtful introspection and reminiscing about the rich life he had led. He mentioned past years to a number of his correspondents, not with longing but with something more like satisfaction for a life well lived. Surely his public years likewise became a subject for dinner-table discussion with his many guests.

He had seen countless changes during his long life. His native land had moved from an odd assortment of individual colonies (each dependent on their mother country) to a loose confederation of thirteen independent states (each viewing itself essentially as a separate nation joining with neighbor nations for mutual benefit) to a strong and proud new republic with sixteen member states. When Washington was born he and his fellow citizens were subject to the whims of the British Crown. Before he died the Americans had established a government by and for the people, solidly built on principles of liberty, justice, equity, and morality.

The man called by his countrymen to serve as founding President over this "great experiment" was a rare one indeed, a man with the courage and character to set a proper precedent for his successors in the long years to follow. That precedent was probably Washington's greatest contribution as President. In a world schooled in the ways of monarchs and dictators, he showed a way to lead without being lordly, a way to represent without ruling.

Although Washington was widely loved, he did have his enemies. Controversy surrounded him from first to last. Some of his fellows had passionately castigated him, criticizing his every political move. Others lionized him, feeling he could do no wrong. Which was the real Washington? How much did early Americans really know about their first President? How much do we know—separated as we are by two hundred years of time, culture, and custom?

The Many Roles of George Washington

Americans know George Washington as the peerless leader of the revolution, signer of the Constitution, first President of the nation. Do those labels constitute the sum of this great man's life? Or was there more?

A simple listing of some of George Washington's roles will partially answer the question. Such a summary will suggest a depth and breadth to Washington that is often not represented, though admittedly it will give only the briefest surface look. In terms of his roles, then, Washington was a:

Son, who respected his mother all his life (even though they did not always agree), who dutifully visited her and helped provide for her in her old age.

Brother, who loved and followed Lawrence as a youth; who corresponded intimately with Jack over the years, keeping the ties strong; who assisted the profligate Samuel when he was in difficult financial straits.

Husband, who shared a long and challenging life with his wife, lovingly and faithfully; who looked hopefully for her letters and encouraged her to join him when he could not be with her at Mount Vernon; who so enjoyed being in her company that more than once he made special note of it in his diary.

Stepfather, who helped raise two children who were not his own, sharing his love and time and means with them and maintaining close contact after they left home.

Uncle and grandfather, who took in two additional children to raise when his stepson died and a third when his brother died; who supported and helped a number of other children over the years.

Friend, who keenly enjoyed the company of those he was close to, earnestly inviting them to join him and Martha for lengthy stays at Mount Vernon, opening the doors to his home so freely that he once called it a "well-resorted tavern."

Correspondent, who wrote letters so faithfully to friends and acquaintances that the combined collection takes up the greater part of a hefty, thirty-seven-volume set.

Diarist, whose journal writings come to six printed volumes, whose diary record of an early part of the French and Indian War was published both in America and in England.

Farmer, who constantly experimented with different crops and different ways of planting, as well as with new kinds of equipment, even engaging in a lengthy correspondence with Arthur Young, one of Great Britain's foremost agriculturalists.

Kind master, taking financial losses rather than split up families of slaves, holding his overseers to strict account for how they treated the slaves in their charge, refusing to buy and sell human beings, and finally freeing them in his will.

Gentleman, in the ultimate sense of the word, treating other people with true kindness and respect while expecting them to return the same to him.

Churchman, attending services as often as he could, even during war, accepting leadership positions of vestryman and church warden, and supporting the church with generous financial offerings.

Christian, looking to the Christian God as the deliverer of the American armies and looking to Jesus Christ as an exemplar whom all could safely follow; he participated in the Communion, fasted, prayed regularly, and repeatedly expressed public gratitude for the providence of God.

Philanthropist, consistently helping those less fortunate than he was, whether they were the poor who lived near his plantation or destitute veterans of the Revolutionary War.

Political philosopher, painstakingly evolving vital principles of liberty and government and sharing his ideas freely with those around him, influencing many to see the need for resistance against the intransigent British (1770s), for a strong federal government (1780s), for neutrality from European nations (1790s).

Reader and thinker, whose personal library numbered in the thousands of volumes, and whose reading habit was strong enough that he lamented when he did not have the time to pursue it.

General, who was able to unite the American forces as no other man could have done, keeping an army together for eight long years of trouble and trial, gradually developing a strategy that defeated the mightiest army on earth.

Statesman, who served as a local representative in the Virginia House of Burgesses, in two Continental Congresses, in the all-important Constitutional Convention, and as founding President of the United States.

Patriot, who time after time gave up the comfortable security of his personal life in order to serve his country. On three separate occasions he retired from public life, fully expecting to live out his days in the quiet of his plantation. And on three separate occasions he answered the call to return to the service of his country, sacrificing his own desires for the peace and safety of America.

The preeminent Washington scholar, Douglas Southall Freeman, who wrote six impressive volumes on George Washington, repeatedly mentioned Washington's personal characteristics in his biography. His extensive index listing gives a further clue to the humanity, breadth, and integrity of the man. Included are such characteristics as amiability, benevolence, common sense, conscientiousness, courage, courtesy, delicacy, dignity, diligence, generosity, honor, humor, intelligence, love of nature, modesty, optimism, orderliness, patience, perseverance, pride, promptness, reserve, self-confidence, self-discipline, and sincerity.[19]

Such lists are only indicators, however; they are not definers. If Washington himself were to give a self-definition, enabling us to look into his own soul (which he essentially did in his many letters), he might simply say: "I was nothing more than a man who was trying to do what was right, believing in the sanctity and virtue of our cause and trusting in Almighty God to help me in it. I made mistakes, but through ignorance or inability only, never willfully. I deeply loved my family, my friends, my country. And although there was always warm satisfaction in public service and public acclaim, my greatest joy came during my quiet hours beside my own fire, with Martha and the grandchildren at my side."

The Final Year

Washington considered 1799 the most financially difficult year of his life. In the previous four years he had sold $50,000 worth of lands, but the money from this source, even when added to income from his leases, had "scarcely been [enough] to keep me afloat."[20] In March, for the first time in his life, he had to negotiate a bank loan. It was, he said after considering the interest charges, "a ruinous mode of obtaining money."[21]

His lack of money was particularly disturbing when he considered his advancing age. His "greatest anxiety," he wrote, was to leave his affairs "in such a clear and distinct form as that no reproach may attach itself to me when I have taken my departure for the land of the spirits."[22]

In the summer of that year, Federalists pleaded with him to once again accept a nomination for President. Gouverneur Morris wrote: "Should you decline, no man will be chosen whom you would wish to see in that high office.... Is retirement in the strict sense of the word a possible thing?... Has it not the disadvantage of leaving you involved in measures which you can neither direct nor control?... From envy and slander no retreat is safe but the grave."[23]

Washington responded to such requests with a firm and vigorous *no*. "Let me ask," he wrote, "what consolation, what satisfaction, what safety should I find in support which depends upon caprice? . . . The favorite today may have the curtain dropped on him tomorrow, while steadiness marks the conduct of the [opposition], and whoever is not on their side must expect to be loaded with all the calumny that malice can invent."

Furthermore, he noted, in the public view he had retired firmly and finally. A return to public office would bring charges of "inconsistency, concealed ambition, dotage, and a thousand more etceteras." Most important of all, the Federalist party was stumbling in the wrong direction. "If principles, instead of men, are not the steady pursuit of the Federalists, their cause will soon be at an end."[24]

Health gave Washington an additional reason for refusing to consider a third term. In 1798 Washington was able to write that his health "never was better."[25] But the years were resting heavily on him. "Although I have abundant cause to be thankful for the good health with which I am blessed," he wrote a year later, "yet I am not insensible to my declination in other respects."[26]

"When the Summons Comes"

In July 1799 he completed and signed a twenty-eight-page will. His Mount Vernon estate had grown to nine thousand acres; he also owned an additional fourteen thousand acres elsewhere. His estimated net worth was $500,000. (Some have placed it closer to one million dollars.)

The will specified that Martha was to have the entire estate, including both real and personal property, until her death (except for small portions allocated elsewhere). The slaves were to be set free at Martha's death, with the old and infirm "comfortably clothed and fed by my heirs while they live," and the children who had no support "taught to read and write, and brought up to some useful occupation." He donated some money to education; forgave some debts owed to him; and gave specific personal items to Dr. James Craik, Lafayette, Tobias Lear, and other friends. After Martha's death the lands were to be divided among family members.[27]

September brought the sad news that Washington's younger brother Charles had died. "I was the first, and am now the last, of my father's children by the second marriage," he wrote soberly. "When I shall be called upon to follow them is known only to the giver of life. When the summons comes I shall endeavor to obey it with good grace."[28]

Now that the specter of death was drawing nearer, Washington referred to it often in his communications, usually through a variety of metaphors. He even felt comfortable in joking about it. Two years earlier, for example, Martha had included this postscript in a letter to a friend in Philadelphia:

> I am now, by desire of the General, to add a few words on his behalf.... Despairing of hearing what may be said of him if he should really go off in an apoplectic or any other fit (for he thinks all fits that issue in death are worse than a love fit, a fit of laughter, and many other kinds which he could name), he is glad to hear beforehand what will be said of him on that occasion, conceiving that nothing extra will happen between this and then to make a change in his character for better or for worse. And besides, as he has entered into an engagement with Mr. [Robert] Morris [the Philadelphia financier] and several other gentlemen not to quit the theater of this world before the year 1800, it may

be relied upon that no breach of contract shall be laid to him on that account, unless dire necessity should bring it about.... In that case, he shall hope that they will do by him as he would by them: excuse it. At present, there seems to be no danger of his giving them the slip, as neither his health nor spirits were ever in greater flow, notwithstanding, he adds, he is descending and has almost reached the bottom of the hill or, in other words, the shades below.[29]

"I Am Not Afraid to Go"

Washington, ever a man of his word, did his best to keep his "engagement" with Robert Morris. He missed seeing the turn of the century by only two weeks.

On December 9, 1799, he was cheerful and seemed healthy. As a nephew said: "He had taken his usual ride, and the clear, healthy flush on his cheek and his spritely manner brought the remark... that we had never seen the General look so well. I have sometimes thought him decidedly the handsomest man I ever saw; and, when in a lively mood, so full of pleasantry, so agreeable to all with whom he associated, that I could hardly realize that he was the same Washington whose dignity awed all who approached him."[30]

Three days later Washington again took a ride around the plantation. He was gone for five difficult hours, trudging his horse through the cold, snowy weather. In the evening he seemed to be "as well as usual."[31] But the next day, December 13, he suffered from a sore throat that was painful enough to keep him from his normal ride. Before retiring he read aloud from a gazette, then asked his secretary, Tobias Lear, to read debates of the recent Virginia General Assembly to him. When they said goodnight, Lear suggested that Washington take something for his throat. Washington declined, saying he preferred to "let it go as it came."[32]

During the night he was seized with chills and a burning fever. Between two and three o'clock in the morning he awakened Martha, hoarsely saying that he was very ill. His voice was weak and low, and he was breathing with difficulty. Martha prepared to rise from the bed to get help, but he stopped her, fearing she might also contract a cold in the freezing house. He lay for several hours in the cold bedroom, shivering miserably from his chills. Finally, about seven o'clock, a maid came into the bedroom to start the morning fire. Martha immediately sent her to get Lear and Albin Rawlins, one of Washington's overseers, to bleed him. When Lear saw Washington's deteriorated condition, he promptly sent his servant for Dr. Craik.

Rawlins arrived before the doctor did, and Washington ordered the man to bleed him. The overseer nervously obeyed, taking half a pint before Martha stopped him from extracting more. Washington showed no improvement. At eight o'clock he got up, dressed (with help), and sat by the fire, trying to get warm. Anxious that Dr. Craik had not arrived, Martha sent a servant to get Dr. Gustavus Brown of Port Tobacco.

Shortly after, around nine, Dr. Craik finally arrived. He administered a variety of remedies, including bleeding the patient once again, but none brought relief. When Washington tried to let a mixture of sage tea and vinegar flow down his swollen throat he almost suffocated. Feeling helpless, Dr. Craik sent for Dr. Elisha Dick to assist him. The three doctors bled him twice more and gave him an emetic of calomel and tartar. All their efforts proved to be fruitless.

Washington looked at Dr. Craik and said weakly, "Doctor, I die hard, but I am not afraid to go."[33]

"Let Me Go Off Quietly"

At half past four in the afternoon Washington instructed Martha to bring in the two wills he had prepared. He briefly examined them, then instructed her to burn one, which was outdated, and to put the other in a safe place. A half hour later he uttered his last words to the doctors: "I feel myself going. I thank you for your attentions, but I pray you to take no more trouble about me. Let me go off quietly; I cannot last long."[34]

Washington's bedroom, where he died on December 14, 1799, "without a struggle or a sigh." The bed shown is the actual bed used by Washington.

About ten o'clock that evening, December 14, 1799, George Washington died "without a struggle or a sigh."[35] He was sixty-seven years old. When Martha saw her beloved husband was gone she said: "'Tis well. All is now over. I shall soon follow him. I have no more trials to pass through."[36] She outlived her husband by two-and-a-half years.

Tobias Lear was present until the end. "His last scene corresponded with the whole tenor of his life," Lear said. "Not a groan or a complaint escaped him in extreme distress. With perfect resignation and full possession of his reason he closed his well-spent life."[37]

At noon on December 18, crowds of mourning friends and neighbors began to gather at Mount Vernon. Later in the afternoon, after formal Episcopal and Masonic services, Washington's body was laid in the family vault on the Mount Vernon property. Echoing artillery fire punctuated the empty feeling of loss shared by people throughout the nation.

The Washington family vault, where George Washington was buried on December 18, 1799. The vault is located at Mount Vernon.

The eulogies for the fallen leader numbered in the hundreds, being offered by John Adams, by Napoleon, and by the U.S. Senate. It was Henry Lee who uttered the most lasting tribute of them all: "First in war, first in peace, and first in the hearts of his countrymen."[38]

Years later Thomas Jefferson wrote, "It may truly be said

that never did nature and fortune combine more perfectly to make a man great, and to place him in the same constellation with whatever worthies have merited from man an everlasting remembrance."[39]

Appendix I

A Personal View of Washington by Thomas Jefferson

I think I knew General Washington intimately and thoroughly; and were I called on to delineate his character, it should be in terms like these.

His mind was great and powerful, without being of the very first order; his penetration strong, though not so acute as that of a Newton, Bacon, or Locke; and as far as he saw, no judgment was ever sounder. It was slow in operation, being little aided by invention or imagination, but sure in conclusion. Hence the common remark of his officers of the advantage he derived from councils of war, where, hearing all suggestions, he selected whatever was best; and certainly no general ever planned his battles more judiciously. But if [the plan was] deranged during the course of the action, if any member of his plan was dislocated by sudden circumstances, he was slow in readjustment. The consequence was that he often failed in the field, and rarely [succeeded] against an enemy in station, as at Boston and York.

"His Integrity Was Most Pure"

He was incapable of fear, meeting personal dangers with the calmest unconcern. Perhaps the strongest feature in his character was prudence, never acting until every circumstance, every consideration, was maturely weighed, refraining if he saw a doubt, but—when once decided—going through with his purpose whatever obstacles opposed.

His integrity was most pure, his justice the most inflexible I have ever known, no motives of interest or consanguinity, of friendship or hatred being able to bias his decision. He was, indeed, in every sense of the words, a wise, a good, and a great man. His temper was naturally irritable and high toned; but reflection and resolution had obtained a firm and habitual ascendency over it. If ever, however, it broke its bonds, he was most tremendous in his wrath. In his expenses he was honorable, but exact, liberal in contributions to whatever promised utility, but frowning and unyielding on all visionary projects and all unworthy calls on his charity. His heart was not warm in its affections, but he exactly calculated every man's value and gave him a solid esteem proportioned to it.

"The Best Horseman of His Age"

His person, you know, was fine, his stature exactly what one would wish, his deportment easy, erect, and noble. [He was] the best horseman of his age, and the most graceful figure that could be seen on horseback.

Although in the circle of his friends, where he might be unreserved with safety, he took a free share in conversation, his colloquial talents were not above mediocrity, possessing neither copiousness of ideas nor fluency of words. In public, when called on for a sudden opinion, he was unready, short, and embarrassed. Yet he wrote readily, rather diffusely, in an easy and correct style. This he had acquired by conversation with the world, for his education was merely reading, writing, and common arithmetic, to which he added surveying at a later day. His time was employed in action chiefly, reading little, and that only in agriculture and English history. His correspondence became necessarily extensive, and, with journalizing his agricultural proceedings, occupied most of his leisure hours within doors.

On the whole, his character was, in its mass, perfect, in nothing bad, in few points indifferent; and it may truly be said that never did nature and fortune combine more perfectly to make a man great and to place him in the same constellation with whatever worthies have merited from man an everlasting remembrance. For his was the singular destiny and merit of leading the armies of his country successfully through an arduous war for the establishment of its independence; of conducting its councils through the birth of a government, new in its forms and principles, until it had settled down into a quiet and orderly train; and of scrupulously obeying the laws through the whole of his career, civil and military, of which the history of the world furnishes no other example. . . .

"A Great Man Hath Fallen"

The soundness of [his judgment] gave him correct views of the rights of man, and his severe justice devoted him to them. He has often declared to me that he considered our new Constitution as an experiment on the practicability of republican government, and with what dose of liberty man could be trusted for his own good; that he was determined the experiment should have a fair trial, and would lose the last drop of his blood in support of it. . . .

These are my opinions of General Washington, which I would vouch at the judgment seat of God, having been formed on an acquaintance of thirty years. I served with him in the Virginia legislature from 1769 to the Revolutionary war, and again, a short time in Congress, until he left us to take command of the army. During the war and after it we corresponded occasionally, and in the four years of my continuance in the office of Secretary of state our intercourse was daily, confidential, and cordial. . . .

I felt on his death, with my countrymen, that "verily a great man hath fallen this day in Israel."[1]

Appendix II

A Personal View of Washington by John Bernard

In July 1798 a British actor named John Bernard met George Washington and left a revealing and engaging sketch of the former President. Bernard had been visiting an acquaintance "on the banks of the Potomac, a few miles below Alexandria, and was returning on horseback." Traveling immediately in front of him was "an old-fashioned chaise" which was going much too fast for the road. Suddenly one of the wheels swerved upon the bank and the chaise flipped over, "flinging out upon the road a young woman who had been its occupant." Here is Bernard's account of what happened next.

The minute before I had perceived a horseman approaching at a gentle trot, who now broke into a gallop, and we reached the scene of the disaster together. The female was our first care. She was insensible, but had sustained no material injury. My companion supported her while I brought some water in the crown of my hat from a spring some way off. The driver of the chaise had landed on his legs, and having ascertained that his spouse was not dead, seemed very well satisfied with the care she was in, and set about extricating his horse. A gush of tears announced the lady's return to sensibility, and then, as her eyes opened, her tongue gradually resumed its office and assured us that she retained at least one faculty in perfection, as she poured forth a volley of invectives on her mate.

The horse was now on his legs, but the vehicle still prostrate, heavy in its frame, and laden with at least half a ton of luggage. My fellow helper set me an example of activity in relieving it of the external weight; and, when all was clear, we grasped the wheel between us and, to the peril of our spinal columns, righted the conveyance. The horse was then put in, and we lent a hand to help up the luggage. All this helping, hauling, and lifting occupied at least half an hour, under a meridian sun in the middle of July, which fairly boiled the perspiration out of our foreheads....

When all was right, and we had assisted the lady to resume her seat, [the driver] begged us to proceed with him to Alexandria and take a drop of "something sociable." Finding, however, that we were unsociable, he extended his hand . . . and, when we had sufficiently *felt* that he was grateful, drove on.

"A Great Man's Claim to ... Reputation"

My companion, after an exclamation at the heat, offered very courteously to dust my coat, a favor the return of which enabled me to take a deliberate survey of his person. He was a tall, erect, well-made man, evidently advanced in years, but who appeared to have retained all the vigor and elasticity resulting from a life of temperance and exercise. His dress was a blue coat buttoned to his chin, and buckskin breeches. Though the instant he took off his hat I could not avoid the recognition of familiar lineaments—which, indeed, I was in the habit of seeing on every signpost and over every fireplace—still I failed to identify him, and, to my surprise, I found that I was an object of equal speculation in his eyes. A smile at length lighted them up, and he exclaimed, "Mr. Bernard, I believe?" I bowed. "I had the pleasure of seeing you perform last winter in Philadelphia." . . .

He then learned the cause of my presence in the neighborhood and remarked, "You must be fatigued. If you will ride up to my house, which is not a mile distant, you can prevent any ill effects from this exertion by a couple of hours' rest." I looked 'round for his dwelling, and he pointed to a building which, the day before, I had spent an hour in contemplating. "Mount Vernon!" I exclaimed; and then, drawing back with a stare of wonder, "Have I the honor of addressing General Washington?" With a smile, whose expression of benevolence I have rarely seen equalled, he offered his hand, and replied, "An odd sort of introduction, Mr. Bernard; but I am pleased to find you can play so active a part in private, and without a prompter." . . . As we rode up to his house we entered freely into conversation, first in reference to his friends at Annapolis, then respecting my own success in America and the impressions I had received of the country.

Flattering as such inquiries were from such a source, I must confess my own reflections on what had just passed were more absorbing. Considering that nine ordinary country gentlemen out of ten, who had seen a chaise upset near their estate, would have thought it savored neither of pride nor ill nature to ride home and send their servants to its assistance, I could not but think that I had witnessed one of the strongest evidences of a great man's claim to his reputation—the prompt, impulsive working of a heart which, having made the good of mankind . . . its religion, was never so happy as in practically displaying it.

"Fashioned by the Hand of Heaven"

On reaching the house (which, in its compact simplicity and commanding elevation, was no bad emblem of its owner's mind), we found that Mrs. Washington was indisposed; but the general ordered refreshments in a parlor whose windows took a noble range of the Potomac. . . .

Though I have ventured to offer some remarks on his less-known contemporaries, I feel it would be an impertinence to say a word on the public merits of a man whose character has been burning as a beacon to Europe till its qualities are as well known as the names and dates of his triumphs. My retrospect of him is purely a social one, and much do I regret . . . that it is confined to a single interview.

The general impression I received from his appearance fully corresponded with the description of him by the Marquis de Chatelluz, who visited America at the close of the war. "The great characteristic of Washington," says he, "is the perfect union which seems to subsist between his moral and physical qualities; so that the selection of one would enable you to judge of all the rest. If you are presented with medals of Trajan or Caesar, the features will lead you to inquire the proportions of their persons; but if you should discover in a heap of ruins the leg or arm of an antique Apollo, you would not be curious about the other parts, but content yourself with the assurance that they were all conformable to those of a god."

Though fourteen years had elapsed since this was written, I could perceive that it was far from being the language of mere enthusiasm. Whether you surveyed his face, open yet well defined, dignified but not arrogant, thoughtful but benign; his frame, towering and muscular, but alert from its good proportion—every feature suggested a resemblance to the spirit it encased, and showed simplicity in alliance with the sublime. The impression, therefore, was that of a most perfect whole; . . . you could not but think you looked upon a wonder, and something sacred as well as wonderful—a man fashioned by the hand of Heaven, with every requisite to achieve a great work. Thus a feeling of awe and veneration stole over you.

In conversation his face had not much variety of expression: a

look of thoughtfulness was given by the compression of the mouth
and the indentation of the brow.... Nor had his voice, so far as I
could discover in our quiet talk, much change or richness of intona-
tion, but he always spoke with earnestness, and his eyes (glorious
conductors of the light within) burned with a steady fire which no
one could mistake for mere affability; they were one grand expression of the well-known line, "I am a man, and interested in all that
concerns humanity."

"An Even Current of Good Sense"

In our hour and a half's conversation he touched on every topic
that I brought before him with an even current of good sense, if he
embellished it with little wit or verbal elegance. He spoke like a man
who had felt as much as he had reflected, and reflected more than
he had spoken, like one who had looked upon society rather in the
mass than in detail, and who regarded the happiness of America
but as the first link in a series of universal victories; for his full faith
in the power of those results of civil liberty which he saw all around
him led him to foresee that it would, ere long, prevail in other
countries, and that the social millennium of Europe would usher in
the political....

When I remarked that his observations were flattering to my
country, he replied, with great good humor, "Yes, yes, Mr.
Bernard, but I consider your country the cradle of free principles,
not their arm chair. Liberty in England is a sort of idol; people are
bred up in the belief and love of it, but see little of its doings. They
walk about freely, but then it is between high walls; and the error
of its government was in supposing that after a portion of their
subjects had crossed the sea to live upon a common, they would
permit their friends at home to build up those walls about them." A
black coming in at this moment with a jug of spring water, I could
not repress a smile, which the general at once interpreted. "This
may seem a contradiction," he continued, "but ... both houses and
slaves were bequeathed to us by Europeans, and time alone can

change them; an event, sir, which, you may believe me, no man desires more heartily than I do. Not only do I pray for it on the score of human dignity, but I can clearly foresee that nothing but the rooting out of slavery can perpetuate the existence of our union, by consolidating it in a common bond of principle."

"Arts of a Practical Nature"

I now referred to the pleasant hours I had passed in Philadelphia, and my agreeable surprise at finding there so many men of talent, at which his face lit up vividly. "I am glad to hear you, sir, who are an Englishman, say so, because you must now perceive how ungenerous are the assertions people are always making on your side of the water. One gentleman of high literary standing...has demanded whether America has yet produced one great poet, statesman, or philosopher. The question shows anything but observation, because it is easy to perceive the causes which have combined to render the genius of this country scientific rather than imaginative. And, in this respect, America has surely furnished her quota. Franklin, Rittenhouse, and Rush are no mean names, to which, without shame, I may append those of Jefferson and Adams as politicians; while I am told that the works of President Edwards of Rhode Island are a textbook in polemics in many European colleges."

Of the replies which I made to his inquiries respecting England, he listened to none with so much interest as to those which described the character of my royal patron, the Prince of Wales. "He holds out every promise," remarked the general, "of a brilliant career. He has been well educated by *events*, and I doubt not that, in his time, England will receive the benefit of her child's [America's] emancipation. She is at present bent double, and has to walk with crutches; but her offspring may teach her the secret of regaining strength, erectness, and independence."

In reference to my own pursuits he repeated the sentiments of Franklin: he feared the country was too poor to be a patron of the drama, and that only arts of a practical nature would for some time be esteemed. The stage he considered to be an indispensable resource for settled society and a chief refiner, not merely interesting as a comment on the history of social happiness by its exhibition of manners, but an agent of good as a school for poetry, in holding up to honor the noblest principles. "I am too old and too far removed," he added, "to seek for or require this pleasure myself, but the cause is not to droop on my account. There's my friend, Mr. Jefferson, has time and taste; he goes always to the play, and I'll introduce you to him," a promise which he kept, and which proved to me the source of the greatest benefit and pleasure.

As I was engaged to dine at home, I at length rose to take my leave, not without receiving from the general a very flattering request to call on him whenever I rode by. I had the pleasure of meeting him once after this in Annapolis, and I dined with him on a public occasion at Alexandria, my impressions each time improving into a higher degree of respect and admiration.[2]

PART II

Timeless Treasures
from
George Washington

Prepared by
Andrew M. Allison,
Jay A. Parry,
and
W. Cleon Skousen

Introduction

Modern Americans generally regard George Washington as a man of action, not a man of reflection.

Over the years an assortment of historians and commentators, often borrowing their ideas from other authors, have fostered and perpetuated the view that Washington was neither an insightful thinker nor a forceful writer. He is widely admired as a military hero, a wise administrator, and a man whose personal reputation and influence were vital to the founding of the United States as a free nation. But one thing he was not, we are told, was a man of letters.

As it turns out, this traditional image of the "father of our country" finds very little support in the historical record.

It is true that, unlike many of his contemporaries, Washington never penned a political treatise, the memoirs of his public career, or any other book. When he was invited in 1785 to write a history of the Revolutionary War, he declined by noting that his "defective education" had "unfit" him for such an undertaking.[1] He later discouraged those who sought to publish his agricultural correspondence, explaining that "I have endeavored . . . to keep myself as much from the eye of the world as I possibly could" and that such a work "might be imputed to me as a piece of ostentation."[2]

Neither did he relish public speaking. While serving in the Virginia House of Burgesses and the First Continental Congress, he seldom participated in debate. (However, when he did speak, others listened. Patrick Henry, another congressional delegate from Virginia and perhaps the most powerful orator on the continent, called Washington "a man of more solid judgment and information than any man on the floor.")[3]

Even after many years in public life, when he was sworn in as the first American President, he was said to be visibly uncomfortable in addressing the large crowd that attended the inaugural ceremonies.

He was also reserved in conversations with strangers. A few, in fact, accused him of being downright cold. (When he was alone with his closest associates, however, he spoke freely. James Madison remembered that, though Washington "was inclined to be taciturn in general society, . . . in the company of two or three intimate friends he was talkative, and when a little excited was sometimes fluent and even eloquent.")[4] As with his reluctance to write for publication, this usual reserve was apparently a product of his natural modesty and his sense of having been inadequately educated.

But none of this justifies the current misconception that Washington's writings made little or no contribution to American thought.

Although his formal schooling was indeed limited, he taught himself extensively through his lifelong habit of independent study. His personal library, one of the largest in America at that time, contained over a thousand books on government, history, biography, military affairs, and agriculture.

This broad-based knowledge is best reflected in his seemingly innumerable public and private letters, which now fill more than four hundred volumes of manuscripts in the Library of Congress.[5] *The Papers of George Washington,* which the University Press of Virginia began publishing in 1976, is expected to eventually run to more than sixty printed volumes.

Thus Washington may well have been the most prolific

letter writer of his time. Over half of his letters and public papers were produced during the Revolutionary War years (1775-83), and a great many were written during his two terms in the presidency (1789-97); but the collection also includes a large volume of his private correspondence with family members, friends, and others.

In describing Washington's writing style, some of his biographers speak of such things as "his awkwardness in phrasing."⁶ But while his typical eighteenth-century syntax may seem hopelessly convoluted to the uninitiated modern reader, he should in fairness be judged by the standards of his own generation.

Thomas Jefferson, who knew the General well for many years, said that he "wrote readily, rather diffusely, in an easy and correct style. This he had acquired by conversation with the world, for his education was merely reading, writing, and common arithmetic, to which he added surveying at a later date.... His correspondence became necessarily extensive."⁷

Another assessment comes from Henrietta Liston, wife of the British minister to the United States. During the 1790s the Listons became close friends with the Washingtons. In her memoirs, Mrs. Liston wrote that the President "knew no language but his own, and he expressed himself in that language rather forcibly than elegantly.... Letter writing seemed in him a peculiar talent. His style was plain, correct, and nervous [i.e., vigorous]. Ill-natured people said that Washington did not write his own public letters, answers to addresses, etc. This is not true. I have known him to write in his usual impressive manner when no person was near to aid him; and what may seem conclusive, he has always written better than the gentlemen to whom the merit of his letters was ascribed."[8]

Some modern detractors have asserted that Washington was "curiously remote from the realm of abstract ideas."[9] "Ideas had only a small part in his life," sniffed an aspiring debunker. "He did not consider them important."[10] But these charges are either the products of prejudice or the vehicles of self-aggrandizement, not the fruits of sound and honest scholarship. Although Washington is often considered a practical rather than a philosophical man, the content of his letters reflects a balance between the two. One of his biographers aptly observed that "he was not the theorist of the Revolution but its born leader."[11] Yet it is equally true that, as James Madison once wrote, Washington's mind was "capable of grand views."[12]

Even a quick perusal of the following pages will demonstrate that Washington wrote intelligently and decisively on a wide range of topics. His letters and public papers reflect his insightful thinking on such diverse subjects as education, marriage and human relations, economics, farming, morality and religion, political philosophy, the U.S. Constitution, national politics, foreign affairs, and war and military science. Especially impressive are his well-developed ideas on liberty and government; indeed, the dates listed with these quotations show that he was sometimes among the first of the Founders to take the positions he did in America's struggle for independence and human freedom.

Some of the excerpts in these pages give us a fascinating glimpse of the private man. The reader may be surprised, for instance, to discover the humorous side of our first President—an aspect of his character that is unknown to most Americans today. According to Madison, "The story so often repeated of his never laughing [is] wholly untrue; no man seemed more to enjoy gay conversation, though he took little part in it himself. He was particularly pleased with the jokes, good humor, and hilarity of his companions."[13] And one of the most eminent Washington scholars of this century, John C. Fitzpatrick, stated that "there are more examples of honest humor in George Washington's letters than can be found in those of ... any one of the [Founding] Fathers except Benjamin Franklin."[14]

Washington also speaks of himself and many of his famous contemporaries with refreshing openness. Of particular interest may be his views on family life, reflected in the passages from letters written to his wife, stepchildren, and other relatives. (His letters to Martha are largely lost to us, however. Shortly before her death she destroyed most of her private correspondence with her husband, "probably motivated by a desire to keep this intimate part of her relationship from the eyes of a world which had so perpetually intruded in her marriage.")[15]

"Timeless Treasures from George Washington" brings together the most important passages from Washington's voluminous writings. For the convenience of the user, these excerpts are arranged alphabetically by subject matter and are extensively cross-referenced. Most of the selections are from *The Writings of George Washington*, ed. John C. Fitzpatrick, 39 vols. (Washington: U.S. Government Printing Office, 1931–44). Several quotations are taken from *The Writings of George Washington*, ed. Jared Sparks, 12 vols. (Boston: American Stationers' Co., 1834–37), and a few others are from additional sources which are cited fully where they appear in the text. Spelling, capitalization, and punctuation have been modernized in some cases for the sake of clarity and readability.

ANDREW M. ALLISON

Timeless Treasures
from
George Washington

Prepared by
Andrew M. Allison,
Jay A. Parry,
and W. Cleon Skousen

A

ADAMS (John), A Good Choice for the Vice Presidency.—From different channels of information, it seemed probable to me...that Mr. John Adams would be chosen Vice President. He will doubtless make a very good one; and let whoever may occupy the first seat, I shall be entirely satisfied with that arrangement for filling the second office.—To the Secretary of War. Fitzpatrick 30:174. (1789.)

ADAMS (John Quincy), An Able Diplomat.—Mr. Adams is the most valuable public character we have abroad, and...he will prove himself to be the ablest of all our diplomatic corps.—To John Adams. Fitzpatrick 35:394. (1797.)

ADVANCEMENT, Should Stem from Own Efforts.—Let your promotion result from your own application and from intrinsic merit, not from the labors of others. The last would prove fallacious and expose you to the re-proach of the daw in borrowed feathers.—To George Washington Parke Custis. Fitzpatrick 35:282. (1796.)

ADVICE, A Proof of Friendship.—The opinion and advice of my friends I receive at all times as a proof of their friendship and am thankful when they are offered.—To Robert R. Livingston. Fitzpatrick 19:91. (1780.)

AFFLICTION, And Christian Fortitude.—Time *alone* can blunt the keen edge of afflictions; philosophy and our religion holds out to us such hopes as will, upon proper reflection, enable us to bear with fortitude the most calamitous incidents of life, and these are all that can be expected from the feelings of humanity.—To Benjamin Lincoln. Fitzpatrick 29:413. (1788.)

AGRICULTURAL SOCIETIES, Praise for.—The Agricultural Society lately established in Philadelphia promises extensi[ve] usefulness if it is prosecuted with spirit. I wish most sincerely that every state in the union would institute similar ones, and that these societies would correspond fully and freely with each other, and communicate all useful discoveries founded on practice, with a due attention to climate, soil, and seasons, to the public. —To James Warren. Fitzpatrick 28:291. (1785.)

AGRICULTURE, And Worms.—Our growing prosperity, meaning the tobacco, is assailed by every villainous worm that has had an existence since the days of Noah (how unkind it was of Noah, now I have mentioned his name, to suffer such a brood of vermin to get a berth in the ark), but perhaps you may be as well off as we are—that is, have no tobacco for them to eat; and there, I think, we nicked the dogs.—To Burwell Bassett. Fitzpatrick 37:485. (1762.)

AGRICULTURE, Scientific Farming Needed.—Nothing, in my opinion, would contribute more to the welfare of these states than the proper management of our lands; and nothing, in this state particularly, seems to be less understood. The present mode of cropping practiced among us is destructive to landed property, and must, if persisted in much longer, ultimately ruin the holders of it.—To William Drayton. Fitzpatrick 28:394. (1786.)

AGRICULTURE, Washington's Love for.—Agriculture has ever been among the most favorite amusements of my life.—To Arthur Young. Fitzpatrick 28:510. (1786.)

The more I am acquainted with agricultural affairs, the better I am pleased with them; insomuch that I can nowhere find so great satisfaction as in

those innocent and useful pursuits. In indulging these feelings, I am led to reflect how much more delightful to an undebauched mind is the task of making improvements on the earth than all the vain glory which can be acquired from ravaging it by the most uninterrupted career of conquest.—To Arthur Young. Fitzpatrick 30:150. (1788.)

AGRICULTURE, Importance of.—Agriculture ... is, in my opinion, an object of infinite importance to the country; I consider it to be the proper source of American wealth and happiness.—To Theodorick Bland. Fitzpatrick 28:517. (1786.)

AGRICULTURE, And Manufacturing.—There are many articles of manufacture which we stand absolutely in need of and shall continue to have occasion for, so long as we remain an agricultural people, which will be while lands are so cheap and plenty, that is to say, for ages to come.—To the Marquis de Lafayette. Fitzpatrick 28:519. (1786.)

AGRICULTURE, Rewards of.—It is certainly among the most rational avocations of life, for what can be more pleasing than to see the work of one's own hands, fostered by care and attention, rising to maturity in a beautiful display of those advantages and ornaments which, by the combination of nature and taste of the projector in the disposal of them, is always regaling to the eye at the same time in their season they are a grateful |gift| to the palate. —To Sir Edward Newenham. Fitzpatrick 29:205. (1787.)

AGRICULTURE, And Speculation.—An extensive speculation, a spirit of gambling, or the introduction of anything which will divert our attention from agriculture must be extremely prejudicial, if not ruinous, to us.—To Thomas Jefferson. Fitzpatrick 29:351. (1788.)

AGRICULTURE, Advantages of Farm Life.—The life of a husbandman, of all others, is the most delectable. It is honorable, it is amusing, and with judicious management it is profitable. —To Alexander Spotswood. Fitzpatrick 29:414. (1788.)

AGRICULTURE, And War.—For the sake of humanity it is devoutly to be wished that the manly employment of agriculture and the humanizing benefits of commerce would supersede the waste of war and the rage of conquest, that the swords might be turned into plowshares, the spears into pruning hooks, and, as the Scripture expresses it, "the nations learn war no more." To the Marquis de Chastellux. Fitzpatrick 29:485. (1788.)

AGRICULTURE, A Principal Resource.—Within our territories there are no mines, either of gold or silver, and this young nation, just recovering from the waste and desolation of a long war, |has| not as yet had time to acquire riches by agriculture and commerce. But our soil is bountiful and our people industrious; and we have reason to flatter ourselves that we shall gradually become useful to our friends.—To the Emperor of Morocco. Fitzpatrick 30:475. (1789.)

AGRICULTURE, Importance of.—I know of no pursuit in which more real and important services can be rendered to any country than by improving its agriculture, its breed of useful animals, and other branches of a husbandman's cares.—To Sir John Sinclair. Fitzpatrick 33:437. (1794.)

AGRICULTURE, Vital to National Welfare.—It will not be doubted that with reference either to individual or national welfare, agriculture is of primary importance. In proportion as nations advance in population and other circumstances of maturity, this truth becomes more apparent, and renders the cultivation of the soil more and more an object of public patronage.—Eighth Annual Address to Congress. Fitzpatrick 35:315. (1796.)

AGRICULTURE. See also FARMING; MANUFACTURES; WASHINGTON (George), Enjoyed Farming.

ALCOHOL. See DRUNKENNESS; LIQUOR; TAVERNS; VICES.

ALEXANDRIA ACADEMY, Money Willed to.—To the trustees . . . of the academy in the town of Alexandria, I give and bequeath, in trust, four thousand dollars . . . towards the support of a free school established at, and annexed to, the said academy, for the purpose of educating such orphan children, or the children of such other poor and indigent persons, as are unable to accomplish it with their own means, and who, in the judgment of the trustees of the said seminary, are best entitled to the benefit of this donation.—Last Will and Testament. Fitzpatrick 37:278. (1799.)

ALLIANCES. See FOREIGN RELATIONS; NEUTRALITY; TREATIES.

AMERICA, A Great Honor to Help Found.—Happy, thrice happy shall they be pronounced hereafter who have contributed anything, who have performed the meanest office, in erecting this stupendous *fabric of freedom and empire* on the broad basis of independence; who have assisted in protecting the rights of human nature and establishing an asylum for the poor and oppressed of all nations and religions. —General Orders. Fitzpatrick 26:335. (1783.)

AMERICA, Its Prospects for Greatness and Happiness.—The citizens of America, placed in the most enviable condition as the sole lords and proprietors of a vast tract of continent, comprehending all the various soils and climates of the world and abounding with all the necessaries and conveniences of life, are now, by the late satisfactory pacification, acknowledged to be possessed of absolute freedom and independence. They are, from this period, to be considered as the actors on a most conspicuous theater, which seems to be peculiarly designated by Providence for the display of human greatness and felicity. Here they are not only surrounded with everything which can contribute to the completion of private and domestic enjoyment, but Heaven has crowned all its other blessings by giving a fairer opportunity for political happiness than any other nation has ever been favored with —Circular to the States. Fitzpatrick 26:484. (1783.)

I begin to look forward, with a kind of political faith, to scenes of national happiness which have not heretofore been offered for the fruition of the most favored nations. The natural, political, and moral circumstances of

our nascent empire justify the anticipation.... We have an almost unbounded territory whose natural advantages for agriculture and commerce equal those of any on the globe. In a civil point of view we have [an] unequalled privilege of choosing our own political institutions and of improving upon the experience of mankind in the formation of a confederated government, where due energy will not be incompatible with unalienable rights of freemen. To complete the picture, I may observe that the information and morals of our citizens appear to be peculiarly favorable for the introduction of such a plan of government.—To Sir Edward Newenham. Fitzpatrick 30:72. (1788.)

If this country can steer clear of European politics...and be wise and temperate in its government, it bids fair to be one of the greatest and happiest nations in the world.—To Sarah Cary Fairfax. Fitzpatrick 36:264. (1798.)

AMERICA, Founded at a Most Auspicious Time.—The foundation of our empire was not laid in the gloomy age of ignorance and superstition, but at an epoch when the rights of mankind were better understood and more clearly defined than at any former period. The researches of the human mind after social happiness have been carried to a great extent; the treasures of knowledge, acquired by the labors of philosophers, sages, and legislatures through a long succession of years, are laid open for our use, and their collected wisdom may be happily applied in the establishment of our forms of government. The free cultivation of letters, the unbounded extension of commerce, the progressive refinement of manners, the growing liberality of sentiment, and, above all, the pure and benign light of revelation have had a meliorating influence on mankind and increased the blessings of society. At this auspicious period, the United States came into existence as a nation, and if their citizens should not be completely free and happy, the fault will be entirely their own.—Circular to the States. Fitzpatrick 26:485. (1783.)

AMERICA, Powerful Only When United.—It is only in our united character as an empire that our independence is acknowledged, that our power can be regarded, or our credit supported among foreign nations. The treaties of the European powers with the United States of America will have no validity on a dissolution of the Union. We shall be left nearly in a state of nature, or we may find by our own unhappy experience that there is a natural and necessary progression from the extreme of anarchy to the extreme of tyranny, and that arbitrary power is most easily established on the ruins of liberty abused to licentiousness.—Circular to the States. Fitzpatrick 26:488. (1783.)

AMERICA, Its Early Missteps Needed Correction.—That the prospect before us is ... fair, none can deny; but what use we shall make of it is exceedingly problematical—not but that I believe all things will come right at last; but like a young heir come a little prematurely to a large inheritance, we shall wanton and run riot until we

Washington in May 1772 (age 40). Portrait by Charles Willson Peale. Washington's grandson, George Washington Parke Custis, said this portrait, along with a painting by James Sharples in 1796, was "the finest and purest likeness of the Chief . . . in the world."

have brought our reputation to the brink of ruin, and then like him shall have to labor with the current of opinion when *compelled*, perhaps, to do what prudence and common policy pointed out ... in the first instance.—To Benjamin Harrison. Fitzpatrick 27:305. (1784.)

AMERICA, To Be Preserved by God.—It is indeed a pleasure, from the walks of private life, to view in retrospect all the meanderings of our past labors, the difficulties through which we have waded, and the fortunate haven to which the ship has been brought! Is it possible after this that it should founder? Will not the all-wise and all-powerful Director of human events preserve it? I think he will. He may, however (for wise purposes not discoverable by finite minds), suffer our indiscretions and folly to place our national character low in the political scale; and this, unless more wisdom and less prejudice take the lead in our governments, will most assuredly be the case.—To Jonathan Trumbull. Fitzpatrick 27:399. (1784.)

AMERICA, Future of.—However unimportant America may be considered at present, and however Britain may affect to despise her trade, there will assuredly come a day when this country will have some weight in the scales of empires.—To the Marquis de Lafayette. Fitzpatrick 28:520. (1786.)

The prospect of national prosperity now before us is truly animating, and ought to excite the exertions of all good men to establish and secure the happiness of their country in the permanent duration of its freedom and independence. America, under the smiles of a divine Providence, the protection of a good government, the cultivation of manners, morals, and piety, can hardly fail of attaining an uncommon degree of eminence in literature, commerce, agriculture, improvements at home, and respectability abroad.—To the Roman Catholics in the United States. Sparks 12:178. (1789.)

AMERICA, An Asylum for the Oppressed.—Under an energetic general government such regulations might be made, and such measures taken, as would render this country the asylum of pacific and industrious characters

from all parts of Europe, would encourage the cultivation of the earth by the high price which its products would command, and would draw the wealth, and wealthy men, of other nations into our bosom by giving security to property and liberty to its holders.—To Thomas Jefferson. Fitzpatrick 29:351. (1788.)

It is a flattering and consolatory reflection that our rising republics have the good wishes of all the philosophers, patriots, and virtuous men in all nations, and that they look upon them as a kind of asylum for mankind. God grant that we may not disappoint their honest expectations by our folly or perverseness.—To the Marquis de Chastellux. Fitzpatrick 29:485. (1788.)

AMERICA, Land of Opportunity for All Classes.—It is a point conceded that America, under an efficient government, will be the most favorable country of any in the world for persons of industry and frugality, possessed of a moderate capital, to inhabit. It is also believed that it will not be less advantageous to the happiness of the lowest class of people, because of the equal distribution of property, the great plenty of unoccupied lands, and the facility of procuring the means of subsistence.—To Richard Henderson. Fitzpatrick 29:520. (1788.)

AMERICA, To Become the World's Storehouse.—I hope, some day or another, we shall become a storehouse and granary for the world.—To the Marquis de Lafayette. Fitzpatrick 29:526. (1788.)

AMERICA, Particularly Favorable to a Republic.—We have an almost unbounded territory whose natural advantages for agriculture and commerce equal those of any on the globe. In a civil point of view we have [the] unequalled privilege of choosing our own political institutions and of improving upon the experience of mankind in the formation of a confederated government, where due energy will not be incompatible with unalienable rights of freemen. To complete the picture, I may observe that the information and morals of our citizens appear to be peculiarly favorable for the introduction of such a plan of government.—To Sir Edward Newenham. Fitzpatrick 30:72. (1788.)

AMERICA, To Be an Example to All the World.—It should be the highest ambition of every American to extend his views beyond himself, and to bear in mind that his conduct will not only affect himself, his country, and his immediate posterity, but that its influence may be co-extensive with the world and stamp political happiness or misery on ages yet unborn. To establish this desirable end, and to establish [a] government of *laws*, the union of these states is absolutely necessary; therefore in every proceeding, this great, this important object should ever be kept in view; and so long as our measures tend to this, and are marked with the wisdom of a well-informed and enlightened people, we may reasonably hope, under the smiles of Heaven, to convince the world that the happiness of nations can be accomplished by pacific revolutions in their political systems, without the destructive intervention of the sword.—To

the legislature of Pennsylvania. Fitzpatrick 30:395*n*. (1789.)

The virtue, moderation, and patriotism which marked the steps of the American people in framing, adopting, and thus far carrying into effect our present system of government has excited the admiration of nations; and it only now remains for us to act up to those principles which should characterize a free and enlightened people, that we may gain respect abroad and ensure happiness to ourselves and our posterity.—To the representatives of the freemen of the commonwealth of Pennsylvania. Sparks 12:165. (1789.)

AMERICA, Prosperous Under New Constitution.—Every part of the Union displays indications of rapid and various improvement; and with burdens so light as scarcely to be perceived, with resources fully adequate to our present exigencies, with governments founded on genuine principles of rational liberty, and with mild and wholesome laws, is it too much to say that our country exhibits a spectacle of national happiness never surpassed if ever before equalled?

Placed in a situation every way so auspicious, motives of commanding force impel us, with sincere acknowledgment to Heaven and pure love to our country, to unite our efforts to preserve, prolong, and improve our immense advantages.—Seventh Annual Address to Congress. Fitzpatrick 34:389. (1795.)

AMERICA. See also COLONIES (American); PATRIOTISM; UNION; UNITED STATES.

AMERICAN REVOLUTION, Brought

On by Necessity.—[The American] Revolution,...I can truly aver, was not in the beginning premeditated, but the result of dire necessity brought about by the persecuting spirit of the British government.—To George William Fairfax. Fitzpatrick 27:58. (1783.)

AMERICAN REVOLUTION, Its Effect on Other Nations.—From the public papers it appears that the parliaments of the several provinces [of France], and particularly that of Paris, have acted with great spirit and resolution. Indeed, the rights of mankind, the privileges of the people, and the true principles of liberty seem to have been more generally discussed and better understood throughout Europe since the American Revolution than they were at any former period.—To Thomas Jefferson. Fitzpatrick 29:350. (1788.)

The American Revolution, or the peculiar light of the age, seems to have opened the eyes of almost every nation in Europe.—To Hector St. John de Crevecoeur. Fitzpatrick 30:281. (1789.)

AMERICAN REVOLUTION, Moderation and Virtue in.—Our revolution was so distinguished for moderation, virtue, and humanity as to merit the eulogium...of being unsullied with a crime.—To Governor John Hawkins Stone. Fitzpatrick 35:343. (1796.)

AMERICAN REVOLUTION. See also DECLARATION OF INDEPENDENCE; GREAT BRITAIN; INDEPENDENCE; REVOLUTIONARY WAR.

APPOINTMENTS, Washington's Guidelines in Making Political.—

Washington in 1776 (age 44). Portrait by Charles Willson Peale. This portrait was painted at the request of John Hancock, then president of the Continental Congress.

Scarcely a day passes in which applications of one kind or another do not arrive, insomuch that, had I not early adopted some general principles, I should before this time have been wholly occupied in this business. As it is, I have found the number of answers which I have been necessitated to give in my own hand an almost unsupportable burden to me. The points in which all these answers have agreed in substance are: that should it be my lot to go again into public office, I would go into it without being under any possible engagements of any nature whatsoever; that, so far as I know my own heart, I would not be in the remotest degree influenced, in making nominations, by motives arising from the ties of amity or blood; and that, on the other hand, three things, in my opinion, ought principally to be regarded, [namely], the fitness of characters to fill offices, the comparative claims from the former merits and sufferings in service of the different candidates, and the distribution of appointments in as equal a proportion as might be to persons belonging to the different states in the Union; for without precautions of this kind, I clearly foresaw the endless jealousies, and possibly the fatal consequences, to which a government depending altogether on the good will of the people for its establishment would certainly be exposed in its early stages.—To Samuel Vaughan. Fitzpatrick 30:238. (1789.)

I must be permitted, with the best ligts I can obtain and upon a general view of characters and circumstances, to nominate such persons alone to offices as, in my judgment, shall be the best qualified to discharge the functions of the departments to which they shall be appointed.—To Mary Wooster. Fitzpatrick 30:327. (1789.)

In every nomination to office I have endeavored, as far as my own knowledge extended or information could be obtained, to make fitness of character my primary object.—To Joseph Jones. Fitzpatrick 30:469. (1789.)

Of two men equally well affected to the true interest of their country, of equal abilities and equally disposed to lend their support, it is the part of prudence to give a preference to him against whom the *least* clamor can be excited.—To the Acting Secretary of State. Fitzpatrick 34:315. (1795.)

I shall not, while I have the honor to administer the government, bring a man into my office of consequence, knowingly, whose political tenets are adverse to the measures which the *general* government are pursuing; for this, in my opinion, would be a sort of political suicide.—To the Acting Secretary of State. Fitzpatrick 34:315. (1795.)

In the appointments to the great offices of the government, my aim has been to combine geographical situations, and sometimes other considerations, with abilities and fitness of *known* characters.—To Edward Carrington Fitzpatrick 34:331. (1795.)

[In making appointments] esteem, love, and friendship can have no influence on my mind.—To John Adams. Fitzpatrick 36:461. (1798.)

APPOINTMENTS. See also PUBLIC OFFICIALS.

APPROBATION, Of a Good Man, a Great Satisfaction.—Nothing in human life can afford a liberal mind more rational and exquisite satisfaction than the approbation of a wise, a great and virtuous man.—To Mrs. Sarah Bache. Fitzpatrick 21:102. (1781.)

APPROBATION, The Best Reward.—The confidence and affection of his fellow citizens is the most valuable and agreeable reward a citizen can receive. Next to the happiness of my country, this is the most powerful inducement I can have to exert myself in its service.—To the inhabitants of Providence. Fitzpatrick 21:337. (1781.)

Next to the approbation of my own mind, arising from a consciousness of having uniformly, diligently, and sincerely aimed, by doing my duty, to promote the true interests of my country, the approbation of my fellow citizens is dear to my heart. In a free country, such approbation *should* be a citizen's best reward; and so it *would* be, if truth and candor were always to estimate the conduct of public men. But the reverse is so often the case that he who, wishing to serve his country, is not influenced by higher motives, runs the risk of being miserably disappointed. Under such discouragements, the good citizen will look beyond the applauses and reproaches of men, and, persevering in his duty, stand firm in conscious rectitude and in the hope of [an] approving Heaven. —To the citizens of Frederick County, Virginia. Fitzpatrick 34:395. (1795.)

APPROBATION. See also MERIT; REPUTATION.

ARITHMETIC, Importance of.— Without arithmetic, the common [affairs of] life are not to be managed with success.—To the Reverend Jonathan Boucher. Fitzpatrick 3:36. (1771.)

ARMY, Discipline Essential in.— Discipline is the soul of an army. It makes small numbers formidable, procures success to the weak, and esteem to all.—Instructions to officers. Fitzpatrick 2:114. (1757.)

An army without order, regularity, and discipline is no better than a commissioned mob. Let us, therefore, . . . endeavor by all the skill and discipline in our power to acquire that knowledge and conduct which [are]

necessary in war. Our men are brave and good, . . . but it is subordination and discipline (the life and soul of an army) which, next under Providence, is to make us formidable to our enemies, honorable in ourselves, and respected in the world.—General Orders. Fitzpatrick 4:202. (1776.)

Nothing can be more hurtful to the service than the neglect of discipline, for . . . discipline, more than numbers, gives one army the superiority over another.—General Orders. Fitzpatrick 8:359. (1777.)

A refusal to obey the commands of a superior officer, especially where the duty required was evidently calculated for the good of the service, cannot be justified without involving consequences subversive of all military discipline.—To Josias C. Hall. Fitzpatrick 11:204. (1778.)

ARMY, Washington's Code of Behavior for.—Be very particular in restraining not only your own troops, but the Indians, from all acts of cruelty and insult, which will disgrace the American army and irritate our fellow subjects against us.—Instructions to Benedict Arnold. Fitzpatrick 3:495. (1775.)

ARMY, Need for a Standing.—The cost of marching home one set of men [and] bringing in another, the havoc and waste occasioned by the first, [and] the repairs necessary for the second, with a thousand incidental charges and inconveniences which have arisen, and which it is scarce possible either to recollect or describe, amounts to near as much as the keeping up a respectable body of troops the whole time, ready for any emergency, would have done. To this may be added that you never can have a well-disciplined army. To bring men well acquainted with the duties of a soldier requires time; to bring them under proper discipline and subordination not only requires time, but is a work of great difficulty, and in this army, where there is so little distinction between the officers and soldiers, requires an uncommon degree of attention. To expect, then, the same service from raw and undisciplined recruits as from veteran soldiers is to expect what never did and perhaps never will happen. Men who are familiarized to danger meet it without shrinking, whereas those who have never seen service often apprehend danger where no danger is. Three things prompt men to a regular discharge of their duty in time of action: natural bravery, hope of reward, and fear of punishment. The two first are common to the untutored and the disciplined soldiers, but the latter most obviously distinguishes the one from the other. A coward, when taught to believe that if he breaks his ranks and abandons his colors [he] will be punished with death by his own party, will take his chance against the enemy; but the man who thinks little of the one, and is fearful of the other, acts from present feelings regardless of consequences. Again, men of a day's standing will not look forward, and from experience we find that as the time approaches for their discharge they grow careless of their arms, ammunition, camp utensils, etc.; nay, even the barracks themselves have felt un-

common marks of wanton depredation, and lay us under fresh trouble and additional expense in providing for every fresh set, when we find it next to impossible to procure such articles as are absolutely necessary in the first instance. To this may be added the seasoning which new recruits must have to a camp, and the loss consequent therefrom. But this is not all. Men engaged for a short, limited time only have the officers too much in their power; for to obtain a degree of popularity, in order to induce a second enlistment, a kind of familiarity takes place which brings on a relaxation of discipline, unlicensed furloughs, and other indulgences incompatible with order and good government, by which means the latter part of the time for which the soldier was engaged is spent in undoing what you were aiming to inculcate in the first.... Congress... would save money and have infinitely better troops if they were, even at the bounty of twenty, thirty, or more dollars, to engage the men already enlisted,... and such others as may be wanted to complete... the establishment, for [the duration of] the war.... The trouble and perplexity of disbanding one army and raising another at the same instant, and in such a critical situation as the last was, is scarcely in the power of words to describe, and such as no man who has experienced it once will ever undergo again.—To the President of Congress. Fitzpatrick 4:316. (1776.)

I am persuaded, and as fully convinced as I am of any one fact that has happened, that our liberties must of necessity be greatly hazarded, if not entirely lost, if their defense is left to any but a permanent standing army; I mean one to exist during the war.—To the President of Congress. Fitzpatrick 6:5. (1776.)

The misfortune of short enlistments and an unhappy dependence upon militia have shown their baneful influence at every period, and almost upon every occasion, throughout the whole course of this war.... All our movements have been made with inferior numbers, and with a mixed, motley crew who were here today [and] gone tomorrow without assigning a reason or even apprising [us] of it.... How we shall be able to rub along till the new army is raised, I know not.—To John Parke Curtis. Fitzpatrick 7:52. (1777.)

Had we kept a permanent army on foot, the enemy would have had nothing to hope for and would, in all probability, have listened to terms long since. —To the President of Congress. Fitzpatrick 19:410. (1780.)

We are always without an army, or have a raw and undisciplined one, engaged for so short a time that we are not fit either for the purposes of offense or defense, much less is it in our power to project schemes and execute plans which depend upon well-disciplined and permanent troops. One half [of] the year is spent in getting troops into the field, the other half is lost in discharging them from their limited service and the manner and time in which they come and go; the public in the meanwhile incurring an immense expense in paying two sets, that is, the

comers and goers, at the same instant, [and] in a waste of provisions, stores, arms, and a thousand things which can scarce be enumerated. In a word, short enlistments have been the primary cause of the continuance of the war, and [of] every evil which has been experienced in the course of it.—To Samuel Washington. Fitzpatrick 19:481. (1780.)

I most firmly believe that the independence of the United States never will be established till there is an army on foot for the war; that if we are to rely on occasional or annual levies we must sink under the expense; and ruin must follow.—To John Mathews. Fitzpatrick 20:113. (1780.)

From long experience and the fullest conviction, I have been and now am decidedly in favor of a permanent force.—To John Mathews. Fitzpatrick 20:115. (1780.)

To suppose that this great revolution can be accomplished by a temporary army, that this army will be subsisted by state supplies, and that taxation alone is adequate to our wants is, in my opinion, absurd and as unreasonable as to expect an inversion in the order of nature to accommodate itself to our views.—To John Cadwalader. Fitzpatrick 20:122. (1780.)

Nothing can be more obvious than [the fact that] a sound military establishment and the interests of economy are the same.—To the President of Congress. Fitzpatrick 20:159. (1780.)

ARMY, An Appeal for Christian Soldiers.—The General hopes and trusts that every officer and man will endeavor so to live and act as becomes a

Washington in 1777 (age 45). Miniature portrait by Charles Willson Peale.

Christian soldier defending the dearest rights and liberties of his country. —General Orders. Fitzpatrick 5:245. (1776.)

ARMY, Should Act with Honor.— Men ... who are not employed as mere hirelings but have stepped forth in defense of everything that is dear and valuable, not only to themselves but to posterity, should take uncommon pains to conduct themselves with uncommon propriety and good order, as their honor, reputation, etc., call loudly upon them for it.—To Israel Putnam. Fitzpatrick 5:489. (1776.)

ARMY, Giving Rank in.— The consequence of giving rank indiscriminately is much to be dreaded.... The too great liberality practiced in this respect will destroy the pride of rank where it ought to exist and will not only render it cheap but contemptible.—To a committee of Congress. Fitzpatrick 8:442. (1777.)

ARMY, Military Pride in.— |Without| military pride ... nothing can be expected from any army.—To a committee of Congress. Fitzpatrick 8:442. (1777.)

ARMY, Necessity of Supplies to.— It is a maxim. that nothing can be of more importance in an army than the clothing and feeding it well.—To a committee of Congress. Fitzpatrick 8:442. (1777.)

ARMY, Guidelines for Discipline in. —Orders, unless they are followed by close attention to the performance of them, are of little avail. They are read by some, only heard of by others, and inaccurately attended to by all, while by a few they are totally disregarded.
. . .

Example, whether it be good or bad, has a powerful influence, and the higher in rank the officer is who sets it, the more striking it is. Hence, and from all military experience, it has been found necessary for officers of every denomination to inspect narrowly the conduct of such parts of the army and corps as are committed to their care.... Of course, neglect of discipline, want of order, irregularity, waste, abuse, and embezzlement of public property insensibly creep in.... But, if the persons issuing |orders| would devote, as duty indispensably requires, a reasonable portion of their time to a personal and close inspection into the affairs of their respective commands; would frequently parade their regiments and compare the actual strength of them, their arms, accoutrements, and clothes, with the returns, and have the deficiencies (if any there be) satisfactorily accounted for and provided; . . . would see that the regulations, the general orders, and their own [orders] were carried into execution where practicable, or report the cause of failure when they cannot; that all returns are made in due form, in proper time, and correctly, comparing one return with another, in order to prevent mistakes, correct abuses, and do justice to the public; and that, in visiting such parts of the line and such particular corps as are entrusted to their care, praise is bestowed on the deserving, reprehension and (where necessary) punishment on the negligent; the good effect would be almost instantaneously felt. Frequent visits and inspection into matters of this kind would produce more real good in one month than volumes of the best digested orders that the wit of man can devise would accomplish in seven years.—To Lord Stirling. Fitzpatrick 18:71. (1780.)

ARMY, Military vs. Civilian Control of.—If a commanding officer is amenable to private calls for the discharge of public duty, he has a dagger always at his breast, and can turn neither to the right nor to the left without meeting its point; in a word, he is no longer a free agent in office, as there are few military decisions which are not offensive to one party or the other.—To Nathanael Greene. Fitzpatrick 28:144. (1785.)

ARMY, Subject to Civil Authority.— It may be proper constantly and strongly to impress upon the army that they are mere agents of civil power, that out of camp they have no other authority than other citizens, that offenses against the laws are to be examined, not by a military officer, but by a magistrate, that they are not exempt from arrests and indictments for violations of the law.—To Daniel Morgan. Fitzpatrick 34:160. (1795.)

ARMY, Choosing a General Staff in. —A good choice [of general staff] is of . . . immense consequence. . . . The inspector general, quartermaster general, adjutant general, and officer commanding the corps of artillerists and engineers ought to be men of the most respectable character, and of first-rate abilities; because, from the nature of their respective offices, and from their being always about the commander-in-chief, who is obliged to entrust many things to them confidentially, scarcely any movement can take place without their knowledge. . . . Besides possessing the qualifications just mentioned, they ought to have those of integrity and prudence in an eminent degree, that entire confidence might be reposed in them. Without these, and their being on good terms with the commanding general, his measures, if not designedly thwarted, may be so embarrassed as to make them move heavily on.—To James McHenry. Fitzpatrick 36:308. (1798.)

ARMY, Quality More Important Than Quantity in.—It is infinitely better to have a *few* good men [in an army] than *many* indifferent ones.—To James McHenry. Fitzpatrick 36:403. (1798.)

ARMY. See also CHAPLAIN; DEFENSE; FURLOUGHS; MILITARY ACADEMY; MILITIA; NATIONAL DEFENSE; NAVY; OFFICERS; PEACE; REVOLUTIONARY WAR; WAR.

ARNOLD (Benedict), Treason of.—Treason of the blackest dye was yesterday discovered! General Arnold, who commanded at West Point, lost to every sentiment of honor or public and private obligation, was about to deliver up that important post into the hands of the enemy. Such an event must have given the American cause a deadly wound if not a fatal stab. Happily, the treason has been timely discovered to prevent the fatal misfortune. The providential train of circumstances which led to it affords the most convincing proof that the liberties of America are the object of divine protection.

At the same time that the treason is to be regretted, the General cannot help congratulating the army on the happy discovery. Our enemies, despairing of carrying their point by force, are practicing every base art to effect by bribery and corruption what they cannot accomplish in a manly way.—General Orders. Fitzpatrick 20:95. (1780.)

ARNOLD (Benedict), Villainous Character of.—I am mistaken if, at *this* time, "Arnold is undergoing the torment of a mental hell."* He wants feeling. From some traits of his character which have lately come to my knowl-

edge, he seems to have been so hackneyed in villainy and so lost to all sense of honor and shame that, while his faculties will enable him to continue his sordid pursuits, there will be no time for remorse.—To John Laurens. Fitzpatrick 20:173. (1780.)

*A week earlier Laurens had written to Washington, "Arnold must undergo a [severe] punishment...in the permanent, increasing torment of a mental hell."—Editor.

ARTICLES OF CONFEDERATION, Too Weak to Build Unity.—I see one head gradually changing into thirteen. I see one army branching into thirteen; and instead of looking up to Congress as the supreme controlling power of the United States, [these armies] are considering themselves as dependent on their respective states. In a word, I see the powers of Congress declining too fast for the consequence and respect which is due to them as the grand representative body of America, and am fearful of the consequences of it.—To Joseph Jones. Fitzpatrick 18:453. (1780.)

ARTICLES OF CONFEDERATION, Inadequate During Revolutionary War.—Our civil government must... undergo a reform; ample powers must be lodged in Congress as the head of the federal union, adequate to all the purposes of war.—To George Mason. Fitzpatrick 20:242. (1780.)

No man in the United States is or can be more deeply impressed with the necessity of a reform in our present confederation than myself. No man, perhaps, has felt the bad effects of it more sensibly; for to the defects thereof, and want of powers in Congress, may justly be ascribed the prolongation of the war and consequently the expenses occasioned by it. More than half the perplexities I have experienced in the course of my command, and almost the whole of the difficulties and distress of the army, have their origin here. But still, the prejudices of some, the designs of others, and the mere machinery of the majority make address [i.e., attention] and management necessary to give weight to opinions which are to combat the doctrines of those different classes of men in the field of politics.—To Alexander Hamilton. Fitzpatrick 26:277. (1783.)

ARTICLES OF CONFEDERATION, Must Be Revised.—That it is necessary to revise and amend the Articles of Confederation, I entertain no doubt; but what may be the consequences of such an attempt is doubtful. Yet something must be done, or the fabric must fall, for it certainly is tottering.—To John Jay. Fitzpatrick 28:431. (1786.)

Fain would I hope that the great and most important of all subjects, the federal government, may be considered with that calm and deliberate attention which the magnitude of it so critically and loudly calls for at this critical moment. Let prejudices, unreasonable jealousies, and local interests yield to reason and liberality. Let us look to our national character, and to things beyond the present moment. No morn ever dawned more favorably than ours did; and no day was ever more clouded than the present. Wisdom and good examples are necessary at this time to rescue the political machine from the impending storm. Virginia has now an opportunity to... take the lead in promoting this great and arduous work. Without an alteration in our political creed, the superstructure we have been seven years in raising, at the expense of so much treasure and blood, must fall. We are fast verging to anarchy and confusion. ... Thirteen sovereignties pulling against each other, and all tugging at the federal head, will soon bring ruin on the whole; whereas a liberal and energetic constitution, well guarded and closely watched to prevent encroachments, might restore us to that degree of respectability and consequences to which we had a fair claim and the brightest prospect of attaining. —To James Madison. Fitzpatrick 29:51 (1786.)

The business of [the Constitutional] Convention is as yet too much in embryo to form any opinion of the result. Much is expected from it by some, but little by others, and nothing by a few. That something is necessary all will agree; for the situation of the general government (if it can be called a government) is shaken to its foundation, and liable to be overset by every blast. In a word, it is at an end, and unless a remedy is soon applied, anarchy and confusion will inevitably ensue.— To Thomas Jefferson. Fitzpatrick 29:224. (1787.)

ARTICLES OF CONFEDERATION, Violations of.—Let the reins of government ... be braced and held with a steady hand, and every violation of the constitution be reprehended; if defec-

tive, let it be amended, but not suffered to be trampled upon while it has an existence.—To Henry Lee. Fitzpatrick 29:34. (1786.)
ARTICLES OF CONFEDERATION, Needed Radical Change.—My wish is that the convention may adopt no temporizing expedient, but probe the defects of the constitution [i.e., the Articles of Confederation] to the bottom and provide radical cures.—To James Madison. Fitzpatrick 29:191. (1787.)
ARTICLES OF CONFEDERATION. See also CONGRESS; CONSTITUTION (U.S.); FEDERAL GOVERNMENT.
ARTS, Promotion of the.—To promote literature in this rising empire, and to encourage the arts, have ever been among the warmest wishes of my heart.—To the trustees of Washington Academy. Fitzpatrick 36:293. (1798.)
ARTS AND SCIENCES, Of National Interest.—The arts and sciences essential to the prosperity of the state and to the ornament and happiness of human life have a primary claim to the encouragement of every lover of his country and mankind.—To Joseph Willard. Fitzpatrick 21:352. (1781.)

There is nothing which can better deserve your patronage than the promotion of science and literature.—First Annual Address to Congress. Fitzpatrick 30:493. (1790.)
ASSISTANCE, Asking for.—It is a maxim with me not to ask what, under similar circumstances, I would not grant.—To the Emperor of Germany. Fitzpatrick 35:45. (1796.)

B

BEHAVIOR, Judging Human.—However it may be the practice of the world ... to consider that only as meritorious which is attended with success, I have accustomed myself to judge of human actions very differently, and to appreciate them by the manner in which they are conducted more than by the *events,* which it is not in the power of human foresight or prudence to command.—To Benjamin Tallmadge. Fitzpatrick 25:415. (1782.)
BOOKS, Basis of Knowledge.—I conceive a knowledge of books is the basis upon which other knowledge is to be built.—To the Reverend Jonathan Boucher. Fitzpatrick 3:50. (1771.)
BOOKS. See also PERIODICALS; PUBLICATIONS; READING.
BORROWING, A Dangerous Practice.—There is no practice more dangerous than that of borrowing money; ... for when money can be had in this way, repayment is seldom thought of in time, the interest becomes a moth, exertions to raise it by dint of industry cease, it comes easy and is spent freely, and many things indulged in that would never be thought of if [they were] to be purchased by the sweat of the brow. In the meantime, the debt is accumulating like a snowball in rolling.—To Samuel Washington. Fitzpatrick 35:498. (1797.)
BORROWING. See also DEBT; FINANCES; NATIONAL DEBT.
BRADDOCK (General Edward), Washington's Observations of.—The general, by frequent breaches of contract, has lost all patience, and, for

Washington in 1777–79 (age 45–47). Miniature portrait by Charles Willson Peale. This portrait was painted at the request of Martha Washington.

want of that temper and moderation which should be used by a man of *sense* upon these occasions, will, I fear, represent us in a light we little deserve; for, instead of blaming the individuals, as he ought, he charges all his disappointments to public supineness and looks upon the country, I believe, as void of honor and honesty. We have frequent disputes on this head, which are maintained with warmth on both sides, especially on his, who is incapable of arguing without, or giving up any point he asserts, let it be ever so incompatible with reason or common sense.—To William Fairfax. Fitzpatrick 1:133. (1755.)

BRADDOCK (General Edward),

Character of.—[His] good and bad qualities were intimately blended. He was brave even to a fault, and in regular service would have done honor to his profession. His attachments were warm, his enmities were strong, and, having no disguise about him, both appeared in full force. He was generous and disinterested, but plain and blunt in his manner even to rudeness.—Biographical memoranda. Fitzpatrick 29:45. (1786.)

C

CALUMNY, The Best Answer to.— To persevere in one's duty and be silent is the best answer to calumny.—To William Livingston. Fitzpatrick 17:225. (1779.)

CALUMNY. See also CENSURE; CRITICISM; NEWSPAPERS.

CANADA, Plea for Alliance with.— We rejoice that our enemies have been deceived with regard to you. They have persuaded themselves, they have even dared to say, that the Canadians were not capable of distinguishing between the blessings of liberty and the wretchedness of slavery, that gratifying the vanity of a little circle of nobility would blind the eyes of the people of Canada. By such artifices they hoped to bend you to their view; but they have been deceived. Instead of finding in you that poverty of soul and baseness of spirit, they see with a chagrin equal to our joy that you are enlightened, generous, and virtuous, that you will not renounce your own rights or serve as instruments to deprive your fellow subjects of theirs. Come then, my brethren, unite with us in an indissoluble union. Let us run together to the same goal. We have taken up arms in defense of our liberty, our property, our wives, and our children. We are determined to preserve them or die. We look forward with pleasure to that day, not far remote (we hope), when the inhabitants of America shall have one sentiment and the full enjoyment of the blessings of a free government.—To the inhabitants of Canada. Fitzpatrick 3:479. (1775.)

CANADA, Accession of.—It is a measure much to be wished, and I believe would not be displeasing to the body of that people; but while Carleton remains among them, with three or four thousand regular troops, they dare not avow their sentiments (if they really are favorable) without a strong support.—To Landon Carter. Fitzpatrick 11:492. (1778.)

CAPITAL PUNISHMENT, Necessary But Unfortunate.—I always hear of capital executions with concern, and regret that there should occur so many instances in which they are necessary. —To James Clinton. Fitzpatrick 13:471. (1778.)

CAPITAL PUNISHMENT. See also PARDON.

CENSURE, The Lot of the Prominent. —Why should I expect to be exempt from censure, the unfailing lot of an elevated station? Merits and talents with which I can have no pretensions of rivalship have ever been subject to it.—To Henry Laurens. Fitzpatrick 10:411. (1778.)

CENSURE, And Duty.—While doing what my conscience informed me was right, as it respected my God, my country, and myself, I could despise all the party clamor and unjust censure which must be expected from some whose personal enmity might be occasioned by their hostility to the government.—To Henry Lee. Fitzpatrick 30:98. (1788.)

CENSURE. See also CALUMNY; CRITICISM.

CENSUS, Results of First National.— The completion of the census of the inhabitants, for which provision was made by law, has been duly notified (excepting one instance in which the return has been informal, and another in which it has been omitted or miscarried), and the returns of the officers who were charged with this duty, which will be laid before you, will give you the pleasing assurance that the present population of the United States borders on four million persons. —Third Annual Address to Congress. Fitzpatrick 31:400. (1791.)

CHAPLAIN, Needed in Army.—The want of a chaplain does, I humbly conceive, reflect dishonor upon the regiment, as all other officers are allowed. The gentlemen of the corps are sensible of this and did propose to support one at their private expense. But I think it would have a more graceful appearance were he appointed as others are.—To Governor Robert Dinwiddie. Fitzpatrick 1:470. (1756.)

CHARITY, Advice on Giving.—Let your *heart* feel for the affliction and distresses of everyone; let your *hand* give in proportion to your purse, remembering always the estimation of the widow's mite. But...it is not everyone who asketh that deserveth charity; all, however, are worthy of the inquiry, or the deserving may suffer.—To Bushrod Washington. Fitzpatrick 26:40. (1783.)

CHARITY, Need for, in Government. —How unfortunate...that internal dissensions should be harrowing and tearing our vitals.... Without more charity,...the fairest prospect of happiness and prosperity that ever was presented to man will be lost.—To Thomas Jefferson. Fitzpatrick 32:130. (1792.)

CHARITY. See also HUMANITARIANISM; POOR.

CHECKS AND BALANCES. See CONSTITUTION (U.S.); SEPARATION OF POWERS.

CHRISTIANITY, Apostasy Within. —The blessed religion revealed in th word of God will remain an eternal and awful monument to prove that the best institutions may be abused by human depravity, and that they may even, in some instances, be made subservient to the vilest of purposes.— Proposed address to Congress (never delivered). Fitzpatrick 30:301. (1789.)

CHRISTIANITY, True, Requires Moral Behavior.—While all men within our territories are protected in worshipping the Deity according to the dictates of their consciences, it is rationally to be expected from them in return that they will all be emulous of evincing the sanctity of their professions by the innocence of their lives and the beneficence of their actions; for no man who is profligate in his morals, or a bad member of the civil

community, can possibly be a true Christian or a credit to his own religious society.—Sparks 12:152. (1789.)

CHRISTIANITY. See also GOD; INDIANS, Christian Missions to; JESUS CHRIST; MORALITY; RELIGION.

CHURCH. See CLERGY; RELIGIOUS SERVICES.

CITIZENSHIP, Vigilant, Needed to Keep America Strong.—No wish in my retirement can exceed that of seeing our country happy; and I can entertain no doubt of its being so if all of us act the part of good citizens, contributing our best endeavors to maintain the Constitution, support the laws, and guard our independence against all assaults, from whatsoever quarter they may come. Clouds may and doubtless often will, in the vicissitudes of events, hover over our political concerns, but a steady adherence to these principles will not only dispel them but render our prospects the brighter by such temporary obscurities.—To the citizens of Alexandria and its neighborhood. Fitzpatrick 35:423. (1797.)

CITIZENSHIP. See also PUBLIC SERVICE.

CLERGY, Harmony Among the.— Believing as I do that *religion* and *morality* are the essential pillars of civil society, I view with unspeakable pleasure that harmony and brotherly love which characterizes the clergy of different denominations, as well in this as in other parts of the United States; exhibiting to the world a new and interesting spectacle, at once the pride of our country and the surest basis of universal harmony.—To the clergy of different denominations residing in and near the city of Philadelphia. Fitzpatrick 35:416. (1797.)

CLOTHING, Moderation in.—Do not conceive that fine clothes make fine men, any more than fine feathers make fine birds. A plain, genteel dress is more admired and obtains more credit than lace and embroidery in the eyes of the judicious and sensible.—To Bushrod Washington. Fitzpatrick 26:40. (1783.)

Decency and cleanliness will always be the first objects in the dress of a judicious and sensible man; a conformity to the prevailing fashion in a certain degree is necessary, but it does not from thence follow that a man should always get a new coat or other clothes upon every trifling change in the mode, when perhaps he has two or three very good ones by him. A person who is anxious to be a leader of the fashion, or one of the first to follow it, will certainly appear in the eyes of judicious men to have nothing better than a frequent change of dress to recommend him to notice.—To George Steptoe Washington. Fitzpatrick 30:247. (1789.)

COLONIES (American), Their Petitions to Great Britain Unheeded.—As to your political sentiments, I would heartily join you in them, so far as relates to a humble and dutiful petition to the throne, provided there was the most distant hope of success. But have we not tried this already? Have we not addressed the Lords, and remonstrated to the Commons? And to what end? Did they deign to look at our petitions? —To Bryan Fairfax. Fitzpatrick 3:228. (1774.)

COLONIES (American), Must Assert Rights or Become Slaves.—An innate spirit of freedom first told me that the measures which [the British] administration has for some time been, and now are, most violently pursuing are repugnant to every principle of natural justice; while much abler heads than my own have fully convinced me that [these measures are] not only repugnant to natural right, but subversive of the laws and constitution of Great Britain itself, in the establishment of which some of the best blood in the kingdom has been spilt.... I shall not undertake to say where the line between Great Britain and the colonies should be drawn; but I am clearly of opinion that one ought to be drawn, and our rights clearly ascertained. I could wish, I own, that the dispute had been left to posterity to determine, but the crisis is arrived when we must assert our rights or submit to every imposition that can be heaped upon us, till custom and use shall make us as tame and abject slaves as the blacks we rule over with such arbitrary sway.— To Bryan Fairfax. Fitzpatrick 3:240. (1774.)

COLONIES (American). See also DECLARATION OF INDEPENDENCE; GREAT BRITAIN; IMPORTS; INDEPENDENCE; NON-IMPORTATION; REVOLUTIONARY WAR; STAMP ACT; TAXATION.

COMMERCE, Civilizing Influence of International.—Although I pretend to no peculiar information respecting commercial affairs, nor any foresight into the scenes of futurity, yet as [a] member of an infant empire, as a philanthropist by character, and (if I may be allowed the expression) as a citizen of the great republic of humanity at large, . . . I cannot avoid reflecting with pleasure on the probable influence that commerce may hereafter have on human manners and society in general. On these occasions I consider how mankind may be connected like one great family in fraternal ties. I indulge a fond, perhaps an enthusiastic, idea that as the world is evidently much less barbarous than it has been, its melioration must still be progressive; that nations are becoming more humanized in their policy; that the subjects of ambition and causes for hostility are daily diminishing; and, in fine, that the period is not very remote when the benefits of a liberal and free commerce will, pretty generally, succeed . . . the devastations and horrors of war.—To the Marquis de Lafayette. Fitzpatrick 28:520. (1786.)

COMMERCE. See also FOREIGN TRADE; IMPORTS; INDIANS; INTERSTATE COMMERCE; NAVY; NONIMPORTATION; PRICE CONTROLS.

CONGRESS, Washington's Obedience to.—While I have the honor to remain in the service of the United States, [I will] obey to the utmost of my power and to the best of my abilities all orders of Congress with a scrupulous exactness.—To the Board of War and Ordnance. Fitzpatrick 5:347. (1776.)

CONGRESS, Ablest Leaders Should Attend.—As there can be no harm in a pious wish for the good of one's country, I shall offer it as mine that each state would not only choose, but absolutely compel, their ablest men to attend Congress; that they would instruct them to go into a thorough investigation of the causes that have produced so many disagreeable effects in the army and country; in a word, that public abuses should be corrected.—To Benjamin Harrison. Fitzpatrick 13:464. (1778.)

CONGRESS, Need for Adequate Powers in.—Unless Congress speaks in a more decisive tone; unless they are vested with powers by the several states competent to the great purposes of war, or assume them as [a] matter of right; and [unless] they, and the states respectively, act with more energy than they hitherto have done, . . . our cause is lost. We can no longer drudge on in the old way. . . . I see one head gradually changing into thirteen. I see one army branching into thirteen; and instead of looking up to Congress as the supreme controlling power of the United States, [they] are considering themselves as dependent on their respective states. In a word, I see the powers of Congress declining too fast for the consequence and respect which is due to them as the grand representative body of America, and am fearful of the consequences of it.—To Joseph Jones. Fitzpatrick 18:453. (1780.)

It is clearly my opinion, unless Congress have powers competent to all general purposes, that the distresses we have encountered, the expense w have incurred, and the blood we have spilt in the course of an eight years' war will avail us nothing.—To Alexander Hamilton. Fitzpatrick 26:188. (1783.)

For Heaven's sake, who are Congress? Are they not the creatures of the people, amenable to them for their conduct, and dependent from day to day on their breath? Where, then, can be the danger of giving them such powers as are adequate to the great ends of government, and to all the general purposes of the Confederation (I repeat the word *general* because I am no advocate for their having to do with the particular policy of any state, further than it concerns the Union at large)? What may be the consequences if they have not these powers, I am at no loss to guess.—To the Reverend William Gordon. Fitzpatrick 27:51. (1783.)

CONGRESS, During the Revolutionary War.—All the business is now attempted, for it is not done, by a timid kind of recommendation from Congress to the states; ... [it is] a many-headed monster, a heterogeneous mass, that never will, or can, come to the same point.—To Fielding Lewis. Fitzpatrick 19:131. (1780.)

If I may be allowed to speak figuratively, our assemblies in politics are to be compared to the wheels of a clock in mechanics; the whole for the general purposes of war should be set in motion by the great wheel (Congress), and if all will do their parts the machine works easy. But a failure in one disorders the whole, and without the large one (which set the whole in motion) nothing can be done; it is ... the united wisdom and exertions of the whole in Congress ... that we are

Washington in 1779 (age 47). Portrait by Charles Willson Peale.

to depend upon. Without this we are no better than a rope of sand, and are as easily broken asunder.—To Archibald Cary. Fitzpatrick 24:347. (1782.)

CONGRESS, The People's Representatives.—Congress are in fact but the people; they return to them at certain short periods [and] are amenable at all times for their conduct.... What interest, therefore, can a man have, under these circumstances, distinct from his constituents?—To Governor Benjamin Harrison. Fitzpatrick 26:184. (1783.)

CONGRESS, Guidelines for Effectiveness in.—My political creed ... is to be wise in the choice of delegates, support them like gentlemen while they are our representatives, give them competent powers for all federal purposes, support them in the due exercise thereof, and lastly, to compel them to close attendance in Congress during their delegation. These things, under the present mode for and termination of elections, aided by annual instead of constant sessions, would, or I am exceedingly mistaken, make us one of the most wealthy, happy, respectable, and powerful nations that ever inhabited the terrestrial globe; without them, we shall, in my opinion, soon be everything which is the direct reverse of them.—To Governor Benjamin Harrison. Fitzpatrick 27:306. (1784.)

CONGRESS, Length of Sessions in. —The incertitude which prevails in Congress, [as well as] the nonattendance of its members, is discouraging to those who are willing and ready to discharge the trust which is reposed in them, while it is disgraceful in a high degree to our country. But I believe the case will never be otherwise so long as that body persist in their present mode of doing business, and...hold constant instead of annual sessions.... Annual sessions would always produce a full representation, and alertness at business. The delegates, after a recess of eight or ten months, would meet each other with glad countenances; they would be complaisant; they would yield to each other as much as the duty they owed their constituents would permit; and they better acquainted with the sentiments of [their constituents] and removing their prejudices during the recess.

Men who are always together get tired of each other's company; they throw off the proper restraint; they say and do things which are personally disgusting; this begets opposition; opposition begets faction; and so it goes on till business is impeded, often at a stand. I am sure (having the business prepared by proper boards or a committee) an annual session of two months would dispatch more business than is now done in twelve; and this by a full representation of the Union.—To Thomas Jefferson. Fitzpatrick 27:376. (1784.)

CONGRESS, Quality of First, Under the Constitution.—The new Congress, on account of the self-created respectability and various talents of its members, will not be inferior to any assembly in the world.—To the Marquis de Lafayette. Fitzpatrick 30:185. (1789.)

CONGRESS, Advice to.—To secure the blessings which a gracious Providence has placed within our reach will, in the course of the present important session, call for the cool and deliberate exertion of your patriotism, firmness, and wisdom.—First Annual Address to Congress. Fitzpatrick 30:491. (1790.)

CONGRESS. See also ARTICLES OF CONFEDERATION; CONSTITUTION (U.S.); FEDERAL GOVERNMENT; LEGISLATURES.

CONGRESSMEN, To Represent the People.—Representatives ought to be the mouth of their constituents.—To Bushrod Washington. Fitzpatrick 29:67. (1786.)

CONSCIENCE, Often Comes Too

Late.—Conscience ... seldom comes to a man's aid while he is in the zenith of health and revelling in pomp and luxury upon ill-gotten spoils; it is generally the *last* act of his life, and comes too late to be of much service to others here, or to himself hereafter.—To John Price Posey. Fitzpatrick 24:986. (1782.)

CONSTITUTION (U.S.), Must Be Framed on Correct Principles.—If, to please the people, we offer what we ourselves disapprove, how can we afterwards defend our work? Let us raise a standard to which the wise and the honest can repair. The event is in the hand of God.—Stated to delegates to the Constitutional Convention, as quoted by Gouverneur Morris in *An Oration upon the Death of General Washington* (delivered in New York, 31 Dec. 1799), pp. 20-21; in Max Farrand, ed., *The Records of the Federal Convention of 1787*, rev. ed., 4 vols. (New Haven, Conn.: Yale University Press, 1937), 3:382. (1787.)

CONSTITUTION (U.S.), Submitted to Congress for Approval.—It is liable to as few exceptions as could reasonably have been expected, ... |and| that it may promote the lasting welfare of that country so dear to us all, and secure her freedom and happiness, is our most ardent wish.—To the President of Congress. Max Farrand, ed., *The Records of the Federal Convention of 1787*, rev. ed., 4 vols. (New Haven, Conn.: Yale University Press, 1937), 2:667. (1787.)

CONSTITUTION (U.S.), Worthy of Acceptance.—The Constitution that is submitted is not free from imperfec-

tions, but there are as few radical defects in it as could well be expected, considering the heterogeneous mass of which the convention was composed and the diversity of interests that are to be attended to. As a constitutional door is opened for future amendments and alterations, I think it would be wise in the people to accept what is offered to them, and I wish it may be by as great a majority of them as it was by that of the convention.—To David Humphreys. Fitzpatrick 29:287. (1787.)

CONSTITUTION (U.S.), Ratification of.—The Constitution is now before the judgment seat. It has, as was expected, its adversaries and supporters. Which will preponderate is yet to be decided. The former more than probably will be most active, as the major part of them will, it is to be feared, be governed by sinister and self-important motives, to which everything in their breasts must yield. The opposition from another class of them may perhaps (if they should be men of reflection, candor, and information) subside in the solution of the following simple questions.... Is the Constitution which is submitted by the convention preferable to the government (if it can be called one) under which we now live?... Is it probable that more confidence would ... be placed in another convention, provided the experiment should be tried, than was placed in the last one, and is it likely that a better agreement would take place therein? What would be the consequences if these should not happen, or even from the delay which must inevitably follow such an experiment? Is there not a constitutional door open for alterations or amendments? And is it not likely that real defects will be as readily discovered after as before trial? And will not our successors be as ready to apply the remedy as ourselves, if occasion should require it?—To Henry Knox. Fitzpatrick 29:288. (1787.)

A few short weeks will determine the political fate of America for the present generation, and probably produce no small influence on the happiness of society through a long succession of ages to come.... It will demonstrate as visibly the finger of Providence as any possible event in the course of human affairs.—To the Marquis de Lafayette. Fitzpatrick 29:507. (1788.)

No one *can* rejoice more than I do at every step the people of this great country take to preserve the Union, establish good order and government, and to render the nation happy at home and respectable abroad. No country upon earth ever had it more in its power to attain these blessings than united America. Wondrously strange, then, and much to be regretted indeed would it be, were we to neglect the means and to depart from the road which Providence has pointed us to so plainly; I cannot believe it will ever come to pass. The great Governor of the Universe has led us too long and too far on the road to happiness and glory to forsake us in the midst of it.—To Benjamin Lincoln. Fitzpatrick 30:11. (1788.)

CONSTITUTION (U.S.), Future

Generations Qualified to Amend.—Is there not a constitutional door open for alterations or amendments? And is it not likely that real defects will be as readily discovered after as before trial? And will not our successors be as ready to apply the remedy as ourselves, if occasion should require it? To think otherwise will, in my judgment, be ascribing more of the *amor patria,* more wisdom, and more virtue to ourselves than I think we deserve.—To Henry Knox. Fitzpatrick 29:289. (1787.)

The warmest friends and the best supporters the Constitution has do not contend that it is free from imperfections; but they found them unavoidable, and are sensible, if evil is likely to arise therefrom, |that| the remedy must come hereafter; for in the present moment it is not to be obtained. And as there is a constitutional door open for it, I think the people (for it is with them to judge) can, as they will have the advantage of experience on their side, decide with as much propriety on the alterations and amendments which are necessary |as| ourselves. I do not think we are more inspired, have more wisdom, or possess more virtue than those who will come after us.—To Bushrod Washington. Fitzpatrick 29:311. (1787.)

CONSTITUTION (U.S.), Opponents of.—The opponents I expected (for it ever has been that the adversaries to a measure are more active than its friends) would endeavor to stamp it with unfavorable impressions, in order to bias the judgment that is ultimately to decide on it. This is evidently the case with the writers in opposition, whose objections are better calculated to alarm the fears than to convince the judgment of their readers. They build their objections upon principles that do not exist, which the Constitution does not support them in, and the existence of which has been, by an appeal to the Constitution itself, flatly denied; and then, as if they were unanswerable, draw all the dreadful consequences that are necessary to alarm the apprehensions of the ignorant or unthinking. It is not the interest of the major part of those characters to be convinced, nor will their local views yield to arguments which do not accord with their present or future prospects. —To Bushrod Washington. Fitzpatrick 29:309. (1787.)

CONSTITUTION (U.S.), Accommodation Required for Ratification.—Is it best for the states to unite or not to unite? If there are men who prefer the latter, then unquestionably the constitution which is offered must, in their estimation, be wrong from the words "We the people" to the signature, inclusively; but those who think differently, and yet object to parts of it, would do well to consider that it does not lie with any one state, or the minority of the states, to superstruct a constitution for the whole. The separate interests, as far as it is practicable, must be consolidated; and local views must be attended to as far as the nature of the case will admit. Hence it is that every state has some objection to the present form, and these objections are directed to different points. That which is most pleasing to one is obnoxious to another, and so vice

versa. If, then, the union of the whole is a desirable object, the component parts must yield a little in order to accomplish it.—To Bushrod Washington. Fitzpatrick 29:310. (1787.)

CONSTITUTION (U.S.), Power of, Rests in the People.—The power under the Constitution will always be in the people. It is entrusted for certain defined purposes, and for a certain limited period, to representatives of their own choosing; and whenever it is executed contrary to their interest, or not agreeable to their wishes, their servants can, and undoubtedly will, be recalled.—To Bushrod Washington. Fitzpatrick 29:311. (1787.)

CONSTITUTION (U.S.), Unanimity in Its Adoption. The various and opposite interests which were to be conciliated, the local prejudices which were to be subdued, the diversity of opinions and sentiments which were to be reconciled, and, in fine, the sacrifices wl ich were necessary to be made on all sides for the general welfare, combined to make it a work of so intricate and difficult a nature that I think it is much to be wondered at that anything could have been produced with such unanimity as the Constitution proposed.—To Mrs. Catharine Macaulay Graham. Fitzpatrick 29:316. (1787.)

CONSTITUTION (U.S.), Only Alternative to National Ruin.—I…most firmly believe that in the aggregate it is the best constitution that can be obtained at this epocha, and that this or a dissolution of the Union awaits our choice, and are the only alternatives before us.—To Governor Edmund

Washington in 1779 (age 47). Engraving from pencil drawing by Pierre Eugene du Simitiere.

Randolph. Fitzpatrick 29:358. (1788.)
CONSTITUTION (U.S.), "Little Short of a Miracle."—It appears to me ...little short of a miracle that the delegates from so many different states (which states...are also different from each other in their manners, circumstances, and prejudices) should unite in forming a system of national government so little liable to well-founded objections.—To the Marquis de Lafayette. Fitzpatrick 29:409. (1788.)
CONSTITUTION (U.S.), Provides Barriers Against Tyranny.—With regard to the two great points, the pivots upon which the whole machine must move, my creed is simply:

1st. That the general government is not invested with more powers than are indispensably necessary to perform the functions of a good government; and consequently that no objection ought to be made against the quantity of power delegated to it.

2nd. That these powers (as the appointment of all rulers will forever arise from, and at short, stated intervals recur to, the free suffrage of the people) are so distributed among the legislative, executive, and judicial branches, into which the general government is arranged, that it can never be in danger of degenerating into a monarchy, an oligarchy, an aristocracy, or any other despotic or oppressive form, so long as there shall remain any virtue in the body of the people.

I would not be understood...to speak of consequences which may be produced in the revolution of ages, by corruption of morals, profligacy of manners, and listlessness for the preservation of the natural and unalienable rights of mankind, nor of the successful usurpations that may be established at such an unpropitious juncture upon the ruins of liberty, however providently guarded and secured; as these are contingencies against which no human prudence can effectually provide. It will at least be a recommendation to the proposed constitution that it is provided with more checks and barriers against the introduction of tyranny, and those of a nature less liable to be surmounted, than any government hitherto instituted among mortals has possessed.—To the Marquis de Lafayette. Fitzpatrick 29:410. (1788.)

CONSTITUTION (U.S.), Will Cause America to "Lift Up Her Head."—There has been much greater unanimity in favor of the proposed government than could have reasonably been expected. Should it be adopted (and I think it will be), America will lift up her head again and in a few years become respectable among the nations. It is a flattering and consolatory reflection that our rising republics have the good wishes of all the philosophers, patriots, and virtuous men in all nations, and that they look upon them as a kind of asylum for mankind. God grant that we may not disappoint their honest expectations.—To the Marquis de Chastellux. Fitzpatrick 29:485. (1788.)

CONSTITUTION (U.S.), God's Hand in Framing and Adoption of.—Maryland has ratified the federal Constitution by a majority of 63 to 11 voices. That makes the seventh state which has adopted it. Next Monday the convention in Virginia will assemble; we have still good hopes of its adoption here, though by no great plurality of votes. South Carolina has probably decided favorably before this time. The plot thickens fast. A few short weeks will determine the political fate of America for the present generation and [will] probably produce no small influence on the happiness of society through a long succession of ages to come. Should everything proceed with harmony and consent according to our actual wishes and expectations, I will confess to you sincerely, my dear Marquis, it will be so much beyond anything we had a right to imagine or

expect eighteen months ago that it will demonstrate as visibly the finger of Providence as any possible event in the course of human affairs can ever designate it. It is impracticable for you or anyone who has not been on the spot to realize the change in men's minds and the progress towards rectitude in thinking and acting which will then have been made.—To the Marquis de Lafayette. Fitzpatrick 29:507. (1788.)

We may, with a kind of pious and grateful exultation, trace the fingers of Providence through those dark and mysterious events which first induced the states to appoint a general convention, and then led them one after another...into an adoption of the system recommended by that general convention, thereby, in all human probability, laying a lasting foundation for tranquility and happiness, when we had but too much reason to fear that confusion and misery were coming rapidly upon us. That the same good Providence may still continue to protect us, and prevent us from dashing the cup of national felicity just as it has been lifted to our lips, is [my] earnest prayer.—To Jonathan Trumbull. Fitzpatrick 30:22. (1788.)

CONSTITUTION (U.S.), Most Perfect Ever Written.—The Constitution recommended by the federal convention [of 1787]...approache[s] nearer to perfection than any government hitherto instituted among men.—To Sir Edward Newenham. Fitzpatrick 30:73. (1788.)

This Constitution is really, in its formation, a government of the people, that is to say, a government in which all power is derived from and at stated periods reverts to them; and... in its operation it is purely a government of laws made and executed by the fair substitutes of the people alone. The election of the different branches of Congress by the [nation's] freemen, either directly or indirectly, is the pivot on which turns the first wheel of the government, a wheel which communicates motion to all the rest. At the same time, the exercise of this right of election seems to be so regulated as to afford less opportunity for corruption and influence, and more for stability and system, than has usually been incident to popular governments.... Hence I have been induced to conclude that this government must be less [subject] to well-founded objections than most which have existed in the world. And in that opinion I am confirmed on three accounts: first, because every government ought to be possessed of power adequate to the purposes for which it was instituted; secondly, because no other or greater powers appear to me to be delegated to this government than are essential to accomplish the objects for which it was instituted, to wit, the safety and happiness of the governed; and thirdly, because it is clear to my conception that no government before introduced among mankind ever contained so many checks and such efficacious restraints to prevent it from degenerating into any species of oppression.... The balances arising from the distribution of the legislative, executive, and judicial powers are the best that have been instituted.—Proposed address to

Congress (never delivered). Fitzpatrick 30:299. (1789.)

CONSTITUTION (U.S.), The Guide for the President.—The Constitution of the United States, and the laws made under it, must mark the line of my official conduct.—To Edmund Randolph. Fitzpatrick 31:9. (1790.)

The Constitution is the guide which I never will abandon.—To the Boston selectmen. Fitzpatrick 34:253. (1795.)

CONSTITUTION (U.S.), Demonstrates Stability of Republicanism— To complete the American character, it remains for the citizens of the United States to show to the world that the reproach heretofore cast on republican governments, for their want of stability, is without foundation when that government is the deliberate choice of an enlightened people; and I am fully persuaded that every well-wisher to the happiness and prosperity of this country will evince by his conduct that we live under a government of laws, and that, while we preserve inviolate our national faith, we are desirous to live in amity with all mankind.—To the inhabitants of Alexandria. Fitzpatrick 33:3. (1793.)

CONSTITUTION (U.S.), A Result of Amity and Concession.—It is a fact declared by the [federal] convention [of 1787], and universally understood, that the Constitution of the United States was the result of a spirit of amity and mutual concession. And it is well known that under this influence the smaller states were admitted to an equal representation in the Senate with the larger states, and that this branch of the government was invested with great powers, for on the equal participation of those powers the sovereignty and political safety of the smaller states were deemed essentially to depend.—To the House of Representatives. Fitzpatrick 35:4. (1796.)

CONSTITUTION (U.S.), Has Just Claim for Support.—This government, the offspring of our own choice, uninfluenced and unawed, adopted upon full investigation and mature deliberation, completely free in its principles, in the distribution of its powers, uniting security with energy, and containing within itself a provision for its own amendment, has a just claim to your confidence and your support. Respect for its authority, compliance with its laws, acquiescence in its measures, are duties enjoined by the fundamental maxims of true liberty.—Farewell Address. Fitzpatrick 35:224. (1796.)

CONSTITUTION (U.S.), Binding Until Changed by Majority.—The basis of our political systems is the right of the people to make and to alter their constitutions of government. But the constitution which at any time exists, till changed by an explicit and authentic act of the whole people, is sacredly obligatory upon all. The very idea of the power and the right of the people to establish government presupposes the duty of every individual to obey the established government.—Farewell Address. Fitzpatrick 35:224. (1796.)

CONSTITUTION (U.S.), Avoid Innovation on Its Principles.—Towards the preservation of your government and the permanency of your present

happy state, it is requisite, not only that you steadily discountenance irregular oppositions to its acknowledged authority, but also that you resist with care the spirit of innovation upon its principles, however specious the pretexts. One method of assault may be to effect, in the forms of the Constitution, alterations which will impair the energy of the system, and thus to undermine what cannot be directly overthrown.—Farewell Address. Fitzpatrick 35:225. (1796.)

CONSTITUTION (U.S.), Changes in, to Be Made with Care.—In all the changes to which you may be invited, remember that time and habit are at least as necessary to fix the true character of governments as of other human institutions; that experience is the surest standard by which to test the real tendency of the existing constitution of a country; that facility in changes upon the credit of mere hypotheses and opinion exposes to perpetual change, from the endless variety of hypotheses and opinion. And remember, especially, that for the efficient management of your common interests in a country so extensive as ours, a government of as much vigor as is consistent with the perfect security of liberty is indispensable. Liberty itself will find in such a government, with powers properly distributed and adjusted, its surest guardian.—Farewell Address. Fitzpatrick 35:225. (1796.)

CONSTITUTION (U.S.), Change Only by Amendment.—If, in the opinion of the people, the distribution or modification of the constitutional powers be in any particular wrong, let it be corrected by an amendment in the way which the Constitution designates. But let there be no change by usurpation; for though this, in one instance, may be the instrument of good, it is the customary weapon by which free governments are destroyed.—Farewell Address. Fitzpatrick 35:229. (1796).

CONSTITUTION (U.S.). See also ARTICLES OF CONFEDERATION; CONGRESS; EXECUTIVE BRANCH FEDERAL GOVERNMENT; GOVERNMENT; JUDICIARY; MAJORITY RULE; PEOPLE; PRESIDENT; SEPARATION OF POWERS.

CONSTITUTIONAL CONVENTION, Needed.—A thorough reform of the present system is indispensable, ...and with hand (and heart) I hope the business will be essayed in a full convention.—To James Madison. Fitzpatrick 29:190. (1787.)

CONSTITUTIONS, Framing of New, Requires Great Care.—To form a new government requires infinite care and unbounded attention; for if the foundation is badly laid, the superstructure must be bad. Too much time, therefore, cannot be bestowed in weighing and digesting matters well. We have, no doubt, some good parts in our present [Virginia] constitution; many bad ones we know we have. Wherefore, no time can be misspent that is employed in separating the wheat from the tares. My fear is that you will all get tired and homesick; the consequence of which will be that you will patch up some kind of a constitution as defective as the present. This should be avoided. Every man should consider that he is lending his aid to frame a constitution which is to render millions happy or miserable, and that a matter of such moment cannot be the work of a day.—To John Augustine Washington. Fitzpatrick 5:92. (1776.)

CONSTITUTIONS, Should Be Obeyed Until Amended.—Precedents are dangerous things. Let the reins of government then be braced and held with a steady hand, and every violation of the constitution be reprehended; if defective, let it be amended, but not suffered to be trampled upon while it has an existence.—To Henry Lee. Fitzpatrick 29:34. (1786.)

CONTROVERSIES, Dealing with Political.—To be disgusted at the decision of questions because they are not consonant to [our] own ideas, and to withdraw ourselves from public assemblies or to neglect our attendance at them upon suspicion that there is a party formed who are inimical to our cause and to the true interest of our country, is wrong, because these things may originate in a difference of opinion; but supposing the fact is otherwise and that our suspicions are well founded, it is the indispensable duty of every patriot to counteract them by the most steady and uniform opposition.—To John Parke Custis. Fitzpatrick 21:318. (1781.)

CONTROVERSIES. See also DISPUTES; OPINION; POLITICAL OPINIONS.

CONWAY CABAL, Washington's Reaction to.—My enemies take an ungenerous advantage of me.... They

Washington in August 1783 (age 51). Portrait by Joseph Wright.

know I cannot combat their insinuations...without disclosing secrets it is of the utmost moment to conceal.... Why should I expect to be exempt from censure, the unfailing lot of an elevated station?...My heart tells me it has been my unremitted aim to do the best circumstances would permit. Yet I may have been very often mistaken in my judgment of the means, and may, in many instances, deserve the imputation of error.—To Henry Laurens. Fitzpatrick 10:410. (1777.)

CRITICISM, Part of Human Nature. —It is the nature of man to be displeased with everything that disappoints a favorite hope or flattering project; and it is the folly of too many

of them to condemn without investigating circumstances.—To the Marquis de Lafayette. Fitzpatrick 12:383. (1778.)

CRITICISM. See also CALUMNY; CENSURE.

CURRENCY, Should Be Backed by Gold and Silver.—I am well aware that appearances ought to be upheld, and that we should avoid as much as possible recognizing by any public act the depreciation of our currency; but I conceive this end would be answered, as far as might be necessary, by stipulating that all money payments should be made in gold and silver, being the common medium of commerce among nations. To the President of Congress. Fitzpatrick 11:217. (1778).

CURRENCY, Need for Fixed Value of.—It is...our interest and truest policy to give a currency, to fix a value, as far as it may be practicable, upon all occasions, upon that which is to be the medium of our internal commerce and the support of the war.—To Gouverneur Morris. Fitzpatrick 12:404. (1778.)

CURRENCY, A Strong, Basic to National Well-being.—Every other effort is in vain unless something can be done to restore [the currency's] credit. Congress, the states individually, and individuals of each state should exert themselves to effect this great end. [Its failure] is the only hope, the last resource, of the enemy; and nothing but our want of public virtue can induce a continuance of the war. Let them once see that, as it is in our power, so it is our inclination and intention to overcome this difficulty, and the idea of conquest or hope of bringing us back to a state of dependence will vanish like the morning dew; they can no more encounter this kind of opposition than the hoarfrost can withstand the rays of an all-cheering sun. The liberties and safety of this country depend upon it; the way is plain; the means are in our power. But it is virtue alone that can effect it.—To Edmund Pendleton. Fitzpatrick 17:52. (1779.)

CURRENCY, Must Have Underlying Value.—Experience has demonstrated the impracticality long to maintain a paper credit without funds for its redemption. The long depreciation of our currency was in the main a necessary effect of the want of those funds. —To John Laurens. Fitzpatrick 21:106. (1781.)

CURRENCY, Need for Uniform.— Uniformity in the currency [and in the] weights and measures of the United States is an object of great importance, and will, I am persuaded, be duly attended to.—First Annual Address to Congress. Fitzpatrick 30:493. (1790.)

CURRENCY. See also INFLATION; MONEY.

CUSTIS (Martha), Washington Expresses Love for His Fiancee.—We have begun our march for the Ohio. A courier is starting for Williamsburg, and I embrace the opportunity to send a few words to one whose life is now inseparable from mine. Since that happy hour when we made our pledges to each other, my thoughts have been continually going to you as another self. That an all-powerful Providence may keep us both in safety

is the prayer of your ever faithful and affectionate friend.—To Martha Custis. Fitzpatrick 2:242. (1758.)

CUSTIS (Martha). See also WASHINGTON (Martha).

CUSTIS (Patsy), Death of.—It is an easier matter to conceive than to describe the distress of this family, especially that of the unhappy parent of our dear Pasty Custis, when I inform you that yesterday... the sweet, innocent girl entered into a more happy and peaceful abode than any she has met with in the afflicted path she hitherto has trod. She rose from dinner about four o'clock in better health and spirits than she appeared to have been in for some time; soon after which she was seized with one of her usual fits, and expired in it in less than two minutes without uttering a word, a groan, or scarce a sigh. This sudden and unexpected blow, I scarce need add, has almost reduced my poor wife to the lowest ebb of misery.—To Burwell Bassett. Fitzpatrick 3:138. (1773.)

D

DEATH, Proper Reaction to.—The ways of Providence being inscrutable, and the justice of [a loved one's death] not to be scanned by the shallow eye of humanity, nor to be counteracted by the utmost efforts of human power or wisdom, resignation and, as far as the strength of our reason and religion can carry us, a cheerful acquiescence to the Divine Will [are] what we are to aim [for].—To Burwell Bassett. Fitzpatrick 3:133. (1773.)

DEATH, Preparations for.—Life is always uncertain, and common prudence dictates to every man the necessity of settling his temporal concerns while it is in his power, and while the mind is calm and undisturbed.—To Mrs. Martha Washington. Fitzpatrick 3:294. (1775.)

DEATH. See also CAPITAL PUNISHMENT; MOURNING.

DEBT, Repayment of.—To contract new debts is not the way to pay old ones.—To James Welch. Fitzpatrick 37:177. (1799.)

DEBT. See also BORROWING; FINANCES; NATIONAL DEBT.

DECISIONS, Washington's Method of Making.—Having no other wish than to promote the true and permanent interests of this country, I am anxious, always, to compare the opinions of those in whom I confide with one another; and those again (without being bound by them) with my own, that I may extract all the good I can.—To John Jay. Fitzpatrick 35:103. (1796.)

DECLARATION OF INDEPENDENCE, Brought On by Necessity.—You will perceive by the enclosed Declaration, which I have the honor to transmit you, that Congress of late have been employed in deliberating on matters of the utmost importance. Impelled by necessity and a repetition of injuries unsufferable, without the most distant prospect of relief, they have asserted the claims of the American colonies to the rights of humanity and declared them free and independent states.—To the Massachusetts legislature. Fitzpatrick 5:238. (1776.)

DECLARATION OF INDEPEN-

DENCE, Announced to American Army.—The Continental Congress, impelled by the dictates of duty, policy, and necessity, having been pleased to dissolve the connection which subsisted between this country and Great Britain, and to declare the united colonies of North America free and independent states, the several brigades are to be drawn up this evening on their respective parades at six o'clock, when the declaration of Congress, showing the grounds and reasons of this measure, is to be read with an audible voice. The General hopes this important event will serve as a fresh incentive to every officer and soldier to act with fidelity and courage, as knowing that now the peace and safety of his country depends (under God) solely on the success of our arms, and that he is now in the service of a state possessed of sufficient power to reward his merit and advance him to the highest honors of a free country.—General Orders. Fitzpatrick 5:245. (1776.)

DECLARATION OF INDEPENDENCE. See also INDEPENDENCE.

DEFENSE, Best Policy of.—To be prepared for war is one of the most effectual means of preserving peace.—First Annual Address to Congress. Fitzpatrick 30:491. (1790.)

DEFENSE, Necessary for Maintaining Peace.—I cannot recommend to your notice measures for the fulfillment of our duties to the rest of the world without again pressing upon you the necessity of placing ourselves in a condition of complete defense, and of exacting from them the fulfillment of their duties towards us. The United States ought not to indulge a persuasion that, contrary to the order of human events, they will forever keep at a distance those painful appeals to arms with which the history of every other nation abounds. There is a rank due to the United States among nations which will be withheld, if not absolutely lost, by the reputation of weakness. If we desire to avoid insult, we must be able to repel it; if we desire to secure peace, one of the most powerful instruments of our rising prosperity, it must be known that we are at all times ready for war.—Fifth Annual Address to Congress. Fitzpatrick 33:165. (1793.)

DEFENSE. See also ARMY; MILITARY ACADEMY; MILITIA; NATIONAL DEFENSE; NAVY; PEACE; REVOLUTIONARY WAR; WAR.

DEMOCRACY, Limitation of.—It is among the evils, and perhaps is not the smallest [evil], of democratical governments that the people must *feel* before they will *see;* when this happens they are roused to action. Hence it is that this form of government is so slow.— To Henry Knox. Fitzpatrick 29:171. (1787.)

DEMOCRACY. See also GOVERNMENT; PEOPLE; REPUBLICANISM; SELF-GOVERNMENT.

DEMOCRATIC SOCIETIES, Cause of the Whiskey Rebellion.—I consider this insurrection as the first *formidable* fruit of the democratic societies, brought forth, I believe, too prematurely for their own views, which may contribute to the annihilation of them.

That these societies were instituted by the *artful* and *designing* members (many of their body I have no doubt mean well, but know little of the real plan), primarily to sow the seeds of jealousy and distrust among the people, of the government, by destroying all confidence in the administration of it, and that these doctrines have been budding and blowing ever since, is not new to anyone who is acquainted with the characters of their leaders, and has been attentive to their maneuvers. I early gave it as my opinion to the confidential characters around me, that, if these societies were not counteracted (not by prosecutions, the ready way to make them grow stronger), or did not fall into disesteem from the knowledge of their origin and the views with which they had been instituted by their father, [French diplomat Edmond] Genet, for purposes well known to the government, ... they would shake the government to its foundation. Time and circumstances have confirmed me in this opinion, and I deeply regret the probable consequences, not as they will affect me personally (for I have not long to act on this theatre, and sure I am that not a man among them can be more anxious to put me aside than I am to sink into the profoundest retirement), but because I see, under a display of popular and fascinating guises, the most diabolical attempts to destroy the best fabric of human government and happiness that has ever been presented for the acceptance of mankind. —To Governor Henry Lee. Fitzpatrick 33:475. (1794.)

DIFFICULTIES, Should Not Be

Overestimated—We ought not to convert trifling difficulties into insuperable obstacles.—To the Marquis de Malmedy. Fitzpatrick 8:69. (1777.)
DIFFICULTIES. See also MISFORTUNES; TRIBULATIONS.
DISCONTENTED, No Safeguard Against the.—Against the malignancy of the discontented, the turbulent, and the vicious, no abilities, no exertions, nor the most unshaken integrity are any safeguard.—To John Jay. Fitzpatrick 34:16. (1794.)
DISPUTES, Dealing with.—To constitute a dispute there must be two parties. To understand it well, both parties, and all the circumstances, must be fully heard; and, to accommodate differences, temper and mutual forbearance are requisite.—To David Stuart. Fitzpatrick 31:29. (1790.)
DISPUTES. See also CONTROVERSIES; OPINION; POLITICAL OPINIONS.
DISSENSIONS, Internal, Are Greatest Threat.—I am under more apprehensions on account of our own dissensions than of the efforts of the enemy.—To Benedict Arnold. Fitzpatrick 13:393. (1778.)
DISTRICT OF COLUMBIA, Beginnings of.—Pursuant to the authority contained in the several acts on that subject, a district of ten miles square for the permanent seat of the government of the United States has been fixed and announced by proclamation, which district will comprehend lands on both sides of the river Potomac and the towns of Alexandria and Georgetown. A city has also been laid out agreeably to a plan which will be placed

Washington in August 1783 (age 51) Portrait by William Dunlap.

before Congress, and as there is a prospect, favored by the rate of sales which have already taken place, of ample funds for carrying on the necessary public buildings, there is every expectation of their due progress.—Third Annual Address to Congress. Fitzpatrick 31:400. (1791.)
DISTRICT OF COLUMBIA. See also NATIONAL UNIVERSITY; WASHINGTON, D.C.
DRESS. See CLOTHING; INDIAN DRESS.
DRUNKENNESS, Ill Effects of.—Consider how little a drunken man differs from a beast. The latter is not endowed with reason; the former deprives himself of it, and when that is

the case acts like a brute, annoying and disturbing everyone around him. But this is not...the worst of it. By degrees [drunkenness] renders a person feeble and not only unable to serve others but to help himself; and, [its] being an act of his own, he falls from a state of usefulness into contempt and at length suffers, if not perishes, in penury and want.—To John Christian Ehler. Fitzpatrick 33:215. (1793.)

DRUNKENNESS. See also LIQUOR; TAVERNS; VICES.

E

EASE, Not to Be Found.—It is in vain, I perceive, to look for ease and happiness in a world of troubles.—To Henry Knox. Fitzpatrick 36:345. (1798.)

ECONOMICS. See AGRICULTURE; BORROWING; COMMERCE; CURRENCY; DEBT; FINANCES; FOREIGN TRADE; INFLATION; INTERSTATE COMMERCE; MANUFACTURES; MONEY; NATIONAL DEBT; PRICE CONTROLS; PROPERTY; TAXATION; WORK.

EDUCATION, Vital in a Republic.—Education generally [is] one of the surest means of enlightening and giving just ways of thinking to our citizens.—To Alexander Hamilton. Fitzpatrick 35:199. (1796.)

Promote,...as an object of primary importance, institutions for the general diffusion of knowledge. In proportion as the structure of a government gives force to public opinion, it is essential that public opinion should be en-

lightened.—Farewell Address. Fitzpatrick 35:230. (1796.)

EDUCATION, Study of Government Should Be Preeminent.—A primary object...should be the education of our youth in the science of *government*. In a republic, what species of knowledge can be equally important? and what duty more pressing on its legislature than to patronize a plan for communicating it to those who are to be the future guardians of the liberties of the country?—Eighth Annual Address to Congress. Fitzpatrick 35:316. (1796.)

EDUCATION, Evils of Foreign.—It has always been a source of serious regret with me to see the youth of these United States sent to foreign countries for the purpose of education, often before their minds were formed or they had imbibed any adequate ideas of the happiness of their own, contracting, too frequently, not only habits of dissipation and extravagance, but principles unfriendly to republican government and to the true and genuine liberties of mankind, which thereafter are rarely overcome.—Last Will and Testament. Fitzpatrick 37:279. (1799.)

EDUCATION. See also ALEXANDRIA ACADEMY; ARTS AND SCIENCES; BOOKS; INFORMATION; KNOWLEDGE; MILITARY ACADEMY; NATIONAL UNIVERSITY; SELF-GOVERNMENT.

ELECTIONS, Avoid Foreign Influence in.—In all free governments, contention in elections will take place, and while it is confined to our own citizens it is not to be regretted; but

severely indeed ought it to be repro-
bated when occasioned by foreign
machinations. I trust, however, that
the good sense of our countrymen will
guard the public weal against this and
every other innovation; and that, although we may be a little wrong now
and then, we shall return to the right
path with more avidity.—To Jonathan
Trumbull. Fitzpatrick 35:412. (1797.)
ELECTIONS. See also FACTIONS;
POLITICAL PARTIES; POLITICS.
ENEMIES, Public and Private.—It is a
tax, however severe, which all those
must pay who are called to eminent
stations of trust, not only to be held up
as conspicuous marks to the enmity of
the public adversaries to their country,
but the malice of secret traitors and
the envious intrigues of false friends
and factions.—To William Livingston.
Fitzpatrick 10:415. (1778.)
**ENEMY, Conversations with, Prohi-
bited.**—Notwithstanding the orders
already given, the General hears with
astonishment that not only soldiers
but officers, unauthorized, are continually conversing with the officers
and sentries of the enemy. Any officer,
non-commissioned officer, or soldier,
or any person whatsoever, who is
detected holding any conversation or
carrying on any correspondence with
any of the officers or sentries of the
advanced posts of the enemy, will be
immediately brought before a general
court-martial and punished with the
utmost severity.—General Orders.
Fitzpatrick 3:340. (1775.)
**ENEMY, Washington's Rebuke When
His Caretaker Assisted the.**—That
which gives me most concern is that

you should go on board the enemy's
vessels and furnish them with refreshments. It would have been a less painful circumstance to me to have heard
that in consequence of your non-
compliance with their request, they
had burnt my house and laid the plantation in ruins. You ought to have considered yourself as my representative,
and should have reflected on the bad
example of communicating with the
enemy and making a voluntary offer
of refreshments to them with a view
to prevent a conflagration.

It was not in your power, I acknowledge, to prevent them from sending a
flag on shore, and you did right to
meet it; but you should, in the same
instant that the business of it was unfolded, have declared explicitly that it
was improper for you to yield to the
request; after which, if they had proceeded to help themselves *by force,* you
could but have submitted (and being
unprovided for defense, this was to be
preferred to a feeble opposition which
only serves as a pretext to burn and
destroy).

I am thoroughly persuaded that you
acted from your best judgment and
believe that your desire to preserve my
property, and rescue the buildings
from impending danger, were your
governing motives. But to go on board
their vessels, carry them refreshments, commune with a parcel of
plundering scoundrels, and request a
favor by asking the surrender of my
Negroes was exceedingly ill-judged,
and, it is to be feared, will be unhappy
in its consequences, as it will be a precedent for others and may become a

Washington in January 1785 (age 58). Medallion profile by Joseph Wright.

subject of animadversion.—To Lund Washington. Fitzpatrick 22:14. (1781.)

ENEMY. See also GREAT BRITAIN; HESSIANS; PRISONERS OF WAR; REVOLUTIONARY WAR; TORIES; WAR.

ENGLAND. See COLONIES (American); GREAT BRITAIN; INDEPENDENCE; REVOLUTIONARY WAR.

ENMITY, Difference Between National and Personal.—I was opposed to the policy of Great Britain and became an enemy to her measures; but I always distinguished between a cause and individuals; and while the latter supported their opinion upon liberal and generous grounds, personally I never could be an enemy to them.—To

John Joiner Ellis. Fitzpatrick 27:56. (1783.)

ERRORS, Willful vs. Unintentional.—A man may err once, and he may err twice, but when those who possess more than a common share of abilities persevere in a regular course of destructive policy, one is more apt to suspect their hearts than their heads.—To Fielding Lewis. Fitzpatrick 22:283. (1781.)

If the enlightened and virtuous part of the community will make allowances for my involuntary errors, I will promise they shall have no cause to accuse me of willful ones.—To Oliver Wolcott. Fitzpatrick 34:447. (1796.)

ERRORS. See also EXCUSES; FAULTS; MISTAKES.

EUROPE, Contrasted with the United States.—The complete establishment of our public credit is a strong mark of the confidence of the people in the virtue of their representatives and the wisdom of their measures; and, while in Europe wars or commotions seem to agitate almost every nation, peace and tranquility prevail among us, except on some parts of our western frontiers where the Indians have been troublesome, to reclaim or chastise whom proper measures are now pursuing. This contrast between the situation of the people of the United States and those of Europe is too striking to be passed over, even by the most superficial observer, and may, I believe, be considered as one great cause of leading the people here to reflect more attentively on their own prosperous state and to examine more minutely, and consequently approve more fully of, the government under which they live than they otherwise would have done. But we do not wish to be the only people who may taste the sweets of an equal and good government; we look with an anxious eye to the time when happiness and tranquillity shall prevail in your country, and when all Europe shall be freed from commotions, tumults, and alarms.—To the Marquis de Lafayette. Fitzpatrick 31:326. (1791.)

While many of the nations of Europe, with their American dependencies, have been involved in a contest unusually bloody, exhausting, and calamitous, in which the evils of foreign war have been aggravated by domestic convulsion and insurrection; in which many of the arts most useful to society have been exposed to discouragement and decay; in which scarcity of subsistence has embittered other sufferings, while even the anticipations of a return of the blessings of peace and repose are alloyed by the sense of heavy and accumulating burdens, which press upon all the departments of industry and threaten to clog the future springs of government—our favored country, happy in a striking contrast, has enjoyed general tranquility, a tranquility the more satisfactory because maintained at the expense of no duty. Faithful to ourselves, we have violated no obligation to others.—Seventh Annual Address to Congress. Fitzpatrick 34:388. (1795.)

EUROPE, Difficulties in.—With respect to the nations of Europe, their situation appears so awful that nothing short of Omnipotence can predict the issue, although every humane mind must feel for the miseries they endure. Our course is plain; they who run may read it. [Europe's] is so bewildered and dark, so entangled and embarrassed, and so obviously under the influence of intrigue that one would suppose if anything could open the eyes of our misled citizens, the deplorable situation of those people could not fail to accomplish it.—To the Secretary of the Treasury. Fitzpatrick 35:457. (1797.)

EUROPE. See also FOREIGN RELATIONS; FRANCE; GREAT BRITAIN; NEUTRALITY; SPAIN.

EXAMPLE, The Power of.—Example, whether it be good or bad, has a powerful influence, and the higher in rank the officer is who sets it, the more striking it is.—To Lord Stirling. Fitzpatrick 18:72. (1780.)

EXCUSES, Avoid Making.—It is better to offer no excuse than a bad one if at any time you should happen to fall into error.—To Harriett Washington. Fitzpatrick 31:408. (1791.)

EXECUTIVE BRANCH, Accountability of Officers in.—In a government as free as ours, where the people are at liberty and will express their sentiments, oftentimes imprudently and for want of information sometimes unjustly, allowances must be made for occasional effervescences; but . . . the executive branch of this government never has [suffered], nor will suffer, while I preside, any improper conduct of its officers to escape with impunity, or will give its sanctions to any disorderly proceedings of its citizens.—To Gouverneur Morris. Fitzpatrick 34:402. (1795.)

EXECUTIVE BRANCH. See also PRESIDENT; PUBLIC OFFICIALS.

EXPERIENCE, Learning from.—We ought not to look back unless it is to derive useful lessons from past errors, and for the purpose of profiting by dear-bought experience. To inveigh against things that are past and irremedial is unpleasing; but to steer clear of the shelves and rocks we have struck upon is the part of wisdom, equally incumbent on political as other men.—To John Armstrong. Fitzpatrick 21:378. (1781.)

EXPERIENCE, Personal, the Only Effective Teacher.—Unfortunately, the nature of man is such that the experience of others is not attended to as it ought to be; we must *feel ourselves* before we can think or perceive the danger which threatens.—To John Marshall. Fitzpatrick 36:93. (1797.)

F

FACTIONS, Subversive to Free Government.—All obstructions to the execution of the laws, all combinations and associations, under whatever plausible character, with the real design to control, counteract, or awe the regular deliberation and action of the constituted authorities, are destructive of this fundamental principle and of fatal tendency. They serve to organize faction, to give it an artificial and extraordinary force, to put in the place of the delegated will of the nation the will of a party, often a small but artful and enterprising minority of the community; and, according to the alternate triumphs of different parties, to make the public administration the mirror of the ill-concerted and incongruous projects of faction, rather than the organ of consistent and wholesome plans digested by common councils and modified by mutual interests. However combinations or associations of the above description may now and then answer popular ends, they are likely, in the course of time and things, to become potent engines by which cunning, ambitious, and unprincipled men will be enabled to subvert the power of the people, and to usurp for themselves the reins of government, destroying afterwards the very engines which have lifted them to unjust dominion.—Farewell Address. Fitzpatrick 35:224. (1796.)

This spirit [of party], unfortunately, is inseparable from our nature, having its root in the strongest passions of the human mind. It exists under different shapes in all governments, more or less stifled, controlled, or repressed; but in those of the popular form it is seen in its greatest rankness and is truly their worst enemy. The alternate domination of one faction over another, sharpened by the spirit of revenge natural to party dissension, which in different ages and countries has perpetrated the most horrid enormities, is itself a frightful despotism. But this leads at length to a more formal and permanent despotism. The disorders and miseries which result gradually incline the minds of men to seek security and repose in the absolute power of an individual; and sooner or later the chief of some prevailing faction, more able or more fortunate than his competitors, turns this disposition to the purposes of his own elevation on the ruins of public liberty.... The common and continual mischiefs of the spirit of party are sufficient to make it the interest and duty of a wise people to discourage and restrain it. It serves always to distract the public councils and enfeeble the public administration. It agitates the community with ill-founded jealousies and false alarms, kindles the animosity of one part against another, foments occasionally riot and insurrection. It opens the door to foreign influence and corruption, which find a facilitated access to the government itself through the channels of party passions. Thus the policy and the will of one country are subjected to the policy and will of another.—Farewell Address. Fitzpatrick 35:226. (1796.)

FACTIONS. See also POLITICAL PARTIES.

FARMING, Washington's Desire for an English Overseer.—Our course of husbandry in this country, and more especially in this state [i.e., Virginia], is not only exceedingly unprofitable, but so destructive to our lands that it is my earnest wish to adopt a better; and as I believe no country has carried the improvement of land and the benefits of agriculture to greater perfection than England, I have asked myself frequently of late whether a thoroughbred practical English farmer, from a part of England where husbandry seems to be best understood and is most advantageously practiced, could not be obtained.... When I speak of a knowing farmer, I mean one who understands the best course of crops; how to plow, to sow, to mow, to hedge, to ditch, and above all, Midas-like, one who can convert everything he touches into manure as the first transmutation towards gold.*—To George William Fairfax. Fitzpatrick 28:185. (1785.)

*Washington did eventually hire an English farmer named James Bloxham, who worked at Mount Vernon from 1786 to 1790.—Editor.

FARMING, Washington's Description of Planting Wheat.—Began...to sow the Siberian wheat, which I had obtained from Baltimore by means of Col. Tilghman, at the Ferry Plantation in the ground laid apart there for experiments. This was done upon ground which some time ago had been marked off by furrows 8 feet apart, in which a second furrow had been run to deepen them, 4 furrows were then plowed to these, which made the whole 5 furrow ridges. These being done some time ago and...[having gotten] hard, I therefore, before the seed was sowed, split these ridges again by running twice in the same furrow, after which I harrowed the ridges; and where the ground was lumpy [I ran] my spiked roller with the harrow at the [tail] over it, which I found very efficacious in breaking the clods and pulverizing the earth, and would have done it perfectly if there had not been too much moisture remaining of the late rains. After this harrowing and rolling where necessary, I sowed the wheat with my drill plow on the reduced ridges in rows 8 feet apart. But I should have observed that, after the ridges were split by the furrow in the middle, and before the furrows were closed again by the harrow, I sprinkled a little dung in them. Finding [that] the barrel discharged the wheat too fast... after sowing 9 of the shortest (for we began at the farthest corner of the field) rows, I stopped every other hole in the barrel, and in this manner sowed 5 rows more, and still thinking the seed too liberally bestowed, I stopped 2 and left one hole open, alternately, by which 4 out of 12 holes only discharged seeds; and this, as I had taken the strap of leather off, seemed to give seed enough (though not so regular as were to be wished) to the ground.—Diary entry. Donald Jackson and Dorothy Twohig, eds., *The Diaries of George Washington*, 6 vols. (Charlottesville, Va: University Press of Virginia, 1976–79), 4:307. (1786.)

FARMING, Six-Year Crop Rotation System.—By the usual mode... we have three fields, [namely] one in corn, one in wheat, and one in hay. By my plan these three fields are divided into six. In 1788, for instance, one of them (say No. 1) is planted with corn 8 feet by 2, single stalks, with Irish potatoes or carrots, or partly both, between. That corn planted in this manner will yield as much to the acre as in any other, that the quantity of potatoes will at least quadruple the quantity of corn, and that the potatoes do not exhaust the soil are facts well established in my mind. In April 1789 it is sown with buckwheat for manure, which is

plowed in before harvest when the seed begins to ripen and there is a sufficiency of it to seed the ground a second time. In July it is again plowed, which gives two dressings to the land at the expense of a bushel of buckwheat and the plowing which would otherwise be essential for a summer fallow. In August, after the putrefaction and fermentation [are] over, wheat is sown, and in 1790 harvested. In 1791 the best and earliest kind of Indian peas are sown broadcast, to be mowed when generally ripe. Since the adoption of this course and progress that has been made to carry it into effect, I have had too much cause to be convinced that peas harvested in this manner [are] a considerable exhaustion of the soil; I have some thoughts, therefore, of substituting a medley of peas, buckwheat for seed, turnips, ... etc., in such parts of the field as best suit them; they will be useful and serve as preparatives. In 1792 spring barley or oats, or equal quantities of each, will be sown with red clover, the latter to be fed with light stock the first year after harvest. In 1793 the field remains in clover for hay, or grazing according to circumstances, and in 1794 comes into corn again, and goes on as before.—To John Beale Bordley. Fitzpatrick 30:49. (1788.)

FARMING, Description of a Threshing Machine.—Called in my ride... to see the operation of his [Winlaw's] threshing machine. The effect was, the heads of the wheat being separated from the straw, as much of the first was run through the mill in 15 minutes as made half a bushel of clean wheat—allowing 8 working hours in the 24, this would yield 16 bushels per day. Two boys are sufficient to turn the wheel, feed the mill, and remove the threshed grain after it has passed through it. Two men were unable, by winnowing, to clean the wheat as it passed through the mill, but a common Dutch fan, with the usual attendance, would be more than sufficient to do it. The grain passes through without bruising and is well separated from the chaff. Women, or boys of 12, to 14 years of age, are fully adequate to the management of the mill or threshing machine. Upon the whole, it appears to be an easier, more expeditious, and much cleaner way of getting out grain than by the usual mode of threshing; and vastly to be preferred to treading, which is hurtful to horses, filthy to the wheat, and not more expeditious, considering the numbers that are employed in the process from the time the head is begun to be formed until the grain has passed finally through the fan.—Diary entry. Donald Jackson and Dorothy Twohig, eds., *The Diaries of George Washington,* 6 vols. (Charlottesville, Va.: University Press of Virginia, 1976–79), 6:12. (1790.)

FARMING, American Approach to, Shortsighted.—The aim of the farmers of this country (if they can be called farmers) is not to make the most they can from the land, which is or has been cheap, but the most of the labor, which is dear; the consequence of which has been [that] much ground has been scratched over, and none cultivated or improved as it ought to have been; whereas a farmer in England,

Washington in April–May 1785 (age 53). Portrait by Robert Edge Pine.

where land is dear and labor cheap, finds it his interest to improve and cultivate highly, that he may reap large crops from a small quantity of ground. That the last is the true, and the first an erroneous policy, I will readily grant; but it requires time to conquer bad habits, and hardly anything short of necessity is able to accomplish it. That necessity is approaching by pretty rapid strides.—To Arthur Young. Fitzpatrick 31:440. (1791.)

FARMING, Washington's Love of Order in.—I shall begrudge no reasonable expense that will contribute to the improvement and neatness of my farms, for nothing pleases me better than to see them in good order, and everything trim, handsome, and thriving about them; nor nothing hurts me more than to find them otherwise.— To William Pearce. Fitzpatrick 33:111. (1793.)

FARMING. See also AGRICULTURE; MANUFACTURES; VIRGINIA.

FAULTS, Palliating One's Own, by Attacking Others.—I shall never attempt to palliate my own faults by exposing those of another.—To Joseph Reed. Fitzpatrick 16:151. (1779.)

FEDERAL GOVERNMENT, Need for a Strong.—It is clearly my opinion, unless Congress have powers competent to all *general* purposes, that the distresses we have encountered, the expense we have incurred, and the blood we have spilt in the course of an eight years' war will avail us nothing.—To Alexander Hamilton. Fitzpatrick 26:188. (1783.)

Unless the states will suffer Congress to exercise those prerogatives they are undoubtedly invested with by the Constitution, everything must very rapidly tend to anarchy and confusion.... It is indispensable to the happiness of the individual states that there should be lodged somewhere a supreme power to regulate and govern the general concerns of the confederated republic, without which the Union cannot be of long duration....
There must be a faithful and pointed compliance on the part of every state with the late proposals and demands of Congress, or the most fatal consequences will ensue.... Whatever measures have a tendency to dissolve the Union, or contribute to violate or

lessen the sovereign authority, ought to be considered as hostile to the liberty and independence of America, and the authors of them treated accordingly.... Unless we can be enabled, by the concurrence of the states, to participate in the fruits of the Revolution and enjoy the essential benefits of civil society, under a form of government so free and uncorrupted, so happily guarded against the danger of oppression, as has been devised and adopted by the Articles of Confederation, it will be a subject of regret that so much blood and treasure have been lavished for no purpose, that so many sufferings have been encountered without a compensation, and that so many sacrifices have been made in vain.—Circular to the States. Fitzpatrick 26:488. (1783.)

It now rests with the confederated powers, by the line of conduct they mean to adopt, to make this country great, happy, and respectable, or to sink it into littleness; worse, perhaps into anarchy and confusion; for certain I am that unless adequate powers are given to Congress for the general purposes of the federal Union, ... we shall soon molder into dust and become contemptible in the eyes of Europe, if we are not made the sport of their politics. To suppose that the general concern of this country can be directed by thirteen heads, or one head without competent powers, is a solecism, the bad effects of which every man who has had the practical knowledge to judge from that I have is fully convinced of, though none perhaps has felt them in so forcible and distressing a degree.... [The slow progress and enormous expense of the Revolutionary War have resulted largely] from that want of energy in the federal constitution which I am complaining of, and which I wish to see given to it by a convention of the people.—To the Reverend William Gordon. Fitzpatrick 27:49. (1783.)

The disinclination of the individual states to yield competent powers to Congress for the federal government, their unreasonable jealousy of that body and of one another, and the disposition, which seems to pervade each, of being all-wise and all-powerful within itself, will, if there is not a change in the system, be our downfall as a nation. This is as clear to me as the A, B, C; and I think we have opposed Great Britain, and have arrived at the present state of peace and independence, to very little purpose if we cannot conquer our own prejudices.... For my own part, although I am returned to and am now mingled with the class of private citizens, and like them must suffer all the evils of a tyranny, or of too great an extension of federal powers, I have no fears arising from this source in my mind; but I have many, and powerful ones indeed, which predict the worst consequences from a half-starved, limping government that appears to be always moving upon crutches, and tottering at every step. Men chosen as the delegates in Congress are cannot officially be dangerous. They depend upon the breath, nay, they are so much the creatures of the people, under the present constitution, that they can

have no views (which could possibly be carried into execution) nor any interests distinct from those of their constituents. My political creed, therefore, is to be wise in the choice of delegates, support them like gentlemen while they are our representatives, give them competent powers for all federal purposes, support them in the due exercise thereof, and, lastly, to compel them to close attendance in Congress during their delegation. These things, under the present mode for and termination of elections, aided by annual instead of constant sessions, would, or I am exceedingly mistaken, make us one of the most wealthy, happy, respectable, and powerful nations that ever inhabited the terrestrial globe. Without them, we shall, in my opinion, soon be everything which is the direct reverse of them.—To Governor Benjamin Harrison. Fitzpatrick 27:305. (1784.)

To *me* it is a solecism in politics, indeed it is one of the most extraordinary things in nature, that we should confederate as a nation and yet be afraid to give the rulers of that nation (who are the creatures of our making, appointed for a limited and short duration, and woo are amenable for every action and recallable at any moment, and are subject to all the evils which they may be instrumental in producing) sufficient powers to order and direct the affairs of the same. By such policy as this the wheels of government are clogged, and our brightest prospects, and that high expectation which was entertained of us by the wondering world, are turned into astonishment; and from the high ground on which we stood, we are descending into the vale of confusion and darkness.—To James Warren. Fitzpatrick 28:290. (1785.)

I do not conceive we can exist long as a nation without having lodged somewhere a power which will pervade the whole union in as energetic a manner as the authority of the state governments extends over the several states. —To John Jay. Fitzpatrick 28:502. (1786.)

You talk, my good sir, of employing influence to appease the present tumults in Massachusetts. I know not where that influence is to be found, or, if attainable, that it would be a proper remedy for the disorders. Influence is no government. Let us have one by which our lives, liberties, and properties will be secured, or let us know the worst at once.—To Henry Lee. Fitzpatrick 29:34. (1786.)

Thirteen sovereignties pulling against each other, and all tugging at the federal head, will soon bring ruin on the whole; whereas a liberal and energetic constitution, well guarded and closely watched to prevent encroachments, might restore us to that degree of respectability and consequence to which we had a fair claim and the brightest prospect of attaining. —To James Madison. Fitzpatrick 29:52. (1786.)

It is agreed on all hands that no government can be well administered without powers; yet the instant these are delegated—although those who are entrusted with the administration are no more than the creatures of the people, act as it were but for a day, and

are amenable for every false step they take—they are, from the moment they receive it, set down as tyrants, their natures, they would conceive from this, immediately changed, and that they can have no other disposition but to oppress.... No man is a warmer advocate for proper restraints and wholesome checks in every department of government than I am; but I have never yet been able to discover the propriety of placing it absolutely out of the power of men to render essential services, because a possibility remains of their doing ill.—To Bushrod Washington. Fitzpatrick 29:311. (1787.)

FEDERAL GOVERNMENT, Must Be Stronger Than States.—We are known by no other character among nations than as the United States. Massachusetts or Virginia is no better defined, nor any more thought of by foreign powers, than the county of Worcester in Massachusetts is by Virginia, or Gloucester County in Virginia is by Massachusetts (respectable as they are); and yet these counties with as much propriety might oppose themselves to the laws of the state in which they are, as an individual state can oppose itself to the federal government, by which it is, or ought to be, bound. Each of these counties has, no doubt, its local polity and interests. These should be attended to and brought before their respective legislatures with all the force their importance merits; but when they come in contact with the general interest of the state, when superior considerations preponderate in favor of the whole, their voices should be heard no more. So should it be with individual states when compared to the Union; otherwise I think it may properly be asked, for what purpose do we farcically pretend to be united? Why do Congress spend months together in deliberating upon, debating, and digesting plans which are made as palatable and as wholesome to the constitution of this country as the nature of things will admit of, when some states will pay no attention to them and others regard them but partially, by which means all those evils which proceed from delay are felt by the whole, while the compliant states are not only suffering by these neglects, but in many instances are injured most capitally by their own exertions, which are wasted for want of the united effort. A hundred thousand men, coming one after another, cannot move a ton weight, but the united strength of fifty would transport it with ease. So has it been with [a] great part of the expense which has been incurred [in] this war. In a word, I think the blood and treasure which has been spent in it has been lavished to little purpose unless we can be better cemented, and that is not to be effected while so little attention is paid to the recommendations of the sovereign power.—To the Reverend William Gordon. Fitzpatrick 27:50. (1783.)

Happy indeed would it be if the [Constitutional] Convention shall be able to recommend such a firm and permanent government for this Union that all who live under it may be secure in their lives, liberty, and property; and thrice happy would it be if such a recommendation should obtain. Everybody wishes, everybody expects something from the convention; but what will be the final result of its deliberation, the book of fate must disclose. Persuaded I am, that the primary cause of all our disorders lies in the different state governments and in the tenacity of that power which pervades the whole of their systems. While independent sovereignty is so ardently contended for, while the local views of each state and separate interests by which they are too much governed will not yield to a more enlarged scale of politics, incompatibility in the laws of different states and disrespect to those of the general government must render the situation of this great country weak, inefficient, and disgraceful. It has already done so, almost to the final dissolution of it. Weak at home and disregarded abroad is our present condition, and contemptible enough it is.—To David Stuart. Fitzpatrick 29:238. (1787.)

FEDERAL GOVERNMENT, Should Not Interfere in State Policies.—I am no advocate for [the federal government's] having to do with the particular policy of any state, further than it concerns the Union at large.—To the Reverend William Gordon. Fitzpatrick 27:51. (1783.)

FEDERAL GOVERNMENT, Must Have Power of Coercion.—I confess . . . that my opinion of public virtue is so far changed that I have my doubts whether any system without the means of coercion in the sovereign [i.e., the federal government] will enforce obedience to the ordinances of a general government, without which everything else fails.—To James Madison. Fitzpatrick 29:190. (1787.)

FEDERAL GOVERNMENT, And Happiness of Citizens.—I consider the successful administration of the general government as an object of almost infinite consequence to the present and future happiness of the citizens of the United States.—To Thomas Jefferson. Fitzpatrick 30:510. (1789.)

FEDERAL GOVERNMENT. See also APPOINTMENTS; ARTICLES OF CONFEDERATION; CONGRESS; CONSTITUTION (U.S.); DISTRICT OF COLUMBIA; EXECUTIVE BRANCH; FOREIGN RELATIONS; GOVERNMENT; JUDICIARY; NATIONAL DEBT; PRESIDENT; PUBLIC OFFICIALS; SEPARATION OF POWERS.

FEDERALIST PAPERS, Washington's Response to.—As the perusal of the political papers under the signature of Publius has afforded me great satisfaction, I shall certainly consider them as claiming a most distinguished place in my library.... That work will merit the notice of posterity, because in it are candidly and ably discussed the principles of freedom and the topics of government which will be always interesting to mankind so long as they shall be connected in civil society.—To Alexander Hamilton. Fitzpatrick 30:66. (1788.)

FINANCES, Importance of Public Credit.—An adequate provision for the support of the public credit is a matter of high importance to the national honor and prosperity.—To the House of Representatives. Fitzpatrick

30:494. (1790.)

FINANCES, Policies for National.—As a very important source of strength and security, cherish public credit. One method of preserving it is to use it as sparingly as possible, avoiding occasions of expense by cultivating peace, but remembering also that timely disbursements to prepare for danger frequently prevent much greater disbursements to repel it; avoiding likewise the accumulation of debt, not only by shunning occasions of expense, but by vigorous exertions in time of peace to discharge the debts which unavoidable wars may have occasioned, not ungenerously throwing upon posterity the burden which we ourselves ought to bear. The execution of these maxims belongs to your representatives, but it is necessary that public opinion should cooperate. To facilitate to them the performance of their duty, it is essential that you should practically bear in mind that towards the payment of debts there must be revenue; that to have revenue there must be taxes; that no taxes can be devised which are not more or less inconvenient and unpleasant; that the intrinsic embarrassment inseparable from the selection of the proper objects (which is always a choice of difficulties) ought to be a decisive motive for a candid construction of the conduct of the government in making it, and for a spirit of acquiescence in the measures for obtaining revenue which the public exigencies may at any time dictate.—Farewell Address. Fitzpatrick 35:230. (1796.)

FINANCES. See also BORROWING;

CURRENCY; DEBT; INFLATION; MONEY; NATIONAL DEBT.

FOREIGN RELATIONS, A Guiding Principle in.—It is a maxim founded on the universal experience of mankind that no nation is to be trusted farther than it is bounded by its interests.—To Henry Laurens. Fitzpatrick 13:256. (1778.)

FOREIGN RELATIONS, Subject to Ministerial Caprice.—The change or caprice of a single minister is capable of altering the whole system of Europe. —To the President of Congress. Fitzpatrick 19:407. (1780.)

FOREIGN RELATIONS, A Policy of Neutrality.—I hope the United States of America will be able to keep disengaged from the labyrinth of European politics and wars.... It should be the policy of united America to administer to [other nations'] wants without being engaged in their quarrels. And it is not in the ability of the proudest and most potent people on earth to prevent us from becoming a great, a respectable, and a commercial nation, if we shall continue united and faithful to ourselves.—To Sir Edward Newenham. Fitzpatrick 30:71. (1788.)

I can most religiously aver I have no wish that is incompatible with the dignity, happiness, and true interest of the people of this country. My ardent desire is, and my aim has been (as far as depended upon the executive department), to comply strictly with *all* our engagements, foreign and domestic, but to keep the United States free from *political* connections with *every* other country; to see that they *may be* independent of *all* and under the in-

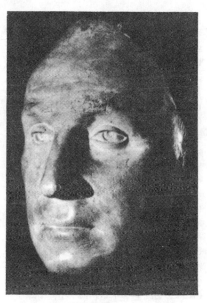

Washington in October 1784 (age 52). Plaster life mask by Jean Antoine Houdon.

fluence of *none*. In a word, I want an *American* character, that the powers of Europe may be convinced we act for *ourselves* and not for *others;* this, in my judgment, is the only way to be respected abroad and happy at home, and not, by becoming the partisans of Great Britain or France, create dissensions, disturb the public tranquility, and destroy, perhaps forever, the cement which binds the Union.—To Patrick Henry. Fitzpatrick 34:335. (1795.)

My policy has been and will continue to be, while I have the honor to remain in the administration of the government, to be upon friendly terms with, but independent of, all the nations of the earth. To share in the broils of none. To fulfill our own engagements. To supply the wants and be carriers for them all, being thoroughly convinced that it is our policy and interest to do so.—To Gouverneur Morris. Fitzpatrick 34:401. (1795.)

I have always given it as my decided opinion that no nation had a right to intermeddle in the internal concerns of another; that everyone had a right to form and adopt whatever government they like best to live under themselves; and that if this country could, consistently with its engagements, maintain a strict neutrality and thereby preserve peace, it was bound to do so by motives of policy, interest, and every other consideration that ought to actuate a people situated and circumstanced as we are, already deeply in debt, and in a convalescent state from the struggle we have been engaged in ourselves.—To James Monroe. Fitzpatrick 35:189. (1796.)

Our detached and distant situation invites and enables us to pursue a different course. If we remain one people, under an efficient government, the period is not far off when we may defy material injury from external annoyance; when we may take such an attitude as will cause the neutrality we may at any time resolve upon to be scrupulously respected; when belligerent nations, under the impossibility of making acquisitions upon us, will not lightly hazard the giving us provocation; when we may choose peace or war, as our interest guided by our justice shall counsel. Why forgo the

advantages of so peculiar a situation? Why quit our own to stand upon foreign ground? Why, by interweaving our destiny with that of any part of Europe, entangle our peace and prosperity in the toils of European ambition, rivalship, interest, humor, or caprice?—Farewell Address. Fitzpatrick 35:234. (1796.)

FOREIGN RELATIONS, Washington's Policy in.—My policy in our foreign transactions has been to cultivate peace with all the world; to observe treaties with pure and absolute faith; to check every deviation from the line of impartiality; to explain what may have been misapprehended, and correct what may have been injurious to any nation; and having thus acquired the right, to lose no time in acquiring the ability to insist upon justice being done to ourselves.—To the House of Representatives. Fitzpatrick 34:37. (1794.)

FOREIGN RELATIONS, And Need for Secrecy in Negotiations.—The nature of foreign negotiations requires caution, and their success must often depend on secrecy; and even when brought to a conclusion, a full disclosure of all the measures, demands, or eventual concessions which have been proposed or contemplated should be extremely impolitic, for this might have a pernicious influence on future negotiations or produce immediate inconveniences, perhaps danger or mischief, in relation to other powers.—To the House of Representatives. Fitzpatrick 35:2. (1796.)

FOREIGN RELATIONS, America

Must Maintain Independence.—We are an independent nation, and act for ourselves. Having fulfilled and being willing to fulfill (as far as we are able) our engagements with other nations, and having decided on and strictly observed a neutral conduct towards... belligerent powers, from an unwillingness to involve ourselves in war, we will not be dictated to by the politics of any nation under heaven, farther than treaties require of us.—To Alexander Hamilton. Fitzpatrick 35:40. (1796.)

FOREIGN RELATIONS, Do Not Permanently Favor One Nation over Another.—Observe good faith and justice towards all nations.... In the execution of such a plan nothing is more essential than that permanent, inveterate antipathies against particular nations and passionate attachments for others should be excluded; and that, in place of them, just and amicable feelings towards all should be cultivated. The nation which indulges towards another an habitual hatred, or an habitual fondness, is in some degree a slave. It is a slave to its animosity or to its affection, either of which is sufficient to lead it astray from its duty and its interest.—Farewell Address. Fitzpatrick 35:231. (1796.)

FOREIGN RELATIONS, And Foreign Influence.—Against the insidious wiles of foreign influence (I conjure you to believe me, fellow citizens), the jealousy of a free people ought to be *constantly* awake, since history and experience prove that foreign influence is one of the most baneful foes of republican government. But that jealousy to be useful must be impartial,

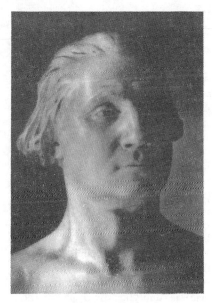

Washington in October 1784 (age 52). Bust by Jean Antoine Houdon.

else it becomes the instrument of the very influence to be avoided, instead of a defense against it.—Farewell Address. Fitzpatrick 35:233. (1796.)

FOREIGN RELATIONS, Avoid Entangling Alliances.—The great rule of conduct for us in regard to foreign nations is in extending our commercial relations to have with them as little *political* connection as possible. So far as we have already formed engagements, let them be fulfilled with perfect good faith. Here let us stop.—Farewell Address. Fitzpatrick 35:233. (1796.)

It is our true policy to steer clear of permanent alliances with any portion of the foreign world. So far, I mean, as we are now at liberty to do it, for let me not be understood as capable of patronizing infidelity to existing engagements (I hold the maxim no less applicable to public than to private affairs that honesty is always the best policy). I repeat it, therefore: let those engagements be observed in their genuine sense. But, in my opinion, it is unnecessary and would be unwise to extend them. Taking care always to keep ourselves, by suitable establishments, on a respectably defensive posture, we may safely trust to temporary alliances for extraordinary emergencies.—Farewell Address. Fitzpatrick 35:234. (1796.)

No policy, in my opinion, can be more clearly demonstrated than that we should do justice to *all* but have no political connections with *any* of the European powers, beyond those which result from and serve to regulate our commerce with them.—To William Heath. Fitzpatrick 35:449. (1797.)

FOREIGN RELATIONS, And European Affairs—Europe has a set of primary interests which to us have none, or a very remote relation. Hence she must be engaged in frequent controversies, the causes of which are essentially foreign to our concerns. Hence therefore it must be unwise in us to implicate ourselves, by artificial ties, in the ordinary vicissitudes of her politics, or the ordinary combinations and collisions of her friendships or enmities.—Farewell Address. Fitzpatrick 35:234. (1796.)

FOREIGN RELATIONS, And "Disinterested" Nations.—Our own experience (if it has not already had this effect) will soon convince us that *disinterested* favors or friendship from any nation whatever is too novel to be calculated on; and there will always be found a wide difference between the words and actions of them.—To William Heath. Fitzpatrick 35:449. (1797.)

FOREIGN RELATIONS. See also CANADA; EUROPE; FRANCE; GREAT BRITAIN; INDIANS; JAY TREATY; NEUTRALITY; PEACE; TREATIES; WAR.

FOREIGN TRADE, A Mixed Blessing.—It has long been a speculative question among philosophers and wise men, whether foreign commerce is of real advantage to any country; that is, whether the luxury, effeminacy, and corruptions which are introduced along with it are counterbalanced by the convenience and wealth which it brings.—To James Warren. Fitzpatrick 28:290. (1785.)

FOREIGN TRADE, A Prophecy.—However unimportant America may be considered at present, and however Britain may affect to despise her trade, there will assuredly come a day when this country will have some weight in the scale of empires.—To the Marquis de Lafayette. Fitzpatrick 28:520. (1786.)

FOREIGN TRADE, Increase of.—The maritime genius of this country is now steering our vessels in every ocean: to the East Indies, the northwest coasts of America, and the extremities of the globe.—To the Comte de Moustier. Fitzpatrick 30:46. (1788.)

FOREIGN TRADE, American Policy in.—Harmony |and| liberal intercourse with all nations are recommended by policy, humanity, and interest. But even our commercial policy should hold an equal and impartial hand, neither seeking nor granting exclusive favors or preferences; consulting the natural course of things; diffusing and diversifying by gentle means the stream of commerce, but forcing nothing; establishing with powers so disposed, in order to give trade a stable course, to define the rights of our merchants, and to enable the government to support them, conventional rules of intercourse, the best that present circumstances and mutual opinion will permit, but temporary and liable to be from time to time abandoned or varied, as experience and circumstances shall dictate; constantly keeping in view that it is folly in one nation to look for disinterested favors from another; that it must pay with a portion of its independence for whatever it may accept under that character; that, by such acceptance, it may place itself in the condition of having given equivalents for nominal favors and yet of being reproached with ingratitude for not giving more. There can be no greater error than to expect or calculate upon real favors from nation to nation. It is an illusion which experience must cure, which a just pride ought to discard.—Farewell Address. Fitzpatrick 35:235. (1796.)

FOREIGN TRADE. See also COMMERCE; NAVY.

FRANCE, Advantages of an American Alliance with.—An immediate declaration of war against Great Britain [by France], in all probability, could not fail to extricate us from our difficulties, and to cement the bond of friendship so firmly between France and America as to produce the most permanent advantage to both. Certainly nothing can be more the true interest of France than to have a weight of such magnitude as America taken out of the scale of British power and opulence and thrown into her own.—To the Chevalier d'Anmours. Fitzpatrick 8:266. (1777.)

FRANCE, America's Responsibility Under Its Alliance with.—I very much fear that we, taking it for granted that we have nothing more to do because France has acknowledged our independence and formed an alliance with us, shall relapse into a state of supineness and perfect security.—To Alexander McDougall. Fitzpatrick 11:352. (1778.)

The court of France has made a glorious effort for our deliverance, and if we disappoint its intentions by our supineness we must become contemptible in the eyes of all mankind; nor can we after that venture to confide that our allies will persist in an attempt to establish what it will appear we want inclination or ability to assist them in.—To Joseph Reed. Fitzpatrick 18:435. (1780.)

FRANCE, Washington's Feelings Toward.—[France is] a country to which I shall ever feel a warm affection.—To the Marquis de Lafayette. Fitzpatrick 26:299. (1783.)

FRANCE, Pending Revolution in.—I like not much the situation of affairs in France. The bold demands of the parliaments and the decisive tone of the

king show that but little more irritation would be necessary to blow up the
spark of discontent into a flame that
might not easily be quenched. If I were
to advise, I should say that great moderation should be used on both sides.
Let it not, my dear Marquis, be considered as a derogation from the good
opinion that I entertain of your prudence when I caution you, as an individual desirous of signalizing yourself in the cause of your country and
freedom, against running into extremes and prejudicing your cause.
The king, though I think from everything I have been able to learn [that he]
is really a good-hearted though a
warm-spirited man, if thwarted in-
judiciously in the execution of prerogatives that belonged to the crown
and in plans which he conceives calculated to promote the national good,
may disclose qualities he has been little
thought to possess. On the other
hand, such a spirit seems to be awakened in the kingdom as, if managed
with extreme prudence, may produce
a gradual and tacit revolution much in
favor of the subjects, by abolishing
lettres de cachet and defining more accurately the powers of government. It is
a wonder to me there should be found
a single monarch who does not realize
that his own glory and felicity must
depend on the prosperity and happiness of his people. How easy is it for a
sovereign to do that which shall not
only immortalize his name, but attract
the blessings of millions.—To the
Marquis de Lafayette. Fitzpatrick
29:524. (1788.)

FRANCE, Tribute to Her Armies.—

To call your nation brave were to pronounce but common praise. Wonderful people! Ages to come will read with
astonishment the history of your brilliant exploits!—Reply to the French
minister. Fitzpatrick 34:413. (1796.)

**FRANCE, Tactics for Threatened War
with.**—It was not difficult for me to
perceive that if we entered into a serious contest with France, . . . the character of the war would differ materially from the last we were engaged in. In
the latter, time, caution, and worrying
the enemy until we could be better
provided with arms and other means,
and had better disciplined troops to
carry it on, was the plan for us. But if
we should be engaged with the
former, they ought to be attacked at
every step, and, if possible, not suffered to make an establishment in the
country.—To the President of the
United States. Fitzpatrick 36:457.
(1798.)

FRANCE. See also EUROPE;
FOREIGN RELATIONS; FRENCH
REVOLUTION; INDIANS; JAY
TREATY; LAFAYETTE (Marquis de);
REVOLUTIONARY WAR.

**FRANKLIN (Benjamin), Washing-
ton's Last Letter to.**—Would to God,
my dear sir, that I could congratulate
you upon the removal of that excruciating pain under which you labor!
and that your existence might close
with as much ease to yourself as its
continuance has been beneficial to our
country and useful to mankind! Or, if
the united wishes of a free people,
joined with the earnest prayers of
every friend to science and humanity,
could relieve the body from pains or in-

firmities, you could claim an exemption on this score. But this cannot be, and you have within yourself the only resource to which we can confidently apply for relief: *a philosophic mind.*

If to be venerated for benevolence, if to be admired for talents, if to be esteemed for patriotism, if to be beloved for philanthropy can gratify the the human mind, you must have the pleasing consolation to know that you have not lived in vain; and I flatter myself that it will not be ranked among the least grateful occurrences of your life to be assured that so long as I retain my memory, you will be thought on with respect, veneration, and affection by your sincere friend.—Fitzpatrick 30:409. (1789.)

FREEDOM, Based on Equal Representation.—I always believed that an unequivocally free and equal representation of the people in the legislature, together with an efficient and responsible executive, were the great pillars on which the preservation of American freedom must depend.—To Mrs. Catharine Macaulay Graham. Fitzpatrick 30:496. (1790.)

FREEDOM, Washington's Love of.—Born, sir, in a land of liberty, having early learned its value, having engaged in a perilous conflict to defend it, having, in a word, devoted the best years of my life to secure its permanent establishment in my own country, my anxious recollections, my sympathetic feelings, and my best wishes are irresistibly excited whensoever, in any country, I see an oppressed nation unfurl the banners of freedom.—To the French minister. Fitzpatrick 34:413.

(1796.)

FREEDOM. See also INDEPENDENCE; LIBERTY; PEACE; RELIGIOUS FREEDOM; SELF-GOVERNMENT.

FRENCH AND INDIAN WAR. See INDIANS.

FRENCH REVOLUTION, Washington's Hopes for.—The revolution which has taken place with you is of such magnitude and of so momentous a nature that we hardly yet dare to form a conjecture about it. We however trust, and fervently pray, that its consequences may prove happy to a nation in whose fate we have so much cause to be interested, and that its influence may be felt with pleasure by future generations.—To the Marquis de Lafayette. Fitzpatrick 30:448. (1789.)

FRENCH REVOLUTION, Washington's Apprehension Concerning.—My greatest fear has been that the nation [i.e., France] would not be sufficiently cool and moderate in making arrangements for the security of that liberty of which it seems to be fully possessed.—To Mrs. Catharine Macaulay Graham. Fitzpatrick 30:498. (1790.)

FRENCH REVOLUTION, And French Patriots' Zeal for Liberty.—The little anecdote which you recall to mind, my dear count, of your countrymen at Rhode Island who burnt their mouths with the hot soup, while mine waited leisurely for it to cool, perhaps, when politically applied in the manner you have done, has not less truth than pleasantry in its resemblance of national characters. But if there shall

Washington in July 1787 (age 55). Portrait by Charles Willson Peale. Washington sat for this portrait while he was attending the Constitutional Convention in Philadelphia.

be no worse consequence resulting from too great eagerness in swallowing something so delightful as liberty than that of suffering a momentary pain or making a ridiculous figure with a scalded mouth, upon the whole it may be said you Frenchmen have come off well, considering how immoderately you thirsted for the cup of liberty. And no wonder, as you drank it to the bottom, that some licentiousness should have been mingled with the dregs.—To the Comte de Rochambeau. Fitzpatrick 31:82. (1790.)

FRENCH REVOLUTION. See also FRANCE.

FRIENDS, Advice on Choosing.— The company in which you will im-

prove most will be least expensive to you.... It is easy to make acquaintances, but very difficult to shake them off, however irksome and unprofitable they are found after we have once committed ourselves to them.... Be courteous to all, but intimate with few, and let those few be well tried before you give them your confidence; true friendship is a plant of slow growth, and must undergo and withstand the shocks of adversity before it is entitled to the appellation.—To Bushrod Washington. Fitzpatrick 26:39. (1783.)

When you have leisure to go into company, ... it should always be of the best kind that the place you are in will afford; by this means you will be constantly improving your manners and cultivating your mind, ... and good company will always be found much less expensive than bad.—To George Steptoe Washington. Fitzpatrick 30:246. (1789.)

FRIENDS, Correspondence with.—It is not the letters from my friends which give me trouble, or add aught to my perplexity.... To correspond with those I love is among my highest gratifications.—To Henry Knox. Fitzpatrick 28:23. (1785.)

FRIENDSHIP, Honesty in.—The arts of dissimulation ... I despise, and my feelings will not permit me to make professions of friendship to the man I deem my enemy, and whose system of conduct forbids it.—To the President of Congress. Fitzpatrick 10:249. (1778.)

FRIENDSHIP, Not Impaired by Political Differences.—The friendship I ever professed and felt for you met with no diminution from the difference in our political sentiments. I know the rectitude of my own intentions and, believing in the sincerity of yours, lamented, though I did not condemn, your renunciation of the creed I had adopted. Nor do I think any person or power ought to do it, while your conduct is not opposed to the general interest of the people and the measures they are pursuing; the latter, that is our actions, depending upon ourselves, may be controlled, while the powers of thinking, originating in higher causes, cannot always be molded to our wishes.—To Bryan Fairfax. Fitzpatrick 11:2. (1778.)

FRIENDSHIP, To Be Measured by Actions, Not Words.—A slender acquaintance with the world must convince every man that actions, not words, are the true criterion of the attachment of his friends, and that the most liberal professions of goodwill are very far from being the surest marks of it. I should be happy that my own experience had afforded fewer examples of the little dependence to be placed on them.—To John Sullivan. Fitzpatrick 17:266. (1779.)

FRIENDSHIP, Perpetuating.—It is my wish [that] the mutual friendship and esteem which have been planted and fostered in the tumult of public life may not wither and die in the serenity of retirement.... We should rather amuse our evening hours of life in cultivating the tender plants, and bringing them to perfection, before they are transplanted to a happier clime.—To Jonathan Trumbull. Fitzpatrick 27:294. (1784.)

FURLOUGHS, Requests for.—The General hears with astonishment the very frequent applications that are made to him, as well by officers as soldiers, for furloughs. Brave men who are engaged in the noble cause of liberty should never think of removing from their camp while the enemy is in sight, and anxious to take every advantage any indiscretion on our side may give them. The General doubts not but the commanding officers of corps will anticipate his wishes, and discourage those under them [from] disgracefully desiring to go home until the campaign is ended.—General Orders. Fitzpatrick 3:346. (1775.)

G

GAMBLING, Ruinous Effects of.—Avoid gaming. This is a vice which is productive of every possible evil, equally injurious to the morals and health of its votaries. It is the child of avarice, the brother of inequity, and [the] father of mischief. It has been the ruin of many worthy families, the loss of many a man's honor, and the cause of suicide. To all those who enter the list, it is equally fascinating; the successful gamester pushes his good fortune till it is overtaken by a reverse; the losing gamester, in hopes of retrieving past misfortunes, goes on from bad to worse, till, grown desperate, he pushes at everything, and loses his all.... Few gain by this abominable practice (the profit, if any, being diffused), while thousands are injured. —To Bushrod Washington. Fitzpatrick 26:40. (1783.)

GAMES OF CHANCE, Forbidden in the Army.—All officers, non-commissioned officers, and soldiers are positively forbidden playing at cards and other games of chance. At this time of public distress, men may find enough to do in the service of their God and their country without abandoning themselves to vice and immorality.—General Orders. Fitzpatrick 4:347. (1776.)

GERMANS, Washington's Assessment of.—They are known to be a steady, laborious people.—To commissioners of the federal district. Fitzpatrick 32:271. (1792.)

GERMANS. See also HESSIANS.

GOD, Washington's Life Preserved by.—By the miraculous care of Providence, that protected me beyond all human expectation, I had four bullets through my coat and two horses shot under me, and yet escaped unhurt.—To John Augustine Washington. Fitzpatrick 1:152. (1755.)

GOD, Washington's Gratitude to.—The General hopes such frequent favors from Divine Providence will animate every American to continue to exert his utmost in the defense of the liberties of his country, as it would now be basest ingratitude to the Almighty, and to their country, to show ... the least backwardness in the public cause.—General Orders. Fitzpatrick 4:119. (1775.)

Providence has a ... claim to my humble and grateful thanks for its protection and direction of me through the many difficult and intricate scenes which this contest has produced, and for the constant interposition in our behalf when the clouds were heaviest and seemed ready to burst upon us.—To Landon Carter. Fitzpatrick 11:492. (1778).

I am ... grateful to that Providence which has directed my steps, and shielded me through the various changes and chances through which I have passed, from my youth to the present moment.—To the Reverend William Gordon. Fitzpatrick 36:49. (1797.)

GOD, Faith in, Must Be Combined with Personal Effort.—To trust altogether in the justice of our cause, without our own utmost exertions, would be tempting Providence.—To Jonathan Trumbull. Fitzpatrick 5:390. (1776.)

The honor and safety of our bleeding country, and every other motive that can influence the brave and heroic patriot, call loudly upon us to acquit ourselves with spirit. In short, we must now determine to be enslaved or free. If we make freedom our choice, we must obtain it by the blessings of Heaven on our united and vigorous efforts.—To the officers and soldiers of the Pennsylvania Associators. Fitzpatrick 5:398. (1776.)

I trust in that Providence which has saved us in six troubles, yea, in seven, to rescue us again from any imminent, though unseen, dangers. Nothing, however, on our part ought to be left undone.—To Benjamin Lincoln. Fitzpatrick 30:63. (1788.)

GOD, Washington's Trust in.—Liberty, honor, and safety are all at stake, and I trust Providence will smile upon our efforts and establish us once more the inhabitants of a free and happy country.—To the officers and soldiers of the Pennsylvania Associators. Fitzpatrick 5:398. (1776.)

No man has a more perfect reliance on the all-wise and powerful dispensations of the Supreme Being than I have, nor thinks His aid more necessary.—To the Reverend William Gordon. Fitzpatrick 37:526. (1776.)

A superintending Providence is ordering everything for the best, and ... in due time all will end well.—To Landon Carter. Fitzpatrick 9:454. (1777.)

Providence has heretofore taken us up when all other means and hope seemed to be departing from us; in this I will confide.—To Benjamin Harrison. Fitzpatrick 13:468. (1778.)

Our affairs are brought to an awful crisis, that the hand of Providence, I trust, may be more conspicuous in our deliverance. The many remarkable interpositions of the divine government in the hours of our deepest distress and darkness have been too luminous to suffer me to doubt the happy issue of the present contest.—To John Armstrong. Fitzpatrick 21:378. (1781.)

As the All-wise Disposer of events has hitherto watched over my steps, I trust that in the important one I may soon be called upon to take [i.e., commencing a second term as President], he will mark the course so plainly as that I cannot mistake the way.—To the Attorney General. Fitzpatrick 32:136. (1792.)

Satisfied, therefore, that you have sincerely wished and endeavored to avert war and exhausted to the last drop the cup of reconciliation, we can with pure hearts appeal to Heaven for the justice of our cause, and may confidently trust the final result to that kind Providence who has heretofore, and so often, signally favored the people of these United States.—To the President of the United States. Fitzpatrick 36:328. (1798.)

GOD, His Will and Purposes.—The determinations of Providence are always wise, often inscrutable, and, though its decrees appear to bear hard upon us at times, [are] nevertheless meant for gracious purposes.—To Bryan Fairfax. Fitzpatrick 11:3. (1778.)

A wise Providence ... no doubt directs [events] for the best of purposes, and to bring round the greatest degree of happiness to the greatest number of his people.—To Governor Jonathan Trumbull. Fitzpatrick 12:406. (1778.)

GOD, Dependence on.—It will ever be the first wish of my heart to aid your pious endeavors to inculcate a due sense of the dependence we ought to place in that all-wise and powerful Being on whom alone our success depends.—To the Reverend Israel Evans. Fitzpatrick 11:78. (1778.)

We have ... abundant reason to thank Providence for its many favorable interpositions in our behalf. It has at times been my only dependence, for all other resources seemed to have failed us.—To the Reverend William Gordon. Fitzpatrick 21:332. (1781.)

I know the delicate nature of the duties incident to the part which I am called to perform; and I feel my incompetence, without the singular assistance of Providence, to discharge them in a satisfactory manner.—To the citizens of Baltimore. Fitzpatrick 30:288. (1789.)

GOD, Intervention of, in Establishing America.—It having pleased the Almighty Ruler of the Universe propitiously to defend the cause of the united American states, and finally, by raising us up a powerful friend among the princes of the earth [i.e., France], to establish our liberty and independence [upon] lasting foundations, it becomes us to set apart a day for gratefully acknowledging the divine goodness and celebrating the important event which we owe to his benign interposition.—General Orders. Fitzpatrick 11:354. (1778.)

It is not a little pleasing, nor less wonderful, to contemplate that after two years' maneuvering and undergoing the strangest vicissitudes that perhaps ever attended any one contest since the creation, both armies are brought back to the very point they set out from, and that that which was the offending party in the beginning is now reduced to the use of the spade and pick-axe for defense. The hand of Providence has been so conspicuous in all this that he must be worse than an infidel that lacks faith, and more than wicked that has not gratitude enough to acknowledge his obligations.—To Thomas Nelson. Fitzpatrick 12:343. (1778.)

We may, with a kind of grateful and pious exultation, trace the finger of Providence through those dark and mysterious events which first induced the states to appoint a general convention and then led them one after another (by such steps as were best calculated to effect the object) into an adoption of the system recommended by that general convention, thereby, in all human probability, laying a lasting foundation for tranquility and happiness, when we had but too much reason to fear that confusion and misery were coming rapidly upon us. That the same good Providence may still continue to protect us and prevent us from dashing the cup of national felicity just as it has been lifted to our lips is [my] earnest prayer.—To Jonathan Trumbull. Fitzpatrick 30:22. (1788.)

When I contemplate the interposition of Providence, as it was manifested in guiding us through the revolution, in preparing us for the reception of a general government, and in conciliating the good will of the people of America towards one another after its adoption, I feel myself...almost overwhelmed with a sense of the divine munificence.—To the mayor, recorder, aldermen, and common council of Philadelphia. Sparks 12:145. (1789.)

No people can be bound to acknowledge and adore the invisible hand, which conducts the affairs of men, more than the people of the United States. Every step by which they have advanced to the character of an independent nation seems to have been distinguished by some token of providential agency.—First Inaugural Address. Fitzpatrick 30:292. (1789.)

Washington in 1788 (age 56). Miniature portrait by James Peale.

The success which has hitherto attended our united efforts we owe to the gracious interposition of Heaven, and to that interposition let us gratefully ascribe the praise of victory and the blessings of peace.—To the Executive of New Hampshire. Fitzpatrick 30:453. (1789.)

I am sure there never was a people who had more reason to acknowledge a divine interposition in their affairs than those of the United States; and I should be pained to believe that they have forgotten that agency which was so often manifested during our revolution, or that they failed to consider the omnipotence of that God who is alone able to protect them.—To John Arm-

strong. Fitzpatrick 32:2. (1792.)

Without the beneficent interposition of the Supreme Ruler of the universe, we could not have reached the distinguished situation which we have attained with such unprecedented rapidity. To him, therefore, should we bow with gratitude and reverence, and endeavor to merit a continuance of his special favors.—To the General Assembly of Rhode Island. Fitzpatrick 35:431. (1797.)

GOD, Acts of, Washington's Attitude Toward.—I look upon every dispensation of Providence as designed to answer some valuable purpose, and I hope I shall always possess a sufficient degree of fortitude to bear without murmuring any stroke which may happen either to my person or [my] estate from that quarter.—To Lund Washington. Fitzpatrick 15:180. (1779.)

At disappointments and losses which are the effects of Providential acts I never repine, because I am sure the divine disposer of events knows better than we do what is best for us, or what we deserve.—To William Pearce. Fitzpatrick 33:375. (1794.)

GOD, Washington's Pleas to, for America.—I consider it an indispensable duty to close this last solemn act of my official life by commending the interests of our dearest country to the protection of Almighty God, and those who have the superintendence of them to his holy keeping.—Address to Congress on resigning his commission. Fitzpatrick 27:285. (1783.)

I earnestly pray that the Omnipotent Being who has not deserted the cause of America in the hour of its extremest hazard will never yield so fair a heritage of freedom a prey to anarchy or despotism.—To the Secretary of War. Fitzpatrick 30:30. (1788.)

It would be peculiarly improper to omit in this first official act my fervent supplications to that Almighty Being who rules over the universe, who presides in the councils of nations, and whose providential aids can supply every human defect, that his benediction may consecrate to the liberties and happiness of the people of the United States a government instituted by themselves for these essential purposes, and may enable every instrument employed in its administration to execute with success the functions allotted to his charge.—First Inaugural Address. Fitzpatrick 30:292. (1789.)

Having thus imparted to you my sentiments, as they have been awakened by the occasion which brings us together, I shall take my present leave; but not without resorting once more to the benign parent of the human race, in humble supplication that, since he has been pleased to favor the American people with opportunities for deliberating in perfect tranquility, and dispositions for deciding with unparalleled unanimity on a form of government for the security of their union and the advancement of their happiness, so his divine blessing may be equally *conspicuous* in the enlarged views, the temperate consultations, and the wise measures on which the success of this government must depend.—First Inaugural Address. Fitzpatrick 30:296. (1789.)

We may ... unite in most humbly offering our prayers and supplications to the great Lord and Ruler of Nations and beseech him to pardon our national and other transgressions; to enable us all, whether in public or private stations, to perform our several and relative duties properly and punctually; to render our national government a blessing to all the people by constantly being a government of wise, just, and constitutional laws, discreetly and faithfully executed and obeyed; to protect and guide all sovereigns and nations (especially such as have shown kindness unto us) and to bless them with good government, peace, and concord; to promote the knowledge and practice of true religion and virtue and the increase of science among them and us; and generally to grant unto all mankind such a degree of temporal prosperity as he alone knows to be best.—Thanksgiving Proclamation. Fitzpatrick 30:428. (1789.)

Let us unite ... in imploring the Supreme Ruler of nations to spread his holy protection over these United States, to turn the machinations of the wicked to the confirming of our Constitution, to enable us at all times to root out internal sedition and put invasion to flight, to perpetuate to our country that prosperity which his goodness has already conferred, and to verify the anticipation of this government being a safeguard to human rights.—To the Senate and the House of Representatives. Fitzpatrick 34:37. (1794.)

The situation in which I now stand,

for the last time, in the midst of the representatives of the people of the United States, naturally recalls the period when the administration of the present form of government commenced; and I cannot omit the occasion to congratulate you and my country on the success of the experiment, nor to repeat my fervent supplications to the Supreme Ruler of the Universe and Sovereign Arbiter of Nations that his Providential care may still be extended to the United States, that the virtue and happiness of the people may be preserved, and that the government which they have instituted for the protection of their liberties may be perpetual.—To the Senate and the House of Representatives. Fitzpatrick 35:319. (1796).

GOD, National Righteousness Required for Blessings of.—There is no truth more thoroughly established than that there exists... an indissoluble union between virtue and happiness.... The propitious smiles of Heaven can never be expected on a nation that disregards the eternal rules of order and right which Heaven itself has ordained.—First Inaugural Address. Fitzpatrick 30:294. (1789.)

GOD, All Nations Should Pay Homage to.—It is the duty of all nations to acknowledge the providence of Almighty God, to obey his will, to be grateful for his benefits, and humbly to implore his protection and favor.— Thanksgiving Proclamation. Fitzpatrick 30:427. (1789.)

GOD, The Author of All Good.— That great and glorious Being ... is the beneficent Author of all the good that

was, that is, or that will be.—Thanksgiving Proclamation. Fitzpatrick 30:427. (1789.)

GOD, Washington Ascribes His Success to.—If such talents as I possess have been called into action by great events, and those events have terminated happily for our country, the glory should be ascribed to the manifest interposition of an overruling Providence.—To the synod of the Reformed Dutch Church in North America. Sparks 12:167. (1789.)

I was but the humble agent of favoring Heaven, whose benign interference was so often manifested in our behalf, and to whom the praise of victory alone is due.—To the legislature of the state of Connecticut. Sparks 12:169. (1789.)

To the great Ruler of events, not to any exertions of mine, is to be ascribed the favorable termination of our late contest for liberty. I never considered the fortunate issue of any measure in any other light than as the ordering of a kind Providence.—To Jonathan Williams. Fitzpatrick 34:130. (1795.)

GOD, Submission to.—The will of Heaven is not to be controverted or scrutinized by the children of this world. It therefore becomes the creatures of it to submit with patience and resignation to the will of the Creator, whether it be to prolong or to shorten the number of our days, to bless them with health or afflict them with pain.—To George Augustine Washington. Fitzpatrick 32:315. (1793.)

I thank you for your kind condolence on the death of my nephew. It is a loss I sincerely regret, but as it is the will of Heaven, whose decrees are always just and wise, I submit to it without a murmur.—To the Reverend Bryan Fairfax. Fitzpatrick 32:376. (1793.)

[It] is not for man to scan the wisdom of Providence. The best he can do is to submit to its decrees. Reason, religion, and philosophy teach us to do this; but it is time alone that can ameliorate the pangs of humanity, and soften its woes.—To Henry Knox. Fitzpatrick 35:409. (1797.)

The ways of Providence are inscrutable, and mortals must submit.—To Thaddeus Kosciuszko. Fitzpatrick 36:22. (1797.)

GOD. See also JESUS CHRIST; MORALITY; PRAYER; RELIGION; REVELATION; THANKSGIVING PROCLAMATION OF 1789.

GOVERNMENT, National vs. State. —I have often regretted the pernicious (and what appears to me fatal) policy of having our able men engaged in the formation of the more local governments and filling offices in their respective states, leaving the great national concern, on which the superstructure of all and every [one] of them does absolutely depend, and without which none can exist, to be managed by men of more contracted abilities.— To John Augustine Washington. Fitzpatrick 11:501. (1778.)

That representatives ought to be the mouth of their constituents, I do not deny; nor do I mean to call in question the right of the latter to instruct them. It is to the embarrassment into which they may be thrown by

Washington in November 1789 (age 57). Portrait by Christian Gulager.

these instructions in national matters that my objections lie. In speaking of national matters I look to the federal government, which, in my opinion, it is the interest of every state to support; and to do this, as there are a variety of interests in the Union, there must be a yielding of the parts to coalesce the whole. Now a county, a district, or even a state might decide on a measure which, though apparently for the benefit of it in its unconnected state, may be repugnant to the interests of the nation, and eventually to the state itself, as part of the confederation.... In local matters which concern the district, or things which respect the internal policy of the state, there may be nothing amiss in instructions. In national matters also the sense, but not the law, of the district may be given, leaving the delegates to judge from the nature of the case and the evidence before them.—To Bushrod Washington. Fitzpatrick 29:67. (1786.)

GOVERNMENT, Avoid Extremes of Anarchy and Tyranny.—There is a natural and necessary progression from the extreme of anarchy to the extreme of tyranny; and... arbitrary power is most easily established on the ruins of liberty abused to licentiousness.—Circular to the States. Fitzpatrick 26:489. (1783.)

We are...anxious that... the rights of man [be] so well understood and so permanently fixed [that], while despotic oppression is avoided on the one hand, licentiousness may not be substituted for liberty nor confusion take [the] place of order on the other. The just medium cannot be expected to be found in a moment; the first vibrations always go to the extremes, and cool reason, which can alone establish a permanent and equal government, is as little to be expected in the tumults of popular commotion as an attention to the liberties of the people is to be found in the dark divan of a despotic tyrant. —To the Marquis de Lafayette. Fitzpatrick 32:54. (1792.)

GOVERNMENT, Effects of Ignorance and Wickedness in.—We are certainly in a delicate situation; but my fear is that the people are not yet sufficiently *misled* to retract from error. To be plainer, I think there is more wickedness than ignorance mixed in our councils....

Ignorance and design are difficult to combat. Out of these proceed illiberal sentiments, improper jealousies, and a train of evils which oftentimes in republican governments must be sorely felt before they can be removed. The former, that is ignorance, being a fit soil for the latter to work in, tools are employed by them which a generous mind would disdain to use, and which nothing but time, and their own puerile or wicked productions, can show the inefficacy and dangerous tendency of. I think often of our situation, and view it with concern. From the high ground we stood upon, from the plain path which invited our footsteps, to be so fallen! so lost! it is really mortifying. But virtue, I fear, has in a great degree taken its departure from our land, and the want of a disposition to do justice is the source of the national embarrassments; for, whatever guise or colorings are given to them, this I apprehend is the origin of the evils we now feel, and probably shall labor under for some time yet.—To John Jay. Fitzpatrick 28:431. (1786.)

GOVERNMENT, God Will Perfect American.—The foundation of a great empire is laid, and I please myself with a persuasion that Providence will not leave its work imperfect.—To the Chevalier de la Luzerne. Fitzpatrick 28:501. (1786.)

GOVERNMENT, Must Be Well Founded.—You talk...of employing influence.... I know not where that influence is to be found ... Influence is no government. Let us have one by which our lives, liberties, and properties will be secured, or let us know the worst at once.—To Henry Lee. Fitzpatrick 29:34. (1786.)

GOVERNMENT, Must Have Both Power and Restraints.—No man is a warmer advocate for proper restraints and wholesome checks in every department of government than I am; but I have never yet been able to discover the propriety of placing it absolutely out of the power of men to render essential services because a possibility remains of their doing ill.— To Bushrod Washington. Fitzpatrick 29:312. (1787.)

GOVERNMENT, Principles of Good. —As, on one side, no local prejudices or attachments, no separate views nor party animosities, will misdirect the comprehensive and equal eye which ought to watch over this great assemblage of communities and interests; so, on another, . . . the foundations of our national policy will be laid in the pure and immutable principles of private morality, and the preeminence of a free government be exemplified by all the attributes which can win the affections of its citizens and command the respect of the world.—First Inaugural Address. Fitzpatrick 30:294. (1789.)

GOVERNMENT, And Religion.— While just government protects all in their religious rights, true religion affords to government its surest support.—To the synod of the Dutch Reformed Church in North America. Sparks 12:167. (1789.)

GOVERNMENT, Must Prevent Oppression.—Government being, among other purposes, instituted to

protect the persons and consciences of men from oppression, it certainly is the duty of rulers, not only to abstain from it themselves, but, according to their stations, to prevent it in others.— To the religious society called Quakers. Sparks 12:168. (1789.)

GOVERNMENT, All Are Entitled to Protection of.—As mankind become more liberal, they will be more apt to allow that all those who conduct themselves as worthy members of the community are equally entitled to the protection of civil government. I hope ever to see America among the foremost nations in examples of justice and liberality.—To the Roman Catholics in the United States. Sparks 12:178. (1789.)

GOVERNMENT, American, a Great Experiment.—The establishment of our new government seemed to be the last great experiment for promoting human happiness by reasonable compact in civil society. It was to be, in the first instance, in a considerable degree a government of accommodation as well as a government of laws.—To Mrs. Catharine Macaulay Graham. Fitzpatrick 30:496. (1790.)

GOVERNMENT, Changes in, Require Care.—A spirit for political improvements seems to be rapidly and extensively spreading through the European countries. I shall rejoice in seeing the condition of the human race happier than ever it has hitherto been. But I should be sorry to see that those who are for prematurely accelerating those improvements were making *more haste than good speed* in their innovations. So much prudence, so much perseverance, so much disinterestedness, and so much patriotism are necessary among the leaders of a nation in order to promote the national felicity that sometimes my fears nearly preponderate over my expectations.—To the Marquis de la Luzerne. Fitzpatrick 31:40. (1790.)

GOVERNMENT, Of United States, Changed by Reason Alone.—A change in the national Constitution, conformed to experience and the circumstances of our country, has been most happily effected by the influence of reason alone; in this change the liberty of the citizen continues unimpaired, while the energy of government is so increased as to promise full protection to all the pursuits of science and industry, together with the firm establishment of public credit and the vindication of our national character.—To the Rhode Island legislature. Fitzpatrick 31:94. (1790.)

GOVERNMENT, Object of.—The aggregate happiness of the society, which is best promoted by the practice of a virtuous policy, is, or ought to be, the end of all government.—To the Comte de Moustier. Fitzpatrick 31:142. (1790.)

GOVERNMENT, Should Be Based on the Will of the People.—It is desirable on all occasions to unite, with a steady and firm adherence to constitutional and necessary acts of government, the fullest evidence of a disposition, as far as may be practicable, to consult the wishes of every part of the community, and to lay the foundations of the public administration in the affection of the people.—Third Annual Address to Congress. Fitzpatrick 31:400. (1791.)

As it is the right of the people that [their will] should be carried into effect, their sentiments ought to be unequivocally known, that the principles on which the government has acted, and which from the President's speech are likely to be continued, may either be changed, or the opposition that is endeavoring to embarrass every measure of the Executive may meet effectual discountenance. Things cannot, ought not, to remain any longer in their present disagreeable state. Nor should the idea that the government and the people have different views be suffered any longer to prevail, at home or abroad; for it is not only injurious to us, but disgraceful also, that a government constituted as ours is should be administered contrary to their interest and will, if the fact be so.—To Thomas Pinckney. Fitzpatrick 35:453. (1797.)

GOVERNMENT, Feeble, Is Little Government at All.—It is indeed little else than a name where the government is too feeble to withstand the enterprises of faction, to confine each member of the society within the limits prescribed by the laws, and to maintain all in the secure and tranquil enjoyment of the rights of person and property.—Farewell Address. Fitzpatrick 35:226. (1796.)

GOVERNMENT, Each Nation Should Establish Its Own.—I wish well to all nations and to all men. My politics are plain and simple. I think every nation has a right to establish that form of government under which it conceives it shall live most happy, provided it infracts no right or is not dangerous to others, and that no governments ought to interfere with the internal concerns of another, except for the security of what is due to themselves.—To the Marquis de Lafayette. Fitzpatrick 37:70. (1798.)

GOVERNMENT. See also CONSTITUTION (U.S.); CONSTITUTIONS; DEMOCRACY; EDUCATION; ELECTIONS; FEDERAL GOVERNMENT; LAWS; LEGISLATURES; LIBERTY; MAJORITY RULE; MONARCHIES; OPPRESSION; PEOPLE; POLITICS; POWER; PUBLIC OFFICIALS; REPUBLICANISM; SELF-GOVERNMENT; SEPARATION OF POWERS.

GREAT BRITAIN, War with, the Last Resort.—At a time when our lordly masters in Great Britain will be satisfied with nothing less than the deprication [sic] of American freedom, it seems highly necessary that something should be done to avert the stroke and maintain the liberty which we have derived from our ancestors; but the manner of doing it to answer the purpose effectually is the point in question.

That no man should scruple or hesitate a moment to use arms in defense of so valuable a blessing, on which all the good and evil of life depends, is clearly my opinion; yet arms, I would beg leave to add, should be the last resource, the *dernier resort.* Addresses to the throne and remonstrances to Parliament we have already, it is said, proved the inefficacy of; how far, then, their attention to

our rights and privileges is to be awakened or alarmed by starving their trade and manufactures remains to be tried.—To George Mason. Fitzpatrick 2:500. (1769.)

GREAT BRITAIN, Ought to Be a Friend Rather Than an Enemy.—The [British] ministry may rely on it that Americans will never be taxed without their own consent. The cause of Boston now is and ever will be considered as the cause of America (not that we approve their conduct in destroying the tea). We shall not suffer ourselves to be sacrificed piecemeal, though God only knows what is to become of us, threatened as we are with so many hovering evils as hang over us at present, having a cruel and bloodthirsty enemy upon our backs, the Indians, between whom and our frontier inhabitants many skirmishes have happened and with whom a general war is inevitable, while those from whom we have a right to seek protection are endeavoring by every piece of art and despotism to fix the shackles of slavery upon us.—To George William Fairfax. Fitzpatrick 3:224. (1774.)

GREAT BRITAIN, Washington's Attitude Toward, in Early 1776.—With respect to myself, I have never entertained an idea of an accommodation [with Great Britain] since I heard of the measures which were adopted in consequence of the Bunker's Hill fight. The king's speech has confirmed the sentiments I entertained upon the news of that affair; and if every man was of my mind, the ministers of Great Britain should know, in a few words, upon what issue

Washington in December 1789 January 1790 (age 58). Portrait by Edward Savage.

the cause should be put. I would not be deceived by artful declarations, nor specious pretenses; nor would I be amused by unmeaning propositions; but in open, undisguised, and manly terms proclaim our wrongs and our resolution to be redressed. I would tell them that we had borne much, that we had long and ardently sought for reconciliation upon honorable terms, that it had been denied us, that all our attempts after peace had proved abortive and had been grossly misrepresented, that we had done everything which could be expected from the best of subjects, that the spirit of freedom beat too high in us to submit to slavery, and that, if nothing else could satisfy a tyrant and his diabolical ministry, we are determined to shake off all connections with a state so unjust and unnatural. This I would tell them, not under covert, but in words as clear as the sun in its meridian brightness.— To Joseph Reed. Fitzpatrick 4:321. (1776.)

GREAT BRITAIN, Sought to Provoke American Rebellion.—Great Britain understood herself perfectly well in this dispute, but did not comprehend America. She meant, as Lord Campden in his late speech in Parliament clearly and explicitly declared, to drive America into rebellion, that her own purposes might be more fully answered by it;... this plan, originating in a firm belief, founded on misinformation, that no effectual opposition would or could be made, they little dreamt of what has happened and are disappointed in their views.... They meant to drive us into what they termed rebellion, that they might be furnished with a pretext to disarm and then strip us of the rights and privileges of Englishmen and citizens.... What name does such conduct as this deserve? And what punishment is there in store for the men who have distressed millions, involved thousands in ruin, and plunged numberless families in inextricable woe?—To Bryan Fairfax. Fitzpatrick 11:3. (1778.)

GREAT BRITAIN, Villainy of, During Revolutionary War.—They must either be wantonly wicked and cruel, or (which is only another mode of describing the same thing) under false colors to endeavor to deceive the great body of the people by industriously propagating a belief that Great Britain is willing to offer any [terms], and that we will accept of no terms, thereby hoping to poison and disaffect the minds of those who wish for peace, and create feuds and dissensions among ourselves. In a word, having less dependence now in their arms than their arts, they are practicing such low and dirty tricks that men of sentiment and honor must blush at their villainy. Among other maneuvers, . . . they are counterfeiting letters and publishing them as intercepted ones of mine to prove that I am an enemy to the present measures [for independence] and have been led into them step by step, still hoping that Congress would recede from their present claims.—To Bryan Fairfax. Fitzpatrick 11:4. (1778.)

The drafts of bills as mentioned by you, and which have since passed into acts of British legislation, are so strongly marked with folly and villainy that one can scarce tell which predominates, or how to be surprised at any act of a British minister. This last trite performance of Master North's* is neither more nor less than an insult to common sense, and shows to what extremity of folly wicked men in a bad cause are sometimes driven.—To Landon Carter. Fitzpatrick 11:494. (1778.)

*Lord North, Prime Minister of England, with the approval of Parliament, offered Americans pardon and cessation of taxes—but not independence. —Editor.

The arts of the enemy, and the low dirty tricks which they are daily practicing, is an evincing proof that they will stick at nothing, however incompatible with truth and manliness, to carry their points.—To John Augustine Washington. Fitzpatrick 11:500. (1778.)

GREAT BRITAIN, Financial Resources of, During the War.—In modern wars the longest purse must chiefly determine the event. I fear that of the enemy will be found to be so. Though the [British] government is deeply in debt and of course poor, the nation is rich and their riches afford a fund which will not be easily exhausted. Besides, their system of public credit is such that it is capable of greater exertions than that of any other nation. Speculators have been a long time foretelling its downfall, but we see no symptoms of the catastrophe being very near. I am persuaded it will at least last out the war, and then, in the opinion of many of the best politicians, it will be a national advantage. If the war should terminate successfully, the crown will have acquired such influence and power that it may attempt anything, and a bankruptcy will probably be made the ladder to climb to absolute authority. Administration may perhaps wish to drive matters to this issue; at any rate, they will not be restrained by an apprehension of it from forcing the resources of the state. It will promote their present purposes, on which their all is at stake, and it may pave the way to triumph more effectually over the constitution. With this disposition I have no doubt that ample means will be found to prosecute the war with the greatest vigor.—To Joseph Reed. Fitzpatrick 18:436. (1780.)

GREAT BRITAIN, Its Power on the Seas.—The maritime resources of Great Britain are more substantial and real than those of France and Spain united. Her commerce is more extensive than that of both her rivals; and it is an axiom that the nation which has the most extensive commerce will always have the most powerful marine.—To Joseph Reed. Fitzpatrick 18:436. (1780.)

GREAT BRITAIN. See also COLONIES (American); DECLARATION OF INDEPENDENCE; ENEMY; EUROPE; FOREIGN RELATIONS; IMPORTS; INDEPENDENCE; JAY TREATY; NONIMPORTATION; REVOLUTIONARY WAR; STAMP ACT; TAXATION.

GREED, a Hindrance to the War Effort.—It gives me very sincere pleasure to [hear of] your endeavors in bringing those murderers of our cause the monopolizers, forestallers, and engrossers—to condign punishment. It is much to be lamented that each state long ere this has not hunted them down as the pests of society and the greatest enemies we have to the happiness of America. I would to God that one of the most atrocious of each state was hung in gibbets upon a gallows five times as high as the one prepared by Haman [of the Old Testament]. No punishment, in my opinion, is too great for the man who can build his greatness upon his country's ruin.—To Joseph Reed. Fitzpatrick 13:383. (1778.)

Nothing, I am convinced, but the depreciation of our currency, ... aided by stockjobbing and party dissensions, has fed the hopes of the enemy and kept the British arms in America to this day. They do not scruple to declare this themselves, and add that we shall be our own conquerers. Cannot our common country, America, possess virtue enough to disappoint them? Is the paltry consideration of a little dirty pelf to individuals to be placed in competition with the essential rights and liberties of the present generation, and of millions yet unborn? Shall a few designing men, for their own aggrandizement and to gratify their own avarice, overset the goodly fabric we have been rearing at the expense of so much time, blood, and treasure? and shall we at last become the victims of our own abominable lust of gain? Forbid it, heaven! forbid it all and every state in the Union! by enacting and enforcing efficacious laws for checking the growth of these monstrous evils and restoring matters, in some degree, to the pristine state they were in at the commencement of the war.—To James Warren. Fitzpatrick 14:312. (1779.)

GUARDIANS, Face More Constraints Than Parents.—I conceive there is much greater circumspection to [be observed] by a guardian than a natural parent, who is only accountable to his own conscience for his conduct, whereas any *faux pas* in a guardian, however well meant the action, seldom fails to meet with malicious construction.—To the Reverend Jonathan Boucher. Fitzpatrick 3:44. (1771.)

H

HAMILTON (Alexander), Washington's Confidence in.—After so long an experience of your public services, I am naturally led, at this moment of your departure from office, which it has always been my wish to prevent, to review them. In every relation which you have borne to me, I have found that my confidence in your talents, exertions, and integrity has been well placed. I the more freely render this testimony of my approbation because I speak from opportunities of information which cannot deceive me, and which furnish satisfactory proof of your title to public regard. My most earnest wishes for your happiness will attend you in your retirement, and you may assure yourself of [my] sincere esteem, regard, and friendship.—To Alexander Hamilton. Fitzpatrick 34:109. (1795.)

HAMILTON (Alexander), Character of.—By some he is considered as an ambitious man, and therefore a dangerous one. That he is ambitious I shall readily grant, but it is of that laudable kind which prompts a man to excel in whatever he takes in hand. He is enterprising, quick in his perceptions, and his judgment intuitively great, qualities essential to a military character.—To President John Adams. Fitzpatrick 36:460. (1798.)

HAMILTON (Alexander). See also JEFFERSON (Thomas); POLITICAL OPINIONS.

HAPPINESS, Source of.—Happiness depends more upon the internal frame of a person's mind than on the externals in the world.—To Mary Ball Washington. Fitzpatrick 29:162. (1787.)

HAPPINESS, Pillars of National.—Nothing but harmony, honesty, industry, and frugality are necessary to make us a great and happy people. Happily, the present posture of affairs and the prevailing disposition of my countrymen promise to cooperate in establishing those four great and essential pillars of public felicity.—To the Marquis de Lafayette. Fitzpatrick 30:186. (1789.)

It appears to me that little more than common sense and common honesty, in the transactions of the community at large, would be necessary to make us a great and a happy nation.—To the citizens of Baltimore. Fitzpatrick 30:288. (1789.)

Your love of liberty, your respect for the laws, your habits of industry, and your practice of the moral and religious obligations are the strongest claims to national and individual happiness.—To the inhabitants of the town of Boston. Sparks 12:172. (1789.)

HAPPINESS, And Morality.—The consideration that human happiness and moral duty are inseparably connected will always continue to prompt me to promote the progress of the former by inculcating the practice of the latter.—To the bishops, clergy, and laity of the Protestant Episcopal Church in New York. Sparks 12:162. (1789.)

HAPPINESS, The Object of Government.—The aggregate happiness of society . . . is, or ought to be, the end of all government.—To the Comte de

Moustier. Fitzpatrick 31:142. (1790.)
**HAPPINESS, Washington's Desire
for Mankind.**—No one can feel a
greater interest in the happiness of
mankind than I do.... It is the first
wish of my heart that the enlightened
policy of the present age may diffuse to
all men those blessings to which they
are entitled, and lay the foundation of
happiness for future generations.—To
Thomas Paine. Fitzpatrick 32:39.
(1792.)
HENRY (Patrick), Death of.—In the
death of Mr. Henry,... not only Virginia but our country at large has sus
tained a very serious loss. I sincerely
lament his death as a friend, and the
loss of his eminent talents as a patriot.
To John Marshall. Fitzpatrick
37:235 (1799.)
**HESSIANS, In the Revolutionary
War.**—One thing I must remark in
favor of the Hessians, and that is that
our people who have been prisoners
generally agree that they receive much
kinder treatment from them than
from the British officers and soldiers.
—To Samuel Chase. Fitzpatrick 7:108.
(1777.)
HONESTY, In Government.—It is an
old adage that *honesty is the best policy.*
This applies to public as well as private
life, to states as well as individuals.—
To James Madison. Fitzpatrick 28:366.
(1785.)

Honesty in states as well as individuals will ever be found the soundest
policy.—To David Stuart. Fitzpatrick
29:302. (1787.)
HONESTY, And Good Sense.—
These are qualities too rare and too
precious not to merit one's particular

*Washington in 1790 (age 58). Detail from
The Surrender of Cornwallis by John
Trumbull.*

esteem.— To the Marquis de Lafayette. Fitzpatrick 29:409. (1788.)
**HONESTY, The Most Enviable Char-
acter Trait.**—I hope I shall always
possess firmness and virtue enough to
maintain (what I consider the most
enviable of all titles) the character of *an
honest man.*—To Alexander Hamilton.
Fitzpatrick 30:67. (1788.)
**HONESTY, And Common Sense,
Needed for a Nation to Prosper.**—It
appears to me that little more than
common sense and common honesty
in the transactions of the community
at large would be necessary to make us
a great and a happy nation. For if the
general government lately adopted
shall be arranged and administered in

such a manner as to acquire the full confidence of the American people, I sincerely believe they will have greater advantages, from their natural, moral, and political circumstances, for public felicity than any other people ever possessed.—To the citizens of Baltimore. Fitzpatrick 30:288. (1789.)

HONESTY. See also INTEGRITY; MORAL CHARACTER; VIRTUE.

HUMANITARIANISM, Lauded.—How pitiful, in the eye of reason and religion, is that false ambition which desolates the world with fire and sword for the purposes of conquest and fame, when compared to the milder virtues of making our neighbors and our fellow men as happy as their frail conditions and perishable natures will permit them to be!—To the Reverend John Lathrop. Fitzpatrick 30:5. (1788.)

HUMANITARIANISM. See also CHARITY; POOR.

I

IMMODESTY, In Bathing, Condemned.—The General does not mean to discourage the practice of bathing while the weather is warm enough to continue it, but he expressly forbids any persons doing it at or near the bridge in Cambridge, where it has been observed and complained of that many men, lost to all sense of decency and common modesty, are running about naked upon the bridge, while passengers, and even ladies of the first fashion in the neighborhood, are pass-

ing over it, as if they meant to glory in their shame.—General Orders. Fitzpatrick 3:440. (1775.)

IMPERFECTION, Human.—It is to be lamented... that great characters are seldom without a blot.—To the Marquis de Lafayette. Fitzpatrick 28:420. (1786.)

IMPORTS, Problems with British.—Instead of getting things good and fashionable in their several kinds, we often have articles sent us that could only have been used by our forefathers in the days of yore. It is a custom, I have some reason to believe, with many shopkeepers and tradesmen in London, when they know goods are bespoken for exportation, to palm sometimes old, and sometimes very slight and indifferent goods upon us, taking care at the same time to advance 10, 15, or perhaps 20 percent upon them.—To Robert Cary & Co. Fitzpatrick 2:350. (1870.)

IMPORTS. See also NONIMPORTATION.

INDEPENDENCE, Not Contemplated in Late 1774.—It is not the wish or interest of |the Massachusetts| government, or any other upon this continent, separately or collectively, to set up for independence; but this you may at the same time rely on, that none of them will ever submit to the loss of those valuable rights and privileges which are essential to the happiness of every free state, and without which life, liberty, and property are rendered totally insecure.... Give me leave to add, as my opinion, that more blood will be spilt on this occasion, if the |British| ministry are determined to push matters to extremity, than history has ever yet furnished instances of in the annals of North America, and such a vital wound given to the peace of this great country as time itself cannot cure or eradicate the remembrance of.... I am as well satisfied as I can be of my existence that no such thing [as independence] is desired by any thinking man in all North America; on the contrary,... it is the ardent wish of the warmest advocates for liberty that peace and tranquility, upon constitutional grounds, may be restored, and the horrors of civil discord prevented.—To Robert MacKenzie. Fitzpatrick 3:246. (1774.)

INDEPENDENCE, Movements Toward, Welcomed by Washington.— I am very glad to find that the Virginia Convention have passed so noble a vote, and with so much unanimity [i.e., instructing the Virginia delegates in Congress to propose that the American colonies declare themselves "free and independent states"]. Things have come to that pass now as to convince us that we have nothing more to expect from the justice of Great Britain; also, that she is capable of the most delusive arts, for I am satisfied that no [British peace] commissioners ever were designed, except Hessians and other foreigners, and that the idea was only to deceive and throw us off our guard. The first it has too effectually accomplished, as many members of Congress—in short, the representation of whole provinces—are still feeding themselves upon the dainty food of reconciliation; and though they will not allow that the expectation of it has

any influence upon their judgments (with respect to their preparations for defense), it is but too obvious that it has an operation upon every part of their conduct and is a clog to their proceedings. It is not in the nature of things to be otherwise, for no man that entertains a hope of seeing this dispute speedily and equitably adjusted by commissioners will go to the same expense and run the same hazards to prepare for the worst event as he who believes that he must conquer or submit to unconditional terms and [their] concomitants, such as confiscation, hanging, etc.—To John Augustine Washington. Fitzpatrick 5:91. (1776.)

INDEPENDENCE, The Cause of Mankind.—Our cause is noble; it is the cause of mankind! and the danger to it is to be apprehended from ourselves. Shall we slumber and sleep, then, while we should be punishing those miscreants who have brought these troubles upon us and who are aiming to continue us in them, while we should be striving to fill our battalions, and devising ways and means to appreciate the currency, on the credit of which everything depends? I hope not.—To James Warren. Fitzpatrick 14:313. (1779.)

INDEPENDENCE, All Conditions Favorable for.—I am happy to be informed by accounts, from all parts of the continent, of the agreeable prospect of a very plentiful supply of almost all the productions of the earth. Blessed as we are with the bounties of Providence necessary for our support and defense, the fault must surely be our own (and great indeed will it be) if

Washington in 1791–95 (age 59–63). Classical-style marble bust by Giuseppe Ceracchi.

we do not, by a proper use of them, attain the noble prize for which we have so long been contending, the establishment of peace, liberty, and independence.—To Thomas McKean. Fitzpatrick 22:405. (1781.)

INDEPENDENCE, Brings Great Blessings.—When we consider the magnitude of the prize we contended for, the doubtful nature of the contest, and the favorable manner in which it has terminated, we shall find the greatest possible reason for gratitude and rejoicing; this is a theme that will afford infinite delight to every benevolent and liberal mind, whether the event in contemplation be considered as the source of present enjoyment or

the parent of future happiness; and we shall have equal occasion to felicitate ourselves on the lot which Providence has assigned us, whether we view it in a natural, a political, or moral point of light.—Circular to the States. Fitzpatrick 26:484. (1783.)

It is universally acknowledged that the enlarged prospects of happiness, opened by the confirmation of our independence and sovereignty, almost exceed the power of description.—Farewell Orders to the Armies of the United States. Fitzpatrick 27:224. (1783.)

INDEPENDENCE, Four Pillars of.—There are four things which I humbly conceive are essential to the well-being, I may even venture to say to the existence, of the United States as an independent power:

1st. An indissoluble union of the states under one federal head.

2dly. A sacred regard to public justice.

3dly. The adoption of a proper peace establishment, and

4thly. The prevalence of that pacific and friendly disposition among the people of the United States which will induce them to forget their local prejudices and policies, to make those mutual concessions which are requisite to the general prosperity, and in some instances to sacrifice their individual advantages to the interest of the community.

These are the pillars on which the glorious fabric of our independence and national character must be supported; liberty is the basis, and whoever would dare to sap the foundation or overturn the structure, under whatever specious pretexts he may attempt it, will merit the bitterest execration and the severest punishment which can be inflicted by his injured country.—Circular to the States. Fitzpatrick 26:487. (1783.)

INDEPENDENCE. See also AMERICAN REVOLUTION; COLONIES (American); DECLARATION OF INDEPENDENCE; FREEDOM; GREAT BRITAIN; LIBERTY; REVOLUTIONARY WAR; SELF-GOVERNMENT.

INDIAN DRESS, Used During French and Indian War.—It gives me great pleasure to find you approve of the dress I have put my men into. It is evident |that| soldiers in that trim are better able to carry their provisions, are fitted for the active service we must engage in, less liable to sink under the fatigues of a march, and by this means |can| get rid of much baggage that would consequently, if carried, protract our line of march; |these|, and not whim or caprice, are really my reasons for ordering them into it.—To Henry Bouquet. Fitzpatrick 2:235. (1758.)

INDIAN DRESS, Used During Revolutionary War.—It occurs to me that if you were to dress a company or two of true woodsmen in the right Indian style and let them make the attack accompanied with screaming and yelling as the Indians do, it would have very good consequences.—To Daniel Morgan. Fitzpatrick 8:236. (1777.)

INDIANS, Their Mode of Warfare.—However absurd it may appear, it is nevertheless certain that five hundred Indians have it more in their power to annoy the inhabitants than ten times their number of regulars. For besides the advantageous way they have of fighting in the woods, their cunning and craft are not to be equalled, neither their activity and indefatigable sufferings. They prowl about like wolves, and, like them, do their mischief by stealth. They depend upon their dexterity in hunting and upon the cattle of the inhabitants for provisions.—To Governor Robert Dinwiddie. Fitzpatrick 1:300. (1756.)

INDIANS, Need for Help of, in French and Indian War.—Without Indians to oppose Indians, we may expect but small success. To Governor Robert Dinwiddie. Fitzpatrick 1:330. (1756.)

A small number, just to point out the wiles and tracks of the enemy, is better than none.—To Governor Robert Dinwiddie. Fitzpatrick 1:341. (1756.)

INDIANS, Pleas for Alliances with, During French and Indian War.—Brothers, you can be no strangers to the many murders and cruelties committed on our countrymen and friends by that false and faithless people, the French, who are constantly endeavoring to corrupt the minds of our friendly Indians, and have stirred up the Shawnees and Delawares, with several other nations, to take up the hatchet against us.... Many of these Indians have invaded our country, laid waste our lands, plundered our plantations, murdered defenseless women and children, and burnt and destroyed wherever they came, which has enraged our friends the Six Nations, Cherokees, Nottoways, Catawbas, and all our Indian allies, and prompted them to take up the hatchet in our defense against these disturbers of the common peace. I hope, brothers, you will likewise take up the hatchet against the French and their Indians, as our other friends have done, and send us some of your young men to protect our frontiers and go to war with us against our restless and ambitious foes. And to encourage your brave warriors, I promise to furnish them with arms, ammunition, clothes, provision, and every necessary for war. And the sooner you send them to our assistance, the greater mark will you give us of your friendship, and the better shall we be enabled to take just revenge of |our enemies'| cruelties.— Speech to the Tuscaroras. Fitzpatrick 1:414. (1756.)

We desire you to go to the Cherokees and tell them the road is now clear and open. We expected them to war last spring, and love them so well that our governor sent some few men to build a fort among them. But we are mighty sorry that they hearken so much to lies French tell as to break their promise and not come to war, when they might have got a great deal of honor and killed a great many of the French, whose hearts are false and rotten as an old stump. If they continue to listen to what the French say much longer they will have great cause to be sorry, as the French have no match-locks, powder, and lead but what they got from King George our father before the war began, and that

will soon be out, when they will get no more, and all French Indians will be starving with cold and must take to bows and arrows again for want of ammunition. Tell them we long to shake hands with them. Let them get their knives and tomahawks sharp. We will go before them, and show them the way to honor, scalps, prisoners, and money enough. We are mighty sorry they stay at home idle when they should go to war and become great men and a terror and dread to their enemies. Tell them they shall have victuals enough, and |shall be| used very kindly.—Speech to Captain Johnne, Catawbas. Fitzpatrick 1:486. (1756.)

INDIANS, Trade with.—A trade with the Indians should be upon such terms and transacted by men of such principles as would at the same time turn out to the reciprocal advantage of the colony |of Virginia| and the Indians, and which would effectually remove those bad impressions that the Indians received from the conduct of a set of rascally fellows, divested of all faith and honor, and give us such an early opportunity of establishing an interest with them as would be productive of the most beneficial consequences, by getting a large share of the fur trade, not only of the Ohio Indians, but, in time, of the numerous nations possessing the back countries westward of it. And to prevent this advantageous commerce from suffering in its infancy by the sinister views of designing, selfish men of the different provinces, I humbly conceive it absolutely necessary that commissioners from each of the colonies be appointed to regulate the mode of that trade, and fix it on such a basis that all the attempts of one colony undermining another, and thereby weakening and diminishing the general system, might be frustrated.—To Francis Fauquier. Fitzpatrick 2:313. (1758.)

Next to a rigorous execution of justice on the violators of peace, the establishment of commerce with the Indian nations in behalf of the United States is most likely to conciliate their attachment. But it ought to be conducted without fraud, without extortion, with constant and plentiful supplies, with a ready market for the commodities of the Indians and a stated price for what they give in payment and receive in exchange. Individuals will not pursue such a traffic unless they be allured by the hope of profit.—Fifth Annual Address to Congress. Fitzpatrick 33:167. (1793.)

INDIANS, Use of, in Revolutionary War.—By...a resolve of Congress,... I am empowered to employ a body of four hundred Indians, if they can be procured upon proper terms. Divesting them of the savage customs exercised in their wars against each other, I think they may be made of excellent use as scouts and light troops, mixed with our own parties. I propose to raise about one half the number among the southern and the remainder among the northern Indians. I have sent Colonel Nathaniel Gist, who is well acquainted with the Cherokees and their allies, to bring as many as he can from thence, and I must depend upon you to employ suitable persons to procure the stipulated number or as near as may be from the northern tribes. The terms made with them should be such as you think we can comply with, and persons well acquainted with their language, manners, and customs, and who have gained an influence over them, should accompany them.—To the Commissioners of Indian Affairs. Fitzpatrick 11:76. (1778.)

INDIANS, Plea for Support of, in Revolutionary War.—Brothers, I am a warrior. My words are few and plain; but I will make good what I say. It is my business to destroy all the enemies of these states and to protect their friends. You have seen how we have withstood the English for four years, and how their great armies have dwindled away and come to very little, and how what remains of them in this part of our great country are glad to stay upon two or three little islands, where the waters and their ships hinder us from going to destroy them. The English, brothers, are a boasting people. They talk of doing a good deal; but they do very little. They fly away on their ships from one part of our country to another; but as soon as our warriors get together they leave it and go to some other part. They took Boston and Philadelphia, two of our greatest towns; but when they saw our warriors in a great body ready to fall upon them, they were forced to leave them.

Brothers, we have till lately fought the English all alone. Now the great king of France is became our good brother and ally. He has taken up the hatchet with us, and we have sworn never to bury it till we have punished the English and made them sorry for all the wicked things they had in their hearts to do against these States. And there are other great kings and nations on the other side of the big waters who love us and wish us well and will not suffer the English to hurt us.

Brothers, listen well to what I tell you and let it sink deep into your hearts. We love our friends and will be faithful to them as long as they will be faithful to us. We are sure our good brothers the Delawares will always be so. But we have sworn to take vengeance on our enemies and on false friends.—Speech to the Delaware Chiefs. Fitzpatrick 15:54. (1779.)

INDIANS, Should Learn Christianity.—Brothers, . . . you do well to wish to learn our arts and ways of life, and above all, the religion of Jesus Christ. These will make you a greater and happier people than you are.—Speech to the Delaware Chiefs. Fitzpatrick 15:55. (1779.)

INDIANS, Best Method of Attacking. —I beg leave to suggest as general rules that ought to govern your operations, to make rather than receive attacks, attended with as much impetuosity, shouting, and noise as possible, and to make the troops act in as loose and dispersed a way as is consistent with a proper degree of government concert and mutual support. It should be previously impressed upon the minds of the men, whenever they have an opportunity, to rush on with the war whoop and fixed bayonet.

Nothing will disconcert and terrify the Indians more than this.—To John Sullivan. Fitzpatrick 15:190. (1779.)

INDIANS, Their Lands Should Be Obtained by Purchase, Not Force.— Policy and economy point very strongly to the expediency of being upon good terms with the Indians, and the propriety of purchasing their lands in preference to attempting to drive them by force of arms out of their country; which, as we have already experienced, is like driving the wild beasts of the forest, which will return as soon as the pursuit is at an end, and fall perhaps upon those that are left there; when the gradual extension of our settlements will as certainly cause the savage as the wolf to retire, both being beasts of prey, though they differ in shape. In a word, there is nothing to be obtained by an Indian war but the soil they live on, and this can be had by purchase at less expense, and without that bloodshed and those distresses which helpless women and children are made partakers of in all kinds of disputes with them.—To James Duane. Fitzpatrick 27:140. (1783.)

INDIANS, Languages of.—To know the affinity of tongues seems to be one step towards promoting the affinity of nations. . . . Should the present or any other efforts of mine to procure information respecting the different dialects of the aborigines in America serve to reflect a ray of light on the obscure subject of language in general, I shall be highly gratified. For I love to indulge the contemplation of human nature in a progressive state of improvement and melioration; and if the

Washington in spring or summer 1790 (age 58). Portrait by Joseph Wright.

idea would not be considered visionary and chimerical, I could fondly hope that the present plan of the great Potentate of the North* might, in some measure, lay the foundation for that assimilation of language which, producing assimilation of manners and interests, should one day remove many of the causes of hostility from among mankind.—To the Marquis de Lafayette. Fitzpatrick 29:374. (1788.)

*The "Potentate of the North" was Catherine the Great, empress of Russia, who was compiling a Universal Dictionary. Washington supplied her with vocabularies of the Delaware and Shawnee languages.—Editor.

INDIANS, Christian Missions to.—If an event so long and so earnestly desired as that of converting the Indians to Christianity, and consequently to civilization, can be effected,

the Society of Bethlehem bids fair to bear a very considerable part in it.—To the Reverend John Ettwein. Fitzpatrick 29:489. (1788.)

In proportion as the general government of the United States shall acquire strength by duration, it is probable they may have it in their power to extend a salutary influence to the aborigines in the extremities of their territory. In the meantime, it will be a desirable thing for the protection of the Union to cooperate, as far as circumstances may conveniently admit, with the disinterested endeavors of your society to civilize and Christianize the savages of the wilderness.—To the Society of United Brethren for Propagating the Gospel Among the Heathen. Fitzpatrick 30:355. (1789.)

A system corresponding with the mild principles of religion and philanthropy towards an unenlightened race of men, whose happiness materially depends on the conduct of the United States, would be as honorable to the national character as conformable to the dictates of sound policy.—Third Annual Address to Congress. Fitzpatrick 31:399. (1791.)

INDIANS, Have Claim to Justice and Humanity.—While the measures of government ought to be calculated to protect its citizens from all injury and violence, a due regard should be extended to those Indians whose happiness in the course of events so materially depends on the national justice and humanity of the United States.—To the Senate and the House of Representatives. Fitzpatrick 30:372. (1789.)

INDIANS, Dealt With in Justice.— The basis of our proceedings with the Indian nations has been and shall be *justice* during the period in which I may have anything to do in the administration of this government.—To the Marquis de Lafayette. Fitzpatrick 31:87. (1790.)

INDIANS, Should Be Taught Husbandry.—Humanity and good policy must make it the wish of every good citizen of the United States that husbandry, and consequently civilization, should be introduced among the Indians. So strongly am I impressed with the beneficial effects which our country would receive from such a thing that I shall always take a singular pleasure in promoting, as far as may be in my power, every measure which may tend to ensure it.—To Timothy Pickering. Fitzpatrick 31:199. (1791.)

INDIANS, Equal Rights of, Should Be Respected.—I must confess I cannot see much prospect of living in tranquility with |the Indians| so long as a spirit of land-jobbing prevails, and our frontier settlers entertain the opinion that there is not the same crime (or indeed no crime at all) in killing an Indian as in killing a white man.—To David Humphreys. Fitzpatrick 31:320. (1791.)

INDIANS, Federal Policies Toward. —It is sincerely to be desired that all need of coercion, in future, may cease, and that an intimate intercourse may succeed, calculated to advance the happiness of the Indians and to attach them firmly to the United States. In order to do this it seems necessary that they should experience the benefits of an impartial administration of justice; that the mode of alienating their lands, the main source of discontent and war, should be so defined and regulated as to obviate imposition and, as far as may be practicable, controversy concerning the reality and extent of the alienations which are made; that commerce with them should be promoted under regulations tending to secure an equitable deportment towards them, and that such rational experiments should be made for imparting to them the blessings of civilization as may, from time to time, suit their condition; that the Executive of the United States should be enabled to employ the means to which the Indians have been long accustomed for uniting their immediate interests with the preservation of peace; and that efficacious provision should be made for inflicting adequate penalties upon all those who, by violating their rights, shall infringe the treaties and endanger the peace of the Union.—Third Annual Address to Congress. Fitzpatrick 31:398. (1791.)

INDIANS, Appointment of Agents to.—To enable, by competent rewards, the employment of qualified and trusty persons to reside among them, as agents, would also contribute to the preservation of peace and good neighborhood. If, in addition to these expedients, an eligible plan could be devised for promoting civilization among the friendly tribes, and for carrying on trade with them upon a scale equal to their wants and under regulations calculated to protect them from imposition and extortion, its influence in cementing their interests with ours could not but be considerable.—Fourth Annual Address to Congress. Fitzpatrick 32:208. (1792.)

INDIANS, Victims of Injustice.—I accord fully in my opinion with you that the plan of annual presents in an abstract view, unaccompanied with other measures, is not the best mode of treating ignorant savages from whose hostile conduct we experience much distress; but it is not to be overlooked that they, in turn, are not without serious causes of complaint from the encroachments which are made on their lands by our people, who are not to be restrained by any law now in being or likely to be enacted. They, poor wretches, have no press through which their grievances are related; and it is well known that when one side only of a story is heard, and often repeated, the human mind becomes impressed with it insensibly. The annual presents, however, which you allude to, are not given so much with a view to purchase peace as by way of retribution for injuries, not otherwise to be redressed. These people are very much irritated by the continual pressure of land speculators and settlers on one hand, and by the impositions of unauthorized and unprincipled traders (who rob them in a manner of their hunting) on the other. Nothing but the strong arm of the Union, or in other words energetic laws, can correct these abuses; but ... jealousies and prejudices (from which I apprehend more fatal consequences to this government than from any other source), aided by local situations and

perhaps by interested considerations, always oppose themselves to efficient measures.

My communications to Congress at the last and present session have proceeded upon similar ideas with those expressed in your letter, namely, to make fair treaties with the savage tribes (by this I mean that they shall perfectly understand every article and clause of them, from correct and repeated interpretations); that these treaties shall be held sacred, and the infractors on either side punished exemplarily; and to furnish them plentifully with goods under wholesome regulations, without aiming at higher prices than |are| adequate to cover the cost and charges. If measures like these were adopted, we might hope to live in peace and amity with these borderers; but not while our citizens, in violation of law and justice, are guilty of the offenses I have mentioned, and are carrying on unauthorized expeditions against them; and when, for the most atrocious murders, even of those of whom we have the least cause of complaint, a jury on the frontiers can hardly be got to listen to a charge, much less to convict a culprit. —To Edmund Pendleton. Fitzpatrick 34:99. (1795.)

INDIANS. See also INDIAN DRESS.

INFLATION, During Revolutionary War.—Can *we* carry on the war much longer? Certainly *no*, unless some measures can be devised, and speedily executed, to restore the credit of our currency, restrain extortion, and punish forestallers. |Unless| these can be effected, what funds can stand the present expenses of the army? And what officer can bear the weight of prices that every necessary article is now got to? A rat in the shape of a horse is not to be bought at this time for less than two hundred pounds, a saddle under thirty or forty, boots twenty, and shoes and other articles in like proportion. How is it possible, therefore, for officers to stand this without an increase of pay? And how is it possible to advance their pay when flour is selling (at different places) from five to fifteen pounds per hundredweight, hay from ten to thirty pounds per ton, and beef and other essentials in this proportion.—To Gouverneur Morris. Fitzpatrick 13:21. (1778.)

INFLATION, Need to Curb.—Let vigorous measures be adopted, not to limit the prices of articles, for this I believe is inconsistent with the very nature of things and impracticable in itself, but to punish speculators, forestallers, and extortioners, and above all ... to promote public and private economy, encourage manufacturers, etc. Measures of this sort, gone heartily into by the several states, would strike at once at the root of all our evils and give the coup de grace to British hope of subjugating this continent, either by their arms or their arts. The first, as I have before observed, they acknowledge is unequal to the task; the latter I am sure will be so if we are not lost to everything that is good and virtuous.—To James Warren. Fitzpatrick 14:313. (1779.)

INFLATION. See also CURRENCY; FINANCES; MONEY.

INFORMATION, Vital Need for Correct, in a Republic.—I am *sure* the mass of citizens in these United States *mean well*, and I firmly believe they will always *act well* whenever they can obtain a right understanding of matters; but in some parts of the Union, where the sentiments of their delegates and leaders are adverse to the government, and great pains are taken to inculcate a belief that their rights are assailed and their liberties endangered, it is not easy to accomplish this, especially, as is the case invariably, when the inventors and abetters of pernicious measures use infinitely more industry in disseminating the poison than the welldisposed part of the community |use| to furnish the antidote. To this source all our discontents may be traced, and from it our embarrassments proceed. Hence serious misfortunes originating in misrepresentation frequently flow and spread before they can be dissipated by truth.—To Governor John Jay. Fitzpatrick 35:37. (1796.)

INFORMATION. See also KNOWLEDGE; NEWSPAPERS; PROPAGANDA; PUBLIC OPINION.

INGRATITUDE, Abhorred by Washington.—Nothing is a greater stranger to my breast, or a sin that my soul [more] abhors, than that black and detestable one, ingratitude.—To Governor Robert Dinwiddie. Fitzpatrick 1:60. (1754.)

Ingratitude ... I hope will never constitute a part of my character, nor find a place in my bosom.—To Landon Carter. Fitzpatrick 11:492. (1778.)

INSURGENCY, Proper Response to.—Know precisely what the insurgents aim at. If they have real grievances, redress them if possible; or acknowledge the justice of them, and your inability to do it in the present moment. If they have not, employ the force of government against them at once.—To Henry Lee. Fitzpatrick 29:34. (1786)

INSURGENCY. See also REVOLUTIONS; SHAYS'S REBELLION.

INTEGRITY, Should Be the Policy of Government.—Let us...as a nation be just; let us fulfill the public contracts, which Congress had undoubtedly a right to make for the purpose of carrying on the war, with the same good faith we suppose ourselves bound to perform our private engagements.—Circular to the States. Fitzpatrick 26:489. (1783.)

INTEGRITY. See also HONESTY; MORAL CHARACTER; MORALITY; VIRTUE.

INTERNATIONAL RELATIONS. See EUROPE; FOREIGN RELATIONS; JAY TREATY; NEUTRALITY; TREATIES.

INTERNATIONAL TRADE. See COMMERCE; FOREIGN TRADE.

INTERSTATE COMMERCE, Federal Control Needed.—We have abundant reason to be convinced that the spirit for trade which pervades these states is not to be restrained; it behooves us, then, to establish just principles; and this, any more than other matters of national concern, cannot be done by thirteen heads differently constructed and organized. The necessity, therefore, of a controlling power is obvious, and why it should be withheld is beyond my comprehension.—To James Warren. Fitzpatrick 28:290. (1785.)

INTERSTATE NAVIGATION, To Provide Great Benefit.—It gives me pleasure to find a spirit for inland navigation prevailing so generally. No country is more capable of improvements in this way than our own, none ...will be more benefited by them; and to begin well, as you justly observe, is all in all.—To Governor William Moultrie. Fitzpatrick 28:439. (1786.)

INTOXICATION. See DRUNKENNESS; LIQUOR; TAVERNS; VICES.

J

JAY TREATY, Washington's Opinion of.—My opinion respecting the treaty is the same now that it was: namely, not favorable to it, but that it is better to ratify it in the manner the Senate have advised...than to suffer matters to remain as they are, unsettled. I find endeavors are not wanting to place it in all the odious points of view of which it is susceptible, and in some which it will not admit.—To the Secretary of State. Fitzpatrick 34:244. (1795.)

JAY TREATY, Opposition to.—I view the opposition which the treaty is receiving from the meetings in different parts of the Union in a very serious light. Not because there is *more* weight in *any* of the objections which are made to it than were foreseen at first, for there are *none* in *some* of them and *gross* misrepresentations in *others*. Nor as it respects myself personally, for this shall have no influence on my conduct, plainly perceiving, and I am accordingly preparing my mind for, the obloquy which disappointment and malice are collecting to heap upon my character. But I am alarmed on account of the effect it may have on, and the advantage the French government may be disposed to make of, the spirit which is at work to cherish a belief in them that the treaty is calculated to favor Great Britain at their expense. Whether they believe or disbelieve these tales, the effect... will be nearly the same; for while they are at war with that power, or so long as the animosity between the two nations exists, it will, no matter at whose expense, be their policy, and it is feared it will be their conduct, to prevent us from being on good terms with Great Britain.... To what length this policy and interest may carry them is problematical; but when they see the people of this country divided, and such a violent opposition given to the measures of their own government, pretendedly in their favor, it may be extremely embarrassing, to say no more of it.

To sum the whole up in a few words, I have never, since I have been in the administration of the government, seen a crisis which, in my judgment, has been so pregnant of interesting events; nor one from which more is to be apprehended.—To the Secretary of State. Fitzpatrick 34:256. (1795.)

JAY TREATY, Widely Scorned and Misrepresented.—At present the cry against the treaty is like that against a mad dog, and everyone, in a manner, seems engaged in running it down....

Washington in 1792 (age 60). Detail from a Revolutionary War depiction by John Trumbull.

It has received the most tortured interpretation, and... the writings against it (which are very industriously circulated) are pregnant of the most abominable misrepresentations.—To Alexander Hamilton. Fitzpatrick 34:262. (1795.)

JEFFERSON (Thomas), His Dispute with Alexander Hamilton.—I regret, deeply regret, the differences in opinion which have arisen and divided you and another principal officer of the government, and wish devoutly there could be an accommodation of them by mutual yieldings.

A measure of this sort would produce harmony and consequent good in our public councils; the contrary will inevitably introduce confusion and serious mischiefs; and for what? because mankind cannot think alike, but would adopt different means to attain the same end. For I will frankly and solemnly declare that I believe the views of both of you are pure and well meant, and that experience alone will decide with respect to the salubrity of the measures which are the subjects of dispute. Why, then, when some of the best citizens in the United States, men of discernment, uniform and tried patriots who have no sinister views to promote but are chaste in their ways of thinking and acting, are to be found some on one side and some on the other of the questions which have caused these agitations, should either of you be so tenacious of your opinions as to make no allowances for those of the other?...I have a great, a sincere esteem and regard for you both, and ardently wish that some line could be marked out by which both of you could walk.—To Thomas Jefferson. Fitzpatrick 32:185. (1792.)

JEFFERSON (Thomas), Washington's Esteem for.—I yesterday received, with sincere regret, your resignation of the office of Secretary of State. Since it has been impossible to prevail upon you to forgo any longer the indulgence of your desire for private life, the event, however anxious I am to avert it, must be submitted to. But I cannot suffer you to leave your station without assuring you that the opinion which I had formed of your integrity and talents, and which dictated your original nomination, has been confirmed by the fullest experience; and

that both have been eminently displayed in the discharge of your duties. Let a conviction of my most earnest prayers for your happiness accompany you in your retirement.—To Thomas Jefferson. Fitzpatrick 33:231. (1794.)

JEFFERSON (Thomas). See also POLITICAL OPINIONS.

JESUS CHRIST, Characteristics of, an Example for National Happiness.—I now make it my earnest prayer that God would have you, and the state over which you preside, in his holy protection; that he would incline the hearts of the citizens to cultivate a spirit of subordination and obedience to government, to entertain a brotherly affection and love for one another, for their fellow citizens of the United States at large, and particularly for their brethren who have served in the field; and finally, that he would most graciously be pleased to dispose us all to do justice, to love mercy, and to demean ourselves with that charity, humility, and pacific temper of mind which were the characteristics of the Divine Author of our blessed religion, and without an humble imitation of whose example in these things we can never hope to be a happy nation.— Circular to the States. Fitzpatrick 26:496. (1783.)

JESUS CHRIST. See also CHRISTIANITY; MORALITY; RELIGION.

JEWS, Washington's Good Wishes for.—May the same wonder-working Deity who long since delivered the Hebrews from their Egyptian oppressors and planted them in the promised land, whose providential agency has lately been conspicuous in establishing

Washington in 1792 (age 60). Water color portrait by Archibald Robertson.

these United States as an independent nation, still continue to water them with the dews of Heaven, and to make the inhabitants of every denomination participate in the temporal and spiritual blessings of that people whose God is Jehovah.—To the Hebrew congregation of the city of Savannah. Sparks 12:186. (1790.)

May the children of the stock of Abraham who dwell in this land continue to merit and enjoy the good will of the other inhabitants, while everyone shall sit in safety under his own vine and fig tree, and there shall be none to make him afraid. May the Father of all mercies scatter light and not darkness in our paths, and make us

all in our several vocations useful here, and in his own due time and way everlastingly happy.—To the Hebrew congregation of Newport, Rhode Island. Philip S. Foner, ed., *George Washington: Selections from His Writings* (New York: International Publishers, 1944), p. 87. (1790.)

JUDICIARY, A Key to National Stability.—I have always been persuaded that the stability and success of the national government, and consequently the happiness of the people of the United States, would depend in a considerable degree on the interpretation and execution of its laws. In my opinion, therefore, it is important that the judiciary system should not only be independent in its operations, but as perfect as possible in its formation.—To the Supreme Court. Fitzpatrick 31:31. (1790.)

K

KNOWLEDGE, Should Be Encouraged.—In my opinion, every effort of genius and all attempts towards improving useful knowledge ought to meet with encouragement in this country.—To Nicholas Pike. Fitzpatrick 28:463. (1786.)

KNOWLEDGE, Essential in a Republic.—Knowledge is in every country the surest basis of public happiness. In one in which the measures of government receive their impression so immediately from the sense of the community as in ours, it is proportionably essential. To the security of a free Constitution it contributes in various ways: by convincing those who are entrusted with the public administration that every valuable end of government is best answered by the enlightened confidence of the people, and by teaching the people themselves to know and to value their own rights; to discern and provide against invasions of them; to distinguish between oppression and the necessary exercise of lawful authority, between burdens proceeding from a disregard to their convenience and those resulting from the inevitable exigencies of society; to discriminate the spirit of liberty from that of licentiousness, cherishing the first, avoiding the last, and uniting a speedy but temperate vigilance against encroachments, with an inviolable respect to the laws.—First Annual Address to Congress. Fitzpatrick 30:493. (1790.)

KNOWLEDGE. See also ARTS AND SCIENCES; BOOKS; EDUCATION; INFORMATION; PERIODICALS; PUBLIC OPINION; REVELATION; SELF-GOVERNMENT.

KNOX (Gen. Henry), Washington's Friendship with.—With respect to General Knox, I can say with truth, there is no man in the United States with whom I have been in habits of greater intimacy, no one whom I have loved more sincerely, nor any for whom I have had a greater friendship.—To President John Adams. Fitzpatrick 36:461. (1798.)

L

LAFAYETTE (Marquis de), Washing-

ton's Love for.—The sentiments of affection and attachment which breathe so conspicuously in all your letters to me are at once pleasing and honorable, and afford me abundant cause to rejoice at the happiness of my acquaintance with you. Your love of liberty, the just sense you entertain of this valuable blessing, and your noble and disinterested exertions in the cause of it, added to the innate goodness of your heart, conspire to render you dear to me; and I think myself happy in being linked with you in bonds of strictest friendship.—To the Marquis de Lafayette. Fitzpatrick 12:50. (1778.)

Your forward zeal in the cause of liberty; your singular attachment to this infant world; your ardent and persevering efforts, not only in America but since your return to France, to serve the United States; your polite attention to Americans; and your strict and uniform friendship for me |have| ripened the first impressions of esteem and attachment which I imbibed for you into such perfect love and gratitude that neither time nor absence can impair.—To the Marquis de Lafayette. Fitzpatrick 16:369. (1779.)

LAFAYETTE (Marquis de), Washington's Emotions on Parting with.—In the moment of our separation upon the road as I traveled, and every hour since, I felt all that love, respect, and attachment for you with which length of years, close connection, and your merits have inspired me. I often asked myself, as our carriages distended, whether that was the last sight I ever should have of you. And though I wished to say no, my fears answered yes. I called to mind the days of my youth, and found they had long since fled to return no more; that I was now descending the hill I had been 52 years climbing and that, though I was blessed with a good constitution, I was of a short-lived family and might soon expect to be entombed in the dreary mansions of my fathers. These things darkened the shades and gave a gloom to the picture, consequently to my prospects of seeing you again; but I will not repine, I have had my day.—To the Marquis de Lafayette. Fitzpatrick 28:7. (1784.)

LAND. See INDIANS; PUBLIC LAND; WEST.

LAWS, Must Be Observed.—Laws or ordinances unobserved, or partially attended to, had better never have been made, because the first is a mere nihil, and the second is productive of much jealousy and discontent.—To James Madison. Fitzpatrick 29:191. (1787.)

If the laws are to be so trampled upon with impunity, and a minority (a small one too) is to dictate to the majority, there is an end put... to republican government, and nothing but anarchy and confusion is to be expected thereafter; for some other man or society may dislike another law, and oppose it with equal propriety, until all laws are prostrate, and everyone (the strongest, I presume) will carve for himself.—To Charles Mynn Thruston. Fitzpatrick 33:465. (1794.)

LAWS, Cannot Please All.—There never was a law yet made... that hit the taste exactly of every man, or every part of the community.—To Daniel Morgan. Fitzpatrick 33:523. (1794.)

LEGISLATURES, Speaking in.— Speak seldom [in legislative bodies] but to important subjects, except such as particularly relate to your constituents, and in the former case make yourself *perfectly* master of the subject. Never exceed a *decent* warmth, and submit your sentiments with diffidence. A dictatorial style, though it may carry conviction, is always accompanied with disgust.—To Bushrod Washington. Fitzpatrick 29:313. (1787.)

LEGISLATURES. See also CONGRESS.

LIBERTY, Must Be Defended.—That no man should scruple or hesitate a moment to use arms in defense of so valuable a blessing [as liberty], on which all the good and evil of life depends, is clearly my opinion; yet arms, I would beg leave to add, should be the last resource, the *dernier resort.*— To George Mason. Fitzpatrick 2:500. (1769.)

LIBERTY, Universal Cause of.—The cause of virtue and liberty is confined to no continent or climate; it comprehends within its capacious limits the wise and good, however dispersed and separated in space or distance.—To the inhabitants of the island of Bermuda. Fitzpatrick 3:475. (1775.)

LIBERTY, The Cause of America.— The cause we are engaged in is so just and righteous that we must try to rise superior to every obstacle in its support.—To Philip Schuyler. Fitzpatrick 4:148. (1775.)

LIBERTY, Spirit of, Since American Revolution.—The rights of mankind, the privileges of the people, and the true principles of liberty seem to have been more generally discussed and better understood throughout Europe since the American Revolution than they were at any former period.—To Thomas Jefferson. Fitzpatrick 29:350. (788.) (1788.)

LIBERTY, Grows Rapidly Once Established.—Liberty, when it begins to take root, is a plant of rapid growth. —To James Madison. Fitzpatrick 29:431. (1788.)

LIBERTY, Future of, Depends on American Experiment. The preservation of the sacred fire of liberty and the destiny of the republican model of government are justly considered as deeply, perhaps as finally, staked on the experiment entrusted to the hands of the American people.—First Inaugural Address. Fitzpatrick 30:294. (1789.)

LIBERTY, Desired for All Mankind. —The impressions naturally produced by similarity of political sentiment are justly to be regarded as causes of national sympathy, calculated to confirm the amicable ties which may otherwise subsist between nations. This reflection, independent of its more particular reference, must dispose every benevolent mind to unite in the wish that a general diffusion of true principles of liberty, assimilating as well as ameliorating the condition of mankind and fostering the maxims of

an ingenuous and virtuous policy, may tend to strengthen the fraternity of the human race, to assuage the jealousies and animosities of its various subdivisions, and to convince them more and more that their true interest and felicity will best be promoted by mutual good will and universal harmony.—To the President of the National Assembly of France. Fitzpatrick 31:206. (1791.)

LIBERTY, Washington's Desire for All to Enjoy.—We do not wish to be the only people who may taste the sweets of an equal and good government; we look with an anxious eye to the time when happiness and tranquility shall prevail in your country, and when all Europe shall be freed from commotions, tumults, and alarms.— To the Marquis de Lafayette. Fitzpatrick 31:326. (1791.)

LIBERTY, American Love of.— Interwoven as is the love of liberty with every ligament of your hearts, no recommendation of mine is necessary to fortify or confirm the attachment. —Farewell Address. Fitzpatrick 35:218. (1796.)

LIBERTY, Safeguarded Best by Stable Government.— For the efficient management of your common interests, in a country so extensive as ours, a government of as much vigor as is consistent with the perfect security of liberty is indispensable. Liberty itself will find in such a government, with powers properly distributed and adjusted, its surest guardian. It is indeed little else than a name where the government is too feeble to withstand the enterprises of faction, to confine each member of the society within the limits prescribed by the laws, and to maintain all in the secure and tranquil enjoyment of the rights of person and property.—Farewell Address. Fitzpatrick 35:226. (1796.)

LIBERTY. See also FREEDOM; INDEPENDENCE; RELIGIOUS FREEDOM; SELF-GOVERNMENT.

LIQUOR, Evils of.—The quantity of spirituous liquors which is a component part of the ration is so large as to endanger, where they might not before exist, habits of intemperance, alike fatal to health and discipline. Experience has repeatedly shown that many soldiers will exchange their rum for other articles, which is productive of the double mischief of subjecting those with whom the exchange is made to the loss of what is far more necessary and to all the consequences of brutal intoxication. The step having been once taken, a change is delicate; but it is believed to be indispensable, and that the temporary evils of a change can bear no proportion to the permanent and immense evils of a continuance of the error.—To the Secretary of War. Fitzpatrick 37:55. (1798.)

LIQUOR. See also DRUNKENNESS; TAVERNS; VICES.

LOVE, Washington's Advice on.—Do not...in your contemplation of the marriage state look for perfect felicity before you consent to wed. Nor conceive, from the fine tales the poets and lovers of old have told us of the transports of mutual love, that heaven has taken its abode on earth. Nor... deceive yourself in supposing that the

only means by which these are to be obtained is to drink deep of the cup and revel in an ocean of love. Love is a mighty pretty thing; but like all other delicious things, it is cloying; and when the first transports of the passion begin to subside, which [they] assuredly will do, and yield, oftentimes too late, to more sober reflections, it serves to evince that love is too dainty a food to live upon *alone*, and ought not to be considered farther than as a necessary ingredient for that matrimonial happiness which results from a combination of causes, none of which are of greater importance than that the object on whom it is placed should possess good sense, good dispositions, and the means of supporting you in the way you have been brought up.... Without these, whatever may be your first impressions of the man, they will end in disappointment; for be assured, and experience will convince you, that there is no truth more certain than that all our enjoyments fall short of our expectations; and to none does it apply with more force than to the gratification of the passions.—To Elizabeth Parke Custis. Fitzpatrick 33:501. (1794.)

Men and women feel the same inclinations towards each other *now* that they always have done, and which they will continue to do until there is a new order of things, and *you*, as others have done, may find, perhaps, that the passions of your sex are easier raised than allayed. Do not, therefore, boast too soon or too strongly of your insensibility to, or resistance of, its powers. In the composition of the human frame there is a good deal of inflammable matter, however dormant it may lie for a time, and like an intimate acquaintance of yours, when the torch is put to it, that which is within you may burst into a blaze. . . .

Love is said to be an involuntary passion, and it is therefore contended that it cannot be resisted. This is true in part only, for like all things else, when nourished and supplied plentifully with aliment, it is rapid in its progress; but let these be withdrawn and it may be stifled in its birth or much stinted in its growth. For example, a woman (the same may be said of the other sex), all beautiful and accomplished, will, while her hand and heart are undisposed of, turn the heads and set the circle in which she moves on fire. Let her marry, and what is the consequence? The madness ceases and all is quiet again. Why? Not because there is any diminution in the charms of the lady, but because there is an end of hope. Hence it follows that love may and therefore ought to be under the guidance of reason, for although we cannot avoid first impressions, we may assuredly place them under guard; and my motives for treating on this subject are to show you, while you remain |single| and retain the resolution to love with moderation, the propriety of adhering to the latter resolution, at least until you have secured your game, and the way by which it may be accomplished.

When the fire is beginning to kindle, and your heart growing warm, propound these questions to it. Who is this invader? Have I a competent

Washington in May 1793 (age 61). Portrait by John Trumbull.

knowledge of him? Is he a man of good character, a man of sense? For, be assured, a sensible woman can never be happy with a fool. What has been his walk in life? Is he a gambler, a spendthrift, or drunkard? Is his fortune sufficient to maintain me in the manner I have been accustomed to live, . . . and is he one to whom my friends can have no reasonable objection? If these interrogatories can be satisfactorily answered, there will remain but one more to be asked; that however, is an important one. Have I sufficient ground to conclude that his affections are engaged by me? Without this the heart of sensibility will struggle against a passion that is not reciprocated—delicacy, custom, or call it by what epithet you will, having precluded all advances on your part. The declaration, without the *most indirect* invitation of yours, must proceed from the man, to render it permanent and valuable, and nothing short of good sense and an easy, unaffected conduct can draw the line between prudery and coquetry. It would be no great departure from truth to say that it rarely happens otherwise than that a thorough-faced coquette dies in celibacy, as a punishment for her attempts to mislead others, by encouraging looks, words, or actions, given for no other purpose than to draw men on to make overtures that they may be rejected.—To Eleanor Parke Curtis. Fitzpatrick 34:91. (1795.)

LOVE. See also MARRIAGE.

M

MAGAZINES. See PERIODICALS.

MAJORITY RULE, Essential to Republican Government.—If the laws are to be . . . trampled upon with impunity, and a minority . . . is to dictate to the majority, there is an end put, at one stroke, to republican government; and nothing but anarchy and confusion is to be expected thereafter. — To Charles Mynn Thruston. Fitzpatrick 33:465. (1794.)

MAJORITY RULE, Fundamental to U.S. Constitution.—|To| yield to the treasonable fury of |a| small . . . portion of the United States would be to violate the fundamental principle of our Constitution, which enjoins that the will of the majority shall prevail.— Sixth Annual Address to Congress. Fitzpatrick 34:30. (1794.)

MAN, Usually Governed by Own Interest.—A small knowledge of human nature will convince us that, with far the greatest part of mankind, interest is the governing principle, and that almost every man is more or less under its influence.—To a committee of Congress. Fitzpatrick 10:363. (1778.)

It is not the public |interest|, but private interest, which influences the generality of mankind, nor can the Americans any longer boast an exception.—To John Laurens. Fitzpatrick 24:421. (1782.)

MAN, Requires Some Regulation.— We have probably had too good an opinion of human nature in forming our confederation. Experience has taught us that men will not adopt and carry into execution measures the best calculated for their own good without the intervention of a coercive power. —To the Secretary for Foreign Affairs. Fitzpatrick 28:502. (1786.)

MAN. See also IMPERFECTION; PASSIONS.

MANUFACTURES, And Agriculture.—Though I would not force the introduction of manufactures by extravagant encouragements and to the prejudice of agriculture, yet I conceive much might be done in that way by women, children, and others without taking one really necessary hand from tilling the earth.—To the Marquis de Lafayette. Fitzpatrick 30:186. (1789.)

MANUFACTURES, Promotion of

Domestic.—I have been writing to our friend General Knox this day, to procure me homespun broadcloth... to make a suit of clothes for myself. I hope it will not be a great while before it will be unfashionable for a gentleman to appear in any other dress. Indeed, we have already been too long subject to British prejudices. I use no porter or cheese in my family but such as is made in America; both those articles may now be purchased of an excellent quality.—To the Marquis de Lafayette. Fitzpatrick 30:187. (1789.)

The promotion of domestic manufactures will, in my conception, be among the swift consequences which may naturally be expected to flow from an energetic government. For myself, having an equal regard for the prosperity of the farming, trading, and manufacturing interests, I will only observe that I cannot conceive the extension of the latter (so far as it may afford employment to a great number of hands which would be otherwise in a manner idle) can be detrimental to the former.—To the Delaware Society for Promoting Domestic Manufactures. Fitzpatrick 30:289. (1789.)

MARRIAGE, Preparation Needed for.—I am now set down to write to you on a subject of importance, and of no small embarrassment to me. My son-in-law and ward, Mr. [John Parke] Custis, has, as I have been informed, paid his addresses to your second daughter [Eleanor Calvert], and having made some progress in her affections has required her in marriage. How far a union of this sort may be agreeable to you, you best can tell, but

I should think myself wanting in candor [were] I not to acknowledge that Miss Nellie's amiable qualifications stand confessed at all hands; and that an alliance with your family will be pleasing to his.

This acknowledgment being made, you must permit me to add, sir, that at this or in any short time, his youth, inexperience, and unripened education [are] and will be insuperable obstacles, in my eye, to the completion of the marriage. As his guardian, I conceive it to be my indispensable duty to endeavor to carry him through a regular course of education, many branches of which, sorry I am to add, he is totally deficient of; and to guard his youth to a more advanced age before an event on which his own peace and the happiness of another [are] to depend takes place—not that I have any doubt of the warmth of his affections, nor, I hope I may add, any fears of a change in them; but at present, I do not conceive that he is capable of bestowing that due attention to the important consequences of a marriage state which [are] necessary to be done by those who are inclined to enter into it; and, of course, am unwilling he should do it till he is. If the affection which they have avowed for each other is fixed upon a solid basis, it will receive no diminution in the course of two or three years, in which time he may prosecute his studies and thereby render himself more deserving of the lady, and useful to society; if, unfortunately (as they are both young), there should be an abatement of affection on either side, or both, it had better precede than follow after marriage.

Delivering my sentiments thus will not, I hope, lead you into a belief that I am desirous of breaking off the match; to postpone it is all I have in view; for I shall recommend it to the young gentleman with the warmth that becomes a man of honor (notwithstanding he did not vouchsafe to consult either his mother or me on the occasion) to consider himself as much engaged to your daughter as if the indissoluble knot |were| tied; and, as the surest means of effecting this, to stick close to his studies (in which |recommendation| I flatter myself you will join me), by which he will, in a great measure, avoid those little flirtations with other girls which may, by dividing the attention, contribute not a little to divide the affection.—To Benedict Calvert. Fitzpatrick 3:129. (1773.)

MARRIAGE, Advice on.—I never did, nor do I believe I ever shall, give advice to a woman who is setting out on a matrimonial voyage; first, because I never could advise one to marry without her own consent; and secondly, because I know it is to no purpose to advise her to refrain when she has obtained it. A woman very rarely asks an opinion or requires advice on such an occasion till her resolution is formed; and then it is with the hope and expectation of obtaining a sanction, not that she means to be governed by your disapprobation, that she applies. In a word, the plain English of the application may be summed up in these words: "I wish you to think as I do; but if unhappily you differ from me in opinion, my heart, I must confess, is

Washington in 1793–94 (age 61–62). Portrait by William Williams. This portrait was ordered by Washington's Masonic lodge; Williams was to "paint him as he is." The painting shows a black mole under the right ear, a scar on the left cheek (said to have come from lancing an ulcerated tooth), and smallpox scars on Washington's nose and cheeks.

fixed, and I have gone too far now to retract."...I will give her my opinion of the measure, not of the man, with candor, and to the following effect: I never expected you would spend the residue of your days in widowhood; but in a matter so important, and so interesting to yourself, children, and connections, I wish you would make a prudent choice, to do which, many considerations are necessary, such as the family and connections of the man, his fortune (which is not the most essential in my eye), the line of conduct he has observed, and disposition and frame of his mind. You should consider what prospect there is of his proving kind and affectionate to you;

just, generous, and attentive to your children; and how far his connections will be agreeable to you; for when they are once formed, agreeable or not, the die being cast, your fate is fixed.—To Lund Washington. Fitzpatrick 27:157. (1783.)

MARRIAGE, The Foundation of Happiness.—I have always considered marriage as the most interesting event of one's life, the foundation of happiness or misery.—To Burwell Bassett. Fitzpatrick 28:152. (1785.)

MARRIAGE, Joy of.—In my estimation, more permanent and genuine happiness is to be found in the sequestered walks of connubial life than in the giddy rounds of promiscuous pleasure, or the more tumultuous and imposing scenes of successful ambition.—To Charles Armand-Tuffin. Fitzpatrick 28:514. (1786.)

MARRIAGE, Washington's Humorous Comments on.—A wife! Well, my dear Marquis, I can hardly refrain from smiling to find you are caught at last. I saw, by the eulogium you often made on the happiness of domestic life in America, that you had swallowed the bait and that you would as surely be taken, one day or another, as that you were a philosopher and a soldier. So your day has at length come. I am glad of it, with all my heart and soul. It is quite good enough for you. Now you are well served for coming to fight in favor of the American rebels, all the way across the Atlantic Ocean, by catching that terrible contagion—domestic felicity—which,... like the smallpox or the plague, a man can have only once in his life, because it

commonly lasts him (at least with us in America—I don't know how you manage these matters in France) for his whole lifetime. And yet after all the maledictions you so richly merit on the subject, the worst wish which I can find in my heart to make against Madame de Chastellux and yourself is that you may neither of you ever get the better of this same—domestic felicity—during the entire course of your mortal existence.—To the Marquis de Chastellux. Fitzpatrick 29:183. (1788.)

MARRIAGE. See also LOVE.

MERIT, Rarely Unrewarded.—Merit rarely goes unrewarded.—To Bushrod Washington. Fitzpatrick 26:40. (1783.)

MILITARY ACADEMY, Establishment of a.—The institution of a military academy is...recommended by cogent reasons. However pacific the general policy of a nation may be, it ought never to be without an adequate stock of military knowledge for emergencies. The first would impair the energy of its character, and both would hazard its safety, or expose it to greater evils when war could not be avoided. Besides that, war might often not depend upon its own choice. In proportion as the observance of pacific maxims might exempt a nation from the necessity of practicing the rules of the military art ought to be its care in preserving, and transmitting by proper establishments, the knowledge of that art. Whatever arguments may be drawn from particular examples, superficially viewed, a thorough examination of the subject will evince that the art of war is at once comprehensive and complicated; that it demands much previous study; and that the possession of it, in its most improved and perfect state, is always of great moment to the security of a nation. This, therefore, ought to be a serious care of every government; and for this purpose an academy, where a regular course of instruction is given, is an obvious expedient, which different nations have successfully employed.—Eighth Annual Address to Congress. Fitzpatrick 35:317. (1796.)

The establishment of an institution of this kind, upon a respectable and extensive basis, has ever been considered by me as an object of primary importance to this country; and while I was in the chair of government I omitted no proper opportunity of recommending it, in my public speeches and other ways, to the attention of the [Congress].—To Alexander Hamilton. Fitzpatrick 37:473. (1799.)

MILITIA, In French and Indian War. —The waste of provision they make is unaccountable; no method or order in being served or purchasing at the best rates, but quite the reverse. Allowance for each man, as other soldiers do, they look upon as the highest indignity, and would sooner starve than carry a few days' provision on their backs for convenience. But upon their march, when breakfast is wanted, [they] knock down the first beef etc. they meet with, and, after regaling themselves, march on until dinner, when they take the same method, and so for supper likewise, to the great oppression of the people. Or, if they chance to impress cattle for provision, the valuation is left

to ignorant and indifferent neighbors, who have suffered by those practices and, despairing of their pay, exact high prices, and thus the public is imposed on at all events. I might add [that] I believe that for the want of proper laws to govern the militia by (for I cannot ascribe it to any other cause), they are obstinate, self-willed, perverse, of little or no service to the people, and very burdensome to the country. Every mean individual has his own crude notions of things and must undertake to direct. If his advice is neglected, he thinks himself slighted, abased, and injured; and, to redress his wrongs, will depart for his home. These, sir, are literally matters of fact, partly from persons of undoubted veracity, but chiefly from my own observations.—To Governor Robert Dinwiddie. Fitzpatrick 1:493. (1756.)

MILITIA, Problems with, in Revolutionary War.—The dependence which the Congress has placed upon the militia has already greatly injured, and I fear will totally ruin, our cause. Being subject to no control themselves, they introduce disorder among the troops [we] have attempted to discipline, while the change in their living brings on sickness; this makes them impatient to get home, which spreads universally and introduces abominable desertion. —To John Augustine Washington. Fitzpatrick 6:96. (1776.)

To place any dependence upon the militia is, assuredly, resting upon a broken staff. Men just dragged from the tender scenes of domestic life, unaccustomed to the din of arms, totally unacquainted with every kind of military skill, which being followed by a want of confidence in themselves when opposed to troops regularly trained, disciplined, and appointed, superior in knowledge and superior in arms, makes them timid and ready to fly from their own shadows. Besides, the sudden change in their manner of living (particularly in the lodging) brings on sickness in many, impatience in all, and such an unconquerable desire of returning to their respective homes that it produces not only shameful and scandalous desertions among themselves, but infuses the like spirit in others. Again, men accustomed to unbounded freedom and no control cannot brook the restraint which is indispensably necessary to the good order and government of any army.— To the President of Congress. Fitzpatrick 6:110. (1776.)

My first wish is that Congress may be convinced of the propriety of relying as little as possible upon militia, and of the necessity of raising a larger standing army than they have voted. The saving in the article of stores, provisions, and in a thousand other things by having nothing to do with militia would amply support a large army which (well officered) would daily be improving instead of continuing a destructive, expensive, and disorderly mob. I am clearly of opinion that if forty thousand men had been kept in constant pay since the first commencement of hostilities, and the militia had been excused doing duty during that period, the continent would have saved money. When I reflect on the losses we have sustained for want of good troops, the certainty of this is placed beyond a doubt in my mind.... In my opinion, if any dependence is placed on militia another year, the Congress will deceive themselves. When danger is a little removed from them, they will not turn out at all. When it comes home to them, the well affected, instead of flying to arms to defend themselves, are busily employed in removing their families and effects, while the disaffected are concerting measures to make their submission [to the enemy], and spread terror and dismay all around to induce others to follow [their] example.—To the President of Congress. Fitzpatrick 6:332. (1776.)

We find, sir, that the enemy are daily gathering strength from the disaffected; this strength, like a snowball, by rolling will increase unless some means can be devised to check effectually the progress of the enemy's arms. Militia may possibly do it for a little while; but in a little while also, the militia of those states which have been frequently called upon will not turn out at all, or with so much reluctance and sloth as to amount to the same thing. Instance New Jersey! Witness Pennsylvania! Could anything but the River Delaware have saved Philadelphia? Can anything... be more destructive to the recruiting service than giving ten dollars' bounty for six weeks' service of the militia, who come in you cannot tell how; go, you cannot tell when; and act, you cannot tell where; consume your provisions, exhaust your stores, and leave you at last in a critical moment.—To the President of Congress. Fitzpatrick 6:403. (1776.)

MILITIA, Not Adequate by Itself for Modern Warfare.—Regular troops alone are equal to the exigencies of modern war, as well for defense as offense, and whenever a substitute is attempted it must prove illusory and ruinous. No militia will ever acquire the habits necessary to resist a regular force. Even those nearest the seat of war are only valuable as light troops to be scattered in the woods and plague rather than do serious injury to the enemy.... The firmness requisite for the real business of fighting is only to be attained by a constant course of discipline and service. I have never yet been witness to a single instance that can justify a different opinion; and it is most earnestly to be wished [that] the liberties of America may no longer be trusted in any material degree to so precarious a dependence.—To the President of Congress. Fitzpatrick 20:49. (1780.)

MILITIA, Important to the United States.—There can be little doubt but [that] Congress will recommend a proper peace establishment for the United States, in which a due attention will be paid to the importance of placing the militia of the Union upon a regular and respectable footing. If this should be the case, I would beg leave to urge the great advantage of it in the strongest terms. The militia of this country must be considered as the palladium of our security and the first effectual resort in case of hostility. It is essential, therefore, that the same system should pervade the whole; that

the formation and discipline of the militia of the continent should be absolutely uniform, and the same species of arms, accoutrements, and military apparatus should be introduced in every part of the United States.—Circular to the States. Fitzpatrick 26:494. (1783.)

The militia... is certainly an object of primary importance, whether viewed in reference to the national security, to the satisfaction of the community, or to the preservation of order.—To the Senate and the House of Representatives. Fitzpatrick 31:402. (1791.)

MILITIA. See also ARMY; REVOLUTIONARY WAR.

MISFORTUNES, Proper Response to. —It is our duty to make the best of our misfortunes, and not to suffer passion to interfere with our interest and the public good.—To William Heath. Fitzpatrick 12:365. (1778.)

MISFORTUNES. See also TRIBULATIONS.

MISTAKES, Easier to Prevent Than to Correct.—It is easier to prevent than to remedy an evil.—To Richard Henry Lee. Fitzpatrick 28:12. (1784.)

MISTAKES. See also ERRORS.

MOBOCRACY, To Be Dreaded.— The tumultous populace of large cities are ever to be dreaded. Their indiscriminate violence prostrates for the time all public authority, and its consequences are sometimes extensive and terrible.—To the Marquis de Lafayette. Fitzpatrick 31:324. (1791.)

MOBOCRACY, Leads to Extremes. —The just medium cannot be expected to be found in a moment; the

Washington in about 1794 (age 62?). Miniature portrait by Walter Robertson.

spectable characters speak of a monarchial form of government without horror. From thinking proceeds speaking; thence to acting is often but a single step. But how irrevocable and tremendous! what a triumph for our enemies to verify their predictions! what a triumph for the advocates of despotism to find that we are incapable of governing ourselves, and that systems founded on the basis of equal liberty are merely ideal and fallacious! —To the Secretary for Foreign Affairs. Fitzpatrick 28:503. (1786.)

I am fully of opinion that those who lean to a monarchial government have either not consulted the public mind, or...they live in a region...much more productive of monarchial ideas than...the southern states, where, from the habitual distinctions which have always existed among the people, one would have expected the first generation [of monarchists], and the most rapid growth of them.—To James Madison. Fitzpatrick 29:190. (1787.)

MONARCHS, Glory of, Depends on People's Prosperity.—It is a wonder to me there should be found a single monarch who does not realize that his own glory and felicity must depend on the prosperity and happiness of his people. How easy is it for a sovereign to do that which shall not only immortalize his name, but attract the blessings of millions.—To the Marquis de Lafayette. Fitzpatrick 29:524. (1788.)

MONEY, Need for Coinage.—A coinage of gold, silver, and copper [is] a measure which in my opinion is become indispensably necessary....

first vibrations always go to the extremes, and cool reason, which can alone establish a permanent and equal government, is as little to be expected in the tumults of popular commotion as an attention to the liberties of the people is to be found in the dark divan of a despotic tyrant.—To the Marquis de Lafayette. Fitzpatrick 32:54. (1792.)

MONARCHIES, Often Ruled by Whim.—The politics of princes are fluctuating, more guided often by a particular prejudice, whim, or interest than by extensive views of policy.—To the President of Congress. Fitzpatrick 19:407. (1780.)

MONARCHISM, American Supporters of.—I am told that even re-

Without a coinage, or [unless] some stop can be put to the cutting and clipping of money, our dollars, pistareens, etc. will be converted (as Teague says) into *five* quarters; and a man must travel with a pair of money scales in his pocket or run the risk of receiving gold at one-fourth less by weight than it counts.—To William Grayson. Fitzpatrick 28:233. (1785.)

MONEY, Borrowing.—There is no practice more dangerous than that of borrowing money.—To Samuel Washington. Fitzpatrick 35:498. (1797.)

MONEY. See also CURRENCY; INFLATION.

MORAL CHARACTER, Of Greatest Importance.—A good moral character is the first essential in a man.... It is therefore highly important that you should endeavor not only to be learned but virtuous.—To George Steptoe Washington. Fitzpatrick 31:163. (1790.)

MORAL CHARACTER. See also HONESTY; INTEGRITY.

MORALITY, Only Sure Foundation of National Happiness.—Purity of morals [is] the only sure foundation of public happiness in any country.— General Orders. Fitzpatrick 13:118. (1778.)

MORALITY, The Duty of a Free People.—While I reiterate the professions of my dependence upon Heaven as the source of all public and private blessings, I will observe that the general prevalence of piety, philanthropy, honesty, industry, and economy seems, in the ordinary course of

human affairs, particularly necessary for advancing and confirming the happiness of our country. While all men within our territories are protected in worshipping the Deity according to the dictates of their consciences, it is rationally to be expected from them in return that they will be emulous of evincing the sanctity of their professions by the innocence of their lives and the beneficence of their actions; for no man who is profligate in his morals, or a bad member of the civil community, can possibly be a true Christian or a credit to his own religious society.—To the General Assembly of the Presbyterian Church in the United States. Sparks 12:152. (1789.)

MORALITY, Inseparable from Religion.—Let us with caution indulge the supposition that morality can be maintained without religion. Whatever may be conceded to the influence of refined education on minds of peculiar structure, reason and experience both forbid us to expect that national morality can prevail in exclusion of religious principle.—Farewell Address. Fitzpatrick 35:229. (1796.)

MORALITY. See also HAPPINESS; RELIGION; VIRTUE.

MORRIS (Gouverneur), Objections to Diplomatic Service of.—While your abilities, knowledge in the affairs of this country, and disposition to serve it were adduced and asserted on one hand [by the U.S. Senate, on President Washington's nomination of Morris as American minister to France], you were charged on the other hand with levity and imprudence of conversation and conduct. It was urged that your habits of expression indicated a hauteur disgusting to those who happen to differ from you in sentiment; and among a people who study civility and politeness more than any other nation, it must be displeasing. [It was also urged] that in France you were considered as a favorer of aristocracy, and unfriendly to its revolution (I suppose they meant constitution); that under this impression you could not be an acceptable public character, [and] of consequence would not be able, however willing, to promote the interest of this country in an essential degree; ... that the promptitude with which your lively and brilliant imagination is displayed allows too little time for deliberation and correction, and is the primary cause of those sallies which too often offend, and of that ridicule of characters which begets enmity not easy to be forgotten, but which might easily be avoided if it [were] under the control of more caution and prudence; in a word, that it is indispensably necessary that more circumspection should be observed by our representatives abroad than they conceive you are inclined to adopt.

In this statement you have the pros and cons; by reciting them I give you a proof of my friendship, if I give none of my policy or judgment. I do it on the presumption that a mind conscious of its own rectitude fears not what is said of it, but will bid defiance to and despise shafts that are not barbed with accusations against honor or integrity; and because I have the fullest confidence (supposing the allegations to be founded in whole or part) that you would find no difficulty, being apprised of the exceptionable light in which they are viewed, and considering yourself as the representative of this country, to effect a change, and thereby silence, in the most unequivocal and satisfactory manner, your political opponents.—To Gouverneur Morris. Fitzpatrick 31:468. (1792.)

MOUNT VERNON, Visitors at.— My house may be compared to a well-resorted tavern, as scarcely any strangers who are going from north to south, or from south to north, do not spend a day or two at it.—To Mary Ball Washington. Fitzpatrick 29:160. (1787.)

MOUNT VERNON, Description of Estate at.—No estate in united America is more pleasantly situated than this. It lies in a high, dry, and healthy country three hundred miles by water from the sea, and ... on one of the finest rivers in the world. Its margin is washed by more than ten miles of tidewater, from the bed of which, and the innumerable coves, inlets, and small marshes with which it abounds, an inexhaustible fund of rich mud may be drawn as a manure, either to be used separately or in a compost, according to the judgment of the farmer. It is situated in a latitude between the extremes of heat and cold, and is the same distance by land and water, with good roads and the best navigation (to and) from the federal city, Alexandria, and Georgetown; distant from the first twelve, from the second nine, and from the last sixteen miles....

The soil of the tract I am speaking [of] is a good loam, more inclined however to clay than sand. From use, and I might add abuse, it is become more and more consolidated, and of course heavier to work. The greater part is a grayish clay; some part is a dark mould; a very little is inclined to sand; and scarcely any to stone. A husbandman's wish would not lay the farms more level than they are, and yet some of the fields (but in no great degree) are washed into gullies, from which all of them have not as yet been recovered.

[The Potomac] River, which encompasses the land the distance above mentioned, is well supplied with various kinds of fish at all seasons of the year, and in the spring with the greatest profusion of shad, herring, bass, carp, perch, sturgeon, etc. Several valuable fisheries appertain to the estate; the whole shore, in short, is one entire fishery.

There are . . . four farms besides that at the mansion house; these four contain 3260 acres of cultivable land, to which some hundreds more adjoining . . . might be added if a greater quantity should be required.

On what is called Union Farm (containing 928 acres of arable and meadow) there is a newly erected brick barn, equal perhaps to any in America, and for conveniences of all sorts, particularly for sheltering and feeding horses, cattle, etc., scarcely to be exceeded anywhere. A new house is now building in a central position, not far from the barn, for the overlooker; which will have two rooms 16 by 18 feet below, and one or two above

nearly of the same size. Convenient thereto is sufficient accommodation for fifty-odd Negroes (old and young). . . .

Besides these, a little without the limits of the farm . . . are one or two other houses, very pleasantly situated, and which, in case this farm should be divided into two (as it formerly was), would answer well for the eastern division. The buildings thus enumerated are all that stand on the premises.

Dogue Run Farm (650 acres) has a small but new building for the overlooker, one room only below and the same above, sixteen by twenty feet each, decent and comfortable for its size. It has also covering for forty-odd Negroes, similar to what is mentioned on Union Farm. It has a new circular barn, now finishing, on a new construction; well calculated, it is conceived, for getting grain out of the straw more expeditiously than in the usual mode of threshing. There are good sheds also erecting, sufficient to cover thirty work horses and oxen.

Muddy Hole Farm (476 acres) has a house for the overlooker, in size and appearance nearly like that at Dogue Run, but older, the same kind of covering for about thirty Negroes, and a tolerably good barn, with stables for the work horses.

River Farm, which is the largest of the four and separated from the others by Little Hunting Creek, contains 1207 acres of plowable land, has an overlooker's house of one large and two small rooms below, and one or two above; sufficient covering for fifty or sixty Negroes, like those before mentioned; a large barn and stables, gone much to decay, but |these| will be replaced next year with new ones....

On the four farms there are fifty-four draft horses, twelve working mules, and a sufficiency of oxen broken to the yoke; the precise number I am unable this moment to ascertain, as they are comprehended in the aggregate of the black cattle. Of the latter there are 317; of sheep, 634; of hogs, many; but as these run pretty much at large in the woodland (which is all under fence), the number is uncertain.—To Arthur Young. Fitzpatrick 33:175. (1793.)

MOURNING, Requires Time.—Nature, no doubt, must feel severely before *calm* resignation will overcome it.—To Henry Knox. Fitzpatrick 29:261. (1787.)

MOURNING. See also DEATH.

N

NATIONAL DEBT, Resources to Repay.—No nation will have it more in its power to repay what it borrows than this. Our debts are hitherto small. The vast and valuable tracts of unlocated lands, the variety and fertility of climates and soils, |and| the advantages of every kind which we possess for commerce insure to this country a rapid advancement in population and prosperity, and a certainty, its independence being established, of redeeming in a short term of years the comparatively inconsiderable debts it may have occasion to contract.—To John Laurens. Fitzpatrick 21:109. (1781.)

NATIONAL DEBT, Should Be Paid Without Delay.—I entertain a strong hope that the state of the national finances is now sufficiently matured to enable you to enter upon a systematic and effectual arrangement for the regular redemption and discharge of the public debt, according to the right which has been reserved to the government. No measure can be more desirable, whether viewed with an eye to its intrinsic importance or to the general sentiment and wish of the nation.—Fourth Annual Address to Congress. Fitzpatrick 32:211. (1792.)

No pecuniary consideration is more urgent than the regular redemption and discharge of the public debt; on none can delay be more injurious, or an economy of time more valuable.—Fifth Annual Address to Congress. Fitzpatrick 33:168. (1793.)

The time which has elapsed since the commencement of our fiscal measures has developed our pecuniary resources so as to open a way for a definitive plan for the redemption of the public debt. It is believed that the result is such as to encourage Congress to consummate this work without delay. Nothing can more promote the permanent welfare of the nation, and nothing would be more grateful to our constituents. Indeed, whatsoever is unfinished of our system of public credit cannot be benefited by procrastination; and as far as may be practicable, we ought to place that credit on grounds which cannot be disturbed, and to prevent that progressive accumulation of debt which must ultimately endanger all governments.

Washington in November 1794 (age 62). Portrait by Adolf Ulric Wertmuller.

—Sixth Annual Address to Congress. Fitzpatrick 34:36. (1794.)

It will afford me heartfelt satisfaction to concur in such further measures as will ascertain to our country the prospect of a speedy extinguishment of the debt. Posterity may have cause to regret if, from any motive, intervals of tranquility are left unimproved for accelerating this valuable end.—Eighth Annual Address to Congress. Fitzpatrick 35:319. (1796.)

NATIONAL DEBT, Avoid When Possible, Repay When Incurred.—As a very important source of strength and security, cherish public credit. One method of preserving it is to use it as sparingly as possible, avoiding occa-

sions of expense by cultivating peace, but remembering also that timely disbursements to prepare for danger frequently prevent much greater disbursements to repel it; avoiding likewise the accumulation of debt, not only by shunning occasions of expense, but by vigorous exertions in time of peace to discharge the debts which unavoidable wars may have occasioned, not ungenerously throwing upon posterity the burden which we ourselves ought to bear.—Farewell Address. Fitzpatrick 35:230. (1796.)

NATIONAL DEBT. See also BORROWING; DEBT; FINANCES; PUBLIC LAND.

NATIONAL DEFENSE, A Solemn Duty.—Although we cannot, by the best concerted plans, absolutely command success, although the race is not always to the swift or the battle to the strong, yet without presumptuously waiting for the miracles to be wrought in our favor, it is our *indispensable duty*, with the deepest gratitude to Heaven for the past and humble confidence in its smiles on our future operations, to make use of all the means in our power for our defense and security.—Circular to the States. Fitzpatrick 23:478. (1782.)

NATIONAL DEFENSE, A Key to Peace.—There is nothing which will so soon produce a speedy and honorable peace as a state of preparation for war, and we must either do this or lay our account for a patched-up, inglorious peace, after all the toil, blood, and treasure we have spent. This has been my uniform opinion, a doctrine I have endeavored, amid the torrent of expectation of an approaching peace, to inculcate; the event, I am sure, will justify me in it.—To James McHenry. Fitzpatrick 25:151. (1782.)

NATIONAL DEFENSE, And Readiness for War.—To be prepared for war is one of the most effectual means of preserving peace.—First Annual Address to Congress. Fitzpatrick 30:491. (1790.)

The United States ought not to indulge a persuasion that, contrary to the order of human events, they will forever keep at a distance those painful appeals to arms with which the history of every other nation abounds. There is a rank due to the United States among nations which will be withheld, if not absolutely lost, by the reputation of weakness. If we desire to avoid insult, we must be able to repel it; if we desire to secure peace, one of the most powerful instruments of our rising prosperity, it must be known that we are at all times ready for war.—Fifth Annual Address to Congress. Fitzpatrick 33:165. (1793.)

NATIONAL DEFENSE, Relies on Manufactures.—A free [people's]... safety and interest require that they should promote such manufactories as tend to render them independent [of] others for essential, particularly for military, supplies.—First Annual Address to Congress. Fitzpatrick 30:491. (1790.)

NATIONAL DEFENSE, Requires a High State of Preparedness.—The safety of the United States, under divine protection, ought to rest on the basis of systematic and solid arrangements, exposed as little as possible to

the hazard of fortuitous circumstances.—To the Senate and the House of Representatives. Fitzpatrick 31:403. (1791.)

NATIONAL DEFENSE. See also ARMY; DEFENSE; MILITIA; NAVY; PLACE; REVOLUTIONARY WAR; WAR.

NATIONAL UNIVERSITY, Desirable.—That a national university in this country is a thing to be desired has always been my decided opinion; and the appropriation of ground and funds for it in the federal city have long been contemplated and talked of.—To the Vice President. Fitzpatrick 34:23. (1794.)

NATIONAL UNIVERSITY, Establishment of, Recommended.—A plan for the establishment of a university in the federal city has frequently been the subject of conversation.... It has always been a source of serious reflection and sincere regret with me that the youth of the United States should be sent to foreign countries for the purpose of education. Although there are doubtless many under these circumstances who escape the danger of contracting principles unfriendly to republican government, yet we ought to deprecate the hazard attending ardent and susceptible minds from being too strongly and too early prepossessed in favor of other political systems, before they are capable of appreciating their own. For this reason I have greatly wished to see a plan adopted by which the arts, sciences, and belles lettres could be taught in their fullest extent, thereby embracing all the advantages of European tuition with the means of acquiring the liberal knowledge which is necessary to qualify our citizens for the exigencies of public as well as private life; and (which with me is a consideration of great magnitude), by assembling the youth from the different parts of this rising republic, contributing, from their intercourse and interchange of information, to the removal of prejudices which might perhaps sometimes arise from local circumstances. The federal city, from its centrality and the advantages which in other respects it must have over any other place in the United States, ought to be preferred as a proper site for such a university. And if a plan can be adopted upon a scale as extensive as I have described, and the execution of it shall commence under favorable auspices, in a reasonable time, with a fair prospect of success, I will grant, in perpetuity, fifty shares in the navigation of [the] Potomac River towards the endowment of it.—To the commissioners of the District of Columbia. Fitzpatrick 34:106. (1795.)

I have heretofore proposed to the consideration of Congress the expediency of establishing a national university.... The assembly to which I address myself is too enlightened not to be fully sensible how much a flourishing state of the arts and sciences contributes to national prosperity and reputation. True it is that our country, much to its honor, contains many seminaries of learning highly respectable and useful; but the funds upon which they rest are too narrow to command the ablest professors in the different departments of liberal knowledge for the institution contemplated, though they would be excellent auxiliaries. Among the motives to such an institution, the assimilation of the principles, opinions, and manners of our countrymen by the common education of a portion of our youth from every quarter well deserves attention. The more homogeneous our citizens can be made in these particulars, the greater will be our prospect of permanent union; and a primary object of such a national institution should be the education of our youth in the science of *government*. In a republic, what species of knowledge can be equally important? and what duty more pressing on its legislature than to patronize a plan for communicating it to those who are to be the future guardians of the liberties of the country?—Eighth Annual Address to Congress. Fitzpatrick 35:316. (1796.)

NATIONAL UNIVERSITY, Should Be in Nation's Capital.—I had but little hesitation in giving the federal district a preference of all other places for this institution.... As this seminary is contemplated for the completion of education and study of the sciences (not for boys in their rudiments), it will afford the students an opportunity of attending the debates in Congress, and thereby becoming more liberally and better acquainted with the principles of law and government.—To Thomas Jefferson. Fitzpatrick 34:147. (1795.)

NATIONAL UNIVERSITY, Could Reduce Local Prejudices.—That which would render it of the highest importance, in my opinion, is that [in] the juvenile period of life, when friendships are formed and habits established that will stick by one, the youth or young men from different parts of the United States would be assembled together, and would by degrees discover that there was not that cause for those jealousies and prejudices which one part of the Union had imbibed against another part; of course, sentiments of more liberality in the general policy of the country would result from it. What but the mixing of people from different parts of the United States during the |Revolutionary| War rubbed off these impressions? A century in the ordinary intercourse would not have accomplished what the seven years' association in arms did; but that ceasing, prejudices are beginning to revive again, and never will be eradicated so effectually by any other means as the intimate intercourse of characters in early life who, in all probability, will be at the head of the councils of this country in a more advanced stage of it.—To Alexander Hamilton. Fitzpatrick 35:199. (1796.)

NATIONAL UNIVERSITY, Money Willed to.—I give and bequeath in perpetuity the fifty shares which I hold in the Potomac Company . . . towards the endowment of a *university* to be established within the limits of the District of Columbia, under the auspices of the general government, if that government should incline to extend a fostering hand towards it.— Last Will and Testament. Fitzpatrick 37:280. (1799.)

NATIONAL UNIVERSITY. See also EDUCATION.

NAVY, Beginning of American, During Revolutionary War.—I am glad to hear the vessels for the lakes are going on with such industry. Maintaining the superiority over the water is certainly of infinite importance. I trust neither courage nor activity will be wanting in those to whom the business is committed.—To Horatio Gates. Fitzpatrick 5:433. (1776.)

NAVY, Necessary to Protect Commerce.—To an active external commerce, the protection of a naval force is indispensable.—Eighth Annual Address to Congress. Fitzpatrick 35:314. (1796.)

NAVY, Helps Protect Neutrality.—It is in our own experience that the most sincere neutrality is not a sufficient guard against the depredation of nations at war. To secure respect to a neutral flag requires a naval force, organized and ready to vindicate it from insult or aggression. This may even prevent the necessity of going to war, by discouraging belligerent powers from committing such violations of the rights of the neutral party as may, first or last, leave no other option.—Eighth Annual Address to Congress. Fitzpatrick 35:314. (1796.)

NAVY, Should Be Created.—These considerations invite the United States to look to the means, and to set about the gradual creation of a navy. The increasing progress of their navigation promises them, at no distant period, the requisite supply of seamen; and their means, in other respects, favor the undertaking. It is an encouragement, likewise, that their particular situation will give weight and influ-

ence to a moderate naval force in their hands. Eighth Annual Address to Congress. Fitzpatrick 35:314. (1796.)
NEUTRALITY, The Course of Wisdom.—Separated as we are by a world of water from other nations, if we are wise we shall surely avoid being drawn into the labyrinth of their politics and involved in their destructive wars.— To the Chevalier de la Luzerne. Fitzpatrick 29:406. (1788.)
NEUTRALITY, The Desire of America.—I believe it is the sincere wish of united America to have nothing to do with the political intrigues or the squabbles of European nations; but, on the contrary, to exchange commodities and live in peace and amity with all the inhabitants of the earth.—To the Earl of Buchan. Fitzpatrick 32:428. (1793.)
NEUTRALITY, Requires Discipline and Restraint.—Having determined, as far as lay within the power of the executive, to keep this country in a state of neutrality, I have made my public conduct accord with the system; and while so acting as a public character, consistency and propriety as a private man forbid those intemperate expressions in favor of one nation, or to the prejudice of another, which many have indulged themselves in, and I will venture to add, to the embarrassment of government, without producing any good to the country.— To Governor Henry Lee. Fitzpatrick 33:479. (1794.)
NEUTRALITY, Allowed Constitutional Government to Mature.—With me, a predominant motive has been to endeavor to gain time to our country

to settle and mature its yet recent institutions, and to progress without interruption to that degree of strength and consistency which is necessary to give it, humanly speaking, the command of its own fortunes.—Farewell Address. Fitzpatrick 35:237. (1796.)
NEUTRALITY. See also EUROPE; FOREIGN RELATIONS.
NEW YORK, Congress Prohibited Burning of.—Had I been left to the dictates of my own judgment, New York should have been laid in ashes before I |retreated from| it; to this end I applied to Congress, but was absolutely forbidden. That they will have cause to repent the order, I have not a moment's doubt of, nor ever had, as it was obvious to me (covered as it may be by their ships) that it will be next to impossible for us to dispossess |the British| of it again, as all their supplies come by water, while ours were derived by land. Besides this, by |our| leaving it standing, the enemy are furnished with warm and comfortable barracks in which their whole force may be concentrated, the place secured by a small garrison (if they choose it) having their ships around it, and only a narrow neck of land to defend, and their principal force left at large to act against us or to remove to any other place for the purpose of harassing us. This, in my judgment, may be set down |as| one of the capital errors of Congress.... In speaking of New York, I...forgot to mention that Providence, or some good honest fellow, has done more for us than we were disposed to do for ourselves, as near one-fourth of the city is supposed to be

consumed |by a recent fire|. However, enough of it remains to answer |the enemy's| purposes.—To Lund Washington. Fitzpatrick 37:532. (1776.)

NEWSPAPERS, Abuse in.—If the government and the officers of it are to be the constant theme for newspaper abuse, and this too without condescending to investigate the motives or the facts, it will be impossible, I conceive, for any man living to manage the helm or to keep the machine together.—To Edmund Randolph. Fitzpatrick 32:137. (1792.)

NEWSPAPERS, Unreliability of.—There is so little dependence on newspaper publications, which take whatever complexion the editors please to give them, that persons at a distance, who have no other means of information, are oftentimes at a loss to form an opinion on the most important occurrences.—To Oliver Wolcott. Fitzpatrick 35:447. (1797.)

NEWSPAPERS. See also PERIODICALS; PROPAGANDA; PUBLICATIONS.

NOBILITY, Titles of.—It appears to be incompatible with the principles of our national constitution to admit the introduction of any kind of nobility, knighthood, or distinctions of a similar nature among the citizens of our republic.—To Jean de Heintz. Fitzpatrick 27:310. (1784.)

NONIMPORTATION, Washington's Support of.—If there are any articles contained in either of the respective invoices (paper only excepted) which are taxed by act of Parliament for the purpose of raising a revenue in America, it is my express

Washington in early 1795 (age 63). Portrait by Gilbert Stuart.

desire and request that they may not be sent, as I have very heartily entered into an association not to import any article which now is or hereafter shall be taxed for this purpose until the said act or acts are repealed. I am therefore particular in mentioning this matter, as I am fully determined to adhere religiously to it, and may perhaps have written for some things unwittingly which may be under these circumstances.—To Robert Cary & Company. Fitzpatrick 2:512. (1769.)

NONIMPORTATION, Of British Goods.—With you I think it a folly to attempt more than we can execute, as that will not only bring disgrace upon us, but weaken our cause; yet I think we may do more than is generally believed in respect to the non-importation scheme. As to the withholding of our remittances, that is another point in which I own I have my doubts on several accounts, but principally on that of justice; for I think, while we are accusing others of injustice, we should be just ourselves; and how this can be, while we owe a considerable debt and refuse payment of it to Great Britain, is to me inconceivable. Nothing but the last extremity, I think, can justify it. Whether this is now come is the question.—To Bryan Fairfax. Fitzpatrick 3:228. (1774.)

NONIMPORTATION. See also TAXATION.

O

OFFICERS, Should Study Military Texts.—Remember that it is the actions, and not the commission, that make the officer, and that there is more expected from him than the title. Do not forget that there ought to be a time appropriated to attain this knowledge, as well as to indulge pleasure. And as we now have no opportunities to improve from example, let us read for this desirable end.—Orders. Fitzpatrick 1:271. (1756.)

Devote some part of your leisure hours to the study of your profession, a knowledge of which cannot be attained without application; nor [is] any merit or applause to be achieved without a certain knowledge thereof. —Instructions to officers. Fitzpatrick 2:114. (1757.)

OFFICERS, Instructions to Military.
—Be strict in your discipline; that is, . . . require nothing unreasonable of your officers and men, but see that whatever is required be punctually complied with. Reward and punish every man according to his merit, without partiality or prejudice; hear his complaints; if well founded, redress them; if otherwise, discourage them in order to prevent frivolous ones. Discourage vice in every shape and impress upon the mind of every man, from the first to the lowest, the importance of the cause, and what it is they are contending for. . . . Be easy and condescending in your deportment to your officers, but not too familiar, lest you subject yourself to a want of that respect which is necessary to support a proper command.—To William Woodford. Fitzpatrick 4:80. (1775.)

The true distinction, sir, between what is called a fine regiment and an indifferent only will ever . . . be found to originate in, and depend upon, the care or the inattention of the officers. . . . That regiment whose officers are watchful of their men and attentive to their wants; who will see that proper use is made and a proper account taken of whatever is drawn for them, and that regimental and company inspections are frequent in order to examine into the state of their arms, ammunition, clothing, and other necessaries, to prevent loss or embezzlement; who will see that the soldiers' clothes are well made, kept whole, and clean, that their huts are swept and purified, that the trash and all kinds of offal [are] either burnt or buried, that vaults or proper necessaries are erected and every person punished who shall on those occasions go elsewhere in the camp, that their provision is in good order, well cooked, and eaten at proper hours—those officers, I say, who attend to these things—and their duty strictly enjoins it on them—give health, comfort, and a military pride to their men, which fires and fits them for everything great and noble. It is by this means [that] the character of a regiment is exalted, while sloth, inattention, and neglect produce the reverse of these in every particular and must infallibly lessen the reputation of the corps.—To Thomas Lansdale. Fitzpatrick 26:68. (1783.)

OFFICERS, Should Receive Adequate Pay.—It becomes evidently clear... that as this contest is not likely to be the work of a day, as the war must be carried on systematically, and to do it you must have good officers, there are, in my judgment, no other possible means to obtain them but by establishing your army upon a permanent footing and giving your officers good pay. This will induce gentlemen and men of character to engage; and till the bulk of your officers are composed of such persons as are actuated by principles of honor and a spirit of enterprise, you have little to expect from them. They ought to have such allowances as will enable them to live like and support the characters of gentlemen; and not be driven by a scanty pittance to the low and dirty arts which many of them practice, to filch the public of more than the difference of pay would amount to upon an ample allowance.

Besides, something is due to the man who puts his life in his hands, hazards his health, and forsakes the sweets of domestic enjoyments.... There is nothing that gives a man consequence and renders him fit for command like a support that renders him independent of everybody but the state he serves. —To the President of Congress. Fitzpatrick 6:108. (1776.)

OFFICERS, Selection of.—One circumstance in this important business ought to be cautiously guarded against, and that is the soldier and officer being too nearly on a level. Discipline and subordination add life and vigor to military movements. The person commanded yields but a reluctant obedience to those he conceives are undeservedly made his superiors. The degrees of rank are frequently transferred from civil life into the departments of the army. The true criterion to judge by (when past services do not enter into the competition) is to consider whether the candidate for office has a just pretension to the character of a gentleman, a proper sense of honor, and some reputation to lose.—To Governor Patrick Henry. Fitzpatrick 6:167. (1776.)

OFFICERS, Sacrifices of, in Revolutionary War.—It does not require... argument... to prove that there is no set of men in the United States (considered as a body) that have made the same sacrifices of their interest in support of the common cause as the officers of the American army; that nothing but a love of their country, of honor, and a desire of seeing their labors crowned with success could

possibly induce them to continue one
moment in service; that no officer can
live upon his pay; that hundreds, having spent their little, all in addition to
their scant public allowance, have
resigned because they could no longer
support themselves as officers; that
numbers are, at this moment, rendered unfit for duty for want of clothing, while the rest are wasting their
property and some of them verging
fast to the gulf of poverty and distress.
—To Joseph Jones. Fitzpatrick 19:368.
(1780.)

OFFICERS. See also ARMY; REVO-
LUTIONARY WAR.

**OLD AGE, Washington's Thoughts
on.** —I will only repeat to you the
assurances of my friendship and of the
pleasure I should feel in seeing you in
the shade of those trees which my
hands have planted, and which by
their rapid growth at once indicate a
knowledge of my declination and their
disposition to spread their mantles
over me before I go hence to return no
more; for this, their gratitude, I will
nurture them while I stay.—To the
Chevalier de Chastellux. Fitzpatrick
27:113. (1784.)

OPINION, Differences of.—My
friendship [for you] is not in the least
lessened by the difference which has
taken place in our political sentiments.
... Men's minds are as variant as their
faces, and where the motives to their
actions are pure, the operation of the
former is no more to be imputed to
them as a crime than the appearance of
the latter; for both, being the work of
nature, are equally unavoidable. Liberality and charity ... ought to govern

*Washington in September 1795 (age 63).
Portrait by Charles Willson Peale.*

all disputes.—To Benjamin Harrison.
Fitzpatrick 30:223. (1789.)

A difference of opinion on political
points is not to be imputed to freemen
as a fault, since it is to be presumed
that they are all actuated by an equally
laudable and sacred regard for the
liberties of their country. If the mind is
so formed in different persons as to
consider the same object to be somewhat different in its nature and consequences as it happens to be placed in
different points of view, and if the
oldest, the ablest, and the most virtuous statesmen have often differed in
judgment as to the best forms of
government, we ought indeed rather
to rejoice that so much has been

effected than to regret that more could not all at once be accomplished.—To the governor and council of North Carolina. Fitzpatrick 30:347n. (1789.)

OPINION. See also CONTROVERSIES; DISPUTES; POLITICAL OPINIONS; PUBLIC OPINION.

OPPRESSION, Leaders Should Prevent.—Government being, among other purposes, instituted to protect the persons and consciences of men from oppression, it certainly is the duty of rulers not only to abstain from it themselves but, according to their stations, to prevent it in others.—To the religious society called Quakers. Fitzpatrick 30:416n. (1789.)

P

PAINE (Thomas), Effect of His 1776 Pamphlet.—By private letters ... I find *Common Sense* is working a powerful change ... in the minds of many men. —To Joseph Reed. Fitzpatrick 4:455. (1776.)

PAINE (Thomas), Washington's Plea for.—Sir, can nothing be done in our [Virginia] Assembly for poor Paine? Must the merits and services of *Common Sense* continue to glide down the stream of time unrewarded by this country? His writings certainly have had a powerful effect upon the public mind. Ought they not, then, to meet an adequate return? He is poor, he is chagrined, and almost, if not altogether, in despair of relief. New York, not the least distressed nor best able state in the Union, has done something for him. This kind of provision he prefers to an allowance from Congress.

He has reasons for it which to him are conclusive, and such, I think, as may be approved by others. His views are moderate; a decent independence is, I believe, all he aims at. Ought he to be disappointed of this?—To James Madison. Fitzpatrick 27:420. (1784.)

PARDON, Exercised by President Washington.—It is a valuable ingredient in the general estimate of our welfare that the part of our country which was lately the scene of disorder and insurrection now enjoys the blessings of quiet and order. The misled have abandoned their errors, and pay the respect to our Constitution and laws which is due from good citizens to the public authorities of the society. These circumstances have induced me to pardon generally the offenders here referred to, and to extend forgiveness to those who had been adjudged to capital punishment. For though I shall always think it a sacred duty to exercise with firmness and energy the constitutional powers with which I am vested, yet it appears to me no less consistent with the public end than it is with my personal feelings to mingle in the operations of government every degree of moderation and tenderness which the national justice, dignity, and safety may permit.—Seventh Annual Address to Congress. Fitzpatrick 34:390. (1795.)

PASSIONS, Part of Man's Nature.—The various passions and motives by which men are influenced are concomitants of fallibility, engrafted into our nature.—To Edmund Randolph. Fitzpatrick 29:357. (1788.)

PATIENCE, A Noble Virtue.—

Patience is a noble virtue, and when rightly exercised does not fail of its reward.—To the Reverend John Rodgers. Fitzpatrick 27:1. (1783.)

PATRIOTISM, And Service to Country.—Every post is honorable in which a man can serve his country.—To Benedict Arnold. Fitzpatrick 3:494. (1775.)

I am clearly in sentiment with you that every man who is in the vigor of life ought to serve his country in whatever line it requires and he is fit for.—To David Humphreys. Fitzpatrick 35:480. (1797.)

PATRIOTISM, And Self-Interest.—Men may speculate as they will; they may talk of patriotism; they may draw a few examples from ancient |history| of great achievements performed by its influence; but whoever builds upon it as a sufficient basis for conducting a long and bloody war will find |himself| deceived in the end.... We must take the passions of men as nature has given them, and those principles as a guide which are generally the rule of action. I do not mean to exclude altogether the idea of patriotism. I know it exists, and I know it has done much in the present contest. But I will venture to assert that a great and lasting war can never be supported on this principle alone. It must be aided by a prospect of interest or some reward. For a time it may of itself push men to action, to bear much, to encounter difficulties, but it will not endure unassisted by interest.—To John Banister. Fitzpatrick 11:286. (1778.)

PATRIOTISM, Of American Women.—Amid all the distresses and sufferings of the army, from whatever sources they have arisen, it must be a consolation to our virtuous countrywomen that they have never been accused of withholding their most zealous efforts to support the cause we are engaged in and |to| encourage those who are defending them in the field. The army do not want gratitude, nor do they misplace it in this instance.—To Mrs. Sarah Bache. Fitzpatrick 21:102. (1781.)

PATRIOTISM, Each American Must Engender Spirit of.—Citizens by birth or choice of a common country, that country has a right to concentrate your affections. The name of AMERICAN, which belongs to you in your national capacity, must always exalt the just pride of patriotism more than any appellation derived from local discriminations. With slight shades of difference, you have the same religion, manners, habits, and political principles. You have in a common cause fought and triumphed together. The independence and liberty you possess are the work of joint councils and joint efforts, of common dangers, sufferings, and successes.—Farewell Address. Fitzpatrick 35:219. (1796.)

PATRIOTISM. See also AMERICA; WHISKEY REBELLION.

PATRIOTS, America's Need for.—It appears as clear to me as ever the sun did in its meridian brightness that America never stood in more eminent need of the wise, patriotic, and spirited exertions of her sons than at this period; and if it is not a sufficient cause for general lamentation, my misconception of the matter impresses it too strongly upon me that the states separately are too much engaged in their local concerns, and have too many of their ablest men withdrawn from the general council for the good of the common weal.—To Benjamin Harrison. Fitzpatrick 13:464. (1778.)

PEACE, Washington's Prayer for.— That the God of armies may enable me to bring the present contest to a speedy and happy conclusion, thereby gratifying me in a retirement to the calm and sweet enjoyment of domestic happiness, is the fervent prayer and most ardent wish of my soul.—To Edmund Pendleton. Fitzpatrick 7:394. (1777.)

PEACE, Without Freedom, Is Unacceptable.—To discerning men, nothing can be more evident than that a peace on the principles of dependence, however limited, after what has happened, would be to the last degree dishonorable and ruinous.—To John Banister. Fitzpatrick 11.287. (1778.)

PEACE, Without Freedom, Would Lead to War.—Nothing short of independence, it appears to me, can possibly do. A peace on other terms would, if I may be allowed the expression, be a peace of war. The injuries we have received from the British nation were so unprovoked, have been so great and so many, that they can never be forgotten. Besides the feuds, the jealousies, the animosities that would ever attend a union with them; besides the importance |and| the advantages we should derive from an unrestricted commerce; our fidelity as a people, our gratitude, our character as men are opposed to a coalition with them as

subjects, but in case of the last extremity. Were we easily to accede to terms of dependence, no nation, upon future occasions, let the oppressions of Britain be never so flagrant and unjust, would interpose for our relief, or at least they would do it with a cautious reluctance and upon conditions, most probably, that would be hard if not dishonorable to us. France, by her supplies, has saved us from the yoke thus far, and a wise and virtuous perseverence would, and I trust will, free us entirely.—To John Banister. Fitzpatrick 11:289. (1778.)

PEACE, And Military Preparedness. —If we are wise, let us prepare for the worst; there is nothing which will so soon produce a speedy and honorable peace as a state of preparation for war. —To James McHenry. Fitzpatrick 25:151. (1782.)

My primary objects, to which I have steadily adhered, have been to preserve the country in peace if I can, and to be prepared for war if I cannot; to effect the first upon terms consistent with the respect which is due to ourselves, and with honor, justice, and good faith to all the world.—To Gouverneur Morris. Fitzpatrick 33:414. (1794.)

PEACE, Washington's First Desire.— My first wish is...to see the whole world in peace, and the inhabitants of it as one band of brothers, striving who should contribute most to the happiness of mankind.—To Charles Armand-Tuffin. Fitzpatrick 28:259. (1785.)

PEACE, Should Be Guarded Against Unwise Acts of Citizens.—Observations on the value of peace with other nations are unnecessary. It would be wise, however, by timely provisions, to guard against those acts of our own citizens which might tend to disturb it, and to put ourselves in a condition to give that satisfaction to foreign nations which we may sometimes have occasion to require from them. I particularly recommend to your consideration the means of preventing those aggressions by our citizens on the territory of other nations, and other infractions of the law of nations, which, furnishing just subject of complaint, might endanger our peace with them.—Fourth Annual Address to Congress. Fitzpatrick 32:209. (1792.)

PEACE, Object of Foreign Relations. —My policy in our foreign transactions has been to cultivate peace with all the world.—Sixth Annual Address to Congress. Fitzpatrick 34:37. (1794.)

PEACE. See also DEFENSE; FOREIGN RELATIONS; NATIONAL DEFENSE; NEUTRALITY; WAR.

PEOPLE, Wishes of, Not Always in Harmony with National Interest.— The wishes of the people, seldom founded in deep disquisitions or resulting from other reasonings than their present feeling, may not entirely accord with our true policy and interest. If they do not, to observe a proper line of conduct for promoting the one and avoiding offense to the other will be a work of great difficulty. —To John Banister. Fitzpatrick 11:288. (1778.)

PEOPLE, Slow to Support New Public

Measures.—The people must *feel* before they will *see*, |and| consequently are brought slowly into measures of public utility.—To George William Fairfax. Fitzpatrick 28:183. (1785.)

PEOPLE, The Underlying Power of the Constitution.—The power under the Constitution will always be in the people. It is entrusted for certain defined purposes, and for a certain limited period, to representatives of their own choosing; and whenever it is executed contrary to their interest, or not agreeable to their wishes, their servants can, and undoubtedly will, be recalled.—To Bushrod Washington. Fitzpatrick 29:311. (1787.)

PEOPLE, Duties of the.—It remains with the people themselves to preserve and promote the great advantages of their political and natural situation; nor ought a doubt to be entertained that men who so well understand the value of social happiness will ever cease to appreciate the blessings of a free, equal, and efficient government.—To the Rhode Island legislature. Fitzpatrick 31:94n. (1790.)

PEOPLE, Source of Independence and Prosperity.—As, under the smiles of Heaven, America is indebted for freedom and independence rather to the joint exertions of the citizens of the several states, in which it may be your boast to have borne no inconsiderable share, than to the conduct of the commander-in-chief, so is she indebted for their support rather to a continuation of those exertions, than to the prudence and ability manifested in the exercise of the powers delegated to the President of the United States.

Washington in September 1795 (age 63). Portrait by Rembrandt Peale.

—To the inhabitants of Providence. Sparks 12:192. (1790.)

From the gallantry and fortitude of her citizens, under the auspices of heaven, America has derived her independence. To their industry and the natural advantages of the country she is indebted for her prosperous situation. From their virtue she may expect long to share the protection of a free and equal government, which their wisdom has established and which experience justifies as admirably adapted to our social wants and individual felicity.—To the Congregational Church and Society at Midway. Sparks 12:198. (1791.)

PEOPLE, Government Should Consult Wishes of.—It is desirable on all occasions to unite with a steady and firm adherence to constitutional and necessary acts of government the fullest evidence of a disposition, as far as may be practicable, to consult the wishes of every part of the community, and to lay the foundations of the public administration in the affections of the people.—Third Annual Address to Congress. Fitzpatrick 31:400. (1791.)

PEOPLE, Voice of the.—Whatever my own opinion may be on this or any other subject, interesting to the community at large, it always has been and will continue to be my earnest desire to learn and to comply, as far as is consistent, with the public sentiment; but it is on *great* occasions *only,* and after time has been given for cool and deliberate reflection, that the *real* voice of the people can be known.—To Edward Carrington. Fitzpatrick 35:31. (1796.)

PEOPLE, Will Act Well When Correctly Informed.—I am sure the mass of citizens in these United States *mean well,* and I firmly believe they will always *act well* whenever they can obtain a right understanding of matters.—To John Jay. Fitzpatrick 35:37. (1796.)

PEOPLE. See also DEMOCRACY; GOVERNMENT; MAJORITY RULE; PUBLIC CONFIDENCE; PUBLIC OPINION; REPUBLICANISM; SELF-GOVERNMENT.

PERIODICALS, Have Great Potential to Improve Society.—I entertain a high idea of the utility of periodical publications, insomuch that I could heartily desire |that| copies of ... magazines, as well as common gazettes, might be spread through every city, town, and village in America. I consider such easy vehicles of knowledge more happily calculated than any other to preserve the liberty, stimulate the industry, and meliorate the morals of an enlightened and free people.—To Mathew Carey. Fitzpatrick 30:7. (1788.)

PERIODICALS. See also NEWSPAPERS; PUBLICATIONS.

POETRY, Written by Young Washington.—

O ye Gods, why should my poor resistless heart
Stand to oppose thy might and power,
At last surrender to cupid's feather'd dart
And now lays bleeding every hour
For her that's pityless of my grief and woes
And will not on me pity take.
I'll sleep amongst my most inveterate foes
And with gladness never wish to wake,
In deluding sleepings let my eyelids close
That in an enraptured dream I may,
In a soft lulling sleep and gentle repose,
Possess those joys denied by day.
—To Frances Alexander. Fitzpatrick 1:19. (1749-50.)

POLITICAL OPINIONS, Differences in.—Differences in political opinions are as unavoidable as, to a certain point, they may perhaps be necessary; but it is exceedingly to be regretted that subjects cannot be discussed with temper on the one hand, or decisions submitted to without having the motives which led to them improperly implicated on the other. And this regret borders on chagrin when we find that men of abilities, zealous patriots, having the same general objects in view and the same upright intentions to prosecute them, will not exercise more charity in deciding on the opinions and actions of one another. When matters get to such lengths, the natural inference is that both sides have strained the cords beyond their bearing and that a middle course would be found the best, until experience shall have decided on the right way; or, which is not to be expected because it is denied to mortals, there shall be some *infallible* rule by which we could *forejudge* events.—To Alexander Hamilton. Fitzpatrick 32:132. (1792.)

POLITICAL OPINIONS. See also CONTROVERSIES; DISPUTES; JEFFERSON (Thomas); OPINION.

POLITICAL PARTIES, A Threat to Liberty.—If we mean to support the liberty and independence which it has cost us so much blood and treasure to establish, we must drive far away the demon of party spirit and local reproach.—To Governor Arthur Fenner. Fitzpatrick 31:48. (1790.)

POLITICAL PARTIES, Useful But Must Be Controlled.—There is an opinion that parties in free countries are useful checks upon the administration of the government and serve to keep alive the spirit of liberty. This within certain limits is probably true, and in governments of a monarchial cast patriotism may look with indulgence, if not with favor, upon the spirit of party. But in those of the popular character, in governments purely elective, it is a spirit not to be encouraged. From their natural tendency, it is certain there will always be enough of that spirit for every salutary purpose. And there being constant danger of excess, the effort ought to be, by force of public opinion, to mitigate and assuage it. A fire not to be quenched, it demands a uniform vigilance to prevent its bursting into a flame, lest, instead of warming, it should consume.—Farewell Address. Fitzpatrick 35:228. (1796.)

POLITICAL PARTIES. See also FACTIONS.

POLITICS, Opponents More Active Than Supporters.—It has ever been that the adversaries to a measure are more active than its friends.—To Bushrod Washington. Fitzpatrick 29:309. (1787.)

POLITICS, Truth Should Be Prized Above Victory in.—Such (for wise purposes, it is presumed) is the turbulence of human passions in party disputes |that| when victory, more than truth, is the palm contended for, . . . the post of honor is a private station.—To the Secretary of War. Fitzpatrick 34:251. (1795.)

The difference . . . between the friends and foes of order and good government is . . . that the latter are always working like bees to distill their poison, while the former |depend| *too much* and *too long* upon the sense and good dispositions of the people.—To Alexander Hamilton. Fitzpatrick 34:264. (1795.)

POLITICS, No Infallibility in.—If any power on earth could, or the great power above would, erect the standard of infallibility in political opinions, there is no being that inhabits this terrestrial globe that would resort to it with more eagerness than myself, so long as I remain a servant of the public. But as I have found no better guide hitherto than upright intentions and close investigation, I shall adhere to these maxims while I keep the watch, leaving it to those who will come after me to explore new ways, if they like, or think them better.—To Henry Knox. Fitzpatrick 34:311. (1795.)

POLITICS, Washington's Guiding Principle in.—I have no object separated from the general welfare to promote. I have no predilections, no prejudices to gratify, no friends whose interests or views I wish to advance at the expense of propriety.—To James McHenry. Fitzpatrick 37:193. (1799.)

POLITICS. See also CONTROVERSIES; ELECTIONS; GOVERNMENT; PUBLIC OFFICE; PUBLIC SERVICE.

POOR, Care of the.—Never let an indigent person ask without receiving *something*, if you have the means; always recollecting in what light the widow's mite was viewed.—To George Washington Parke Custis. Fitzpatrick 35:283. (1796.)

POOR. See also CHARITY; HUMANITARIANISM.

POPULATION, Growth of, an Asset. —Our population advances with a celerity which, exceeding the most

Washington in September 1795 (age 63). Water color miniature portrait by Raphaelle Peale.

sanguine calculations, proportionally augments our strength and resources, and guarantees our future security.— Seventh Annual Address to Congress. Fitzpatrick 34:389. (1795.)

POPULATION. See also CENSUS.

POSTAL SYSTEM, Important to National Welfare.—I cannot forbear intimating to you the expediency of . . . facilitating the intercourse between the distant parts of our country by a due attention to the post office and post roads.—First Annual Address to Congress. Fitzpatrick 30:493. (1790.)

The importance of the post office and post roads, on a plan sufficiently liberal and comprehensive, as they respect the expedition, safety, and

facility of communication, is increased by the instrumentality in diffusing a knowledge of the laws and proceedings of the government; which, while it contributes to the security of the people, serves also to guard them against the effects of misrepresentation and misconception.—To the Senate and the House of Representatives. Fitzpatrick 31:403. (1791.)

POWER, Should Be Exercised When Necessary.—Extensive powers not exercised as far as was necessary have, I believe, scarcely ever failed to ruin the possessor.—To Joseph Reed. Fitzpatrick 19:114. (1780.)

POWER. See also GOVERNMENT; SEPARATION OF POWERS.

PRAYER, Required of Soldiers.—The Continental Congress having ordered Friday to be observed as a day of "fasting, humiliation and prayer, humbly to supplicate the mercy of Almighty God, that it would please him to pardon all our manifold sins and transgressions, and to prosper the arms of the united colonies, and finally, establish the peace and freedom of America upon a solid and lasting foundation"—the General commands all officers and soldiers to pay strict obedience to the orders of the Continental Congress, and by their unfeigned and pious observance of their religious duties, incline the Lord, and Giver of Victory, to prosper our arms.—General Orders. Fitzpatrick 5:43. (1776.)

PRAYER. See also GOD; RELIGION; REVELATION; THANKSGIVING PROCLAMATION OF 1789.

PRECEDENTS, Can Be Dangerous. —Precedents are dangerous things.—

To Henry Lee. Fitzpatrick 29:34. (1786.)

PRECEDENTS, Should Be Based on True Principles.—As the first of everything in our situation will serve to establish a precedent |for future American presidents|, it is devoutly wished on my part that these precedents may be fixed on true principles. —To James Madison. Fitzpatrick 30:310. (1789.)

PRECEDENTS, Importance of Correct, in the Presidency.—In our progress towards political happiness my station is new; and, if I may use the expression, I walk on untrodden ground. There is scarcely any part of my conduct which may not hereafter be drawn into precedent. Under such a view of the duties inherent to my arduous office, I could not but feel... an anxiety for the |nation| that every new arrangement should be made in the best possible manner.—To Mrs Catharine Macaulay Graham. Fitzpatrick 30:496. (1790.)

PRESIDENT, Limiting Terms of, Unadvisable.—There cannot, in my judgment, be the least danger that the President will by any practicable intrigue ever be able to continue himself one moment in office, much less perpetuate himself in it, but in the last stage of corrupted morals and political depravity |among the people|; and even then there is as much danger that any other species of domination would prevail. Though, when a people shall have become incapable of governing themselves, and fit for a master, it is of little consequence from what quarter he comes. Under an extended view of this part of the subject, I can see no propriety in precluding ourselves from the services of any man who on some great emergency shall be deemed universally most capable of serving the public.—To the Marquis de Lafayette. Fitzpatrick 29:479. (1788.)

PRESIDENT, Governed by the People.—I only wish, while I am a servant of the public, to know the will of my masters, that I may govern myself accordingly.—To Edmund Pendleton. Fitzpatrick 33:96. (1793.)

PRESIDENT, Should Lead with a National Perspective.—In every act of my administration, I have sought the happiness of my fellow citizens. My system for the attainment of this object has uniformly been to overlook all personal, local, and partial considerations; to contemplate the United States as one great whole;...and to consult only the substantial and permanent interests of our country.—To the selectmen of Boston. Fitzpatrick 34:252. (1795.)

PRESIDENT, Should Exercise Power in Moderation.—Though I shall always think it a sacred duty to exercise with firmness and energy the constitutional powers with which I am vested, yet it appears to me no less consistent with the public good than it is with my personal feelings to mingle in the operations of government every degree of moderation and tenderness which the national justice, dignity, and safety may permit.—Seventh Annual Address to Congress. Fitzpatrick 34:390. (1795.)

PRESIDENT. See also EXECUTIVE BRANCH; PRECEDENTS.

PRICE CONTROLS, Unnatural and Impractical.—To limit the prices of articles . . . I believe is inconsistent with the very nature of things and impracticable in itself.—To James Warren. Fitzpatrick 14:313. (1779.)

PRINCIPLE, Will Triumph.—In times of turbulence, when the passions are afloat, calm reason is swallowed up in the extremes to which measures are attempted to be carried; but when those subside and the empire of |reason| is resumed, the man who acts from principle, who pursues the paths of truth, moderation, and justice, will regain his influence.—To John Luzac. Fitzpatrick 36:84. (1797.)

PRINCIPLES, More Important Than Party.—It is . . . most devoutly to be wished that faction|were|at an end, and that those to whom everything dear and valuable is entrusted would lay aside party views and return to first principles. Happy, happy, thrice happy |our| country if such |were| the government of it, but alas! we are not to expect that the path is to be strewed with flowers. That great and good Being who rules the universe has disposed matters otherwise, and for wise purposes, I am persuaded.—To Joseph Reed. Fitzpatrick 13:348. (1778.)

PRISONERS OF WAR, Washington's Kindness to.—I have shown all the respect I could to them here, and have given some necessary clothing, by which I have disfurnished myself, for, having brought no more than two or three shirts from Will Creek that we might be light, I was ill provided to furnish them.—To Governor Robert Dinwiddie. Fitzpatrick 1:67. (1754.)

PRISONERS OF WAR, Treatment of, in Revolutionary War.—Any other prisoners who may fall into your hands, you will treat with as much humanity and kindness as may be consistent with your own safety and the public interest.—Instructions to Benedict Arnold. Fitzpatrick 3:494. (1775.)

It is not my wish that severity should be exercised towards any whom the fortune of war has thrown, or shall throw, into our hands. On the contrary, it is my desire that the utmost humanity should be shown them. I am convinced the latter has been the prevailing line of conduct to prisoners.—To Sir William Howe. Fitzpatrick 6:260. (1776.)

PRISONERS OF WAR. See also HESSIANS; RETALIATION.

PROCRASTINATION, An Undesirable Practice.—Put off nothing till the morrow that you can do today, |for| the habit of postponing things is among the worst in the world.—To Howell Lewis. Fitzpatrick 33:148. (1793.)

PROFANITY, Condemnation of.—The General is sorry to be informed that the foolish and wicked practice of profane cursing and swearing (a vice heretofore little known in an American army) is growing into fashion. He hopes the officers will, by example as well as influence, endeavor to check it, and that both they and the men will reflect that we can have little hopes of the blessing of Heaven on our arms if we insult it by our impiety and folly; added to this, it is a vice so mean and low, without any temptation, that every man of sense and character detests and despises it.—General Orders. Fitzpatrick 5:367. (1776.)

It is much to be lamented that the foolish and scandalous practice of profane swearing is exceedingly prevalent in the American army. Officers of every rank are bound to discourage it, first by their example, and then by punishing offenders. As a means to abolish this and every other species of immorality, brigadiers are enjoined to take effectual care to have divine service duly performed in their respective brigades.—General Orders. Fitzpatrick 8:152. (1777.)

The wanton practice of swearing [is] a vice productive of neither advantage nor pleasure.—General Orders. Fitzpatrick 13:119. (1778.)

PROFANITY. See also VICES.

PROPAGANDA, Effects of.—It is well known that when one side only of a story is heard and often repeated, the human mind becomes impressed with it insensibly.—To Edmund Pendleton. Fitzpatrick 34:99. (1795.)

PROPERTY, Man Desires Mastery of Own.—It is . . . natural for man to wish to be the absolute lord and master of what he holds in occupancy.—To William Strickland. Fitzpatrick 35:500. (1797.)

PUBLIC CONFIDENCE, How to Preserve.—In general I esteem it a good maxim that the best way to preserve the confidence of the people durably is to promote their true interest.—To Joseph Reed. Fitzpatrick 19:114. (1780.)

PUBLIC LAND, A Refuge for the Poor.—Rather than quarrel about territory, let the poor, the needy and

oppressed of the earth, and those who want land resort to the fertile plains of our western country, the second land of promise, and there dwell in peace, fulfilling the first and great commandment.—To David Humphreys. Fitzpatrick 28:202. (1785.)

PUBLIC LAND, Should Be Sold to Repay National Debt.—A provision for the sale of the vacant lands of the United States is particularly urged, among other reasons, by the important considerations that they are pledged as a fund for reimbursing the public debt [and] that, if timely and judiciously applied, they may save the necessity of burdening our citizens with new taxes for the extinguishment of the principal.—Third Annual Address to Congress. Fitzpatrick 31:403. (1791.)

PUBLIC LAND. See also WEST.

PUBLIC OFFICE, An Opportunity to Do Good.—All see, and most admire, the glare which hovers round the external trappings of elevated office. To me there is nothing in it beyond the luster which may be reflected from its connection with a power of promoting human felicity.—To Mrs. Catharine Macaulay Graham. Fitzpatrick 30:496. (1790.)

PUBLIC OFFICE. See also POLITICS.

PUBLIC OFFICIALS, Guidelines for.—In general I esteem it a good maxim that the best way to preserve the confidence of the people durably is to promote their true interest; there are particular exigencies when this maxim has peculiar force. When any great object is in view, the popular mind is roused into expectation and prepared to make sacrifices both of ease and property; if those to whom they confide the management of their affairs do not call them to make these sacrifices, and the object is not attained, or they are involved in the reproach of not having contributed as much as they ought to have done towards it, they will be mortified at the disappointment, they will feel the censure, and their resentment will rise against those who with sufficient authority have omitted to do what their interest and their honor required. —To Joseph Reed. Fitzpatrick 19:114. (1780.)

Let me, in a friendly way, impress the following maxims upon the executive officers. In all important matters, to deliberate maturely, but to execute promptly and vigorously. And not to put things off until the morrow which can be done, and require to be done, today. Without an adherence to these rules, business never will be well done, or done in an easy manner; but will always be in arrears, with one thing treading upon the heels of another. —To the Secretary of War. Fitzpatrick 35:138. (1796.)

Good measures should always be executed as soon as they are conceived and circumstances will permit. —To the Secretary of State. Fitzpatrick 35:161. (1796.)

PUBLIC OFFICIALS, Accountable to the People.—Men in responsible positions cannot, like those in private life, be governed *solely* by the dictates of their own inclinations, or by such motives as can only affect themselves. ... A man in public office ... is account-

able for the consequences of his measures to others, and one in private life...has no other check than the rectitude of his own actions.—To the Duke de Liancourt. Fitzpatrick 35:167. (1796.)

PUBLIC OFFICIALS, Should Not Have to Be Wealthy.—The compensations to the officers of the United States...appear to call for legislative revision. The consequences of a defective provision are of serious import to the government. If private wealth is to supply the defect of public [compensation], it will greatly contract the sphere within which the selection of characters for office is to be made, and will proportionally diminish the probability of a choice of men [who are] able as well as upright. Besides that, it would be repugnant to the vital principles of our government virtually to exclude from public trusts [those with] talents and virtue unless accompanied by wealth.—Eighth Annual Address to Congress. Fitzpatrick 35:318. (1796.)

PUBLIC OFFICIALS. See also APPOINTMENTS; ENEMIES; EXECUTIVE BRANCH; GOVERNMENT.

PUBLIC OPINION, Weakened by Ignorance.—In a free and republican government, you cannot restrain the voice of the multitude; every man will speak as he thinks, or more properly without thinking, [and] consequently will judge of effects without attending to the causes.—To the Marquis de Lafayette. Fitzpatrick 12:383. (1778.)

PUBLIC OPINION, Should Generally Direct Public Officials.—Whatever my own opinion may be on this or any other subject interesting to the community at large, it always has been and will continue to be my earnest desire to learn and to comply, as far as is consistent, with the public sentiment; but it is on *great* occasions *only,* and after time has been given for cool and deliberate reflection, that the *real* voice of the people can be known.—To Edward Carrington. Fitzpatrick 35:31. (1796.)

PUBLIC OPINION, Needs to Be Enlightened.—Promote,...as an object of primary importance, institutions for the general diffusion of knowledge. In proportion as the structure of a government gives force to public opinion, it is essential that public opinion should be enlightened.—Farewell Address. Fitzpatrick 35:230. (1796.)

PUBLIC OPINION, Should Be Known.—As it is the right of the people that [their will] should be carried into effect, their sentiments ought to be unequivocally known, that the principles on which the government has acted...may either be changed, or the opposition...may meet effectual discountenance.—To Thomas Pinckney. Fitzpatrick 35:453. (1797.)

PUBLIC OPINION. See also INFORMATION; KNOWLEDGE; NEWSPAPERS; OPINION; PEOPLE; PROPAGANDA; SELF-GOVERNMENT.

PUBLIC SERVICE, A Citizen's Duty.—The share you have taken in [recent] public disputes is commendable and praiseworthy; it is a duty we owe our country, a claim posterity has on us. It is not sufficient for a man to be a pas-

Washington in late summer or fall 1796 (age 64). Portrait by Gilbert Stuart. An engraving of this portrait, in reverse, appears on our dollar bill. Martha Washington said this painting was not a "true resemblance."

sive friend and well-wisher to the cause.—To John Augustine Washington. Fitzpatrick 4:450. (1776.)

PUBLICATIONS, Unsatisfactory, Proper Response to.—Should anything present itself in this or any other publication, I shall never undertake the painful task of recrimination, nor do I know that I should ever enter upon my justification.—To William Goddard. Fitzpatrick 28:162. (1785.)

With those who are disposed to cavil, or who have the itch of writing strongly upon them, nothing can be made to suit their palates; the best way, therefore, to disconcert and defeat them is to take no notice of their publications; all else is but food for declamation.—To Samuel Vaughan. Fitzpatrick 28:327. (1785.)

PUBLICATIONS. See also BOOKS; NEWSPAPERS; PERIODICALS.

R

READING, Light.—Light reading (by this I mean books of little importance) may amuse for the moment, but leaves nothing solid behind.—To George Washington Parke Custis. Fitzpatrick 35:341. (1796.)

READING. See also BOOKS; NEWSPAPERS; PERIODICALS; PUBLICATIONS.

RELIGION, And Morality, Pillars of Human Happiness.—Of all the dispositions and habits which lead to political prosperity, religion and morality are indispensable supports. In vain would that man claim the tribute of patriotism who should labor to subvert these great pillars of human happiness, these firmest props of the duties of men and citizens. The mere politician, equally with the pious man, ought to respect and to cherish them. A volume could not trace all their connections with private and public felicity. Let it simply be asked, where is the security for property, for reputation, for life, if the sense of religious obligation desert the oaths which are the instruments of investigation in courts of justice?—Farewell Address. Fitzpatrick 35:229. (1796.)

RELIGION. See also CHARITY; CHRISTIANITY; CLERGY; GOD; JESUS CHRIST; JEWS; MORALITY; PRAYER; REVELATION; THANKS-GIVING PROCLAMATION OF 1789; VIRTUE.

RELIGIOUS FREEDOM, Washington's Commitment to.—If I could conceive that the general government might ever be so administered as to render the liberty of conscience insecure, I beg you will be persuaded that no one would be more zealous than myself to establish effectual barriers against the horrors of spiritual tyranny, and every species of religious persecution.—To the General Committee of the United Baptist Churches in Virginia. Fitzpatrick 30:321*n*. (1789.)

RELIGIOUS FREEDOM, Every American Should Enjoy.—I have often expressed my sentiments that every man, conducting himself as a good citizen, and being accountable to God alone for his religious opinions, ought to be protected in worshipping the Deity according to the dictates of his own conscience.—To the General Committee of the United Baptist Churches in Virginia. Fitzpatrick 30:321*n*. (1789.)

The citizens of the United States of America have a right to applaud themselves for having given to mankind examples of an enlarged and liberal policy, a policy worthy of imitation. All profess alike liberty of conscience and immunities of citizenship. It is now no more that toleration is spoken of, as if it [were] by the indulgence of one class of people that another enjoyed the exercise of their inherent natural rights. For happily the government of the United States, which gives to bigotry no sanction, to persecution no assistance, requires only that they

who live under its protection should demean themselves as good citizens, in giving it on all occasions their effectual support.—To the Hebrew congregation of Newport, Rhode Island. Philip S. Foner, ed., *George Washington: Selections from His Writings* (New York: International Publishers, 1944), p. 87. (1790.)
RELIGIOUS FREEDOM, A Blessing to America.—The liberty enjoyed by the people of these states of worshipping Almighty God agreeably to their consciences is not only among the choicest of their *blessings*, but also of their *rights*. While men perform their social duties faithfully, they do all that society or the state can with propriety demand or expect, and remain responsible only to their Maker for the religion or modes of faith which they may prefer or profess.—To the religious society called Quakers. Sparks 12:168. (1789.)

We have abundant reason to rejoice that in this land the light of truth and reason has triumphed over the power of bigotry and superstition, and that every person may here worship God according to the dictates of his own heart. In this enlightened age and in this land of equal liberty, it is our boast that a man's religious tenets will not forfeit the protection of the laws, nor deprive him of the right of attaining and holding the highest offices that are known in the United States.—To the members of the New Church in Baltimore. Fitzpatrick 32:315. (1793.)
RELIGIOUS SERVICES, Officers and Soldiers Expected to Attend.—The General most earnestly requires and expects . . . of all officers and sol-

diers, not engaged on actual duty, a punctual attendance on divine service, to implore the blessings of heaven upon the means used for our safety and defense. —General Orders. Fitzpatrick 3:309. (1775.)

The honorable Continental Congress having been pleased to allow a chaplain to each regiment, . . . the colonels or commanding officers of each regiment are directed to procure chaplains accordingly, persons of good characters and exemplary lives, |and| to see that all inferior officers and soldiers pay them a suitable respect and attend carefully upon religious exercises. The blessing and protection of Heaven are at all times necessary, but especially so in times of public distress and danger.—General Orders. Fitzpatrick 5:244. (1776.)

The commander-in-chief directs that divine service be performed every Sunday at eleven o'clock in those brigades |in| which there are chaplains; those which have none |are| to attend the places of worship nearest to them. It is expected that officers of all ranks will by their attendance set an example to their men. While we are zealously performing the duties of good citizens and soldiers, we certainly ought not to be inattentive to the higher duties of religion. To the distinguished character of patriot, it should be our highest glory to add the more distinguished character of Christian. The signal instances of providential goodness which we have experienced, and which have now almost crowned our labors with complete success, demand from us in a peculiar manner the warmest returns of gratitude and piety to the Supreme Author of all good.—General Orders. Fitzpatrick 11:342. (1778.)

Divine service is to be performed tomorrow in the several brigades or divisions. The commander-in-chief earnestly recommends that the troops not on duty should universally attend with that seriousness of deportment and gratitude of heart which the recognition of such reiterated and astonishing interpositions of Providence demand of us.—General Orders. Fitzpatrick 23:247. (1781.)

RELIGIOUS TOLERATION, And Leaving Judgment to God.—Avoid all disrespect to or contempt of the religion of the country and its ceremonies. Prudence, policy, and a true Christian spirit will lead us to look with compassion upon their errors without insulting them. While we are contending for our own liberty, we should be very cautious of violating the rights of conscience in others, ever considering that God alone is the judge of the hearts of men, and to him only in this case they are answerable.—Instructions to Benedict Arnold. Fitzpatrick 3:492. (1775.)

RELIGIOUS TOLERATION, Practiced by Washington.—Being no bigot myself to any mode of worship, I am disposed to indulge the professors of Christianity in the church that road to heaven which to them shall seem the most direct, plainest, easiest, and least liable to exception.—To the Marquis de Lafayette. Fitzpatrick 29:259. (1787.)

REPUBLICANISM, A Superior Form

of Government.—Republicanism is not the phantom of a deluded imagination. On the contrary,...under no form of government will laws be better supported, liberty and property better secured, or happiness be more effectually dispensed to mankind.—To Edmund Pendleton. Fitzpatrick 34:99. (1795.)

REPUBLICANISM. See also DEMOCRACY; GOVERNMENT; PEOPLE; SELF-GOVERNMENT.

REPUTATION, Good, Brings Happiness.—To stand well in the estimation of one's country is a happiness that no rational creature can be insensible of.—To Joseph Reed. Fitzpatrick 16:8. (1779.)

REPUTATION, The Kind to Seek.—The good opinion of honest men, friends to freedom and well-wishers to mankind, wherever they may be born or happen to reside, is the only kind of reputation a wise man would ever desire.—To Edward Pemberton. Fitzpatrick 30:1. (1788.)

REPUTATION. See also APPROBATION; MERIT.

RETALIATION, In War.—Retaliation is certainly just and sometimes necessary, even where attended with the severest penalties. But when the evils which may and must result from it exceed those intended to be redressed, prudence and policy require that it should be avoided.—To the President of Congress. Fitzpatrick 7:211. (1777.)

I really know not what to say on the subject of retaliation. Congress have it under consideration and we must await their determination. Of this I am convinced, that of all laws it is the most difficult to execute, where you have not the transgressor himself in your possession. Humanity will ever interfere and plead strongly against the sacrifice of an innocent person for the guilt of another.—To Nathanael Greene. Fitzpatrick 23:391. (1781.)

The enemy, persisting in that barbarous line of conduct they have pursued during the course of this war, have lately most inhumanly executed Captain Joshua Huddy of the Jersey State troops, taken prisoner by them at a post on Tom's River; and in consequence I have written to the British commander-in-chief that unless the perpetrators of that horrid deed were delivered up, I should be under the disagreeable necessity of retaliating as the only means left to put a stop to such inhuman proceedings. You will therefore immediately, on receipt of this, designate by lot for the above purpose a British captain who is an unconditional prisoner, if such a one is in your possession.... I need not mention to you that every possible tenderness, that is consistent with the security of him, should be shown to the person whose unfortunate lot it may be to suffer.—To Moses Hazen. Fitzpatrick 24:217. (1782.)

RETALIATION. See also PRISONERS OF WAR.

REVELATION, A Blessing to Society. —The free cultivation of letters, the unbounded extension of commerce, the progressive refinement of manners, the growing liberality of sentiment, and, above all, the pure and benign light of revelation have had a meliorating influence on mankind and increased the blessings of society.— Circular to the States. Fitzpatrick 26:485. (1783.)

REVOLUTIONARY WAR, Washington's Feelings at Outbreak of.—Unhappy it is ... to reflect that a brother's sword has been sheathed in a brother's breast, and that the once happy and peaceful plains of America are either to be drenched with blood or inhabited by slaves. Sad alternative! But can a virtuous man hesitate in his choice?—To George William Fairfax. Fitzpatrick 3:22. (1775.)

REVOLUTIONARY WAR, Citizen-Soldiers in.—When we assumed the soldier, we did not lay aside the citizen; and we shall most sincerely rejoice with you in that happy hour when the establishment of American liberty upon the most firm and solid foundations shall enable us to return to our private stations in the bosom of a free, peaceful, and happy country.—To the New York legislature. Fitzpatrick 3:305. (1775.)

REVOLUTIONARY WAR, Fought for Posterity.—Under |God's| providence, those who influence the councils of America and all the other inhabitants of the united colonies, at the hazard of their lives, are determined to hand down to posterity those just and invaluable privileges which they received from their ancestors.—To Thomas Gage. Fitzpatrick 3:431. (1775.)

REVOLUTIONARY WAR, Localism in.—Connecticut wants no Massachusetts man in their corps; Massachusetts thinks there is no necessity for a Rhode Islander to be introduced

Washington in 1796 (age 64). Pastel portrait by James Sharples. Washington's grandson, George Washington Parke Custis, later pronounced this "the best likeness of the man extant."

among them; and New Hampshire says it's very hard that her valuable and experienced officers (who are willing to serve) should be discarded because her own regiments, under the new establishment, cannot provide for them.—To Joseph Reed. Fitzpatrick 4:77. (1775.)

I have labored ever since I have been in the service to discourage all kinds of local attachments and distinctions of country, denominating the whole by the greater name of American; but I found it impossible to overcome prejudices.—To the President of Congress. Fitzpatrick 6:405. (1776.)

REVOLUTIONARY WAR, Enlisting Free Negroes in.—It has been represented to me that the free Negroes who have served in this army are very much dissatisfied at being discarded. As it is to be apprehended that they may seek employ in the |British| army, I have presumed to depart from the resolution respecting them and have given license for their being enlisted.— To the President of Congress. Fitzpatrick 4:195. (1775.)

REVOLUTIONARY WAR, Washington Credits Soldiers for His Success in.—They were indeed, at first, "a band of undisciplined husbandmen," but it is (under God) to their bravery and attention to their duty that I am indebted for that success which has procured me the only reward I wish to receive: the affection and esteem of my countrymen.—To the President of Congress. Fitzpatrick 4:489. (1776.)

REVOLUTIONARY WAR, To Decide American Freedom or Slavery.— The time is now near at hand which must probably determine whether Americans are to be freemen or slaves; whether they are to have any property they can call their own; whether their houses and farms are to be pillaged and destroyed, and they consigned to a state of wretchedness from which no human efforts will probably deliver them. The fate of unborn millions will now depend, under God, on the courage and conduct of this army. Our cruel and unrelenting enemy leaves us no choice but a brave resistance or the most abject submission. This is all we can expect; we have therefore to resolve to conquer or die. Our own country's honor ... call|s| upon us for a vigorous and manly exertion, and if we now shamefully fail we shall become infamous to the whole world. Let us therefore rely upon the goodness of the cause, and the aid of the Supreme Being in whose hands victory is, to animate and encourage us to great and noble actions. The eyes of all our countrymen are now upon us, and we shall have their blessings and praises if happily we are the instruments of saving them from the tyranny meditated against them. Let us therefore animate and encourage each other, and show the whole world that a freeman contending for *liberty* on his own ground is superior to any slavish mercenary on earth.—General Orders. Fitzpatrick 5:211. (1776.)

The honor and safety of our bleeding country, and every other motive that can influence the brave and heroic patriot, call loudly upon us to acquit ourselves with spirit. In short, we must now determine to be enslaved or free. If we make freedom our choice, we must obtain it by the blessings of Heaven on our united and vigorous efforts.—Address to the officers and soldiers of the Pennsylvania Associators. Fitzpatrick 5:398. (1776.)

The General hopes...every man's mind and arms will be prepared for action and, when called to it, |will| show our enemies, and the whole world, that freemen contending on their own land are superior to any mercenaries on earth.—General Orders. Fitzpatrick 5:469. (1776.)

The hour is fast approaching on which the honor and success of this army and the safety of our bleeding country depend. Remember, officers and soldiers, that you are freemen, fighting for the blessings of liberty—that slavery will be your portion, and that of your posterity, if you do not acquit yourselves like men.... Remember how your courage and spirit have been despised and traduced by your cruel invaders, though they have found by dear experience at Boston, Charlestown, and other places what a few brave men contending in their own land and in the best of causes can do against base hirelings and mercenaries.—General Orders. Fitzpatrick 5:479. (1776.)

REVOLUTIONARY WAR, Need for Harmony Among Troops.—Enjoin... upon the officers, and let them inculcate and press home to the soldiery, the necessity of order and harmony among them, who are embarked in one common cause and mutually contending for all that freemen hold dear. I am persuaded |that| if the officers will but exert themselves, these animosities, this disorder, will in a great measure subside; and nothing being more essential to the service than that it should, I am hopeful nothing on their parts will be wanting to effect it.—To Philip Schuyler. Fitzpatrick 5:290. (1776.)

It is with great concern the General understands that jealousies etc. are arisen among the troops from the different provinces, of reflections frequently thrown out which can only tend to irritate each other and injure the noble cause in which we are engaged, and which we ought to support with one hand and one heart. The General most earnestly entreats the officers and soldiers to consider the consequences; that they can |in| no way assist our cruel enemies more effectually than |by| making division among ourselves; that the honor and success of the army, and the safety of our bleeding country, depend upon harmony and good agreement with each other; that the provinces are all united to oppose the common enemy, and all distinctions sunk in the name of an American. To make this |name| honorable, and preserve the liberty of our country, ought to be our only emulation, and he will be the best soldier and the best patriot who contributes most to this glorious work, whatever his station, or from whatever part of the continent he may come. Let all distinctions of nations, countries, and provinces therefore be lost in the generous contest |of| who shall behave with the most courage against the enemy, and the most kindness and good humor to each other. If there are any officers or soldiers so lost to virtue and a love of their country as to continue in such practices after this order, the General assures them, and is directed by Congress to declare to the whole army, that such persons shall be severely punished and dismissed |from| the service with disgrace.—General Orders. Fitzpatrick 5:361. (1776.)

REVOLUTIONARY WAR, Duty of Each Soldier.—With ... hope and confidence ... that this army will have its equal share of honor and success, the General most earnestly exhorts every officer and soldier to pay the utmost attention to his arms and health; to have the former in the best order for action, and by cleanliness and care to preserve the latter; to be exact in their discipline, obedient to their superiors, and vigilant on duty. With such preparation and a suitable spirit, there can be no doubt but |that|, by the blessing of heaven, we shall repel our cruel invaders, preserve our country, and gain the greatest honor.—General Orders. Fitzpatrick 5:315. (1776.)

REVOLUTIONARY WAR, Concern About Fighting in New York.—When I consider that the city of New York will in all human probability very soon be the scene of a bloody conflict, I cannot but view the great numbers of women, children, and infirm persons remaining in it with the most melancholy concern.... It would relieve me from great anxiety if your honorable body would immediately deliberate upon it and form and execute some plan for their removal and relief, in which I will cooperate and assist to the utmost of my power.—To the New York legislature. Fitzpatrick 5:444. (1776.)

REVOLUTIONARY WAR, Orders Against Cowardice.—It is the General's express order that if any man attempts to skulk, lay down, or retreat without orders he be instantly shot down as an example. He hopes no such scoundrel will be found in this army; but on the contrary, everyone for himself resolving to conquer or die, and trusting to the smiles of heaven upon so just a cause, will behave with bravery and resolution. Those who are distinguished for their gallantry and good conduct may depend upon being honorably noticed, and suitably rewarded; and if this army will but emulate and imitate their brave countrymen in other parts of America, he has no doubt they will, by a glorious victory, save their country and acquire to themselves immortal honor.— General Orders. Fitzpatrick 5:480. (1776.)

REVOLUTIONARY WAR, Plundering Forbidden.—The burning of houses, where the apparent good of the service is not promoted by it, and the pillaging of them, at all times and upon all occasions, is to be discountenanced and punished with the utmost severity. In short, it is to be hoped that men who have property of their own, and a regard for the rights of others, will shudder at the thought of rendering any man's situation, to whose protection he had come, more insufferable than his open and avowed enemy would make it, when by duty and every rule of humanity they ought to aid and not oppress the distressed in their habitations. The distinction between a well-regulated army and a mob is the good order and discipline of the first, and the licentious and disorderly behavior of the latter.—To Israel Putnam. Fitzpatrick 5:488. (1776.)

The General does not admit of any pretense for plundering; whether it is Tory property taken beyond the lines or not, it is equally a breach of orders, and to be punished in the officer who gives orders or the soldier who goes without.—General Orders. Fitzpatrick 6:105. (1776.)

Notwithstanding all the cautions, the earnest requests, and the positive orders of the commander-in-chief to prevent our own army from plundering our own friends and fellow citizens, yet to his astonishment and grief, fresh complaints are made to him that so wicked, infamous, and cruel a practice is still continued, and that, too, in circumstances most distressing: where the wretched inhabitants, dreading the enemy's vengeance for their adherence to our cause, have left all and fled to us for refuge! We complain of the cruelty and barbarity of our enemies; but does it equal ours? They sometimes spare the property of their friends. But some among us, beyond expression barbarous, rob even them! Why did we assemble in arms? Was it not, in one capital point, to protect the property of our countrymen? And shall we, to our eternal reproach, be the first to pillage and destroy? Will no motives of humanity, of zeal, [of] interest, and of honor restrain the violence of the soldiers, or induce officers to keep so strict a watch over the ill-disposed as effectually to prevent the execution of their evil designs and the gratification of their savage inclinations? Or, if these powerful motives are too weak, will they pay no regard to their own safety? How many noble designs have miscarried, how many victories have been lost, how many armies ruined by an indulgence of soldiers in plundering?—General Orders. Fitzpatrick 9:178. (1777.)

REVOLUTIONARY WAR, A War of Posts.—On our side the war should be defensive. It has even been called a war of posts.... We should on all occasions avoid a general action or put anything to the risk unless compelled by a necessity, into which we ought never to be drawn.—To the President of Congress. Fitzpatrick 6:28. (1776.)

REVOLUTIONARY WAR, Sickness in Army.—The case of our sick is also worthy of much consideration; their number by the returns form at least one-fourth of the army. Policy and humanity require they should be made as comfortable as possible.—To the President of Congress. Fitzpatrick 6:30. (1776.)

REVOLUTIONARY WAR, Policy of Retreat in.—I am sensible [that] a retreating army is encircled with difficulties, that the declining an engagement subjects a general to reproach, and that the common cause may be in some measure affected by the discouragements which it throws over the minds of many; nor am I insensible of the contrary effects, if a brilliant stroke could be made with any probability of success, especially after our loss upon Long Island; but when the fate of America may be at stake on the issue, when the wisdom of cooler moments and experienced men have decided that we should protract the war if possible, I cannot think it safe or wise to adopt a different system, when the season for action draws so near a close.—To the President of Congress. Fitzpatrick 6:31. (1776.)

REVOLUTIONARY WAR, Military Policy Toward Citizenry.—It is our business to give protection and support to the poor, distressed inhabitants, not to multiply and increase

their calamities.—General Orders. Fitzpatrick 7:47. (1777.)

REVOLUTIONARY WAR, Desertion in.—Several of our officers have broken their paroles and stolen away. This practice, ignominious to themselves, dishonorable to the service, and injurious to the officers of sentiment and delicacy who remain behind to experience the rigors of resentment and distrust on their account, cannot be tolerated, whatever be the pretense. I have made a point of sending those back that have come under my observation, and I must desire you will do the same towards those who fall under yours.—To Alexander McDougall. Fitzpatrick 8:108. (1777.)

[If any officers] leave their post or command before they are regularly drawn off or relieved, or shall directly or indirectly cause any soldier to do the like, they shall be punished as far as martial law will extend, without favor or mitigation.—To Charles Scott. Fitzpatrick 13:166. (1778.)

REVOLUTIONARY WAR, Problem of Foreign Officers in.—Our corps being already formed and fully officered,...the number of foreign gentlemen already commissioned and continually arriving with fresh applications throw such obstacles in the way of any future appointments that every new arrival is only a new source of embarrassment to Congress and myself, and of disappointment and chagrin to the gentlemen who came over. Had there been only a few to provide for, we might have found employment for them in a way advantageous to the service and honorable to themselves; but as they have come over in such crowds, we either must not employ them, or we must do it at the expense of one-half the officers of the army, which you must be sensible would be attended with the most ruinous effects and could not fail to occasion a general discontent.—To Benjamin Franklin. Fitzpatrick 9:85. (1777.)

The ambition of these men . . . is unlimited and unbounded; and the singular instances of rank, which have been conferred upon them in but too many cases, have occasioned general dissatisfaction and general complaint. The feelings of our own officers have been much hurt by it, and their ardor and love for the service greatly dampened. Should a like proceeding still be practiced, it is not easy to say what extensive murmurings and consequences may ensue. I will further add that we have already a full proportion of foreign officers in our general councils, and should their number be increased it may happen upon many occasions that their voices may equal, if not exceed, the rest.—To Henry Laurens. Fitzpatrick 12:224. (1778.)

I trust you think me so much a citizen of the world as to believe that I am not easily warped or led away by attachments merely local or American. Yet I confess I am not entirely without them, nor does it appear to me that they are unwarrantable, if confined within proper limits. Fewer promotions in the foreign line would have been productive of more harmony and made our warfare more agreeable to all parties. The frequency of them is

the source of jealousy and of disunion. We have many, very many, deserving officers who are not opposed to merit wheresoever it is found, nor insensible of the advantages derived from a long service in an experienced army, nor to the principles of policy. Where any of these principles mark the way to rank, I am persuaded, they yield a becoming and willing acquiescence; but where they are not the basis, they feel severely.—To Henry Laurens. Fitzpatrick 12:224. (1778.)

I do most sincerely wish that we had not a single foreigner among us, except the Marquis de Lafayette, who acts upon very different principles from those which govern the rest.—To Gouverneur Morris. Fitzpatrick 12:227. (1778.)

They may be divided into three classes, namely, mere adventurers without recommendation, or recommended by persons who do not know how else to dispose of or provide for them; men of great ambition, who would sacrifice everything to promote their own personal glory; or mere spies, who are sent here to obtain a thorough knowledge of our situation and circumstances, in the execution of which, I am persuaded, some of them are faithful emissaries, as I do not believe a single matter escapes unnoticed or unadvised at a foreign court.—To Gouverneur Morris. Fitzpatrick 12:227. (1778.)

REVOLUTIONARY WAR, Incentives for Bravery of American Soldiers.—Let it never be said that in a day of action you turned your backs on the foe. Let the enemy no longer triumph. They brand you with ignominious epithets. Will you patiently endure that reproach? Will you suffer the wounds given to your country to go unrevenged? Will you resign your parents, wives, children, and friends to be the wretched vassals of a proud, insulting foe? And your own necks to the halter?...Nothing, then, remains but nobly to contend for all that is dear to us. Every motive that can touch the human breast calls us to the most vigorous exertions. Our dearest rights, our dearest friends, and our own lives, honor, glory, and even shame urge us to fight. And my fellow soldiers, when an opportunity presents, be firm, be brave. Show yourselves men, and the victory is yours.— General Orders. Fitzpatrick 9:306. (1777.)

REVOLUTIONARY WAR, Distrust of Military Power During.—I confess I have felt myself greatly embarrassed with respect to a vigorous exercise of military power. I have been well aware of the prevalent jealousy of military power, and that this has been considered as an evil much to be apprehended even by the best and most sensible among us. Under this idea, I have been cautious and wished to avoid as much as possible any act that might improve it.... The people at large are governed much by custom. To acts of legislation or civil authority they have been ever taught to yield a willing obedience without reasoning about their propriety On those of military power, whether immediate or derived originally from another source, they have ever looked with a jealous and suspicious eye.—To the President of Congress. Fitzpatrick 10:159. (1777.)

REVOLUTIONARY WAR, Severe Difficulties of.—Unless some great and capital change suddenly takes place,...this army must inevitably be reduced to one or other of these three things: starve, dissolve, or disperse in order to obtain subsistence in the best manner they can.... Three or four days' bad weather would prove our destruction. What, then, is to become of the army this winter? And if we are as often without provisions now as with them, what is to become of us in the spring, when our forces will be collected, with the aid perhaps of militia, to take advantage of an early campaign before the enemy can be reinforced?...Few men |have| more than one shirt, many only the |half| of one, and some none at all.... Besides a number of men confined to hospitals, ...we have...no less than 2898 men now in camp unfit for duty because they are barefoot and otherwise naked. Notwithstanding which,...we find gentlemen...reprobating the measure |of putting the army into winter quarters| as much as if they thought the soldiery were made of stocks or stones and equally insensible of frost and snow; and, moreover, as if they conceived it easily practicable for an inferior army under the disadvantages I have described...to confine a superior one (in all respects well appointed, and provided for a winter's campaign) within the city of Philadelphia, and to cover from depredation and waste the states of Pennsylvania,

[New] Jersey, etc. But what makes this matter still more extraordinary in my eye is that these very gentlemen, who were well apprised of the nakedness of the troops, . . . should think a winter's campaign and the covering these states from the invasion of an enemy so easy and practicable a business. I can assure those gentlemen that it is a much easier and less distressing thing to draw remonstrances in a comfortable room by a good fireside than to occupy a cold, bleak hill and sleep under frost and snow without clothes or blankets; however, although they seem to have little feeling for the naked and distressed soldier[s], I feel superabundantly for them, and from my soul pity those miseries which it is neither in my power to relieve [nor] prevent. It is for these reasons, therefore, I have dwelt upon the subject; and it adds not a little to my other difficulties and distress to find that much more is expected of me than is possible to be performed, and that upon the ground of safety and policy I am obliged to conceal the true state of the army from public view and thereby expose myself to detraction and calumny.—To the President of Congress. Fitzpatrick 10:192. (1777.)

We are without money, and have been so for a great length of time; without provision and forage, except what is taken by impress; without clothing; and shortly shall be (in a manner) without men. In a word, we have lived upon expedients till we can live no longer, and it may truly be said that the history of this war is a history of false hopes and temporary devices.

—To George Mason. Fitzpatrick 20:242. (1780.)

It was known that . . . the expense in comparison with our circumstances as colonists must be enormous, the struggle protracted, dubious, and severe. . . . Not then organized as a nation, or known as a people upon the earth, we had no preparation. Money, the nerve of war, was wanting. The sword was to be forged on the anvil of necessity.—Proposed address to Congress (never delivered). Fitzpatrick 30:297. (1789.)

REVOLUTIONARY WAR, Suffering of American Troops in.—Our sick naked, our well naked, our unfortunate men in captivity naked!—To Governor William Livingston. Fitzpatrick 10:233. (1777.)

The soldiers . . . have been (two or three times) days together without provisions, and once six days without any of the meat kind; could the poor horses tell their tale, it would be in a strain still more lamentable, as numbers have actually died from pure want.—To John Cadwalader. Fitzpatrick 11:117. (1778.)

No history now extant can furnish an instance of an army's suffering such uncommon hardships as ours have done, and bearing them with the same patience and fortitude. To see men without clothes to cover their nakedness, without blankets to [lie] on, without shoes, by which their marches might be traced by the blood from their feet, and almost as often without provisions as with, marching through frost and snow, and at Christmas taking up their winter quarters within a day's march of the enemy without a house or hut to cover them till they could be built, and submitting to it without a murmur, is a mark of patience and obedience which in my opinion can scarce be paralleled.—To John Banister. Fitzpatrick 11:291. (1778.)

REVOLUTIONARY WAR, British Occupation of American Towns.—I am well convinced myself that the enemy, long ere this, are perfectly well satisfied that the possession of our towns, while we have an army in the field, will avail them little. It involves us in difficulty, but does not by any means insure them conquest. They will know that it is our arms, not defenseless towns, they have to subdue before they can arrive at the haven of their wishes, and that, till this end is accomplished, the superstructure they have been endeavoring to raise, "like the baseless fabric of a vision," falls to nothing.—To Henry Laurens. Fitzpatrick 13:15. (1778.)

REVOLUTIONARY WAR, Distressing Circumstances of the.—If I |were| to be called upon to draw a picture of the times and of men, from what I have seen and heard and in part know, I should in one word say that idleness, dissipation, and extravagance seem to have laid fast hold of most of them; that speculation, peculation, and an insatiable thirst for riches seem to have got the better of every other consideration and almost of every order of men; that party disputes and personal quarrels are the great business of the day, while the momentous concerns of an empire—a great and accumulated

Washington in 1796 (age 64). Pastel portrait by James Sharples.

debt, ruined finances, depreciated money, and want of credit (which in their consequences |are| the want of everything)—are but secondary considerations and postponed from day to day, from week to week, as if our affairs wear the most promising aspect. After drawing this picture, which from my soul I believe to be a true one, I need not repeat to you that I am alarmed and wish to see my countrymen roused. I have no resentments, nor do I mean to point at any particular characters,... but in the present situation of things I cannot help asking—where |are| Mason, Wythe, Jefferson, Nicholas, Pendleton, Nelson? ... I feel more real distress on account of the present appearances of things than I have done at any one time since the commencement of the dispute.... Providence has heretofore taken me up when all other means and hope seemed to be departing from me. In this I will confide.—To Benjamin Harrison. Fitzpatrick 13:466. (1778.)

REVOLUTIONARY WAR, Condemnation of Speculators in.—Friends and foes seem now to combine to pull down the goodly fabric we have hitherto been raising at the expense of so much time, blood, and treasure; and unless the bodies politic will exert themselves to bring things back to first principles, correct abuses, and punish our internal foes, inevitable ruin must follow. Indeed, we seem to be verging so fast to destruction that I am filled with sensations to which I have been a stranger till within these three months. It is now consistent with the views of the speculators, various tribes of moneymakers, and stockjobbers of all denominations to continue the war for their own private emolument without considering that their avarice and thirst for gain must plunge everything (including themselves) in one common ruin.—To George Mason. Fitzpatrick 14:300. (1779.)

I cannot with any degree of patience behold the infamous practices of speculators, monopolizers, and all that class of gentry which are preying upon our very vitals and, for the sake of a little dirty pelf, are putting the rights and liberties of the country into the most imminent danger.—To Lund Washington. Fitzpatrick 15:180. (1779.)

REVOLUTIONARY WAR, Decay of Public Virtue During.—Our conflict is not likely to cease so soon as every good man would wish. The measure of iniquity is not yet filled; and unless we can return a little more to first principles and act a little more upon patriotic grounds, I do not know when it will, or what may be the issue of the contest. Speculation, peculation, engrossing, |and| forestalling, with all their concomitants, afford too many melancholy proofs of the decay of public virtue, and too glaring instances of its being the interest and desire of too many, who would wish to be thought friends, to continue the war. Nothing, I am convinced, but the depreciation of our currency, proceeding in a great measure from the foregoing causes, aided by stockjobbing and party dissensions, has fed the hopes of the enemy and kept the British arms in America to this day. They do not scruple to declare this themselves, and add that we shall be our own conquerors. Cannot our common country, America, possess virtue enough to disappoint them? Is the paltry consideration of a little dirty pelf to individuals to be placed in competition with the essential rights and liberties of the present generation, and of millions yet unborn? Shall a few designing men, for their own aggrandizement and to gratify their own avarice, overset the goodly fabric we have been rearing at the expense of so much time, blood, and treasure? And shall we at last become the victims of our own abominable lust of gain? Forbid it, Heaven! Forbid it, all and every state in the Union! by enacting and enforcing efficacious laws for checking the growth of these monstrous evils and restoring matters in some degree to the pristine state they were in at the commencement of the war!—To James Warren. Fitzpatrick 14:312. (1779.)

REVOLUTIONARY WAR, Payment of Soldiers in.—All that the common soldiery of any country can expect is food and clothing. The pay given in other armies is little more than nominal, very low in the first instance and subject to a variety of deductions that reduce it to nothing. This is the case with the British troops, though I believe they receive more than those of any of the European armies. The idea of maintaining [our soldiers'] families at home, at public expense, is peculiar to us and is incompatible with the finances of any government. Our troops have been uniformly better fed than any others; they are at this time very well clad, and I hope will continue to be so. While this is the case they will have no just cause of complaint.—To William Maxwell. Fitzpatrick 15:33. (1779.)

REVOLUTIONARY WAR, Role of Spies in.—Single men in the night will be more likely to ascertain facts than the best glasses in the day.—To Anthony Wayne. Fitzpatrick 15:397. (1779.)

REVOLUTIONARY WAR, Midnight Attack Recommended.—The usual time for exploits of this kind is a little before day, for which reason a vigilant officer is then more on the watch; I therefore recommend a midnight

hour. . . . A dark night and even a rainy one, if you can find the way, will contribute to your success.—To Anthony Wayne. Fitzpatrick 15:398. (1779.)

REVOLUTIONARY WAR, Support from States Sometimes Lacking.—The contest among the different states now is not which shall do most for the common cause, but which shall do least.—To Fielding Lewis. Fitzpatrick 19:132. (1780.)

REVOLUTIONARY WAR, Ruinous National Policy During.—It has ever been our conduct and misfortune to slumber and sleep while we should be diligent in preparation, and when pressed by irresistible necessity and when we can delay no longer, then to bring ourselves to the brink of destruction by expensive and temporary expedients. In a word, we have no system, and seem determined not to profit by experience. We are, during the winter, dreaming of independence and peace, without using the means to [achieve them]. In the spring, when our recruits should be with the army and in training, we have just discovered the necessity of calling for them; and by the fall, after a distressed and inglorious campaign for want of them, we begin to get a few men, which come in just in time enough to eat our provisions and consume our stores without rendering any service. Thus it is, one year rolls over another, and without some change we are hastening to our ruin.—To John Augustine Washington. Fitzpatrick 19:135. (1780.)

I lament most sincerely the system of policy which has been but too generally adopted in all the states, to wit, that of temporary expedients, which, like quack medicines, are so far from removing the causes of complaint that they only serve to increase the disorder. This has, in a most remarkable manner, been the case with respect to short enlistments, which |have| been the primary cause of all our misfortunes.—To Fielding Lewis. Fitzpatrick 22:282. (1781.)

REVOLUTIONARY WAR, False Security in.—The satisfaction I have in any successes that attend us, or even in the alleviation of misfortunes, is always allayed by a fear that it will lull us into security. Supineness and a disposition to flatter ourselves seem to make parts of our national character; when we receive a check and are not quite undone, we are apt to fancy we have gained a victory; and when we do gain any little advantage, we imagine it decisive and expect the war is immediately to end. The history of the war is a history of false hopes and temporary expedients. Would to God they were to end here!—To James Duane. Fitzpatrick 20:117. (1780.)

REVOLUTIONARY WAR, Victory Evasive.—The favorable disposition of Spain, the promised succor from France, the combined force in the West Indies, the declaration of Russia (acceded to by other powers of Europe, humiliating to the naval pride and power of Great Britain), the superiority of France and Spain by sea in Europe, the Irish claims and English disturbances, formed, in the aggregate, an opinion in my breast (which is not very susceptible of peaceful

dreams) that the hour of deliverance was not far distant; for... however unwilling Great Britain might be to yield the point, it would not be in her power to continue the contest. But alas! these prospects, flattering as they were, have proved delusory, and I see nothing before us but accumulating distress.—To John Cadwalader. Fitzpatrick 20:121. (1780.)

REVOLUTIONARY WAR, National Reforms Needed During.—If we mean to continue our struggles (and it is to be hoped we shall not relinquish our claim), we must do it upon an entire new plan. We must have a permanent force, not a force that is constantly fluctuating and sliding from under us as a pedestal of ice would do from a statue in a summer's day.... We must at the same time contrive ways and means to aid our taxes by loans and put our finance|s| upon a more certain and stable footing than they are at present. Our civil government must likewise undergo a reform; ample powers must be lodged in Congress as the head of the federal union, adequate to all the purposes of war. Unless these things are done, our efforts will be in vain, and |will| only serve to accumulate expense, add to our perplexities, and dissatisfy the people without a prospect of obtaining the prize in view.—To George Mason. Fitzpatrick 20:242. (1780.)

REVOLUTIONARY WAR, Military Punishment in.—It appears to me indispensable there should be an extension of the present corporal punishment; and also that it would be useful to authorize courts-martial to sentence delinquents to labor at public works; perhaps even for some crimes, particularly desertion, to transfer them from the land to the sea service, where they have less opportunity to indulge their inconstancy. A variety in punishments is of utility, as well as a proportion. The number of lashes may either be indefinite, left to the discretion of the court to fix, or limited to a larger number; in this case, I would recommend five hundred.—To the President of Congress. Fitzpatrick 21:179. (1781.)

REVOLUTIONARY WAR, Washington Certain of Victory in.—We must not despair; the game is yet in our own hands; to play it well is all we have to do, and I trust the experience of error will enable us to act better in the future. A cloud may yet pass over us; individuals may be ruined; and the country at large, or particular states, undergo temporary distress; but certain I am that it is in our power to bring the war to a happy conclusion.—To John Mathews. Fitzpatrick 22:176. (1781.)

REVOLUTIONARY WAR, Settlement of Back Pay to Army.—Painful as the task is to describe the dark side of our affairs, it sometimes becomes a matter of indispensable necessity. Without disguise or palliation, I will inform you candidly of the discontents which, at this moment, prevail universally throughout the army. The complaint of evils which they suppose almost remediless are the total want of money or the means of existing from one day to another, the heavy debts they have already incurred, the loss of

credit, the distress of their families ... at home, and the prospect of poverty and misery before them.... The officers also complain of ... the leaving the compensation for their services in a loose, equivocal state, without |the government's| ascertaining their claims upon the public or making provision for the future payment of them. ... Though no one that I have seen or heard of appears opposed to the principle of reducing the army as circumstances may require, yet I cannot help fearing the result of |this| measure ... under present circumstances, when I see such a number of men goaded by a thousand stings of reflection on the past, and of anticipation on the future, about to be turned into the world, soured by penury and what they call the ingratitude of the public, involved in debts, without one farthing of money to carry them home, after having spent the flower of their days (and many of them their patrimonies) in establishing the freedom and independence of their country, and |having| suffered everything human nature is capable of enduring on this side of death. I repeat it, |in view of| these irritable circumstances, without one thing to soothe their feelings or frighten the gloomy prospects, I cannot avoid apprehending that a train of evils will follow of a very serious and distressing nature.... The patience and long-suffering of this army are almost exhausted, and ... there never was so great a spirit of discontent as at this instant. While |we are| in the field I think it may be kept from breaking out into acts of outrage, but when we retire into winter quarters ... I cannot be at ease respecting the consequences.—To the Secretary of War. Fitzpatrick 25:226. (1782.)

The establishment of funds and security of the payment of all the just demands of the army will be the most certain means of preserving the national faith and future tranquility of this extensive continent.... If this country should not ... perform everything, which has been requested in the |army's| late memorial to Congress, then will my belief become vain, and the hope that has been excited void of foundation. And "if (as has been suggested for the purpose of inflaming their passions) the officers of the army are to be the only sufferers by this |revolution|, if retiring from the field they are to grow old in poverty, wretchedness, and contempt, if they are to wade through the vile mire of dependency and owe the miserable remnant of that life to charity which has hitherto been spent in honor," then shall I have learned what ingratitude is; then shall I have realized a tale which will embitter every moment of my future life. But I am under no such apprehensions; a country rescued by their arms from impending ruin will never leave unpaid the debt of gratitude.—To the President of Congress. Fitzpatrick 26:231. (1783.)

I fix it as an *indispensable* measure that, previous to the disbanding |of| the army, all their accounts should be completely liquidated and settled, and that every person shall be ascertained of the balance due to him.... But after settlement is formed, there remains another circumstance of more importance still, and without which it will be of little consequence to have the sums due them ascertained; that is, the payment of some part of the balance The distresses of officers and soldiers are now driven to the extreme, and without this provision will not be lessened by the prospect of dissolution |of the army|. It is therefore universally expected that three months' pay at least must be given them before they are disbanded; this sum it is confidently imagined may be procured, and is absolutely indispensable.... I repeat ... that this sum at least must by some means be procured. Without this provision it will be absolutely impossible for many to get from camp, or to return to their friends; and driven to such necessities, it is impossible to foresee what may be the consequences of their not obtaining it.... To be disbanded at last without this little pittance,... like a set of beggars—needy, distressed, and without prospect—will not only blast the expectations of their creditors and expose the officers to the utmost indignity and the worst of consequences, but will drive every man of honor and sensibility to the extremest horrors of despair.—To Theodorick Bland. Fitzpatrick 26:286. (1783.)

REVOLUTIONARY WAR, Harmony Between French and American Armies.—It may, I believe, with much truth be said that a greater harmony between two armies never subsisted than that which has prevailed between the French and American since the first junction of them last year.—To the Marquis de Lafayette. Fitzpatrick

25:279. (1782.)

REVOLUTIONARY WAR, American Victory Almost Unbelievable.—If historiographers should be hardy enough to fill the page of history with the advantages that have been gained with unequal numbers (on the part of America) in the course of this contest, and attempt to relate the distressing circumstances under which they have been obtained, it is more than probable that posterity will bestow on their labors the epithet and marks of fiction; for it will not be believed that such a force as Great Britain has employed for eight years in this country could be baffled in their plan of subjugating it by numbers infinitely less, composed of men oftentimes half starved, always in rags, without pay, and experiencing, at times, every species of distress which human nature is capable of undergoing.—To Nathanael Greene. Fitzpatrick 26:104. (1783.)

REVOLUTIONARY WAR, Mutiny Prevented by Washington.—Let me entreat you, gentlemen, . . . not to take any measures which, viewed in the calm light of reason, will lessen the dignity and sully the glory you have hitherto maintained; let me request you to rely on the plighted faith of your country, and place a full confidence in the purity of the intentions of Congress. . . . And let me conjure you, in the name of our common country, as you value your own sacred honor, as you respect the rights of humanity, and as you regard the military and national character of America, to express your utmost horror and detestation of the man who wishes, under any spe-

cious pretenses, to overturn the liberties of our country, and who wickedly attempts to open the floodgates of civil discord and deluge our rising empire in blood. By thus determining, and thus acting, you will . . . give one more distinguished proof of unexampled patriotism and patient virtue, rising superior to the pressure of the most complicated sufferings; and you will, by the dignity of your conduct, afford occasion for posterity to say, when speaking of the glorious example you have exhibited to mankind, "Had this day been wanting, the world had never seen the last stage of perfection to which human nature is capable of attaining."*—To the officers of the army. Fitzpatrick 26:226. (1783.)

*Excerpted from Washington's famous Newburgh Address, given in response to an inflammatory and anonymous circular urging officers and soldiers to march on Congress and force them to issue back pay and fulfill other overdue promises to the army.—Editor.

REVOLUTIONARY WAR, Giving Arms to Soldiers at Close of.—I must beg the liberty to suggest to Congress an idea which has been hinted to me and which has affected my mind very forcibly. That is, that at the discharge of the men engaged for [the duration of] the war, Congress should be pleased to suffer those men, noncommissioned officers and soldiers, to take with them as their own property, and as a gratuity, the arms and accoutrements they now hold. This act would raise pleasing sensations in the minds of those worthy and faithful men who, from their early engaging in the war at moderate bounties and

from their patient continuing under innumerable distresses, have not only deserved nobly from their country, but have obtained an honorable distinction over those who, with shorter terms, have gained large pecuniary rewards. This act, at a comparatively small expense, would be deemed an honorable testimonial from Congress of the regard they bear to those distinguished worthies and the sense they have of their suffering virtues and services, which have been so happily instrumental towards the security and establishment of the rights, liberties, and independence of this rising empire. These constant companions of their toils and dangers, preserved with sacred care, would be handed down from the present possessors to their children as honorable badges of bravery and military merit, and would probably be brought forth on some future occasion, with pride and exultation, to be improved, with the same military ardor and emulation, in the hands of posterity, as they have been used by their forefathers in the present establishment and foundation of our national independence and glory. — To the President of Congress. Fitzpatrick 26:332. (1783.)

REVOLUTIONARY WAR, End of Hostilities Proclaimed.— The commander-in-chief orders the cessation of hostilities between the United States of America and the king of Great Britain to be publicly proclaimed tomorrow at twelve o'clock,...after which the chaplains with the several brigades will render thanks to almighty God for all his mercies, partic-

ularly for his overruling the wrath of man to his own glory, and causing the rage of war to cease among the nations. . . .

The proclamation...must afford the most rational and sincere satisfaction to every benevolent mind, as it puts a period to a long and doubtful contest, stops the effusion of human blood, opens the prospect to a more splendid scene, and, like another morning star, promises the approach of a brighter day than has hitherto illuminated the Western Hemisphere; on such a happy day, a day which is the harbinger of peace, a day which completes the eighth year of the war, it would be ingratitude not to rejoice!— General Orders. Fitzpatrick 26:334. (1783.)

REVOLUTIONARY WAR, Eulogy to Troops at End of.— While the General recollects the almost infinite variety of scenes through which we have passed with a mixture of pleasure, astonishment, and gratitude, while he contemplates the prospects before us with rapture, he cannot help wishing that all the brave men...who have shared in the toils and dangers of effecting this glorious revolution, of rescuing millions from the hand of oppression, and of laying the foundation of a great empire, might be impressed with a proper idea of the dignified part they have been called to act...on the stage of human affairs; for happy, thrice happy shall they be pronounced hereafter who have contributed anything, who have performed the meanest office, in erecting this stupendous fabric of freedom and empire on the broad basis of independence, who have assisted in protecting the rights of human nature and establishing an asylum for the poor and oppressed of all nations and religions.

The glorious task for which we first flew to arms being thus accomplished; the liberties of our country being fully acknowledged and firmly secured by the smiles of heaven on the purity of our cause, and |by| the honest exertions of a feeble people (determined to be free) against a powerful nation (disposed to oppress them); and the character of those who have persevered through every extremity of hardship, suffering, and danger being immortalized by the illustrious appellation of the patriot army—nothing now remains but for the actors of this mighty scene to preserve a perfect, unvarying consistency of character through the very last act, to close the drama with applause, and to retire from the military theater with the same approbation of angels and men which have crowned all their former virtuous actions.—General Orders. Fitzpatrick 26:335. (1783.)

REVOLUTIONARY WAR, Causes of Trouble in.—I could demonstrate to every mind open to conviction that in less time, and with much less expense than has been incurred, the war might have been brought to the same happy conclusion, if the resources of the continent could have been properly drawn forth; that the distresses and disappointments which have very often occurred have, in too many instances, resulted more from a want of energy in the continental government than a

deficiency of means in the particular states; that the inefficacy of measures arising from the want of an adequate authority in the supreme power, from a partial compliance with the requisitions of Congress in some of the states, and from a failure of punctuality in others, while it tended to damp the zeal of those which were more willing to exert themselves, served also to accumulate the expenses of the war and to frustrate the best concerted plans; and that the discouragement occasioned by the complicated difficulties and embarrassments in which our affairs were by this means involved would have long ago produced the dissolution of any army less patient, less virtuous, and less perservering than that which I have had the honor to command.—Circular to the States. Fitzpatrick 26:495. (1783.)

REVOLUTIONARY WAR, Condemnation of Pennsylvania Mutineers.—When we consider that these Pennsylvania levies who have now mutinied are recruits and soldiers of a day, who have not borne the heat and burden of the war and who can have in reality very few hardships to complain of, and when we at the same time recollect that those soldiers who have lately been furloughed from this army are the veterans who have patiently endured hunger, nakedness, and cold, who have suffered and bled without a murmur, and who with perfect good order have retired to their homes without the settlement of their accounts or a farthing of money in their pockets, we shall be as much astonished at the virtues of the latter as we are struck with horror and detestation at the proceedings of the former; and every candid mind, without indulging ill-grounded prejudices, will undoubtedly make the proper discrimination.— To the President of Congress. Fitzpatrick 27:33. (1783.)

REVOLUTIONARY WAR, God the Author of American Victory.—The disadvantageous circumstances on our part, under which the war was undertaken, can never be forgotten. The singular interpositions of Providence in our feeble condition were such as could scarcely escape the attention of the most unobserving, while the unparalleled perseverence of the armies of the United States, through almost every possible suffering and discouragement for the space of eight long years, was little short of a standing miracle.—Farewell Orders to the Armies of the United States. Fitzpatrick 27:223. (1783.)

REVOLUTIONARY WAR, Victory in, Astonishing.—A contemplation of the complete attainment (at a period earlier than could have been expected) of the object for which we contended against so formidable a power cannot but inspire us with astonishment and gratitude.... Every American officer and soldier must now console himself for any unpleasant circumstances which may have occurred by a recollection of the uncommon scenes in which he has been called to act no inglorious part, and the astonishing events of which he has been a witness, events which have seldom if ever before taken place on the stage of human action, nor can they probably

ever happen again. For who has before seen a disciplined army formed at once from such raw materials? Who, that was not a witness, could imagine that the most violent local prejudices would cease so soon, and that men who came from the different parts of the continent, strongly disposed, by the habits of education, to despise and quarrel with each other, would instantly become but one patriotic band of brothers; or who, that was not on the spot, can trace the steps by which such a wonderful revolution has been effected, and such a glorious period put to all our warlike toils?—Farewell Orders to the Armies of the United States. Fitzpatrick 27:223. (1783.)

REVOLUTIONARY WAR, Washington's Farewell to the Army.—To bid a final adieu to the armies he has so long had the honor to command, [the commander-in-chief] can only again offer in their behalf his recommendations to their grateful country, and his prayers to the God of armies. May ample justice be done them here, and may the choicest of heaven's favors, both here and hereafter, attend those who, under the divine auspices, have secured innumerable blessings for others; with these wishes, and this benediction, the commander-in-chief is about to retire from service. The curtain of separation will soon be drawn, and the military scene to him will be closed forever.—Farewell Orders to the Armies of the United States. Fitzpatrick 27:227. (1783.)

REVOLUTIONARY WAR, America's Secret Resource in.—If we had a secret resource of a nature unknown to the enemy, it was in the unconquerable resolution of our citizens, the conscious rectitude of our cause, and a confident trust that we should not be forsaken by Heaven.—Proposed address to Congress (never delivered). Fitzpatrick 30:297. (1789.)

REVOLUTIONARY WAR, Sacrifices in.—The tempest of war having at length been succeeded by the sunshine of peace, our citizen-soldiers impressed a useful lesson of patriotism on mankind by nobly returning with impaired constitutions and unsatisfied claims, after such long sufferings and severe disappointments, to their former occupations. Posterity as well as the present age will doubtless regard with admiration and gratitude the patience, perseverance, and valor which achieved our revolution. They will cherish the remembrance of virtues which had but few parallels in former times, and which will add new luster to the most splendid page of history.—To the people of the state of South Carolina. Sparks 12:187. (1790.)

REVOLUTIONARY WAR. See also AMERICAN REVOLUTION; ARMY; ENEMY; GOD; GREAT BRITAIN; HESSIANS; INDEPENDENCE; INDIANS; MILITIA; NAVY; NEW YORK; OFFICERS; PRISONERS OF WAR; TORIES; TREASON; WAR; YORKTOWN.

REVOLUTIONS, Among Nations.—The rapidity of national revolutions appears no less astonishing than their magnitude. In what they will terminate is known only to the great Ruler of events; and confiding in his wisdom and goodness, we may safely trust the

issue to him without perplexing ourselves to seek for that which is beyond human ken, only taking care to perform the parts assigned us in a way that reason and our own consciences approve of.—To David Humphreys. Fitzpatrick 32:398. (1793.)

REVOLUTIONS. See also AMERICAN REVOLUTION; FRENCH REVOLUTION; INSURGENCY.

RUMORS, Washington's Response to.—I never suffer reports unsupported by proofs to have weight in my mind.—To Richard Henry Lee. Fitzpatrick 22:382. (1781.)

S

SELF-GOVERNMENT, American, a Unique Development in History.—A greater drama is now acting on this theater than has heretofore been brought on the American stage, or any other in the world. We exhibit at present the novel and astonishing spectacle of a whole people deliberating calmly on what form of government will be most conducive to their happiness, and deciding with an unexpected degree of unanimity in favor of a system which they conceive calculated to answer the purpose.—To Sir Edward Newenham. Fitzpatrick 30:73. (1788.)

SELF-GOVERNMENT, Importance of Enlightened Citizenry in.—I am sure the mass of citizens in these United States *mean well*, and I firmly believe they will always *act well* whenever they can obtain a right understanding of matters.—To John Jay. Fitzpatrick 35:36. (1796.)

SELF-GOVERNMENT. See also

Washington in 1796 (age 64). Pastel portrait by James Sharples.

DEMOCRACY; EDUCATION; FREEDOM; GOVERNMENT; INDE-PENDENCE; INFORMATION; KNOWLEDGE; LIBERTY; PEOPLE; PUBLIC OPINION; REPUBLICAN-ISM.
SEPARATION OF POWERS, Guards Against Tyranny.—These powers |of the federal government|...are so distributed among the legislative, executive, and judicial branches... that it can never be in danger of degenerating into a monarchy, an oligarchy, an aristocracy, or any other despotic or oppressive form so long as there shall remain any virtue in the body of the people.... It is provided with more checks and barriers against the intro-

duction of tyranny...than any government hitherto instituted among mortals.—To the Marquis de Lafayette. Fitzpatrick 29:410. (1788.)
SEPARATION OF POWERS, Essential for Preservation of Freedom.—I have always believed that an unequivocally free and equal representation of the people in the legislature, together with an efficient and responsible executive, were the great pillars on which the preservation of American freedom must depend.—To Mrs. Catharine Macaulay Graham Fitzpatrick 30:496. (1790.)
SEPARATION OF POWERS, Must Be Preserved.—It is important...that the habits of thinking in a free country should inspire caution in those entrusted with its administration to confine themselves within their respective constitutional spheres, avoiding in the exercise of the powers of one department to encroach upon another. The spirit of encroachment tends to consolidate the powers of all the departments in one, and thus to create, whatever the form of government, a real despotism. A just estimate of that love of power, and proneness to abuse it, which predominates in the human heart is sufficient to satisfy us of the truth of this position. The necessity of reciprocal checks in the exercise of political power, by dividing and distributing it into different depositories and constituting each the guardian of the public weal against invasions by the others, has been evinced by experiments ancient and modern, some of them in our country and under our own eyes. To preserve them must be

as necessary as to institute them. If in
the opinion of the people the distribution or modification of the constitutional powers be in any particular
wrong, let it be corrected by an
amendment in the way which the
Constitution designates. But let there
be no change by usurpation; for
though this, in one instance, may be
the instrument of good, it is the
customary weapon by which free
governments are destroyed. The precedent must always greatly over-
balance in permanent evil any partial
or transient benefit which the use can
at any time yield.—Farewell Address.
Fitzpatrick 35:228. (1796.)

SEPARATION OF POWERS. See
also CONSTITUTION (U.S.); FED-
ERAL GOVERNMENT.

**SHAYS'S REBELLION, Washing-
ton's Reaction to.**—What is the cause
of all these commotions? Do they
proceed from licentiousness, British
influence disseminated by the Tories,
or real grievances which admit of
redress? If the latter, why were they
delayed till the public mind had become
so much agitated? If the former, why
are not the powers of government
tried at once? It is as well to be without
|them| as not to live under their exer-
cise. Commotions of this sort, like
snowballs, gather strength as they roll
if there is no opposition in the way to
divide and crumble them.—To David
Humphreys. Fitzpatrick 29:27. (1786.)

I am mortified beyond expression
when I view the clouds that have
spread over the brightest morn that
ever dawned upon any country....
My humble opinion is that there is a

call for decision. Know precisely what
the insurgents aim at. If they have real
grievances, redress them if possible, or
acknowledge the justice of them and
your inability to do it in the present
moment. If they have not, employ the
force of government against them at
once. If this is inadequate, all will be
convinced that the superstructure is
bad, or wants support. To be more
exposed in the eyes of the world, and
more contemptible than we already
are, is hardly possible.—To Henry Lee.
Fitzpatrick 29:34. (1786.)

**SLAVERY, Washington's Aversion
to.**—I every day long more and more
to get clear of |my Negro slaves|.—To
Lund Washington. Fitzpatrick 12:327.
(1778.)

Were it not...that I am principled
against selling Negroes, as you would
do cattle in the market, I would not in
twelve months from this date be
possessed of one as a slave.—To
Alexander Spotswood. Fitzpatrick
34:47. (1794.)

On this estate (Mount Vernon) I
have more working Negroes, by a full
|half|, than can be employed to any
advantage.... |But| to sell the over-
plus I cannot, because I am principled
against this kind of traffic in the
human species. To hire them out is
almost as bad, because they could not
be disposed of in families to any advantage, and to disperse the families I have
an aversion.—To Robert Lewis. Fitzpatrick 37:338. (1799.)

SLAVERY, Abolition of.—There is
not a man living who wishes more
sincerely than I do to see a plan adopted
for the abolition of |slavery|; but there

is only one proper and effectual mode by which it can be accomplished, and that is by legislative authority; and this, as far as my suffrage will go, shall never be wanting.—To Robert Morris. Fitzpatrick 28:408. (1786.)

Your late purchase of an estate in the colony of Cayenne, with a view of emancipating the slaves on it, is a generous and noble proof of your humanity. Would to God a like spirit would diffuse itself generally into the minds of the people of this country; but I despair of seeing it. Some petitions were presented to the [Virginia] Assembly at its last session for the abolition of slavery, but they could scarcely obtain a reading. To set [the slaves] afloat at once would, I really believe, be productive of much inconvenience and mischief; but by degrees it certainly might, and assuredly ought, to be effected; and that, too, by legislative authority.—To the Marquis de Lafayette. Fitzpatrick 28:424. (1786.)

I never mean (unless some particular circumstance should compel me to it) to possess another slave by purchase, it being among my first wishes to see some plan adopted by which slavery in this country may be abolished by slow, sure, and imperceptible degrees.—To John Francis Mercer. Fitzpatrick 29:5. (1786.)

I wish from my soul that the legislature of this state [Virginia] could see the policy of a gradual abolition of slavery; it would prevent much future mischief.—To Lawrence Lewis. Fitzpatrick 36:2. (1797.)

SLAVERY, Must Be Abandoned to

Perpetuate Union.—I can clearly foresee that nothing but the rooting out of slavery can perpetuate the existence of our Union, by consolidating it in a common bond of principle.—Spoken to John Bernard, as quoted by Bernard in *Retrospections of America* (New York: Harper & Brothers, 1887), p. 91. (1798.)

SLAVES, Washington's Kindness to.
—It is foremost in my thoughts to desire you will be particularly attentive to my Negroes in their sickness, and to order every overseer positively to be so likewise; for I am sorry to observe that the generality of them view these poor creatures in scarcely any other light than they do a draft horse or ox, neglecting them as much when they are unable to work, instead of comforting and nursing them when they lie on a sickbed.—To Anthony Whiting. Fitzpatrick 32:184. (1792.)

SLAVES, Liberated in Washington's Will.—Upon the decease of my wife, it is my will and desire that all the slaves which I hold in my own right shall receive their freedom. To emancipate them during her life would, though earnestly wished by me, be attended with such insuperable difficulties, on account of their intermixture by marriages with the dower Negroes, as to excite the most painful sensations, if not disagreeable consequences, from the latter,. . . it not being in my power, under the tenure by which the dower Negroes are held, to manumit them.—Last Will and Testament. Fitzpatrick 37:276. (1799.)

SLAVES, Old and Infirm, Provided for in Washington's Will.—And whereas, among those who will receive freedom according to this device, there may be some who from old age or bodily infirmities...will be unable to support themselves, it is my will and desire that all...shall be comfortably clothed and fed by my heirs while they live.—Last Will and Testament. Fitzpatrick 37:276. (1799.)

SLEEP, Rise Early from.—Rise early, that by habit it may become familiar, agreeable, healthy, and profitable. It may for a while be irksome to do this; but that will wear off, and the practice will produce a rich harvest forever thereafter, whether in public or private walks of life.—To George Washington Parke Custis. Fitzpatrick 36:118. (1798.)

SOCIETY OF THE CINCINNATI, Support for.—There is not, I conceive, an unbiased mind that would refuse the officers of the late army the right of associating for the purpose of establishing a fund for the support of the poor and distressed of their fraternity, when many of them, it is well known, are reduced to their last shifts by the ungenerous conduct of their country in not adopting more vigorous measures to render their certificates productive.—To Samuel Vaughan. Fitzpatrick 28:327. (1785.)

SOLUTIONS, Temporary, to Be Avoided.—It has ever been our conduct and misfortune to slumber and sleep while we should be diligent in preparation, and when pressed by irresistible necessity and when we can delay no longer, then to bring ourselves to the brink of destruction by expensive and temporary expedients.

In a word, we have no system, and seem determined not to profit by experience.—To John Augustine Washington. Fitzpatrick 19:135. (1780.)

I lament most sincerely the system of policy which has been but too generally adopted in all the states, to wit, that of temporary expedients, which, like quack medicines, are so far from removing the causes of complaint that they only serve to increase the disorder.—To Fielding Lewis. Fitzpatrick 22:282. (1781.)

SPAIN, Behind Other Nations in Liberality.—In this age of free inquiry and enlightened reason it is to be hoped that the condition of the people in every country will be bettered, and the happiness of mankind promoted. Spain appears to be so much behind the other nations of Europe in liberal policy that a long time will undoubtedly elapse before the people of that kingdom can taste the sweets of liberty, and enjoy the natural advantages of their country.—To David Humphreys. Fitzpatrick 31:318. (1791.)

STAMP ACT, Arguments Against.—The Stamp Act imposed on the colonies by the Parliament of Great Britain engrosses the conversation of the speculative part of the colonists, who look upon this unconstitutional method of taxation as a direful attack upon their liberties, and loudly exclaim against the violations. What may be the result of this and some other (I think I may add) ill-judged measures, I will not undertake to determine; but this I may venture to affirm, that the advantage accruing to the mother country will fall greatly short of the expectations of the ministry; for certain it is |that| our whole substance does already in a manner flow to Great Britain, and that whatsoever contributes to lessen our importations must be hurtful to their manufactures. And the eyes of our people, already beginning to open, will perceive that many luxuries which we lavish our substance to Great Britain for can well be dispensed with, while the necessaries of life are (mostly) to be had within ourselves. This consequently will introduce frugality, and be a necessary stimulation to industry. If Great Britain therefore loads her manufactures with heavy taxes, will it not facilitate these measures? They will not compel us, I think, to give our money for their exports, whether we will or no, and certain I am |that| none of their traders will part from them without a valuable consideration. Where, then, is the utility of these restrictions?

As to the Stamp Act, taken in a single view, one...bad consequence attending it I take to be this: our courts of judicature must inevitably be shut up, for it is impossible (or next of kin to it) under our present circumstances that the act of Parliament can be complied with, were we ever so willing to enforce the execution; for not to say, which alone would be sufficient, that we have not money to pay |for| the stamps, there are many other cogent reasons to prevent it; and if a stop be put to our judicial proceedings, I fancy the merchants of Great Britain trading to the colonies will not be among the last to wish for a repeal of it.—To

Francis Dandridge. Fitzpatrick 2:425. (1765.)

STAMP ACT, Repeal of.—The repeal of the Stamp Act, to whatsoever causes owing, ought much to be rejoiced at; for had the Parliament of Great Britain resolved upon enforcing it, the consequences, I conceive, would have been more direful than is generally apprehended, both to the mother country and her colonies. All, therefore, who were instrumental in procuring the repeal are entitled to the thanks of every British subject, and have mine cordially.—To Robert Cary & Company. Fitzpatrick 2:440. (1766.)

STAMP ACT. See also TAXATION.

STEUBEN (General Friedrich, Baron von), Character of.—Sensible, sober, and brave, well acquainted with tactics and with the arrangement and discipline of an army; high in his ideas of subordination, impetuous in his temper, ambitious—and a foreigner.—Opinion of the general officers. Fitzpatrick 31:509. (1792.)

SWORDS, Bequeathed in Washington's Will.—To each of my nephews, William Augustine Washington, George Lewis, George Steptoe Washington, Bushrod Washington, and Samuel Washington, I give one of the swords or cutteaux of which I may die possessed; and they are to choose in the order they are named. These swords are accompanied with an injunction not to unsheath them for the purpose of shedding blood, except it be for defense, or in defense of their country and its rights; and in the latter case, to keep them unsheathed and prefer falling with them in their hands to the relinquishment thereof.—*Last Will and Testament.* Fitzpatrick 37:288. (1799.)

T

TAVERNS, Problem of.—I apprehend it will be thought advisable to keep a garrison always at Fort Loudoun; for which reason I would beg leave to represent the great nuisance the number of tippling-houses in Winchester are . . . to the soldiers, who, by this means, in |spite| of the utmost care and vigilance, are, so long as their pay holds good, incessantly drunk and unfit for service.—*To Governor Robert Dinwiddie.* Fitzpatrick 1:470. (1756.)

TAXATION, Great Britain's Policy of.—Does it not appear as clear as the sun in its meridian brightness that there is a regular, systematic plan formed to fix the right and practice of taxation upon us? Does not the uniform conduct of Parliament for some years past confirm this? Do not all the debates, especially those just brought to us, in the House of Commons on the side of government expressly declare that America must be taxed in aid of the British funds, and that she has no longer resources within herself? Is there anything to be expected from petitioning after this? Is not the attack upon the liberty and property of the people of Boston, before restitution of the loss to the India Company was demanded, a plain and self-evident proof of what they are aiming at? Do not the subsequent bills (now, I dare

say, acts) for depriving the Massachusetts Bay of its charter, and for transporting offenders into other colonies or to Great Britain for trial, where it is impossible from the nature of the thing that justice can be obtained, convince us that the administration is determined to stick at nothing to carry its point? Ought we not, then, to put our virtue and fortitude to the severest test?—*To Bryan Fairfax.* Fitzpatrick 3:228. (1774.)

TAXATION, Without Representation.—What further proofs are wanted to satisfy one of the designs of the |British| ministry than their own acts, which are uniform and plainly tending to the same point, nay, if I mistake not, avowedly to fix the right of taxation? What hope, then, from petitioning, when they tell us that now or never is the time to fix the matter? Shall we, after this, whine and cry for relief, when we have already tried it in vain? Or shall we supinely sit and see one province after another fall a prey to despotism? If I |were| in any doubt as to the right which the Parliament of Great Britain had to tax us without our consent, I should most heartily coincide with you in |your| opinion that to petition, and petition only, is the proper method to apply for relief; because we should then be asking a favor, and not claiming a right which, by the law of nature and our |English| constitution, we are, in my opinion, indubitably entitled to. I should even think it criminal to go further than this, under such an idea; but none such I have. I think the Parliament of Great Britain have no more right to put their hands into my pocket, without my consent, than I have to put my hands into yours for money.—To Bryan Fairfax. Fitzpatrick 3:232. (1774.)

TAXATION. See also FINANCES; GREAT BRITAIN; NONIMPORTATION; STAMP ACT.

TENANTS, Treatment of.—Where acts of Providence interfere to disable a tenant, I would be lenient in the exaction of rent; but when the cases are otherwise, I will not be put off; because it is on these my own expenditures depend, and because an accumulation of undischarged rents is a real injury to the tenant.—To Thomas Freeman. Fitzpatrick 27.470. (1784.)

THANKSGIVING PROCLAMATION OF 1789, Text of.—Whereas it is the duty of all nations to acknowledge the providence of the Almighty God, to obey His will, to be grateful for His benefits, and humbly to implore His protection and favor; and whereas both houses of Congress have, by their joint committee, requested me "to recommend to the people of the United States a day of public thanksgiving and prayer, to be observed by acknowledging with grateful hearts the many and signal favors of Almighty God, especially by affording them an opportunity peaceably to establish a form of government for their safety and happiness":

Now, therefore, I do recommend and assign Thursday, the 26th day of November next, to be devoted by the people of these states to the service of that great and glorious Being who is the beneficent author of all the good that was, that is, or that will be; that

we may then all unite in rendering unto Him our sincere and humble thanks for His kind care and protection of the people of this country previous to their becoming a nation; for the signal and manifold mercies and the favorable interpositions of His providence in the course and conclusion of the late war; for the great degree of tranquility, union, and plenty which we have since enjoyed; for the peaceable and rational manner in which we have been enabled to establish constitutions of government for our safety and happiness, and particularly the national one now lately instituted; for the civil and religious liberty with which we are blessed, and the means we have of acquiring and diffusing useful knowledge; and, in general, for the great and various favors which He has been pleased to confer upon us.

And also that we may then unite in most humbly offering our prayers and supplications to the great Lord and Ruler of Nations, and beseech Him to pardon our national and other transgressions; to enable us all, whether in public or private stations, to perform our several and relative duties properly and punctually; to render our national government a blessing to all the people by constantly being a government of wise, just, and constitutional laws, discreetly and faithfully executed and obeyed; to protect and guide all sovereigns and nations (especially such as have shown kindness to us), and to bless them with good governments, peace, and concord; to promote the knowledge and practice of true religion and virtue, and the increase of science among them and us; and, generally, to grant unto all mankind such a degree of temporal prosperity as He alone knows to be best.

Given under my hand, at the city of New York, the 3rd day of October, A.D. 1789.—Fitzpatrick 30:427. (1789.)

TIME, A Revealer of Secrets.—Time may unfold more than prudence ought to disclose.—To Henry Lee. Fitzpatrick 33:24. (1793.)

TORIES, Forgiveness of.—Unhappy wretches! Deluded mortals! Would it not be good policy to grant a generous amnesty, and conquer these people by a generous forgiveness?—To Joseph Reed. Fitzpatrick 4:455. (1776.)

TORIES, Leniency to.—I do,... in behalf of the United States, by virtue of the powers committed to me by Congress, hereby ... |grant| full liberty to all such as prefer the interest and protection of Great Britain to the freedom and happiness of their country, forthwith to withdraw themselves and families within the enemy's lines.—Proclamation. Fitzpatrick 7:62. (1777.)

TRADE. See COMMERCE; FOREIGN TRADE; INDIANS; INTERSTATE COMMERCE; PRICE CONTROLS.

TREASON, In Revolutionary War.—This |Arnold's treason| is an event that occasions me equal regret and mortification; but traitors are the growth of every country, and in a revolution of the present nature it is more to be wondered at that the catalogue is so small than that there have been found a few.—To the Comte de Rochambeau. Fitzpatrick 20:97. (1780.)

TREASON. See also ARNOLD (Benedict).

TREATIES, Should Be Few.—I do not like to add to the number of our national obligations. I would wish as much as possible to avoid giving a foreign power new claims of merit for services performed to the United States, and would ask no assistance that is not indispensable.—To Henry Laurens. Fitzpatrick 13:257. (1778.)

TREATIES, Must Be Fair for All.—Treaties which are not built upon reciprocal benefits are not likely to be of long duration.—To the Comte de Moustier. Fitzpatrick 29:448. (1788.)

I believe it is among nations as with individuals: the party taking advantage of the distresses of another will lose infinitely more in the opinion of mankind and in subsequent events than he will gain by the stroke of the moment.—To Gouverneur Morris. Fitzpatrick 31:328. (1791.)

TREATIES, Power to Make.—It is said to be the general understanding and practice of nations, as a check on the mistakes and indiscretions of ministers or commissioners, not to consider any treaty negotiated and signed by such officers as final and conclusive until ratified by the sovereign or government from whom they derive their powers.—To the Senate. Fitzpatrick 30:406. (1789.)

The Constitution is the guide which I never will abandon. It has assigned to the President the power of making treaties, with the advice and consent of the Senate. It was doubtless supposed that these two branches of government would combine, without passion (and with the best means of information), those facts and principles upon which the success of our foreign relations will always depend, |and| that they ought not to substitute for their own conviction the opinions of others. —To the Boston selectmen. Fitzpatrick 34:253. (1795.)

Having been a member of the general convention and knowing the principles on which the Constitution was formed, I have ever entertained but one opinion on this subject; and from the first establishment of the government to this moment my conduct has exemplified that opinion, that the power of making treaties is exclusively vested in the President, by and with the advice and consent of the Senate, provided two thirds of the Senators present concur, and that every treaty so made and promulgated thenceforward became the law of the land. It is thus that the treaty-making power has been understood by foreign nations; and in all the treaties made with them, we have declared and they have believed that when ratified by the President, with the advice and consent of the Senate, they became obligatory. —To the House of Representatives. Fitzpatrick 35:3. (1796.)

TREATIES, Must Be Made with Caution.—It doubtless is important that all treaties and compacts formed by the United States with other nations, whether civilized or not, should be made with caution and executed with fidelity.—To the Senate. Fitzpatrick 30:406. (1789.)

TREATIES. See also FOREIGN RELATIONS; JAY TREATY.

TRIBULATIONS, To Be Expected in Life.—Human affairs are always checkered, and vicissitudes in this life are rather to be expected than wondered at. -To Robert Stewart. Fitzpatrick 2:396. (1763.)

TRIBULATIONS. See also DIFFICULTIES; MISFORTUNES.

TRUTH, Will Prevail.—Truth will ultimately prevail where there |are| pains taken to bring it to light.—To Charles Mynn Thruston. Fitzpatrick 33:465. (1794.)

U

UNION, Threatened by Local Jealousies.—The disinclination of the individual states to yield competent powers to Congress for the federal government, their unreasonable jealousy of that body and of one another, and the disposition which seems to pervade each, of being all-wise and all-powerful within itself, will, if there is not a change in the system, be our downfall as a nation. This is as clear to me as the A, B, C; and I think we have opposed Great Britain and have arrived at the present state of peace and independence to very little purpose if we cannot conquer our own prejudices. The powers of Europe begin to see this; and our newly acquired friends, the British, are already and professedly acting upon this ground, and wisely too, if we are determined to persevere in our folly. They know that individual opposition to their measures is futile, and *boast* that we are not sufficiently united as a

Washington in 1797 or 1798 (age 65 or 66). Portrait by Edward Savage.

nation to give a general one! Is not the indignity alone of this declaration, while we are in the very act of peace-making and conciliation, sufficient to stimulate us to vest more extensive and adequate powers in the sovereign of these United States?—To Governor Benjamin Harrison. Fitzpatrick 27:305. (1784.)

Contracted ideas, local pursuits, and absurd jealousy are continually leading us from those great and fundamental principles which are characteristic of wise and powerful nations, and without which we are no more than a rope of sand, and shall as easily be broken.—To Henry Knox. Fitzpatrick 28:93. (1785.)

UNION, Requires Accommodation to Majority Rule.—We are either a united people under one head and for federal purposes, or we are thirteen independent sovereignties eternally counteracting each other; if the former, whatever such a majority of the states as the constitution points out conceives to be for the benefit of the whole should, in my humble opinion, be submitted to by the minority. Let the southern states always be represented, let them act more in union, let them declare freely and boldly what is for the interest of, and what is prejudicial to, their constituents, and there will, there must, be an accommodating spirit.—To James McHenry. Fitzpatrick 28:228. (1785.)

UNION, Essential to America.—I confess to you candidly that I can foresee no greater evil than disunion.—To James McHenry. Fitzpatrick 28:228. (1785.)

It should be the highest ambition of every American to extend his views beyond himself, and to bear in mind that his conduct will not only affect himself, his country, and his immediate posterity, but that its influence may be coextensive with the world, and stamp political happiness or misery on ages yet unborn. To establish this desirable end, and to establish |a| government of laws, the union of these states is absolutely necessary; therefore in every proceeding, this great, this important object should ever be kept in view; and so long as our measures tend to this, and are marked with the wisdom of a well-informed and enlightened people, we may reasonably hope, under the smiles of Heaven, to convince the world that the happiness of nations can be accomplished by pacific revolutions in their political systems, without the destructive intervention of the sword.—To the legislature of Pennsylvania. Fitzpatrick 30:395*n*. (1789.)

UNION, Must Be Carefully Protected.—The unity of government which constitutes you one people is also now dear to you. It is justly so, for it is a main pillar in the edifice of your real independence, the support of your tranquility at home |and| your peace abroad, of your safety, of your prosperity, of that very liberty which you so highly prize. But as it is easy to foresee that from different causes and from different quarters much pains will be taken, many artifices employed to weaken in your minds the conviction of this truth; as this is the point in your political fortress against which the batteries of internal and external enemies will be most constantly and actively (though often covertly and insidiously) directed, it is of infinite moment that you should properly estimate the immense value of your national union to your collective and individual happiness.... You should cherish a cordial, habitual, and immovable attachment to it, accustoming yourselves to think and speak of it as of the palladium of your political safety and prosperity, watching for its preservation with jealous anxiety, discountenancing whatever may suggest even a suspicion that it can in any event be abandoned, and indignantly frowning upon the first dawning of every attempt to alienate any portion of our country from the rest, or to enfeeble the sacred ties which now link together the various parts.—Farewell Address. Fitzpatrick 35:218. (1796.)

UNION, Regional Benefits of.—The north, in an unrestrained intercourse with the south, protected by the equal laws of a common government, finds in the productions of the latter great additional resources of maritime and commercial enterprise, and precious materials of manufacturing industry. The south, in the same intercourse, benefiting by the agency of the north, sees its agriculture grow and its commerce expand. Turning partly into its own channels the seamen of the north, it finds its particular navigation invigorated; and while it contributes, in different ways, to nourish and increase the general mass of the national navigation, it looks forward to the protection of a maritime strength to which itself is unequally adapted.

The east, in a like intercourse with the west, already finds, and in the progressive improvement of interior communications by land and water will more and more find, a valuable vent for the commodities which it brings from abroad or manufactures at home. The west derives from the east supplies requisite to its growth and comfort, and what is perhaps of still greater consequence, it must of necessity owe the secure enjoyment of indispensable outlets for its own productions to the weight, influence, and the future maritime strength of the Atlantic side of the Union, directed by an indissoluble community of interest as one nation. Any other tenure by which the west can hold this essential advantage, whether derived from its own separate strength or from an apostate and unnatural connection with any foreign power, must be intrinsically precarious.—Farewell Address. Fitzpatrick 35:220. (1796.)

UNION, General Benefits of.—While ... every part of our country thus feels an immediate and particular interest in union, all the parts combined cannot fail to find in the united mass of means and efforts greater strength, greater resource, proportionably greater security from external danger, a less frequent interruption of their peace by foreign nations; and—what is of inestimable value!—they must derive from union an exemption from those broils and wars between themselves which so frequently afflict neighboring countries not tied together by the same government, which their own rivalships alone would be sufficient to produce, but which opposite foreign alliances, attachments, and intrigues would stimulate and embitter. Hence, likewise, they will avoid the necessity of those overgrown military establishments which under any form of government are inauspicious to liberty, and which are to be regarded as particularly hostile to republican liberty. In this sense it is that your union ought to be considered as a main prop of your liberty, and that the love of the one ought to endear to you the preservation of the other.—Farewell Address. Fitzpatrick 35:221. (1796.)

UNION, A Worthy Experiment.—Is there a doubt whether a common government can embrace so large a sphere? Let experience solve it. To listen to mere speculation in such a case |would be| criminal. We are authorized to hope that a proper organization of the whole, with the auxiliary agency of governments for the respective subdivisions, will afford a happy issue to the experiment. It is well worth a fair and full experiment. With such powerful and obvious motives to union, affecting all parts of our country, while experience shall not have demonstrated its impracticability, there will always be reason to distrust the patriotism of those who in any quarter may endeavor to weaken its bands.—Farewell Address. Fitzpatrick 35:222. (1796.)

UNION, Disrupted by Partisan Misrepresentations.—Designing men may endeavor to excite a belief that there is a real difference of local interests and views |between geographical regions|. One of the expedients of party to acquire influence within particular districts is to misrepresent the opinions and aims of other districts. You cannot shield yourselves too much against the jealousies and heartburnings which spring from these misrepresentations. They tend to render alien to each other those who ought to be bound together by fraternal affection.—Farewell Address. Fitzpatrick 35:223. (1796.)

UNION, Must Be Federal, Not Merely Regional.—To the efficacy and permanency of your union, a government for the whole is indispensable. No alliances, however strict, between the parts can be an adequate substitute. They must inevitably experience the infractions and interruptions which all alliances in all times have experienced.—Farewell Address. Fitzpatrick 35:224. (1796.)

UNION. See also AMERICA; UNITED STATES.

UNITED STATES, Must Set Its Course at End of War.—It remains only for the states to be wise, and to establish their independence on that basis of inviolable, efficacious union and firm confederation which may prevent their being made the sport of European policy. May Heaven give them wisdom to adopt the measures still necessary for this important purpose.—To Nathanael Greene. Fitzpatrick 26:275. (1783.)

Notwithstanding the cup of blessing is thus reached out to us, notwithstanding happiness is ours, if we have a disposition to seize the occasion and make it our own, yet it appears to me there is an option still left to the United States of America, that it is in their choice, and depends upon their conduct, whether they will be respectable and prosperous, or contemptible and miserable, as a nation. This is the time of their political probation; this is the moment when the eyes of the whole world are turned upon them; this is the moment to establish or ruin their national character forever; this is the favorable moment to give such a tone to our federal government as will enable it to answer the ends of its institution, or this may be the ill-fated moment for relaxing the powers of the Union, annihilating the cement of the confederation, and exposing us to become the sport of European politics, which may play one state against another to prevent their growing importance and to serve their own interested purposes. For, according to the system of policy the states shall adopt at this moment, they will stand or fall; and by their confirmation or lapse it is yet to be decided whether the revolution must ultimately be considered as a blessing or a curse—a blessing or a curse not to the present age alone, for with our fate will the destiny of unborn millions be involved.—Circular to the States. Fitzpatrick 26:485. (1783.)

UNITED STATES, Had to Learn How to Govern Itself.—We now stand an independent people, and have yet to learn political tactics. We are placed among the nations of the earth, and have a character to establish; but how we shall acquit ourselves time must discover. The probability [is], at least I fear it is, that local or state politics will interfere too much with that more liberal and extensive plan of government which wisdom and foresight, freed from the mist of prejudice, would dictate; and that we shall be guilty of many blunders in treading this boundless theater before we shall have arrived at any perfection in this art. In a word, that the experience which is purchased at the price of difficulties and distress will alone convince us that the honor, power, and true interest of this country must be measured by a continental scale; and that every departure therefrom weakens the Union, and may ultimately break the band which holds us together. To avert these evils, to form a constitution that will give consistency, stability, and dignity to the Union, and sufficient powers to the great council of the nation for general purposes, is a duty which is incumbent upon every man who wishes well to his country, and will meet with my aid as far as it can be rendered in the private walks of life.—To the Marquis de Lafayette. Fitzpatrick 26:298. (1783.)

I unite my prayers most fervently with yours for wisdom to these United States, and have no doubt [that] after a little while all errors in the present form of their government will be corrected and a happy temper be diffused through the whole. But like young heirs come a little prematurely perhaps to a large inheritance, it is more than probable they will riot for a while; but . . . this, if it should happen, though it is a circumstance which is to be lamented (as I would have the national character of America be pure and immaculate), will work its own cure, as there is virtue at the bottom.—To George William Fairfax. Fitzpatrick 27:58. (1783.)

UNITED STATES, Its Sovereignty Should Be Safeguarded.—Whatever measures have a tendency to dissolve the Union, or contribute to violate or lessen [its] sovereign authority, ought to be considered as hostile to the liberty and independence of America, and the authors of them treated accordingly.—Circular to the States. Fitzpatrick 26:488. (1783.)

UNITED STATES, Must Act As a Nation.—We are either a united

people or we are not. If the former, let us, in all matters of general concern, act as a nation, which [has] national objects to promote and a national character to support. If we are not, let us no longer act a farce by pretending to it.—To James Madison. Fitzpatrick 28:336. (1785.)

UNITED STATES, Prosperity of.—Our internal governments are daily acquiring strength. The laws have their fullest energy; justice is well administered; robbery, violence, or murder is not heard of from New Hampshire to Georgia. The people at large (as far as I can learn) are more industrious than they were before the war. Economy begins, partly from necessity and partly from choice and habit, to prevail. The seeds of population are scattered over an immense tract of western country. In the old states, which were the theatres of hostility, it is wonderful to see how soon the ravages of war are repaired. Houses are rebuilt, fields enclosed, stocks of cattle which were destroyed are replaced, and many a desolated territory assumes again the cheerful appearance of cultivation. In many places the vestiges of conflagration and ruin are hardly to be traced. The arts of peace, such as clearing rivers, building bridges, and establishing conveniences for traveling, etc., are assiduously promoted. In short, the foundation of a great empire is laid, and I please myself with a persuasion that Providence will not leave its work imperfect.—To the Chevalier de la Luzerne. Fitzpatrick 28:500. (1786.)

The United States enjoy a scene of

prosperity and tranquility under the new government [i.e., the Constitution] that could hardly have been hoped for under the old [i.e., the Articles of Confederation].—To Mrs. Catharine Macaulay Graham. Fitzpatrick 31:316. (1791.)

Tranquility reigns among the people, with that disposition towards the general government which is likely to preserve it. They begin to feel the good effects of equal laws and equal protection. The farmer finds a ready market for his produce, and the merchant calculates with more certainty on his payments.... Each day's experience of the government of the United States seems to confirm its establishment, and to render it more popular. ... Our public credit stands on that [high] ground which three years ago it would have been considered as a species of madness to have foretold.—To David Humphreys. Fitzpatrick 31:318. (1791.)

UNITED STATES, And the Fruits of Freedom.—I really believe that there never was so much labor and economy to be found before in the country as at the present moment. If they persist in the habits they are acquiring, the good effects will soon be distinguishable. When the people shall find themselves secure under an energetic government, when foreign nations shall be disposed to give us equal advantages in commerce from dread of retaliation, when the burdens [i.e., debts] of war shall be in a manner done away the sale of western lands, when the seeds of happiness which are sown here shall begin to expand themselves, and when

everyone, under his own vine and fig tree, shall begin to taste the fruits of freedom, then all these blessings (for all these blessings will come) will be referred to the fostering influence of the new government.... Indeed, I do not believe that Providence has done so much for nothing. It has always been my creed that we should not be left as an awful monument to prove "that mankind, under the most favorable circumstances for civil liberty and happiness, are unequal to the task of governing themselves, and therefore made for a master."—To the Marquis de Lafayette. Fitzpatrick 29:525. (1788.)

UNITED STATES, Has One of World's Best Governments.—That the [American] government, though not absolutely perfect, is one of the best in the world, I have little doubt. —To Mrs. Catharine Macaulay Graham. Fitzpatrick 30:496. (1790.)

UNITED STATES, Office Seekers in.—The United States [is] a country where offices bear no proportion to the seekers of them.—To John Jay. Fitzpatrick 34:19. (1794.)

UNITED STATES. See also AMERICA; CENSUS; DECLARATION OF INDEPENDENCE; FEDERAL GOVERNMENT; INDEPENDENCE; POPULATION; UNION; WEST.

UNITY, Need for.—Nothing but disunion can hurt our cause. This will ruin it if great prudence, temper, and moderation [are] not mixed in our counsels and made the governing principles of the contending parties.— To Joseph Reed. Fitzpatrick 4:483. (1776.)

UNITY, Importance of, During a Crisis.—The present situation of public affairs affords abundant causes of distress; we should be very careful how we aggravate or multiply them by private bickerings.... All little differences and animosities calculated to increase the unavoidable evils of the times should be forgotten, or at least postponed.—To Lord Stirling. Fitzpatrick 8:22. (1777.)

UNITY, More Important Than Party Politics During a Crisis.—The hour ...is certainly come when party differences and disputes should subside, when every man (especially those in office) should with one hand and one heart pull the same way and with their whole strength.—To John Armstrong. Fitzpatrick 15:99. (1779.)

UNIVERSITY. See NATIONAL UNIVERSITY.

V

VANITY, Effect of.—There is no restraining men's tongues or pens when charged with a little vanity.—To Joseph Reed. Fitzpatrick 4:166. (1775.)

VICES, Washington's Opposition to.—I have, both by threats and persuasive means, endeavored to discountenance gaming, drinking, swearing, and irregularities of every other kind; while I have, on the other hand, practiced every artifice to inspire a laudable emulation in the officers for the service of their country and to encourage the soldiers in the unerring exercise of their duty.—To Governor Robert Dinwiddie. Fitzpatrick 1:317. (1756.)

The General most earnestly requires and expects a due observance of those articles of war established for the government of the army, which forbid profane cursing, swearing, and drunkenness.—General Orders. Fitzpatrick 3:309. (1775.)

VICES. See also DRUNKENNESS; GAMBLING; GAMES OF CHANCE; IMMODESTY; LIQUOR; PROFANITY; TAVERNS; VIRTUE.

VIRGINIA, Difficulty of Farming in.—The nature of a Virginia estate [is] such that without close application it never fails bringing the proprietors in debt annually, as Negroes must be clothed and fed, taxes paid, etc., etc., whether anything is made or not.—To Edward Montague. Fitzpatrick 3:285. (1775.)

VIRGINIA. See also MOUNT VERNON.

VIRTUE, Trial of.—Few men have virtue to withstand the highest bidder.—To Robert Howe. Fitzpatrick 16:119. (1779.)

VIRTUE, Public, Needed to Safeguard the Constitution.—The [federal] government...can never be in danger of degenerating into a monarchy, an oligarchy, an aristocracy, or any other despotic or oppressive form so long as there shall remain any virtue in the body of the people.—To the Marquis de Lafayette. Fitzpatrick 29:410. (1788.)

VIRTUE, And Happiness.—There is no truth more thoroughly established than that there exists, in the economy and course of nature, an indissoluble union between virtue and happiness, between duty and advantage, between the genuine maxims of an honest and magnanimous policy and the solid rewards of public prosperity and felicity.—First Inaugural Address. Fitzpatrick 30:294. (1789.)

VIRTUE, Required for Free Government.—It is substantially true that virtue or morality is a necessary spring of popular government.—Farewell Address. Fitzpatrick 35:229. (1796.)

VIRTUE, And Talents.—Without virtue and without integrity, the finest talents or the most brilliant accomplishments can never gain the respect or conciliate the esteem of the truly valuable part of mankind.—To Bartholomew Dandridge. Fitzpatrick 35:422. (1797.)

VIRTUE. See also HONESTY; INTEGRITY; MORALITY; PATIENCE; RELIGION; VICES.

VIRTUES, Civilian and Military.—The private virtues of economy, prudence, and industry will not be less amiable in civil life than the more splendid qualities of valor, perseverance, and enterprise were in the field. —Farewell Orders to the Armies of the United States. Fitzpatrick 27:225. (1783.)

W

WANTS, Can Be Insatiable.—Imaginary wants are indefinite and oftentimes insatiable, because they sometimes are boundless, and always changing.—To John Augustine Washington. Fitzpatrick 26:43. (1783.)

WAR, Value of Experienced Soldiers in.—Men who are familiarized to

danger meet it without shrinking, whereas those who have never seen service often apprehend danger where no danger is.—To the President of Congress. Fitzpatrick 4:316. (1776.)

WAR, Incentives in Battle.—Three things prompt men to a regular discharge of their duty in time of action: natural bravery, hope of reward, and fear of punishment.—To the President of Congress. Fitzpatrick 4:316. (1776.)

WAR, Treatment of Cowardice in.— A coward, when taught to believe that if he breaks his ranks and abandons his colors [he] will be punished with death by his own party, will take his chance against the enemy.—To the President of Congress. Fitzpatrick 4:316. (1776.)

WAR, Military Expropriations in, Evil.—It will never answer to procure supplies of clothing or provision by coercive measures.... Such procedures may give a momentary relief, but if repeated will prove of the most pernicious consequences.—To the President of Congress. Fitzpatrick 10:267. (1778.)

WAR, Sacrifices in.—When men are employed and have the incitements of military honor to engage their ambition and pride, they will cheerfully submit to inconveniences which in a state of tranquility would appear insupportable.—To a committee of Congress. Fitzpatrick 14:28. (1779.)

WAR, An Evil.—My first wish is to see this plague to mankind banished from off the earth, and the sons and daughters of this world employed in more pleasing and innocent amusements than in preparing implements and exercising them for the destruction of mankind.—To David Humphreys. Fitzpatrick 28:202. (1785.)

WAR, Condemnation of.—It is more consonant to all the principles of reason and religion (natural and revealed) to replenish the earth with inhabitants rather than to depopulate it by killing those already in existence; besides, it is time for the age of knight-errantry and mad-heroism to be at an end. Your young military men, who want to reap the harvest of laurels, don't care (I suppose) how many seeds of war are sown; but for the sake of humanity it is devoutly to be wished that the manly employment of agriculture and the humanizing benefits of commerce would supersede the waste of war and the rage of conquest; and the swords might be turned into plowshares, the spears into pruning-hooks, and, as the scripture expresses it, "the nations learn war no more."—To the Marquis de Chastellux. Fitzpatrick 29:484. (1788.)

WAR, To Be Avoided If Possible.—The friends of humanity will deprecate war wheresoever it may appear; and we have experienced enough of its evils in this country to know that it should not be wantonly or unnecessarily entered upon. I trust, therefore, that the good citizens of the United States will show to the world that they have as much wisdom in preserving peace...as they have heretofore displayed valor in defending their just rights.—To the merchants and traders of the city of Philadelphia. Fitzpatrick 32:460. (1793.)

The madness of the European powers, and the calamitous situation into which all of them are thrown by the present ruinous war, ought to be a serious warning to us to avoid a similar catastrophe, as long as we can with honor and justice to our national character.—To Edmund Pendleton. Fitzpatrick 34:100. (1795.)

WAR, In the Hands of God.—The vicissitudes of war [are] in the hands of the Supreme Director, where no control is.—To the Secretary of State. Fitzpatrick 36:323. (1798.)

WAR, Need for Unity in.—My first wish would be that my military family, and the whole army, should consider themselves as a band of brothers, willing and ready to die for each other.—To Henry Knox. Fitzpatrick 36:508. (1798.)

WAR, Offense Sometimes the Best Defense.—It has been very properly the policy of our government to cultivate peace. But in contemplating the possibility of our being driven to unqualified war, it will be wise to anticipate that frequently the most effectual way to defend is to attack.—To the Secretary of War. Fitzpatrick 37:37. (1798.)

Offensive operations oftentimes are the surest, if not the only (in some cases), means of defense.—To John Trumbull. Fitzpatrick 37:250. (1799.)

WAR. See also ARMY; DEFENSE; ENEMY; INDIANS; MILITIA; NATIONAL DEFENSE; NAVY; PEACE; PRISONERS OF WAR; RETALIATION; REVOLUTIONARY WAR.

WAR OFFICE, Formation of.—The institution of a war office is certainly an event of great importance, and in all probability will be recorded as such in the historic page. The benefits derived from it, I flatter myself, will be considerable, though the plan upon which it is first formed may not be entirely perfect. This, like other great works in its first edition, may not be entirely free from error. Time will discover its defects and experience |will| suggest the remedy, and such further improvements as may be necessary; but it was right to give it a beginning.—To the President of Congress. Fitzpatrick 5:159. (1776.)

WASHINGTON, D.C., Growth and Prospects of.—A century hence, if this country keeps united (and it is surely its policy and interest to do so), will produce a city, though not as large as London, yet of a magnitude inferior to few others in Europe, on the banks of the Potomac; where one is now establishing for the permanent seat of the government of the United States between Alexandria and Georgetown, on the Maryland side of the river, a situation not excelled for commanding prospect, good water, salubrious air, and safe harbor by any in the world; and where elegant buildings are erecting and in forwardness for the reception of Congress in the year 1800.—To Sarah Cary Fairfax. Fitzpatrick 36:264. (1798.)

WASHINGTON, D.C. See also DISTRICT OF COLUMBIA; NATIONAL UNIVERSITY.

WASHINGTON (George), His Preparation for Military Command.—I flatter myself that under a skillful commander, or man of sense (whom I most sincerely wish to serve under), with my own application and diligent study of my duty, I shall be able to conduct my steps without censure and, in time, render myself worthy of the promotion that I shall be favored with now.—To Richard Corbin. Fitzpatrick 1:34. (1754.)

WASHINGTON (George), Bravery of.—I have a constitution hardy enough to encounter and undergo the most severe trials, and, I flatter myself, resolution to face what any man durst, as shall be proved when it comes to the test.—To Governor Robert Dinwiddie. Fitzpatrick 1:60. (1754.)

WASHINGTON (George), His Life Preserved by God.—As I have heard ...a circumstantial account of my death and dying speech, I take this early opportunity of contradicting both, and of assuring you that I now exist and appear in the land of the living by the miraculous care of Providence, that protected me beyond all human expectation; I had four bullets through my coat, and two horses shot under me, and yet escaped unhurt.—To John Augustine Washington. Fitzpatrick 1:152. (1755.)

WASHINGTON (George), Humility of.—I wish...it were more in my power than it is to answer the favorable opinion my friends have conceived of my abilities. Let them not be deceived; I am unequal to the task [of commanding Virginia's military forces], and do assure you it requires more experience than I am master of to conduct an affair of the importance that this is now arisen to.—To Charles Lewis. Fitzpatrick 1:163. (1755.)

When I contemplate the interposition of Providence, as it was manifested in guiding us through the revolution, in preparing us for the reception of a general government, and in conciliating the good will of the people of America towards one another after its adoption, I feel myself ... almost overwhelmed with a sense of the divine munificence. I feel that nothing is due to my personal agency in all these complicated and wonderful events, except what can simply be attributed to the exertions of an honest zeal for the good of my country.—To the mayor, recorder, aldermen, and common council of Philadelphia. Sparks 12:145. (1789.)

WASHINGTON (George), His Empathy for the Distressed.—I am too little acquainted with pathetic language to attempt a description of the people's distresses [on the Virginia frontier amidst Indian raids], though I have a generous soul, sensible of wrongs and swelling for redress. But what can I do? If bleeding, dying! would glut their insatiate revenge, I would be a willing offering to savage fury, and die by inches to save a people! I see their situation, know their danger, and participate [in] their sufferings, without having it in my power to give them further relief than uncertain promises.—To Governor Robert Dinwiddie. Fitzpatrick 1:324. (1756.)

The supplicating tears of the women and moving petitions from the men melt me into such deadly sorrow that I solemnly declare, if I know my own mind, I could offer myself a willing sacrifice to the butchering enemy, pro-

vided that would contribute to the people's ease.—To Governor Robert Dinwiddie. Fitzpatrick 1:325. (1756.)

Although [some leading Americans] seem to have little feeling for the naked and distressed soldier[s], I feel superabundantly for them, and from my soul pity those miseries which it is neither in my power to relieve [nor] prevent.—To the President of Congress. Fitzpatrick 10:196. (1777.)

WASHINGTON (George), Open and Honest.—Do not think, my lord, that I am going to flatter; notwithstanding I have exalted sentiments of your lordship's character and respect your rank, it is not my intention to adulate. My nature is open and honest and free from guile.—To the Earl of Loudoun. Fitzpatrick 2:18. (1757.)

WASHINGTON (George), Willing to Receive Criticism.—It is with pleasure I receive reproof, when reproof is due, because no person can be readier to accuse me than I am to acknowledge an error, when I am guilty of one; nor more desirous for atoning for a crime, when I am sensible of having committed it.—To Governor Robert Dinwiddie. Fitzpatrick 2:122. (1757.)

The hints you have communicated from time to time not only deserve, but do most sincerely and cordially meet with, my thanks. You cannot render a more acceptable service, nor in my estimation give a more convincing proof of your friendship, than by a free, open, and undisguised account of every matter relative to myself or [my] conduct. I can bear to hear of imputed or real errors. The man who wishes to stand well in the opinion of others must do this, because he is thereby enabled to correct his faults, or remove prejudices which are imbibed against him. For this reason, I shall thank you for giving me the opinions of the world upon such points as you know me to be interested in; for, as I have but one capital object in view, I could wish to make my conduct coincide with the wishes of mankind as far as I can... without departing from |the| great line of duty.—To Joseph Reed. Fitzpatrick 4:240. (1776.)

As I have no other view than to promote the public good, and am unambitious of honors not founded in the approbation of my country, I would not desire in the least degree to suppress a free spirit of inquiry into any part of my conduct that even faction itself may deem reprehensible.—To the President of Congress. Fitzpatrick 10:410. (1778.)

WASHINGTON (George), Happy to Be Married. I am now, I believe, fixed at this seat |Mount Vernon| with an agreeable consort for life, and hope to find more happiness in retirement |from military command| than I ever experienced amid a wide and bustling world.—To Richard Washington. Fitzpatrick 2:337. (1759.)

WASHINGTON (George), Generosity of.—Having once or twice of late heard you speak highly in praise of the Jersey College, as if you had a desire of sending your son William there (who, I am told, is a youth fond of study and instruction, and disposed to a sedentary, studious life; in following... which he may not only promote his own happiness, but the future welfare

of others), I should be glad, if you have no other objection to it than what may arise from the expense, if you would send him there as soon as it is convenient and depend on me for twenty-five pounds...a year for his support so long as it may be necessary for the completion of his education. No other return is expected or wished for this offer than that you will accept it with the same freedom and good will with which it is made, and that you may not even consider it in the light of an obligation, or mention it as such; for be assured that from me it will never be known.—To William Ramsay. Fitzpatrick 2:499. (1769.)

WASHINGTON (George), Angered by Charge of Dishonesty.—Your impertinent letter...was delivered to me yesterday.... As I am not accustomed to receive such from any man, nor would have taken the same language from you personally without letting you feel some marks of my resentment, I would advise you to be cautious in writing me a second |letter| of the same tenor; for though I understand you were drunk when you did it, yet give me leave to tell you that drunkenness is no excuse for rudeness; and that but for your stupidity and sottishness you might have known, by attending to the public gazettes,...that you had your full quantity of ten thousand acres of land allowed you |for service in the French and Indian War under Washington's command|.—To George Muse. Fitzpatrick 3:179. (1774.)

WASHINGTON (George), His Attitude Toward Requests for Help.—I never deny or even hesitate in granting any request that is made to me (especially by persons I esteem, and in matters of moment) without feeling inexpressible uneasiness.—To John West. Fitzpatrick 3:262. (1775.)

WASHINGTON (George), His Devotion to the Cause of Liberty.—It is my full intention to devote my life and fortune in the cause we are engaged in, if need be.—To John Augustine Washington. Fitzpatrick 3:277. (1775.)

As the Congress desires, I will enter upon the momentous duty, and exert every power I possess in their service for the support of the glorious cause. —Acceptance of appointment as General and Commander-in-Chief. Fitzpatrick 3:292. (1775.)

WASHINGTON (George), Accepts Command of American Army.— Though I am truly sensible of the high honor done me in this appointment, yet I feel great distress from a consciousness that my abilities and military experience may not be equal to the extensive and important trust. However, as the Congress desires, I will enter upon the momentous duty and exert every power I possess in their service for the support of the glorious cause. I beg they will accept my most cordial thanks for this distinguished testimony of their approbation. But lest some unlucky event should happen unfavorable to my reputation, I beg it may be remembered by every gentleman in the room that I this day declare with the utmost sincerity, I do not think myself equal to the command I am honored with. As to pay,...I beg leave to assure the

Congress that, as no pecuniary consideration could have tempted me to have accepted this arduous employment at the expense of my domestic ease and happiness, I do not wish to make any profit from it. I will keep an exact account of my expenses; those I doubt not they will discharge, and that is all I desire.—Acceptance of appointment as General and Commander-in-Chief. Fitzpatrick 3:292. (1775.)

My Dearest: I am now set down to write to you on a subject which fills me with inexpressible concern, and this concern is greatly aggravated and increased when I reflect upon the uneasiness I know it will give you. It has been determined in Congress that the whole army raised for the defense of the American cause shall be put under my care, and that it is necessary for me to proceed immediately to Boston to take upon me the command of it. You may believe me, my dear Patsy, when I assure you in the most solemn manner that, so far from seeking this appointment, I have used every endeavor in my power to avoid it, not only from my unwillingness to part with you and the family, but from a consciousness of its being a trust too great for my capacity, and that I should enjoy more real happiness in one month with you at home than I have the most distant prospect of finding abroad, if my stay were to be seven times seven years. But as it has been a kind of destiny that has thrown me upon this sevice, I shall hope that my undertaking it is designed to answer some good purpose. You might and I suppose did perceive, from the tenor of my letters, that I was apprehensive I could not avoid this appointment, as I did not pretend to intimate when I should return. That was the case. It was utterly out of my power to refuse this appointment without exposing my character to such censures as would have reflected dishonor upon myself and given pain to my friends. This, I am sure, could not, and ought not, to be pleasing to you, and must have lessened me considerably in my own esteem. I shall rely, therefore, confidently on that Providence which has heretofore preserved and been bountiful to me, not doubting but that I shall return safe to you in the fall. I shall feel no pain from the toil or the danger of the campaign; my unhappiness will flow from the uneasiness I know you will feel from being left alone. I therefore beg that you will summon your whole fortitude, and pass your time as agreeably as possible.—To Mrs. Martha Washington. Fitzpatrick 3:293. (1775.)

I am now embarked on a tempestuous ocean, from whence perhaps no friendly harbor is to be found. I have been called upon by the unanimous voice of the colonies to the command of the Continental Army. It is an honor I by no means aspired to. It is an honor I wished to avoid, as well from an unwillingness to quit the peaceful enjoyment of my family as from a thorough conviction of my own incapacity and want of experience in the conduct of so momentous a concern; but the partiality of the Congress, added to some political motives, left me without a choice. May God grant, therefore, that my acceptance of it

may be attended with some good to the common cause, and without injury (from want of knowledge) to my own reputation. I can answer but for three things: a firm belief [in] the justice of our cause, close attention in the prosecution of it, and the strictest integrity. If these cannot supply the place of ability and experience, the cause will suffer, and more than probably my character along with it, as reputation derives its principal support from successes; but it will be remembered, I hope, that no desire or insinuation of mine placed me in this situation. I shall not be deprived, therefore, of a comfort in the worst event if I retain a consciousness of having acted to the best of my judgment.—To Burwell Bassett. Fitzpatrick 3:296. (1775.)

WASHINGTON (George), His Sense of Destiny.—As it has been a kind of destiny that has thrown me upon this service, I shall hope that my undertaking it is designed to answer some good purpose.... I shall rely, therefore, confidently on that Providence which has heretofore preserved and been bountiful to me.—To Mrs. Martha Washington. Fitzpatrick 3:294. (1775.)

WASHINGTON (George), Distressed During Revolutionary War.—There have been so many great and capital errors and abuses to rectify, so many examples to make, and so little inclination in the officers of inferior rank to contribute their aid to accomplish this work, that my life has been nothing else (since I came here) but one continued round of *annoyance* and *fatigue;* in short, no pecuniary recompense could induce me to undergo what I have, especially as I expect, by showing so little countenance to irregularities and public abuses, to render myself very obnoxious to a greater part of these people.—To Richard Henry Lee. Fitzpatrick 3:454. (1775.)

The reflection on my situation, and that of this army, [give me] an uneasy hour when all around me are wrapped in sleep. Few people know the predicament we are in.... How much happier I should have been if... I had taken my musket on my shoulder and entered the ranks.—To Joseph Reed. Fitzpatrick 4:243. (1776.)

It is not in the power of words to describe the task I have to act.... Fifty thousand pounds should not induce me again to undergo what I have done. —To John Augustine Washington. Fitzpatrick 6:96. (1776.)

Such is my situation that if I were to wish the bitterest curse to an enemy on this side of the grave, I should put him in my stead with my feelings.... I never was in such an unhappy, divided state since I was born.—To Lund Washington. Fitzpatrick 6:138. (1776.)

I am wearied almost to death with the retrograde motion of things, and I solemnly protest that a pecuniary reward of twenty thousand pounds a year would not induce me to undergo what I do; and after all, perhaps, to lose my character [i.e., reputation], as it is impossible under such a variety of distressing circumstances to conduct matters agreeably to public expectation, or even of those who employ me, as they will not make proper allow-

Washington in November 1798 (age 66). Crayon drawing by Charles Fevret de Saint-Memin. This is the last known portrait of Washington drawn from life.

ances for the difficulties their own errors have occasioned.—To John Augustine Washington. Fitzpatrick 6:246. (1776.)

The predicament in which I stand as citizen and soldier is as critical and delicate as can well be conceived. It has been the subject of many contemplative hours. The sufferings of a complaining army on one hand, and the inability of Congress and tardiness of the states on the other, are the forebodings of evil, and may be productive of events which are more to be deprecated than prevented; but I am not without hope.—To Alexander Hamilton. Fitzpatrick 26:186. (1783.)

WASHINGTON (George), Thought-

fulness of.—I can never think of promoting my convenience at the expense of your interest and inclination.—To Joseph Reed. Fitzpatrick 4:104. (1775.)

WASHINGTON (George), A Benefactor to the Poor.—Let the hospitality of the house, with respect to the poor, be kept up; let no one go hungry away. If any of these kind of people should be in want of corn, supply their necessities, provided it does not encourage them in idleness; and I have no objection to your giving my money in charity, to the amount of forty or fifty pounds a year, when you think it well bestowed. What I mean by having no objection is that it is my desire that it should be done. You are to consider that neither myself [nor my] wife [is] now in the way to do these good offices. In all other respects I recommend it to you, and have no doubts of your observing the greatest economy and frugality, as I suppose you know that I do not get a farthing for my services here more than my expenses; it becomes necessary, therefore, for me to be saving at home.—To Lund Washington. Fitzpatrick 4:115. (1775.)

I am at a loss, however, for whose benefits to apply the little I can give, and into whose hands to place it; whether for the use of the fatherless children and widows (made so by the late calamity) who may find it difficult, while provisions, wood, and other necessaries are so dear, to support themselves; or to other and better purpose (if any) I know not, and therefore have taken the liberty of asking your advice.—To the Reverend

William White. Fitzpatrick 33:221. (1793.)

I... will direct my manager, Mr. Pearce, to pay my annual donation for the education of orphan children, or the children of indigent parents who are unable to be at the expense themselves. I [have] pleasure in appropriating this money to such uses, as I always shall in... paying it.—To the Reverend James Muir. Fitzpatrick 33:281. (1794.)

Mrs. Haney should endeavor to do what she can for herself; this is a duty incumbent on everyone. But you must not let her suffer, as she has thrown herself upon me. Your advances on this account will be allowed always, at settlement, and I agree readily to furnish her with provisions; and for the good character you give of her daughter, make the latter a present, in my name, of a handsome but not costly gown, and other things which she may stand mostly in need of. You may charge me also with the worth of your tenement on which she is placed, and where perhaps it is better she should be than at a great distance from your attentions to her.—To Robert Lewis. Fitzpatrick 34:123. (1795.)

WASHINGTON (George), Not Guilty of Incivility.—I cannot charge myself with incivility or, what in my opinion is tantamount, ceremonious civility.—To Joseph Reed. Fitzpatrick 4:165. (1775.)

WASHINGTON (George), Valued His Countrymen's Esteem.—Nothing would give more real satisfaction than to know the sentiments which are entertained of me by the public, whether they be favorable or otherwise.... The man who wishe[s] to steer clear of shelves and rocks must know where they [lie]. I know—but to declare it, unless to a friend, may be an argument of vanity—the integrity of my own heart. I know the unhappy predicament I stand in; I know that much is expected of me; I know that without men, without arms, without ammunition, without anything fit for the accommodation of a soldier, little is to be done; and, which is mortifying, I know that I cannot stand justified to the world without exposing my own weakness and injuring the cause by declaring my wants, which I am determined not to do further than unavoidable necessity brings every man acquainted with them. If, under these disadvantages, I am able to keep above water (as it were) in the esteem of mankind, I shall feel myself happy; but if, from the unknown peculiarity of my circumstances, I suffer in the opinion of the world, I shall not think you take the freedom of a friend if you conceal the reflections that may be cast upon my conduct. My own situation feels so irksome to me at times that, if I did not consult the public good more than my own tranquility, I should long ere this have put everything to the cast of a die.—To Joseph Reed. Fitzpatrick 4:319. (1776.)

To stand well in the good opinion of my countrymen constitutes my chiefest happiness; and will be my best support under the perplexities and difficulties of my present station.—To Benjamin Harrison. Fitzpatrick 13:463 (1778.)

Having performed duties (which I conceive every country has a right to require of its citizens), I claim no merit; but no man can feel more sensibly the reward of approbation for such services than I do. Next to the consciousness of having acted faithfully in discharging the several trusts to which I have been called, the thanks of one's country and the esteem of good men [are] the highest gratification my mind is susceptible of.—To the Earl of Radnor. Fitzpatrick 35:493. (1797.)

The favorable sentiments which others, you say, have expressed respecting me cannot but be pleasing to [one] who always walked on a straight line and endeavored, as far as human frailties and perhaps strong passions would enable him, to discharge the relative duties to his Maker and fellowmen, without seeking any indirect or left-handed attempts to acquire popularity.—To Bryan Fairfax. Fitzpatrick 37:94. (1799.)

WASHINGTON (George), Patriotism of.—When the councils of the British nation had formed a plan for enslaving America and depriving her sons of their most sacred and invaluable privileges, against the clearest remonstrances of the [English] constitution, of justice, and of truth, and, to execute their schemes, had appealed to the sword, I esteemed it my duty to take a part in the contest, and more especially on account of my being called thereto by the unsolicited suffrages of the representatives of a free people; wishing for no other reward than that arising from a conscientious discharge of the important trust, and that my services might contribute to the establishment of freedom and peace upon a permanent foundation, and merit the applause of my countrymen and every virtuous citizen.— Answer to an address from the Massachusetts legislature. Fitzpatrick 4:440. (1776.)

WASHINGTON (George), Did Not Seek Power.—I have no lust for power.—To the President of Congress. Fitzpatrick 6:402. (1776.)

WASHINGTON (George), Perseverance of.—We should never despair; our situation before has been unpromising and has changed for the better; so, I trust, it will again. If new difficulties arise, we must only put forth new exertions and proportion our efforts to the exigency of the times.—To Philip Schuyler. Fitzpatrick 8:408. (1777.)

WASHINGTON (George), Good Humor of.—It is much to be lamented that things are not now as they formerly were |before the Conway Cabal|; but we must not, in so great a contest, expect to meet with nothing but sunshine. I have no doubt but that everything happens so for the best, that we shall triumph over all our misfortunes, and shall, in the end, be ultimately happy; when, my dear Marquis, if you will give me your company in Virginia, we will laugh at our past difficulties and the folly of others.—To the Marquis de Lafayette. Fitzpatrick 10:237. (1777.)

WASHINGTON (George), Willing to Relinquish Military Command.— Neither interested nor ambitious views led me into the service; I did not solicit the command |of the American army|, but accepted it after much entreaty, with all that diffidence which a conscious want of ability and experience equal to the discharge of so important a trust must naturally create in a mind not quite devoid of thought. And after I did engage, |I| pursued the great line of my duty and the object in view (as far as my judgment could direct) as pointedly as the needle to the pole. So soon, then, as the public gets dissatisfied with my services, or a person is found better qualified to answer her expectation, I shall quit the helm with as much satisfaction, and retire to a private station with as much content, as ever the wearied pilgrim felt upon his safe arrival in the Holy Land,... and shall wish most devoutly that those who come after may meet with more prosperous gales than I have done, and less difficulty.—To the Reverend William Gordon. Fitzpatrick 10:338. (1778.)

WASHINGTON (George), Loyal to His Leaders.—No expressions of personal politeness to me can be acceptable |when| accompanied by reflections on the representatives of a free people, under whose authority I have the honor to act. The delicacy I have observed in refraining from everything offensive in this way entitled me to expect a similar treatment from you. I have not indulged myself in invective against the present rulers of Great Britain, in the course of our correspondence, nor will I even now avail myself of so fruitful a theme.— To Sir William Howe. Fitzpatrick 10:409. (1778.)

WASHINGTON (George), His Aversion to Discord.—I am as averse to controversy as any man, ... willing to |bury differences| in silence and ... oblivion. My temper leads me to peace and harmony with all men; and it is particularly my wish to avoid any personal feuds or dissensions with those who are embarked in the same great national interest with myself, as every difference of this kind must in its consequences be very injurious.—To Horatio Gates. Fitzpatrick 10:508. (1778.)

I have happily had but few differences with those with whom I have the honor of being connected in the service.... I bore much for the sake of peace and the public good. My conscience tells me I acted rightly in these transactions, and should they ever come to the knowledge of the world, I trust I shall stand acquitted by it.—To Nathanael Greene. Fitzpatrick 23:190. (1781.)

WASHINGTON (George), His Devotion to Duty.—There is nothing I have more at heart than to discharge the great duties incumbent on me, with the strictest attention to the ease and convenience of the people.—To Thomas Wharton. Fitzpatrick 11:45. (1778.)

You ask how I am to be rewarded for all this? There is one reward that nothing can deprive me of, and that is the consciousness of having done my duty with the strictest rectitude and most scrupulous exactness; that if we should ultimately fail in the present contest, it is not owing to the want of exertion in me.—To Lund Washing-

ton. Fitzpatrick 18:392. (1780.)

The want of regular exercise, |together| with the cares of office, will, I have no doubt, hasten my departure for that country from whence no traveller returns; but a faithful discharge of whatsoever trust I accept, as it ever has |been|, so it always will be the primary consideration in every transaction of my life, be the consequences what they may.—To Dr. James Craik. Fitzpatrick 30:396. (1789.)

Nothing short of imperious necessity can justify my being absent from the seat of government while Congress is in session.—To John Clark. Fitzpatrick 33:520. (1794.)

To leave home so soon will be inconvenient.... But while I am in office, I shall never suffer private convenience to interfere with what I consider to be my official duties.—To Edmund Randolph. Fitzpatrick 34:255. (1795.)

WASHINGTON (George), His Sense of Honor.—I feel everything that hurts the sensibility of a gentleman.—To the Marquis de Lafayette. Fitzpatrick 12:382. (1778.)

WASHINGTON (George), Eager to Conclude the War.—As peace and retirement are my ultimate aim and the most pleasing and flattering hope of my soul, everything advancive of this end contributes to my satisfaction, however difficult and inconvenient in the attainment, and will reconcile any place and all circumstances to my feelings while I continue in service.—To Joseph Reed. Fitzpatrick 13:385. (1778.)

I pant for retirement, and am persuaded that an end of our warfare is not to be obtained but by vigorous exertions.... I can truly say that the first wish of my soul is to return speedily into the bosom of that country which gave me birth, and, in the sweet enjoyment of domestic happiness and the company of a few friends, to end my days in quiet, when I shall be called from this stage.—To Archibald Cary. Fitzpatrick 24:347. (1782.)

I only wait (and with anxious impatience) the arrival of the definitive treaty, that I may take leave of my military employments and, by bidding adieu to public life, forever enjoy in the shades of retirement that ease and tranquility to which, for more than eight years, I have been an entire stranger, and for which a mind which has been constantly on the stretch during that period, and perplexed with a thousand embarrassing circumstances, oftentimes without a ray of light to guide it, stands much in need.—To Robert Stewart. Fitzpatrick 27:89. (1783.)

WASHINGTON (George), Willing to Suffer with His Troops.—To share a common lot and participate [in] the inconveniences which the army (from the peculiarity of our circumstances) are obliged to undergo has, with me, been a fundamental principle.—To Nathanael Greene. Fitzpatrick 17:423. (1780.)

WASHINGTON (George), His Refusal to Be King.—With a mixture of great surprise and astonishment, I have read with attention the sentiments you have submitted to my perusal. Be assured, sir, no occurrence in the course of the war has given me more painful sensations than your information of there being such ideas existing in the army as you have expressed, and I must view [these ideas] with abhorrence and reprehend [them] with severity....

I am much at a loss to conceive what part of my conduct could have given encouragement to an address which to me seems big with the greatest mischiefs that can befall my country. If I am not deceived in the knowledge of myself, you could not have found a person to whom your schemes are more disagreeable.... Let me conjure you, then, if you have any regard for your country, concern for yourself or posterity, or respect for me, to banish these thoughts from your mind, and never communicate, as from yourself or anyone else, a sentiment of the like nature.—To Lewis Nicola. Fitzpatrick 24:272. (1782.)

WASHINGTON (George), His Sense of Rectitude.—The consciousness of having attempted faithfully to discharge my duty, and the approbation of my country, will be a sufficient recompense for my services.—To the President of Congress. Fitzpatrick 26:232. (1783.)

WASHINGTON (George), His Feelings at End of Revolutionary War.—I anticipate with pleasure the day, and that I trust [is] not far off, when I shall quit the busy scenes of ... military employment and retire to the more tranquil walks of domestic life. In that, or whatever other situation Providence may dispose of my future days, the remembrance of the many friendships and connections I have had the happiness to contract with the gentlemen of the army will be one of my most grateful reflections.—To Israel Putnam. Fitzpatrick 26:463. (1783.)

The great object for which I had the honor to hold an appointment in the service of my country being accomplished, I am now preparing to resign it into the hands of Congress, and to return to that domestic retirement which, it is well known, I left with the greatest reluctance, a retirement for which I have never ceased to sigh through a long and painful absence, and in which (remote from the noise and trouble of the world) I meditate to pass the remainder of life in a state of undisturbed repose.—Circular to the States. Fitzpatrick 26:483. (1783.)

The scene is at last closed. I feel myself eased of a load of public care. I hope to spend the remainder of my days in cultivating the affections of good men and in the practice of the domestic virtues.—To George Clinton. Fitzpatrick 27:288. (1783.)

At length . . . I am become a private citizen on the banks of the Potomac, and under the shadow of my own vine and my own fig tree, free from the bustle of a camp and the busy scenes of public life, I am solacing myself with those tranquil enjoyments of which the soldier who is ever in pursuit of fame, the statesman whose watchful days and sleepless nights are spent in devising schemes to promote the welfare of his own |country or| perhaps the ruin of other countries, as if this globe was insufficient for us all, and the courtier who is always watching

the countenance of his prince, in hopes of catching a gracious smile, can have very little conception. I am not only retired from all public employments, but I am retiring within myself, and shall be able to view the solitary walk and tread the paths of private life with heartfelt satisfaction. Envious of none, I am determined to be pleased with all; and this, my dear friend, being the order for my march, I will move gently down the stream of life until I sleep with my fathers.—To the Marquis de Lafayette. Fitzpatrick 27:317. (1784.)

I am just beginning to experience that ease and freedom from public cares which, however desirable, takes some time to realize; for strange as it may |seem|, it is nevertheless true that it was not till lately I could get the better of my usual custom of ruminating as soon as I |awoke| in the morning on the business of the ensuing day, and of my surprise, after having revolved many things in my mind, to find that I was no longer a public man, or had anything to do with public transactions. I feel now, however, as I conceive a wearied traveler must do who, after treading many a painful step, with a heavy burden on his shoulders, is eased of the latter, having reached the goal to which all the former were directed; and from his housetop is looking back and tracing with a grateful eye the meanders by which he escaped the quicksands and mires which lay in his way, and into which none but the all-powerful Guide and great Disposer of human events could have prevented his falling.—To Henry Knox. Fitzpatrick

27:340. (1784.)

WASHINGTON (George), His Lack of Enmity.—Personal enmity I bear none, to any man.—To the Reverend Jacob Duche. Fitzpatrick 27:91. (1783.)

WASHINGTON (George), Too Modest to Write His Memoirs.—Any memoirs of my life, distinct and unconnected with the general history of the war, would rather hurt my feelings than tickle my pride while I lived. I had rather glide gently down the stream of life, leaving it to posterity to think and say what they please of me, than by any act of mine to have vanity or ostentation imputed to me.... I do not think vanity is a trait of my character.—To Dr. James Craik. Fitzpatrick 27:371. (1784.)

WASHINGTON (George), Learned to Sit for Portraits.—I am so hackneyed to the touches of the painter's pencil that I am now altogether at their beck, and sit "like Patience on a monument" while they are delineating the lines of my face. It is a proof, among many others, of what habit and custom can accomplish. At first I was as impatient at the request, and as restive under the operation, as a colt is of the saddle. The next time I submitted very reluctantly, but with less flouncing. Now, no dray horse moves more readily to his thill than I to the painter's chair.—To Frances Hopkinson. Fitzpatrick 28:140. (1785.)

WASHINGTON (George), Declined to Write a History of the War.—If I had talents for it, I have not leisure to turn my thoughts to commentaries; a consciousness of a defective education and a certainty of the want of time unfit me for such an undertaking.—To David Humphreys. Fitzpatrick 28:203. (1785.)

WASHINGTON (George), Optimism of.—It is assuredly better to go laughing than crying through the rough journey of life.—To Theodorick Bland. Fitzpatrick 28:516. (1786.)

WASHINGTON (George), A Philanthropist by Nature.—[I am] a philanthropist by character, and (if I may be allowed the expression)...a citizen of the great republic of humanity at large.—To the Marquis de Lafayette. Fitzpatrick 28:520. (1786.)

WASHINGTON (George), Integrity of.—I do not recollect that in the course of my life I ever forfeited my word, or broke a promise made to anyone.—To William Triplet. Fitzpatrick 2:18. (1786.)

29:18. (1786.)

While I feel the most lively gratitude for the many instances of approbation from my country, I can no otherwise deserve it than by obeying the dictates of my conscience.—To the Boston selectmen. Fitzpatrick 34:254. (1795.)

Conscious integrity has been my unceasing support; and while it gave me confidence in the measures I pursued, the belief of it, by acquiring to me the confidence of my fellow citizens, ensured the success which they have had. This consciousness will accompany me in my retirement; without it, public applauses could be viewed only as proofs of public error, and felt as the upbraidings of personal demerit.—To the Pennsylvania Senate. Fitzpatrick 35:366. (1797.)

WASHINGTON (George), Not

Driven by Ambition.—In answer to the observations you make on the probability of my election to the presidency, ... I need only say that it has no enticing charms and no fascinating allurements for me.... The increasing infirmities of nature and the growing love of retirement do not permit me to entertain a wish beyond that of living and dying an honest man on my own farm. Let those follow the pursuits of ambition and fame who have a keener relish for them, or who may have more years in store for the enjoyment.—To the Marquis de Lafayette. Fitzpatrick 29:479. (1788.)

I have a consolation within that no earthly efforts can deprive me of, and that is that neither ambitious nor interested motives have influenced my conduct.—To Governor Henry Lee. Fitzpatrick 33:23. (1793.)

WASHINGTON (George), His Love for Private Life.—The great Searcher of human hearts is my witness that I have no wish which aspires beyond the humble and happy lot of living and dying a private citizen on my own farm.—To Charles Pettit. Fitzpatrick 30:42. (1788.)

I had rather be at Mount Vernon, with a friend or two about me, than to be attended at the seat of government by the officers of state and the representatives of every power in Europe.—To David Stuart. Fitzpatrick 31:54. (1790.)

WASHINGTON (George), Placed Duty and Virtue Before Popularity.—Though I prize, as I ought, the good opinion of my fellow citizens, yet, if I know myself, I would not seek or re-

tain popularity at the expense of one social duty or moral virtue.—To Henry Lee. Fitzpatrick 30:97. (1788.)

WASHINGTON (George), Reluctant to Accept the Presidency.—I should unfeignedly rejoice in case the electors, by giving their votes in favor of some other person, would save me from the dreaded dilemma of being forced to accept or refuse. If that may not be, I am, in the next place, earnestly desirous ... of knowing whether there does not exist a probability that the government would be just as happily and effectually carried into execution without my aid as with it.... I have always felt a kind of gloom upon my mind as often as I have been taught to expect |that| I might, and perhaps must ere long, be called to make a decision. You will, I am well assured, believe the assertion (though I have little expectation it would gain credit from those who are less acquainted with me) that if I should receive the appointment and if I should be prevailed upon to accept it, the acceptance would be attended with more diffidence and reluctance than I ever experienced before in my life. It would be, however, with a fixed and sole determination of lending whatever assistance might be in my power to promote the public weal, in hopes that at a convenient and early period my services might be dispensed with, and that I might be permitted once more to retire, to pass an unclouded evening after the stormy day of life, in the bosom of domestic tranquility.—To Alexander Hamilton. Fitzpatrick 30:110. (1788.)

Every personal consideration conspires to rivet me (if I may use the expression) to retirement. At my time of life, and under my circumstances, nothing in this world can ever draw me from it unless it be a conviction that the partiality of my countrymen had made my services absolutely necessary, joined to a fear that my refusal might induce a belief that I preferred the conservation of my own reputation and private ease to the good of my country. After all, if I should conceive myself in a manner constrained to accept, I call Heaven to witness that this very act would be the greatest sacrifice of my personal feelings and wishes that ever I have been called upon to make. It would be to forgo repose and domestic enjoyment for trouble, perhaps for public obloquy. For I should consider myself as entering upon an unexplored field, enveloped on every side with clouds and darkness.—To Benjamin Lincoln. Fitzpatrick 30:119. (1788.)

The event which I have long dreaded, I am at last constrained to believe is now likely to happen.... From the moment when the necessity had become more apparent, and as it were inevitable, I anticipated, in a heart filled with distress, the ten thousand embarrassments, perplexities, and troubles to which I must again be exposed in the evening of a life already nearly consumed in public cares.—To Samuel Vaughan. Fitzpatrick 30:237. (1789.)

My movements to the chair of government will be accompanied by feelings not unlike those of a culprit who is going to the place of his execution, so

unwilling am I, in the evening of a life nearly consumed in public cares, to quit a peaceful abode for an ocean of difficulties, without that competency of political skill, abilities, and inclination which is necessary to manage the helm. I am sensible that I am embarking the voice of my countrymen, and a good name of my own, on this voyage, but what returns will be made for them, Heaven alone can foretell. Integrity and firmness is all I can promise; these, be the voyage long or short, never shall forsake me although I may be deserted by all men. For of the consolations which are to be derived from these, under any circumstances, the world cannot deprive me.—To the Acting Secretary of War. Fitzpatrick 30:268. (1789.)

Among the vicissitudes incident to life, no event could have filled me with greater anxieties than that of which the notification was transmitted by your order, and received on the fourteenth day of the present month. On the one hand, I was summoned by my country, whose voice I can never hear but with veneration and love, from a retreat which I had chosen with the fondest predilection, and, in my flattering hopes, with an immutable decision, as the asylum of my declining years, a retreat which was rendered every day more necessary as well as more dear to me, by the addition of habit to inclination, and of frequent interruptions in my health to the gradual waste committed on it by time. On the other hand, the magnitude and difficulty of the trust to which the voice of my country called me, being sufficient to awaken the wisest and most experienced of her citizens, could not but overwhelm with despondence one who, inheriting inferior endowments from nature and unpracticed in the duties of civil administration, ought to be peculiarly conscious of his own deficiencies. In this conflict of emotions, all I dare aver is that it has been my faithful study to collect my duty from a just appreciation of every circumstance by which it might be affected. All I dare hope is that, if in executing this task [i.e., accepting the presidency] I have been too much swayed by... the confidence of my fellow citizens, and have thence too little consulted my incapacity as well as disinclination for the weighty and untried cares before me, my error will be palliated by the motives which misled me, and its consequences be judged by my country with some share of the partiality in which they originated.—First Inaugural Address. Fitzpatrick 30:291. (1789.)

WASHINGTON (George), Accepts Election to the Presidency.—I have been long accustomed to entertain so great a respect for the opinion of my fellow citizens that the knowledge of the unanimous suffrages having been given in my favor scarcely leaves me the alternative for an option.... While I realize the arduous nature of the task which is imposed upon me, and feel my own inability to perform it, I wish there may not be reason for regretting the choice. All I can promise is only that which can be accomplished by an honest zeal.—To Charles Thomson. Fitzpatrick 30:285. (1789.)

Accustomed as I have been to pay a respectful regard to the opinion of my countrymen, I did not think myself at liberty to decline the acceptance of the high office to which I have been called by their united suffrage.... If I have distressing apprehensions that I shall not be able to justify the too exalted expectations of my countrymen, I am supported under the pressure of such uneasy reflections by a confidence that the most gracious Being, who has hitherto watched over the interests and averted the perils of the United States, will never suffer so fair an inheritance to become a prey to anarchy, despotism, or any other species of oppression.—To the mayor, recorder, aldermen, and common council of Philadelphia. Sparks 12:145. (1789.)

WASHINGTON (George), Considered a Man of Learning.—I am not a little flattered by being considered by the patrons of literature as one in their number. Fully apprised of the influence which sound learning has on laws, I shall only lament my want of abilities to make it still more extensive.—To the president and faculty of the University of the State of Pennsylvania. Fitzpatrick 30:289. (1789.)

WASHINGTON (George), His Love for His Country.—I was summoned by my country, whose voice I can never hear but with veneration and love.—First Inaugural Address. Fitzpatrick 30:292. (1789.)

Should it please God... to grant me health and long life, my greatest enjoyment will be to behold the prosperity of my country;... while the belief... of my fellow citizens... that I have been the happy instrument of much good to my country and to mankind will be a source of unceasing gratitude to Heaven.—To the Massachusetts Senators. Fitzpatrick 35:398. (1797.)

Retired from noise myself, and the responsibility attached to public employment, my hours will glide smoothly on. My best wishes, however, for the prosperity of our country will always have the first place in my affections.—To William Heath. Fitzpatrick 35:450. (1797.)

WASHINGTON (George), Broadmindedness of.—Shall I . . . set up my judgment as the standard of perfection? And shall I arrogantly pronounce that whosoever differs from me must discern the subject through a distorting medium, or be influenced by some nefarious design? The mind is so formed in different persons as to contemplate the same object in different points of view. Hence originates the difference on questions of the greatest import, both human and divine. In all institutions of the former kind, great allowances are doubtless to be made for the fallibility and imperfection of the authors.—Proposed address to Congress (never delivered). Fitzpatrick 30:299. (1789.)

WASHINGTON (George), Did Not Let Formalities Impede Business.—Everyone who has any knowledge of my manner of acting in public life will be persuaded that I am not accustomed to impede the dispatch or frustrate the success of business by a ceremonious attention to idle forms.—To the Comte de Moustier. Fitzpatrick 30:334. (1789.)

WASHINGTON (George), His Attitude Toward Death.—Do not flatter me with vain hopes; I am not afraid to die, and therefore can bear the worst. . . . Whether tonight or twenty years hence makes no difference; I know that I am in the hands of a good Providence.—Spoken to Dr. Samuel Bard, attending surgeon, as quoted in George Washington Parke Custis, *Recollections and Private Memoirs of Washington,* ed. Benson J. Lossing (New York: Derby & Jackson, 1860), p. 398n. (1790.)

I was the first and am now the last of my father's children by the second marriage who remain. When I shall be called upon to follow them is known only to the giver of life. When the summons comes, I shall endeavor to obey it with a good grace.—To Burgess Ball. Fitzpatrick 37:372. (1799.)

I die hard, but I am not afraid to go. —Spoken from his deathbed to Dr. James Craik, as quoted in Tobias Lear, *Letters and Recollections of George Washington* (Garden City, N.Y.: Doubleday, Doran & Company, 1932), p. 133. (1799.)

WASHINGTON (George), Shunned Ostentation.—[Mrs. Washington's] wishes coincide with my own as to simplicity of dress, and everything which can tend to support propriety of character without partaking of the follies of luxury and ostentation.—To Mrs. Catharine Macaulay Graham. Fitzpatrick 31:498. (1790.)

WASHINGTON (George), Longed for Retirement.—I have not been . . . able to dispose my mind to a longer continuation in the office I have now the honor to hold. I ... still look forward to the fulfillment of my fondest and most ardent wishes to spend the remainder of my days (which I cannot expect will be many) in ease and tranquility. Nothing short of conviction that my dereliction of the chair of government (if it should be the desire of the people to continue me in it) would involve the country in serious disputes respecting the chief magistrate, and the disagreeable consequences which might result therefrom in the floating and divided opinions which seem to prevail at present, could in any wise induce me to relinquish the determination I have formed |to retire|.—To James Madison. Fitzpatrick 32:45. (1792.)

I can religiously aver that no man was ever more tired of public life, or more devoutly wished for retirement than I do.—To Edmund Pendleton. Fitzpatrick 34:98. (1795.)

To the wearied traveller who sees a resting place, and is bending his body to lean thereon, I now compare myself. ... The remainder of my life (which in the course of nature cannot be long) will be occupied in rural amusements, and ... I shall seclude myself as much as possible from the noisy and bustling crowd.—To Henry Knox. Fitzpatrick 35:409. (1797.)

WASHINGTON (George), His Reaction to Censure.—In what will this abuse terminate? The result, as it respects myself, I care not; for I have a consolation within that no earthly efforts can deprive me of, and that is that neither ambitious nor interested motives have influenced my conduct.

The arrows of malevolence, therefore, however barbed and well pointed, never can reach the most vulnerable part of me; though, while I am up as a mark, they will be continually aimed. —To Governor Henry Lee. Fitzpatrick 33:23. (1793.)

The gazettes ... will bring you pretty well acquainted with the state of politics and of parties in this country, and show you in what manner I am attacked for a steady opposition to every measure which has a tendency to disturb the peace and tranquility of it. But these attacks, unjust and unpleasant as they are, will occasion no change in my conduct; nor will they work any other effect in my mind than to increase the anxious desire which has long possessed my breast to enjoy in the shades of retirement the consolation of having rendered my country every service my abilities were competent to, uninfluenced by pecuniary or ambitious considerations. ... Malignity, therefore, may dart her shafts; but no earthly power can deprive me of the consolation of knowing that I have not in the course of my administration been guilty of a willful error, however numerous they may have been from other causes.—To David Humphreys. Fitzpatrick 35:91. (1796.)

For the divisions which have taken place among us with respect to our political concerns, for the attacks which have been made upon those to whom the administration of the government has been entrusted by the people, and for the calumnies which are leveled at all those who are disposed to support the measures thereof, I feel, on public account, as much as any man can do, because (in my opinion) much evil and no good can result from such conduct, to this country. So far as these attacks are aimed at me personally, it is, I can assure you, sir, a misconception if it be supposed I feel the venom of the darts. Within me I have a consolation which proves an antidote against their utmost malignity, rendering my mind in the retirement I have long panted after perfectly tranquil. To "John Langhorne" [Peter Carr?]. Fitzpatrick 36:52. (1797.)

WASHINGTON (George), Belonged to No Party.—[I am] of no party.... [My] sole wish is to pursue, with undeviating steps, a path which would lead this country to respectability, wealth, and happiness.—To the Secretary of War. Fitzpatrick 34:251. (1795.)

I [am] no believer in the infallibility of the politics or measures of any man living. In short, ... I [am] no party man myself, and the first wish of my heart [is], if parties [do] exist, to reconcile them.—To Thomas Jefferson. Fitzpatrick 35:119. (1796.)

WASHINGTON (George), Guideposts of His Presidency.—As I have found no better guide hitherto than upright intentions and close investigation, I shall adhere to these maxims while I keep the watch.—To Henry Knox. Fitzpatrick 34:310. (1795.)

WASHINGTON (George), Misrepresented by Political Foes.—Until within the last year or two, ... I had no conception that parties would or even could go the length I have been witness to; nor did I believe until lately

that it was within the [bounds] of probability, hardly within those of possibility, that while I was using my utmost exertions to establish a national character of our own, independent, as far as our obligations and justice would permit, of every nation of the earth, and wished by steering a steady course to preserve this country from the horrors of a desolating war, ...I should be accused of being the enemy of one nation [i.e., France] and subject to the influence of another [i.e., Great Britain]; and, to prove it, that every act of my administration would be tortured, and the grossest and most insidious misrepresentations of them be made, by giving one side only of a subject, and that too in such exaggerated and indecent terms as could scarcely be applied to a Nero, a notorious defaulter, or even to a common pickpocket—To Thomas Jefferson. Fitzpatrick 35:120. (1796.)

WASHINGTON (George), His Feelings at End of His Presidency.—In looking forward to the moment which is intended to terminate the career of my public life, my feelings do not permit me to suspend the deep acknowledgment of that debt of gratitude which I owe to my beloved country for the many honors it has conferred upon me; still more for the steadfast confidence with which it has supported me; and for the opportunities I have thence enjoyed of manifesting my inviolable attachment, by services faithful and persevering, though in usefulness unequal to my zeal. If benefits have resulted to our country from these services, let it always be remembered to your praise, and as an instructive example in our annals that, under circumstances in which the passions agitated in every direction were liable to mislead, amid appearances sometimes dubious, viscissitudes of fortune often discouraging, in situations in which not unfrequently want of success has countenanced the spirit of criticism, the constancy of your support was the essential prop of the efforts, and a guarantee of the plans by which they were effected. Profoundly penetrated with this idea, I shall carry it with me to my grave as a strong incitement to unceasing vows that Heaven may continue to you the choicest tokens of its beneficence; that your union and brotherly affection may be perpetual; that the free Constitution, which is the work of your hands, may be sacredly maintained; that its administration in every department may be stamped with wisdom and virtue; that, in fine, the happiness of the people of these states, under the auspices of liberty, may be made complete, by so careful a preservation and so prudent a use of this blessing as will acquire to them the glory of recommending it to the applause, the affection, and adoption of every nation which is yet a stranger to it.—Farewell Address. Fitzpatrick 35:217. (1796.)

Though in reviewing the incidents of my administration I am unconscious of intentional error, I am nevertheless too sensible of my defects not to think it probable that I may have committed many errors. Whatever they may be, I fervently beseech the Almighty to avert or mitigate the evils to which

they may tend. I shall also carry with me the hope that my country will never cease to view them with indulgence; and that after forty-five years of my life dedicated to its service, with an upright zeal, the faults of incompetent abilities will be consigned to oblivion, as myself must soon be to the mansions of rest. Relying on |my country's| kindness in this as in other things, and actuated by that fervent love towards it which is so natural to a man who views in it the native soil of himself and his progenitors for several generations, I anticipate with pleasing expectation that |retirement| in which I promise myself to realize, without alloy, the sweet enjoyment of partaking, in the midst of my fellow citizens, the benign influence of good laws under a free government, the ever favorite object of my heart and the happy reward, as I trust, of our mutual cares, labors, and dangers.—Farewell Address. Fitzpatrick 35:237. (1796.)

When, in the decline of life, I gratify the fond wish of my heart in retiring from public labors, and find the language of approbation and fervent prayers for future happiness following that event, my heart expands with gratitude and my feelings become unutterable.—To the General Assembly of the state of Rhode Island. Fitzpatrick 35:431. (1797.)

WASHINGTON (George), Enjoyed Farming.—A few months more will put an end to my political existence and place me in the shades of Mount Vernon under my vine and fig tree.... It is true (as you have heard) that to be a cultivator of land has been my favorite amusement; but it is equally true that I have made very little proficiency in acquiring knowledge either in the principles or practice of husbandry. My employments through life have been so diversified, my absences from home have been so frequent and so long at a time, as to have prevented me from bestowing the attention and from making the experiments which are necessary to establish facts in the science of agriculture. And now, though I may amuse myself in that way for the short time I may remain on this theater, it is too late in the day for me to commence a scientific course of experiments.—To Landon Carter. Fitzpatrick 35:246. (1796.)

At no period have I been more closely employed than within the three months I have been at home, in repairing the ravages which an eight years' absence (except occasional short visits which were inadequate to investigation) have produced on my farms, buildings, and everything around them.... At the age of sixty-five I am recommencing my agricultural pursuits and rural amusements, which at all times have been the most pleasing occupation of my life, and most congenial with my temper, notwithstanding a small proportion of it has been spent in this way.—To the Earl of Buchan. Fitzpatrick 35:487. (1797.)

WASHINGTON (George), His Activities in Retirement.—For myself, having turned aside from the broad walks of political |life| into the narrow paths of private life, I shall leave it with those whose duty it is to consider subjects of this sort |i.e., public affairs|,

and (as every good citizen ought to do) conform to whatsoever the ruling powers shall decide. To make and sell a little flour annually, to repair houses (going fast to ruin), to build one for the security of my papers of a public nature, and to amuse myself in agricultural and rural pursuits will constitute employment for the few years I have to remain on this terrestrial globe. If, |in addition| to these, I could now and then meet the friends I esteem, it would fill the measure and add zest to my enjoyments; but, if ever this happens, it must be under my own vine and fig tree.—To Oliver Wolcott. Fitzpatrick 35:447. (1797.)

I have nothing to say that could either inform or amuse a Secretary of War in Philadelphia. I might tell him that I begin my diurnal course with the sun; that, if my hirelings are not in their places at that time, I send them messages expressive of my sorrow for their indisposition; that, having put these wheels in motion, I examine the state of things further, and the more they are probed, the deeper I find the wounds are which my buildings have sustained by an absence and neglect of eight years. By the time I have accomplished these matters, breakfast (a little after seven o'clock, about the time I presume you are taking leave of Mrs. McHenry) is ready.... This being over, I mount my horse and ride round my farms, which employs me until it is time to dress for dinner, at which I rarely miss seeing strange faces, come as they say out of respect for me. Pray, would not the word curiosity answer as well? And how different this from having a few social friends at a cheerful board! The usual time of sitting at table, a walk, and tea brings me within the dawn of candlelight; previous to which, if not prevented by company, I resolve that, as soon as the glimmering taper supplies the place of the great luminary, I will retire to my writing table and acknowledge the letters I have received; but when the lights are brought, I feel tired and disinclined to engage in this work, conceiving that the next night will do as well. The next comes, and with it the same causes for postponement, and effect, and so on. ... Having given you the history of a day, it will serve for a year, and I am persuaded you will not require a second edition of it. But it may strike you that in this detail no mention is made of any portion of time allotted for reading. The remark would be just, for I have not looked into a book since I came home; nor shall I be able to do it until I have discharged my workmen, probably not before the nights grow longer, when possibly I may be looking in Doomsday Book.—To James McHenry. Fitzpatrick 35:455. (1797.)

WASHINGTON (George), His Post-Retirement View of Public Affairs.—I am now seated in the shade of my vine and fig tree, and although I look with regret on many transactions which do not comport with my ideas, I shall, notwithstanding, "view them in the calm lights of mild philosophy," persuaded, if any great crisis should occur to require it, that the good sense and spirit of the major part of the people of this country will direct them properly. —To Charles Cotesworth Pinckney.

Fitzpatrick 35:471. (1797.)

WASHINGTON (George), Thankful for Divine Help.—I am ... grateful to that Providence which has directed my steps, and shielded me in the various changes and chances through which I have passed, from my youth to the present moment.—To the Reverend William Gordon. Fitzpatrick 36:49. (1797.)

WASHINGTON (George), Concerned About Financial Affairs.—A sixteen years' absence from home (with short intervals only) could not fail to derange |my private concerns| considerably, and to require all the time I can spare from the usual avocations of life to bring them into tune again. But this is not all, nor the worst, for being the executor, the administrator, and trustee of and for other estates, my greatest anxiety is to leave all these concerns in such a clear and distinct form as that no reproach may attach itself to me when I have taken my departure for the land of spirits.— To the Secretary of War. Fitzpatrick 37:158. (1799.)

WASHINGTON (George), Provisions for His Burial.—The family vault at Mount Vernon requiring repairs, and being improperly situated besides, I desire that a new one of brick, and upon a larger scale, may be built at the foot of what is commonly called the Vineyard Enclosure, on the ground which is marked out; in which my remains, with those of my deceased relatives (now in the old vault) and such others of my family as may choose to be entombed there, may be deposited. And it is my express desire that my corpse may be interred in a private manner, without parade or funeral oration.—Last Will and Testament. Fitzpatrick 37:293. (1799.) **WASHINGTON (Martha), Washington's Love for.**—You may believe me, my dear Patsy, when I assure you in the most solemn manner that, so far from seeking this appointment |as commander-in-chief|, I have used every endeavor in my power to avoid it, not only from my unwillingness to part with you and the family, but from a consciousness of its being a trust too great for my capacity; and that I should enjoy more real happiness in one month with you at home than I have the most distant prospect of finding abroad, if my stay were to be seven times seven years.—To Mrs. Martha Washington. Fitzpatrick 3:293. (1775.)

I shall rely, therefore, confidently on that Providence which has heretofore preserved and been bountiful to me, not doubting but that I shall return safe to you in the fall. I shall feel no pain from the toil or the danger of the campaign; my unhappiness will flow from the uneasiness I know you will feel from being left alone.—To Mrs. Martha Washington. Fitzpatrick 3:294. (1775.)

I shall hope that my friends will visit and endeavor to keep up the spirits of my wife as much as they can, as my departure will, I know, be a cutting stroke upon her.—To John Augustine Washington. Fitzpatrick 3:300. (1775.) **WASHINGTON (Martha).** See also CUSTIS (Martha).

WASHINGTON (Mary), Washington's Feelings on Death of.—Awful and affecting as the death of a parent is, there is consolation in knowing that Heaven has spared ours to an age beyond which few attain, and favored her with the full enjoyment of her mental faculties and as much bodily strength as usually falls to the lot of fourscore. Under these considerations, and a hope that she is translated to a happier place, it is the duty of her relatives to yield due submission to the decrees of the Creator.—To Elizabeth Washington Lewis. Fitzpatrick 30:399. (1789.)

WAYNE (General Anthony), Character of.—More active and enterprising than judicious and cautious. No economist, it is feared. Open to flattery, vain, easily imposed upon and liable to be drawn into scrapes. Too indulgent (the effect perhaps of some of the causes just mentioned) to his officers and men. Whether sober or a little addicted to the bottle, I know not. —Opinion of the general officers. Fitzpatrick 31:510. (1792.) **WEST, Settlement of the.**—To suffer a wide-extended country to be overrun with land jobbers, speculators, and monopolizers, or even with scattered settlers, is in my opinion inconsistent with that wisdom and policy which our true interest dictates, or that an enlightened people ought to adopt; and, besides, is pregnant of disputes both with the savages and among ourselves, the evils of which are easier to be conceived than described. And for what, but to aggrandize a few avaricious men, to the prejudice of many and the embarrassment of government? For the people engaged in these pursuits, without contributing in the smallest degree to the support of government, or considering themselves as amenable to its laws, will involve it, by their unrestrained conduct, in inextricable perplexities, and more than probably in a great deal of bloodshed.—To James Duane. Fitzpatrick 27:133. (1783.)

WEST. See also PUBLIC LAND.

WHISKEY REBELLION, A Challenge to Law and Government.— What may be the consequences of such violent and outrageous proceedings is painful in a high degree even in contemplation. But if the laws are to be so trampled upon with impunity, and a minority (a small one too) is to dictate to the majority, there is an end put, at one stroke, to republican government, and nothing but anarchy and confusion is to be expected thereafter; for some other man or society may dislike another law and oppose it with equal propriety until all laws are prostrate, and everyone (the strongest, I presume) will carve for himself.—To Charles Mynn Thruston. Fitzpatrick 33:465. (1794.)

WHISKEY REBELLION, Patriotism in.—The spirit which blazed out on this occasion, as soon as the object was fully understood and the lenient measures of the government were made known to the people, deserve[s] to be communicated. For there are instances of general officers going at the head of a single troop and of light companies; of field officers, when they came to the places of rendezvous and found no command for them in that grade, turning into the ranks and

proceeding as private soldiers under their own captains; and of numbers, possessing the first fortunes in the country, standing in the ranks as private men and marching day by day with their knapsacks and haversacks at their backs, sleeping on straw with a single blanket, in a soldier's tent, during the frosty nights which we have had. By way of example to others, nay more, many young Quakers (not discouraged by the elders) of the first families, characters, and property [have] turned into the ranks and are marching with the troops.—To John Jay. Fitzpatrick 34:17. (1794.)

[The recent insurrection] has demonstrated that our prosperity rests on solid foundations, by furnishing an additional proof that my fellow citizens understand the true principles of government and liberty; that they feel their inseparable union; that notwithstanding all the devices which have been used to sway them from their interest of duty, they are now as ready to maintain the authority of the laws against licentious invasions as they were to defend their rights against usurpation. It has been a spectacle, displaying to the highest advantage the value of republican government, to behold the most and least wealthy of our citizens standing in the same ranks as private soldiers; preeminently distinguished by being the army of the Constitution; undeterred by a march of three hundred miles over rugged mountains, by the approach of an inclement season, or by any other discouragement. Nor ought I to omit to acknowledge the efficacious and patriotic cooperation which I have experienced from the chief magistrates of the states, to which my requisitions have been addressed. To every description, indeed, of citizens let praise be given. But let them persevere in their affectionate vigilance over that precious depository of American happiness, the Constitution of the United States. Let them cherish it, too, for the sake of those who from every clime are daily seeking a dwelling in our land.—Sixth Annual Address to Congress. Fitzpatrick 34:34. (1794.)

WHISKEY REBELLION. See also DEMOCRATIC SOCIETIES.

WOMEN, Patriotism of American.— Nor would I rob the fairer sex of their share in the glory of a revolution so honorable to human nature, for indeed I think you ladies are in the number of the best patriots America can boast.— To Annis Boudinot Stockton. Fitzpatrick 30:76. (1788.)

WORK, Economy in.—My observation on every employment in life is that wherever and whenever one person is found adequate to the discharge of a duty by close application thereto, it is worse executed by two persons, and scarcely done at all if three or more are employed therein.— To Henry Knox. Fitzpatrick 32:160. (1792.)

tions for this operation has been most conspicuous and remarkable.—To Thomas McKean. Fitzpatrick 23:343. (1781.)

Y

YORKTOWN, Hand of God in American Victory at.—The interposing Hand of Heaven in the various instances of our extensive prepara-

Selected Bibliography

Andrist, Ralph K., ed. *George Washington: A Biography in His Own Words.* New York: Newsweek, 1972.

Bellamy, Francis Rufus. *The Private Life of George Washington.* New York: Thomas Y. Crowell Company, 1951.

Boatner, Mark Mayo, III. *Encyclopedia of the American Revolution.* New York: David McKay Company, 1966.

Burnett, Edmund C., ed. *Letters of Members of the Continental Congress.* 8 vols. Washington: Carnegie Institution of Washington, 1921–36.

Commager, Henry Steele, and Morris, Richard B., eds. *The Spirit of 'Seventy-Six: The Story of the American Revolution As Told by Participants.* 2 vols. Indianapolis: Bobbs-Merrill Company, 1958.

Custis, George Washington Parke. *Recollections and Private Memoirs of Washington.* Edited by Benson J. Lossing. New York: Derby & Jackson, 1860.

Fitzpatrick, John C. *George Washington Himself.* Indianapolis: Bobbs-Merrill Company, 1933.

Flexner, James Thomas. *George Washington: The Forge of Experience (1732–1775).* Boston: Little, Brown and Company, 1965.

————. *George Washington in the American Revolution (1775–1783).* Boston: Little, Brown and Company, 1968.

————. *George Washington and the New Nation (1783–1793).* Boston: Little, Bown and Company, 1970.

————. *George Washington: Anguish and Farewell (1793–1799).* Boston: Little, Brown and Company, 1972.

Freeman, Douglas Southall. *George Washington.* 7 vols. New York: Charles Scribner's Sons, 1948–57. (Vol. 7 by John A. Carroll and Mary W. Ashworth.)

Hamilton, Alexander. *The Papers of Alexander Hamilton.* Edited by Harold C. Syrett. 26 vols. New York: Columbia University Press, 1961–79.

Hamilton, Stanislaus Murray, ed. *Letters to Washington and Accompanying Papers.* 5 vols. Boston: Houghton Mifflin Company, 1898–1902.

Jefferson, Thomas. *The Writings of Thomas Jefferson*. Edited by Albert Ellery Bergh. 20 vols. Washington: Thomas Jefferson Memorial Association, 1907.

Lear, Tobias. *Letters and Recollections of George Washington*. Garden City, N.Y.: Doubleday, Doran & Company, 1932.

Scheer, George F., and Rankin, Hugh F. *Rebels and Redcoats*. Cleveland and New York: World Publishing Company, 1957.

Sparks, Jared, ed. *Correspondence of the American Revolution, Being Letters of Eminent Men to George Washington*. 4 vols. 1853. Reprint. Freeport, N.Y.: Books for Libraries Press, 1970.

Ward, Christopher. *The War of the Revolution*. Edited by John Richard Alden. 2 vols. New York: Macmillan Company, 1952.

Washington, George. *The Diaries of George Washington*. Edited by Donald Jackson and Dorothy Twohig. 6 vols. Charlottesville, Va.: University Press of Virginia, 1976–79.

————. *The Diaries of George Washington, 1748–1799*. Edited by John C. Fitzpatrick. 4 vols. Boston and New York: Houghton Mifflin Company, 1925.

————. *The Papers of George Washington: Colonial Series*. Edited by W. W. Abbot. 4 vols. by 1984. Charlottesville, Va.: University Press of Virginia, 1983–.

————. *The Writings of George Washington*. Edited by Worthington Chauncey Ford. 14 vols. New York: G. P. Putnam's Sons, 1889–93.

————. *The Writings of George Washington from the Original Manuscript Sources, 1745–1799*. Edited by John C. Fitzpatrick. 39 vols. Washington: United States Government Printing Office, 1931–44.

————. *The Writings of George Washington . . . with a Life of the Author*. Edited by Jared Sparks. 12 vols. Boston: American Stationers' Company, 1834–37.

Notes and References

Preface

1. James Elliot Cabot, ed., *The Complete Works of Ralph Waldo Emerson*. 12 vols. (New York: Wm. H. Wise & Company, 1926), 2:10.

2. Quoted in John C. Fitzpatrick, *George Washington Himself* (Indianapolis: Bobbs-Merrill Company, 1933), p. 409.

3. Lyman H. Butterfield, ed., *Letters of Benjamin Rush*, 2 vols. (Princeton, N.J.: Princeton University Press, 1951), 1:92.

4. Quoted in James Morton Smith, ed., *George Washington: A Profile* (New York: Hill and Wang, 1969), p. x.

5. Thomas Jefferson, *Notes on the State of Virginia* (1782), in *The Writings of Thomas Jefferson*, ed. Albert Ellery Bergh, 20 vols. (Washington: The Thomas Jefferson Memorial Association, 1907), 2:94.

6. Scott MacFarland, ed., *Subject Guide to Books in Print—1989-1990*, 4 vols. (New York and London: R.R. Bowker Company, 1989), 4:7230-31.

7. In 1965, for example, there were around 3,000 publications about George Washington in the New York Public Library. James Thomas Flexner, *George Washington: The Forge of Experience (1732-1775)* (Boston: Little, Brown and Company, 1965), p. 353.

8. James Thomas Flexner, *Washington: The Indispensable Man* (Boston: Little, Brown and Company, 1974), p. xvi.

9. Douglas Southall Freeman, *George Washington*, 7 vols. (New York: Charles Scribner's Sons, 1948-57), 6:xxx-xxxi.

10. Flexner, *Washington: The Indispensable Man*, p. xvi.

Chapter 1—A Virginia Boyhood

1. Letter from GW to Joseph Reed (8 Nov. 1775), in John C. Fitzpatrick, ed., *The Writings of George Washington*, 39 vols. (Washington: United States Government Printing Office, 1931–44), 4:77. Hereafter cited as Fitzpatrick.

2. James Sullivan (then a member of the Massachusetts legislature and later governor of Massachusetts), quoted in Thomas C. Amory, *Life of James Sullivan, with Selections from His Writings*, 2 vols. (Boston: Phillips, Sampson and Company, 1859), 1:69-70.

3. Saul K. Padover, ed., *The Washington Papers* (New York: Harper & Brothers, 1955), pp. 7-8.

4. Albert Welles, *The Pedigree and History of the Washington Family* (New York: Society Library, 1879), introduction, pp. iv-vi. Welles also recorded this interesting observation: "The remarkable resemblance of character between Odin and his descendant Washington, separated by a period of eighteen centuries, is so great as to excite the profound and devout astonishment of the genealogical student—one the founder of the most eminent race of kings and conquerors, and the other of the grand Republic of America." Ibid., introduction, p. iv.

5. Ibid., preface, p. iv; introduction, pp. xxxii-xxxiii.

6. See Douglas Southall Freeman, *George Washington*, 7 vols. (New York: Charles Scribner's Sons, 1948-57), 1:15-20. Hereafter cited as Freeman.

7. The baby was named after Major George Eskridge, who had served as Mary's guardian when she was orphaned as a child. Eskridge was a lawyer of distinction who was well known throughout the Northern Neck.

8. This description, given by a Mr. Withers, is quoted from Freeman 1:33.

9. The familiar "cherry tree" episode, like several others often retold about Washington's youth, was apparently invented by Mason Locke ("Parson") Weems several years after the President's death—or at least there is no available evidence that it was drawn from a reliable source. The story first appeared in the fifth edition (1806) of Weems's *Life of George Washington, with Curious Anecdotes Equally Honorable to Himself and Exemplary to His Young Countrymen* (originally published in 1800). Weems is regarded by historians as "a persuasive fictionalizer" who was "continually expanding his text with new imaginings." James Thomas Flexner, *George Washington: The Forge of Experience (1732-1775)* (Boston: Little, Brown and Company, 1965), p. 357. This may be a disappointment to those of us who have grown up admiring the little fellow who supposedly declared, "I can't tell a lie, Pa.... I did cut it with my hatchet." But the following observation by an eminent Washington scholar seems significant in this regard: "It is not necessary to strain for effects in the story of George Washington. Everything for which documentary proof does not exist may be discarded without regret, for the provable facts that remain support a life and character more than satisfactory to the most ardent admirer." John C. Fitzpatrick, *George Washington Himself* (Indianapolis: Bobbs-Merrill Company, 1933), p. 19.

10. GW to Henry Knox (27 April 1787), Fitzpatrick 29:209.

11. In a letter written to Washington in June 1756, fellow Virginian George Mason referred to a Sergeant Piper as "my neighbor and your old schoolfellow," implying that Washington had indeed attended a school. Robert A. Rutland, ed., *The Papers of George Mason, 1725-1792*, 3 vols. (Chapel Hill, N.C.: University of North Carolina Press, 1970), 1:38. Colonel David Humphreys, one of Washington's aides during the Revolutionary War, reported in an unfinished 1786 manuscript entitled "The Life of General Washington" (prepared largely at

Mount Vernon with Washington's own assistance) that "his education was principally conducted by a private tutor." Quoted in Flexner, *George Washington: The Forge of Experience*, p. 24. See also Freeman 1:64n, 78n.

12. Fitzpatrick, *George Washington Himself*, pp. 19-21, 517n; William H. Wilbur, *The Making of George Washington*, 2d ed. rev. (DeLand, Fla.. Patriotic Education, 1973), pp. 60-61.

13. GW to David Humphreys (25 July 1785), Fitzpatrick 28:203.

14. GW to Francis Hopkinson (5 Feb. 1789), Fitzpatrick 30:196-97; see also Fitzpatrick, *George Washington Himself*, pp. 122-23.

15. See Fitzpatrick, *George Washington Himself*, pp. 23-28 for a useful overview of Washington's education, including various extracts from his exercise books.

16. Moncure D. Conway, *George Washington's Rules of Civility* (New York: John W. Lovell Co., 1890), passim. For examples of Washington's application of these maxims in his adult life, see Fitzpatrick, *George Washington Himself*, pp. 22-23.

17 Lawrence Washington to Augustine Washington (30 May 1741), in Freeman 1:69.

18. The cause of Augustine's death was described as "gout of the stomach." See Freeman 1:72n.

19. GW to the mayor and citizens of Fredericksburg, Virginia (14 Feb. 1784), Fitzpatrick 27:332.

20. Humphreys, "The Life of General Washington," quoted in Flexner, *George Washington: The Forge of Experience*, p. 30.

21. Robert Jackson to Lawrence Washington (18 Sept. 1746), quoted in Freeman 1:195.

22. Humphreys, "The Life of General Washington," quoted in Flexner, *George Washington: The Forge of Experience*, p. 30.

Chapter 2—Expanding Horizons

1. Fitzpatrick, *George Washington Himself*, pp. 40, 519n. Even at this early date, Washington carefully recorded all income and expenses in a personal account book. He continued the practice throughout his life.

2. Diary entry (15 Mar. 1748), in Donald Jackson and Dorothy Twohig, eds., *The Diaries of George Washington*, 6 vols. (Charlottesville, Va: University Press of Virginia, 1976-79), 1:9-10. Hereafter cited as *Diaries*. Isaac Pennington was one of the earliest settlers in the Shenandoah Valley. Spelling, capitalization, and punctuation have been modernized here and in other quotations in this biography.

3. Diary entry (16 Mar. 1748), *Diaries* 1:11.

4. Diary entry (21 Mar. 1748), *Diaries* 1:12.

5. Diary entry (23 Mar. 1748), *Diaries* 1:13.

6. Diary entry (12 Apr. 1748), *Diaries* 1:23.

7. Buckner Stith to GW (1748?), in John Corbin, *The Unknown Washington: Biographic Origins of the Republic* (New York: Charles Scribner's Sons, 1930), p. 54.

8. Thomas, Lord Fairfax, to Mary Ball Washington (1748?), in Frank Donovan, ed., *The George Washington Papers* (New York: Dodd, Mead & Company, 1964), p. 7.

9. Freeman 1:229 and *n*.

10. GW to Lawrence Washington (5 May 1749), Fitzpatrick 1:13.

11. GW to Robin _____ [1749-50], Fitzpatrick 1:15-16. The "very agreeable young lady" mentioned in this letter was a sister-in-law to George William Fairfax, who had accompanied Washington on the surveying expedition to the South Branch of the Potomac. The "Lowland Beauty" has not been identified.

12. GW to Captain John Posey (24 June 1767), Fitzpatrick 2:458.

13. Diary entry (5 Nov. 1751), *Diaries* 1:73.

14. Diary entry (17 Nov. 1751), *Diaries* 1:82.

15. Diary entry (23 Dec. 1751), *Diaries* 1:93.

16. Lawrence Washington to an unknown correspondent (Apr.? 1752), in Jared Sparks, ed., *The Writings of George Washington... with a Life of the Author,* 12 vols. (Boston: American Stationers' Company, 1834-37), 2:423. Hereafter cited as Sparks.

17. GW to Mrs. Lawrence Washington [1749-50], Fitzpatrick 1:18.

18. GW to William Fauntleroy, Sr. (20 May 1752), Fitzpatrick 1:22.

19. Despite his great physical strength, Washington was a frequent victim of illnesses during his life. For a summary of these see Paul Leicester Ford, *The True George Washington* (Philadelphia: J.B. Lippincott Company, 1896), pp. 48-59.

20. Quoted in Thomas J. Fleming, *First in Their Hearts: A Biography of George Washington* (New York: W. W. Norton & Company, 1968), p. 17.

Chapter 3—A Dangerous Journey

1. Diary entry (4 Dec. 1753), *Diaries* 1:144.

2. Diary entry (15 Dec. 1753), *Diaries* 1:152.

3. Ibid.

4. Gist journal entry (22 Dec. 1753), in William M. Darlington, ed., *Christopher Gist's Journals* (Pittsburgh: J. R. Weldin & Co., 1893), p. 84.

5. Diary entry (26 Dec. 1753), *Diaries* 1:155.

6. Diary entry (27 Dec. 1753), *Diaries* 1:155; Gist journal entry (27 Dec. 1753), Darlington, pp. 85–86.

7. Diary entry (29 Dec. 1753), *Diaries* 1:155.

8. Ibid., p. 156.

9. Gist journal entry (29 Dec. 1753), Darlington, p. 86.

10. Reprinted in *Diaries* 1:130–61.

11. Fitzpatrick, *George Washington Himself*, p. 50.

Chapter 4—The Thick of Battle

1. GW to Governor Robert Dinwiddie (9 Mar. 1754), Fitzpatrick 1:32.

2. GW to Governor Robert Dinwiddie (20 Mar. 1754), Fitzpatrick 1:35.

3. GW to Governor Horatio Sharpe of Maryland (27 Apr. 1754), Fitzpatrick 1:44.

4. Quoted in GW diary entry (22 Apr. 1754), *Diaries* 1:178.

5. This was the same Indian name that had been given to Washington's great-grandfather in the previous century. See GW's biographical memoranda (Oct. 1786), Fitzpatrick 29:37; *Diaries* 1:183n; Freeman 1:317n.

6. GW to John Augustine Washington (31 May 1754), Fitzpatrick 1:70. After this letter was published in the *London Magazine* the following August, King George II reportedly observed, "He would not say so if he had been used to hear many." Quoted in Horace Walpole, *Memoires of the Last Ten Years of the Reign of George the Second,* 2 vols. (London: John Murray, 1822), 1:347. During the Revolutionary War an acquaintance asked Washington if it was true that he found charm in the whistling of bullets. "If I said so," he answered, "it was when I was young." Quoted in William Gordon, *The History of the Rise, Progress, and Establishment of the Independence of the United States of America,* 4 vols. (London: Printed for the author, 1788), 2:203.

7. GW to Governor Robert Dinwiddie (3 June 1754), Fitzpatrick 1:73.

8. GW to Colonel Joshua Fry (29 May 1754), Fitzpatrick 1:58–59.

9. GW to John Augustine Washington (31 May 1754), Fitzpatrick 1:70.

10. Biographical memoranda (Oct. 1786), Fitzpatrick 29:40.

11. Ibid.

12. From a letter of Captain Adam Stephen to Benjamin Rush (1775), quoted in Freeman 1:405.

13. See John Robinson to GW (15 Sept. 1754), in Stanislaus Murray Hamilton, ed., *Letters to Washington and Accompanying Papers,* 5 vols. (Boston: Houghton Mifflin

Company, 1898–1902), 1:45–46.

14. GW to Colonel William Fitzhugh (15 Nov. 1754), Fitzpatrick 1:105–6.

15. Ibid., pp. 106–7.

16. Biographical memoranda (Oct. 1786), Fitzpatrick 29:41.

17. John Peyton to Henry Peyton (25 Feb. 1755), in John Lewis Peyton, *The Adventures of My Grandfather* (New York: Argonaut Press, 1966), pp. 231–32.

18. Quoted in Thomas J. Fleming, *First in Their Hearts: A Biography of George Washington* (New York: W. W. Norton & Company, 1968), p. 22.

19. Quoted in ibid.

20. Robert Leckie, *The Wars of America* (New York: Harper and Row, 1968), p. 45.

21. Ibid.

22. GW to John Augustine Washington (28 June 1755), Fitzpatrick 1:141–42.

23. Ibid., p. 144.

24. GW to Mary Ball Washington (18 July 1755), Fitzpatrick 1:151.

25. GW to John Augustine Washington (18 July 1755), Fitzpatrick 1:152. See also biographical memoranda (Oct. 1786), Fitzpatrick 29:43.

26. Biographical memoranda (Oct. 1786), Fitzpatrick 29:43.

27. GW to Mary Ball Washington (18 July 1755), Fitzpatrick 1:151.

28. GW to John Augustine Washington (18 July 1755), Fitzpatrick 1:153.

29. Ibid., p. 152.

30. These figures are from Freeman 2:86.

31. GW to Robert Jackson (2 Aug. 1755), Fitzpatrick 1:155. Washington believed that Braddock's army had been defeated by no more than three hundred men, but in actuality the enemy may have been almost three times as numerous. GW to Mary Ball Washington (18 July 1755), Fitzpatrick 1:151; Freeman 2:94, 101.

32. George Washington Parke Custis, *Recollections and Private Memoirs of Washington*, ed. Benson J. Lossing (New York: Derby & Jackson, 1860), p. 302.

33. Ibid., pp. 303–4. This incident was related personally by Dr. James Craik, an eyewitness, to G. W. P. Custis, Martha Washington's grandson and GW's adopted son. It is interesting to note that Washington never received the slightest injury in battle during his life.

34. Quoted in Flexner, *George Washington: The Forge of Experience*, p. 134.

35. Charles Lewis to GW (Aug. 1755?), Hamilton, *Letters to Washington and Accompanying Papers*, 1:75–76.

36. Christopher Gist to GW (15 Oct. 1755), Hamilton, *Letters to Washington and Accompanying Papers*, 1:110.

37. From a sermon entitled "Religion and Patriotism the Constituents of a Good Soldier" (17 Aug. 1755), which was published in Philadelphia and London; quoted in Sparks 2:89–90*n*. In 1759 Davies became president of Princeton College, afterward Princeton University.

38. GW to Augustine Washington (2 Aug. 1755), Fitzpatrick 1:157.

Chapter 5—Defending the Frontier

1. GW to Charles Lewis (14 Aug. 1755), Fitzpatrick 1:163.

2. Governor Robert Dinwiddie to GW (14 Aug. 1755), in W. W. Abbot, ed., *The Papers of George Washington: Colonial Series*, 4 vols. by 1984 (Charlottesville, Va.: University of Virginia, 1983–), 2:4.

3. GW to Governor Robert Dinwiddie (24 Apr. 1756), Fitzpatrick 1:329.

4. GW to Governor Robert Dinwiddie (27 Apr. 1756), Fitzpatrick 1:342.

5. GW to Governor Robert Dinwiddie (22 Apr. 1756), Fitzpatrick 1:324–25.

6. Ibid., p. 325.

7. GW to Colonel John Stanwix (8 Oct. 1757), Fitzpatrick 2:145. Three decades later Washington wrote, "The frontiers were continually harassed; but not having force enough to carry the war to the gates of [Fort] Duquesne, [I] could do no more than distribute the troops along the frontiers in the stockaded forts, more with a view to quiet the fears of the inhabitants than from any expectation of giving securities in so extensive a line to the settlements." Biographical memoranda (Oct. 1786), Fitzpatrick 29:46.

8. Edward C. McGuire, *The Religious Opinions and Character of Washington* (New York: Harper & Brothers, 1836), pp. 330–31; see also Freeman 2:146 and *n*.

9. GW to John Robinson (5 Aug. 1756), Fitzpatrick 1:430–31.

10. Ibid., p. 431.

11. This journey, which acquainted Washington for the first time with the more populous areas of the northern provinces (including Philadelphia and New York), took place in February and March of 1756. Shirley ignored a petition from Virginia's officers for inclusion in the regular establishment, but he did declare that Washington outranked Dagworthy. See Freeman 2:157–68.

12. GW to Governor Robert Dinwiddie (11 Oct. 1755), Fitzpatrick 1:200–201.

13. GW to Governor Robert Dinwiddie (18 Apr. 1756), Fitzpatrick 1:317.

14. Orders (7 July 1756), Fitzpatrick 1:396.

15. Orders (30 Aug. 1756), Fitzpatrick 1:450–51.

16. Orders (1 May 1756), Fitzpatrick 1:353.

17. Orders (25 Dec. 1755), Fitzpatrick 1:258. After executing two deserters in

1757, Washington wrote to the governor: "Your Honor will, I hope, excuse my hanging instead of shooting them. It conveyed much more terror to others, and it was for example's sake we did it." GW to Governor Robert Dinwiddie (3 Aug. 1757), Fitzpatrick 2:118.

18. For example, see orders (25 Sept. 1756), Fitzpatrick 1:473.

19. General instructions to all the captains of companies (29 July 1757), Fitzpatrick 2:114. Washington followed his own advice, frequently studying books on military science and taking fencing lessons from a Sergeant Wood while at Winchester. See Fitzpatrick 1:254–55n; Freeman 2:204.

20. GW to Governor Robert Dinwiddie (4 Aug. 1756), Fitzpatrick 1:423.

21. GW to Captain James Cunningham (28 Jan. 1757), Fitzpatrick 2:5.

22. See Freeman 2:274–75.

23. GW to Colonel John Stanwix (4 Mar. 1758), Fitzpatrick 2:166–67.

24. Biographical memoranda (Oct. 1786), Fitzpatrick 29:48.

25. David Humphreys, "The Life of General Washington" (unfinished 1786 manuscript prepared at Mount Vernon with GW's assistance), quoted in Flexner, *George Washington: The Forge of Experience*, p. 222.

26. Officers of the Virginia Regiment to GW (31 Dec. 1758), Hamilton, *Letters to Washington and Accompanying Papers*, 3:143–45; also in Sparks 2:477–78.

27. GW to the officers of the Virginia Regiment (10 Jan. 1759), in Flexner, *George Washington: The Forge of Experience*, pp. 349–50.

28. Ibid., p. 350.

Chapter 6—Marrying into a Ready-Made Family

1. Estimates and recorded measurements of Washington's height differ somewhat. He once described himself as approximately "six feet high." GW to Charles Lawrence (26 Apr. 1763), Fitzpatrick 2:395. However, at the time of his death the length of the body was measured at "6 feet 3½ inches exact." Diary of Tobias Lear (15 Dec. 1799), in Lear, *Letters and Recollections of George Washington* (Garden City, N.Y.: Doubleday, Doran & Company, 1932), p. 137. In old age he stated, "My weight in my best days . . . never exceeded from two hundred and ten to twenty." Quoted in Custis, *Recollections and Private Memoirs of Washington*, p. 527. He may have weighed less in 1759 because of his youth or because of the illness he had suffered during the preceding months.

2. The Marquis de Lafayette once said of Washington, "I never saw so large a hand on any human being." Quoted in Custis, *Recollections and Private Memoirs of*

Washington, p. 484. Washington's adopted son, George Washington Parke Custis, wrote: "Could a cast have been made from his right hand (so far did its dimensions exceed nature's model), it would have been preserved in museums for ages as the anatomical wonder of the eighteenth century." Ibid., p. 527.

3. In ordering clothes, Washington described himself as "proportionably made; if anything, rather slender than thick...with pretty long arms and thighs." GW to Charles Lawrence (26 Apr. 1763), Fitzpatrick 2:395-96.

4. "Washington's tooth difficulties may have been due to his hard frontier fare and the nervous tension under which he worked, for they began at the age of twenty-two or twenty-three and continued throughout his life. He was, as his ledger accounts show, unusually careful of his teeth; the purchases of 'spunge' toothbrushes by the dozen, of tinctures of myrrh and other dentifrices, and bills for dental work are too numerous to admit of any other conclusion. His first tooth was extracted in April 1756, and one by one he lost the others, though he fought a hard but losing fight to retain them. The last one went in 1790." Fitzpatrick, *George Washington Himself*, p. 73.

5. Description by George Mercer (1760), quoted in Freeman 3:6. Over the years, many others praised Washington's horsemanship. One of these was Thomas Jefferson, who called him "the best horseman of his age, and the most graceful figure that could be seen on horseback." Jefferson to Dr. Walter Jones (2 Jan. 1814), in Albert Ellery Bergh, ed., *The Writings of Thomas Jefferson*, 20 vols. (Washington: Thomas Jefferson Memorial Association, 1907), 14:49.

6. See GW to William Fauntleroy, Sr. (20 May 1752), Fitzpatrick 1:22; on Mary Philipse see Freeman 2:160 and *n*, 167.

7. John Corbin, *The Unknown Washington: Biographic Origins of the Republic* (New York and London: Charles Scribner's Sons, 1930), p. 51.

8. GW to Mrs. George William Fairfax (12 Sept. 1758), Fitzpatrick 2:288.

9. See Paul Leicester Ford, *The True George Washington* (Philadelphia: J. B. Lippincott Company, 1896), pp. 91-92; Fitzpatrick, *George Washington Himself*, pp. 110-14.

10. See Bishop William Meade, *Old Churches, Ministers, and Families of Virginia*, 2 vols. (Philadelphia: J. B. Lippincott & Co., 1861), 1:108-9; William H. Wilbur, *The Making of George Washington*, 2d ed. rev. (DeLand, Fla.: Patriotic Education, 1973), p. 150.

11. For example, see Freeman 2:338n; Flexner, *George Washington: The Forge of Experience*, pp. 199-205; Corbin, *The Unknown Washington*, pp. 64-66.

12. Postscript by Sally Fairfax, Ann Spearing [Spears?], and Elizabeth Dent in letter from George William Fairfax to GW (26 July 1755), Hamilton, *Letters to Washington and Accompanying Papers*, 1:74.

13. Freeman 1:235a; see also 2:388; 5:498.

14. See Corbin, *The Unknown Washington*, pp. 51, 70-71. Some writers have

asserted that Sally Fairfax was "the great love" of Washington's life and remained so until he died. As evidence they cite a letter he wrote her in old age, recollecting "those happy moments, the happiest in my life, which I have enjoyed in your company." GW to Sarah Cary Fairfax (16 May 1798), Fitzpatrick 36:263. What most of these writers overlook is that Washington used almost the same phrase several years earlier in a letter to Sally's husband. See GW to George William Fairfax (27 Feb. 1785), Fitzpatrick 28:83.

15. Custis, *Recollections and Private Memoirs of Washington*, p. 499. For a discussion of the time of their first acquaintance, see Freeman 2:401-4.

16. Daniel Parke Custis married Martha Dandridge in 1749. They had four children altogether, but the first two died in childhood. Custis passed away at the age of forty-five, possibly of a heart attack. Martha was only twenty-six years old at the time. See Freeman 2:294, 298-99.

17. Custis, *Recollections and Private Memoirs of Washington,* p. 500.

18. Ibid.

19. See Joseph Jackson, "Washington in Philadelphia," *Pennsylvania Magazine of History and Biography* 56 (1932):115.

20. GW to Martha Custis (20 July 1758), Fitzpatrick 2:242. Biographer Douglas Freeman questioned the authenticity of this letter, or at least the version that appears in published sources. See Freeman 2:405-6. However, most Washington scholars have accepted it as authentic. (The original manuscript, extant in the mid-1800s but since lost, has not yet been rediscovered.)

21. The ceremony was performed by an Episcopal minister, the Reverend David Mossom. On the location of the wedding see Freeman 3:1-2*n*.

22. "Old Cully," an "ancient family servant," interviewed by G. W. P. Custis "in his hundredth year." Custis, *Recollections and Private Memoirs of Washington,* pp. 501-2.

23. Francis Rufus Bellamy, *The Private Life of George Washington* (New York: Thomas Y. Crowell Company, 1951), p. 135.

24. GW to Richard Washington (20 Sept. 1759), Fitzpatrick 2:337.

25. The Washingtons probably lived in another Custis home in Williamsburg during this session of the Burgesses. See Freeman 3:2-3 and *n*.

26. Quoted in ibid., p. 6.

27. Recounted by Edmund Randolph in William Wirt, *Sketches of the Life and Character of Patrick Henry* (Philadelphia: Porter and Coates, 1817), p. 45. On the credibility of this account see Freeman 3:7*n*.

28. GW to Bushrod Washington (10 Nov. 1787), Fitzpatrick 29:313. This nephew later became an Associate Justice of the U.S. Supreme Court. Thomas Jefferson once observed that he had "served with General Washington in the legislature of Virginia before the Revolution, and, during it, with Dr. Franklin in

Congress. I never heard either of them speak ten minutes at a time, nor to any but the main point which was to decide the question. They laid their shoulders to the great points, knowing that the little ones would follow of themselves." Autobiography of Thomas Jefferson (1821), Bergh, *The Writings of Thomas Jefferson*, 1:87. And Charles Willson Peale, who was "well acquainted" with Washington, noted that he was "a man of very few words, but when he speaks it is to the purpose." Peale to Edmond Jennings (29 Aug. 1775), in Charles Coleman Sellers, *Charles Willson Peale*, 2 vols. (Philadelphia: American Philosophical Society, 1947), 1:122.

29. GW to John Alton (1 Apr. 1759), Fitzpatrick 2:318-19.

30. See Flexner, *George Washington: The Forge of Experience*, pp. 195-96.

31. Ibid., p. 246; see also Mount Vernon Ladies' Association of the Union, *Mount Vernon: An Illustrated Handbook* (Mount Vernon, Va., 1967).

32. GW to the Marchioness de Lafayette (4 Apr. 1784), Fitzpatrick 27:385.

Chapter 7— A Gentleman Farmer

1. GW to Arthur Young (12 Dec. 1793), Fitzpatrick 33:175.

2. Bellamy, *The Private Life of George Washington*, p. 154. Many of Washington's properties in the West were rented to tenants who did not have the means to purchase their own farmland.

3. GW to Alexander Spotswood (13 Feb. 1788), Fitzpatrick 29:414.

4. GW to Robert Stewart (27 Apr. 1763), Fitzpatrick 2:397.

5. GW to William Augustine Washington (5 Apr. 1798), Fitzpatrick 36:240.

6. GW to Robert Cary & Company (22 Jan. 1764), Fitzpatrick 2:412.

7. GW to Burwell Bassett (28 Aug. 1762), Fitzpatrick 37:485. This kind of jesting was a common characteristic in Washington's personal correspondence. According to John C. Fitzpatrick, "There are more examples of honest humor in George Washington's letters than can be found in those of Jefferson, Madison, Hamilton or any one of the [Founding] Fathers except Benjamin Franklin." *George Washington Himself*, p. 446.

8. GW to Edward Montague (5 Apr. 1775), Fitzpatrick 3:285.

9. David M. Matteson, "Washington the Farmer," pamphlet number 4 in the series *Honor to George Washington*, ed. Albert Bushnell Hart (Washington: United States George Washington Bicentennial Commission, 1932), p. 38. In 1780 Washington was elected a member of the American Philosophical Society, at that time the leading scientific organization in the country. The following year he was elected to the American Academy of Arts and Sciences at Boston. During his

life he became an honorary member of several agricultural societies, including the Board of Agriculture of Great Britain.

10. James Thomas Flexner, *Washington: The Indispensable Man* (Boston: Little, Brown and Company, 1974), pp. 48–49.

11. GW to the Reverend Jonathan Boucher (5 June 1771), Fitzpatrick 3:44.

12. GW to Lund Washington (20 Sept. 1783), Fitzpatrick 27:158.

13. Invoice of sundries to be shipped by Robert Cary & Company (20 Sept. 1759), Fitzpatrick 2:335.

14. GW to Burwell Bassett (20 June 1773), Fitzpatrick 3:138.

15. Ibid.

16. GW to Burwell Bassett (25 Apr. 1773), Fitzpatrick 3:133. Bassett, a brother-in-law to Martha Washington, had lost his own daughter that spring.

17. GW to the Reverend Myles Cooper (15 Dec. 1773), Fitzpatrick 3:167. Cooper was then the president of King's College.

18. Martha Washington to Nelly Calvert (Dec. 1773?), quoted in James Hosmer Penniman, "Washington, Proprietor of Mount Vernon," pamphlet number 9 in the series *Honor to George Washington,* ed. Albert Bushnell Hart (Washington: United States George Washington Bicentennial Commission, 1932), p. 99.

19. Flexner, *George Washington: The Forge of Experience,* p. 234.

20. Fitzpatrick, *George Washington Himself,* p. 152.

21. GW to Richard Washington (20 Oct. 1761), Fitzpatrick 2:371.

22. GW to Archdeacon Andrew Burnaby (27 July 1761), in *William and Mary College Quarterly Historical Magazine* 22 (1942):222.

23. GW to Richard Washington (20 Oct. 1761), Fitzpatrick 2:371.

24. Quoted in Charles Coleman Sellers, *Charles Willson Peale,* 2 vols. (Philadelphia: American Philosophical Society, 1947), 1:108–9. See also Custis, *Recollections and Private Memoirs of Washington,* pp. 482 84 for other interesting anecdotes. Of his first experience in sitting for a portrait painter, Washington remarked that he was "in so grave, so sullen a mood, and now and then under the influence of Morpheus [i.e., sleepy] when some critical strokes are making, that I fancy the skill of this gentleman's pencil will be put to it in describing to the world what manner of man I am." GW to the Reverend Jonathan Boucher (21 May 1772), Fitzpatrick 3:84.

25. GW to the Reverend Jonathan Boucher (9 July 1771), Fitzpatrick 3:50-51. The breadth of Washington's knowledge of books, together with some idea of his educational philosophy, can be gathered from the impressive list of approximately one hundred volumes he ordered for his stepson in 1769. See his "Catalogue of Books for Master Custis" sent to Capel and Osgood Hanbury (25

July 1769), Fitzpatrick 2:515–17. "The inventory of Washington's books made at the time of his death by the appraisers of his estate shows that his library then numbered about nine hundred volumes." Appleton P. C. Griffin and William Coolidge Lane, ed., *A Catalogue of the Washington Collection in the Boston Athenaeum* (Boston: The Boston Athenaeum, 1897), p. vii; see catalog and inventory on pp. 1–233, 479–566.

26. GW to George Muse (29 Jan. 1774), Fitzpatrick 3:179–80.

27. Diary entry (3 Jan. 1760), *Diaries* 1:214.

28. Diary entry (6 Jan. 1760), *Diaries* 1:215.

29. GW to John West (13 Jan. 1775), Fitzpatrick 3:262.

30. GW to Lund Washington (26 Nov. 1775), Fitzpatrick 4:115.

31. GW to George Washington Parke Custis (15 Nov. 1796), Fitzpatrick 35:283. This reference to the "widow's mite" pertains to a biblical passage in the 12th chapter of St. Mark. Washington wrote similarly to one of his nephews: "Let your *heart* feel for the affliction and distresses of everyone, |and| let your *hand* give in proportion to your purse, remembering always the estimation of the widow's mite.... It is not everyone who asketh that deserveth charity; all, however, are worthy of the inquiry, or the deserving may suffer." GW to Bushrod Washington (15 Jan. 1783), Fitzpatrick 26:40.

32. Account book entries, quoted in Fitzpatrick, *George Washington Himself*, p. 91.

33. GW to William Ramsay (29 Jan. 1769), Fitzpatrick 2:500.

34. GW to John West (13 Jan. 1775), Fitzpatrick 3:262.

Chapter 8—Seeds of Rebellion

1. GW to Robert Cary & Company (10 Aug. 1760), Fitzpatrick 2:347–48.

2. GW to Robert Cary & Company (28 Sept. 1760), Fitzpatrick 2:350.

3. GW to Francis Dandridge (20 Sept. 1765), Fitzpatrick 2:425–26.

4. GW to Robert Cary & Company (21 July 1766), Fitzpatrick 2:440. Recalling a year later the abandonment of that "act of oppression," Washington observed that "a contrary measure would have introduced very unhappy consequences. Those, therefore, who wisely foresaw this and were instrumental in procuring the repeal...must reflect with pleasure that, through their means, many scenes of confusion and distress have been avoided." GW to Capel and Osgood Hanbury (25 July 1767), Fitzpatrick 2:466.

5. Quoted in Freeman 3:164.

6. GW to George Mason (5 Apr. 1769), Fitzpatrick 2:500–501.

7. Ibid., p. 501.

8. GW to Robert Cary & Company (25 July 1769), Fitzpatrick 2:512-13.

9. Quoted by Thomas Lynch, a South Carolina delegate to the First Continental Congress, in a diary entry by John Adams (31 Aug. 1774), Lyman H. Butterfield, ed., *Diary and Autobiography of John Adams*, 4 vols. (Cambridge, Mass.: Harvard University Press, Belknap Press, 1961), 2:117. See also a contemporary letter from Silas Deane, a Connecticut delegate, to his wife (10 Sept. 1774), in Edmund C. Burnett, ed., *Letters of Members of the Continental Congress*, 8 vols. (Washington: Carnegie Institution of Washington, 1921-36), 1:28.

10. Proceedings (24 May 1774), in John Pendleton Kennedy and H. R. McIlwaine, eds., *Journals of the House of Burgesses of Virginia*, 13 vols. (Richmond, Va.: Virginia State Library, 1905-15), 13:124.

11. Articles of association signed in Raleigh Tavern (27 May 1774), Kennedy and McIlwaine, *Journals of the House of Burgesses of Virginia*, 13:xiii-xiv.

12. Diary entry (1 June 1774), *Diaries* 3:254.

13. GW to George William Fairfax (10 June 1774), Fitzpatrick 3:224.

14. GW to Bryan Fairfax (4 July 1774), Fitzpatrick 3:228-29. Although Washington strongly favored the nonimportation association, he disapproved of proposals by some Americans to repudiate debts owed by the colonists to British merchants. "While we are accusing others of injustice," he said, "we should be just ourselves." Ibid., p. 229.

15. GW to Bryan Fairfax (20 July 1774), Fitzpatrick 3:233.

16. Ibid., pp. 231-34.

17. GW to Bryan Fairfax (24 Aug. 1774), Fitzpatrick 3:240, 242.

Chapter 9—America Protests

1. Fairfax County Resolves (18 July 1774), in Robert A. Rutland, ed., *The Papers of George Mason, 1725-1792*, 3 vols. (Chapel Hill, N.C.: University of North Carolina Press, 1970), 1:201-3. The entire text of Mason's twenty-four resolutions extends to page 209; see page 210 for a note on authorship.

2. Freeman 3:370.

3. Quoted in Fitzpatrick, *George Washington Himself*, p. 160.

4. Freeman 3:380.

5. Worthington Chauncey Ford et al., eds., *Journals of the Continental Congress, 1774-1789*, 34 vols. (Washington: U.S. Government Printing Office, 1904-37), 1:39-40.

6. GW to Captain Robert Mackenzie (9 Oct. 1774), Fitzpatrick 3:245-46. In the same letter Washington stated: "I am as well satisfied as I can be of my

existence that no such thing [as independence] is desired by any thinking man in all North America. On the contrary,...it is the ardent wish of the warmest advocates for liberty that peace and tranquility, upon constitutional grounds, may be restored, and the horrors of civil discord prevented." Ibid., pp. 246–47. Even after the Revolutionary War had been raging for three years, an American officer reported that he had heard Washington declare "a thousand times, and he does it every day in the most public company, that independence [had been] farthest of anything from his thoughts, and that he never [had] entertained the idea until he plainly saw that absolute conquest was the aim and unconditional submission the terms which Britain meant to grant." Tench Tilghman to his father (24 Apr. 1778), in Samuel Alexander Harrison, comp., *Memoir of Lieutenant Colonel Tench Tilghman* (Albany: J. Munsell, 1876), p. 166.

7. Freeman 3:392.

8. Speech in Virginia Convention of Delegates (23 Mar. 1775), quoted in Norine Dickson Campbell, *Patrick Henry: Patriot and Statesman* (Old Greenwich, Conn: Devin-Adair, 1969), p. 130.

9. GW to John Augustine Washington (25 Mar. 1775), Fitzpatrick 3:277.

10. See Ethan Allen, *A Narrative of Colonel Ethan Allen's Captivity* (Philadelphia: Robert Bell, 1779), pp. 5–11.

11. Freeman 3:426 and *n*.

12. John Adams to Abigail Adams (29 May 1775), in Lyman H. Butterfield, ed., *Adams Family Correspondence*, 4 vols. (Cambridge, Mass.: Harvard University Press, 1963–73), 1:207.

13. GW to George William Fairfax (31 May 1775), Fitzpatrick 3:292.

Chapter 10—A General to the Generals

1. Elbridge Gerry to the Massachusetts delegates in Congress (4 June 1775), in James T. Austin, *The Life of Elbridge Gerry*, 2 vols. (Boston: Wells and Lilly, 1828–29), 1:79.

2. See Freeman 3:433–34 and *n*. Edmund Pendleton was the delegate referred to here. Pendleton did voice some opposition during the debate on this question, but when the vote was taken he joined his colleagues in unanimous approval of Washington.

3. Autobiography of John Adams (1802-7), in Lyman H. Butterfield, ed., *Diary and Autobiography of John Adams*, 4 vols. (Cambridge, Mass.: Harvard University Press, Belknap Press, 1961), 3:322-23. It should be noted that Adams was not making the formal nomination in this speech. Washington was nominated the next day by Thomas Johnson of Maryland.

4. Worthington Chauncey Ford et al., eds., *Journals of the Continental Congress, 1774–1789,* 34 vols. (Washington: U.S. Government Printing Office, 1904–37), 2:91. Washington's commission, which was to continue in force "until revoked by this or a future Congress," gave him "full power and authority to act as you shall think for the good and welfare of the service"—subject only to "such orders and directions, from time to time, as you shall receive from . . . Congress." Ibid., p. 96. The original document is reproduced in Fitzpatrick 3:292a.

5. Ford et al., *Journals of the Continental Congress,* 2:97.

6. Following his election, Washington reportedly said to Patrick Henry, "Remember, Mr. Henry, what I now tell you: from the day I enter upon the command of the American armies, I date my fall and the ruin of my reputation." Quoted by Henry in George W. Corner, ed., *The Autobiography of Benjamin Rush* (Princeton, N.J.: Princeton University Press, 1948), p. 113. As one modern biographer has observed, "Seldom in American history, if ever, has achievement been in such amazing contrast to a man's expectations." Freeman 3:435a.

7. Acceptance of Appointment as General and commander in chief (16 June 1775), Fitzpatrick 3:292–93. A recent book by a "noted humorist" (Marvin Kitman, *George Washington's Expense Account* [New York: Simon and Schuster, 1970]) has attempted to cast doubt on the integrity of Washington's financial transactions during the war. The object of this satirical publication, which first appeared as an article in *Playboy* magazine, is to portray the commander in chief as "the inventor of the padded expense account." However, the author has come under severe criticism for ignoring several obvious historical facts, such as Washington's obligation to bear the costs of his entire headquarters operation, or the extremely rapid devaluation of American currency during that period. (See *Virginia Quarterly Review,* Autumn 1970, p. cliii; *Chicago Tribune Book World,* 19 July 1970, p. 4.) It has also been shown that the author is guilty of gross miscalculations in converting Washington's figures into terms of today's dollars. (See William H. Wilbur, *The Making of George Washington,* 2d ed. rev. [DeLand, Fla.: Patriotic Education, 1973], pp. 246–52.) A more accurate assessment of the General's wartime expenditures is reflected in the fact that when the public audit of his financial records was completed in 1784, "the skilled accountants of the Treasury found that there was a discrepancy of 89/90 of one dollar more due to Washington than his accounts showed." John C. Fitzpatrick, ed., *George Washington's Accounts of Expenses While Commander-in-Chief of the Continental Army, 1775–1783* (Boston and New York: Houghton Mifflin Company, 1917), p. 142. See Jay A. Parry, "Did Washington Cheat on His Expense Account?" *Freemen Digest,* February 1984, pp. 34–37.

8. John Adams to Abigail Adams (17 June 1775), in Lyman H. Butterfield, ed., *Adams Family Correspondence,* 4 vols. (Cambridge, Mass.: Harvard University Press, 1963–73), 1:215.

9. GW to John Augustine Washington (20 June 1775), Fitzpatrick 3:299.

10. Ibid.

11. GW to Burwell Bassett (19 June 1775), Fitzpatrick 3:297.

12. GW to Mrs. Martha Washington (18 June 1775), Fitzpatrick 3:293-94. As suggested by this and other communications, Washington initially thought that the outcome of the war would be determined by a single military campaign. In the event of an unfavorable outcome, he had considered seeking refuge on his western lands in the Ohio Valley. See GW to Burwell Bassett (28 Feb. 1776), Fitzpatrick 4:539.

13. GW to Mrs. Martha Washington (18 June 1775), Fitzpatrick 3:294-95.

14. GW to Mrs. Martha Washington (23 June 1775), Fitzpatrick 3:301.

15. GW to the New York legislature (26 June 1775), Fitzpatrick 3:305.

16. GW to George William Fairfax (31 May 1775), Fitzpatrick 3:291.

17. GW to John Augustine Washington (27 July 1775), Fitzpatrick 3:371.

18. Ibid., p. 372. Although the American forces (then about 16,000) outnumbered the British troops in and around Boston, they were woefully inferior in terms of position, arms, and martial discipline.

19. Ibid., p. 371.

20. Committee of the Massachusetts Provincial Congress to GW (2 July 1775), in Peter Force, ed., *American Archives . . . A Documentary History of the Origin and Progress of the North American Colonies*, 9 vols. (Washington: M. St. Clair Clarke and Peter Force, 1837-53), 2:1472-73.

21. GW to the President of Congress (10 July 1775), Fitzpatrick 3:327-28.

22. General Orders (4 July 1775), Fitzpatrick 3:309.

23. Ibid.

24. The Reverend William Emerson to his wife (17 July 1775), in Sparks 3:491-92.

25. GW to Major General Philip Schuyler (28 July 1775), Fitzpatrick 3:374.

26. Quoted in Freeman 3:520.

Chapter 11—A Troubled Command

1. GW to John Augustine Washington (27 July 1775), Fitzpatrick 3:373.

2. GW to Governor Jonathan Trumbull [of Connecticut] (4 Aug. 1775), Fitzpatrick 3:389.

3. Shelby Little, *George Washington* (London: George Routledge & Sons, 1931), p. 123.

4. GW to the President of Congress (4 Aug. 1775), Fitzpatrick 3:395.

5. Ibid.

6. GW to John Augustine Washington (10 Sept. 1775), Fitzpatrick 3:487–88.

7. Ibid., p. 488.

8. GW to Richard Henry Lee (29 Aug. 1775), Fitzpatrick 3:450.

9. "The Connecticut and Rhode Island troops stand engaged to the 1st |of| December only, and none longer than to the 1st |of| January. A dissolution, therefore, of the present army will take place unless some early provision is made against such an event." GW to the President of Congress (21 Sept. 1775), Fitzpatrick 3:506.

10. Ibid., p. 512.

11. Ibid.

12. General Orders (26 Oct. 1775), Fitzpatrick 4:44. Washington had learned just two days before this that four British warships had wantonly destroyed the coastal town of Falmouth, Maine, on October 18.

13. GW to the President of Congress (11 Nov. 1775), Fitzpatrick 4:82.

14. GW to Joseph Reed (28 Nov. 1775), Fitzpatrick 4:124–25.

15. James Warren to John Adams (3 Dec. 1775), in Robert J. Taylor, ed., *Papers of John Adams,* 6 vols. by 1983 (Cambridge, Mass.: Harvard University Press, Belknap Press, 1977–), 3:347. About the same time he wrote to Adams that "the General has many difficulties with officers and soldiers. His judgment and firmness, I hope, will carry him through them." Ibid. (16 Nov. 1775), pp. 305–6.

16. GW to Richard Henry Lee (29 Aug. 1775), Fitzpatrick 3:454.

17. GW to Major General Philip Schuyler (5 Dec. 1775), Fitzpatrick 4:148.

18. Henry Knox to Lucy Knox (9 July 1775), in Francis Samuel Drake, *Life and Correspondence of Henry Knox* (Boston: S. G. Drake, 1873), p. 15.

19. GW to Colonel William Woodford (10 Nov. 1775), Fitzpatrick 4:80.

20. Abigail Adams to John Adams (16 July 1775), in Charles Francis Adams, ed., *Familiar Letters of John Adams and His Wife Abigail Adams During the Revolution* (New York: Ayer Co., 1875), p. 78.

21. Journal entry (20 July 1775), in James Thacher, *A Military Journal During the American Revolutionary War* (Boston: Richardson and Lord, 1823), p. 37.

22. Benjamin Rush to Thomas Rushton (29 Oct. 1775), in Lyman H. Butterfield, ed., *Letters of Benjamin Rush,* 2 vols. (Princeton, N.J.: Princeton University Press, 1951), 1:92.

23. James Warren to John Adams (16 Nov. 1775), Taylor, *Papers of John Adams,* 3:306.

24. Martha Washington to Miss Ramsay (30 Dec. 1775), in Freeman 3:581.

25. Martha Washington to Miss Ramsay (30 Dec. 1775), in James Thomas Flexner, *George Washington in the American Revolution (1775-1783)* (Boston: Little, Brown and Company, 1968), pp. 59-60.

26. Letter of Mercy Warren (1776), in Worthington Chauncey Ford, ed., *The Warren-Adams Letters, Being Chiefly a Correspondence Among John Adams, Samuel Adams, and James Warren*, 2 vols. (Boston: Massachusetts Historical Society, 1917, 1925), 1:228.

27. Nathanael Greene to Samuel Ward (31 Dec. 1775), in Richard K. Showman, ed., *The Papers of General Nathanael Greene*, 3 vols. by 1983 (Chapel Hill, N.C.: University of North Carolina Press, 1976-), 1:173-74.

28. GW to John Sullivan (10 Jan. 1776), Fitzpatrick 4:225.

29. GW to Joseph Reed (4 Jan. 1776), Fitzpatrick 4:211-12.

30. GW to Joseph Reed (14 Jan. 1776), Fitzpatrick 4:243.

31. GW to the President of Congress (9 Feb. 1776), Fitzpatrick 4:316-18.

32. Samuel Adams gave voice to the reluctance of many of his congressional colleagues when he wrote that standing armies were "always dangerous to the liberties of the people." Samuel Adams to James Warren (7 Jan. 1776), in Harry Alonzo Cushing, ed., *The Writings of Samuel Adams*, 4 vols. (1904-8; reprint ed., New York: Octagon Books, 1968), 3:250.

33. GW to Joseph Reed (10 Feb. 1776), Fitzpatrick 4:319.

34. GW to Joseph Reed (4 Jan. 1776), Fitzpatrick 4:210.

35. GW to Joseph Reed (31 Jan. 1776), Fitzpatrick 4:297. This mention of Falmouth was a reference to the unprovoked British destruction of a coastal village in Maine the preceding October.

36. GW to Joseph Reed (10 Feb. 1776), Fitzpatrick 4:321.

37. General Orders (27 Feb. 1776), Fitzpatrick 4:355.

38. Robert Leckie, *The Wars of America* (New York: Harper and Row, 1968), pp. 127-28.

39. Christopher Ward, *The War of the Revolution*, ed. John Richard Alden, 2 vols. (New York: Macmillan Co., 1952), 1:194.

Chapter 12—A Moment of Triumph

1. GW to Joseph Reed (14 Jan. 1776), Fitzpatrick 4:243.

2. GW to Burwell Bassett (28 Feb. 1776), Fitzpatrick 4:359.

3. Quoted in Peter Force, ed., *American Archives . . . A Documentary History of the Origin and Progress of the North American Colonies*, 9 vols. (Washington: M. St. Clair Clarke and Peter Force, 1837-53), 5:425.

4. GW to John Augustine Washington (31 Mar. 1776), Fitzpatrick 4:448.

5. Ibid.

6. GW to Joseph Reed (1 Apr. 1776), Fitzpatrick 4:456.

7. GW to Joseph Reed (19 Mar. 1776), Fitzpatrick 4:406.

8. Flexner, *Washington: The Indispensable Man*, p. 75.

9. GW to John Hancock (18 Apr. 1776), Fitzpatrick 4:489. Washington received many other "rewards" during his lifetime, of course. It is significant to note that he received five honorary doctoral degrees, each an LL.D.: Harvard, 1776; Yale, 1781; University of Pennsylvania, 1783; Washington College, 1789; and Brown University, 1790.

10. Worthington Chauncey Ford et al., eds., *Journals of the Continental Congress, 1774-1789*, 34 vols. (Washington: U.S. Government Printing Office, 1904-37), 4:388.

11. GW to John Augustine Washington (31 May 1776), Fitzpatrick 5:93.

12. GW to the President of Congress (10 July 1776), Fitzpatrick 5:250.

13. General Orders (28 June 1776), Fitzpatrick 5:195.

14. GW to the Reverend William Gordon (13 May 1776), Fitzpatrick 37:526.

15. General Orders (9 July 1776), Fitzpatrick 5:245.

16. On Washington's religious beliefs and practices, see Sparks 12:399-411; William J. Johnson, *George Washington the Christian* (1919; reprint ed., Milford, Mich.: Mott Media, 1976); Edward C. McGuire, *The Religious Opinions and Character of Washington* (New York: Harper and Brothers, 1836); Joseph Buffington, *The Soul of George Washington* (Philadelphia: Dorrance & Company, 1936); Paul F. Boller, Jr., *George Washington and Religion* (Dallas, Tex.: Southern Methodist University Press, 1963); John C. Fitzpatrick, "Washington As a Religious Man," pamphlet number 5 in the series *Honor to George Washington*, ed. Albert Bushnell Hart (Washington: United States George Washington Bicentennial Commission, 1932), pp. 46-55.

17. GW to Joseph Reed (1 Apr. 1776), Fitzpatrick 4:455.

18. GW to John Augustine Washington (31 May 1776), Fitzpatrick 5:91-92.

19. General Orders (2 July 1776), Fitzpatrick 5:211.

20. General Orders (9 July 1776), Fitzpatrick 5:245.

21. John Adams to James Lloyd (Jan. 1815) in Charles Francis Adams, ed., *The Works of John Adams*, 10 vols. (Boston: Little, Brown and Co., 1850-56), 10:110-11. There is some uncertainty about whether Adams's statement refers to the French Revolution or to the American Revolutionary War, and reading the statement in context confuses rather than clarifies. Nevertheless, many historians think Adams's estimate is a fair one when applied to America's war for independence.

22. GW to the President of Congress (2 Sept. 1776), Fitzpatrick 6:5.

23. GW to the President of Congress (8 Sept. 1776), Fitzpatrick 6:28-29.

24. For examples of Washington's intelligence activities see Flexner, *George Washington in the American Revolution,* pp. 44, 50, 204, 231, 285, 296, 350-51, 545.

Chapter 13—Disaster at New York

1. Flexner, *Washington: The Indispensable Man,* p. 79.

2. Daniel McCurtin, journal entry (29 June 1776), in Thomas Balch, ed., *Papers Relating Chiefly to the Maryland Line During the Revolution* (Philadelphia: Printed for the Seventy-six Society, 1857), p. 40.

3. General Orders (1 Aug. 1776), Fitzpatrick 5:362.

4. General Orders (3 Aug. 1776), Fitzpatrick 5:367.

5. General Orders (13 Aug. 1776), Fitzpatrick 5:424-25.

6. GW to the New York legislature (17 Aug. 1776), Fitzpatrick 5:444.

7. GW to Lund Washington (19 Aug. 1776), Fitzpatrick 5:458.

8. Quoted in Thomas Warren Field, *The Battle of Long Island* (Brooklyn, N.Y.: 1869), p. 502.

9. Quoted by an unknown patriot soldier in Henry Onderdonk, *Revolutionary Incidents of Suffolk and Kings Counties* (New York: Leavitt & Company, 1849), p. 148; reprinted in Henry Steele Commager and Richard B. Morris, eds., *The Spirit of 'Seventy-Six: The Story of the American Revolution As Told by Participants,* 2 vols. (Indianapolis: Bobbs-Merrill Company, 1958), 1:440.

10. Fitzpatrick, *George Washington Himself,* pp. 248-49.

11. Noemie Emery, *Washington: A Biography* (New York: G. P. Putnam's Sons, 1976), pp. 195-96.

12. GW to the President of Congress (2 Sept. 1776), Fitzpatrick 6:4.

13. GW to the President of Congress (8 Sept. 1776), Fitzpatrick 6:30.

14. GW to the President of Congress (15 Sept. 1776), Fitzpatrick 6:58.

15. William Heath, *Heath's Memoirs of the American War,* ed. Rufus R. Wilson (1798; reprint ed., Freeport, N.Y.: Books for Libraries Press, 1970), p. 70.

16. William B. Reed, ed., *The Life and Correspondence of Joseph Reed,* 2 vols. (Philadelphia: Lindsay and Blakiston, 1847), 1:236; quoted in Flexner, *George Washington in the American Revolution,* p. 123.

17. GW to the President of Congress (18 Sept. 1776), Fitzpatrick 6:69.

18. Diary entry (20 Sept. 1776), *Diary of Frederick Mackenzie,* 2 vols. (Cambridge, Mass.: Harvard University Press, 1930), 1:60.

19. GW to Lund Washington (6 Oct. 1776), Fitzpatrick 37:533.

20. Maria Hull Campbell, *Revolutionary Services and Civil Life of General William Hull, Prepared from His Manuscripts* (New York: D. Appleton and Co., 1848), p. 38.

Chapter 14—"I Shall Continue to Retreat"

1. GW to the President of Congress (6 Nov. 1776), Fitzpatrick 6:250.

2. GW to John Augustine Washington (19 Nov. 1776), Fitzpatrick 6:246.

3. Francis, Lord Rawdon, to Robert Auchmuty (25 Nov. 1776), in Great Britain Historical Manuscripts Commission, *Report on the Manuscripts of the Late Reginald Rawdon Hastings,* 4 vols. (London: H. M. Stationery Office, 1930-47), 3:192; quoted in Commager and Morris, *The Spirit of 'Seventy-Six,* 1:497.

4. GW to Charles Lee (30 Nov. 1776), in Commager and Morris, *The Spirit of 'Seventy-Six,* 1:499.

5. Quoted in Commager and Morris, *The Spirit of 'Seventy-Six,* 1:496.

6. Charles Lee to Joseph Reed (24 Nov. 1776), in *The Lee Papers,* 4 vols. (New York: New York Historical Society, 1872-75), 2:305-6.

7. GW to Governor William Livingston of New Jersey (30 Nov. 1776), Fitzpatrick 6:313.

8. GW to Lund Washington (17 Dec. 1776), Fitzpatrick 6:347.

9. Diary entry (2 Dec. 1776), in Frank Moore, ed., *Diary of the American Revolution,* 2 vols. (New York: Charles Scribner, 1859-60), 1:357-58.

10. Thomas Paine, *The American Crisis* (Dec. 1776), in Moncure Daniel Conway, ed., *The Writings of Thomas Paine,* 4 vols. (New York: G. P. Putnam's Sons, 1894-96), 1:170-73.

11. General Charles Lee to General Horatio Gates (13 Dec. 1776), in Commager and Morris, *The Spirit of 'Seventy-Six,* 1:500.

12. Fitzpatrick, *George Washington Himself,* p. 272.

Chapter 15—A Season of Success and Suffering

1. GW to Joseph Reed or John Cadwalader (23 Dec. 1776), Sparks 4:241. Fitzpatrick doubts the authenticity of this letter, though it certainly does describe both the situation and Washington's state of mind. See Fitzpatrick 6:427n.

2. Thomas Paine, *The American Crisis* (Dec. 1776), in Moncure Daniel Conway, ed., *The Writings of Thomas Paine,* 4 vols. (New York: G. P. Putnam's Sons, 1894-96), 1:172-73.

3. "Diary of an Officer on Washington's Staff" (25 Dec. 1776), in William S. Stryker, *The Battles of Trenton and Princeton* (1898; reprint ed., Spartanburg, S.C.: Reprint Co., 1967), pp. 361–64.

4. Quoted in ibid. (26 Dec. 1776).

5. Thomas Rodney to Caesar Rodney (30 Dec. 1776), in Hezekiah Niles, ed., *Principles and Acts of the Revolution in America* (New York: A. S. Barnes & Co., 1876), p. 249.

6. GW to the President of Congress (27 Dec. 1776), Fitzpatrick 6:443–44.

7. Ibid.

8. GW to the President of Congress (20 Dec. 1776), Fitzpatrick 6:402.

9. GW to a committee of Congress (1 Jan. 1777), Fitzpatrick 6:464.

10. Quoted in Howard LaFay, "George Washington: The Man Behind the Myths," *National Geographic,* July 1976, p. 101.

11. Freeman 4:236–37.

12. GW to Lund Washington (17 Dec. 1776), Fitzpatrick 6:347.

13. GW to the President of Congress (20 Sept. 1776), Fitzpatrick 6:85.

14. Quoted in Philip S. Foner, ed., *George Washington: Selections from His Writings* (New York: International Publishers, 1944), p. 18.

15. GW to the President of Congress (5 Dec. 1776), Fitzpatrick 6:332.

16. GW to the President of Congress (20 Dec. 1776), Fitzpatrick 6:403.

17. GW to the President of Congress (24 Sept. 1776), Fitzpatrick 6:110–12.

18. Henry Knox to his brother (23 Sept. 1776), in Francis Samuel Drake, *Life and Correspondence of Henry Knox* (Boston: S. G. Drake, 1873), pp. 31–32; quoted in Commager and Morris, *The Spirit of 'Seventy-Six,* 1:479.

19. GW to Lund Washington (30 Sept. 1776), Fitzpatrick 6:138.

20. GW to John Augustine Washington (22 Sept. 1776), Fitzpatrick 6:96.

21. GW to the President of Congress (22 Dec. 1776), Fitzpatrick 6:420–21.

Chapter 16—Vexations and Perplexities

1. Quoted in James Wilkinson, *Memoirs of My Own Time,* 3 vols. (Philadelphia, 1816), 1:145.

2. GW to the President of Congress (5 Jan. 1777), Fitzpatrick 6:470.

3. Henry Knox, quoted in Freeman 4:357.

4. Robert Leckie, *The Wars of America* (New York: Harper and Row, 1968), p. 162.

5. Ibid.

6. Quoted in John C. Miller, *Triumph of Freedom: 1775–1783* (Boston: Little, Brown and Co., 1948), pp. 164–65.

7. Journal entry (7 Jan. 1777), in *The Journal of Nicholas Cresswell, 1774–1777*, 2d ed. (New York: Dial Press, 1928), p. 180.

8. William Harcourt to Simon Harcourt (17 Mar. 1777), in Edward W. Harcourt, ed., *The Harcourt Papers*, 14 vols. (Oxford, 1880–1905?), 11:208; quoted in George F. Scheer and Hugh F. Rankin, *Rebels and Redcoats* (Cleveland and New York: World Publishing Co., 1957), p. 221.

9. Bartholomew Dandridge to GW (16 Jan. 1777), in Fitzpatrick, *George Washington Himself*, p. 286.

10. *Pennsylvania Journal*, 19 February 1777, in Frank Moore, ed., *Diary of the American Revolution*, 2 vols. (New York: Charles Scribner, 1859–60), 1:396–97.

11. GW to Joseph Reed (23 Feb. 1777), Fitzpatrick 7:192.

12. GW to the President of Congress (31 Jan. 1777), Fitzpatrick 7:81.

13. GW to Robert Morris (2 Mar. 1777), Fitzpatrick 7:225.

14. GW to Samuel H. Parsons (3 Apr. 1777), Fitzpatrick 7:354.

15. General Orders (28 June 1777), Fitzpatrick 8:308.

16. John Hancock to GW (24 June 1777), in Jared Sparks, ed., *Correspondence of the American Revolution, Being Letters of Eminent Men to George Washington*, 4 vols. (1853; reprint ed., Freeport, N.Y.: Books for Libraries Press, 1970), 1:391.

17. GW to the President of Congress (9 July 1777), Fitzpatrick 8:373.

18. GW to the President of Congress (12 July 1777), Fitzpatrick 8:384.

19. Quoted in Mark Mayo Boatner III, *Encyclopedia of the American Revolution* (New York: David McKay Co., 1966), pp. 1103, 1107.

20. GW to the President of Congress (25 July 1777), Fitzpatrick 8:470.

21. Freeman 4:463.

22. GW to Gen. William Heath (30 Sept. 1777), Fitzpatrick 9:287.

23. General Orders (3 Oct. 1777), Fitzpatrick 9:306.

24. Diary of Lieutenant Sir Martin Hunter (Oct. 1777), in Leckie, *The Wars of America*, p. 167; see also Commager and Morris, *The Spirit of 'Seventy-Six*, 1:625.

25. GW to the President of Congress (5 Oct. 1777), Fitzpatrick 9:310.

26. General Orders (5 Oct. 1777), Fitzpatrick 9:312.

27. GW to Landon Carter (27 Oct. 1777), Fitzpatrick 9:454.

Chapter 17—Surrender at Saratoga

1. Robert Leckie, *The Wars of America* (New York: Harper and Row, 1968), p. 170.

2. Ibid.

3. Quoted in Burton E. Stevenson, ed., *The Home Book of Quotations, Classical and Modern*, 9th ed. (New York: Dodd, Mead, and Co., 1958), p. 62.

4. For a full discussion of the battles leading up to Saratoga, as well as the final battle itself, see Ward, *The War of the Revolution*, 1:398-431, 2:477-542; and Boatner, *Encyclopedia of the American Revolution*, pp. 67-76, 133-42, 970-80.

Chapter 18—The Conway Cabal

1. Quoted in John Stockton Littell, ed., *Memoirs of His Own Time... by Alexander Graydon* (Philadelphia: Lindsay & Blakiston, 1846), pp. 299-300; quoted in Freeman 4:547.

2. Quoted in Howard LaFay, "George Washington: The Man Behind the Myths," *National Geographic*, July 1976, p. 107.

3. See GW to Thomas Conway (9 Nov. 1777), Fitzpatrick 10:29.

4. James Craik to GW (6 Jan. 1778), Sparks 5:493-95.

5. GW to the President of Congress (2 Jan. 1778), Fitzpatrick 10:249.

6. GW to Horatio Gates (9 Feb. 1778), Fitzpatrick 10:440.

7. GW to Henry Laurens (31 Jan. 1778), Fitzpatrick 10:410-11.

8. Ibid.

9. GW to the Reverend William Gordon (23 Jan. 1778), Fitzpatrick 10:338.

10. GW to the Marquis de Lafayette (31 Dec. 1777), Fitzpatrick 10:237.

11. GW to Horatio Gates (24 Feb. 1778), Fitzpatrick 10:508-9.

Chapter 19—The Depths of Valley Forge

1. GW to Israel Putnam (11 Nov. 1777), Fitzpatrick 10:42.

2. Nathanael Greene to Henry Marchant (17 Nov. 1777), in Richard K. Showman, ed., *The Papers of Nathanael Greene*, 3 vols. by 1983 (Chapel Hill, N.C.: University of North Carolina Press, 1976-), 2:199.

3. Attributed to James Sullivan Martin, in Joseph Plumb Martin, *Private Yankee Doodle, Being a Narrative of Some of the Adventures, Dangers, and Sufferings of a Revolutionary Soldier*, ed., George F. Scheer (Boston: Little, Brown and Co., 1962), pp. 101-3.

4. Albigence Waldo, "Valley Forge, 1777-1778," *Pennsylvania Magazine of History and Biography*, 21 (1896): 305-10.

5. GW to John Banister (21 Apr. 1778), Fitzpatrick 11:291.

6. General Orders (17 Dec. 1777), Fitzpatrick 10:167-68.

7. GW to the President of Congress (23 Dec. 1777), Fitzpatrick 10:196.

8. GW to the President of Congress (23 Dec. 1777), Fitzpatrick 10:193-96.

9. GW to Governor William Livingston of New Jersey (31 Dec. 1777), Fitzpatrick 10:233.

10. Colonel William Shepard to Captain David Mosely (25 Jan. 1778), in Freeman 4:579.

11. Mrs. Westlake (a neighbor to the Potts family in 1778), quoted in Benson J. Lossing, *Mary and Martha: The Mother and the Wife of George Washington* (New York: Harper & Brothers, 1886), pp. 168, 171.

12. GW to Landon Carter (30 May 1778), Fitzpatrick 11:492.

13. See William J. Johnson, *George Washington the Christian* (1919; reprint ed., Milford, Mich.: Mott Media, 1976), pp. 102-7; Edward C. McGuire, *The Religious Opinions and Character of Washington* (New York: Harper and Brothers, 1836), pp. 158-59.

14. Custis, *Recollections and Private Memoirs of Washington*, p. 493.

15. For example, see Sparks 12:406, 407; Johnson, *George Washington the Christian*, pp. 128-31, 229-30; McGuire, *The Religious Opinions and Character of Washington*, p. 168.

16. Boatner, *Encyclopedia of the American Revolution*, p. 1137.

Chapter 20—A Year of Hope and Deceit

1. GW to Henry Laurens (30 Apr. 1778), Fitzpatrick 11:326-27.

2. GW to the President of Congress (1 May 1778), Fitzpatrick 11:332-33.

3. General Orders (6 May 1778), Fitzpatrick 11:354.

4. Charles Lee to Benjamin Rush (4 June 1778), in Boatner, *Encyclopedia of the American Revolution*, pp. 525-26.

5. Quoted in ibid., p. 526.

6. Quoted in Carl Van Doren, *Secret History of the American Revolution* (New York: Popular Library, 1941), p. 34.

7. Alexander Hamilton to Elias Boudinot (5 July 1778), in Harold C. Syrett, ed., *The Papers of Alexander Hamilton*, 26 vols. (New York: Columbia University Press, 1961-79), 1:510.

8. *The Lee Papers*, 4 vols. (New York: New York Historical Society, 1872-75), 3:78, 81, 112, 147, 191-92. A myth has been perpetuated that Washington swore profusely at Lee on that occasion. Historians, however, have been able to find no reliable evidence that Washington swore on that or any other day. There were, in fact, eyewitnesses who denied any claims that Washington swore at

Monmouth. See William J. Johnson, *George Washington the Christian* (1919; reprint ed., Milford, Mich.: Mott Media, 1976), pp. 115-17. The General was opposed to swearing as a matter of principle and repeatedly issued general orders against the practice.

9. GW to John Augustine Washington (4 July 1778), Fitzpatrick 12:157.

10. *Memoirs, Correspondence, and Manuscripts of General Lafayette, Published by His Family*, 3 vols. (London: Saunders and Otley, 1837), 1:54 and *n.*

11. GW to John Augustine Washington (4 July 1778), Fitzpatrick 12:157.

12. Alexander Hamilton to Elias Boudinot (5 July 1778), Syrett, *The Papers of Alexander Hamilton*, 1:512.

13. GW to the President of Congress (1 July 1778), Fitzpatrick 12:143-45.

14. General Orders (30 June 1778), Fitzpatrick 12:131.

15. Quoted in Freeman 5:59.

Chapter 21—Help from Abroad, Troubles at Home

1. GW to Gouverneur Morris (24 July 1778), Fitzpatrick 12:226-28.

2. Quoted in Howard LaFay, "George Washington: The Man Behind the Myths," *National Geographic*, July 1976, p. 104.

3. Quoted in Bellamy, *The Private Life of George Washington*, p. 266.

4. GW to Lafayette (25 Sept. 1778), Fitzpatrick 12:500.

5. Quoted in Bellamy, *The Private Life of George Washington*, p. 262.

6. GW to Thomas Nelson (20 July 1778), Fitzpatrick 12:343.

7. GW to John Augustine Washington (26 Nov. 1778), Fitzpatrick 13:335.

8. GW to Lord Stirling (19 Nov. 1778), Fitzpatrick 13:284.

9. GW to Joseph Reed (12 Dec. 1778), Fitzpatrick 13:385.

10. GW to Benjamin Harrison (5-7 May 1779), Fitzpatrick 15:5.

11. GW to James Wilkinson (22 Dec. 1779), Fitzpatrick 17:300.

12. GW to Philip Schuyler (30 Jan. 1780), Fitzpatrick 17:467.

13. Circular to the governors of the middle states (16 Dec. 1779), Fitzpatrick 17:273-74.

14. Nathanael Greene to Moore Furman (4 Jan. 1780), in Freeman 5:144.

15. James Thacher, *A Military Journal During the American Revolutionary War* (Boston: Richardson and Lord, 1823), p. 221.

16. Joseph Walker to Samuel B. Webb (6 Feb. 1780), in Worthington C. Ford, ed., *Correspondence and Journals of Samuel Blachley Webb*, 3 vols. (1893; reprint ed., New

York: New York Times, 1969), 2:245.

17. Friedrich Kapp, *The Life of John Kalb* (New York, 1884), pp. 182–83.

18. GW to the Board of War (25 Mar. 1780), Fitzpatrick 18:150.

19. GW to Henry Champion (12 Apr. 1780), Fitzpatrick 18:252.

20. A committee of Congress to Congress (10 May 1780), in Burnett, *Letters of Members of the Continental Congress*, 5:133.

21. GW to Joseph Reed (28 May 1780), Fitzpatrick 18:434–35.

22. Lafayette to Joseph Reed (31 May 1780), in William B. Reed, ed., *The Life and Correspondence of Joseph Reed*, 2 vols. (Philadelphia: Lindsay and Blakiston, 1847), 2:207; quoted in Freeman 5:166.

23. Ebenezer Huntington to Andrew Huntington (7 July 1780), in *Letters Written by Ebenezer Huntington During the American Revolution* (New York: Printed for C. F. Heartman, 1915), pp. 87–88.

24. Circular to several states (27 Aug. 1780), Fitzpatrick 19:451.

25. Circular to governors of the middle states (16 Dec. 1779), Fitzpatrick 17:273.

26. GW to Gouverneur Morris (4 Oct. 1778), Fitzpatrick 13:21.

27. Kapp, *The Life of John Kalb*, p. 184.

28. Benson J. Lossing, *The Pictorial Field-Book of the Revolution*, 2 vols. (1859; reprint ed., Rutland, Vt.: Charles E. Tuttle Company, 1972), 1:319n.

29. Worthington Chauncey Ford et al., eds., *Journals of the Continental Congress, 1774–1789*, 34 vols. (Washington: U.S. Government Printing Office, 1904–37), 15:1039.

30. GW to William Fitzhugh (10 Apr. 1779), Fitzpatrick 14:365.

31. GW to Lund Washington (29 May 1779), Fitzpatrick 15:180.

32. GW to John Jay (23 Apr. 1779), Fitzpatrick 14:437.

33. Quoted in Robert Leckie, *The Wars of America* (New York: Harper and Row, 1968), p. 197.

Chapter 22—"A History of False Hopes"

1. See Fitzpatrick 18:203, 264–65, 299, 307.

2. Ward, *The War of the Revolution*, 2:728.

3. Alexander Hamilton to James Duane (6 Sept. 1780), Syrett, *The Papers of Alexander Hamilton*, 2:421.

4. See discussion in Boatner, *Encyclopedia of the American Revolution*, pp. 168–69.

5. GW to Jonathan Trumbull (11 June 1780), Fitzpatrick 18:509.

6. Circular to several states (30 June 1780), Fitzpatrick 19:104-5.

7. Count de Rochambeau to Count de Vergennes (16 July 1780), in Sparks 7:506.

8. GW to Fielding Lewis (6 July 1780), Fitzpatrick 19:132.

9. GW to James Duane (4 Oct. 1780), Fitzpatrick 20:118.

10. GW to George Mason (22 Oct. 1780), Fitzpatrick 20:242.

11. GW to the Committee of Cooperation (13 July 1780), Fitzpatrick 19:166.

12. GW to John Augustine Washington (6 July 1780), Fitzpatrick 19:135-36.

13. GW to George Mason (22 Oct. 1780), Fitzpatrick 20:242.

14. GW to Joseph Jones (31 May 1780), Fitzpatrick 18:453.

15. GW to Gouverneur Morris (10 Dec. 1780), Fitzpatrick 20:458-59.

Chapter 23—Treachery in the North, Battles in the South

1. GW to Richard Henry Lee (6 Mar. 1777), Fitzpatrick 7:252.

2. General Orders (6 Apr. 1780), Fitzpatrick 18:225.

3. Quoted in Richard Rush, *Occasional Productions* (Philadelphia, 1860), p. 83; reprinted in Flexner, *George Washington in the American Revolution*, p. 386.

4. General Orders (26 Sept. 1780), Fitzpatrick 20:95.

5. GW to John Laurens (13 Oct. 1780), Fitzpatrick 20:173.

6. Quoted in Ward, *The War of the Revolution*, 2:741.

7. Quoted in ibid., p. 742.

8. Quoted in ibid.

9. Anthony Wayne to Joseph Reed (16 Dec. 1780), in William B. Reed, ed., *The Life and Correspondence of Joseph Reed*, 2 vols. (Philadelphia: Lindsay and Blakiston, 1847), 2:315-17; quoted in Commager and Morris, *The Spirit of 'Seventy-Six*, 2:768.

10. General Orders (30 Jan. 1781), Fitzpatrick 21:158-59.

11. Nathanael Greene to Joseph Reed (9 Jan. 1781), Reed, *The Life and Correspondence of Joseph Reed*, 2:334-35; quoted in Commager and Morris, *The Spirit of 'Seventy-Six*, 2:1152.

12. Robert Leckie, *The Wars of America* (New York: Harper and Row, 1968), p. 207.

13. Quoted in Boatner, *Encyclopedia of the American Revolution*, p. 1030.

14. For a complete discussion of the southern battles covered in this chapter, see Ward, *The War of the Revolution*, 2:748-801, 823-34; Boatner, *Encyclopedia of the American Revolution*, pp. 1018-39.

Chapter 24—The Great Strike at Yorktown

1. GW to John Laurens (30 Jan. 1781), Fitzpatrick 31:162.

2. GW to Lund Washington (30 Apr. 1781), Fitzpatrick 22:14-15.

3. GW to John Armstrong (26 Mar. 1781), Fitzpatrick 21:378.

4. GW to John Laurens (9 Apr. 1781), Fitzpatrick 21:439.

5. GW to John Matthews (7 June 1781), Fitzpatrick 22:176.

6. Benjamin Franklin to GW (5 Mar. 1780), in Albert Henry Smyth, ed., *The Writings of Benjamin Franklin,* 10 vols. (New York: Macmillan Company, 1905-7), 8:28-29.

7. GW to Thomas Lee (28 Aug. 1781), Fitzpatrick 23:58.

8. Nathanael Greene to Henry Knox (Aug. or Sept. 1781), quoted in Scheer and Rankin, *Rebels and Redcoats,* p. 493.

9. Comments by Guillaume de Deux-Ponts and Duc de Lauzun, quoted in Bellamy, *The Private Life of George Washington,* p. 323.

10. Journal entry (10-15 Oct. 1781), in James Thacher, *A Military Journal During the American Revolutionary War* (Boston: Richardson and Lord, 1823), pp. 340-41.

11. Earl Cornwallis to Sir Henry Clinton (11 Oct. 1781), in Benjamin Franklin Stevens, ed., *The Campaign in Virginia, 1781,* 2 vols. (London, 1888), 2:177.

12. Ibid. (15 Oct. 1781), p. 188.

13. Johann C. Dohla, *Tagebuch eines Bayreuther Soldaten* (Bayreuth, Germany, 1913), p. 148; quoted in Scheer and Rankin, *Rebels and Redcoats,* p. 490.

14. GW to Charles, Earl Cornwallis (18 Oct. 1781), Fitzpatrick 23:237-38.

15. Custis, *Recollections and Private Memoirs of Washington,* pp. 245-47.

16. Quoted in Scheer and Rankin, *Rebels and Redcoats,* p. 495.

17. Oscar Brand, *Songs of '76* (New York: M. Evans and Co., 1972), pp. 156-57.

18. GW to the President of Congress (19 Oct. 1781), Fitzpatrick 23:241. The messenger who carried this dispatch, Lieutenant Colonel Tench Tilghman, required reimbursement for his travel expenses—but the treasury was inadequate even for so small an expense. The members of Congress pitched in and paid Tilghman out of their own pockets, each contributing one dollar.

19. General Orders (20 Oct. 1781), Fitzpatrick 23:247.

20. Quoted in Thomas J. Fleming, *First in Their Hearts: A Biography of George Washington* (New York: W. W. Norton & Company, 1968), p. 99.

21. *The Historical and Posthumous Memoirs of Sir Nathaniel William Wraxall, 1772-1784,* ed. Henry B. Wheatley, 5 vols. (New York: Scribner and Welford, 1884), 2:138-40; quoted in Commager and Morris, *The Spirit of 'Seventy-Six,* 2:1243-44.

22. GW to Thomas Nelson (27 Oct. 81), Fitzpatrick 23:271.

23. GW to the President of Congress (28 Nov. 1781), Fitzpatrick 23:360-61.

24. GW to Nathanael Greene (16 Nov. 1781), Fitzpatrick 23:347.

25. Quoted in James Thacher journal entry (3 and 4 Oct. 1781), Thacher, *A Military Journal*, p. 336.

26. Ibid. (10-15 Oct. 1781), p. 342.

27. Quoted in Custis, *Recollections and Private Memoirs of Washington*, pp. 191-92.

28. Benjamin Harrison to Robert Morris (Jan. 1777?), quoted in Fleming, *First in Their Hearts*, p. 66.

29. Quoted in Saxe Commins, ed., *Basic Writings of George Washington* (New York: Random House, 1948), p. 272n.

30. Lafayette to GW (30 Dec. 1777), in Louis Gottschalk, ed., *The Letters of Lafayette to Washington, 1777-1799*, 2d ed. (Philadelphia: American Philosophical Society, 1976), p. 14.

31. Jacob Duche to GW (8 Oct. 1777), Sparks, *Correspondence of the American Revolution*, 1:453.

32. GW to Lewis Nicola (22 May 1782), Fitzpatrick 24:272.

33. GW to Archibald Cary (15 June 1782), Fitzpatrick 24:347-48.

34. Quoted in Scheer and Rankin, *Rebels and Redcoats*, p. 498.

35. Quoted in ibid., p. 499.

36. GW to James McHenry (12 Sept. 1782), Fitzpatrick 25:151.

37. GW to John Augustine Washington (16 Jan. 1783), Fitzpatrick 26:44.

38. GW to Thomas Jefferson (10 Feb. 1783), Fitzpatrick 26:118.

39. GW to the Marquis de Lafayette (13 Dec. 1782), Fitzpatrick 25:434.

Chapter 25—"A Gulf of Civil Horror"

1. GW to James McHenry (17 Oct. 1782), Fitzpatrick 25:269.

2. Ibid.

3. GW to Benjamin Lincoln (2 Oct. 1782), Fitzpatrick 25:228.

4. GW to Joseph Jones (14 Dec. 1782), Fitzpatrick 25:430.

5. GW to John Augustine Washington (16 Jan. 1783), Fitzpatrick 26:44; cf. GW to John Armstrong (10 Jan. 1783), Fitzpatrick 26:26-27.

6. GW to Alexander Hamilton (4 Mar. 1783), Fitzpatrick 26:186.

7. Alexander Hamilton to GW (13 Feb. 1783), Syrett, *The Papers of Alexander Hamilton*, 3:253-55.

8. GW to Alexander Hamilton (4 Mar. 1783), Fitzpatrick 26:186.

9. Quoted in John F. Schroeder and Benson J. Lossing, *Life and Times of Washington*, rev. ed., 4 vols. (Albany, N.Y.: M. M. Belcher Publishing Co., 1903), 3:1467–68.

10. GW to Alexander Hamilton (12 Mar. 1783), Fitzpatrick 26:216–18.

11. GW to the officers of the army (15 Mar. 1783), Fitzpatrick 26:222–27.

12. Josiah Quincy, *The Journals of Major Samuel Shaw, with a Life of the Author* (Boston: William Crosby and H. P. Nichols, 1847), p. 104.

13. Ibid., pp. 104–5.

14. GW to Lund Washington (19 Mar. 1783), Fitzpatrick 26:245.

15. GW to the President of Congress (18 Mar. 1783), Fitzpatrick 26:229–32.

16. Flexner, *George Washington in the American Revolution*, p. 508.

17. Thomas Jefferson to GW (16 Apr. 1783), Bergh, *The Writings of Thomas Jefferson*, 4:218.

Chapter 26—The Closing Days of War

1. GW to the Chevalier de la Luzerne (29 Mar. 1783), Fitzpatrick 26:264–65.

2. General Orders (18 Apr. 1783), Fitzpatrick 26:335–36.

3. Ibid., pp. 334–35.

4. GW to Nathanael Greene (6 Feb. 1783), Fitzpatrick 26:104.

5. GW to the President of Congress (16 July 1783), Fitzpatrick 27:70.

6. Circular to the States (8 June 1783), Fitzpatrick 26:483–96.

7. David Howell to Governor William Greene (9? Sept. 1783), Burnett, *Letters of Members of the Continental Congress*, 7:292.

8. Quoted in ibid.

9. General Orders (2 Nov. 1783), Fitzpatrick 27:223–27.

10. Quoted in Washington Irving, *Life of George Washington*, ed. Allen Guttmann and James A. Sappenfield, 5 vols. in 3 (Boston: Twayne Publishers, 1982), 4:246.

11. Citizens of New York to GW (26 Nov. 1783), in Hugh Hastings and J. A. Holden, eds., *Public Papers of George Clinton, First Governor of New York*, 10 vols. (New York and Albany, N.Y.: State of New York, 1899–1914), 8:300–301.

12. *Memoir of Colonel Benjamin Tallmadge* (1858; reprint ed., New York: New York Times and Arno Press, 1968), pp. 63–64.

13. Ibid., p. 64.

14. Ibid.

Chapter 27—Victory Over the Mighty British Empire

1. Boatner, *Encyclopedia of the American Revolution*, pp. 264, 882.

2. See Commager and Morris, *The Spirit of 'Seventy-Six*, 1:227-64.

3. Claude H. Van Tyne, *England and America—Rivals in the American Revolution* (New York: Macmillan Company, 1927), p. 124.

4. See Commager and Morris, *The Spirit of 'Seventy-Six*, 1:239; Boatner, *Encyclopedia of the American Revolution*, pp. 523-24.

5. See Commager and Morris, *The Spirit of 'Seventy-Six*, 1:325-26.

6. Ibid.

7. Commager and Morris, *The Spirit of 'Seventy-Six*, 1:326; Boatner, *Encyclopedia of the American Revolution*, p. 663; H. E. Egerton, *The Causes and Character of the American Revolution* (Oxford: Clarendon Press, 1923), p. 178.

8. Commager and Morris, *The Spirit of 'Seventy-Six*, 1:333-34; Robert Leckie, *The Wars of America* (New York: Harper and Row, 1968), pp. 134-35.

9. George C. Neumann and Frank J. Kravic, *Collector's Illustrated Encyclopedia of the American Revolution* (Harrisburg, Penn.: Stackpole Books, 1975), p. 164.

10. Boatner, *Encyclopedia of the American Revolution*, p. 264.

11. Edward J. Lowell, *The Hessians...in the Revolutionary War* (1884; reprint ed., Port Washington, N.Y.: Kennikat Press, 1965), p. 300.

12. Boatner, *Encyclopedia of the American Revolution*, p. 897.

13. Ibid., pp. 756-57.

14. Neumann and Kravic, *Collector's Illustrated Encyclopedia of the American Revolution*, p. 186.

15. Ibid.

16. Samuel Wigglesworth to the New Hampshire Committee of Safety (27 Sept. 1776), in Commager and Morris, *The Spirit of 'Seventy-Six*, 2:825.

17. Neumann and Kravic, *Collector's Illustrated Encyclopedia of the American Revolution*, p. 186.

18. Commager and Morris, *The Spirit of 'Seventy-Six*, 2:854.

19. William Slade diary (13-28 Dec. 1776), in ibid., pp. 856-57.

20. For further discussion on Washington's abilities as a general, see Flexner, *George Washington in the American Revolution*, pp. 531-52.

21. GW to Landon Carter (30 May 1778), Fitzpatrick 11:492.

22. GW to the Reverend William Gordon (9 Mar. 1781), Fitzpatrick 21:332.

23. GW to the legislature of the state of Connecticut (17 Oct. 1789), Sparks 12:169-70.

24. GW to Jonathan Williams (2 Mar. 1795), Fitzpatrick 34:130.

Chapter 28—Whatever Became of the Leaders in the War?

1. Oration in the city of Philadelphia (26 Dec. 1799), quoted in Albert Bushnell Hart, comp., "Tributes to Washington," pamphlet number 3 in the series *Honor to George Washington,* ed. Albert Bushnell Hart (Washington: United States George Washington Bicentennial Commission, 1932), p. 30.

2. A convenient reference for further information on the major figures of the war is Boatner, *Encyclopedia of the American Revolution.* Entries are arranged alphabetically by last name. See also J. T. Headley, *Washington and His Generals* (New York: E. B. Treat, 1865); and George Athan Billias, ed., *George Washington's Generals* (New York: William Morrow and Co., 1964).

Chapter 29—The General Retires

1. Worthington Chauncey Ford et al., eds., *Journals of the Continental Congress, 1774-1789,* 34 vols. (Washington: U.S. Government Printing Office, 1904-37), 25:820.

2. Address to Congress (23 Dec. 1783), Fitzpatrick 27:284.

3. James McHenry to his fiancee (23 Dec. 1783), in Bernard C. Steiner, *Life and Correspondence of James McHenry* (Cleveland, 1907), pp. 69-70.

4. Address to Congress (23 Dec. 1783), Fitzpatrick 27:285.

5. Freeman 5:477-78.

6. GW to David Humphreys (25 July 1785), Fitzpatrick 28:202-3.

7. GW to Charles Armand-Tuffin (7 Oct. 1785), Fitzpatrick 28:289.

8. Thomas Jefferson to William Johnson (27 Oct. 1822), in Paul Leicester Ford, ed., *The Writings of Thomas Jefferson,* 10 vols. (New York: G. P. Putnam's Sons, 1892-99), 10:222.

9. GW to George William Fairfax (10 July 1783), Fitzpatrick 27:60.

10. GW to Robert Stewart (10 Aug. 1783), Fitzpatrick 27:89.

11. Quoted in James Hosmer Penniman, "Washington, Proprietor of Mount Vernon," pamphlet number 9 in the series *Honor to George Washington,* ed. Albert Bushnell Hart (Washington: United States George Washington Bicentennial Commission, 1932), p. 99.

12. GW to the learned professions of Philadelphia (13 Dec. 1783), Fitzpatrick 27:269.

13. GW to Lund Washington (11 June 1783), Fitzpatrick 27:3.

14. GW to Lund Washington (19 May 1780), Fitzpatrick 18:392.

15. GW to the mayor of Annapolis (22 Dec. 1783), Fitzpatrick 27:281.

16. GW to Thomas Jefferson (10 Feb. 1783), Fitzpatrick 26:118.

17. GW to the Marquis de Lafayette (5 Apr. 1783), Fitzpatrick 26:298.

18. GW to the Chevalier de Chastellux (12 Oct. 1783), Fitzpatrick 27:188-90.

19. GW to George Clinton (28 Dec. 1783), Fitzpatrick 27:288.

20. GW to Alexander Hamilton (4 Mar. 1783), Fitzpatrick 26:188.

21. GW to Alexander Hamilton (30 Mar. 1783), Fitzpatrick 26:277.

22. GW to the Marquis de Lafayette (5 Apr. 1783), Fitzpatrick 26:297-98.

23. GW to John Augustine Washington (31 May 1776), Fitzpatrick 5:92.

24. GW to the Reverend William Gordon (8 July 1783), Fitzpatrick 27:49-50.

Chapter 30—Life at Mount Vernon

1. GW to the Marquis de Lafayette (1 Feb. 1784), Fitzpatrick 27:317-18.

2. GW to Henry Knox (20 Feb 1784), Fitzpatrick 27:340-41.

3. GW to Lund Washington (12 Feb. 1783), Fitzpatrick 26:127.

4. GW to Fielding Lewis (27 Feb. 1784), Fitzpatrick 27:345.

5. William H. Wilbur, *The Making of George Washington*, 2d ed. rev. (DeLand, Fla.: Patriotic Education, 1953), pp. 251-52.

6. GW to Lund Washington (7 May 1787), Fitzpatrick 29:212.

7. GW to Mary Ball Washington (15 Feb. 1787), Fitzpatrick 29:160-61.

8. Diary entry (30 June 1785), *Diaries* 4:157.

9. GW to George William Fairfax (27 Feb. 1785), Fitzpatrick 28:83-84.

10. GW to David Humphreys (7 Feb. 1785), Fitzpatrick 28:65.

11. GW to Arthur Young (4 Dec. 1788), Fitzpatrick 30:150.

12. GW to Alexander Spotswood (13 Feb. 1788), Fitzpatrick 29:414.

13. GW to Arthur Young (6 Aug. 1787), in *Diaries* 1:xxix.

14. GW to George William Fairfax (10 Nov. 1785), Fitzpatrick 28:313.

15. GW to Charles Carter (20 Jan. 1788), Fitzpatrick 29:388.

16. GW to John Beale Bordley (17 Aug. 1788), Fitzpatrick 30:48.

17. GW to Charles Carter (20 Jan. 1788), Fitzpatrick 29:388.

18. GW to William Pierce (18 Jan. 1795), Fitzpatrick 34:97.

19. Dixon Wecter, "President Washington and Parson Weems," in James Morton Smith, ed., *George Washington: A Profile* (New York: Hill and Wang, 1969), p. 4.

20. Robert Hunter, *Quebec to Carolina in 1785-86: Travel Diary of Robert Hunter*, ed. Louis B. Wright and Marion Tinling (San Marino, Cal.: Huntington Library, 1943), pp. 143, 195.

21. GW to George William Fairfax (30 June 1785), Fitzpatrick 28:185-86.

22. GW to Lund Washington (15 Aug. 1778), Fitzpatrick 12:327.

23. Flexner, *George Washington in the American Revolution*, p. 342.

24. Flexner, *George Washington: Anguish and Farewell*, p. 123.

25. GW to Robert Lewis (18 Aug. 1799), Fitzpatrick 37:338.

26. GW to Robert Morris (12 Apr. 1786), Fitzpatrick 27:407-8.

27. GW to the Marquis de Lafayette (10 May 1786), Fitzpatrick 27:424.

28. GW to John Francis Mercer (9 Sept. 1786), Fitzpatrick 29:5.

29. Quoted in David Humphreys, "The Life of General Washington," as printed in Flexner, *George Washington: Anguish and Farewell*, p. 121.

30. Quoted in John Bernard, *Retrospections of America* (New York: Harper & Brothers, 1887), p. 91.

31. James Hosmer Penniman, "Washington, Proprietor of Mount Vernon," pamphlet number 9 in the series *Honor to George Washington*, ed. Albert Bushnell Hart (Washington: United States George Washington Bicentennial Commission, 1932), p. 97.

32. Quoted in Paul Leicester Ford, *The True George Washington* (Philadelphia: J.B. Lippincott Company, 1896), p. 94.

33. Hunter, *Quebec to Carolina in 1785-86*, p. 194.

34. James Madison to Jared Sparks (n.d.), in Ford, *The True George Washington*, p. 179.

35. Winslow C. Watson, ed., *Men and Times of the Revolution; or Memoirs of Elkanah Watson* (New York: Dana and Company, 1856), p. 244.

36. Quoted in Penniman, "Washington, Proprietor of Mount Vernon," p. 96.

37. GW to Francis Hopkinson (16 May 1785), Fitzpatrick 28:140-41.

38. GW to the Marquis de Lafayette (8 Dec. 1784), Fitzpatrick 28:7.

39. GW to James Craik (25 Mar. 1784), Fitzpatrick 27:371.

40. GW to David Humphreys (25 July 1785), Fitzpatrick 28:203.

41. Quoted in Ford, *The True George Washington*, p. 64.

42. GW to the State Societies of the Cincinnati (31 Oct. 1786), Fitzpatrick 29:32.

43. GW to Henry Knox (2 Apr. 1787), Fitzpatrick 29:195.

44. GW to the Marquis de Lafayette (8 Dec. 1784), Fitzpatrick 28:7.

45. GW to the Marchionesse de Lafayette (10 May 1786), Fitzpatrick 28:419.

46. See GW to Mary Ball Washington (15 Feb. 1787), Fitzpatrick 29:158.

47. GW to Lund Washington (7 May 1787), Fitzpatrick 29:213.

48. GW to James Craik (4 Aug. 1788), Fitzpatrick 30:36.

49. GW to Mary Ball Washington (15 Feb. 1787), Fitzpatrick 29:158.

50. GW to Theodorick Bland (15 Aug. 1786), Fitzpatrick 28:516.

Chapter 31—"A Half-Starved, Limping Government"

1. GW to Sir Edward Newenham (10 June 1784), Fitzpatrick 27:417.
2. GW to Benjamin Harrison (18 Jan. 1784), Fitzpatrick 27:305.
3. GW to James Warren (7 Oct. 1785), Fitzpatrick 28:290.
4. GW to Benjamin Harrison (18 Jan. 1784), Fitzpatrick 27:305-6.
5. GW to Nathanael Greene (31 Mar. 1783), Fitzpatrick 26:275.
6. GW to Benjamin Harrison (18 Jan. 1784), Fitzpatrick 27:306.
7. GW to Henry Knox (28 Feb. 1785), Fitzpatrick 28:93.
8. GW to James Madison (30 Nov. 1785), Fitzpatrick 28:336.
9. GW to James Warren (7 Oct. 1785), Fitzpatrick 28:290.
10. GW to David Stuart (30 Nov. 1785), Fitzpatrick 28:328.
11. GW to John Jay (1 Aug. 1786), Fitzpatrick 28:502.
12. GW to the Chevalier de la Luzerne (1 Aug. 1786), Fitzpatrick 28:500-501.
13. GW to James Madison (5 Nov. 1786), Fitzpatrick 29:51-52.
14. Ibid, p. 52.
15. GW to Henry Lee (31 Oct. 1786), Fitzpatrick 29:34-35.
16. Ibid, p. 35.
17. Jonathan Elliot, ed., *The Debates in the Several State Conventions on the Adoption of the Federal Constitution,* 2d ed. rev., 5 vols. (Philadelphia: J. B. Lippincott Company, 1907), 1:118.
18. GW to John Jay (1 Aug. 1786), Fitzpatrick 28:503-4.
19. GW to James Madison (18 Nov. 1786), Fitzpatrick 29:72.
20. GW to Edmund Randolph (21 Dec. 1786), Fitzpatrick 29:120.
21. GW to John Jay (1 Aug. 1786), Fitzpatrick 28:504.
22. Worthington Chauncey Ford et al., eds., *Journals of the Continental Congress, 1774-1789,* 34 vols. (Washington: U.S. Government Printing Office, 1904-37), 32:73-74.
23. Henry Knox to GW (Mar. or Apr. 1787), quoted in Freeman 6:85.
24. Quoted in John Jay Smith, *American Historical and Literary Curiosities,* 2d series (New York, 1860), sec. II, pp. 20-21; reprinted in James Thomas Flexner, *George Washington and the New Nation (1783-1793)* (Boston: Little, Brown and Co., 1969), p. 108.
25. GW to David Humphreys (26 Dec. 1786), Fitzpatrick 29:128.
26. GW to James Madison (31 Mar. 1787), Fitzpatrick 29:190.

27. Ibid., pp. 190–92.

28. James Monroe to Thomas Jefferson (12 July 1788), in Stanislaus Murray Hamilton, ed., *The Writings of James Monroe,* 7 vols. (1898–1903; reprint ed., New York: AMS Press, 1969), 1:186.

29. Henry Knox to the Marquis de Lafayette (25 July 1787), quoted in Freeman 6:87.

30. *Pennsylvania Herald,* 12 May 1787, p. 3; quoted in Freeman 6:87.

Chapter 32—Forming a New Constitution

1. William Pierce, "Character Sketches of Delegates to the Federal Convention," in Max Farrand, ed., *The Records of the Federal Convention of 1787,* rev. ed., 4 vols. (New Haven, Conn.: Yale University Press, 1937), 3:91.

2. Ibid., p. 94.

3. Thomas Jefferson to John Adams (30 Aug. 1787), Bergh, *The Writings of Thomas Jefferson,* 6:289.

4. Pierce, "Character Sketches of Delegates to the Federal Convention," Farrand, *The Records of the Federal Convention of 1787,* 3:92.

5. Ibid., p. 89.

6. Ibid., p. 94.

7. Ibid.

8. Ibid., p. 92.

9. Ibid., p. 91.

10. Ibid., p. 96.

11. Ibid., p. 95.

12. Ibid., p. 89.

13. Ibid., pp. 91-92.

14. Ibid., p. 94.

15. Samuel Eliot Morison, *Oxford History of the American People* (New York: Oxford University Press, 1965), p. 305.

16. GW to Thomas Jefferson (30 May 1787), Fitzpatrick 29:224.

17. GW to George Augustine Washington (3 June 1787), Fitzpatrick 29:228.

18. *Massachusetts Centinel,* 13 June 1787, p. 3; quoted in Freeman 6:95.

19. Resolutions proposed by Mr. Randolph in convention (29 May 1787), Farrand, *The Records of the Federal Convention of 1787,* 1:22.

20. Quoted in Farrand, *The Records of the Federal Convention of 1787,* 3:86-87.

21. GW to George Augustine Washington (10 June 1787), Fitzpatrick 29:233.

22. GW to George Augustine Washington (3 June 1787), Fitzpatrick 29:228.

23. GW to Alexander Hamilton (10 July 1787), Fitzpatrick 29:245. It should be noted that Hamilton's discouragement with the convention stemmed partly from his failure to win support for his own proposed plan of government. Hamilton's plan had definite monarchical tendencies and was not well received by his fellow delegates. See Farrand, *The Records of the Federal Convention of 1787*, 1:282-311; 3:617-30.

24. Convention debate (2 July 1787), Farrand, *The Records of the Federal Convention of 1787*, 1:511.

25. GW to Alexander Hamilton (10 July 1787), Fitzpatrick 29:245-46.

26. GW to David Stuart (1 July 1787), Fitzpatrick 29:239.

27. Convention debate (17 July 1787), Farrand, *The Records of the Federal Convention of 1787*, 2:28-29.

28. Pierce Butler to Weedon Butler (5 May 1788), in Farrand, *The Records of the Federal Convention of 1787*, 3:302.

29. Convention debate (17 Sept. 1787), Farrand, *The Records of the Federal Convention of 1787*, 2:643-44.

30. Ibid., p. 644.

31. Quoted in Saul K. Padover, ed., *The Washington Papers* (New York: Harper & Brothers, 1955), p. 388.

32. Quoted in Farrand, *The Records of the Federal Convention of 1787*, 2:648.

33. Diary entry (17 Sept. 1787), *Diaries* 5:185.

34. Proposed address to Congress, never delivered (Apr.? 1789), Fitzpatrick 30:299-300.

35. James Madison to Thomas Jefferson (9 Dec. 1787), in Robert A. Rutland, ed., *The Papers of James Madison*, 14 vols. by 1983 (Chicago: University of Chicago Press, 1962-), 10:208.

36. GW to the Marquis de Lafayette (7 Feb. 1788), Fitzpatrick 29:409.

37. Alexander Hamilton, James Madison, and John Jay, *The Federalist Papers* (New York: Mentor Books, 1961), No. 45.

38. Remarks in the House of Representatives (6 Feb. 1792), Farrand, *The Records of the Federal Convention of 1787*, 3:366.

39. Thomas Jefferson to Albert Gallatin (16 June 1817), Bergh, *The Writings of Thomas Jefferson*, 15:133.

40. Benjamin Franklin to the Abbes Chalut and Arnaud (17 Apr. 1787), in Albert Henry Smyth, ed., *The Writings of Benjamin Franklin*, 10 vols. (New York: The Macmillan Co., 1905-7), 9:569.

41. GW to the Marquis de Lafayette (7 Feb. 1788), Fitzpatrick 29:410.

42. Farewell Address (17 Sept. 1796), Fitzpatrick 35:229.

43. Hamilton, Madison, and Jay, *The Federalist Papers*, No. 22.

44. Ibid., No. 46.

45. GW to Bushrod Washington (10 Nov. 1787), Fitzpatrick 29:311.

46. John Adams, "The Massachusetts Declaration of Rights" (1 Sept. 1779), in George A. Peek, Jr., ed., *The Political Writings of John Adams* (New York: Liberal Arts Press, 1954), p. 96.

47. Jonathan Dayton, as quoted in William Steele to Jonathan D. Steele (Sept. 1825), Farrand, *The Records of the Federal Convention of 1787*, 3:471.

48. For a discussion on this point see Flexner, *George Washington and the New Nation*, pp. 123-24.

49. Samuel S. Forman, *Narrative of a Journey Down the Ohio and Mississippi in 1789-90*, ed. Lyman C. Draper (Cincinnati: Robert Clarke & Co., 1888), p. 15.

50. GW to the Marquis de Lafayette (17 Aug. 1787), Fitzpatrick 29:260.

51. Gouverneur Morris, "An Oration upon the Death of General Washington" (31 Dec. 1799), Farrand, *The Records of the Federal Convention of 1787*, 3:381-82. The language used by Morris in describing this incident makes it impossible to establish precisely when Washington made the statement. Freeman used the quotation in connection with the Great Compromise (mid-July), while noting that "this incident may have occurred before the Convention began its work." See Freeman 6:98.

52. *New York Daily Advertiser*, 26 July 1787, p. 2; quoted in Freeman 6:114.

53. *Pennsylvania Packet*, 23 August 1787, p. 3; quoted in Freeman 6:114.

Chapter 33—The Ratification Fight

1. GW to the Marquis de Lafayette (18 Sept. 1787), Fitzpatrick 29:277.

2. GW to Bushrod Washington (10 Nov. 1787), Fitzpatrick 29:310.

3. GW to Patrick Henry (24 Sept. 1787), Fitzpatrick 29:278.

4. GW to the Marquis de Lafayette (7 Feb. 1788), Fitzpatrick 29:409-10.

5. GW to Benjamin Harrison (9 Mar. 1789), Fitzpatrick 30:223-24.

6. GW to the Marquis de Lafayette (7 Feb. 1788), Fitzpatrick 29:410-11.

7. GW to James McHenry (27 Apr. 1788), Fitzpatrick 29:471.

8. *Pennsylvania Packet*, quoted in Frank Donovan, ed., *The George Washington Papers* (New York: Dodd, Mead and Co., 1964), p. 200.

9. *Independent Gazetteer*, 15 October 1787, p. 2; quoted in Freeman 6:119.

10. GW to Rufus King (29 Feb. 1788), Fitzpatrick 29:428

11. GW to the Marquis de Lafayette (28 May 1788), Fitzpatrick 29:507-8.

12. GW to the Reverend John Lathrop (22 June 1788), Fitzpatrick 30:5.

13. GW to Benjamin Lincoln (29 June 1788), Fitzpatrick 30:11.

14. GW to Jonathan Trumbull (20 July 1788), Fitzpatrick 30:22.

15. James Monroe to Thomas Jefferson (12 July 1788), in Stanislaus Murray Hamilton, ed., *The Writings of James Monroe*, 7 vols. (1898–1903; reprint ed., New York: AMS Press, 1969), 1:186.

Chapter 34—"Best Fitted" for the Presidency

1. David Humphreys to GW (28 Sept. 1787), quoted in Freeman 6:120.

2. *Pennsylvania Packet*, 5 August 1788, p. 2; quoted in Freeman 6:147.

3. Gouverneur Morris to GW (30 Oct. 1787), in Samuel Eliot Morison, ed., *Sources and Documents Illustrating the American Revolution*, 2d ed. (New York: Oxford University Press, 1965), pp. 306–7.

4. GW to Henry Lee (22 Sept. 1788), Fitzpatrick 30:98.

5. GW to the Marquis de Lafayette (28 Apr. 1788), Fitzpatrick 29:479–80.

6. GW to Alexander Hamilton (3 Oct. 1788), Fitzpatrick 30:111.

7. GW to Benjamin Lincoln (26 Oct. 1788), Fitzpatrick 30:119.

8. GW to Jonathan Trumbull (4 Dec. 1788), Fitzpatrick 30:149.

9. GW to Samuel Vaughan (21 Mar. 1789), Fitzpatrick 30:238.

10. GW to Henry Knox (1 Apr. 1789), Fitzpatrick 30:268.

11. GW to Charles Thomson (14 Apr. 1789), Fitzpatrick 30:285–86.

12. Diary entry (16 Apr. 1789), *Diaries* 5:445.

13. Frank Monaghan, *Notes on the Inaugural Journey and the Inaugural Ceremonies of George Washington as First President of the United States* (mimeograph, 1939), p. 9; quoted in Freeman 6:166.

14. To the mayor, corporation, and citizens of Alexandria (16 Apr. 1789), Fitzpatrick 30:287.

15. GW to the citizens of Baltimore (17 Apr. 1789), Fitzpatrick 30:288.

16. Freeman 6:171.

17. Ibid., p. 172.

18. Jacob Hiltzheimer, some twenty miles away in Bristol, recorded in his diary that he heard the "great guns" sounding their welcome in Philadelphia. See Jacob C. Parsons, ed., *Extracts from the Diary of Jacob Hiltzheimer, 1765–1798* (Philadelphia, 1893), p. 152; quoted in Freeman 6:172*n*.

19. Address to the leaders of the city of Philadelphia (20 Apr. 1789), Sparks 12:145.

20. Quoted in Freeman 6:175–76.

21. Quoted in George Adams Boyd, *Elias Boudinot: Patriot and Statesman, 1740–1821* (Princeton, N.J.: Princeton University Press, 1952), p. 164.

22. Diary entry (23 Apr. 1789), *Diaries* 5:447.

Chapter 35—"God Bless Our President!"

1. Freeman 6:189.

2. Tobias Lear to George Augustine Washington (3 May 1789), quoted in Freeman 6:192.

3. First inaugural address (30 Apr. 1789), Fitzpatrick 30:292–96.

4. Fisher Ames to George Richards Minot (3 May 1789), in Seth Ames, ed., *Works of Fisher Ames*, ed. and enl. by W. B. Allen, 2 vols. (Indianapolis: Liberty Classics, 1983), 1:568.

5. GW to Catharine Macaulay Graham (9 Jan. 1790), Fitzpatrick 30:496.

6. GW to James Madison (5 May 1789), Fitzpatrick 30:311.

7. GW to Henry Knox (1 Apr. 1789), Fitzpatrick 30:268.

8. GW to Benjamin Harrison (9 Mar. 1789), Fitzpatrick 30:224–25.

9. GW to Edmund Randolph (11 Feb. 1790), Fitzpatrick 31:9.

10. Martha Washington to Frances Bassett Washington (8 June 1789), in Stephen Decatur, Jr., *Private Affairs of George Washington from the Records and Accounts of Tobias Lear, Esquire, His Secretary* (Boston, 1933), pp. 20–21.

11. Ibid., p. 21.

12. Abigail Adams to her sister (28 June 1789), in Stewart Mitchell, ed., *New Letters of Abigail Adams, 1788–1801* (Boston: Houghton Mifflin Co., 1947), p. 13.

13. Abigail Adams to Mary Cranch (12 July 1789), Mitchell, *New Letters of Abigail Adams*, p. 15.

14. Quoted in Frank B. Freidel, Jr., "Profiles of the Presidents, Part I: The Presidency and How It Grew," *National Geographic*, November 1964, p. 650.

15. William Maclay, journal entry (27 Aug. 1789), in Edgar S. Maclay, ed., *The Journal of William Maclay* (New York: Albert & Charles Boni, 1927), p. 134.

16. Reminiscence by the Reverend Ashbel Greene, in Custis, *Recollections and Private Memoirs of Washington*, p. 435n.

17. Quoted in Custis, *Recollections and Private Memoirs of Washington*, p. 398n.

18. John Brett Langstaff, *Doctor Bard of Hyde Park* (New York: E.P. Dutton & Co., 1942), pp. 168–76.

19. GW to James Craik (8 Sept. 1789), Fitzpatrick 30:396.

20. Some have suggested that Washington's relationship with his mother was

strained. While there is some truth to that claim, the matter has been greatly exaggerated by certain modern writers. Washington was a strong-willed man who was not always willing to bow to the sometimes unreasonable wishes of his equally strong-willed mother. But there is every evidence that George Washington was a loving and dutiful son. His attitude is summed up in one statement he made during the Revolutionary War. When he learned that his mother was complaining of not being adequately cared for, he promptly wrote to his brother: "Inquire into her real wants and see what is necessary to make her comfortable.... While I have anything, I will part with it to make her so, and wish you to take measures in my behalf accordingly." GW to John Augustine Washington (16 Jan. 1783), Fitzpatrick 26:44.

21. GW to Elizabeth Washington Lewis (13 Sept. 1789), Fitzpatrick 30:399.

22. Ibid.

23. Thomas Jefferson to Martha J. Randolph (16 May 1790), Bergh, *The Writings of Thomas Jefferson*, 18:185.

24. Martha Washington to Mercy Warren (12 June 1790), in Worthington Chauncey Ford, ed., *The Warren-Adams Letters, Being Chiefly a Correspondence Among John Adams, Samuel Adams, and Mercy Warren*, 2 vols. (Boston: Massachusetts Historical Society, 1917, 1925), 2:319.

25. GW to David Stuart (15 June 1790), Fitzpatrick 31:55.

26. GW to Samuel Vaughan (21 Mar. 1789), Fitzpatrick 30:238.

27. Ibid.

28. John Adams to Silvanus Bourn (30 Aug. 1789), in Charles Francis Adams, ed., *The Works of John Adams*, 10 vols. (Boston: Little, Brown and Co., 1850-56), 9:561.

29. Thomas Jefferson to the heads of the [executive] departments (6 Nov. 1801), Bergh, *The Writings of Thomas Jefferson*, 10:289-90.

30. GW to Alexander Hamilton (26 June 1796), Fitzpatrick 35:103.

31. Proposed address to Congress, never delivered (Apr. 1789), Fitzpatrick 30:299.

32. GW to Benjamin Harrison (9 Mar. 1789), Fitzpatrick 30:223.

33. Thomas Jefferson to the heads of the [executive] departments (6 Nov. 1801), Bergh, *The Writings of Thomas Jefferson*, 10:290.

34. *Essex Journal*, 10 March 1790; quoted in Freeman 6:226-27.

35. Freeman 6:186; see also Maclay, *The Journal of William Maclay*, pp. 23-37.

36. Thomas Jefferson to James Madison (29 July 1789), in Julian P. Boyd, ed., *The Papers of Thomas Jefferson*, 20 vols. by 1982 (Princeton, N.J.: Princeton University Press, 1950-), 15:315.

37. GW to Gouverneur Morris (13 Oct. 1789), Fitzpatrick 30:442.

Chapter 36—"All Things . . . Seem to Succeed"

1. Historical Statistics of the United States, 1789-1945 (Washington: U.S. Bureau of the Census, 1949), p. 25.

2. Diary entry (20 Oct. 1789), Diaries 5:468.

3. First Annual Address to Congress (8 Jan. 1790), Fitzpatrick 30:491-93.

4. Report Relative to a Provision for the Support of Public Credit (9 Jan. 1790), in Syrett, The Papers of Alexander Hamilton, 6:86.

5. For a detailed discussion of Hamilton's plan see Broadus Mitchell, Alexander Hamilton: The National Adventure (1788-1804) (New York: Macmillan Company, 1962), pp. 47-53.

6. The Anas (4 Feb. 1818), Bergh, The Writings of Thomas Jefferson, 1:273-77.

7. GW to the Comte de Rochambeau (10 Aug. 1790), Fitzpatrick 31:83-84.

8. Second Report on the Further Provision Necessary for Establishing Public Credit (13 Dec. 1790), Syrett, The Papers of Alexander Hamilton, 7:331. Emphasis in original.

9. Opinion on the constitutionality of an act to establish a bank (23 Feb. 1791), Syrett, The Papers of Alexander Hamilton, 8:98.

10. Opinion against the constitutionality of a national bank (15 Feb. 1791), Bergh, The Writings of Thomas Jefferson, 3:153.

11. Fourth Annual Address to Congress (6 Nov. 1792), Fitzpatrick 32:211-12.

12. GW to John Adams, John Jay, and Alexander Hamilton (10 May 1789), Fitzpatrick 30:320.

13. Gazette of the United States, 28 October 1789, p. 3; quoted in Freeman 6:243n.

14. GW to Tobias Lear (30 July 1792), Fitzpatrick 32:101.

15. GW to Governor Alexander Martin of North Carolina (14 Nov. 1791), Fitzpatrick 31:415.

16. GW to David Humphreys (20 June 1791), Fitzpatrick 31:318.

17. Diary entry (3 July 1791), Diaries 6:168.

18. The Anas (29 Feb. 1792), Bergh, The Writings of Thomas Jefferson, 1:287-88.

19. Ibid. (10 July 1792), p. 309.

20. GW to James Madison (20 May 1792), Fitzpatrick 32:45-46.

21. The Anas (1 Oct. 1792), Bergh, The Writings of Thomas Jefferson, 1:317.

22. Thomas Jefferson to GW (23 May 1792), Bergh, The Writings of Thomas Jefferson, 8:347.

Chapter 37—The Jefferson-Hamilton Feud

1. GW to the Marquis de Lafayette (3 June 1790), Fitzpatrick 31:46.

2. *National Gazette*, 4 July 1792, p. 2; quoted in Freeman 6:361.

3. GW to Gouverneur Morris (21 June 1792), Fitzpatrick 32:63.

4. The Anas (10 July 1792), Bergh, *The Writings of Thomas Jefferson*, 1:310.

5. Journal entry (14 Dec. 1790), in Edgar S. Maclay, ed., *The Journal of William Maclay* (New York: Albert & Charles Boni, 1927), p. 341.

6. The Anas (1 Oct. 1792), Bergh, *The Writings of Thomas Jefferson*, 1:316.

7. Thomas Jefferson to GW (23 May 1792), Bergh, *The Writings of Thomas Jefferson*, 8:344; Paul Leicester Ford, *The Writings of Thomas Jefferson*, 10 vols. (New York: G.P. Putnam's Sons, 1892-99), 1:214-16.

8. Alexander Hamilton to GW (9 Sept. 1792), Syrett, *The Papers of Alexander Hamilton*, 12:348.

9. GW to Thomas Jefferson (23 Aug. 1792), Fitzpatrick 32.130-31. An almost identical letter went to Alexander Hamilton on August 26; see Fitzpatrick 32.132-34.

10. GW to Thomas Jefferson (18 Oct. 1792), Fitzpatrick 32:185-86.

11. GW to Thomas Jefferson (1 Jan. 1794), Fitzpatrick 33:231.

12. Thomas Jefferson to Martin Van Buren (29 June 1824), Bergh, *The Writings of Thomas Jefferson*, 16:66.

13. GW to Timothy Pickering (27 July 1795), Fitzpatrick 34:251.

14. GW to Alexander Hamilton (29 Oct. 1795), Fitzpatrick 34:348-49.

15. John Adams to Abigail Adams (8 Feb. 1796), in Charles Francis Adams, ed., *Letters of John Adams Addressed to His Wife*, 2 vols. (Boston: Charles C. Little and James Brown, 1841), 2:195.

Chapter 38—Foreign Troubles, Domestic Strife

1. Thomas Jefferson to Monsieur de Ternant (23 Feb. 1793), Bergh, *The Writings of Thomas Jefferson*, 9:33.

2. Proclamation of Neutrality (22 Apr. 1793), Fitzpatrick 32:430-31.

3. GW to Sir Edward Newenham (29 Aug. 1788), Fitzpatrick 30:71-72.

4. GW to Patrick Henry (9 Oct. 1795), Fitzpatrick 35:334-35.

5. Thomas Jefferson to James Madison (9 June 1793), Bergh, *The Writings of Thomas Jefferson*, 9:120.

6. Edmond Charles Genet to Thomas Jefferson (8 June 1793), in Freeman 7:88.

7. John Adams to Thomas Jefferson (30 June 1813), in Charles Francis Adams, ed., *The Works of John Adams*, 10 vols. (Boston: Little, Brown and Company, 1850-56), 10:47.

8. Edmond Charles Genet to French Foreign Minister Lebrun (19 June 1793), in Frederick J. Turner, ed., *Correspondence of the French Ministers to the United States, 1791-1797*, vol. 2 of *Annual Report of the American Historical Association for the Year 1903* (Washington: U.S. Government Printing Office, 1904), 2:217; translated in Freeman 7:92*n*.

9. GW to Henry Lee (21 July 1793), Fitzpatrick 33:23.

10. GW to Henry Lee (26 Aug. 1794), Fitzpatrick 33:476.

11. GW to Henry Lee (21 July 1793), Fitzpatrick 33:23-24.

12. The Anas (2 Aug. 1793), Bergh, *The Writings of Thomas Jefferson*, 1:382.

13. Thomas Jefferson to James Madison (7 July 1793), Ford, *The Writings of Thomas Jefferson*, 6:338.

14. Thomas Jefferson to James Madison (11 Aug. 1793), in Dumas Malone, *Jefferson and the Ordeal of Liberty* (Boston: Little, Brown and Co., 1962), pp. 134-35.

15. GW to Charles Mynn Thruston (10 Aug. 1794), Fitzpatrick 33:465.

16. Sixth Annual Address to Congress (19 Nov. 1794), Fitzpatrick 34:29-30.

17. GW to Henry Lee (21 July 1793), Fitzpatrick 33:23.

18. GW to William Pearce (27 Mar. 1796), Fitzpatrick 34:507.

19. GW to John Greenwood (20 Jan. 1797), Fitzpatrick 35:370-71.

20. GW to John Ehler (23 Dec. 1793), Fitzpatrick 33:214-15.

21. GW to George Washington Parke Custis (28 Nov. 1796), Fitzpatrick 35:294-95.

22. GW to Elizabeth Parke Custis (14 Sept. 1794), Fitzpatrick 33:501.

Chapter 39—The Controversial Jay Treaty

1. GW to the Senate (16 Apr. 1794), Fitzpatrick 33:332-33.

2. John Jay to Edmund Randolph (7 Mar. 1795), in Henry H. P. Johnston, ed., *The Correspondence and Public Papers of John Jay*, 4 vols. (New York: G. P. Putnam's Sons, 1890-93), 4:138.

3. John Jay to GW (7 Mar. 1795), Johnston, *The Correspondence and Public Papers of John Jay*, 4:133-34.

4. GW to Alexander Hamilton (14 July 1795), Fitzpatrick 34:241 42.

5. GW to the commissioners of the District of Columbia (29 July 1795), Fitzpatrick 34:259.

6. GW to Alexander Hamilton (29 July 1795), Fitzpatrick 34:262-64.

7. GW to Edmund Randolph (22 July 1795), Fitzpatrick 34:224.

8. GW to Edmund Randolph (29 July 1795), Fitzpatrick 34:256.

9. GW to Charles Cotesworth Pinckney (24 Aug. 1795), Fitzpatrick 34:285.

10. Nathaniel Ames, diary entry (14 Aug. 1795), in Charles Warren, *Jacobin and Junto, or Early American Politics as Viewed in the Diary of Dr. Nathaniel Ames, 1785-1822* (Cambridge, Mass.: Harvard University Press, 1931), p. 63.

11. Benjamin Bache in the *Aurora*, 22 August 1795; quoted in Freeman 7:303.

12. GW to the Republicans of Savannah (31 Aug. 1795), Fitzpatrick 34:294-95.

13. GW to Henry Knox (20 Sept. 1795), Fitzpatrick 34:310.

14. Proceedings and debates of the House of Representatives (2 Mar. 1796), *Annals of the Congress of the United States: Fourth Congress*, 2 vols. (Washington: Gales and Seaton, 1849), 1:400-401. However, the House did exclude from its request any such papers "as any existing negotiation may render improper to be disclosed." Ibid., pp. 424, 426.

15. John Adams to Abigail Adams (25 Mar. 1796), in Charles Francis Adams, ed., *Letters of John Adams Addressed to His Wife*, 2 vols. (Boston: Charles C. Little and James Brown, 1841), 2:215.

16. GW to the House of Representatives (30 Mar. 1796), Fitzpatrick 35:3-5.

17. Washington took care not to infringe on the responsibilities reserved to the Supreme Court, but he once did make the mistake of asking the court for an opinion in the area of executive policy. In July 1793, in the midst of the Genet crisis, Washington and his Cabinet sent to the Supreme Court a list of twenty-nine queries relating to the problem of neutrality. The court politely refused to give an opinion, saying it was not in their province to do so. See Freeman 7:104, 108, 110 and *n*.

18. GW to Alexander Hamilton (8 May 1796), Fitzpatrick 35:40.

19. GW to David Humphreys (12 June 1796), Fitzpatrick 35:91-92.

20. GW to Thomas Jefferson (6 July 1796), Fitzpatrick 35:119.

21. Ibid., pp. 120-22.

Chapter 40—The End of Public Life

1. GW to Edmund Pendleton (22 Jan. 1795), Fitzpatrick 34:98.

2. GW to Robert Lewis (26 June 1796), Fitzpatrick 35:99.

3. GW to John Jay (8 May 1796), Fitzpatrick 35:35-37.

4. Isaac Weld (22 Feb. 1796), in his *Travels Through the States of North America*, 4th ed., 2 vols. (1807; reprint ed., New York and London: Johnson Reprint Corporation, 1968), 1:104*n*.

5. Benjamin Henry Latrobe, diary entry (16 July 1796), quoted in Fitzpatrick 35:142*n*.

6. GW to Alexander Hamilton (15 May 1796), Fitzpatrick 35:48-49.

7. For a more detailed discussion of the authorship of the Farewell Address,

see Victor Hugo Paltsits, ed., *Washington's Farewell Address* (New York: New York Public Library, 1935); Flexner, *George Washington: Anguish and Farewell*, pp. 292-307; Freeman 7:381-82, 398-403.

8. Farewell Address (17 Sept. 1796), Fitzpatrick 35:214-38.

9. Eighth Annual Address to Congress (7 Dec. 1796), Fitzpatrick 35:319-20.

10. GW to George Washington Parke Custis (27 Feb. 1797), Fitzpatrick 35:403.

11. GW to Henry Knox (2 Mar. 1797), Fitzpatrick 35:409.

12. Mrs. Susan R. Echard, quoted in Custis, *Recollections and Private Memoirs of Washington*, p. 434n.

13. John Adams to Abigail Adams (5 Mar. 1797), in Charles Francis Adams, ed., *Letters of John Adams Addressed to His Wife*, 2 vols. (Boston: Charles C. Little and James Brown, 1841), 2:244.

14. GW to John Augustine Washington (May 1778), Fitzpatrick 11:500.

15. James Thomas Flexner, *George Washington: Anguish and Farewell (1793-1799)* (Boston: Little, Brown and Co., 1969), p. 443n. Benjamin Harrison's 21 July 1775 letter to GW was first published in the London *Daily Advertiser*, still preserved in official British archives. This original text clearly shows that the paragraph added in the September 1775 *Gentleman's Magazine* was fabricated for propaganda purposes. For discussions of this and other fraudulent attacks on Washington's morality (including the so-called Bew letters), see Dixon Wecter, "President Washington and Parson Weems," in James Morton Smith, ed., *George Washington: A Profile* (New York: Hill and Wang, 1969), pp. 20-22; John C. Fitzpatrick, "The George Washington Slanders," in *Report of the United States George Washington Bicentennial Commission*, 5 vols. (Washington: U.S. George Washington Bicentennial Commission, 1932), 3:313-19; Bellamy, *The Private Life of George Washington*, pp. 259-60, 294; Paul Leicester Ford, *George Washington* (published in 1896 as *The True George Washington*; reprint ed., Port Washington, N.Y.: Kennikat Press, 1970), chap. 4, "Relations with the Fair Sex," pp. 84-111. See also Freeman 1:235a; 2:388; 5:498.

16. For a more complete discussion of this issue, see Jay A. Parry, "Did Washington Cheat on His Expense Account?" *Freemen Digest*, February 1984, pp. 34-37.

17. GW to Bryan, Lord Fairfax (20 Jan. 1799), Fitzpatrick 37:94.

18. GW to William Livingston (7 Dec. 1797), Fitzpatrick 17:225.

Chapter 41—The Final Days

1. William Sullivan, quoted in Paul Leicester Ford, *The True George Washington* (Philadelphia: J. B. Lippincott Company, 1896), p. 41.

2. Nelly Custis to Mrs. Oliver Wolcott, Jr. (19 Mar. 1797), William S. Baker, *Washington After the Revolution, 1784-1799* (Philadelphia, 1898), p. 347; quoted in Freeman 7:447n.

3. Martha Washington to Lucy Knox (1797?), quoted in Bellamy, *The Private Life of George Washington,* p. 380.

4. GW to James McHenry (3 Apr. 1797), Fitzpatrick 35:430-31.

5. J. P. Brissot de Warville, *New Travels in the United States of America* (London: Printed for J. S. Jordan, 1792), p. 429.

6. GW to Lawrence Lewis (4 Aug. 1797), Fitzpatrick 36:2-3.

7. Custis, *Recollections and Private Memoirs of Washington,* p. 168.

8. GW to William Vans Murray (3 Dec. 1797), Fitzpatrick 36:87.

9. GW to James McHenry (29 May 1797), Fitzpatrick 35:455-56.

10. GW to "John Langhorne" (15 Oct. 1797), Fitzpatrick 36:53. After writing this letter Washington learned that John Langhorne was a fictitious name, probably for Peter Carr, an unprincipled nephew of Thomas Jefferson. Carr was likely trying to provoke Washington into making some rash and bitter statements, but the former President did not take the bait.

11. GW to Oliver Wolcott (15 May 1797), Fitzpatrick 35:447.

12. GW to William Heath (20 May 1797), Fitzpatrick 35:449.

13. GW to David Humphreys (26 June 1797), Fitzpatrick 35:481.

14. GW to Robert Lewis (26 June 1796), Fitzpatrick 35:99.

15. GW to the Secretary of the Treasury (15 May 1797), Fitzpatrick 35:447.

16. GW to James McHenry (4 July 1798), Fitzpatrick 36:304-5.

17. Ibid., p. 307. That summer Washington told a visitor to his home: "Submission [to France] is cowardice. Rather than that, America will arouse;...in spite of my age, [I] will give all the blood that remains in my veins." Quoted in W. M. Kozlowski, "A Visit to Mount Vernon a Century Ago: A Few Pages of an Unpublished Diary of the Polish Poet J. U. Niemcewicz," *Century Magazine* 41 (Feb. 1902):521.

18. James Hosmer Penniman, "Washington, Proprietor of Mount Vernon," pamphlet number 9 in the series *Honor to George Washington,* ed. Albert Bushnell Hart (Washington: United States George Washington Bicentennial Commission, 1932), p. 99.

19. See Freeman 2:460; 4:727-29; 5:568; 6:527; 7:725.

20. GW to Robert Lewis (18 Aug. 1799), Fitzpatrick 37:339.

21. GW to Alexander Addison (3 Mar. 1799), Fitzpatrick 37:146.

22. GW to James McHenry (25 Mar. 1799), Fitzpatrick 37:158.

23. Gouverneur Morris to GW (9 Dec. 1799), in Jared Sparks, ed., *The Life of*

Gouverneur Morris, with Selections from His Correspondence, 3 vols. (Boston: Gray and Bowen, 1832), 3:123–24.

24. GW to Jonathan Trumbull (21 July 1799), Fitzpatrick 37:349.

25. GW to Alexander Hamilton (27 May 1798), Fitzpatrick 36:271.

26. GW to Jonathan Trumbull (21 July 1799), Fitzpatrick 37:313.

27. Last Will and Testament (9 July 1799), Fitzpatrick 37:275–94.

28. GW to Burgess Ball (22 Sept. 1799), Fitzpatrick 37:372.

29. Martha Washington to Eliza Powel (17 Dec. 1797), Fitzpatrick 36:109n.

30. Quoted in James K. Paulding, *A Life of Washington,* 2 vols. (1858; reprint ed., Port Washington, N.Y.: Kennikat Press, 1970), 2:196.

31. Lear, *Letters and Recollections of George Washington,* p. 129.

32. Quoted in ibid., p. 130.

33. Quoted in ibid., p. 133.

34. Quoted in ibid., p. 134.

35. Ibid., p. 135.

36. Quoted in ibid.

37. Tobias Lear to John Adams (15 Dec. 1799), in Charles Francis Adams, ed., *The Works of John Adams,* 10 vols. (Boston: Little, Brown and Company, 1850–56), 9:163–64.

38. Oration in the city of Philadelphia (26 Dec. 1799), quoted in Albert Bushnell Hart, comp., "Tributes to Washington," pamphlet number 3 in the series *Honor to George Washington,* ed. Albert Bushnell Hart (Washington: United States George Washington Bicentennial Commission, 1932), p. 30.

39. Thomas Jefferson to Walter Jones (2 Jan. 1814), Bergh, *The Writings of Thomas Jefferson,* 14:52.

Appendixes

1. Thomas Jefferson to Walter Jones (2 Jan. 1814), Bergh, *The Writings of Thomas Jefferson,* 14:48-52

2. John Bernard, *Retrospections of America, 1797-1811* (New York: Harper & Brothers, 1887), pp. 85-93.

Introduction to "Timeless Treasures from George Washington"

1. GW to David Humphreys, 25 July 1785, Fitzpatrick 28:203.

2. GW to Arthur Young, 4 December 1788, Fitzpatrick 30:153.

3. Quoted in John C. Fitzpatrick, *George Washington Himself* (Indianapolis: Bobbs-

Merrill Co., 1933), p. 160.

4. Madison to Jared Sparks, quoted in Paul Leicester Ford, *George Washington* (1896; reprint, Port Washington, N.Y.: Kennikat Press, 1970), p. 179.

5. By 1930 the Library of Congress had thus far collected, according to "a conservative estimate," around seventy-five thousand pages of Washington's letters and other writings. Fitzpatrick 1:xli.

6. Freeman, *George Washington* 3:352.

7. Jefferson to Dr. Walter Jones, 2 January 1814, in *The Writings of Thomas Jefferson*, ed. Albert Ellery Bergh, 20 vols. (Washington: Thomas Jefferson Memorial Association, 1907), 14:49–50.

8. Henrietta Liston, "Journal of Washington's Resignation, Retirement, and Death," ed. James C. Nicholls, *Pennsylvania Magazine* 96 (1971): 514–15. An especially good analysis of Washington's abilities as a writer is found in Henry Cabot Lodge, *George Washington*, 2 vols. (1898; reprint, New York: AMS Press, 1972), 2:337–50.

9. Harold W. Bradley, "The Political Thinking of George Washington," in James Morton Smith, ed., *George Washington: A Profile* (New York: Hill and Wang, 1969), p. 146.

10. W. E. Woodward, *George Washington: The Image and the Man* (New York: Liveright, 1946), p. 454.

11. Bernard Fay, *George Washington: Republican Aristocrat* (Boston: Houghton Mifflin Co., 1931), p. 166.

12. Madison to Thomas Jefferson, 9 January 1785, in *The Writings of James Madison*, ed. Gaillard Hunt, 9 vols. (New York: G. P. Putnam's Sons, 1900–1910), 2:109.

13. Madison to Jared Sparks, quoted in Paul Leicester Ford, *George Washington*, p. 179.

14. Fitzpatrick, *George Washington Himself*, p. 446.

15. James Thomas Flexner, *George Washington: Anguish and Farewell* (Boston: Little, Brown and Co., 1972), p. 345n.

Index

M

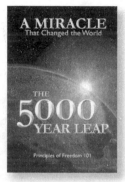

THE REAL THOMAS JEFFERSON
The True Story of America's Philosopher of Freedom
709 pages, 58 illustrations.
$22.95
Visit *nccs.net*

The Real Thomas Jefferson is the true story of America's Philosopher of Freedom. This book lets you meet the man as he really was—rather than as interpreted by historians—as much of his exciting story is told in his own words.

Part II of this book is a compilation of the most salient and insightful passages from Jefferson's writings, listed by subject.

THE REAL BENJAMIN FRANKLIN
The True Story of America's Greatest Diplomat
504 pages, 42 illustrations.
$19.95
Visit *nccs.net*

Meet the real Benjamin Franklin and the true story of America's greatest diplomat. Learn about the businessman, the renowned scientist, the loyal patriot and the man of deep religious convictions—not as historians characterize him—but by letting him tell much of his dramatic story in his own words.

The second portion of this book brings together the most insightful and timeless passages from Franklin's writings, arranged topically.

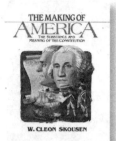

THE MAKING OF AMERICA
The Substance and Meaning of the Constitution
920 pages, hardcover
$29.95
Visit *nccs.net*

The Making of America: The Substance and Meaning of the Constitution provides a wealth of material on the Founding Fathers' intentions when drafting the American Constitution. It is one of the most thorough compilations of statements by the Framers relating to constitutional interpretation.

It addresses the Constitution clause by clause and provides resources on the Founder's intent of each clause.

A MORE PERFECT UNION (DVD)
America Becomes a Nation
Runtime: 1 hour 52 minutes
$19.95
Visit *nccs.net*

A MORE PERFECT UNION: America Becomes A Nation is the first comprehensive re-creation of those stirring debates during the sweltering summer of 1787. Filmed on location at Independence Hall and other historical sites, it dramatically chronicles how America became a nation and those underlying principles that guard our freedoms today.

Officially recognized by the Commission on the Bicentennial of the United States Constitution, who cited the film as being "of exceptional merit." It is used by thousands of schools across America to teach the Constitution.